Dedication

To Rama, Kiran and Jeevan for your understanding
and support during yet another 'book year'.

5th Edition

Research Methods
and Statistics in
Psychology

WITHDRAWN

Hugh Coolican

Acknowledgements

To Alison Wadeley for a very thoughtful and useful review of the fourth edition. To my students whose assignments always show me what's needed and on whom I try out some of the ideas. To tutors and enquirers who have offered suggestions or pointed out errors. A special thanks to all staff involved at Hodder Education but especially Tamsin Smith, Bianca Knights, and to Susan Dunsmore for some painstaking copy-editing.

Every effort has been made to trace and acknowledge the owners of copyright. The publishers will be glad to make suitable arrangements with any copyright holders whom it has not been possible to contact.

First published in Great Britain in 2009 by
Hodder Education, an Hachette UK company,
338 Euston Road, London NW1 3BH

www.hoddereducation.com

Hachette Livre UK's policy is to use papers that are natural, renewable and recyclable products and made from wood grown in sustainable forests. The logging and manufacturing processes are expected to conform to the environmental regulations of the country of origin.

The advice and information in this book are believed to be true and accurate at the date of going to press, but neither the author[s] nor the publisher can accept any legal responsibility or liability for any errors or omissions.

British Library Cataloguing in Publication Data
A catalogue record for this book is available from the British Library

Library of Congress Cataloging-in-Publication Data
A catalog record for this book is available from the Library of Congress

ISBN: 978 0 340 983 447

1 2 3 4 5 6 7 8 9 10

Typeset in 10/13pt StempelSchneidler by Dorchester Typesetting Group Ltd
Printed and bound in Malta

What do you think about this book? Or any other Hodder Education title?
Please send your comments to educationenquiries@hodder.com

ii

Contents

Preface

This book is for anyone starting out on a psychology course which contains a fair amount of hands-on practical research training and the writing up of psychological reports. It will be most useful for those studying for a psychology degree but will also serve students on Masters courses in psychology (where methods knowledge may have become a little rusty), on other social sciences courses, on nursing degrees and in several other related disciplines. The common factor is the need to understand how researchers gather data in a fair and unbiased manner and how they analyse and interpret those data. A feature that I'm sure all such readers would be pleased to find is a friendly common-sense approach that uses clear concrete examples to explain otherwise abstract and sometimes complex notions. In the past this book has been praised for doing just that and I truly hope it continues to do so.

A basic premise of the book has always been that people start out on research methods courses with many of the basic principles already acquired through their experience of everyday life. To some extent the job of tutors and writers is to harness those concepts and to formalise and then elaborate upon them. Before you do psychology you probably know just what a fair experiment would be, what an average is, what it means when people deviate a lot from an average and even the fundamentals of *statistical significance* – you can probably tell intuitively when samples of girls' and boys' reading scores differ by an amount that cannot be explained just by chance variation. Hence you are not really starting out on something you know little about no matter how frightened you may be of numbers and science.

One of the bonuses of studying research methods and statistics is that you greatly enhance what Neil Postman (1987) referred to as your personal 'crap detection' system, to put it rather crudely. That is, a study of methods and statistics at the very least and done properly will enable your ability to spot gross errors in the statistical arguments of advertisers, politicians and charlatans who try to use numbers or 'findings' to bamboozle you. There are several examples of such poor methods or data massaging in the book and hopefully you will later be able to argue 'Ah but,.....' at dinner parties and become everybody's best friend as you point out the flaws in the assumptions people make from 'findings' that have made the news.

Many people start psychology courses with a very strong fear of the statistics that may be involved. This is understandable if, for you, the world of numbers has always been something of a no-go area. However, statistics is one of the easiest areas of maths (it must be, both my children said so, even the one for whom maths was a nightmare).

You should not have to do a lot of by-hand calculating, unless your tutors are sadists! Psychology is not about (re-)learning to do sums; it's about *using* statistical tools to summarise data and to show people that we have found a relationship between the data that supports a particular view or theory about how people work. Where you do have to calculate, be assured that the actual calculation steps for most procedures *never* extend beyond the basic capability of the average 11 year old, and can all be done on a £2 calculator.

In this fifth edition (I can't believe this book started 20 years ago!) there have been several changes. Exercises have been moved so that they follow each substantive piece of work rather than appearing only at the end of a chapter. There are an increased number of stop and think exercises now in boxes called 'Pause for thought'. Instructions for SPSS now cover the latest edition (v.16) as well as the last few previous versions for the most part. In the statistics sections the way to report each statistical test, introduced in the fourth edition, has been augmented in each case by the way to report effect size and confidence limits where appropriate.

Qualitative methods, as ever, are integrated into general chapters (e.g. interviewing, observation and the quantitative–qualitative debate in Chapter 2) and two specialist chapters. The first edition was almost certainly the first general methods text in the UK to pay specific attention to qualitative methods. These have been updated again and there is a new appearance for narrative analysis and an expanded section on thematic analysis. The example qualitative article has been replaced by one that much more clearly follows a grounded theory approach. For qualitative methods in particular, but also in general, there are far more website addresses to consult for further information and resources. There are several attempts to tackle 'psychology myths' such as what the Hawthorne studies really showed, how Zimbardo biased his famous study and, more substantially, a debate on the much misused term 'ecological validity' which is extended on the companion website, www.hodderplus.com/psychology.

This companion website is a major new technology addition and I have used it to post several more extended debates and detailed information that could not have appeared in the book itself for reasons of size. I hope to continue to add to this site, including more exercises, more debates and further links to useful resources as they appear.

I encourage feedback, queries and, yes, people just telling me I'm wrong about something – how else would we learn? This time around you will be able to e-mail me your queries using the website and I will attempt to provide a clear response. Finally I'd like to repeat something from the fourth edition preface. While you toil away, writing those inevitable reports, just keep thinking that none of the truly fascinating ideas about human behaviour and experience and none of the wonderful insights about ourselves that can be gained on a short psychology course would be possible without someone (many committed people in fact) doing exactly as you are doing!

Psychology, science and research

This introduction sets the scene for research in psychology. The key ideas are as follows:

- Psychological researchers *generally follow a scientific approach, developed from the* 'empirical method' *into the* 'hypothetico-deductive' method. This involves careful definition and measurement, and the logic of testing hypotheses produced from falsifiable theories.
- Most people use the rudimentary logic of scientific theory testing quite often in their everyday lives.
- Although scientific thinking is a careful extension of common-sense thinking, common sense on its own can lead to false assumptions.
- Good research is *replicable*; theories are clearly explained and *falsifiable*.
- Theories in science and in psychology are not 'proven' true but are supported or challenged by research evidence. Much research attempts to eliminate variables as possible explanations. It also attempts to broaden the scope of a previously demonstrated effect or to find instances where the effect does not occur.
- Scientific research is a continuous and social activity, involving promotion and checking of ideas among colleagues.
- Research has to be planned carefully, with attention to *design, variables, samples* and subsequent data *analysis*. If all these areas are not thoroughly planned, results may be ambiguous or useless.
- Some researchers have strong objections to the use of traditional scientific methods in the study of persons. They support *qualitative* methods and data gathering, dealing with meaningful verbal data rather than exact measurement and statistical summary.

Why psychology and science?

If you are just starting to read this book, then you have probably started on a course in psychology and may have been surprised, if not daunted, to find your tutors talking about psychology being a 'science'. You will probably have found that you must carry out practical research exercises, make measurements, deal with statistics and write up your findings as a scientific report (or, just maybe, you weren't surprised at all). Many people cannot divorce from their concept of 'science' images of Bunsen burners, retort stands, white coats, complicated mathematical formulae and really unpleasant smells.

Rest assured the psychological 'laboratory' contains none of these things and shouldn't really involve you in difficult maths. There is the use of statistics for sure but (a little later on) I hope to

1

assure you that all statistical calculations can be carried out on a £2 calculator and anyway there are computers to do any serious number crunching.

The main point to put across right here and now, however, is that science is not about retort stands and white coats. It is a system of thought which leads us to a rational explanation of how things work in the world and a process of getting closer to truths and further from myths, fables and unquestioned or 'intuitive' ideas about people. A further point, and one which is central to the approach of this book, is to emphasise that you already do think scientifically even if you thought you didn't (or not very often). We will return to that point too in a moment.

This book, then, is about the ways that psychologists go about establishing evidence for their theories about people. It is about how they do research and the advantages and disadvantages involved in the use of alternative methods. However, it is also about much more than that. In this chapter, we will discuss the reasons why psychology uses the scientific method and ask, what *is* science and what is scientific thinking? We will also briefly introduce a vein within psychological research that largely rejects traditional scientific methods, especially the attempt to measure or predict behaviour.

Isn't a lot of psychology just simple intuition?

But first let's address those readers who are disappointed because they thought that, after all, psychology is not a physical science and we all know so much about people already; surely a lot of it is plain common sense or pure intuition? Intuition is often seen as a handy short cut to truth. Figure 1.1 illustrates the intuitive thinker and the critical thinker considering the proposition that heat makes people aggressive.

Figure 1.1 The intuitive thinker and the critical thinker

Now let's look at something else that is blindingly obvious and 'intuitively' known. **Men are more aggressive than their female partners.**

Well, yes, plenty of psychological and criminological research will back up this statement and it can seem that we don't really need the research because the finding is so obvious. However, we need to be careful with the detail. We would all presumably also assume, as a consequence, that males in partnerships would hit their female partners more often than the other way around. Well, according to a large study by Archer (2000), females in heterosexual partnerships are slightly more likely than men to use acts of physical aggression and to use them more often than men. Males, however, are much more likely to cause injury through physical aggression. This was no result from a very unusual sample of people. The study was an analysis of the results of many studies carried out across Canada, the USA, the UK, Israel, South Korea and New Zealand. This does not dispute many women's dreadful experience of violent partners. It *could* mean that, in ordinary relationships where physical aggression is sometimes used, women use mild aggression where men perhaps hold back, knowing their strength. However, one of the important things about science is that you are able to go and check the findings and perhaps carry out your own research if you are not convinced that what the findings seem to show is genuine.

Why can't we trust intuition?

We can't trust intuition because it depends too much on myth, stereotype, prejudice and received but unchecked wisdom. In addition, when confronted with a new problem intuition is very vulnerable to our tendency to stick with what we know. Try these two problems and don't read any further until you have had a think about them.

Pause for thought

Imagine a rope placed around the circumference of the Earth (and please try to ignore hills, mountains and lakes). Suppose we now want to lift the rope so that it is 1 metre above the Earth all the way around. About how much more rope would we need?

Take a piece of paper and fold it over on itself three times. The paper is now a bit thicker than it was before. We can't physically fold a piece of paper more than about seven times so now just imagine folding it over on itself another 50 times. How thick would the paper now be?

The answer to the first problem is just over 6 metres! How can that be you say because the Earth is so huge. The trouble here is that because part of the problem involves a massive size, we think the answer must be massive … but it isn't. If you'd like to check out the calculation then take a look at p. 26; having promised no awkward maths, it would be unwise of me to put formulae into the main text right now!

Exactly the same process happens with the second problem but in the opposite direction. Here we know paper is very thin so we assume the answer will be a relatively small amount. In fact the paper would be thick enough to stretch from the Earth to the Sun … and back again … and back again with a bit left over! I haven't provided a calculation for this but if you take a piece of paper to be 0.1 mm. thick,[1] then double this thickness 53 times (using Excel, for instance), you'll get a huge

---

[1] Please note that this book uses the British Psychological Society Style Guide recommendation of using a leading zero where a value *could* be greater than one, but not where the highest value possible is one (e.g. $p = .05$).

number of millimetres which you can then divide by 1,000,000 to get kilometres. If you now convert to UK measurement the distance is about 280 million miles!

What has all this to do with psychology? Well, the problem we're dealing with here is that intuition, or 'common sense', gives us 'obvious' answers which are incorrect so we can't rely on it for developing a system of psychological knowledge.

Intuition is an even poorer help when issues are much more personal to us. Ritov and Baron (1990) asked participants a hypothetical question. 'Imagine there is a flu epidemic during which your child has a 10 in 10,000 chance of dying. There is a vaccine which will certainly prevent the disease but it can produce fatalities.' They asked participants to decide the maximum level of risk of death from the vaccine that they would accept for their child. Participants generally would not accept a risk higher than 5 in 10,000. In other words, participants were willing to submit their child to a 1 in 1,000 chance of dying from flu rather take the lower (1/2 in 1,000) risk of death from the vaccine. This is 'magical thinking'. Perhaps people thought that they would rather 'chance' took their child than that any positive decision they made could be linked to the child's death even though the *not* acting carried double the chance of fatality! Something very similar has happened for real in the UK in recent years where very flimsy and in fact discredited evidence (e.g. Honda, Shimizu and Rutter, 2005) that the MMR jab might be a cause of autism has led parents to avoid it and probably contributed to a serious rise in cases of measles, mumps and rubella (Jansen *et al.*, 2003).

Many people are convinced that their 'intuition' tells them reliable truths about the world and about people. Psychologists aren't.

Science – not a subject but a way of thinking

Many students who choose psychology are put off by the idea of 'science' being applied to the study of people. People who are interested in people are not usually terribly interested in laboratory equipment or procedures. However, what we need to be clear of here is that science is not a body of technical knowledge or a boring 'subject' but simply a *way of thinking* that leads us towards testable explanations of what we observe in the world around us. It doesn't deliver the 'truth' but it does provide us with reasonable accounts of what *might* be going on. What's more, *it is a thought system that we all use in our everyday lives.* It is no different from the logic that is used in the following 'everyday' example.

Pause for thought

Imagine that you have a younger brother and that you've been given the task of taking him to the doctor with a rash that he seems to get each week on Monday. The doctor takes one look and asks 'Does he eat broccoli?' 'Yes,' you answer, 'He doesn't like it so he just has to eat it on Sundays when we have a roast dinner with our Gran.' The doctor feels fairly sure that the rash is an allergy. The obvious move now is to banish broccoli from his diet (brother is ecstatic) and watch for the rash. Four weeks later the rash has not re-appeared. The broccoli theory looks good.

Has this 'proved' that broccoli was the problem? Well, no, and here is a point that will be repeated many times in different ways throughout this book. Contrary to popular 'common sense' (and this is not true just for 'soft' psychology but for all sciences, no matter how hard), *scientific research does not prove theories true*. Listen to scientific experts being interviewed in the media and you will hear them use phrases like 'all the evidence so far points towards…' or 'the evidence is consistent with …', no matter how hard the interviewer pushes for a definitive answer to questions like 'Do power lines cause childhood leukaemia?'. Research supplies *evidence* which might support or contradict a theory. If your brother's rash disappears, then we have *support for* (not proof of) the broccoli allergy theory. We don't have proof because it could have been the herbs that Mum always cooks along with the broccoli that were causing the rash. There is always another possible explanation for findings. However, if the rash remains, then we have, as we shall see, a more definite result that appears to knock out the broccoli theory altogether, though again, there is the outside possibility that your brother is allergic to broccoli *and* to something else that Mum always includes in the Sunday meal. By taking out one item at a time though, and leaving all the others, we could be pretty certain, eventually, what item or items cause the rash.

Never use the term 'prove'

So a scientific test never 'proves' a theory to be true. If ever you are tempted to write 'this proves …' always cross out the word 'proves' and use 'supports' instead. The word 'proof' belongs in mathematics, where mathematicians really *do* prove that one side of an equation equals the other, or in detective stories – where the victim's blood on the suspect's shoes is said to 'prove' their guilt. Of course it doesn't. There is always a perhaps stretched but possible innocent explanation of how the blood arrived there ('Oh, he borrowed those last week and I remember he cut himself shaving'). In psychology, as for detective work, if theories are speculative explanations, then 'evidence' can only ever support, not 'prove', anything. We know that the suspect committed the crime if we see unambiguous video tape of the incident. However, we do not now talk of 'evidence' to support a theory since the suspect's guilt is no longer theory – it is fact (but even then it could have been the suspect's twin!).

Info Box 1.1	Findings and conclusions

Be careful always to distinguish between 'FINDINGS' and 'CONCLUSIONS'. Findings are what actually occurred in a study – what the results were. Conclusions are what the researcher may conclude as a result of considering findings in the light of background theory. For instance, the fact that identical twins' IQs correlate quite highly is a *finding*. From this finding a researcher might *conclude* that heredity plays a big part in the development of intelligence. This is not the only possible conclusion, however. Since identical twins also share a very similar environment (they even have the same birthday and sex compared with other pairs of siblings), the finding could *also* be taken as evidence for the role of the environment in the development of intelligence. In Archer's (2000) study mentioned above, the *finding* was a small but significant difference with females using physical aggression slightly more than their male partners. What we *conclude* from this is *perhaps* that most males, knowing their strength, restrain their impulses. However, we do not *know* this until we conduct further research. The lack of a rash is a *finding*; the assumption that broccoli caused it is a *conclusion*. Findings should always be clear, unambiguous and subject to little if any argument. Conclusions on the other hand are very often contentious and disputed.

Thinking scientifically – we can all do it

I claimed above that people use the logic of scientific thinking in their everyday lives. The difference between ordinary and professional scientific thinking is just a matter of practice and the acquisition of some extra formal concepts and procedures. The study of psychology itself will tell you that almost all children begin to seriously question the world, and to test hypotheses about it, from the age of around six or seven. The logic that you will need to cope with science, and all the concepts of methods and statistics in this book, are in place by age 11. Everything else is just more and more complicated use of the same tools. We use these tools every day of our lives. We used the brother's rash example above to demonstrate this. Here is another example. Suppose you find music coming from only one channel of the stereo and you suspect a fault in the CD player, which the cat knocked off its shelf a while back. How to test this theory? Try a new CD player, known to be working. If it works we tend to assume the old CD player was at fault. If it doesn't we look elsewhere, probably at the amplifier. In this everyday situation, we have *predicted* what should happen if our theory is correct that the CD player is broken. We have tested this prediction and seem to have established that the old player *was* bust. Of course, as in science, the result here isn't conclusive. If the new CD player *does* work, this doesn't entirely 'prove' that the old one had failed. Maybe it's the way the leads connect with the player that causes the problem. If the new player doesn't work perhaps it broke only as we installed it. Perhaps the old one is really OK and the problem lies elsewhere. All these theories can be eliminated or strengthened by further testing, which is exactly the way that the scientific method works too.

Pause for thought

Most people fairly frequently use the basic logical principles that underlie all scientific thinking, such as the logic of hypothesis testing which we will explore in more detail shortly. They are usually quite capable of generating several basic research designs used in psychology without having received any formal training.

To have a go at generating basic research designs, try thinking of ways to test the proposal depicted in Figure 1.1: 'Heat makes people aggressive.'

With student colleagues try to think of ways to gather evidence for this idea. If you do the exercise alone, try it on several different occasions in order to come up with quite different approaches to the test.

Some suggestions appear in Table 1.1. (The suggestions that students in workshops produce in answer to this question often predict most of the lecture topics on a first-year course in research methods!)

Suggested designs for testing the theory that heat makes people more aggressive	Methods used (which we will learn more about in Chapters 2–7)
Have people solve difficult problems in a hot room then in a cold room; measure their blood pressure.	Repeated measures experiment; very indirect measure of aggression.
Have one group of people solve problems in a hot room and a different group solve them in a cool room. Have them tear up cardboard afterwards and assess aggression from observation.	Between groups (independent samples) experiment; aggression assessed from direct observation of behaviour but coding will be required.
Observe amount of horn-hooting by drivers in a city on hot and cold days.	Naturalistic observation.
Put people in either a hot or cold room for a while, then interview them using a scale to measure aggression.	Between groups (independent samples) experiment; dependent variable is a measurement by psychological scale.
Approach people on hot and cold days, and administer (if they agree) aggression scale.	Between groups quasi-experiment; aggression is defined as measured on a psychological scale.
Check public records for number of crimes involving aggression committed in hot and cold seasons in the same city.	Use of archival data; a kind of indirect observation.

Table 1.1 Possible ways to test the hypothesis that heat makes people more aggressive

Beyond common sense – the formal scientific method

The discussion and exercises above were intended to convey the idea that most people use the logical thinking that is needed for scientific investigation every day of their lives. Many people believe they are a long way from scientific thinking but they usually are not. However, it is now time to tackle the other side of the coin – the belief that psychology (and psychological science) is all just 'common sense'. Allport argued that psychological science should have the aim of

enhancing – above the levels achieved by common sense – our powers of predicting, understanding and controlling human action (1940: 23).

If we can predict, then we have observed enough to know that what we are observing does not just happen randomly; we have noted a pattern of regularities. For instance we know that broccoli leads to a rash but we may not understand why. Understanding is Allport's next criterion. The final one, *controlling* human action, may sound authoritarian and worrying, which is ironic when you know that Allport was, in the same paragraph as the quotation, arguing against authoritarianism in psychological science. By 'control' he was referring to the fact that science is usually put to good purpose. If we can understand and control events, we can also improve people's lives. In the case of psychology, some of the benefits to society might be: improving teaching and learning, reducing antisocial and prejudicial behaviour, operating the most effective and humane forms of management, alleviating people's disturbed behaviour, enhancing human sporting performance, and so on.

So what is this scientific method then?

Scientific method, as it is popularly described today, is in fact a merger of two historical models of science, the *empirical method*, as espoused by Francis Bacon in the early seventeenth century, and the splendidly named *hypothetico-deductive method*, which is pretty much the kind of logical testing we encountered above but as applied to exploring the unknown rather than solving technical stereo problems or treating a rash.

The empirical method

'Empirical' means 'through experience'. The original empirical method had two stages:

1 Gathering of data, directly, through experience, through our external senses, with no preconceptions as to how they are ordered or what explains them.

2 Induction of patterns and relationships within the data. That is, to see what relationships appear to exist within our data. For instance, it was at some time noted that water boils at 100° at sea level but that this temperature point lowers by some predictable amount as our height above sea level increases.

The reason for this emphasis on starting out to investigate phenomena with no preconceptions was that Bacon, along with later Enlightenment philosophers and scientists, was fighting a battle against explanations of phenomena that rested entirely on mysticism, on ancient belief or, more importantly, on the orthodoxy of the Church of Rome. The empiricists argued that knowledge could only be obtained through personal experience of the world and not through inner contemplation and the acceptance of ancient wisdom (a sophisticated form of 'common sense'). From the time of the early and successful Greek investigations, knowledge in most of the world had been the preserve of the authorities and could only be gained, it was thought, through inner contemplation, not through careful observation of worldly events. In Bacon's era scientists (e.g. Galileo) could be threatened with death for the heresy of going against the Church's word using empirical evidence. Take a look at Box 1.2 to see why ancient wisdom should not be trusted over simple worldly observation.

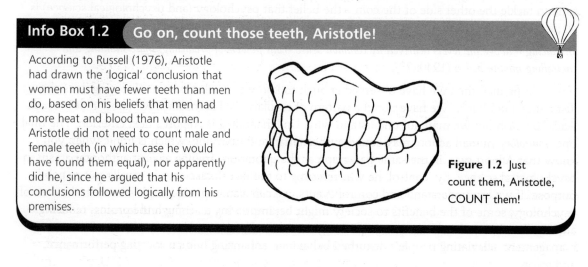

Info Box 1.2   Go on, count those teeth, Aristotle!

According to Russell (1976), Aristotle had drawn the 'logical' conclusion that women must have fewer teeth than men do, based on his beliefs that men had more heat and blood than women. Aristotle did not need to count male and female teeth (in which case he would have found them equal), nor apparently did he, since he argued that his conclusions followed logically from his premises.

Figure 1.2 Just count them, Aristotle, COUNT them!

Observing without preconceptions

The trouble with Bacon's ideal of trying to view events in the world without making any assumptions is that we very rarely can. Whenever, as adults, we come across new events we wish to explain, it is inevitable that we bring to bear on the situation ideas we have gathered, perhaps only roughly, incompletely and unscientifically, through our experience in the world so far, a point made strongly in modern psychology by social constructionists and qualitative researchers. For example, if we lie on the beach looking at the night sky and see a 'star' moving steadily, we know it's a satellite, but only because we have a lot of received astronomical knowledge, from our culture, in our heads thanks to the work of astronomers through the ages. However, there are always alternative theories possible. One Ancient Greek explanation of the night sky, which I am rather partial to, was that it was a great dome-like cover littered with tiny pinholes that let in the sunlight from outside. Without prior knowledge, the theory of the pin-pricked cover and the theory that we are looking at stars and planets are equally acceptable.

We constantly use our knowledge of people in order to explain and predict what they are doing. We are all prejudiced in the sense that we pre-judge. We have a limited amount of information, not enough to guarantee that we are right. In Jerome Bruner's words, one constantly 'goes beyond the information given' (1973: 224) in perceiving and understanding the world.

What do you assume as you read this?

A sudden crash brought me running to the kitchen. The accused was crouched in front of me, eyes wide and fearful. Her hands were red and sticky. A knife lay on the floor …

[continued at the foot of next page]

The example above shows that we can quite differently interpret a scene depending upon the background information we are provided with. Asked to observe a three year old in a nursery, students will often report something like: 'She was nervous. She was insecure.' This is understandable since we are adult humans who are used to going beyond the directly available information and assuming a state that usually accompanies the signs. However, all we can actually observe are the *signs* and people asked *only* to record observable behaviour actually have to be trained to do just this and avoid making assumptions. We don't actually *see* insecurity, we assume it. What we actually observe are darting eyes, solo play, holding on to adults, and so on. We superimpose on this what psychologists would call a 'schema' – a developed notion of what insecurity is and what counts as 'evidence' for it. We end up with a construction of what we are seeing rather than limiting ourselves to the mere available sensory information. We do this constantly and so easily that we are not usually aware of it happening.

Francis Bacon's model advocated that we should simply observe events and record these as descriptions and measurements. Such pieces of information (e.g. lengths, colours, movements) are known as data (the plural of 'datum'). The idea was that if we organised and compared enough data about observed events, we would eventually perceive some regularities. When such regularities are summarised, they become what are known as 'laws' through the process of *induction*, moving from particular instances to a general rule. These laws are mathematical equations that fully describe and predict the behaviour of matter. For instance, Boyle's law says that the pressure multiplied by the volume of a gas is always equal to the same value (or $P \times V = C$). Don't worry!

Psychology has not developed anything like this kind of universal mathematical generalisation … although attempts have been made.

The idea that we should observe behaviour without a background theory was a position advocated by the radical behaviourist B. F. Skinner who felt (in the 1930s) that psychology was too young for grand theories and that the psychological researcher should simply draw up tables of the learning behaviour of animals under various schedules of reward and punishment. The trouble with this approach is that it is much more like practical technology than theoretical science. It tells us, should we ever need to know, just what would be the most efficient way to train a rat to run round a maze and press a lever. It tells us that if we reward a rat *on average* every 20 bar presses we will get a very hard-working rat. It does *not* tell us *how* the rat learns and it certainly tells us little about the complex psychological processes that motivate humans at work. We also end up with mountains of data that *confirm* a 'law' of behaviour but we never know if the law is universal. That is, we don't know if the law is valid for all situations as is the case in physics (well, usually). If we want to test the application of the rat-learning law, we have to think of ways to extend it. We might consider what would happen if we rewarded the rat, not for a number of presses, but simply for the first press made after an interval of 30 seconds. The trouble now with the pure empirical method is that we are in fact working from a background *theory*, otherwise how would we decide what is worth testing? We wouldn't, for instance, think it likely that taping a Suduko puzzle to the ceiling would have much effect on the rat's behaviour.

Asking *why*? Generating theories for laws

A major problem with the pure empirical method is that humans find it hard to just record observations. They inevitably ask '*why* does this occur?' and in fact were probably asking that before they started observing. We do not calmly and neutrally observe. We question as we watch. We learn that individuals will give apparently life-threatening electric shocks to someone they think is another participant and who is screaming out that they have a heart complaint, simply because a 'scientist' orders them to do so. It is impossible to hear of this without, at the same instant, wanting to know why they would do this. Could it be because the scientist is seen as an authority? Could it be that research participants just know that a respectable scientist wouldn't permit harm to another experimental volunteer? Could it be the scientist's white coat that emphasises authority? Some of these ideas are harder to test than others.

Theory, hypothesis, research question and prediction

Suppose a psychologist sets out to test the idea, mentioned earlier, that heat is a cause of aggression. This is a THEORY stated in a very general way. It requires evidence to support it and this will come from the derivation of a HYPOTHESIS (or several) that we can then test. For instance, if heat is a major cause of aggression, then it should be the case that violent crimes are more numerous in

Answer is . . .

. . . so did a jam jar and its contents. The accused was about to lick her tiny fingers.

the hotter months of the year. We can hypothesise that more violent crimes occur in the Summer or we can ask 'Are there more aggressive acts in hotter months than in colder ones?'. This query is a RESEARCH QUESTION. From the question or the hypothesis we can proceed to formulate a precise RESEARCH PREDICTION for a research investigation. This will refer to the specific context in which the researchers are going to conduct their investigation. Suppose they are going to count the numbers of reported physical fights in the playground at Gradgrind Upper School (GUS). The research prediction might be:

More physical fights will be recorded in the GUS playground incidents book during the months of June and July than during the months of December and January.

Notice that this is now a prediction in measurable terms. We have provided aggression with an *operational definition* – a term which will be explained in Chapter 2. For now just note that we do not say 'There will be more aggression at Gradgrind during the Summer' because this is quite imprecise. We state what we will count as a (limited) measure of aggression.

The operationalised prediction follows from the hypothesis that aggressive acts are more numerous in warmer months. In order to properly understand significance testing (see Chapter 14), it is essential that this difference between a hypothesis and the specific test of it – the research prediction – be carefully distinguished. There is less of a clear divide between hypothesis and theory. A hypothesis is a generalised claim about the world. One might propose, for instance, that caffeine shortens reaction times in a simple task or that concrete words are recalled more easily than abstract words. A hypothesis is usually a proposed fact about the world that follows logically from a broader background theory. However, it is as equally acceptable to say 'my theory is that caffeine shortens reaction time' as it is to say 'my hypothesis is that caffeine shortens reaction time' and many *theories* in psychology are called hypotheses, for instance, we have the 'Sapir–Whorf hypothesis' regarding language and thinking, and the 'carpentered world hypothesis' concerned with depth perception, both of which are quite complicated theories.

If we look back to the problem of your brother's rash earlier, we see that the doctor suggested that broccoli was the problem – a hypothesis developed from a more general theory of allergies. The *test* of this hypothesis was to lay off broccoli for a month and the prediction was that the rash would disappear. If it did disappear, the hypothesis was supported.

Having introduced theories, hypotheses and test predictions we can now take a more formal look at the contemporary scientific method as used by psychologists.

The hypothetico-deductive method – testing scientific theories

Mainstream psychological research tends to lean heavily on what has come to be known by the rather cumbersome term HYPOTHETICO-DEDUCTIVE METHOD, the main steps of which are outlined in Box 1.3. Basically it means a method in which theories (general explanations of observed 'laws' or regularities) are evaluated by generating and testing hypotheses. Hypotheses are statements about the world that are derived from more general theories.

Info Box 1.3   The traditional scientific (hypothetico-deductive) method

The scientific method	Example using short- and long-term memory
Observation, gathering and ordering of data	Carry out tests of relatively short-term memory using word lists of varying lengths.
Induction of generalizations or 'laws'	Most people can only recall without error a list of 6 or 7 letters, numbers or words. With longer lists, several items are usually not recalled.
Development of explanatory theories	Suggestion that we have a short-term memory store (STS) and long-term store (LTS) and that list items have to be rehearsed in the ST 'buffer' if they are to be transferred to the LTS.
Deduction of hypothesis to test theory	If this is so, then when a list has just been presented, the last few items should be in the rehearsal buffer and are easier to obtain.
Test hypothesis. Develop research prediction	Have several research participants listen to then attempt to *free recall* (i.e. in any order) all the words in a list. Last 5 or 6 items should be better recalled.
Results of test provide support for or challenge to theory	A recency effect *does* occur; the last few items *are* better recalled. This then supports the ST/LT model.

Note: 'Induction means to move from the particular to the general: having tested enough people we assume that 7 is the average limit for perfect ST memory. Deduction is the process of logical argument that leads from premises to conclusion. For instance, if *there is a black and a brown pencil in a box* and we take out a black one then there must be a brown one still in the box. This MUST be true if the premises of the argument are correct. The 'premise' here is the statement in italics.

As an example of the hypothetico-deductive method, consider the 'social loafing' theory that people working in unfamiliar groups are likely to feel inhibited and, as the group size increases, to feel that their individual effort is less important and less needed. This gives rise to a more specific hypothesis that individuals working in groups put in less effort. If we want to *test* this hypothesis empirically, we can set up a specific experiment where we ask people to pull on a rope either alone or in groups of varying sizes. This was actually done by Ingham, Levinger, Graves and Peckham (1974) where it was *predicted* that the larger the group, the lower would be the average strain readings during the rope-pulling task. These results were confirmed.

Does this then constitute *proof* of the social loafing theory that people work less hard in a group because they are inhibited by feeling less important? Well, no, it doesn't. We said earlier that we do not talk about 'proof' of a theory in psychology or in any science. Why not? The fact is that there is always some alternative explanation of any finding. What else would explain the fact that people pull less hard when in a group? Perhaps it is harder to coordinate your pull when several other people are pulling on it too. Perhaps the other people interfere with concentration. All we can say when our hypothesis is confirmed is that we have *support* for the theory; we have *evidence* for the social loafing explanation.

We can of course run a new experiment where we try to *eliminate* each of these alternative explanations. We could ask participants to pull on a separate rope *each*, telling them that the score will be the combined effort put in by the team as a whole. This way, if group performance is still lower than individual, we can rule out the explanation that loafing is caused by problems of coordination. A very large number of psychological experiments are about attempting to rule out alternative explanations for effects.

What if the effort does *not* drop in a group setting? Does this *disprove* the hypothesis that people work less hard in groups? Well, again, no. Perhaps participants in the experiment guessed what was going on and therefore concentrated on putting in as much effort as they did when working alone. Perhaps they even got to hear about what the experimenter expected and worked against the prediction. In other words, perhaps social loafing really does occur in real-life contexts but the experimental setting fails to produce the effect.

When researchers fail to find an effect,[2] then they look around for reasons why not and then run another study which deals with the possible reasons for the failure. Perhaps not enough caffeine was used in an experiment to demonstrate its effects on memory. Perhaps the rope-pulling task is not hard enough to demonstrate social loafing. On the other hand, when research *fulfils* predictions, researchers may not sit on their laurels and bask in the sunshine of success; there will be other researchers trying to show that the effect does not work or at least that it does not extend very far beyond the context in which it was demonstrated.

Replication

If we run one experiment and get the expected result, it is always possible that this was a fluke, just a statistical quirk. To check this and to guard against fraudulent claims, which do occur from time to time in any science, scientists try to REPLICATE important studies. Science is full of unrepeatable one-off events, about which initially everyone gets very excited. In 1989, Stanley Pons and Martin Fleischmann announced at a press conference that they had observed controlled nuclear fusion in a glass jar. If they had, then this would have provided huge amounts of energy for the world at low cost. Unfortunately their initial findings were never replicated and the discovery of a reliable cold fusion procedure remains a holy grail in physics.

Replication of studies is particularly important in psychology, where claims are made about the extremely varied and flexible behaviour of humans. Because people are so complicated and there are so many of them, and so many different types, we can only make estimates from samples of

---

[2] Psychological research studies usually look for some well-defined and measurable outcome. This will often be a difference between groups or between performances under certain conditions, or it may be some relationship between measures, such as a correlation (see Chapter 17). For ease of explanation, a useful general term for such differences or correlations, which we'll often use from now on, is an 'effect'.

people's behaviour. We cannot test everyone. We have to generalize from small *samples* to whole *populations* – see Chapter 2. For us to be able to be more certain that a demonstrated psychological effect is in fact a real one, we need several psychological researchers to be able to replicate results of studies, just as you would expect me to be able to repeat a stunning snooker shot if you're to be convinced it wasn't a fluke.

In order to replicate, researchers require full details of the original study and it is a strong professional ethic that psychologists communicate their data, procedures and results clearly to one another (see Chapter 23). People are considered charlatans in psychology, as elsewhere, if they claim to demonstrate effects (such as telepathy or exotic forms of psychotherapy) yet will not publish clearly, or at all, the predictions, the methods and the results of their research work so that the research community, and the general public, can check whether outcomes support declared aims. The US psychologist Arthur Jensen, for instance, has long been accused of evading scrutiny of his declared findings in the highly sensitive and controversial area of 'race' differences in intelligence, because he will not provide the raw data from his work on apparent reaction-time differences between members of different 'racial' groups (see Kamin, 1977; 1981; 1995).

Replications do not need to be, and rarely are, an *exact* repeat of the original study. Traditional, scientific method demands replication in order to establish that an effect was not a fluke occurrence. However, this concern about fluke effects tends to be more acute the more controversial or ground-breaking the findings of the original study were. Very often a replication is in effect a slight extension of a demonstrated effect. Replications may vary with the type of people studied, the setting in which the study takes place, the materials used in the study (e.g. a different measurement scale) or the kind of task participants are asked to do.

Disconfirming theories

We have seen that researchers constantly try to challenge findings and to demonstrate the limitations of an effect. Why are scientific researchers such spoilsports? Why are they always trying to show that other researchers are wrong? There are good reasons. Let me explain after this little exercise.

Pause for thought

I am thinking of a rule that generates valid sets of numbers. For instance, if my rule was 'descending odd numbers', then 9, 7, 3 and 7, 3, 1 would fit but 9, 8, 5 would not. Imagine then that I have such a rule in my head and that I tell you that the following sets of numbers fit the rule: 2, 4, 6 and 8, 10, 12.

Suppose that I ask you now to generate more sets of numbers and that I will tell you whether they fit the rule or not. Your task is to do this until you can identify the rule. What would be the next set of numbers you would try?

Chances are that you selected another set of equally spaced ascending numbers such as 14, 16, 18 or 3, 5, 7. Basically did you think of a set of numbers that *would* fit the rule? I ask because really you can't get anywhere unless you find a set of numbers that *don't* fit the rule that you are considering as a possible answer. If you think they go up in twos, then what's the point of asking whether 3, 5 and 7 fit? If they do I'll say 'yes' but you won't know if the rule is 'goes up in twos' or perhaps 'goes up in even amounts' or just 'goes up'. If you want to check out a hunch, then try a set that would *not* fit your hunch. So why not try 1, 3, 7? If *that* fits then you can certainly *reject* 'goes up in twos' and also 'goes up in even amounts'. You then move on to another test that would lead you to reject *another* possibility and so on. If we think the new rule might be 'goes up', then we might try 3, 2, 1 and so on. My rule was, in fact, 'goes up'.

What does this little exercise tell us? Simply this – if we have a scientific 'law' and we keep running investigations that supply yet more *supportive* evidence, then we don't get to know its limitations. If we want to learn more about the causes behind a phenomenon it is fruitful to try to find where it does *not* work. As an example we might note that Gabrenya, Wang and Latané (1985) found that the *opposite* of social loafing occurred in experiments with Chinese children. Whereas US children counting tone patterns were less successful in pairs than when working alone, the Chinese children did *better* in pairs than when alone. Finding this disconfirmation of the social loafing hypothesis enabled researchers to broaden the original theory so that the effect of 'social striving' became included and was more evident where the participants' society was 'collectivist' in nature, that is, it was a society stressing group loyalty and duty rather than the I-go-first nature of many Western societies which are labelled 'individualist'.

Popper (1959) went so far as to say that most scientific investigation is about or should be about the attempted falsification of theories. That is, we find out whether theories are robust by trying to show them to be wrong. We don't have to succeed. It's just that more powerful evidence is provided by falsifying a theory than by continually showing it to be sound. It is a bit like having a law that 'all swans are white' and laboriously adding to our observations that confirm the law each time we spot another white swan. It would be a lot more productive to go looking for a black swan because that will move us on swiftly to reject the original law which cannot now be true (unless someone is being cruel to swans with creosote).

Very many scientific and psychological studies are designed to *challenge* a hypothesis in order to rule it out or at least to show its limits. In the example of the broccoli proposal for your brother's rash, if the rash doesn't disappear after the removal of broccoli test, then we have established that it isn't the broccoli (alone) that is causing the rash. In the case of the cross-cultural disconfirmation of the social loafing effect we have, through failure of the original effect to appear, moved on to a broader, more complex understanding of when people loaf and when they don't. In fact, the findings in collectivist societies corresponded with further studies in the West which showed that if people were in cohesive groups (Karau and Hart, 1998) or even if they had just a few minutes' normal social interaction before performing the group task (Holt, 1987, cited in Brown, 1988), social loafing did not occur and it began to appear that loafing mainly occurred in rarefied experimental groups where individuals had never met or interacted before.

Falsifiability

We have seen that advances in scientific understanding can be made by eliminating alternative explanations for effects. We saw above that a challenge to a theory is far more useful than repetitively providing confirmations of it. If your television keeps getting interference and you suspect the neighbour's electric mower, then if the mower is switched off and the effect persists, you must surely be wrong. The explanation is eliminated.

Because scientific research is often about eliminating possible explanations it follows that these explanations, or theories, must be put forward in terms where we can try to do the crucial test which will eliminate them. Theories, according to Popper (1959), must be phrased in terms that make them FALSIFIABLE. If it is not possible to find a way in which a theory *could* be falsified then it is not a theory fit for science. This does not mean that the theory *must* be falsified, only that we can do tests that *would* falsify it *if* it is indeed false.

Psychoanalytic theory often comes under attack for being unfalsifiable and explaining away any contrary findings in further terms of the theory rather than accepting that the theory cannot explain those findings. For instance, Ernest Jones (1931) analysed the game of chess in psychoanalytic terms, arguing that it was shot through with sexual symbolism and that the grim, underlying, but of course unconscious, motivation for playing the game is the castration of the king, who symbolises the player's father. The intense and rational concentration of the game is in fact a camouflage for seething passions in the resolution of the Oedipus complex! Adjusting one's pawns is apparently evidence of a suppressed desire to masturbate. When Jones presented these explanations to professional chess players, they were shocked, not surprisingly. However, Jones explained that their aggressive reaction to the theory was just more evidence *for* it; Jones argued that the players, rather than genuinely finding his views completely off the wall, were actually demonstrating a 'reaction formation', a kind of over-reaction that gives away our game, as when a child protests its innocence of chocolate stealing so loudly that it is clear that it is indeed guilty. So, angry chess players reacting to Jones' 'explanations' of their behaviour are in fact unconsciously defending against their unacceptable and sexually charged motives for playing!

This explanation by Jones preserves the theory against seemingly contradictory evidence by using the theory to explain the reaction. This way the theory could never be seriously challenged since any attempt to refute it would itself be evidence for the theory. It has been argued that women, according to 'penis envy' theory, should desire their babies to be boys since they are substitutes for their original and unacceptable desire – their father. Evidence for this prediction was provided by Hammer (1970). Suppose, however, that a majority of women were now found to prefer a female baby, a position that was moderately supported by Pooler (1991). This would be easy to explain away as the women suffering embarrassment at the exposure of their sordid secret and therefore as the women using reaction formation to say the opposite of what their unconscious mind 'really' desires. With this sort of explanation, *any* 'evidence', desiring boy babies or desiring girl babies, is taken as support for the theory. So Popper argued that for any theory to count as a theory, we must at least be able to see how it could be falsified. Popper argued that what distinguishes scientific method is:

[its] manner of exposing to falsification, in every conceivable way, the system to be tested. Its aim is not to save the lives of untenable systems but, on the contrary, to select the one which is by comparison the fittest, by exposing them all to the fiercest struggle for survival (1959: 42).

We don't 'prove theories true' – we stay with the ones that have produced the best explanations of the data, and that have so far survived all attacks relatively successfully. Usually at least two, if not several, theories co-exist and are in conflict with one another. Proponents of theory A try to support it with evidence and at the same time try to demonstrate holes in theory B. At the same time opponents of theory A are trying to falsify it and so the theory A proponents will also be trying to reconcile their theory with conflicting findings. In this way a sort of 'survival of the fittest' occurs, with theories falling by the wayside as they have to cope with more and more ill-fitting data and other theories surviving as the best explanation so far.

How psychologists actually do scientific research

The general public could be forgiven for believing that science is all about making dramatic discoveries and breakthroughs. This is indeed often the image projected by the media and by enthusiastic science teachers at school. However, the everyday world of the scientific researcher is much more mundane and tends to plod along largely according to the direction of flow depicted in Figure 1.3. Although it is easy to think about a single project beginning and ending at specific points of time, the reality of research is more like a constant cycle of events.

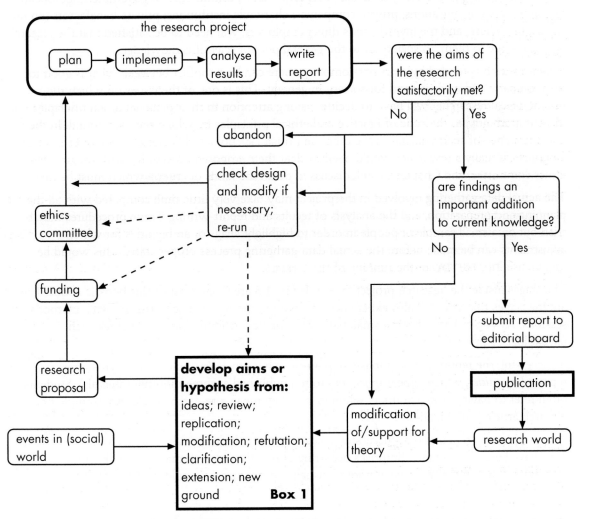

Figure 1.3 The research cycle – start at Box 1

A project can be developed from a combination of the current trends in research theory and methods, from attempts to challenge competing theories, as explained earlier, or, in the case of psychology, from important events in the everyday social world. The investigator might wish to replicate a study by someone else in order to verify it. Typically, they will want to repeat the study but try to demonstrate the limits of an effect as we saw earlier in the case of social loafing. Or they might wish to extend the findings to other areas, or to modify the study because it has design weaknesses. Every now and again, an investigation breaks completely new ground (as did Latané's studies on bystander helping after the murder of Kitty Genovese in 1964 which prompted public outcry at New Yorkers' apparent apathy), but the vast majority of scientific investigations develop out of the current state of play.

Politics and economics enter at the stage of funding. Research staff, in universities, colleges or hospitals, have to justify their salaries and the expense of the project. Funds will usually come from one of the following: university or hospital research funds; central or local government; European Union research organisations; private companies; charitable institutions; private benefactors (on rare occasions). These, and the investigator's direct employers, will need to be satisfied that the research is worthwhile to them, to society or to the general pool of scientific knowledge.

When research is funded by a private company, there can be a conflict between what is good for that company and what is good for society in general. This is one of the issues on which the psychological researcher will have to decide, paying attention to their personal moral principles but, more importantly, to the code of practice and ethical principles by which they are bound. In the UK, the source of such principles would be the British Psychological Society's Code of Ethics and Conduct.[3] Usually a researcher would need to clear their proposed procedures with the university's ethics committee, and Chapter 23 will discuss in detail the kinds of criteria which must be met.

The actual data gathering involved in the project may take very little time compared with all the planning and preparation, and the analysis of results and report-writing. Some procedures may be tried out on a small sample of people in order to highlight snags or ambiguities for which adjustments can be made before the actual data-gathering process proper starts. This would be known as a PILOT STUDY, or the running of PILOT TRIALS.

The stages inside the 'research project' box in Figure 1.3 are what most of this book is about. These are the stages that you will also experience on your psychology course in the 'research methods' sessions. As you can see, this is a small part of the process from the professional research psychologist's point of view.

If successful, the report will be published in a research journal. Psychology research studies are reported in *articles*, which appear in *journals* (often published at three-monthly intervals). Students often refer to having read a 'journal' when in fact they mean a research article. An example of a research article is provided on p. 641.

What is difficult to define is a 'successful' research project. It doesn't always mean that the original aims have been entirely met. Surprises occurring during the research may well make it more important than it might have been, though usually such surprises would lead the investigator to

---

[3] Available at: www.bps.org.uk/the-society/code-of-conduct/code-of-conduct_home.cfm

re-think, re-plan and run again on the basis of the new insights. As we saw earlier, *failure* to confirm a hypothesis can be an important source of information. What matters overall is that the research results are an important or useful contribution to current knowledge and theory development, and that the project is accurately and professionally written up (see Chapter 24). The importance and worth of the project will be decided by the editorial board of an academic journal (such as *The British Journal of Psychology*), which will have the report reviewed, usually by experts (known as 'referees') who should not be aware of the identity of the investigator. Articles subject to such 'peer review' carry more credibility and prestige than those that are not.

Whether or not the research findings are published, they will probably have some small effect on the development of theory, if only as an indication that a promising line of investigation has proved fruitless. If findings are challenging to an existing theory or line of investigation, then some academics may argue that the design was so different from previous research that its inconsistency with their own work can be ignored. Others will wish to query the results and may ask the investigator to provide RAW DATA (all the original results, individual participants' scores on tests, and so on). Some will want to replicate the study, some to modify ... and here we are, back where we started on the research cycle.

What are the main features of a psychological investigation?

This is a huge question and basically an introduction to the rest of this book! Although researchers differ in their views on the appropriate investigative methods for human psychology, there are three central ways to gather information about people. You either ask them, observe them or meddle. By 'meddling', I mean perform some sort of intervention, very often a simple experiment. These three approaches are covered in Chapters 7 and 8, Chapter 6 and Chapter 3 respectively.

Planning research

To get us started, and to allow me to introduce the rest of this book, let's look at the key decision areas facing anyone about to conduct some research. I have identified these in Figure 1.4 and the lack of order for these four areas is intended to emphasise that each aspect is dependent upon the others. When asked to create their own independent investigation, students often say 'Well, I want to use a questionnaire.' Their tutor's initial response should be 'But why? You haven't decided on your research question yet!' The question you pose will to some extent determine the design you have to employ and this design in turn will dictate the kinds of data you can gather and how. You can't ask your tutor 'How many participants will I need?' if you haven't already worked out what design you are going to employ. You can't *know* that you need questionnaires if you haven't already decided what you want to find out.

In Figure 1.4, the four boxes represent the following questions.

- Design – HOW shall we test our hypothesis or answer our research question?
- Variables – WHAT shall we measure? (What human characteristics or behaviour under what conditions?)
- Samples – WHOM shall we study?
- Analysis – WHAT sort of evidence will we get, in what form?

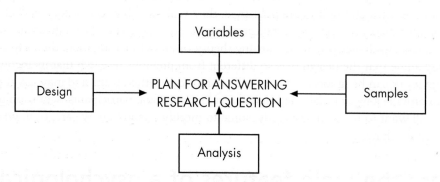

Figure 1.4 Key decision areas in a research project

Before looking at these a little more closely, think again about the method(s) you thought of for testing the hypothesis that heat makes people more aggressive.

Variables

Variables are tricky things. They are the things that alter, and whose changes we can measure, so that we can make comparisons, such as 'Are you tidier than I am?' Heat is a variable in our study. How shall we define and control it? How shall we make sure that it isn't humidity, rather than temperature, that is responsible for any aggression?

The real problem, though, is how to measure 'aggression'. Physical things are always relatively easy to measure. The history of psychology has a lot to do with the attempt to create techniques to measure human behaviour and psychological characteristics. We could devise some sort of questionnaire – more technically known as a psychometric scale of measurement (the construction of these is dealt with in Chapter 8). We could instead observe people's behaviour at work and record the numbers of arguments, or the amount of swearing or shouting. We could ask participants to punch a stuffed pad and record the force. We could even consult school or police records and note numbers of violent incidents. Each of these would be a measure of 'aggression'. The important thing is that we must be clear in our communications with other researchers about *how* exactly we measured our variables. We cannot say 'memory was tested'. We must instead say something like 'participants were asked to recall a 20-word list and the number of items recalled correctly within two minutes was used as a measure of memory task performance'. This clear definition is essential if others wish to replicate our study.

The difficulty of defining variables, stating exactly what it is we mean by a term and how, if at all, we intend to measure it, seemed to me to be so primary that this is tackled in the chapter immediately following this introductory one.

Samples

These are the people we are going to study or work with (but sometimes we sample materials, such as personal ads, rather than people directly). We could conduct a FIELD STUDY (i.e. work outside the laboratory studying people in a real-life setting) and make observations on office workers on hot and cool days. However, could we be sure that builders or nurses would behave in the same way? If we select a sample for our laboratory experiment, what factors shall we take into account in trying to make the group representative of most people in general? Is this possible? These are issues of 'sampling' and are also dealt with in Chapter 2. An important, primary principle to remember is this: in psychological research studies we are usually not specifically interested in the sample that we study (though for some qualitative research studies this *is* the focus). We study a sample because we cannot study the entire population and we assume that the sample is a small representation of the sorts of humans in general that we are interested in (perhaps all of them). This is an obvious point when you consider research in, say, biology where a sample of one species of fly would be studied in order to make generalisations about all flies in that species. However, in psychology classes students often lose sight of this principle. You should always keep in mind (in most quantitative work at least) the problems involved in generalising from the people you have studied in particular to the entire human race – one must learn to be humble in science! As we shall see later (in Chapter 9), a large proportion of psychological research has been conducted only on students, most of these in the United States.

One word on terminology here. It used to be common to refer to the people studied in psychological research, especially in experiments, as 'subjects'. There are objections to this, particularly from those who argue that a false model of the human being is generated by referring to (and possibly treating) research participants in this distant, coolly scientific manner, as if they were laboratory rats. The British Psychological Society now requires all publications to use the term 'research participants' or simply 'participants'. On the grounds of courtesy and gratitude to people who volunteer to participate in psychological research, the terminology used about them should reflect the relationship between researcher and researched as a human *interaction* rather than as a set of procedures carried out on a passive 'subject'. The term is still common, however, in several US journals and in those with a more traditionally hard, 'scientific' background (e.g. *Biopsychology*).

I have used the term 'participant' throughout this book but, in the interests of clarity, I have stuck with the term 'between subjects' in the section on ANOVA calculations in Chapters 18–21 in order not to confuse readers checking my text with others on a difficult statistical topic. The term is used generically in the statistical world and would often refer to mice or even leaves!

Design

The design is the overall structure and strategy of the research study. Decisions on measuring irritability may determine whether we conduct a laboratory study or field research. If we want realistic aggression we might wish to measure it in the field (for example, the office setting) on hot and cold days. If we think we need a carefully controlled environment, we can use the psychology laboratory. We could ask participants to carry out a frustrating task – for instance, balancing pencils on a slightly moving surface – then administer an 'aggression' questionnaire. We could test participants under hot and cold conditions ensuring that exactly the same temperatures were used in each case. In addition, we could control for humidity by making this the same in both hot and cold conditions. Experiments such as this can be run in various ways, each a different design. Shall we have the same group of people perform the frustrating task under the two temperature conditions? If so, mightn't they be getting practice at the task that will make changes in their performance harder to interpret? Perhaps we should use two different samples of people, one in each condition, but then will the groups be equivalent? These are all issues of research design. Experimental designs, in particular, are dealt with in Chapter 3. In Chapter 4 we shall discuss what is and what is not an experiment.

Resources

The nature of the design is determined not just by technical considerations but also by matters of funding and available resources. The researcher may not have the funding, staff or time to carry out a long-term study where this might otherwise be considered most desirable. The most appropriate technical equipment may be just too expensive. Resources may not stretch to testing in different cultures. A study in the natural setting – say, in a hospital – may be too time-consuming or ruled out by lack of permission. The laboratory may just have to do.

Nature of research aim

If the researcher wishes to study the effects of maternal deprivation on a 3-year-old child then certain designs are ruled out. We cannot experiment by artificially depriving children of their mothers (I hope you agree!) and we cannot question a 3 year old in any great depth. We may be left with the best option of simply observing the child's behaviour, although some researchers have turned to experiments on animals in lieu of humans.

Previous research

If we intend to replicate an earlier study, we may need its original design and method. An extension of the study may require the same design, because an extra group is to be added, or it may require use of a different design that complements the first. We may wish to demonstrate that a laboratory-discovered effect can be reproduced in a natural setting, for instance.

The researcher's attitude to scientific investigation

There can be hostile debates between psychologists from different research backgrounds. Some swear by the strictly controlled laboratory setting, seeking to emulate the 'hard' physical sciences in their isolation and precise measurement of variables. Others prefer the more realistic field setting, while there is a growing body of researchers who favour qualitative methods – see Chapters 10 and 22

Analysis

The decisions made about design and measurement will have a direct effect on the statistical or other analysis that is possible at the end of data collection. It is pointless to steam ahead with a particular design and procedure, gather a set of statistical data then find that these data are difficult if not impossible to analyse. This tells us that the design and measures were not well thought out. Usually you should consider the statistical analysis *while* you are designing the study. As a very simple example, if you are interested in people's attitudes to the use of physical punishment and you ask the question 'Do you agree with hitting children as punishment?', you will get no information about the *strength* of people's opinion. You have asked a question that can only be responded to with 'yes' or 'no'. You could instead ask people to express their attitude to hitting on a scale from one to ten. Though this is a very crude measure, you can at least then talk of the *average* strength for two different groups of people rather than just the number of yes and no responses.

There is a principle relating to computer programming that goes 'garbage in – garbage out'. It applies here too. If a questionnaire contains items like 'How do you feel about hitting children?', what is to be done with the largely unquantifiable results? We can't statistically analyse people's reports of their feelings. On the other hand, if we are conducting a qualitative study (see below) and are specifically interested in people's feelings about physical punishment, then it is no use asking a series of questions such as 'Do you agree with hitting children?' since this type of question requires just a 'yes' or 'no' answer. In quantitative studies it is important to think about the analysis when designing the study and its measures, or else it might be difficult to use appropriate statistical methods to draw conclusions from the data. In qualitative studies data gathering and analysis go hand in hand and it is usually necessary to decide on the analytic method before even starting to gather data. Thoughts of the analysis should not stifle creativity, but it is important to keep it central to the planning.

Statistics

Having broached the subject of statistics, it's time to start assuring the mathematically timid that statistics is a lot easier than you think it is, at least to the level you require in basic psychology courses. If you are like the majority of psychology students you will be saying to yourself 'But I'm useless at statistics', 'I don't have a mathematical brain' or similar. It is interesting how most people would be ashamed to admit they were illiterate (if they were) yet being 'non-mathematical' or just being 'bad with numbers' can almost be worn as a badge of honour. Most people *do* have a 'mathematical brain', it's just that possessing mathematical skills just doesn't seem very relevant to many people and then when these skills *are* needed it is perhaps a little late. The good news anyway is that you really should not find yourself working out long, complicated calculations with forbidding formulae (they are provided in this book but you need not fully understand them). We live in an age where the bit that most people hate about maths and numbers is done by slaves (better known as computers). Most tutors thankfully do not believe in getting you to do hard calculations 'because they're good for you'. For now though let's just have a light-hearted discussion of why we need statistics, why we need to know how to use them properly and why they are not so terrifying.

Why do we need statistics at all? Well, we need evidence for our theories and a lot of this is best provided in numerical form. You would not want, for instance, to be treated by a surgeon with a 95% failure rate. You'd want to know the odds of survival and what proportion of patients make a full and healthy recovery. These are all statistics.

Info Box 1.4   Statistics in the news

Shock! Horror! 25% of maths teachers to retire in next ten years!

The media often bamboozle us with statistics and your psychology course should at least help you to be more alert to their tricks in the future. As an example a newspaper claimed with alarm, as part of a 'big worry' article on the shortage of maths teachers, that 25% of maths teachers would retire in the next 10 years. A moment's thought tells us that this is true of just about any profession. You work for around 40 years, often less. Hence in any 10-year period about a quarter of that profession would retire. This is an example of big numbers seeming important. We had an earlier example with the rope around the Earth. Try this spoof headline too:

Millions of Brits have more than the average number of fingers!

Very few people have one extra finger but quite a lot more have lost one through some kind of accident. Hence the *mean* average number of fingers per person must be 9.999 something and therefore millions have more than the average! The problem here is that the wrong kind of average has been selected. If we took the mode (see Chapter 11) then we would get the figure of 10 that we are used to. That is what *most* people have. This is a very simple lesson demonstrating that we need to know how to use statistics appropriately if we are not to produce misleading or meaningless 'results'.

It is my firm belief that you can understand what statistics do, what they are telling you and what you shouldn't try to claim with them, without needing to understand fully the theory of statistics and without being able to do calculations from bewildering algebraic formulae. I think it is rather like knowing what a car can do, knowing how to maintain it and what not to do to it, without knowing in technological detail how the engine works. Of course you will need to cope with very simple and basic numerical procedures, such as the calculation of the mean, which is a kind of average. However, you probably already know about the mean either from school (it is taught at around age 10 these days) or from working out that if three children ate six fish fingers between them then each child had two on average, even though the greedy one, in fact, had four.

The point is that you need to understand *not* what complicated formulae mean but what kind of statistic analysis you should use, how to arrange your data, how to ask a computer to analyse them for you and, especially, how to make sense of the analysis you receive. What you don't want to do is to make silly statements with statistics, use inadequate data or use the wrong tests. Here is another example of a very poor interpretation of data used in a popular publication.

In 1996, the *Reader's Digest* published data showing that of ten wallets, each containing £30 and 'lost' (deliberately dropped) in major cities, eight were returned from Glasgow but only four from Cardiff. On this basis the magazine claimed that 'residents of Glasgow … emerged as Britain's most honest citizens', whereas 'people in Cardiff showed a disappointing tendency to take the money' (reported in *The Guardian*, 17 June 1996).

The leap here from tiny samples of ten people to grand universal claims about the entire populations of Cardiff and Glasgow is of course silly and quite irresponsible of the journalists, who have great influence over public opinion. Your experience of statistics on your psychology course should at least heighten your sensitivity to tricks like these which are used constantly by the media and politicians to falsely present as 'fact' what is only a poorly supported opinion. Statistics only ever support a claim, they do not prove it true. An Indian cricketer once joked that 'statistics are like mini-skirts: what they reveal is exciting but what they conceal is vital'.

Statistics are a useful tool in the investigation of similarities and differences between the behaviour of individuals and groups in different circumstances. They are not something that psychology students should be made to suffer. You should think of them only as a means to obtaining a clear, objective and fair conclusion about the area of psychological research in which you are interested.

Qualitative data and qualitative approaches

You might be pleased to hear that not all data gathered in psychological research studies are numerical. There has been a particular growth over the past 20 years or so in what are called QUALITATIVE APPROACHES which gather QUALITATIVE DATA. As we shall see later on, in Chapters 2, 10 and 22, many researchers in psychology and the social sciences reject the application of the conventional methods of the physical sciences as being inappropriate for work with people and society. It may be all right, they argue, to investigate the expansion of metal, plant growth or chemical reactions using precise measuring equipment and laboratory experiments, but human behaviour is not susceptible to precision measurement, nor is this appropriate. Human experience, being reflective and not passive, is never going to be summarised by neat, mathematically expressed laws. Giving someone a score for a personality characteristic, they would argue, is a travesty of the general concept of personality. Instead, personality can be studied by gathering meaningful verbal information from people which gives a richer, fuller description of the phenomenon of interest. Qualitative data can be text-based or pictorial. Very often they are the contents of interviews or they are an observer's notes.

One last word (for now) on the nature of scientific research

Throughout the book, and in any practical work, can I suggest that the reader keep the following words from Robert Pirsig's *Zen and the Art of Motorcycle Maintenance* in mind?

The real purpose of the scientific method is to make sure nature hasn't misled you into thinking you know something you actually don't know. (1999: 108)

Answer to problem on p. 3

The circumference of the Earth is $2\pi r$ where r is the radius of the Earth. If the rope were 1 m. above the earth all the way round then the new radius would be $r + 1$ m. and the new circumference would be $2\pi (r + 1)$ m. which is $2\pi r + 2\pi$ m. This is just 2π m. more than the original Earth circumference. π is approximately 3.14 so the increase in rope required is 6.28 metres.

Glossary

Note: at the end of each chapter in this book there is a glossary of definitions for terms introduced (unless these are more fully defined in a subsequent chapter). Sub-sets are grouped, as with 'samples' on p. 55.

Analysis	Investigation of data for patterns or evidence of an effect
Data	Relatively uninterpreted information
Deduction	Logical argument using rules to derive a conclusion from premises
Design	Structure and strategy of a piece of research
Effect	A difference or correlation between samples leading to an assumed relationship between variables in the population
Empirical method	Scientific method of gathering information and summarising it in the hope of identifying general patterns
Falsifiability	Principle that theories must be defined in a way that makes it possible to show they are wrong
Field experiment/study	Research study where data are gathered from participants outside the research centre
Hypothesis	Precise statement of assumed relationship between variables
Hypothesis-testing	Research that analyses data for a predicted effect
Hypothetico-deductive method	Method of recording observations, developing explanatory theories and testing predictions from those theories
Induction	Process of moving from particular instances to a generalised pattern
Participant	Person who takes part in a psychological investigation as a member of a sample or individual case
Pilot study/trials; piloting	Preliminary study or trials often carried out to predict snags and assess features of a main study to follow
Population	Whole group or category of people from among whom samples are selected
Qualitative data	Data left in their original forms of meaning (e.g. speech, text) and not quantified
Quantitative data	Data in numerical form, the results of measurement

Raw data	Unprocessed data as gathered in a study
Replication	Repeating a completed study
Research prediction	Prediction in precise terms about how variables should be related in the analysis of data if a hypothesis is to be supported
Research question	The question a researcher is trying to answer in an investigation
Scientific method	General method of investigation using induction and deduction
Variable	Quantity that can change; usually used to refer to a measure of phenomena

Measuring people –
variables, samples and the qualitative critique

2

This chapter is an introduction to the language and concepts of measurement in social science.

- *Variables* are identified events that change in value when measured.
- Many explanatory concepts in psychology are unobservable directly but are treated as *hypothetical* constructs, as in other sciences.
- Under the conventional research paradigm (the 'scientific model'), variables to be measured need precise *operational definitions* (the steps taken to measure the phenomenon) so that researchers can communicate effectively about their findings.
- The concepts of *reliability* of measures (consistency) and of *validity* (whether the instrument measures what is intended) are briefly introduced.

The second part of this chapter looks at how people are selected for study in psychological research. The issues arising are as follows.

- Samples should be representative of the populations to which results may be generalised.
- Equal probability selection provides representative samples if they are large enough.
- Various non-random selection techniques (quota sampling, snowball sampling, critical cases, focus groups, panels) aim to provide representative, or at least useful, small samples. Opportunity and self-selecting samples may well be unacceptably biased.
- Size of samples for experiments is a subject of much debate; large is not always best.
- The concepts of effect size (size of found difference) and statistical power (likelihood of conclusively demonstrating an effect if one exists) are briefly introduced.

The qualitative–quantitative dimension is introduced as a fundamental division within the theory of methods in contemporary psychological research, with a general critique of positivism. The dimension will be referred to throughout as research varies in the extent to which it employs aspects of either approach. Some researchers see the two approaches as complementary rather than conflicting.

Variables

A variable is anything that varies. This is rather a circular definition, I know, but it gets us started. We could also say that variables are observable events which can change and whose changes can be measured in some way. Let's list some things that vary:

1 *Height* – this varies as you grow older and it varies between individuals.

2 *Time* – could be time in seconds to respond with 'yes' or 'no' to questions or to solve a set of anagrams.

3 *The political party people vote for* – note that differences between parties are *qualitative* and cannot be represented by numbers.

4 *Feelings towards your partner or parent* – seems these would be hard to measure but they do change.

5 *Extroversion* – we can measure this using a psychological scale; we get a 'score' for extroversion.

6 *Attitude towards vandals* – we can use an attitude scale as a measure.

7 *Anxiety* – again we can use a psychological scale.

Notice that all of these can vary:

- within yourself from one time to another
- between different individuals in society.

The essence of studying anything (birds, geology, emotion) is the observation of changes in variables. If nothing changed, there would be nothing to observe. The essence of scientific research is to relate these changes in variables to changes in other variables. A first step in this process is to find some way to quantify variables; to find a way to measure changes in them.

Measuring variables

A measure of a variable can take several, perhaps many, values across a range. The value is often numerical but not necessarily so. In example 3 above, the different values of the variable are party names. Variables such as these are known as *categorical variables* because each value of the variable is a discrete and qualitatively separate category. We can say which party a person votes for, but this doesn't measure their political attitude along a scale. Similarly, we can ask people whether they are single/married/cohabiting/divorced/separated, but we can't say 'how married' they are by indicating a number from a scale. Variables like height, time and the number of siblings you have are known as *measured variables* because we can use a number to indicate where along a scale a person lies on this variable. One of the major tasks in attempting to assess psychological variables is often the move from categorical variable (e.g. like/don't like or calm/anxious) to measured variable (degree of liking, how anxious). We will discuss categorical and measured variables further in Chapter 11.

For example 4 we haven't yet decided how we could assess 'feelings'. Some variables are easy to measure and we are familiar with the type of measuring instrument required. Height is one of these and time another, though the equipment required to measure 'reaction times' (as in example 2) can be quite sophisticated, because of the very brief intervals involved.

Some variables are familiar in concept but measuring them numerically seems a very difficult, strange or impossible thing to do, as in the case of extroversion, attitude, anxiety or feelings. However, although people often like to think that they don't, or even can't, make psychological measurements of people, some crude measurement at least is implied in statements such as 'He is very strongly opposed to smoking' or 'She didn't seem particularly averse to the idea of living in Manchester'. If he is strongly opposed, then presumably he is ranked a bit higher than someone who is 'just a bit' opposed. Likewise, there must be people towards whom your feelings are stronger than towards others. Of course you can't *just* put a number on feelings – their qualitative differences are their most important aspect – but you can in some sense talk about *degree*.

In psychology, if we are to work with variables such as attitude and anxiety we must be able to specify them precisely, partly because we want to be accurate in the measurement of their change, and partly because we wish to communicate with others about our findings. If we wish to be taken seriously in our work it must be possible for others to replicate our findings using the same measurement procedures as we used to obtain our findings.

The next section is an introduction to debate among psychologists as to how exactly we can measure, or at least somehow assess, such psychological variables as 'attitude' and 'anxiety'. We can start by asking, just what are these variables?

Defining psychological variables

Pause for thought

First, try to write down your own definition of:

1 intelligence
2 anxiety
3 superstition.

Perhaps that was difficult. Now, give some examples of people displaying these characteristics.

You probably found the definitions quite hard, especially the first. Why is it that we have such difficulty defining terms we use every day with good understanding? You must have used these terms very many times in your communications with others, saying, for instance:

- I think Jenny has a lot of intelligence

- Bob gets anxious whenever a dog comes near him

- Are people today less superstitious than they were?

Psychological constructs

In the exercise above, though finding definitions may have been difficult, I hope you found it relatively easier to give examples of people being intelligent, anxious or superstitious. Chapter 1 argued that information about people must come, somehow, from what they say or do. When we are young, we are little psychologists. We build up a concept of 'intelligence' or 'anxiety' from learning what are signs or manifestations of it. In the case of anxiety this might be: biting lips, shaking hand, tremulous voice in the case of anxiety.

Notice that we learn that certain things are done 'intelligently': getting sums right, doing them quickly, finishing a jigsaw. People who do these things consistently get called 'intelligent' (the adverb has become an adjective). It is one step now to statements like 'she has a lot of intelligence' where we find a noun instead of an adjective. It is easy to think of intelligence as having some thing-like quality, of existing independently, because we can use it as a noun.

The Greek philosopher Plato ran into this sort of trouble, asking questions like 'What is justice?' The problem partly occurs because, in English at least, we can ask the question 'What is X?' It might be better to ask 'What is it to be X?' or even 'What is it to act in an X-like way?' We could ask 'What is it to be intelligent?' or 'What is it to act intelligently?' The tendency to treat an abstract concept as if it had independent existence is known as REIFICATION. Some (e.g. Ryle, 1949) have argued that it is the noun-ridden nature of English that leads us up the garden path looking for things that are just reifications; consider the difference between 'I had that on my mind' or 'In my mind I thought so', compared with 'I was thinking'. The first two statements imply a place, a store, a thing; the last statement is like the phrase 'I was sleeping'. Thinking is something we do. Because, in English, we can do it 'in our mind' does not mean that there is this extra thing that does our thinking for us or a physical place where our thinking goes on.

Some psychologists (especially the behaviourist Skinner, who took an extreme empiricist position) would argue that observable events (like biting lips), and, for anxiety, directly measurable internal ones (like increased heart rate or adrenalin secretion), are *all* there is to anxiety. Anxiety just is all these events. No more. They would say that we don't need to assume extra concepts over and above these things that we can observe and measure. To assume the existence of internal structures or processes, such as anxiety or 'attitude', is seen as 'mentalistic', unobjective and unscientific. This approach of course makes it relatively easy to measure 'anxiety' – we simply count the number of lip-bitings and measure heart rate.

Other psychologists argue that there is more; anxiety is *dispositional* – that is, each person has an internal tendency to behave more or less anxiously in a somewhat predictable pattern. They would argue that the concept is useful in theory development, even if they are unable to trap and measure it in accurate detail. They behave, in fact, like the 'hard' scientists in physics. No physicist has ever directly seen an atom or a quark. This isn't physically possible. (It may be logically impossible ever to 'see' intelligence, but that's another matter). What physicists do is assume that atoms and quarks exist, and then work out how much of known physical evidence is explained by them. Quarks are HYPOTHETICAL CONSTRUCTS. They will survive as part of an overall theory so long as the amount they explain is a good deal more than the amount they fail to explain or which they contradict.

In a tentative way, psychologists treat concepts like intelligence, anxiety or attitude as hypothetical constructs too. They are assumed to exist as factors that explain observable behaviour. If, after research that attempts both to support and refute the existence of the constructs, these explanations remain feasible, then the constructs can remain as theoretical entities. A state of anxiety is assumed from observation of a person's sweating, stuttering and shaking, but we don't see 'anxiety' as such. Anxiety is, then, a hypothetical construct – a reference to an inner state that is assumed to play its part among all the effects on human behaviour.

Organisation of constructs

A psychological construct can be linked to others in an explanatory framework from which further predictions are possible and testable. We might, for instance, argue that people who are low in self-esteem might develop a need to feel better than some other people. This need might be directed towards members of minority ethnic groups since anti-minority prejudice is quite common and may be encouraged among prejudiced peers. We would now hypothesise that self-esteem is linked to hostility towards minority ethnic group members and we could objectively measure hostility by using a psychological scale or, better still, since people can attempt to 'look good' on questionnaires, we could observe directly but discreetly any discriminatory behaviour. We cannot observe low self-esteem directly, though we can use a psychometric scale (see Chapter 8) in an attempt to measure it. However, we might assume from previous research findings that a strict authoritarian upbringing is often related to low self-esteem. 'Authoritarian upbringing' can be assessed relatively easily and openly by observation of parental style and through interview. We might then look for a relationship: do people who have experienced authoritarian rearing tend to exhibit discriminatory behaviour towards members of minority groups? This possible relationship between observable behaviour and hypothetical constructs (self-esteem, superiority need and attitude) is illustrated in Figure 2.1.

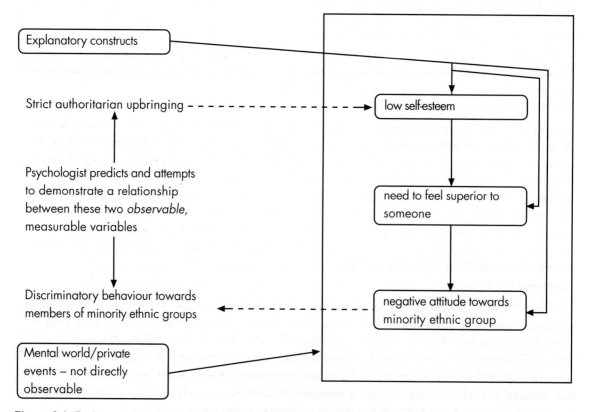

Figure 2.1 Explanatory framework for hypothesised link between strict upbringing and discriminatory behaviour

Operational definitions of psychological constructs

If psychologists are to use hypothetical constructs in their research work and theorising, they must obviously be very careful indeed in explaining how these are to be treated as variables. Psychologists, along with other scientists, recognise that there is a difference between a construct and our measurement of that construct. The 'variables' that we use in psychological research are observable measures of often unobservable constructs. The extent to which our measure actually coincides with the construct is referred to as *construct validity* and is discussed further in Chapter 4. To achieve validity, our measurements must at least be precise. Even for the more easily measurable constructs, such as short-term memory capacity, definitions must be clear. One particular difficulty for psychologists is that a large number of terms for variables they might wish to research already exist in everyday English, with wide variation in possible meaning.

Pause for thought

Discuss with a colleague, or think about, the terms shown below. How could any of these be measured?

Identity	Attention	Reinforcement	Egocentric	Attitude
Neurotic	Instinct	Conformity	Unconscious	Conscience

In search of objectivity, scientists conducting research attempt to 'operationalise' their constructs. An OPERATIONAL DEFINITION of construct X gives us the set of activities required to measure X. It is like a set of instructions. For instance, in physics, pressure is precisely defined as force per unit area. To measure pressure we have to find out the weight impinging on an area and divide by that area. When it comes to measuring humans, things can get a little trickier. Even in measuring a person's height, if we want to agree with others' measurements, we will need to specify conditions such as what to take as the top of the head and how the person should stand. Our definition of height might be 'distance from floor to crown in bare feet and with crown directly above spine'. In general, though, height and time present us with no deep problem since the units of measurement are already clearly and universally defined.

Many definitions in psychological research are made specifically and only for a particular investigative setting. In a particular piece of memory research we might define short-term memory capacity as 'the longest list of digits on which the participant has perfect recall in more than 80% of trials'. Here, on each trial, the participant has to try to recall the digit string presented in the order it was given. Several trials would occur with strings from three to, say, twelve digits in length. At the end of this, it is relatively simple to calculate our measure of short-term memory capacity according to our operational definition.

If a researcher had measured the 'controlling' behaviour of mothers with their children, he or she would have to provide the coding scheme (see Chapter 6) given to assistants for making recordings during observation. This might include categories of 'physical restraint', 'verbal warning', 'verbal demand', and so on, with detailed examples given to observers during training. The coding scheme becomes the operational definition of controlling behaviour.

Psychologists often need some measure of general intelligence but they know that 'intelligence' is too broad a concept to be pinned down by a relatively short test. They state instead that, *for the purposes of their specific investigation*, the test they use will be their operational definition of intelligence. Intelligence then becomes 'that which is measured by this particular intelligence test'. Since intelligence tests differ, we obviously do not have in psychology the universal agreement about measures enjoyed by physicists. It might be argued that physicists have many ways to measure pressure but they know what pressure is. Likewise, can't psychologists have several ways to measure intelligence? Well, in physics there is a gold standard definition for constructs like pressure or viscosity and psychologists are just not in the same position. In psychology there is no agreed standard for intelligence, but several competing measures and many tests which measure only one *aspect* of intelligence. The appropriate measure for intelligence is still the subject of vigorous debate. (See factor analysis on p. 190.)

An operational definition gives us a more or less valid method for measuring some part of a hypothetical construct. It rarely covers the whole of what is usually understood by that construct. It is hard to imagine an operational definition that could express the rich and diverse meaning of 'human intelligence'. For any particular piece of research, though, we must state exactly what we are counting as a measure of the construct we are interested in. As an example, consider a project carried out by some students who placed a ladder against a wall and observed men and women walking round or under it. For this research, 'superstitious behaviour' was (narrowly) operationalised as the avoidance of walking under the ladder.

Pause for thought

First have a look at some sloppy definitions where, if confronted with them, you would have to go back to the author of them and ask 'Yes, but how exactly did you measure that?'

'.......*aggression* will be higher in the hot room condition'.

'.......the trained group will have better *memories*'.

'.......males will be more *sexist* in their attitudes'.

'.......participants will think they are more *intelligent* than their parents'.

The golden rule to follow when writing your own definitions is 'From your description could a naïve reader make the exact measurements that you did?'.

Pause for thought

Imagine you are about to start testing the hypotheses stated below. In each case, try to provide operationalised definitions for the (italicised) variables involved. If it helps, ask yourself 'What will count as (aggression) in this study? How exactly will it be measured?' Think carefully, and then state the exact procedure you would use to carry out the measurement of the variables;

1 *Physically punished* children are more *aggressive*.

2 *Memory deterioration* can be the result of *stress* at work.

3 *Language development* is promoted in infants by parents who provide a lot of *visual and auditory stimulation*.

4 People are more likely to *comply* with a request from a person they *trust*.

5 People told an infant is male are more likely to *describe the infant according to the popular male stereotype* than will those told it is female.

Here are some ideas.

1 *Physical punishment*: number of times parent reports striking per week; questionnaire to parents on attitudes to physical punishment.

Aggression: number of times child initiates rough-and-tumble behaviour observed in playground at school; number of requests for violence-related toys in letters to Father Christmas.

2 *Stress*: occupations defined as more stressful the more sickness, heart attacks, etc. reported within them; there are also many questionnaire measures of stress.

Memory: could be defined as we did for short-term memory capacity, above, or participants could keep a diary of forgetful incidents. 'Deterioration' implies a comparison of at least two measures taken at different times.

3 *Language development (stage of)*: length of child's utterances, size of vocabulary, etc.

Stimulation: number of times parent initiates sensory play, among other things, during home observation.

4 *Compliance*: if target person agrees to researcher's request for change in street.

Trust: might be defined in terms of dress, role and associated status; in one condition, researcher dresses smartly with doctor's bag; in the other, with scruffy clothes. Alternatively, we could ask participants to assess trustworthiness on a scale after the request has been made.

5 *Stereotype response*: number of times participant, in describing the infant, uses terms coming from a list developed by asking a panel of the general public which infant features were typically masculine and which typically feminine.

Reliability and validity

If measures have reliability and validity, then other researchers will treat them with credibility. Without reliable and valid assessments the normal business of research cannot be conducted. If measures are unreliable or invalid, then researchers will find that other findings will conflict with their own. The problem is more acute for psychologists since there is far less agreement among them than among other scientists about the measurement of constructs, or even on what constructs are at all relevant or meaningful to the subject area. A good example of the real dangers involved when researchers use concepts that are not objectively agreed by others is that of so-called 'slow schizophrenia', which was a condition only ever 'observed' by psychiatrists in the former Soviet Union. The only patients who displayed symptoms were dissidents opposed to the existing political system. In addition, the only psychiatrists who observed these symptoms were those trained by just one senior psychiatrist, and the only places of observation were certain clinics under the jurisdiction of the KGB (the government's then security service) (Joravsky, 1989).

Nowadays you can buy a plastic strip that can be placed on a baby's forehead and used to measure temperature. This is a great improvement on attempting to keep a glass thermometer under a wriggling armpit or in even more uncomfortable places! However, the first thing you'd want to check, before laying out money on this new measuring instrument, is whether it truly measures temperature and not, say, perspiration level. In addition, you would not be best pleased if, as you watched the colour of the strip, it kept changing between one shade and the next even though you knew that the baby's temperature could not be oscillating by so much in so little time.

In the first instance, you would be querying the instrument's VALIDITY – Does the instrument measure what it is intended to measure? If the reading kept changing you would be querying the instrument's RELIABILITY – Is it consistent? Does it produce the same readings in the same circumstances? Both reliability and validity will be discussed in some detail in Chapter 8, where they are applied in particular to psychological tests and scales. However, the next few chapters are about overall methods in psychological research and, at times, we will need to refer to the general meaning of these terms, and a few others.

1 *Reliability*: any measure we use in life should be reliable, otherwise it's useless. You wouldn't want your car speedometer to give you different readings for the same actual speed on different occasions. This applies to psychological measures as much as any other. Hence, questionnaires should produce the same results when re-tested on the same people at different times (so long as nothing significant has happened to them); different observers counting aggressive acts made by children should come up with similar tallies; ratings of the intensity of sexual imagery in dream reports should be similar across different judges.

2 *Validity*: in addition to being consistent, we should also be able to have confidence that our measuring device is measuring what it's supposed to measure. You wouldn't want your speedometer to be recording oil pressure or your thermometer to be measuring humidity. In psychology this issue is of absolutely crucial importance since it is often difficult to agree on what a construct 'really is', and things in psychology are not as touchable or 'get-at-able' as things in physics or chemistry. Hence, validity is the issue of whether psychological measures really do make some assessment of the phenomenon under study. A psychological scale may

measure a construct it was not intended to measure or it may measure nothing much at all of interest. A questionnaire intended to measure assertiveness, for instance, may in fact measure something more akin to selfishness. A scale intended to measure 'animism' in dreams, and which counts the number of cats and dogs you report, may simply do that and nothing more! In Chapter 4 we will look more closely at this issue of construct validity along with other forms of validity which are concerned with whether the effect we apparently demonstrated in a research study is in fact a genuine one – the issue of *experimental validity* in general.

Exercises

I Match the following definitions to the construct they operationally define:

Constructs	Definitions
1 Conformity	(a) Number of words correctly recalled
2 Sex-appropriate play	(b) Distance travelled by ruler after experimenter releases it and participant has to catch it (converted to seconds using object acceleration formula).
3 Memory	(c) Difference between participant's estimate of beans in a jar and that 'given by an expert'
4 Reaction time	(d) Number of times child is observed playing with toy associated with its own sex
5 Anxiety	(e) Difference in scores produced when rating oneself as how one is and how one would like to be
6 Self-esteem	(f) Number of fear-related incidents in a participant's story

2 What could be an operational definition of: 'noise', 'span of attention', 'smile', 'frustration', in the following loosely worded hypotheses?

(a) Noise affects efficiency of work

(b) Span of attention varies with the time of day

(c) Smiles given tend to produce smiles in return

(d) Aggression can be the result of frustration

3 A friend says 'My cat hates Beethoven. Every time I put on a symphony she rushes out of the house.' Would you say this measure of the cat's attitude to Beethoven was reliable, valid, both or neither?

Samples

Suppose you had just come back from the airport with an Indian friend who is to stay with you for a few weeks and she switches on the television. To your horror, one of the worst imaginable game shows is on and you hasten to tell her that this is not typical of British TV fare. Suppose, again, that you are measuring attitudes to trades unions and you decide to use the college canteen to select people to answer your questionnaire. Unknown to you, the men and women you select are mainly people with union positions on a training course for negotiation skills. In both these cases an *unrepresentative sample* has been selected. In each case, our view of what is typical can be distorted.

Populations and samples

One of the main aims of scientific study is to be able to generalise from samples. A psychologist might be interested in establishing some quality of all human behaviour, or in the characteristics of a certain group, such as those with strong self-confidence or those who have experienced pre-school education. In each case the POPULATION is all the existing members of that group, more technically referred to as 'cases', and we shall sometimes make use of this term in the explanations that follow. Think of a biologist who wants to establish the properties of a field of beans treated with a new fertiliser. Since the population itself will normally be too large for each case within it to be investigated, we would normally select a SAMPLE from it. The rationale is that if we take a fair enough sample – one that is *representative* of *all* the beans (see below) – then we may generalise our results from the sample, with a certain degree of caution, to the overall population. A population need not consist of people. For the biologist, it is beans. A psychologist might be measuring participants' reaction times, in which case the population is not the people who could be tested but all the times that could ever be produced. A population could even be made up of all the companies in a certain country that run a crèche for employees' children.

A further technical term, often used in relation to surveys, is the SAMPLING FRAME. This refers to the population from which we will sample, but is often more specific than the vague term 'population'. For instance, if we want to assess students' attitudes towards their university, then the sampling frame from which we will need to select our sample will be the population of students at the university. However, if we want to discover something about the problems faced by single-parent students, then we will have single-parent students as our sampling frame but will need to include those at all kinds of university or college.

The sampling frame in this sense can also be referred to as the TARGET POPULATION. It may be useful, when using these concepts, to keep in mind an image of the political pollster trying to estimate how many people will vote for the party in government. The pollster can't ask tens of millions of voters (in the UK) so he or she takes a sample, quite small, but large enough to give a good estimate of how the whole population will vote. Psychologists conducting traditional research ideally select samples from the population to which they would like to generalise any significant results.

Sampling bias

To make reliable estimates we need our sample to be representative of the population to which we wish to generalise results. The pollster would be silly to ask only people living in the prime minister's own constituency about their voting intentions. If we studied male and female driving behaviour by observing drivers in a town at 11.45 am or 3.30 pm, the sample would contain more drivers than usual who are picking up children from school. Since these are more likely to be women, the sample behaviour would be biased because children have an affect on an adult's driving behaviour. More female than male drivers would have their driving behaviour affected by this factor. This weighting of a sample with an over-representation of one particular category of people is known as SAMPLING BIAS. The sample tested in the college canteen was a biased sample, if we assumed we were sampling the general public's current attitude to trades unions.

Pause for thought

A sampling frame is limited by the method used to contact people. If a researcher wants to sample attitudes from all inhabitants of a town, which of the following methods would produce the least bias and why?

(a) Using the telephone directory

(b) Selecting from all houses

(c) Using the electoral roll

(d) Questioning people on the street

I hope you'll agree that the electoral roll will provide us with the widest, least biased section of the population, though it won't include prisoners, the homeless, new residents or persons in long-term psychiatric care. If we use a relatively unbiased sampling method then we should get numbers of men, women, over-60s, people with diabetes, young professionals, members of all cultural groups, and so on, in proportion to their frequency of occurrence in the town as a whole, so long as the sample is fairly large. Use of the telephone directory has inbuilt bias because it eliminates those who are ex-directory or have no phone at all. The house-selection method eliminates those in residential institutions. The street will not contain people at work, people in hospital and so on.

According to Ora (1965), many experimental studies may be biased simply because the sample used contains volunteers. Ora found that where circumstances did not favour volunteering, those that did volunteer were more likely to be unconventional, neurotic and introverted than non-volunteers and also less likely to be aware of social desirability. This does not quite square with Burns (1974: 162) who found that the typical male volunteer, as compared with non-volunteers and those who did volunteer but only after an incentive, would 'be less positive on what he is as he sees himself; have a more healthy capacity for criticism; be lower on subtle defensiveness; tend more toward ascendance, self-seeking ambitiousness and resourcefulness. The female, in addition to all the above, would also be clever, enthusiastic, imaginative, spontaneous; *less* serious, industrious, conforming; less calm, patient, practical, and strict in her own work and expectations of others; *more* independent, self-reliant, forceful, and foresighted; adventurous, humorous, idealistic, egotistic, and concerned with personal pleasure.

In fact, to call many US participants 'volunteers' is somewhat misleading. In US psychology departments the student is often required to participate in a certain number of research projects as part of the departmental 'subject pool' (see Sieber, 1999); the 'volunteering' only concerns which particular projects they choose. Until the mid-1970s at least, it would also be the case that a vast majority of these US students would be white and male.

Banyard and Hunt (2000) investigated the use of students in research published in two major UK journals through 1995 and 1996. They found that only 31 studies (29.0%) used a sample of non-student adults, although six (5.6%) of these studies also used students as part of the sample. In a few of these cases the adults were faculty staff within the university. Of the 18,635 people who made up the samples for the two journals, 44% were undergraduates, 23% were other students, and only 29% were non-student adults.

Does it matter that individuals are not all the same?

It does matter, of course. In fact, this is at the heart of the study of psychology.

Pause for thought

Suppose that we are investigating the effect of noise distraction on memory. We set up an experiment in which one group of participants does a memory task in silence while another group does the same task while a lot of distracting noise is played. Suppose the participants in the noisy condition perform worse than the silent condition participants. Could this difference be caused by anything *other than* the noise distraction?

I hope that one of your possible explanations was that the silent group might just happen to have better memories. This would have occurred by chance when the people were allocated to the respective conditions, but it is an important sampling bias. If so, the study would be said to be 'confounded' (see p. 60) by PARTICIPANT VARIABLES. These are variations between persons acting as participants, and which are relevant to the study at hand – see p. 67. Researchers have to try to make sure, when they conduct this kind of study, that they have *equivalent groups* in each condition. – see p. 67.

In the kind of experiment described above then, the researcher needs 'an average bunch of people' in each condition and we are not specifically interested in the psychological characteristics of the participants; we only make sure that they do not contain any unusual characteristics which might contaminate our experiment. In an experiment on normal memory processes we do not want individuals with special 'photographic memories'. In a study of the effects of colour on perception we do not want people who are colour blind. We are only interested in whether a certain variable has an effect on the normal processes of memory or perception.

In other areas of psychological research, though, the variable under investigation is not one which affects human behaviour in general but one which varies *between* people. Often, the differences between people are precisely what the study is focused on. We might for instance be interested in whether high self-esteem is a factor in job success. We would then want to measure people for self-esteem and then relate this measure somehow to a measure of job success such as level of promotion or customer approval (see the section on 'Group difference studies', p. 110).

Representative samples

If we are investigating differences between categories or groups of people (e.g. between computer owners and non-owners, nurses and doctors, or eight and twelve-year-old children) we need samples REPRESENTATIVE of the populations from which they are drawn (e.g. all computer owners). If we want a small sample of nurses that will tell us fairly accurately what nurses in general think about the status and rewards of their job, then we need the sample to reflect the range of characteristics in the nurse population at large. We do not want, for instance, too many higher-paid nurses or too many mental health nurses. We want a mini-representation of the population of nurses, that is, a good *cross-section*.

If we do select too many highly paid nurses, we will have a sample bias. How do we ensure that the individuals we select will not introduce sampling bias? The simple truth is that a truly representative sample is an abstract ideal probably unachievable in practice. The practical goal we can set ourselves is to remove as much sampling bias as possible. We need to ensure that no particular sub-groups of the members of the target population are under- or over-represented.

Equal probability selection and random sampling

What we need, then, is a sample that is as likely to contain one person as the next. Put more formally, we have the definition of what is known as an EQUAL PROBABILITY SELECTION METHOD (known for short as 'epsem'):

An equal probability selection method is a procedure for producing a sample into which every case in the target population has an equal probability of being selected.

There are several ways of getting as close as possible to this ideal and all of these involve some form of random selection.

The meaning of random

Random is not simply haphazard. The strict meaning of random sequencing is that no event is ever predictable from any of the preceding sequence. Haphazard human choices may have some underlying pattern of which we are unaware. This is not true for the butterfly. Evolution has led it to make an endlessly random sequence of turns in flight (unless injured), which makes prediction impossible for any of its much more powerful predators.

Pause for thought

Which of the following procedures do you think would produce a group of people who would form a random sample?

(a) Picking anybody off the street to answer a questionnaire

(Target population: the general public)

(b) Selecting every fifth home in a street

(Target population: the street)

(c) Selecting every tenth name on the school register

(Target population: the school)

(d) Sticking a pin in a list of names

(Target population: the names on the list)

(e) Selecting well-shuffled slips from a hat containing the names of all Wobbly College students and asking those selected to answer your questionnaire on sexual behaviour

(Target population: Wobbly College students)

The answer is that none of these methods involves pure random selection. In item (a) we may avoid people we don't like the look of, or they may avoid us. In (d) we are less likely to stick our pin at the top or bottom of the paper. In (e) the initial selection *is* random but our sample will not contain those who refuse to take part or who are absent on the day. In items (b) and (c) the definition clearly isn't satisfied. However, in these cases we can, with a little tweak, produce an equal probability sample by using the method of *systematic sampling* described below.

Very few psychological research projects have ever drawn a truly random sample (or 'simple random sample', as described below) from a large population. Common methods are advertising in the local press, using leaflets in clinics, sports centres, etc. as appropriate to the research topic or using personal contacts; by far the most common method is to use students. A very common line in student practical reports is 'a random sample was selected'. This has never been true in my experience, unless the target population was limited to the course year or college and, even then, random selection has been extremely rare.

What students (and other researchers) can reasonably do is to attempt to obtain as unbiased a sample as possible, or to make the sample fairly representative by selecting individuals from important sub-categories (some younger, some older, and so on) as is described under 'stratified sampling', below. Either way, it is very important to discuss this issue when interpreting results and evaluating one's research, otherwise what seems like a general effect could be just the result of careless sampling.

Probability-based sampling methods

The simple random sample

In a SIMPLE RANDOM SAMPLE every case in the target population has an equal chance of selection and so does every possible *combination* of cases. If we require a simple random sample of 20 employees of Wizzo Fireworks in Neasden then we must take all employees' names and use one of the first three methods described in Box 2.1.

The systematic random sample

In a SYSTEMATIC RANDOM SAMPLE we select every n^{th} case from the population, where n is any number (e.g. every fifth person). However, to satisfy the epsem definition, before we start selection, every case must have an equal chance of being in our sample. This was not so in items (b) and (c) of the exercise above. To make those methods use equal probability sampling we select our starting point at random. If we are going to select every tenth case, then we choose at random a number between one and ten; let's say this is seven. We then select the 7th case, the 17th, the 27th and so on. This way, at the start, every individual did have an equal probability of being selected, but every combination of individuals did not, since only ten possible combinations could have been drawn.

Info Box 2.1 | **Random sampling and random ordering**

Selecting a simple random sample

1. Computer selection

The computer can generate an endless string of random numbers. These are numbers that have absolutely no relationship to each other as a sequence and are selected with equal frequency. Given a population of names the computer would use these to select a random set of the required size.

2. Random number tables

Alternatively, we can use the computer to generate a set of random numbers that we record and use to do any selecting ourselves. Such a table appears in the Appendix as Table 1. Starting anywhere in the table and moving either vertically or horizontally, a random sequence of numbers is produced. To select five people at random from a group of 50, give everyone a number from 1 to 50 and enter the table by moving through it vertically or horizontally. Select the people who hold the first five numbers that occur as you move through the table.

3. Manual selection

The numbered balls in a bingo session or the numbers on a roulette wheel are selected randomly, as are raffle tickets drawn from a barrel or hat; so long as they are all well shuffled, the selector can't see the papers and these are all folded so as not to feel any different from one another. You can select a sample of 20 from the college population this way, but you'd need a large box rather than the 'hat' so popular in answers to questions on random selection! Technically, the box should be shuffled each time a single name is drawn.

Other random procedures

Random allocation to experimental groups

In writing up reports it is possible to confuse the distinction between random *sampling* and random *allocation*. The former means selecting cases entirely at random from a population of cases and, as mentioned, this is very difficult to achieve, if it is possible at all. However, if you have obtained 40 participants it is a very easy task to RANDOMLY ALLOCATE these to the conditions of your experiment; if there are two conditions you would select 20 from 40 using tables as described above. This can also be done by tossing a coin for the first participant, to decide in which condition they should participate, and alternating all successive allocations. A slightly messier approach would be to toss a coin for each participant, leaving the possible problem that the last few participants will have to be allocated to one condition that represents the side of the coin that has turned up less frequently.

Random trial ordering and sequencing of stimulus materials

We may wish to put 20 words in a memory list into random order. To do this, give each word a random number as described before. Then put the random numbers into numerical order, keeping the word with each one. The words will now be randomly ordered. If we wanted to test the speed to classify items in an experiment where the words in one set are animals and the others are plants, this procedure would neatly RANDOMISE the individual items into a single list in which it was now not possible to guess which trial was coming next: animal or plant. This prevents participants guessing what the next response should be.

Stratified sampling

If we are taking a relatively small sample from a large population whose characteristics we know, we can ensure good representation in the sample while still using an epsem method. Suppose you wanted a representative sample of students; you might decide to take business studies students, art students, social science and science students in proportion to their numbers. If 24% of the college population comprises art students, then 24% of your sample will be students *selected randomly* from the arts faculty.

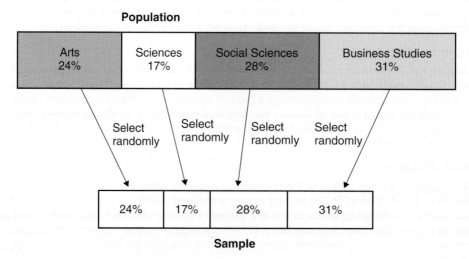

Figure 2.2 Proportions in faculties for a stratified sample

The sub-sections (i.e. strata) of the population we identify as relevant will vary according to the particular research we are conducting. If, for instance, we are researching the subject of attitudes to unemployment, we would want to ensure proportional representation of employed and unemployed, while on abortion we might wish to represent various religions. If the research has a local focus, then the local, not national, proportions would be relevant. In practice, with small-scale research and limited samples, only a few relevant strata can be accommodated. In any case, the strata used must be exhaustive – that is, they must comprise the entire population. We must use, say, x% doctors, y% nursing staff, and z% other staff, where x + y + z = 100. We cannot call our sample stratified if one stratum (e.g. administration staff) has been left out completely. If we sample randomly from the various strata we have identified, then we are using an epsem method. Every individual has the same chance of being selected as they would have if all staff names were shuffled in a box.

Cluster samples

An alternative to stratified sampling that is often more convenient and economical is to select 'clusters' that represent sub-categories. For instance, in a university, instead of obtaining a list of all geography students and then selecting a sample from this stratum at random, the researcher might instead simply select randomly one of the classes – this would be a single cluster and its random selection again serves to make the selection process an epsem method, so long as all classes are roughly the same size. This reduces the need to spend time and effort obtaining a sample of geography students who may be spread throughout the student population. The method is of course open to the criticism that each cluster may not be as representative of the whole sub-group as another.

Non-probability-based sampling methods (non-epsem)

Quota sampling

This method has been popular among market research companies and opinion pollsters. As with stratified sampling, it consists of obtaining people from categories, in proportion to their occurrence in the general population, but with the selection from each category being left entirely to the devices of the interviewer, who would be unlikely to use pure random methods. Interviewers would simply stop asking 18–21-year-old males, for instance, when the quota for this category had been reached. Quota sampling may not always identify an exhaustive set of categories. It can also tend to include only those respondents within each category who are easier to contact or to approach.

The self-selecting sample

I mentioned earlier some students who placed a ladder against a wall and observed how many men and women passed under or around it. In this investigation the sample could not be selected by the researchers. They had to rely on observing those people that happened along the street at that time who are, then, a SELF-SELECTING SAMPLE. Volunteers for an experiment are also self-selecting.

Research Methods and Statistics in **Psychology**

The opportunity or convenience sample (or haphazard samples)

We have seen that much research is carried out on students. These participants are simply the most convenient ones available. A large lecture is an opportunity to test a lot of people at once. For these reasons such samples are often designated as non-random by calling them OPPORTUNITY or CONVENIENCE SAMPLES. The samples available in a natural experiment (see Chapter 5) are also opportunistic in nature. If there is a chance to study children about to undergo an educational innovation, the researcher who takes it has no control over who goes into the sample.

A special kind of opportunity sample is the HAPHAZARD SAMPLE. This is the kind you select if you go to the library and just pick from whoever is present. The title of the method implies the intention *also* to select without conscious bias, although the claim that you would have asked anyone at all often sounds a bit suspect!

Purposive sampling

Kalton (1983) refers to another category of non-random samples termed PURPOSIVE SAMPLES or EXPERT CHOICE SAMPLES. The selection choice here is made by the researcher on the basis of those who are most representative for the issues involved in the research or who are likely to have appropriate expertise in the matter. Some examples should clarify this point.

Snowball sampling

This refers to a technique often employed in qualitative research (see Chapter 10) where information is required, for instance, from key people in an organisation or from those who have personal or professional experiences of, say, alcoholism. A researcher might select several key people for interview and these people in turn may lead the interviewer to further relevant people who could also be contacted for interview.

Critical cases

A special case may sometimes highlight things that can be related back to most non-special cases. Researchers interested in perceptual learning have studied people who have dramatically gained sight at an advanced age. Children who have been seriously deprived of social contact and stimulation can give us insights into what is critical for normal human development. Case studies are looked at in more detail on pages 142 to 146.

Focus groups and panels

Researchers may bring together a panel of either experts, those with a particular interest in a topic or, in the case of focus groups, simply a selection of people who are fairly representative of the general population. These groups will meet more than once, possibly regularly, in order to provide information, as is described in a little more detail in Chapter 7.

Sample size

One of the most popular items in many students' armoury of prepared responses to the instruction 'Suggest modifications to this research' is 'The researcher should have tested more participants'. If a significant difference has been demonstrated between two groups this is not necessary unless (i) we have good reason to suspect sampling bias, or (ii) we are replicating the study (see Chapter 1). If the research has failed to show a significant difference, we may well suspect our samples of bias, but is it a good idea simply to add a lot more to our tested samples?

The argument for large samples

It is easier to produce a biased sample with small samples. I hope the following example will make this clear. If you were to select five people from a group containing five Catholics, five Muslims, five Hindus and five Buddhists, you'd be more likely to get a religious bias in your sample than if you selected ten people. For instance, if you select only five they could all be Catholics, but with ten this isn't possible. In general, the larger the sample the less likely it is that serious sampling bias will occur so long as the selection method is truly random.

When we turn to significance testing of differences between sets of scores we shall see that larger sample sizes increase the 'power' of statistical tests (see Chapter 15). They make it more likely that we will detect an effect if it exists. Small samples may lead us to conclude that there is no real difference between groups or conditions. Suppose there are somewhat more pro- than anti-abortionists in the country as a whole, the ratio being six to five. A small sampling strategy, producing 12 for and 10 against will not convince anyone that this difference represents a real population difference, but a difference of 360 to 300 might. Although we haven't yet covered probability, I hope that your acquired sense of chance factors would agree with this.

Arguments against large samples

Large samples may obscure a weak design

As we shall see, experimental methods are about control of all variables except the ones under investigation. If we need a very large sample to demonstrate a difference between two experimental procedures, then it could be that our measuring system or manipulation of conditions is faulty and we need to tighten it up, to tease out unwanted variables contributing to a lack of clear difference between scores. We need to investigate some of the 'threats to internal and external validity' described in Chapter 4.

Large samples may obscure participant variables

It may be that an effect works on some people but not others (Figure 2.3); it might work for good readers, say, but not weak readers. Taking a large sample will give us an eventual significant difference between groups (caused only by the good readers) but may cause us to ignore an important difference between people relevant to the effect and that would be worth further investigation.

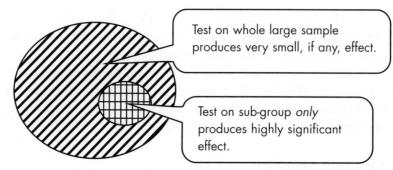

Figure 2.3 Effect works on sub-group who are hidden in larger samples which reduces significance

Large samples are costly and time-consuming

Reasons such as cost should, ideally, never stand in the way of advancing science; however, realistically, it is not always possible to test large samples, and researchers (and psychology students) need to create good designs that don't always require this.

Large samples may produce insignificant differences

Later on, you will learn that you must never use the term 'insignificant' when referring to a difference between samples which fails to reach the criteria for *statistical* significance which we will cover in Chapter 14. Such a difference is said to be 'not significant'. With 'insignificant differences' here, though, I am referring to actual differences between populations that have no real meaning in scientific or psychological terms. If we took all the people in Barnsley whose names begin with 'C' and 'D', we would certainly find some tiny and trivial difference in the mean IQ score of the two populations; there is always some small fluctuation in measurements. A difference here though of, say, 0.03 (when the mean IQ is usually 100) would be meaningless and there would be nothing we would want to do or say about it. With large enough samples (say, thousands), some differences even become statistically significant but are still so small that they provide no useful knowledge.

Power and effect sizes

The issue of whether differences are meaningful or not has a lot to do with the issue of statistical power and effect size. These terms will be dealt with technically in Chapter 15 but, for now, let's just note that these are of central importance when students ask 'How many participants should I test in my study?' Power is the likelihood that you will demonstrate an effect if there is really one there, given the measures, sample sizes and statistical analysis you are using. Effect size is the actual difference you find but is often an estimate of the theoretical difference in the population as a whole, e.g. the average difference in short-term memory size between 8- and 11-year-olds.

Introducing the quantitative/qualitative debate

Up to this point we have largely concentrated on the traditional approach to scientific research in psychology, in which the hypothetico-deductive method entails the topics of this chapter: strict variable definition, measurement and control, along with structured sampling. The approach, largely taken up by psychologists in the early part of the twentieth century, assumes that accurate observation and data analysis will lead us towards the development of 'laws' that account for all relationships between variables. These laws can be validated by making consistently accurate predictions about further variables. A fundamental principle underlying the approach is to assert that the only meaningful phenomena that can be studied scientifically are those that can be directly observed and measured quantitatively – a central principle of the philosophy of POSITIVISM. This philosophy of science, particularly in behaviourism (e.g. Skinner, 1953), dominated psychological research in the middle of the twentieth century and through to the mid-1970s. Around that time, however, and partly triggered by changes in the philosophy of research in sociology, by the expansion of applied psychology into several new areas (e.g. health, disability), and powerfully by feminist psychologists, strong objections were raised against the use of the experimental method in psychological research. There was a more general objection to the emphasis on quantification of any psychological phenomenon in order to give it research credibility. To many researchers, this gave psychology a pseudo-scientific image but worked against the true understanding of people as people rather than scientific 'subjects'.

Prior to this, there had been strong voices, but largely in the wilderness. Lippmann (1922), universally credited with coining the term 'stereotype', had this to say about the attempt to measure intelligence:

If ... the impression takes root that these tests really measure intelligence, that they constitute some sort of last judgment on the child's capacity, that they reveal 'scientifically' his predestined ability, then it would be a thousand times better if all the intelligence testers and all their questionnaires were sunk without warning in the Sargasso Sea. (1922: 19)

Here is a point from Bem and Looren de Jong (1997) concerning the hopes of nineteenth-century European philosophers wishing to make hermeneutics (originally a method for making sense of classical texts in a cultural context) the fundamental method for human sciences:

Wilhelm Dilthey (1833–1911) and others dreamt of making hermeneutics into a strong and central methodology of the human sciences. It was their intention to protect these studies against the obtrusive natural sciences and to guarantee their autonomy. The central idea is that human creations such as literary products ... and behaviour cannot be objectified as things disconnected from human subjects; instead they are laden with values and must be understood in the context of their time and cultural setting. (1997: 23)

Quantification and qualitative experience

'Quantification' means to measure on some numerical basis, if only by counting frequency. Whenever we count, we quantify, and putting people into categories is a prelude to counting. Classifying people by astrological sign entails a crude form of quantification; so does giving a grade to an essay.

Qualitative research, by contrast, emphasises meanings, experiences (often verbally described), descriptions and so on. Raw data will be exactly what people have said (in interview or recorded conversations) or a neutral description of what has been observed (with problems raised about whether any observation can truly be 'neutral' or just factual). Qualitative data can later be quantified to some extent but a 'qualitative approach' usually values the data as qualitative.

It is rather like the difference between counting the shapes and colours of a pile of sweets as against feeling them, playing with them, eating them; or measuring the rays in sunsets rather than appreciating them. The difference between each one may be somehow quantifiable but such measurements will not convey the importance and the special impact of some over others.

By strict definition, a measure of a variable can only be quantitative. As the variable changes so different values are recorded. There may only be two values – for instance, male and female as values of gender. A positivist would argue that psychologists can only study measured variables because contrast and comparison can only be achieved where there is change; what changes is a variable and variables must be quantifiable.

The case against this view is eloquently put by Reason and Rowan (1981) in a statement on what they call 'quantophrenia':

> *There is too much measurement going on. Some things which are numerically precise are not true; and some things which are not numerical are true. Orthodox research produces results which are statistically significant but humanly insignificant; in human inquiry it is much better to be deeply interesting than accurately boring.* (1981: xv)

This is a sweeping statement, making it sound as though all research is 'humanly insignificant' if it does not use the methods preferred by the authors. This is not so. Many, possibly boring but accurate, research exercises have told us a lot about perceptual processes, for instance, and about what prompts us to help others. However, the statement would not have been made without an excess of emphasis within mainstream psychological research on the objective measurement and direct observation of every concept, such that important topics not susceptible to this treatment were devalued.

On the topic of 'emotion', for instance, in mainstream textbooks you will find little that relates to our everyday understanding of that term. You will find strange studies in which people are injected with drugs and put with either a happy or angry actor, and studies in which people are given false information about events they are normally oblivious of – such as their heart or breathing rate. These things are quantifiable, as are questionnaire responses, and you will find an emphasis on fear, aggression, 'emotional intelligence' or recognising emotional expressions because important aspects of these concepts are measurable. However, they represent a very narrow window on the full concept of human emotion.

Varying research contexts and ideological positions

In reviewing the wide and increasing volume of relevant literature it appears possible to identify something like a continuum of positions on the value and role of qualitative methods, as described below.

Pure quantitative position

This view rejects qualitative approaches as inherently lacking in objectivity, reliability and validity. It believes that measurement is fundamental to scientific activity and that, without it, concepts and statements are meaningless.

Qualitative data may be quantified

Quantification of qualitative data is not a new procedure (see the section on 'Content analysis' in Chapter 22). Even strict experiments must often start with a qualitative observation (e.g. 'the rat pressed the lever') and quantify it (e.g. by counting bar-pressing frequencies). Many studies involve the rating of interview responses or story-endings on a scale upon which raters have been trained to a good level of agreement. The incorporation of qualitative data into hypothesis testing research was given the title 'little q' research by Kidder and Fine (1987) as compared to 'big Q' bottom-up pure qualitative research described below.

Quantitative findings can be augmented by or developed from qualitative data

In studies like those on bystander intervention/apathy, and especially those by Milgram (1963) on almost incredible patterns of obedience, post-experimental interviews serve to embellish the quantitative findings, adding explanatory meaning to people's otherwise sometimes incomprehensible behaviour. Data from such interviews can help direct new explanatory hypotheses and new research to test them. For instance, in bystander apathy studies, information from post-experimental interviews may prompt us to try new studies where we make the participant bystander more aware of the social value of helping others.

Qualitative and quantitative methods – different horses for different courses

If you're interested in the accuracy of human perception in detecting colour changes, or in our ability to process incoming sensory information at certain rates, then it seems reasonable to conduct highly controlled experimental investigations using a high degree of accurate quantification. If your area is psychology applied to social work practice, awareness changes in ageing or the experience of mourning, you are very likely to find that qualitative methods are appropriate to your work. In contrast to the previously described position, where qualitative work is viewed as important but subsidiary to final quantitative analysis, the studies of Reicher and Emmler (1986) used an initial quantitative survey to identify appropriate groups of adolescents who were then taken through intensive qualitative interviews concerning attitudes towards formal authority. The position generally holds that qualitative or quantitative methods should be used as appropriate to the subject matter and research aims.

Pure (radical) qualitative position – 'Big Q'

There is no one qualitative position and this stance of using only qualitative methods, as a sort of radical dogma as well as a chosen method, is common to several branches of the qualitative movement. Most qualitative approaches are not just a question of methodological choice but are accompanied by an ideological or philosophical position that absolutely rejects positivism and hypothetico-deductive approaches, on theoretically argued grounds, as being damaging to the proper understanding of human action. A major common qualitative theme has been an emphasis on the role of the researcher in constructing knowledge *through* the process of research contrasted with the conventional idea of the researcher discovering already existent 'facts' about human behaviour and experience. Several of these approaches are 'bottom-up' in that they argue that theory should *emerge* from one's data rather than one's analysis being driven by previous theory. You do not search in the data for features you have already decided upon; you allow the theory to develop from the analysis of data. This is quite the opposite of the traditional hypothesis-testing approach.

Relative values of quantitative and qualitative studies

In general, methods that are 'tighter' and more rigorous give rise to more reliable and internally valid data (see Chapter 4), replicable effects and a claim to greater objectivity. This impression of objectivity, though, can be challenged. Quantitative researchers are not without passion and are perfectly capable of letting their favoured theory guide them in picking this rather than set of variables to concentrate upon. Quantitative results are open to the criticism of giving narrow, unrealistic information using measures that trap only a tiny portion of the concept originally under study (see Figure 2.4). Qualitative enquiries, with looser controls and conducted in more natural, everyday circumstances, give richer results and more realistic information. Advocates feel, therefore, that they are more likely to reflect human thought and action in a natural, cultural context. However, they have also had to defend a vigorous argument that qualitative data make replication very difficult and that there are numerous, sometimes conflicting, ways in which qualitative data can be organised and interpreted. A defence against this argument is of course that statistical data can also be variously interpreted and that different studies come up with quite different results, often dependent on the way in which variables have been constructed and operationalised.

Qualitative methods and data   **Quantitative methods and data**

Rich ◄———————————	**Information**	——————————► Narrow
Subjective[1] ◄———————	**Interpretation**	———————► Objective
Realistic, naturalistic[2] ◄———————	**Setting**	————————► Artificial
Loosely or non-structured ◄———————	**Design**	———————► Highly structured
High ◄———————————	**Realism**	——————————► Low[3]
Low ◄———————————	**Reliability**	——————————► High
High ◄———————————	**Reflexivity** (p. 240)	———————► Low/non-existent

1. Many qualitative proponents argue strongly that their methods do *not* necessarily invoke greater subjectivity at all. Numbers can be used subjectively, as when 'trained raters' use a rating scale to 'code' observed behaviour. A descriptive account of an abused person's experience can be written objectively and can be checked with them for accuracy and true reflection. A person's own reasons for objecting to abortion could be counted as more objective data than a number that places them at point five on a zero to 30 abortion attitude scale.
2. Naturalistic studies (those carried out in natural surroundings) may use fully quantified data-gathering procedures. Qualitative studies, however, will almost always tend to be naturalistic, although interviews could be carried out in an 'artificial' university room.
3. But see mundane and experimental realism on p. 118.

Figure 2.4 Variations across research concepts for qualitative and quantitative research

Loosely controlled methods will produce unpredictable amounts and types of information that the researcher has to sift, organise and select for importance, but such methods leave more room for the researcher to manoeuvre in questioning the participants and in deciding what observations are more worthwhile, thus fostering more natural, less stilted human interaction with more realistic results. The price is a potential for greater individual bias but this is accepted by qualitative researchers as an inevitable aspect of human research, which quantitative researchers mostly ignore or disguise. Where quantitative researchers would see it as a problem that looser wider-ranging studies permit little generalisation across different studies, qualitative researchers see it as a strength that their studies produce rich, unique data, perhaps hard to compare with other findings, but more valid in terms of their reflection of reality and less distorted by the requirements of operationalisation and hard scientific measurement.

Chapter 10 will deal with these issues in greater depth and introduce the range of qualitative approaches currently in use. Chapter 22 will attempt to give advice on how to approach the analysis of qualitative data. It cannot hope to span the range that is covered by texts dedicated to qualitative methods (e.g. Willig, 2008; Smith, 2008; Lyons and Coyle, 2007). However, it can tell you what the major decisions are, what the major pitfalls might be and, most important of all, advise you on checking out thoroughly what kinds of approach there are, and what kinds of procedures you might need to use, before setting out to collect your data.

The reason for this brief introduction, then a return to the subject in Chapter 10, is to alert you early on to the issues so that, as you read the early material in this book, you can question it in terms of this debate. In addition, I would not want you surprised by Chapter 10, thinking 'So the earlier material was all a big waste of time then!' In fact, some qualitative points of view and concepts are integrated into the chapters on questioning methods (particularly the work on interviewing), so that you are aware that not all psychological research methods involve rigid quantification and experimentally strict procedures.

Exercises

1 The aim of a particular investigation is to compare the attitudes of low-, middle- and high-income mothers to discipline in child rearing. What factors should be taken into account in selecting two comparable samples (apart from social class)?

2 A psychologist advertises in the university bulletin for students willing to participate in an experiment concerning the effects of alcohol consumption on appetite. For what reasons might the sample gathered not be a random selection of students?

3 A simple random sample of all students in the Humanities faculty at Suffix University could be drawn by which one of these methods?

(a) Selecting all the students within one randomly selected department of the faculty

(b) Grouping all psychology students in the faculty by surname initial (A, B, … Z) and then selecting one person at random from each initial group

(c) Putting the names of all faculty students into a box, shuffling the box and drawing out names without looking.

4 A researcher wishes to survey young people's attitudes to law and order. Interviewers complete questionnaires with sixth formers who volunteer from the schools that agree to be included in the study. Families are also selected at random from the local telephone directory. Young people are also questioned at local clubs. Discuss several ways in which the complete sample for the study may be biased.

5 A psychology tutor carries out an experiment by allocating the front half of her class to an experimental condition. They are taught special techniques for problem solving. The rear half of the class serve as a control group (see p. 62). The experimental group do better. How might a fault in her procedure be to blame for the observed difference rather than the difference in instructions?

Answers

1 Some factors could be: area lived in, number of children, age, level of education, etc.

2 The students taking part will be volunteers; no teetotallers will be included; the sample is biased towards the type of people reading the bulletin or being told about the study by those who do.

3 Only (c) gives all students, and all combinations, an equal chance of selection.

4 The sixth-formers are volunteers. Only schools that agreed to the study can be sampled from. Those who are ex-directory or who only have a mobile phone cannot be included. Those who use the clubs more frequently are more likely to be selected.

5 She has not randomly allocated participants to conditions. Perhaps the front half of the class are more interested – they select the front of the class because they are more committed – and are therefore already better at this kind of problem solving task.

Glossary

Hypothetical construct	Phenomenon or construct assumed to exist, and used to explain observed effects, but as yet unconfirmed; stays as an explanation of effects while evidence supports it
Operational definition	Definition of phenomenon in terms of the precise procedures taken to measure it
Population	All possible members of a category and from which a sample is drawn.
Positivism	Methodological belief that the world's phenomena, including human experience and social behaviour, are reducible to observable facts and the mathematical relationships between them. Includes the belief that the only phenomena relevant to science are those that can be measured
Qualitative approach	Methodological stance gathering qualitative data which usually holds that information about human events and experience, if reduced to numerical form, loses most of its important meaning for research

Qualitative data	Information gathered that is not in numerical form
Quantitative data	Information about a phenomenon in numerical form i.e. counts or measurements
Random number	Number not predictable from those preceding it
Randomise	To put various trials of an experiment into an unbiased sequence, where prediction is impossible
Randomly allocate	To put people into different conditions of an experiment on a random basis
Reification	Tendency to treat abstract concepts as real entities
Reliability	Extent to which findings or measures can be repeated with similar results; consistency of measures
Sample	Group selected from population for an investigation
Biased	Sample in which members of a sub-group of the target population are over- or under-represented
Cluster	Groups in the population selected at random from among other similar groups and assumed to be representative of a population
Convenience/Opportunity	Sample selected because they are easily available for testing
Haphazard	Sample selected from population with no conscious bias (but likely not to be truly random)
Quota	Sample selected, not randomly, but so that specified groups will appear in numbers proportional to their size in the target population
Representative	Type of sample aimed at if results of research are to be generalised
Self-selecting	Sample selected for study on the basis of members' own action in arriving at the sampling point
Simple random	Sample selected in which every member of the target population has an equal chance of being selected and all possible combinations can be drawn
Stratified	Sample selected so that specified sub-groups will appear in numbers proportional to their size in the target population; within each sub-group cases are randomly selected
Systematic (random)	Sample selected by taking every n^{th} case from a list of the target population; 'random' if starting point for n is selected at random
Sampling bias (or selection bias)	Systematic tendency towards over- or under-representation of some categories in a sample
Validity	Extent to which instruments measure what they were intended to measure. Also, extent to which a research effect can be trusted as real or as not 'contaminated' or confounded
Variable	Phenomenon that varies. In psychology usually refers to phenomenon for which an objective measure has been provided

Experiments and experimental designs
in psychology

This chapter introduces the general concept of an experiment and goes on to outline basic uses of this design in psychological research.

- A *true experiment* attempts to isolate cause and effect, and to eliminate alternative explanations of observed relationships between variables.
- In a true experiment an *independent variable* is manipulated and all other salient variables are controlled, including the *random allocation* of participants to conditions. The effect of the independent variable on a carefully observed and measured *dependent variable* is recorded.
- Simple experimental designs introduced in this chapter are: *independent samples*, *repeated measures*, *matched pairs*, *single participant* and *small n*.
- Problems associated with these experimental designs include: *order effects*, *non-equivalent stimuli*, *participant variables*, *non-equivalent groups*, problems with *matching*.
- The experimental designs are compared and contrasted in terms of their inherent strengths and weaknesses.
- Simple two-condition experiments are rare in published psychological research; most experiments are more complex and the concepts of *factors* and *levels* are introduced.

The role of experiments in gathering evidence – demonstrating cause and effect

We have said that research methods are all about fair and efficient ways of gathering evidence to support theories. The experiment is considered one of the most powerful ways of doing this mainly because it eliminates a lot of alternative explanations which can occur with other kinds of evidence. It is more likely than other methods to demonstrate a relatively unambiguous connection between cause and effect and these connections are what science tries to establish. Let's demonstrate the strength of experiments by moving through types of investigation towards the true experiment.

In Chapter 1, we considered possible ways to gather evidence for the proposal that heat causes aggression. Usually psychologists gather data from people directly but they can also gather evidence *indirectly* by looking at various kinds of social statistics. For instance, if heat causes aggression to increase, what kind of statistics would we expect to see for records of violent crime in any particular area as the temperature increases? Well, presumably we would expect to see an *increase* in such crimes as it gets hotter; that is, in warmer weeks and months we would expect to see more physical assaults, bodily harm and so on than in cooler weeks and months.

Pause for thought

Anderson (1987) gathered data on these kinds of violent crime in several large North American cities. Sure enough they found that the hotter the year, the more the violent crime; he also found that the hotter the quarter of the year, the more the violent crime; he even found that the hotter the city, the more violent crime occurred.

Would you say that the evidence just presented is impressive evidence for the hypothesis that heat causes aggression? Can you think of causes, other than heat, that might be responsible for the rises in aggression as evidenced by violent crimes?

Alternative explanations

There are always alternative interpretations of findings. The trouble here is that as heat goes up, so do certain other factors. For instance, the warmer it is, the more people there are out in public places, the longer are the queues for ice cream, the longer are the traffic jams and so on. It may not be heat at all that causes the aggression but one of these other factors – see Figure 3.1. The trouble is that with this kind of *non-experimental design* we can't exclude these other factors as they operate in everyday life.

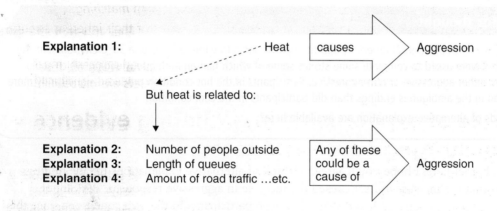

Figure 3.1 Alternative explanations of the heat-aggression link

The point being made here is that we can gather data that *supports* a hypothesis but very often, in studies like these, we cannot rule out *competing explanations*; that is *we cannot confidently point to a clear cause and effect relationship between events and human behaviour* – we can't be at all sure that it is the heat that causes the observed increases in human aggression rather than other variables. As we shall soon see, in a true experiment we can control these other variables.

However, before getting to that point, let's just look at another type of design where more control is involved.

Kenrick and MacFarlane (1986) observed the number of male and female drivers who honked at a car parked (by the researchers) at a green light in Phoenix Arizona while temperatures varied between 88° and 116° Fahrenheit (roughly 31° to 47° Centigrade). There was a direct relationship – horn-honking increased as temperature rose. In fact, this relationship was even stronger when only those who had their windows rolled down were considered, the assumption here being that the discomfort was worse for these drivers since they presumably did not have air conditioners working.

There is more control in this design since the researchers could *observe directly* what the drivers did, they could choose when to park the car and they limited their measure of 'aggression' to one simple and unambiguous piece of behaviour – horn honking. However, they could *not* control the temperature on any particular day and they had no control at all over the people they tested. The people involved in the study had to be just those drivers who happened along on the day – a 'self-selecting' sample. Suppose, by chance, that more aggressive drivers tended to turn up on the hotter days; perhaps less aggressive drivers tend not to go out in the heat. Again we see there are alternative explanations to an apparent causal relationship between heat and aggression. Now have a look at the following study.

Pause for thought

Rule, Taylor and Dobbs (1987) randomly allocated participants to either a 21°C or a 33°C environment. All participants were asked to complete some stories some of which had an ambiguous ending which could have been either aggressive or non-aggressive. Participants in the hot condition produced significantly more aggression in the ambiguous endings than did participants in the cool condition.

What kinds of alternative explanation are available here?

It is much harder here, I hope you'll agree, to think of alternative explanations for the findings other than that the increase in heat caused the increase in aggressive responses. We cannot automatically point to a possible difference between participants in the two conditions since they were allocated to the conditions at random and we saw in Chapter 2 that this should even out any major differences between the two groups. Of course it is *possible* that there is still a difference but it's much more unlikely and we don't have any clear evidence. We could in fact test all participants using an aggression scale and hope to show that there was no significant difference between the two groups before the experiment started, without of course arousing their suspicions over the nature of the experiment.

The stories for each participant are exactly the same so there can't be any difference from these. It is of course possible that the odd story has a special effect on the odd participant which might trigger anger but we are clutching at straws if we make this claim.

I hope you'll agree that the first makes no sense in this experiment, and the second is what the experiment aimed to demonstrate. Two variables are involved in this experiment and one is traditionally known as the INDEPENDENT VARIABLE (or IV), while the other is known as the DEPENDENT VARIABLE (or DV).

Could you decide now which variable (temperature in the room or number of aggressive responses) would be called the *dependent variable*?

The dependent variable is the variable in the experiment whose changes *depend on* the manipulation of the independent variable. Here, then, the number of aggressive responses is the dependent variable and the temperature is the independent variable. The change in numbers of aggressive responses *depends on* the change in temperature – see Figure 3.2. The essential aim of an experiment is to demonstrate an unambiguous 'causal link' between these two variables.

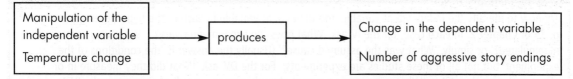

Figure 3.2 The casual link between temperature change (IV) and aggressive responses (DV)

Features of the true experiment; avoiding confounds

In a *true experiment* the researcher:

- manipulates an independent variable

- holds all other variables constant

- measures any change in the dependent variable

The middle point above is crucial and is the heart of scientific experimentation. We saw that in the Rule *et al.* experiment participants were *randomly allocated* to conditions. This was to eliminate any variation between the groups that could be caused by participant variables; there might by accident be more aggressive people in the hot temperature condition. Such a pre-existing difference would CONFOUND our interpretation of the findings. We might conclude that temperature increases aggression when in fact we started off with more aggressive people in the higher temperature condition. Other variables we might hold constant would be the humidity in each room, the amount of noise, the exact instructions given to each group and, of course, the content of the stories they have to respond to. In doing this we try to leave only one variable (the IV) that is changed by the researcher and one other variable (the DV) which changes as a result.

Looking back to the Anderson study, we see that there were changes in temperature but these were not manipulated by the experimenter and many other variables were free to change at the same time thus confounding our interpretation of the related changes in violent crime rates. In the Kenrick and MacFarlane study, the researchers could select the daytime temperatures at which to send out the car but they could not make particular temperatures occur, they could not control a host of other attendant conditions (such as humidity) and they could not control which drivers would form the sample to be tested. They had to use whoever came along and perhaps, as we said, less aggressive drivers avoid the heat. This factor would be a CONFOUNDING VARIABLE.

Asking 'Ah but...'

One of the most valuable habits the psychology student can acquire is always to ask, when presented with a research conclusion (X causes Y) that supports a particular theory, 'Ah, but could some *other* variable have caused Y to change?' This is not being 'negative' or pedantic – it is a vital procedure for checking that we do not accept pseudo-scientific claims and theories. On the positive side, it also stimulates further research leading to clearer knowledge about an area of interest. Simply put, it is the way we can approach truth out of speculation.

Pause for thought

Try now to identify the independent variable and dependent variable in each of the hypotheses given on p. 35 of Chapter 2. In each case, for the IV ask 'What does the experimenter vary?', 'What was controlled or manipulated?' or simply, 'What was the assumed cause?' (Usually the answer is 'the conditions of the experiment' but not all of these studies are experiments). For the DV, ask 'What did they measure in or about each participant?' or 'What measure was expected to change as a result of changes in the IV?'

I hope you came up with something close to the information shown in Table 3.1.

	Independent variable	Dependent variable
Ex. a	physical punishment (degree of)	amount of aggression
Ex. b	work stress (degree of)	amount of memory deterioration
Ex. c	level of stimulation	stage of language development
Ex. d	trustworthiness	comply or not
Ex. e	gender information to participant	masculinity/femininity of description

Table 3.1 Dependent and independent variables in studies to test hypotheses on p. 35

Levels of the independent variable

Independent variables are defined in terms of LEVELS. In the Rule *et al.* experiment, the independent variable had two levels, 21°C and 33°C. Suppose a research study was conducted which submitted participants to three noise intensities: no noise, moderate noise and loud noise. These conditions would represent *three* levels of the IV. IVs can have many levels; in a study conducted by Cialdini, Reno and Kallgren (1990) the researchers arranged for 0, 1, 2, 4, 8 or 16 pieces of litter to be left on the ground to see whether this would affect whether people walking by would drop a leaflet they had just been given. The IV here then has six levels.

The independent variable is usually given a title that covers the *dimension* along which the levels are different values, e.g. 'temperature' or 'litter level'. This can be a little misleading when an IV is named, for instance, 'training' where there are levels of 'mental and physical training', 'mental training only', 'physical training only' but also a level which is 'no training'. However, the point is that there is only *one* IV in each case; we don't say 'the IV was the different temperatures, 21°C and 33°C'. We say 'the IV was *temperature* which had two levels, 21°C and 33°C'.

Having introduced some of the central features of a true experiment have a go at this exercise to see if you can design a sound experimental study.

Pause for thought

Outline the procedures you would use to run a 'fair' experiment testing the hypothesis that people learn a list of 20 words better after consuming caffeine. Identify the IV, DV and procedures employed to deal with possible confounding variables.

Let's hope you got most of the main features which would be:

1 Find willing participants and inform them that they might consume some caffeine if they continue.

2 Divide participants into two groups at random.

3 Administer caffeine to one group and not to the other.

4 Present the words in the list in exactly the same way and with the same exact timing for everyone.

5 Ask participants to recall the words giving the same time for everyone to recall.

6 Thank the participants and explain to them exactly what the experiment was intended to show.

7 Analyse results to see whether the caffeine group recalled significantly more words than the non-caffeine group.

Some points about each of these steps:

1 We must inform potential participants that they might be asked to ingest caffeine since this could be a risk to their health. This is an aspect of the ethics of research with human participants and is included in the Code of Conduct mentioned in Chapter 1, but also see Chapter 23.

2 You may have decided to test the same group of participants twice, once before taking the caffeine and once after. This is a valid approach and is called a *repeated measures* design. We will look at this design in the next section.

3 The group that does *not* get the caffeine is called a *control group* – see below. We need a control condition to see what people would recall without caffeine. This is called a *baseline measure*.

4 If we vary the procedure from one condition to the next, we may produce some bias. If we chat happily to one group and not the other we may motivate the first group to do better in the task. For this reason procedures in strict experiments have to be STANDARDISED – that is, exactly the same procedure is followed with each individual participant. This procedure then would be standardised.

5 This is called *debriefing* and is another standard ethical procedure.

6 The meaning of 'significant' will be explained in Chapter 14. What we mean here is that a very slight difference would be expected even on a chance basis. We need a difference that is large enough to be taken seriously as probably an effect and not just a slight difference easily explained by slight variations in conditions and people within the groups.

Control groups

If we want to see whether a 'treatment' has altered participants' behaviour then we need to compare this behaviour with what would occur without the treatment. Many experiments include a CONTROL GROUP to act as a BASELINE MEASURE of behaviour without treatment. This would be the group *not* given caffeine in the experiment we just considered. In an experiment where we want to know if the presence of an audience reduces performance on a word recognition task we obviously need a control group who perform *without* an audience in order to compare. A control group is not always necessary. If we are noting how people's behaviour alters when they talk to a male baby, as compared with a female baby, then we do not need a control group. It *might* be interesting to know how people talk when they don't know the baby's sex but we can demonstrate changes in behaviour simply by telling participants a baby is male or female.

Placebo groups

In medical trials of new drug treatments, one group of patients is often given an inert substance (a 'placebo') so that the patients *think* they have had the treatment. This is because the researchers want to eliminate an alternative explanation that patients might have improved, not from the drug but because of the psychological expectations of improvement, or the hope given by the new approach. Since we are investigating psychological states it is even more important that psychological researchers rule out the possibility of unwanted psychological expectations being the causal variable responsible for any observed changes in experiments. In the memory experiment just described participants might produce better recall because they *think* the caffeine should affect them rather than it *actually* affecting them. A PLACEBO GROUP is similar to a control group in that they experience exactly the same conditions as the experimental group except for the level of the independent variable that is thought to affect the dependent variable. However, whereas the control group receives nothing, the placebo group receives *something* which is like the active level of the IV but is ineffective.

As an example of placebo group use consider Maltby *et al.* (2002) who worked with 45 participants who had a debilitating fear of flying. The participants were randomly assigned to one of two groups. The *experimental group* were exposed to a virtual reality flying experience. The placebo group received what is termed *attention-placebo treatment*. The participants received the same information and other attention that the experimental group did but they did not get the virtual experience. After these treatments *both* groups improved significantly on several tests of flight anxiety, although the exposure group had better scores on most of the tests and more of them agreed to fly. This last difference was only slight, however, and after six months almost all test differences between the groups had disappeared. This suggests that it might be the simple *knowledge* that one is receiving treatment that reduces anxiety, rather than the specific therapy used in this case.

A strength of the experiment – eliminating causal directions

Suppose experiments were outlawed and that we could only gather information from making observations about what people already do. Such designs are often called 'correlational' since we can only demonstrate that variables are related rather than that one variable is the cause of the other. For instance, we might find that students with high self-esteem obtain higher exam results. However, is it the higher self-esteem that helps high-scoring students to get their marks or is it the effect of getting high marks that gives them their high self-esteem?

Ah, but, … is it that direction?

Another 'Ah, but …' question to add to your critical armoury is the question 'Ah, but could Y have affected X instead?' *whenever* you hear of a correlation between variables. For instance, Kraut *et al.* (1998) found a correlation such that the more people used the internet, the higher were their depression scores. In a report of this study (see p. 119) a conclusion was drawn that internet use (X) causes depression (Y). An alternative interpretation is that depressed people are more likely to use the internet – that is, X might be an *effect* of Y, not its *cause*.

Experiments can identify causal direction

Hence, along with looking for possible confounding variables one should also always query the *direction* of an apparent cause–effect relationship. *The experiment can eliminate one of these directions.* We might observe that people who have better memories also tend to drink more coffee. We can argue that maybe caffeine causes the better memories. However, it is also possible that the kind of people who have good memories are more likely to pass exams, therefore more likely to take up pressurised jobs and hence more likely to drink higher levels of coffee. This is a rather tenuous connection, I know, but we *must* entertain all possibilities. However, with an experiment we can easily demonstrate a *direct* effect and therefore rule out this rather convoluted explanation of the relationship between memory and caffeine. There are two possible directions to explain the relationship: caffeine improves memory or good memory increases caffeine intake. The observational result is ambiguous. An experiment, however, leaves it clear that caffeine improves memory. Very often an experiment can demonstrate the direction of cause where an observation in the field has left the direction ambiguous.

Info Box 3.1	Talking of coffee, couldn't the newspaper make the coffee taste nice?

I said in Chapter 1 that people use scientific thinking naturally in their everyday lives. This starts early, and even toddlers can be shown to be using logic. Here, though, is a personal example that happened when I was completing the fourth edition of this book. At breakfast with my two sons, Jeevan (then eight) said to Kiran (then thirteen) 'I think the reason Daddy likes his newspaper is because he always has his coffee with it.' Surprised, but not missing a trick, I tried 'Couldn't it be that I like my coffee because I always read my newspaper with it?' 'No,' Jeevan came back straight away, 'you like coffee at other times, so it can't be that.'

This was a neat piece of scientific logic that stunned me in one so young. Needless to say, Jeevan (now fourteen), does better in science at present than in any other subject!

Brief critique of the experiment

We can't always do experiments. Often they are quite inappropriate or they are simply unethical. We cannot deprive children of stimulation but we can go out and observe what happens when parents have deprived them. Experiments can be highly artificial and can severely limit the range of what can sensibly be studied. This is because we require that all variables be strictly operationally defined and that they occur in a specific manner in the experimental setting – be it in the laboratory or the field. Non-experimental methods are better suited to the study of naturally occurring phenomena, such as reactions to parental discipline, gender-specific behaviour, large-scale investigation of attitudes and prejudice, everyday health behaviour and so on. Some of these areas are investigated with field experiments (see pp. 119–120) but often an interview or observational approach is far more appropriate given the nature of the topic and target population (e.g. observation of young babies rather than interviews!).

A further disadvantage of experiments is that they can involve *reactivity* effects, where participants react in some way to the knowledge that they are participating in a psychology experiment. We will discuss this issue in Chapter 4. It is possible to conduct experiments where the people involved do not know they are participating but in this case certain ethical issues are raised. However, most experiments require that participants follow specific instructions and hence they must be aware that they are participating and their behaviour may be significantly affected by this knowledge.

Two final critical points would be raised by qualitative researchers. First, the experiment completely prescribes what the participant must do; their behaviour is therefore relatively passive and they cannot give a personal view of the situation (at least as part of the formal quantitative results). Second, the aura of an experiment can invest the exercise with scientific credibility, which sometimes may not be fully deserved. 'Let me do an experiment on you' seems more to imply a known likely result than 'Let me ask you a few questions.' We shall consider a wide range of non-experimental methods in Chapters 5 to 10.

The strengths of experiments	Critique of experiments
• Can isolate cause and effect because independent variable is completely controlled.	• Reactivity effects occur if participants know they are in an experiment; possible ethical problems if they do not.
• Can control many extraneous influences so that validity is high and alternative explanations of events are eliminated or weakened.	• Limits the kind of phenomena that can be investigated because variables must be tight in operational definition, and conditions can therefore be quite artificial.
• Alternative explanations of effects can be investigated/eliminated in extensions of the original experiment because experiments are easier to replicate accurately than many other studies.	• Participants' contribution completely prescribed; no unique view from participants is possible.
	• Can invest results with false 'scientific credibility'.

Table 3.2 Strengths and weaknesses of experimental designs

Exercises

1 Researchers often show baby participants two different patterns and record the time spent looking at each one. The pattern looked at longest is taken to be the one that the baby prefers or at least is more interested in. The idea is to see whether the baby prefers complex patterns to simpler ones. What is the independent variable and what is the dependent variable in this experiment?

2 What are the main features of an experiment?

3 In Milgram's (1963) main demonstration of obedience, it was shown that, if the experimenter insisted, participants would continue to deliver an electric shock to a 'victim' whenever they got a memory trial wrong even though they were screaming in agony. This is a dramatic demonstration but not a true experiment as it stands. What condition(s) could be added to turn it into one?

4 Which method controls more strongly against alternative interpretations of results – experiment or non-experiment?

Answers

1 Independent variable: complexity of pattern. Dependent variable: time spent gazing.

2 Independent variable is manipulated by experimenter, all other possible variables are held constant including random allocation of participants to conditions, dependent variable is measured after controlled changes in the independent variable.

3 As a control group, have people give shocks but experimenter gives no orders to continue (this was done and almost all participants gave up at the first victim complaint, though few textbooks describe this). Milgram also varied the distance of the victim, distance of experimenter, whether confederates also refused or went on with the experiment, among many other variables.

4 Experiment.

Simple experimental designs
The independent samples design

Pause for thought

Students on psychology degree courses often have to design their own study, carry it out and report it. Imagine that two students have decided on their project which will investigate the hypothesis that people are poorer at performing a difficult task when they are being observed by other people. They set up the following specific design. First of all they need operational definitions of the following:

- a sensori-motor task

- an audience

- a measure of performance.

For the performance measure they decide to use one of those wiggly-wire contraptions you see at village fêtes where participants have to move a metal loop along the wire without touching it. When it does touch, a buzzer sounds and the time in contact is recorded. The measure of performance is operationally defined, then, as time in contact and is measured to the nearest tenth of a second. This gives a neatly quantified measure of performance – seconds in contact. If the presence of an audience seriously impairs performance on the wiggly-wire task, the students should find that participants performing with an audience will have longer contact times than participants who perform the task completely on their own. The audience is always the same six student colleagues who do not talk throughout the test session but who always stare at the participant.

Thirteen psychology student participants are invited to complete the task of moving the wire from 'start' to 'home' in front of the audience. The student experimenters carry out the control condition on the following day but find that no psychology students are available. Instead they ask a group of 12 students from a watch repair technician training course to complete the wiggly-wire task in a quiet room. Each student performs the task alone with only the experimenter present, who sits behind a screen.

Results show that time in contact in the audience condition is much greater than in the alone condition.

What is the independent variable in this experiment?

What is the dependent variable in this experiment?

The students here are conducting what is known as an INDEPENDENT SAMPLES design experiment. The title says just what it means. One group of participants is subject to the experimental condition (the presence of an audience) while an entirely different group of people participates in the control (absence of audience) condition. These two conditions are the *levels* of the independent variable which we could name 'audience'. When looking for the independent variable, look for the variable that was *manipulated* by the experimenter. We know the values of this variable before we start the experiment. The dependent variable has values that we *cannot* know before the experiment starts since it is a measure of the participants' performance – time in contact.

The generalised experiment depicted in Figure 3.3 is also an independent samples design. The Maltby *et al.* (2002) and Cialdini *et al.* (1990) studies described earlier are examples of independent samples designs. Other terms for independent samples design are INDEPENDENT GROUPS, UNRELATED GROUPS/DESIGN, BETWEEN GROUPS and BETWEEN SUBJECTS. The latter two terms are very common in the world of more complex experimental designs that use ANOVA and which we will meet in Chapter 18.

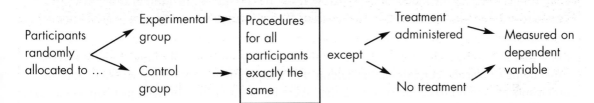

Figure 3.3 The classic two group experimental design with treatment and control (no treatment) groups

Pause for thought

Read the experiment again (if you haven't already spotted the deliberate mistake) and see if you can find a possible confounding variable – that is, something that is not controlled for in the experimental design and which could be responsible for the difference in completion times.

You may have noticed two things. First, one group of participants was comprised of psychology students while the other group contained watch repair trainees. You may also have noticed the slight difference in numbers in each condition, 12 and 13. This difference is trivial and will be dealt with by the statistical analysis employed. *Never* worry about slight sample size differences. Larger differences that might be a problem are dealt with in Chapter 15. What *is* a worry here is that the students asked watch repair trainees to participate. These students are likely to have good control of fine movements. They may do better than the psychology students and if they are in the control condition it may be their special skills that make their times shorter and *not* the fact that they are alone. This difference between samples 'threatens the validity' of the conclusions made from the experiment, an issue to be discussed in Chapter 4.

Participant variables and non-equivalent groups

The difference between psychology and watch repair students is a *participant variable*. These were introduced in Chapter 2 and can be a major weakness of independent samples designs. Differences found might not be caused by the independent variable at all, but may be the result of having too many people with a certain characteristic or skill in one of the conditions of an experiment. The problem is also known as that of NON-EQUIVALENT GROUPS.

Dealing with participant variables

In an independent samples design it would always be difficult to rule out participant differences as a possible source of variation between the results of groups in our study, but there are certain steps we can take to reduce the likelihood that this was the cause of differences found.

Random allocation of participants to conditions

This follows the classic line of experimental design already discussed, and is probably the best move. In biology, a researcher would randomly split a sample of beans and subject one sample to a fertiliser treatment and use the rest as a 'control group'. In psychology, the same line is followed. When results are in, if the independent variable really has no effect, then minor differences between the two samples are simply the result of random variation among people and other non-systematic variables.

Notice that in Maltby *et al.*'s study, described above, participants were allocated *at random* to the virtual flying or placebo conditions. In Cialdini *et al.*'s experiment it was not possible to allocate participants at random to conditions since they were innocent passers-by who just happened along when a particular condition was running. This is a serious flaw in the experimental design, making it a *quasi-experiment*, a topic to be discussed in Chapter 5.

Pre-test of participants

In a more elaborate solution, we can try to show that both groups were similar in relevant performance before the experimental conditions were applied. For instance, the students could pre-test the two groups on the wiggly-wire task. Both groups would be tested first in the quiet room. Here their scores should not differ. If they do, we could either sample again or allocate the existing participants to the two conditions making sure that the two groups are equivalent on wiggly-wire performance.

Representative allocation

Pre-testing is time-consuming and will not eliminate all problems of non-equivalent groups. Both groups might score the same in the pre-test but the group given the audience condition may contain a greater number of people who are particularly inhibited by public performance. What appears to be a general effect may really only be an effect for certain sorts of people. If we knew this, we could have made the two groups equivalent on this inhibition-in-public variable.

Hence we can make our two groups equally representative on several variables. However, we must decide intuitively, given the nature of the research topic and aims, which variables are going to be the most important to balance for. In the present example it would have been sensible, with hindsight, to split the watchmaker and psychology students equally into the two conditions. Within each category chosen as relevant (gender, watch repairer, etc.), allocation of half that category to one condition and half to the other would be performed on as random a basis as possible.

Repeated measures design

The students conducting the audience effect experiment ran into the problem that their two groups of participants might not initially be equivalent. There might have been more people with relevant skills in one group than in the other. Is there a way to eliminate these differences altogether? One of the students comes up with the idea of having the same people do both conditions. This way, all differences between participants become irrelevant and we are really testing whether an audience has an effect on each *individual's* performance, compared with when they were alone. This is why the REPEATED MEASURES design, which we are about to investigate, is sometimes called a WITHIN SUBJECTS design, since we are looking at differences *within* each participant (or 'subject'). The more usual term, 'repeated measures', refers to the fact that the *same measure* is repeated on each participant but under the various conditions of the independent variable. If the participants are the same for both conditions, and all other variables are controlled, any differences *within participants* should be the effect of the manipulated independent variable.

Multiple testing is not repeated measures

It is important to note that in a repeated measures design exactly the same measure is taken under two different conditions of the independent variable. In other studies two measures may be taken. For instance, participants might take a neuroticism test and then an extroversion test. In this case we are not *repeating* measures and all we can do with the subsequent data is to correlate the pairs of scores (see Chapter 17). Such a study is not an 'experiment', nor even a 'quasi-experiment' (see Chapter 5).

Order effects

Pause for thought

Suppose the students run the experiment as a repeated measures design and people perform first in front of an audience, then alone. Suppose they find that, as expected, times in front of an audience are much longer than times produced when doing the task alone.

What could *now* explain this difference apart from the independent variable of being alone or having an audience? What confounding variable is present? What has not been controlled?

You probably realised that people might improve on the second condition simply because they've had some practice (and they may be less anxious about learning a new task). Effects from the order in which people participate in conditions are known as ORDER EFFECTS. It is of course possible that people would perform *worse* in the second condition, perhaps because they were disheartened by failure, through boredom or through fatigue. Either way we must always be aware of the possibility of order effects in a repeated measures design experiment. This possibility is one of the major disadvantages of a repeated measures design.

Pause for thought

Can you make a list now of some solutions to the problem of order effects? How can a researcher design an experiment that avoids the contamination of order effects?

Dealing with order effects

1. Counterbalancing

If participants' performances in the alone condition might have been improved because of their prior experience in the audience condition, it makes sense to have half of them perform alone first and the other half to perform in front of an audience first. This is known as COUNTERBALANCING the conditions and is very often part of the procedure in a repeated measures design. Calling the conditions A and B, one group does the AB order while the other group does the BA order.

Would this in fact eliminate the order effect? Well, no, it wouldn't. However, if practice *does* improve performance, and so long as it does not swamp any other effects, then it will produce improvements for most participants, but this would lead to a little improvement in the 'alone' condition for one group and a little improvement in the 'audience' condition for the other group. Thus, the improvements would cancel each other out, leaving only the effect we are interested in as a noticeable difference between the two groups.

Warning for tests and exams!

It is easy to get fooled into thinking that, because the design involves splitting participants into two groups, we have an independent samples design. The splitting is solely for the purpose of counterbalancing. The question you need to ask yourself is, 'After the experiment is completed, did each participant serve in all conditions?' If yes, you have a repeated measures design.

Asymmetrical (or 'non-symmetrical') order effects

The neat arrangement of counterbalancing may be upset if the practice effect occurring in the AB order is not equivalent to that produced in the BA order. For instance, suppose that there is in fact no audience effect and that people's performance is equal in both conditions in the absence of order effects. Suppose too that in the alone condition it is possible to concentrate on improvement and that this transfers to the audience condition. We see shorter times in the audience condition for this group. However, when the audience is present in the *first* condition, perhaps people concentrate so much on coping with this distraction that no carry-over effect from learning the task is possible, even though performance is as good as in the alone condition. Here we would see no difference between conditions. Overall then, times in the audience condition are shorter. In this example, counterbalancing would lose its error balancing effect and we might wrongly conclude that an audience facilitates performance when, in fact, it has no effect. If we did not inspect our results thoroughly, we might only see the overall higher average time in the alone condition, rather than change in one order group and not in the other.

2. Complex counterbalancing

ABBA

(Not the one-time Swedish pop group!) To balance asymmetrical order effects (to some extent at least), all participants take conditions in the order ABBA. Their score in condition A is taken as the mean of the two A trials and likewise for B.

Multi-condition designs

If an experiment has three conditions (i.e. three levels of the independent variable) we might divide participants into six groups and have them take part in the following orders of condition:

ABC	ACB	BAC
BCA	CAB	CBA

3. Randomisation of condition order

Some experiments involve quite a number of conditions. For instance, we might want participants to solve anagrams with six different levels of complexity. We can present the six conditions to each participant in a different randomly arranged order. This could be arranged by having a computer arrange the numbers 1 to 6 in a random order for each participant and giving the six conditions according to this set of numbers. This should dissipate any order effects still further.

4. Randomisation of stimulus items

A different solution in the last example would be to give participants just one list of anagrams containing all the anagrams from the six conditions in just one list with the anagrams randomly mixed together. This approach does eliminate order effects since, here, participants do not complete one condition then the next.

Typically this is done for experiments on 'levels of processing' where, on each trial, participants have to respond 'True' or 'False' to a statement and a word item. For example:

(i)   has four letters   or

(ii) rhymes with sweet   or

(iii) fits in the sentence 'John was butted by a _____'.

The word that then follows might be 'goat', which should produce the response 'True' in item types (i) and (iii) but 'False' on item type (ii). The items types (i), (ii) and (iii) represent processing at increasingly 'deeper' levels. Instead of presenting all item types (i), then (ii) and finally (iii), we can mix together all the item types in a random order so the participant never knows which kind of item will occur next. Later participants are asked to attempt recognition of all the single words they have seen, and the prediction is tested that they should recall more of the items that they have processed to a 'deeper' level; i.e. more type iii items than type ii or type i.

5. Elapsed time

We can leave enough time between conditions for any learning or fatigue effects to dissipate.

6. Using another design

We may have to give up the idea of using the same group for each condition. We could move to an 'independent samples design', but, since this design has important disadvantages, we might try to resist this more drastic solution to the problem of order effects.

Comparison of repeated measures and independent samples designs

Repeated measures and independent samples designs are very much alter egos. The advantages of one are the disadvantages of the other. They are by far the most commonly used of experimental designs and so it is worth comparing one with the other. In Table 3.3 on p. 75 we list, in briefer form, the advantages and disadvantages of the four basic designs covered in this chapter.

Disadvantages of repeated measures – a strength of independent samples

- Repeated measures design has the problem of possible order effects, described above, which the independent samples design avoids.

- If we lose a participant between conditions of a repeated measures design, we have lost a score from each condition since we can't use just one score from any participant – we must have a pair. In the independent samples design participants are tested just the once so losing a participant means only losing a score from one condition.

- The aim of the experimental research may become obvious to the participant who takes both conditions and this makes 'pleasing the experimenter' (see Chapter 4) or screwing up the results more possible. This is a kind of order effect.

- In a repeated measures design we may have to wait until practice effects have worn off and the participant is ready for another test, whereas with independent samples we can run the two conditions simultaneously with two different groups of participants.

- If each participant experiences both conditions of, say, a memory experiment using word lists, we have to use a different list in each condition. This creates the problem of making *equivalent stimuli,* i.e. lists in this case. It is possible to obtain lists that give the frequency of occurrence of words in the written English language, obtained through literature surveys. You could try looking at www.kilgarriff.co.uk/BNClists/lemma.num. Here the first column is the list number of the word. The second column is how frequently it occurred in a survey, the third column is the word itself and the fourth column is the type of word it is (definite article, verb, noun etc.).

Disadvantage of independent samples – a strength of repeated measures

- The major problem is that of non-equivalence of samples, described above. Differences in performance between conditions can be mainly the results of participant differences.

- With repeated measures we obtain ten scores in each condition using just ten participants, whereas with independent samples we'd need double that number of participants to get ten scores in each condition. Participants can be hard to find and individual testing takes time.

- If there is too great a difference between the statistical variances of independent groups (a lack of *homogeneity of variance,* dealt with in Chapter 15), we have to alter our statistical procedure in carrying out a parametric test. Parametric tests are preferred to their alternatives in terms of their power to provide evidence for real differences. If the numbers of participants in the different conditions are *very* different we may not be able to report a significant difference when, in reality, a real difference exists.

When not to use a repeated measures design

1 When order effects cannot be eliminated or are asymmetrical.

2 Often, people *must* be naïve for each condition. In VIGNETTE studies, for example, a person is shown one of two alternative 'vignettes' varying in one feature only (descriptions of an incident or person) with all other material kept the same. Having read the description, people may be asked to assess a driver's blame under one of two conditions: the vignette describes the damage in an accident as very serious or as slight. In this kind of study, obviously the same participants cannot be used in both conditions, since then the research aim would be transparent to participants.

3 Group difference studies (see Chapter 5) cannot be repeated measures designs, i.e. where the 'independent variable' of interest is a category of persons, such as male/female, working class/middle class or extrovert/introvert.

4 Where an equivalent control group is essential we might pre-test a group of children, apply a programme designed to increase their sensitivity to the needs of people with disabilities, then test again to measure improvement. To check that the children would not have changed anyway, irrespective of the 'treatment', we need to compare their changes with a separate control and/or placebo group.

Info Box 3.2   Example of a vignette study

Lewis, Croft-Jeffreys and David (1990) sent to 139 psychiatrists vignettes that varied the sex and ethnicity of a fictitious client. When the client was described as African-Caribbean the following differences in ratings occurred compared with when the client was supposedly white: the illness was of a shorter duration; fewer drugs were required; the client was potentially more violent; and criminal proceedings were more appropriate.

Matched-pairs design

In the disability attitude example above, we do not *have* to use an independent samples design and introduce the risk that participant variables will 'drown out' any difference from our independent variable. Suppose we suspect that any change in attitude to people with disabilities is likely to be slight. Differences between the children in the two groups might well be so great that any subtle attitude change would remain hidden. However, since we are conducting a pre-test of attitudes, why not compare each child in the 'treatment' group with a child in the control group that is similar to them in attitude to start with? We would hope that, for each such pair of children, the 'treated' one should change while the other paired child should not. This compromise between the two designs so far discussed is known as a MATCHED-PAIRS design.

We would proceed by identifying the two highest scorers on our attitude pre-test. We would randomly allocate these, one to the control group and the other to the programme group. We would then identify the next two highest scorers and allocate in the same way, and so on, through the whole sample. This way, we have most of the advantages of the repeated measures design (we can deal with differences between pairs of scores) while avoiding the worst of the possible participant variables problem. We do not entirely eliminate the problem of participant variables since the matching of one child in the experimental group with one child in the control group just cannot be perfect.

One of nature's most useful gifts to psychological researchers is, some believe, the existence of identical (monozygotic) twins. These represent the perfect matched pair – when they're just born at least – and create the perfect natural experiment (see p. 109). Any differences between them later in life can fairly safely be attributed to differences in environmental experience. The converse is not true, however. *Similarities* cannot easily be attributed to common genetic make-up, since identical twins usually share fairly similar environments as well as their genes. Even when they are reared in separate environments, they still share the same looks, birthday, metabolism, historical culture and so on.

Single participant or small *n* design

To hear of just one person being used for experimental research can make the scientifically minded recoil in horror. Surely this must produce quite unrepresentative results, impossible to generalise from? Quite rightly, they assume, one turns to objective psychological research in order to avoid the many generalisations lay people make from personal anecdotes about single individuals.

However, consider a physical scientist who obtains just one sample of weird moonrock from a returning space mission. The rock could be tested for amount of expansion at different temperatures, in a vacuum and in normal atmosphere, in order to detect significant changes in its behaviour. This would yield valuable scientific knowledge in itself. Further, from our general knowledge of the world of rocks, we could fairly safely assume that similar rock would exist on the moon. In the same way, there are some sorts of things people do that, we know for good reason, are likely to vary according to the same pattern (but not necessarily at the same level) for almost everyone. An example of this might be the experimental situation in which someone has to make decisions from an increasing number of alternatives – say, sorting cards according to colour, then suit and so on. If we had a very patient and accommodating participant we could test out all sorts of hypotheses about how changes in the sorting instructions affect performance.

Ebbinghaus (1913) carried out an enormous number of memory experiments on himself using a wide variation of conditions and lists of nonsense syllables. Many modern studies of memory have used one participant over an extended series of experimental trials. Experiments can also be carried out on one or two people who suffer a particular condition or form of brain damage. Humphreys and Riddock (1993) experimented on two patients with Balint's syndrome (a difficulty in reaching under visual guidance caused by specific brain damage). The patient had to say whether 32 circles on a card were all the same colour or not. One patient performed much better when the circles were closer together, thus supporting a theory that the damage causes difficulty in switching

Design	Advantages	Disadvantages	Remedy (if any)
Independent samples	No order effects	Lack of 'homogeneity of variance' may prevent use of parametric test (Chapter 15)	Ensure roughly equal numbers in each group
	Can use exactly the same stimulus lists etc. in each condition	Participant variables not controlled/Non-equivalent groups	Random allocation of participants to conditions
	Participants can't guess aim of experiment	Less economical on participants than repeated measures	
	No need to wait for participants to 'forget' first condition		
Repeated Measures	Participant acts as own control so participant variables have little effect.	Order effects	Counterbalance or randomise conditions/stimulus materials
			Leave long time gap between conditions
	More economical on participants	Need different stimulus lists etc.	
	Homogeneity of variance not a problem (see Chapter 15)	Loss of participants between conditions	Do independent samples instead
		May not be able to conduct second condition immediately	Ensure conditions are equivalent
		Participants not naïve for second condition and may try to guess aim	Deceive participants as to aim (or leave long time gap)
Matched pairs	No wait for participants to forget first condition	Hard to find perfect matches and therefore time consuming	
	Can use same stimulus lists etc.	Loss of one member of pair entails loss of whole pair	
	Participant variables partly controlled	Some participant variables still present	Randomly allocate pairs to conditions
	No order effects		
	Homogeneity of variance not a problem		
Single participant	Useful where few participants available and/or a lot of time required for training participant in specialised task	Retraining required if original participant leaves project	Treat participant very nicely!

Table 3.3 Advantages and disadvantages of the various experimental designs

attention, although this is only true for some patients. Hence, single participant designs can be very useful in the investigation of cognitive deficits associated with specific medical conditions.

They can also be useful where very long-term training is required that would not be financially or technically possible on a larger sample. For instance, Spelke, Hirst and Neisser (1976) gave five hours of training for many weeks to two students in order to demonstrate that they were eventually able to read text for comprehension at normal speed while writing down, again at normal speed, a separate list of words from dictation and to recall these later having also written down the categories to which the heard words belonged!

Technically this would be a 'small N design' since more than one participant was involved. N is the symbol used to denote the number of participants in a sample and the arguments above would justify the use of a small number of participants in an experimental study. These are also often found in the areas of clinical or counselling psychology where differences in treatment are investigated on small numbers of clients who happen to be available and who suffer from a particular clinical syndrome.

Related and unrelated designs

In a RELATED DESIGN, a score in one condition (e.g. 'hot') is directly paired with a score in the other condition (e.g. 'cold'). This is clearly so in a *repeated measures* design where each pair of scores comes from one person (see Figure 11.12). It is also true for *matched pairs* designs where the score for the 5th child in a group that has experienced a reading enhancement programme ('ChildAreadingscore' in Figure 11.13) is paired directly with the score for the matched 5th child in the control group ('ChildBreadingscore').

The *independent samples* or *'between groups'* design is an UNRELATED DESIGN. We say this simply because each score in one group or condition cannot in any way be related to any specific score in the other groups or conditions. Table 11.10 shows the recorded talking times for two groups of children; one group is male and the other female. In this design there has been no matching of participants so the first male child score of 132 is not linked in any way to a specific score in the female set; we simply have two *independent groups* – a term often used for unrelated designs in place of 'independent samples'. In Figure 11.11 you can see that the data have been entered into the SPSS spreadsheet as two variables; one is the independent variable, denoting whether the participant is male or female, and the other is the dependent variable of talking time in seconds. (Note that SPSS stands for *Statistical Package for the Social Sciences* and instructions for using it commence in Chapter 11.)

In a *single participant* design, very often the participant performs several *trials* in each condition of an experiment. For instance, we might ask one person to recall what they can from several strings of ten digits. Let's suppose that for some trials the digits are written in coloured ink and for others in black ink. We are interested in whether the participant does better on the coloured ink trials. Here, it is tempting to see the design as related. However, because *all* the data come from the same source, *all* the trials in the coloured ink condition are related to *all* the trials in the black ink condition. On the other hand, there is no obvious link between trial 5 in one condition and trial 5 in the other, apart from the fact it *is* trial 5, but we're not interested in the position of trials. We simply want several measures of performance under each condition. Hence rows in the two columns of data are not linked and hence we have an *unrelated design* for the data.

Between groups and within groups designs

Unrelated designs may also be termed BETWEEN GROUPS (or BETWEEN SUBJECTS) since we are investigating the differences between independent groups of participants placed into different conditions of an experiment. Repeated measures designs may also be termed WITHIN GROUPS (or

WITHIN SUBJECTS) designs since the difference that is analysed is that between two performances *within* each participant; differences *between* participants have been eliminated for the analysis, therefore they are not relevant and are not statistically analysed.

More complex experimental designs

Experiments in psychological research are rarely as simple in design as those just outlined. In an experiment studying the effect of caffeine on memory recall, for instance, one group would be given caffeine and one group would not. However, it would make sense *also* to have a placebo group that would be given an inert substance just so that we could see whether merely *thinking* you have been given a drug will affect recall performance. This experiment would have one independent variable with *three* levels.

Factors in an experiment

In the investigation of audience effects we might decide that perhaps the task we gave people was too unfamiliar or too complex, and no wonder people did much worse when being observed: no one ever seems to observe your best car-parking or reversing feats! The literature does indeed support the proposal that simple tasks produce improvement in front of an audience, whereas complex tasks deteriorate. We could therefore conduct an experiment where participants perform a simple *and* a complex task in front of an audience and while alone, if they have the patience. We would then be manipulating *two* independent variables simultaneously. Such complex designs are desirable for several reasons, not just because they are elegant. In Chapter 19, we shall see that there is a statistical advantage in merging two separate experiments into one experimental design. It is also preferable to allocate participants *from the same participant pool*, at random, to several conditions of a complex design rather than to use a different pool at different times.

Independent variables are also known as FACTORS in the experiment and this is the terminology to use when discussing more complex (MULTI-FACTORIAL) designs. Thus the audience and task design just introduced would contain *two* factors each with two *levels*. The *task* factor has levels of *simple* and *complex* while the *audience* factor has the levels of *present* and *absent*. The entire design would be termed a *2 x 2 unrelated design*. Designs such as these will be discussed further from Chapter 19 onwards.

1 Caffeine is given to one group while plain water is given to another. Reaction times are measured. What kind of design is used, with what major weakness?

2 In one version of the 'visual cliff' experiment (Gibson and Walk, 1960), infants are observed while their mothers try to entice them to come to them across a glass sheet with a large drop beneath it. The babies are seated in the middle of the table and there is a 'safe'-looking surface to the other side of the apparently deep drop. What condition can be added to make this a true experiment, and what sort of design would the experiment then be?

3 Your tutor conducts an experiment on your class. Each student is given a set of anagrams to solve and the time to solve each one is taken. You find that some of the anagrams were of concrete words and the others were of abstract words, in no particular order. The tutor was interested in whether concrete word anagrams are easier to solve. What is the independent variable and what is the dependent variable? What experimental design was this, and what special precaution, associated with this design, has your tutor wisely taken and why?

4 Again, your tutor conducts an experiment. Students are in pairs and all are right-handed. You time your partner while she learns a finger maze, first with the left hand, then with the right. She then times you while you learn, first with the right, then the left. The tutor is looking at whether right-handed people learn more quickly with their right hand than with their left. What sort of experimental design is this? What special precaution is taken and why?

5 How is each pair of participants in a matched pairs design experiment allocated to the experimental conditions?

1 Independent samples; possible non-equivalence of groups on participant variables.

2 Add condition with same babies enticed over the shallow side — this gives repeated measures; or have control group enticed over shallow side — independent samples; or match control group with experimental group on stage of crawling — matched pairs.

3 IV: word type; DV: solution time; Design: repeated measures with randomisation of the stimuli to control for order effects.

4 Repeated measures. Counterbalancing. Avoid order effects.

5 They are randomly allocated, for instance by asking them to draw a counter (1 or 2) from a bag.

Glossary

Asymmetrical order effect	Order effect that has greater strength in one particular order and where, therefore, counterbalancing would be ineffective
Baseline comparison	Measure of what would occur if no experimental level of the independent variable were applied; how 'untreated' participants perform
Confounding variable	Variable that is uncontrolled and obscures any effect sought, usually in a systematic manner
Control group	Group used as baseline measure against which performance of experimental group is assessed
Counterbalancing	Half participants do conditions in a particular order and the other half take the conditions in the opposite order – this is done to balance possible order effects
Dependent variable	Variable that is assumed to be directly affected by changes in the independent variable in an experiment
Experiment	Study in which an independent variable is manipulated
Experimental designs	
Factorial design	Experiment in which more than one independent variable is manipulated
Independent samples (between groups; groups/subjects independent/unrelated)	Each condition of the independent variable is experienced by only one group of participants
Matched pairs	Each participant in one group/condition is paired on specific variable(s) with a participant in another group/condition
Repeated measures (within subjects/groups)	Each participant experiences all levels of the independent variable
Related	Design in which individual scores in one condition can be paired with individual scores in other conditions
Single participant	Design in which only one participant is tested in several trials at all independent variable levels
Small *N* design	Design in which there is only a small number of participants, typically in clinical or counselling work but also where participants need substantial training for a highly skilled task
Unrelated	Design in which individual scores in one condition cannot be paired (or linked) in any way with individual scores in any other condition
Independent variable	Variable which experimenter manipulates in an experiment and which is assumed to have a direct effect on the dependent variable
Levels	The different values taken by the independent variable; often, the conditions of an experiment, e.g. levels of caffeine at 50mg, 100mg and 200mg in the investigation of memory recall

Non-equivalent groups	A possible confounding variable where two or more groups in an independent samples design experiment differ on a skill or characteristic relevant to the dependent variable
Order effect	A confounding effect caused by experiencing one condition, then another, such as practice or fatigue
Participant variables	Person variables differing in proportion across different experimental groups, and possibly confounding results
Placebo group	Group of participants who don't receive the critical 'treatment' but everything else the experimental group receives; used in order to eliminate placebo effects – participants may perform differently simply because they *think* they have received an effective treatment
Pre-test	Measure of participants before an experiment in order to balance or compare groups, or to assess change by comparison with scores after the experiment
Randomisation	Putting stimulus items or trial types into random order for the purpose of elimination of order effects
Standardised procedure	Testing or measuring behaviour with exactly the same formalised routine for all participants
Vignette	A story, scenario or other description given to all participants but with certain details altered and this difference constitutes the independent variable – see the example given in the text on p. 73

Validity in psychological research $\quad 4$

This chapter investigates issues of experimental validity and links this with the different threats to validity relevant to experiments, in particular, and to all research methods in general.

- The variation among scores resulting in an experiment can be analysed into variance because of the *treatment* (the *effect* under investigation), *systematic variance* from *confounding* and *unsystematic variance* from *random errors*.

- *Experimental validity* concerns the issue of whether an experimental procedure has isolated a genuine cause–effect relationship and the analysis of systematic variance and errors.

- *Threats to validity* are the many ways in which it is possible for an apparent but false effect to appear, or for a real effect to be obscured.

- *Statistical conclusion validity* concerns whether statistical errors have been made which either lead to a false conclusion that an effect exists when it does not, or to a false conclusion that it does not exist when it does.

- *Internal validity* refers to the issue of whether an apparent effect would have occurred anyway, without the application of the experimental 'treatment'. This can occur through incorrectly applied statistics, sampling biases, history effects and other extraneous variables unconnected with manipulation of the independent variable.

- *Construct validity* concerns generalisation from the particular operational measure of a construct to the construct itself. It includes most examples of confounding, and is intimately connected with the operationalisation of variables. We can ask: Does our measure really assess the construct?

- A major task in experiments is to avoid *confounding*, which can occur through lack of control in variables associated with the independent variable: expectancies, participant reactivity effects, demand characteristics and variables systematically changing with the independent variable.

- *External validity* concerns whether an effect generalises from the specific people, place and measures of variables tested to the population, other populations, other times and other settings.

- One check on validity is *replication;* another is the relatively recent development of *meta-analysis*.

The interpretation of experiments

A little boy once said to another 'Frogs have their ears in their legs, you know. I can prove it.' 'Rubbish!' said the other. 'How could you possibly prove that?' The first boy (nasty little brat) proceeded to chop off a frog's legs and started to shout at the frog 'Jump! Go on jump! . . . See, he can't hear me!'

This 'experiment' of course has several faults that I'm sure the astute reader will have spotted. Apart from being ethically tasteless, the boy has confounded the independent variable (ears) with a variable essential for demonstration of the dependent variable (legs) and has not run a control condition to convince us that hearing frogs *can* understand English and *will* obey commands.

In this chapter we are going to review all the likely sources of error in experiments that might cause us to assume, wrongly, that we have demonstrated an effect when none exists, or that an effect didn't occur when, in fact, it did. Validity concerns whether our conclusions are correct.

Pause for thought

If we run our aggression experiment with some participants in a hot room and some in a cold room, and use a questionnaire to measure consequent aggression, how certain can we be that it was the change in temperature that caused any heightened aggression in the hot room? Try to think of alternative interpretations of the results.

The following alternative explanations are possible:

- The hot room participants were already more aggressive.
- It wasn't the heat but a change in humidity that caused the aggressiveness to increase.
- The experimenter treated the hot room participants more negatively.
- Some participants guessed what the experiment was about because they talked to earlier participants.
- The temperature was so high that some of the hot condition participants guessed what was going on when they saw the subject of the questionnaire.

In this chapter we consider all the factors that can lead to misinterpretation of the results of a study and link these to issues in the design of experiments and other research designs. We look first at general influences on the dependent variable. In the ideal experiment only the manipulation of the independent variable will cause any change in the dependent variable. We want no *alternative* explanation of the effect to be feasible. In reality, of course, there are always several possible influences upon the dependent variable and these can be considered in terms of *sources of variance*.

Sources of variance in the experiment

Whenever we take any sample of measures we end up with *variance*. We will deal with this concept statistically in Chapter 11. However, for the moment, let's just consider it non-technically. If we measure the lengths of matches in a box we will find variance among the lengths around the average. Since all matches are *intended* to be the same length, statisticians often refer to this kind of variance as ERROR VARIANCE. Even if the match-making machine is working at its best, there will still always be a little, perhaps tiny, variance among match lengths. This kind of error variation is *unsystematic*. It is random in its effects on individual matches. Turning to psychology, if we measure the recall of a sample of participants for a 15-item word list we will also obtain variance among their scores. Because psychology relies on statistical theory our analysis, too, assumes that *all* uncontrolled variance is error variance. It may be, however, that children who eat spinach are better memorisers. If we can show this to be so, then we can remove some of the error variance and explain the overall variance as partly caused by the *systematic* variable of spinach eating. That is, *some* of the variance among children's scores is *not* random.

In the perfect experiment, then, there would be *no* error variance. All variance in the dependent variable would be the result of manipulation of the independent variable. If we had asked our participants to recall a word list in hot and cold conditions then all variance in the recall scores should be the result solely of the temperature change. In a real-life experiment, however, there will be many sources of variance – from the independent variable, from confounding variables and from error, as depicted in Figure 4.1. The 'treatment' and the 'confounding' here both have *systematic* effects – they produce a difference in one direction only. The errors (sometimes referred to as RANDOM ERRORS) are *unsystematic* – they affect both groups roughly equally and in unpredictable directions in each instance. *The researcher's aim in a good experiment is to control and/or balance out systematic errors while attempting to keep unsystematic errors down to a minimum.*

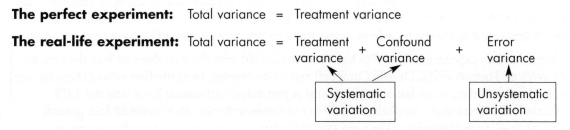

The perfect experiment: Total variance = Treatment variance

The real-life experiment: Total variance = Treatment variance + Confound variance + Error variance

Figure 4.1 Variation in the results of an experiment (after Leary, 1995)

We can consider the sources of variation depicted in Figure 4.1 by looking at an experiment conducted by Johnston and Davey (1997), who showed participants just one of three different news bulletins edited to contain positive, neutral or negative content. The groups were measured before and after the viewing for sadness and anxiety. Results showed that, after the viewing, the participants in the group that saw the negative bulletin were significantly sadder and more anxious than those in the other two groups.

In the perfect experiment we would want any variation in sadness scores to be *entirely* explained by the difference between the bulletins. However, suppose the negative news bulletin reader was, as it happens, more miserable than the other readers. This systematic factor, rather than the content of the news stories, might be responsible for a change in sadness. The confounding variation in scores may cause us to declare the wrong effect. On the other hand, if the *positive* news bulletin reader were the more miserable person, we may declare a failure when there really *is* an effect. For one group, the increase in sadness due to the negative news stories might be matched, in the other group, by an increase in sadness caused by the positive news bulletin reader! Notice here that the confounding variance would *subtract* from any treatment variance – the happier positive news group is brought back nearer to the levels of the neutral and negative news groups by its miserable newsreader and a true effect might be disguised.

In addition to the possible confounding variables in this experiment, there will also be a myriad sources of error variance: amount of physical movement in each story, personal excitement in each story, flicker on the television monitors, ambient temperature, small sounds in the room, fluctuations in light and so on. Unsystematic errors caused by any of these variables are assumed to occur in each condition equally so they do not produce a systematic bias in scores. However, if there are a lot of them, we may find that any subtle treatment effect is buried under so much distorting 'noise'. If people do not concentrate on the message, because of all the distraction, then the message will not have its desired effect.

Validity in experiments and other research designs

EXPERIMENTAL VALIDITY has to do with the *truth* of conclusions we draw about our experiment. Note that, in this section, the concepts apply to *all* kinds of research study and 'experiment' is used as a convenient term. Chapter 5 will distinguish clearly between experiments, quasi-experiments and non-experiments. What we are interested in then is the most fundamental of scientific concepts – did the experiment really work? Did it demonstrate a genuine effect? These and a few other questions require answers if we are to be able to assess the scientific worth of psychological research studies.

The thinking on experimental validity has been dominated over the past three or four decades by the work of Thomas Cook, Donald Campbell and Julian Stanley, with the first two of these having no relation with their more famous namesakes! A particularly influential book was the 1979 publication by Cook and Campbell of *Quasi-experimentation*. In this, they outlined four general types of validity and introduced the term THREATS TO VALIDITY to refer to any influence on our research variables that might provide an alternative explanation of our effect or that might limit the generality of what we appear to have found. In general, threats to validity are limitations on the interpretations of our results. These types of validity have become extremely widely known across fields as diverse as business management, psychology, engineering, economics, sociology and so on but, as with many popular concepts, they are used with varying degrees of accuracy and faithfulness to the original meanings. In 2002, even Cook and Campbell themselves moved the goalposts by redefining some of the validity types (Shadish, Cook and Campbell, 2002).

What we'll do here is to use their four basic types of validity as a basis for outlining many of the problems and unwanted effects that occur in psychological studies but we will not stick to their detailed terminology nor go into the kind of extensive debate they present concerning the precise relationship between the various threats to experimental validity (Figure 4.2). Before we do so, however, you might like to have a go at the task in the Pause for thought box below as a way of becoming familiar with some of the more common 'threats to validity'. Remember we just want to consider the research project example and highlight all the ways in which the design might have produced untrustworthy results.

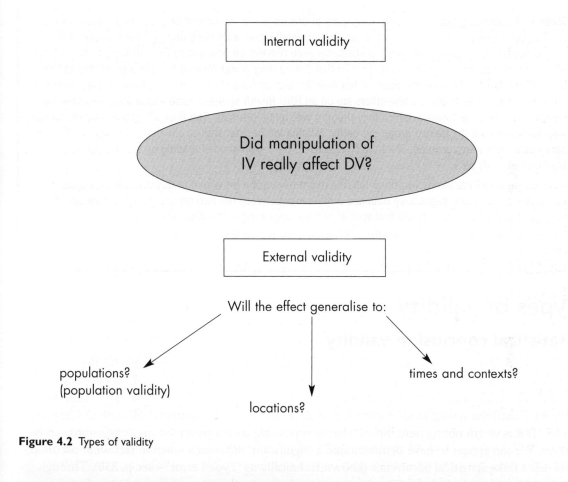

Figure 4.2 Types of validity

Pause for thought

Consider the following research project carried out by a student at Ripoff University College, where staff have responsibility for 60 students per class, one hour a week and therefore have very little time to monitor each student's research project.

Tabatha feels she can train people to draw better. To do this, she asks student friends to be participants in her study, which involves training one group and having the other as a control. She tells friends that the training will take quite some time so those who are rather busy are placed in the control group and need only turn up for the test sessions. Both groups of participants are tested for artistic ability at the beginning and end of the training period, and improvement is measured as the difference between these two scores. The test is to copy a drawing of Mickey Mouse. A slight problem occurs in that Tabatha lost the original pre-test cartoon, but she was fairly confident that her post-test one was much the same. She also found the training was too much for her to conduct on her own so she had to get an artist acquaintance to help, after giving him a rough idea of how her training method worked.

Those in the trained group have had ten sessions of one hour and, at the end of this period, Tabatha feels she has got on very well with her own group, even though rather a lot have dropped out because of the time needed. One of the control group participants even remarks on how matey they all seem to be and that some members of the control group had noted that the training group seemed to have a good time in the bar each week after the sessions. Some of her trainees sign up for a class in drawing because they want to do well in the final test. Quite a few others are on an HND Health Studies course and started a module on creative art during the training, which they thought was quite fortunate. The final difference between groups was quite small but the trained group did better. Tabatha loathes statistics so she decides to present the raw data just as they were recorded. She hasn't yet reached the recommended reading on significance tests* in her RUC self-study pack.

Now, please list all the things you think Tabatha might have got a bit wrong in this study. In particular, list all the reasons why she might have obtained a difference between her two groups *other than* the specific training plan she used. You should find several of these appearing in the discussion of validity below.

* A statistical significance test tells us whether a difference is one that could be expected simply on a chance basis (see Chapter 14).

Types of validity

Statistical conclusion validity

Inappropriate statistical procedures, or other statistical errors, may be responsible for the appearance of a difference or correlation that does not represent reality. We may simply have produced a 'fluke' large difference between samples, we may have entered data incorrectly, we may have used the wrong kind of statistical analysis and so on, all matters dealt with in Chapters 11 to 21. It is worth noting here though that two possible and opposite wrong conclusions can be drawn. We can appear to have demonstrated a 'significant' difference when in fact what occurred was just a fluke statistical occurrence (known technically as 'Type I error' – see p. 338). Through error, we can also conclude from our statistical analysis that there is no effect when in fact there really is one – a 'Type II error' (p. 340).

Internal validity

When we conduct an experiment, we may observe what appears to be an effect of the independent variable on the dependent variable. However, the apparent effect might be caused by something entirely unrelated to the manipulation of the independent variable; in other words, internal validity is concerned with whether there really is a *causal* link between independent variable and dependent variable, even if this link is indirect. If there is no link at all then the experiment lacks internal validity. We have already encountered several threats to internal validity and a pretty clear one would be sampling bias and non-equivalent groups. In Chapter 3 we saw that having psychology students in one condition and watch repair trainees in another might produce a significant difference between the two groups' performance but that *this difference is not in any way caused by the manipulation of the independent variable.* This difference would have occurred even if 'treatment' had not been given.

As another example, events might occur outside the research context that affect one group more than another. For instance, children attending a 'booster' class in school might be expected to gain in reading ability over control-group children. However, members of the booster class may *also* have just started watching a new and effective educational television programme at home. It may be the TV programme that causes the effect not the booster programme. Internal validity threats can work in the opposite direction too. Suppose the control-group children are the ones who mostly watch the TV programme. They might improve their reading too so that the booster programme might be considered ineffective. Some common threats to internal validity are described in Box 4.1.

Info Box 4.1   Some common threats to internal validity

History effects

In field experiments, where a 'treatment' is to be applied that might last quite some time, it is particularly important to use a control group for comparison because something relevant might happen that all participants in the research programme are exposed to. For instance, in the Summer of 2002 two children were abducted and tragically killed in highly publicised circumstances. If a safer parenting programme had been running at the time, then interpretations of the programme's success might have been compromised by the fact that parents *in general* probably paid a lot more attention to the safety of their children during that period. A control group would tell the researchers how large this independent effect might be and this can be subtracted from the apparent programme effect.

Biased selection (sampling)

Suppose your tutor has females in the class solve anagrams of animal words and males solve anagrams of legal terms. Since the animal anagrams were solved more quickly she claims that animal anagrams are easier to solve. You might just point out the possible confounding caused by having females do one task and males do the other. Perhaps females are better at anagrams. It doesn't matter whether females *are*, in fact, better at anagrams. What matters is the *potential* for a sampling bias. As we saw in the independent samples design, it is essential to allocate participants *randomly* to conditions. Many student practical projects lack attention to this 'threat' where, very often, it is easily avoided with a simple allocation procedure. Other selection biases can occur where, for instance, certain types of people are more likely to volunteer for one condition of an experiment than another, or where certain sorts of people are more likely to leave an experiment without completion.

Mortality

This sombre-sounding term simply refers to participant drop-out rate. A stress management programme group might be compared with a control group, and every week all participants asked to attend for various physiological measurements and questionnaire administration. If people dropping out of the control group tend to be the most stressed people, then the final comparison may show little stress reduction for the programme since the baseline comparison group now contains relatively low-stress people.

Maturation

In long-term studies on children some effects can become either accentuated or obscured because children in either the control or experimental groups are maturing at different rates.

Treatment imitation

Participants in a control condition may get to know what those in a 'treatment' condition are doing. For instance, control parents might copy a 'boost to reading' programme so their children do not miss out. This might *deflate* any difference between groups and *disguise* a real effect from the programme.

Rivalry

Control participants may resent treatment participants and try to do better than them; alternatively, they may become demoralised.

Construct validity and the problem of confounding variables

Very often, an effect really *does* occur when the independent variable is manipulated, but not for the reasons the researcher thinks; that is, the independent variable itself is not the variable causing the effect. Something else varies with it and causes the change. The most common type of threat here is from *confounding*, a concept we have already encountered and will investigate in greater detail below. Cook and Campbell (1979) argued that when confounding occurs we make an assumption about the *wrong psychological construct*. For instance we might ask participants to form a vivid mental image of each word in a to-be-learned list and find that these participants recall the words better than participants asked only to 'study' each word. We might interpret this as evidence that imaging words causes better recall whereas, in fact, the instruction to image might merely have made the task more interesting. Hence *task interest* has caused the difference not imagery. CONSTRUCT VALIDITY concerns whether our measures of a construct are really measuring it, and also the extent to which the construct itself is supported by psychological evidence – see p. 200. According to Shadish *et al.* (2002: 21), construct validity in an experiment can apply to samples and settings as well as the variables employed. For instance, we have poor construct validity if a questionnaire intended to measure extroversion in fact only measures sociability; if a sample intended to represent nursing staff in fact includes a good proportion of maintenance staff as well; if a study conducted in a private independent school is taken as representative of all schools.

In this section, because we are concerned with the problems of experimental designs we will mainly be concerned with issues of confounding of the independent variable, in other words, with the construct validity of our independent variables.

Dealing with confounding variables

We saw in Chapter 3 that improvement through therapy might be caused only by the special attention that clients receive, and not the specific therapeutic treatment used. If the researchers assume that it is the specific therapeutic procedures that are producing an effect then they are working with the wrong psychological construct of their independent variable in the model they are presenting. The special attention is completely correlated with the therapeutic treatment (if you get one then you get the other). It is a confounding variable. Using a placebo group who get attention but not the specific treatment, and comparing these two groups with a control group, would cast better light on what is the effective variable – see Figure 4.3.

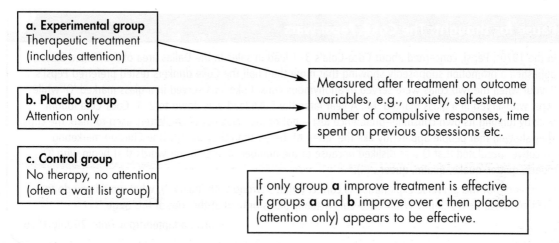

Figure 4.3 Role of placebo group in identifying the confounding variable of attention

Tackling confounds – the heart of science?

Attempts like this to eliminate possible confounding variables as alternative explanations are really the heart of scientific activity. It doesn't matter whether the proposed confounding variable really *does* have an effect. The name of the game is to produce a refined test that simply *rules out* the confounding variable as a competing explanation. Remember from Chapter 1 that all theories need to be falsifiable in principle. If the placebo group do no better than the control group, then the therapeutic procedure is supported and the competing explanation of placebo attention is weakened. If, however, the placebo group do as well as the full therapy group, then it would appear that attention alone might be the explanation of any improvement found using this kind of therapy. We then have to alter the psychological construct which explains therapeutic improvement.

Suppose we wished to test for a difference between people's recall for concrete and for abstract words. We create two lists, one for each type of word. However, it could well turn out, if we don't check thoroughly, that the abstract words we choose are also more uncommon; they occur less frequently in people's speech and in common reading. Any effect we find may be the result of *uncommon* words being harder to learn rather than *abstract* words being harder to learn. We can easily adjust for this by using commonly available surveys of word frequencies in the popular media (see p. 72 for a relevant web address).

The critical student will always be alert for possible confounding variables, as presumably were Coca-Cola's publicity workers when they challenged Pepsi Cola's advertising campaign tactics some years ago, as explained in the following Pause for thought box.

Examples of tackling confounding in psychological research

1. Did you really distort what I saw?

In a famous series of experiments by Elizabeth Loftus and her colleagues (e.g. Loftus and Palmer, 1974), participants were asked leading questions after seeing a film of a car accident. For example, 'How fast were the cars going when they smashed into each other?' was asked in one condition, whereas 'hit' was substituted for 'smashed into' in another condition. The people in the 'smashed into' condition tended to recall a greater speed and this was taken as evidence for the distortion of original memories by leading questions. The argument was later raised, however, that participants may simply have been responding to what they thought was required of them, and were not suffering permanently distorted memories.

Loftus tackled this alleged confounding variable (immediate research demand) by re-doing the experiment but also asking participants to recall, one week after the original test, extra information

[1] As a scientific test, Coca-Cola put its own drink into both the 'M' and 'Q' glasses. Results showed that most people preferred the Coke in the 'M' glass. The consistent use of 'Q' associated with the competitor's drink had apparently confounded Pepsi's advertising 'research'.

about the film. They were asked, for instance, whether they recalled any broken glass in the incident. It was assumed that participants would not recall at this point the exact question they were asked the week before. Those participants who had been in the 'smashed into' condition one week earlier tended to report glass more frequently (there wasn't any in fact) and this supported the view that original memories had been more or less permanently distorted by the questions asked immediately after viewing the incident. Lindsay (1990) even told participants that information given to them after viewing an office robbery was all wrong and to ignore it. Nevertheless, the information appeared to distort the participants' later recall of events in the film.

2. Nice smell – good memory

A rich vein of research from the early 1980s has been the use of 'mood induction' to produce temporary up or down moods in participants, and to measure several types of consequent effects. Typically, one group of participants is either given sad materials (written or filmed) or is instructed explicitly to get into a sad mood, while a second group is induced or instructed into a happy mood. They might then be asked to recall memories (e.g. of childhood) or to recall words from a set of both 'happy' and 'sad' words given earlier in a memory task. Ehrlichman and Halpern (1988) argued that induction or instruction techniques might not only create a temporary mood but also 'set' thought processes in the mood direction. Hence, participants might *not* be recalling sadder things because they were in a sadder mood – they may simply have sad events more readily available because the mood-induction procedure gives 'cues' to this kind of information; the instructions make it clear what is expected.

In order to eliminate this possible confounding variable, Ehrlichman and Halpern attempted to create a mood in participants simply by exposing them to pleasant or unpleasant smells. In support of their predictions, those exposed to a pleasant smell recalled happier memories than did those exposed to an unpleasant smell. This was important as it supports the theory that temporary mood affects mental processes, even when overt mental processes have not been used to *induce* that mood. Interestingly, the reverse procedure works too. Participants induced into a negative mood were more likely to correctly identify previously experienced unpleasant tastes than pleasant tastes, whereas the reverse was true for those undergoing positive mood induction (Pliner and Steverango, 1994).

Threats to validity – a nuisance or a key to discovery?

We are about to look at quite a long list of factors within experimental and other designs that can be threats to validity. Most of these can be considered as problems with constructs; that is, the variable actually responsible for changes observed in the dependent variable are not caused directly by changes in the independent variable but by some other uncontrolled factor in the experimental setting.

Often, the variables involved are seen as 'nuisance' variables that interfere with interpretations of results and can be avoided by more careful design, attention to procedures, materials and so on.

However, as we said earlier, unwanted variables *can* lead to dramatic research developments. When Pavlov was investigating digestive systems in dogs, it was their feeders' footsteps and the sight of their food buckets that acted as confounding variables causing the dogs to dribble before they were given food. These 'nuisance' variables, however, were instrumental in leading Pavlov to his monumental work on classical conditioning.

We should also sound a note of caution before starting out on a discussion of what can possibly bias results and interfere with the optimum performance of participants in an experiment. Some of the proposed effects outlined below, if they exist, are very subtle indeed. However, consider an experiment by Hovey in 1928 where two groups of students were asked to complete an intelligence test. One group was in a quiet room. The other group took the test in a room with 'seven bells, five buzzers, a 500-watt spotlight, a 90,000-volt rotary spark gap, a phonograph, two organ pipes of varying pitch, three metal whistles, a 55-pound circular saw . . . a photographer taking pictures and four students doing acrobatics!' (Rosnow and Rosenthal, 1997: 32). There was no difference in the performance of the two groups!

Confounding variables can lead us to:	Example from the text:
wrongly identify the causal component of the independent variable	concreteness of word seen as producing easier recall rather than frequency
assume the intended independent variable has an effect when it doesn't	therapy doesn't work; attention is effective alone
assume an effect doesn't occur when it does	a miserable positive newsreader might cause moods to stay the same that might otherwise have been 'lifted' by the upbeat news content

Expectancy and the social psychology of the psychology experiment

Experimenter and researcher expectancy

Since psychology experiments are carried out by humans on humans, it has been argued that the necessary social interaction that must occur between experimenter and participant makes the psychological experiment different in kind from those in the natural sciences. Is it possible that, completely beyond the level of conscious awareness, the experimenter's eagerness to 'get a result' could be a confounding variable? Experimenters rarely 'cheat' but they are human and might, without realising it, convey to participants what they are expecting to happen. Rosenthal and Fode (1963) showed that students given groups of 'bright' and 'dull' rats (which actually possessed a random mix of maze-learning abilities) produced results consistent with the labels of their rats: 'bright' rats ran faster! This was originally used to show that experimenter expectancies can even affect the behaviour of laboratory rats. In their legendary publication *Pygmalion in the Classroom*, Rosenthal and Jacobson (1968) reported that (randomly selected) children whose teachers were manipulated to 'overhear' that they were expected to make late gains in academic development, actually made significant gains compared with non-selected children. This suggested that teachers had responded to the 'dropped' information by somehow, unknowingly, giving the 'late bloomers' enriched attention.

Figure 4.4 'Bright' rats run faster!

A total of 40 experiments between 1968 and 1976 failed to show further evidence of experimenters passing on to participants influences that investigators (those running the research project) had 'planted'. However, Rafetto (1967) led one group of experimenters to believe that sensory deprivation produces many reports of hallucinations and another group to believe the opposite. The experimenters then interviewed people who had undergone sensory deprivation. The instructions for interviewing were purposely left vague. Experimenters reported results in accordance with what they had been led to believe. Eden (1990) demonstrated that where army leaders were told (incorrectly) that their subordinates were above average, platoon members performed significantly better than where this information was not given. Some studies have shown that experimenters can affect participants' responses through facial or verbal cues, and that certain participants are more likely to pick up experimenter influence than others, particularly those high in need for approval. Finally, Rosenthal himself (Rosnow and Rosenthal, 1997), has conducted meta-analyses (see p. 100) of hundreds of expectancy studies in several quite different areas and claims to obtain overall effects far above chance levels. In fact, the Rosnow and Rosenthal text is a little gem as a sourcebook for all manner of sometimes unbelievable experimenter and participant expectancy and bias effects, including many features of volunteers, the problems of student dominance in psychology experiments and so on.

Participant expectancy, Hawthorne effects and demand characteristics

If participants who need approval are affected by experimenter influence, as was just mentioned, then this suggests that they perhaps want to get the 'right' result and do well. Participant

---

Info Box 4.2   The Hawthorne studies – what effect?

Among many experimental manipulations and observations carried out during famous work-performance research at the Hawthorne electrical plant in the USA, the productivity of five female workers was assessed under varying conditions of rest breaks and changes to the working day and week. In several other experiments lighting conditions were varied and in one informal condition with only two workers, productivity under extremely low light conditions was investigated. It was found that productivity generally increased with changes to rest breaks and working conditions but sometimes dipped when rest breaks were terminated. Overall there was no reliable relationship between lighting conditions and productivity though it was maintained and even increased under the very low conditions but no more than the researchers had predicted. This last result has 'captivated' textbook authors to the point where it is often reported that *whatever* changes were made to the lighting level, productivity increased. The effects are reported as being mainly the result of the workers being observed by researchers and being unused to this kind of attention. However, the rest break and working week study continued for five years so the workers in fact had plenty of time to get used to being observed. The effects were also confounded by researchers changing pay and incentive systems part-way through the experiment and removing two of the least co-operative of the five workers from the rest break studies. However, despite a lack of clear evidence of its effects in the Hawthorne project, research methods terminology has taken up the term HAWTHORNE EFFECT to refer to the situation where participants' behaviour is affected simply by the knowledge that they are the focus of an investigation and are being observed.

expectancy refers in general to the ways in which research participants interact with the researcher and research context perhaps even guessing what is expected of them. It was used to explain some famously reported effects (see Box 4.2) allegedly demonstrated during a massive applied psychology project conducted in the 1920s at the Hawthorne electrical plant in the USA (Roethlisberger and Dickson, 1939) but recently reported by Olson, Hogan and Santos (2006) to be more myth than reality.

PARTICIPANT EXPECTANCY then refers to the expectation on the part of participants that their behaviour should alter in an experimental situation. Orne (1962) demonstrated hypnosis on a couple of volunteers among a group of students. He untruthfully emphasised that 'catalepsy of the dominant hand' (a kind of paralysis and numbness) was a common reaction of hypnotised subjects. He then asked for more volunteers from the student audience and had them hypnotised by an experimenter. Of these nine students five showed catalepsy of the dominant hand while two showed catalepsy of both hands. Among a control group, not given the initial hypnotism demonstration, none showed catalepsy of the dominant hand while three showed catalepsy of both hands. It was arranged that the experimenter did not know from which group each of his subjects to be hypnotised came. It seems the experimental group students had acted in accordance with what they had been led to expect from the demonstration. The fact that three students in the control group showed non-specific catalepsy was explained by Orne as possibly because he had tested students in general for catalepsy.

Demand characteristics

This last suggestion, that students pick up cues from the experimental setting and procedure as to what is expected in the experiment to be conducted, was further investigated by Orne. If participants wish to behave as expected they would need to know what was required of them. Orne (1962) argued that there are many cues in an experimental situation that give participants an idea of what the study is about, what behaviour is under study and, perhaps, what changes are expected of them. Those cues that may reveal the experimental hypothesis Orne named DEMAND CHARACTERISTICS and offered the following definition of them:

The totality of cues that convey an experimental hypothesis to the subject become significant determinants of the subject's behaviour. We have labelled the sum total of such cues as the 'demand characteristics of the experimental situation'. (1962: 779)

Orne and Scheibe (1964) asked participants to undergo 'sensory deprivation'. Some of the participants were asked to sign a liability release form and were shown a 'panic button' to use if required. These participants reacted in a more extreme manner to the 'stress' (simply sitting alone in a room for four hours) than did a control group. The button and release form presumably acted as cues to the participants that their behaviour was expected to be disturbed. An antidote to the confounding effects of demand characteristics was proposed by Aronson and Carlsmith (1968), who argued that *experimental realism* (see p. 118) should lower the potency of demand characteristics, because participants' attention is entirely grabbed by the interest of the procedure.

One special related problem is that of *enlightenment* referring to the increasing awareness of psychology students (who comprise the significant majority of psychological research participants) and to a lesser extent, the general public, about psychological research findings, even if these are often poorly understood.

Participant reactions to demand characteristics and expectancy

Participants could react to demand characteristics in several ways. They may engage in what is termed 'pleasing the experimenter'. This was the force of the criticism of the Loftus experiment described above. In fact, Weber and Cook (1972) found little evidence that participants do try to respond as they think the experimenter might wish. Masling (1966) even suggested that a 'screw you' effect might occur as participants attempt to alter their behaviour *away from* what is expected!

The concept of the 'good subject'

Contrary to these findings, however, Orne famously demonstrated that participants asked to add up thousands of two digit numbers did not give up after a while, as Orne had thought they would, but tried Orne's stamina by continuing for over five and a half hours. They even continued when told to tear each worksheet up into 32 pieces after completing the sums! Orne argued that research participants are typically very obedient and very concerned to do their best for science.

Evaluation apprehension

Riecken (1962) suggested that research participants have a strong motive to 'look good' – a phenomenon which later became known as SOCIAL DESIRABILITY. Rosenberg (1969) coined the term EVALUATION APPREHENSION to describe participants' anxiety that their performance will be under scrutiny. The interesting question here is, then, do participants behave according to what they think are the requirements of the experiment or do they rather behave in a way which they think will put them in the best light? There seems no clear answer since, in differently designed experiments designed to settle the issue, Sigal, Aronson and Van Hoose (1970) found that participants responded in the direction of creating a favourable self-image rather than follow the strongly hinted at expected behaviour of altruism. Adair and Schachter (1972) critically analysed this study and then produced results suggesting the opposite pattern; participants favoured following the demand characteristics, i.e. cooperate with the scientific aim, rather than behave to look good. Rosnow *et al.* 1973 carried out a further follow-up and found, guess what, results in the opposite direction from Adair and Schachter. Several other studies followed and it seems that the two competing motivations can be manipulated by subtly different research designs and that personality may also play a role.

Reactive and non-reactive studies

What all this tells us is that research participants are *active* in the research situation. We cannot treat them simply as persons to be experimented *upon*. Along with the expectancies of the experimenter these factors show the experimental situation to be unlike those in any other science. Uniquely, in psychology both researcher and researched can interact subtly with one another and *at the same level*. Although biologists may deal with living organisms at least they cannot suspect their laboratory animals of trying to figure out what the experimenter is after with the exception possibly of chimpanzees!

Studies in which the participant is expected to *react* to being studied have been termed REACTIVE designs or they are said to use a 'reactive measure'. It could be argued that the closeness of the researcher and the awesome surroundings and formality of the procedures in a psychological laboratory make reactive measures even more distorting. The general point, however, is that participants are people and people are active, social, enquiring human beings. They are not passive 'subjects' who are simply experimented *on*. Their social adjustments, thoughts and constructions of the world around them will interact with psychological research arrangements designed specifically to investigate the operation of those very thoughts, constructions and behaviour.

It must be emphasised that *any* research study, experimental or not, in so far as participants are aware of being participants, can be affected by all the social and expectancy variables just described. Social desirability, in particular, is probably more potent in surveys and interviews than in many simple experiments.

Dealing with expectancies and other biases

Standardised procedures

In order to reduce the effects of any experimenter bias, and to control random errors in general, researchers usually run their investigations using a set of strictly STANDARDISED PROCEDURES,[2] identical for all participants in a specific condition. In large studies the researcher often directs several experimenters to run the conditions and the standardised procedure should ensure that every participant receives exactly the same instructions as every other participant in that condition. In addition, the procedure should be identical for participants in the common parts of all *other* conditions. For instance, members of an experimental group who receive caffeine, and members of a control group who don't, should all be given exactly the same instructions and treatment for the recall task which is the common part of an investigation into the effects of caffeine on memory.

Student-run practicals are notorious for employing very varied treatments of participants with different information from each student tester. Even for a single tester, with the best will in the world, it is difficult to run an identical procedure with your Dad at tea time and with your boyfriend or girlfriend later that same evening. Paid researchers must do better than this but, nevertheless, it would be naïve to assume that features of the tester (accent, dress, looks, etc.), their behaviour or the surrounding physical environment do not produce unwanted variations.

Even with standardised procedures, experimenters do not always follow them. Friedman (1967) argued that this is partly because experimenters may not recognise that social interaction and non-verbal communication play a crucial role in the procedure of an experiment. Male experimenters, when the participant is female, are more likely to use her name, smile and look directly at her (Rosenthal, 1966). Both males and females take longer to gather data from a participant of the opposite sex than a same-sex participant (Rosnow and Rosenthal, 1997: 26). Written procedures do not usually tell the experimenter exactly how to greet participants, engage in casual pleasantries, arrange seating and how much to smile. Where variations are systematic, as for the male experimenter bias, they may well produce a significant confounding effect.

---

[2] Be careful not to confuse this term with '*standardisation*' when this term is related to the standardisation of psychological scales and tests (see p. 201).

Blind and double blind procedures

Because participants may behave according to expectations, experimental procedures are often organised to keep participants unaware of the aim of the research project. However, this is not always feasible, and participants must realise, for example, that a chemical substance they are asked to ingest has something to do with expected performance on a task they are then asked to perform. On such occasions researchers can employ a SINGLE BLIND procedure in which participants do not know whether they have ingested the drug or an inert *placebo* – see p. 62. In experiments where no placebo is necessary but where different participants have performed in two different conditions, a single blind procedure is used to keep the *experimenter* unaware of which condition a participant was in so that they just cannot lean towards giving higher ratings or observation scores to members of the group expected to score more highly. For instance, a researcher giving aggressiveness ratings to male and female dream content would not be told the sex of each dreamer. This should defeat the Pygmalion effect discussed earlier.

Where both participant *and* experimenter are unaware of the precise treatment given, we have what is known as a DOUBLE BLIND procedure. In the caffeine and memory study briefly mentioned above, neither the participants nor the research assistants who calculate each participant's recall score would know whether caffeine or a placebo had been used. This would matter particularly where the recall score is not just the addition of correctly recalled words from a list but where the dependent variable includes aspects of human judgement, as when assessing the aggressiveness content of a recalled description of a viewed video. In such cases assistants 'rate' the content according to a set of judgement guidelines but there would be plenty of room for judgements to be biased by knowing which condition a participant was in.

One complex and more subtle method of extracting what are likely to be the effects of experimenter expectancy from the effects of an experimental treatment occurs with the use of an EXPECTANCY CONTROL DESIGN. In this design (e.g. Burnham, 1966, in Rosnow and Rosenthal, 1997) half the participants receive the experimental treatment and half do not as in the standard between groups design. However, half of those given the experimental treatment are assessed by data collectors who are told the participant was in the treatment condition, while the other half are assessed by a data collector who is told they were control participants. The same split occurs for the control group. Now, using a 2 x 2 design described later in Chapter 19, we can look at the overall effect of the treatment, the overall effect of expectancy and any interaction between these two variables.

External validity

In a sense, construct validity asks whether the effect demonstrated can be generalised from the measures used in the study (e.g. IQ test) to the fuller construct (e.g. intelligence). External validity asks a similar question. It asks whether the apparent effects demonstrated in an investigation can be generalised *beyond the exact experimental context*. In particular, can effects be generalised from:

- the specific sample tested to other people
- the research setting to other settings
- the period of testing to other periods.

Bracht and Glass (1968) called the first of these POPULATION VALIDITY and the second ECOLOGICAL VALIDITY but see Box 4.1

Population validity

As we saw in Chapter 1, in 1996, the *Guardian* reported a *Reader's Digest* 'experiment' in which ten wallets, each containing £30, were dropped in each of several UK cities. On the basis of numbers of wallets returned intact, the *Guardian* article claimed that Liverpudlians (eight returned) were more honest than people in Cardiff (four returned). Hopefully, most readers would dismiss the ludicrous leap from a sample of ten people to several hundred thousand or more as completely invalid.

POPULATION VALIDITY concerns the extent to which an effect can be generalised from the sample studied to the population from which they were selected and also to other populations. The results of a class experiment can't necessarily be generalised to *all* students, nor can they be generalised to all other groups of people. The matter of how important this issue is varies with the type of study. Work in cross-cultural psychology (see Chapter 9) has shown us that many effects published in US student texts as apparently *universal* are, in fact, largely limited to *individualistic* (mainly 'western') societies, e.g. the 'fundamental attribution error' and the 'self-serving attributional bias'. Note the use of the term 'fundamental' as evidence of the belief that this effect is *universal*. Some psychologists extrapolate to whole continents with terms like 'the African mind' (see Jung's quotation and Lynn's (1991a) estimate of the 'black African IQ' on p. 212). We have already seen that a vast number of psychology experiments have been carried out on students, mainly white, mainly Western and, until the 1970s, mainly male. Things have changed though – 84% of UK psychology students are now female (Stevens and Gielen, 2007: 84).

ECOLOGICAL VALIDITY is referred to by many authors as the extent to which findings generalise to other settings, e.g. from the laboratory to a field setting or from one field setting to another. However, there is much confusion and argument about the 'hijacking' of the term from its original use and it has also become a substitute for the term 'realism' in loose research methods talk, see Info Box 4.3. For an extended discussion, see www.hodderplus.com/psychology.

Info Box 4.3	**The three faces (at least) of ecological validity**

Use of the term 'ecological validity' has become widespread and over-generalised to the point of being somewhat useless. Over ten years ago, Hammond (1998) referred to its use as 'casual' and 'corrupted' and to the robbing of its meaning (away from those who continue to use its original sense) as 'bad science, bad scholarship and bad manners'. There are three relatively distinct and well used uses of the term and I refer to the last as the 'pop version' to signify that this use, though very popular, is a conceptual dead end and tells us nothing useful about validity.

1. The original technical meaning

Brunswik (e.g. 1947) introduced the term 'ecological validity' to psychology as an aspect of his work in perception 'to indicate the degree of correlation between a proximal (e.g. retinal) cue and the distal (e.g. object) variable to which it is related' (Hammond, 1998, para 18). This is a very technical use. The proximal stimulus is the information received directly by the senses – for instance, two lines of differing lengths on our retinas. The distal stimulus is the nature of that actual object in the environment that we are receiving information from. If we know that the two lines are from two telegraph poles at different distances from us, we might *interpret* the two poles as the same size but one further away than the other. The two lines have ecological validity in so far as we know how to usefully interpret them in an environment that we have learned to interpret in terms of perspective cues. The two lines do *not* appear to us as having different lengths because we interpret them in the context of other cues that tell us how far away the two poles are. In that context their ecological validity is high in predicting that we are seeing telegraph poles.

2. The external validity meaning

Bracht and Glass (1968) defined ecological validity as an aspect of external validity and referred to the degree of generalisation that is possible from results in one specific study setting to other different settings. This has usually had an undertone of comparing the paucity of the experimental environment with the greater complexity of a 'real' setting outside the laboratory. In other words people asked how far will the results of this (valid) laboratory experiment generalise to life outside it? Cook and Campbell (1979) also supported this interpretation though they have more recently, and because of the controversy, replaced it with the term 'external validity with regard to settings'. On this view, effects can be said to have demonstrated ecological validity the more they generalise to different settings and this can be established quantitatively by replicating studies in different research contexts.

3. The 'pop' version

The pop version is the definition very often taught on basic psychology courses. It takes the view that a study has (high) ecological validity so long as the setting in which it is conducted is 'realistic', or the materials used are 'realistic', or indeed if the study itself is naturalistic or in a 'natural' setting. The idea is that we are likely to find out more about 'real life' if the study is in some way close to 'real life', begging the question of whether the laboratory is not 'real life'.

The pop version is in fact unnecessary since Brunswik (1947, in Hammond, 1998) also introduced a perfectly adequate term – *representative design*. In a thorough discussion of ecological validity, Kvavilashvili and Ellis (2004) bring the original and external validity usages together by arguing that both representativeness and generalisation are involved but that generalisation improves the more that representativeness is dealt with. However, they argue that a highly artificial and unrealistic experiment can still demonstrate an ecologically valid effect. They cite as an example Ebbinghaus's memory tasks with nonsense syllables. His materials and task were quite unlike everyday memory tasks but the effects Ebbinghaus demonstrated could be shown to operate in everyday life, though they were confounded by many other factors. Araújo, Davids and Passos (2007) argue that the popular 'realism' definition of ecological validity is a confusion of the term with representative design and this is a good paper for understanding what Brunswik actually meant by 'ecological validity'. The term is in regular use in its original meaning by many cognitive psychologists. They are not clinging to a 'dinosaur' interpretation in the face of unstoppable changes in the evolution of human language. It is probably best to leave the term there and specifically refer to 'generalisation to settings' and 'more realistic' when discussing these concepts.

The problem with the pop version is that it has become a knee-jerk mantra – the more realistic, the more ecological validity. There is, however, no way to gauge the extent of this validity. Teaching students that ecological validity refers to the realism of studies or their materials simply adds a new 'floating term' to the psychological glossary that is completely unnecessary since we already have the terminology. The word to use is 'realism'. As it is, students taught the pop version simply have to learn to substitute 'realism' when they see 'ecological validity' in an examination question.

Milgram vs Hofling – which is more 'ecologically valid'?

A problem with the pop version is that it doesn't teach students anything at all about validity as a general concept. It simply teaches them to spot when material or settings are not realistic and encourages them to claim that this is a 'bad thing'. It leads to confusion with the laboratory-field distinction and a clichéd positive evaluation of the latter over the former. For example, let's compare Milgram's famous laboratory studies of obedience (see Chapter 23) with another obedience study by Hofling *et al.* (1966) where nurses working in a hospital, unaware of any experimental procedure, were telephoned by an unknown doctor and broke several hospital regulations by starting to administer, at the doctor's request, a potentially lethal dose of an unknown medicine. The pop version would describe Hofling's study as more 'ecologically valid' because it was carried out in a naturalistic hospital setting on real nurses at work. In fact, this would be quite wrong in terms of generalisation since the effect has *never* been replicated. The finding seems to have been limited to *that* hospital at *that* time with *those* staff members. A partial replication of Hofling's procedures failed to produce the original obedience effect (Rank and Jacobson, 1977[3]), whereas Milgram's study has been successfully replicated in several different countries using a variety of settings and materials. In one of Milgram's variations, validity was demonstrated when it was shown that shifting the entire experiment away from the university laboratory and into a 'seedy' downtown office, apparently run by independent commercial researchers, did not significantly reduce obedience levels. Here, following the pop version, we seem to be in the ludicrous situation of saying that Hofling's effect is more valid even though there is absolutely no replication of it, while Milgram's is not, simply because he used a laboratory! The real problem is that there is no empirical test of 'validity' in the pop notion of ecological validity. It is certainly a somewhat ludicrous notion to propose that, solely on the basis of greater 'naturalness', a field study *must* be more valid than a laboratory one. (For an extended version of this debate, see the companion website.)

Meta-analysis

We have seen that one way to establish the external validity of an effect is to conduct replications of the original study that demonstrated it. Unfortunately for the scientific model of psychology which many psychologists adhere to, it is the exception, rather than the rule, to find a procedure that 'works' reliably every time it is tested. The world of psychological research is littered with conflicting results and areas of theoretical controversy, often bitterly disputed. Confusion occurs because researchers use different constructs, in different research settings, on different populations and at different historical moments.

Here are some areas in which literally hundreds of studies have been carried out, yet without bringing us much closer to a definitive conclusion about the relationships they explore:

- sex differences and origin of differences in sex role
- the origins of intelligence – nature or nurture
- socio-economic position and educational or occupational achievement
- conformity and its relation to other personality variables
- cognitive dissonance (and alternative explanations)
- language development and parental stimulation
- deprivation of parental attachment and related emotional disturbance.

Periodically, it has been the tradition to conduct a literature review of research in these and many other topic areas. Examples of these will be found in the *Annual Review of Psychology*. The problem

---

[3] Unlike in Hofling's study, nurses were familiar with the drug and were able to communicate freely with peers.

here is that reviewers can be highly selective and subjectively weight certain of the studies. They can interpret results with their own theoretical focus and fail to take account of common characteristics of some of the studies which might explain consistencies or oddities. In other words, the traditional review of scientific studies in psychology *can* be relatively unscientific.

META-ANALYSIS is a relatively recent approach to this problem, employing a set of statistical techniques in order to use the results of possibly hundreds of studies of the same or similar hypotheses and constructs. Studies are thoroughly reviewed and sorted as to the suitability of their hypotheses and methods in testing the effect in question. The collated set of acceptable results forms a new 'data set'. The result of each study is treated rather like an individual participant's result in a single study. The statistical procedures are beyond the scope of this book but they do centre on the comparison of *effect sizes* across studies and these are introduced and explained in Chapter 14. Here are some examples of meta-analytic research.

- In one of the most famous and early meta-analytic studies, Smith and Glass (1977) included about 400 studies of the efficacy of psychotherapy (i.e. does it work?). The main findings were that the average therapy patient showed improvement superior to 75% of non-therapy patients, and that behavioural and non-behavioural therapies were not significantly different in their effects.

- Rosnow and Rosenthal (1997) report meta-analytic studies on hundreds of studies of experimenter expectancy following doubts about their classic original work described earlier.

- Fischer and Chalmers (2008) found 213 effect sizes from 171 articles (across 22 countries involving 89,138 participants) that included sufficient statistical information and which used the Life Orientation Test (LOT) on medically fit participants over 18. The LOT was employed as a measure of optimism and the researchers found that there was very little cross-cultural variation in levels of LOT but that higher optimism was consistently related to higher levels of individualism (see p. 216) and egalitarianism.

Meta-analysis takes account of sample size and various statistical features of the data from each study. There are many arguments about features that merge in the analysis, such as Presby's (1978) argument that some non-behavioural therapies covered by Smith and Glass were better than others. The general point, however, is that meta-analysis is a way of gathering together and refining knowledge (a general goal of science) in a subject area where one cannot expect the commonly accepted and standardised techniques of the natural sciences. It also brings into focus the various external threats to validity producing variation in a measured effect.

1 Of the designs outlined below:

(a) Which are not likely to be affected by demand characteristics?

(b) Which might involve looser procedures than the rest?

(c) Which could be subject to researcher bias?

(d) In which could 'blind' data-gathering and/or assessing procedures be employed?

1   A ladder is placed against a street wall to see whether more males or females avoid it.

2   Randomly allocated students are asked to write essays in silence or listening to loud music.

3   Boys with no brother and boys with two brothers are observed under laboratory conditions to see which group exhibits greater aggression.

4   A researcher, dressed either casually or smartly, approaches passengers at a station to ask for directions. The aim is to see whether smarter dress elicits greater help.

5   Under laboratory conditions, people are asked to make a speech, contrary to their own view, first alone and then in front of others. Their attitude strength is measured after each presentation.

6   Drug addicts are compared with a control group on their tolerance of pain, measured in the laboratory.

7   Researchers visit various grades of worker at their place of employment and take them through a questionnaire on their attitude to authority. It is thought that salary level will be related to degree of respect for authority.

8   One of two very similar homes for the elderly passes from local government to private control. Workers in each are compared on job satisfaction over the following year, using informal interviews.

9   Children in one school class are given a six-month trial of an experimental new reading programme using a multi-media approach. A second class of children receive special attention in reading but not the new programme. Improvements in reading are assessed.

10 The number of days off sick for workers in a large factory is measured monthly for one year before and one year after the national introduction of new regulations under which people may 'self-certificate' sicknesses lasting under four days.

2 Which two of the suggestions below might produce more valid measures of the construct of attitude towards the elderly?

(a) answers to a structured questionnaire

(b) what people say to a close friend in conversation

(c) what people say in an informal interview

(d) the number of elderly people a participant counts as close friends

3 Each of the following statements from students discussing their practical work contains a reference to a form of internal or external validity threat. Pick 'statistical conclusion', 'internal', 'construct' or 'external' for each one and, where possible, name or describe the threat.

(a) I mucked up the stats!

(b) Didn't you use the test we were given in class then?

(c) Useless questionnaire; didn't cover aggression – it was more to do with etiquette.

(d) Course they knew what was going on; they know how to hide their prejudices.

(e) I bet you egged them on in the imagery condition!

(f) Bet it wouldn't work on the geography students.

(g) It was noisy in the student refectory; would they dislike that music so much in their own rooms?

(h) We used 20mg of caffeine in one condition and 40mg in the other but I think the 40mg was too low. They didn't show any significant difference in reaction time.

Answers

1 (a) 1, 4, 10 (for 7 and 8 demand characteristics are possible if participants are aware of participating in a scientific study).

(b) 7, 8, 9

(c) all

(d) all; in each case data gatherers need not know the true or full purpose of the research

2 (b) No effects from knowledge of testing, for instance; unlikely to lie or 'look good'.

(d) Probably the most reliable and objective but a narrow measure.

3 (a) statistical conclusion; (b) internal (changed instrument); (c) construct; (d) construct (social desirability/'looking good'); (e) construct (experimenter expectancy/bias); (f) external (population validity); (g) external (setting); (h) construct validity; levels of independent variable too narrow.

Glossary

Demand characteristics	Cues in a study which help the participant to work out what is expected.
Double blind	Experimental procedure where neither participants nor data gatherers know which treatment participants have received.
Error variance	Variance among scores caused by the operation of randomly acting variables
Evaluation apprehension	Participants' concern about being tested, which may affect results

Expectancy control design	Design that isolates treatment effects, expectancy effects and their interaction
Experimenter expectancy	Tendency for experimenter's knowledge of what is being tested to influence the outcome of research
Experimenter reliability	The extent to which the results produced by two or more experimenters are consistent
Extraneous variable	Anything other than the independent variable that could affect the dependent variable; it may or may not have been allowed for and/or controlled
Hawthorne effect	Effect on human performance caused solely by the knowledge that one is being observed
Meta-analysis	Statistical analysis of results of multiple equivalent studies of the same, or very similar, hypotheses in order to assess more thoroughly an effect's validity
Non-reactive study	Study in which people are not aware that they are being researched
Participant expectancy	Effect on study of participants' expectancy about what they think is supposed to happen
Pleasing the experimenter	Tendency of participants to act in accordance with what they think the experimenter would like
Random error	Any error possible in measuring a variable, excluding error that is systematic
Reactive study/design	Study in which participants are required to respond in some way; they are therefore aware of being the subject of assessment
Single blind	Procedure in an experiment where either participants or the experimenters do not know which treatment each participant received
Social desirability	Tendency of research participants to want to 'look good' and provide socially acceptable answers
Standardised procedure	Tightly controlled steps taken by experimenter with each participant and used to avoid experimenter bias or expectancy effects
Validity	The extent to which an effect demonstrated in research is genuine, not produced by spurious variables and not limited to a specific context
Construct	Extent to which operational measures of variables match or encompass the intended theoretical construct
Internal	Extent to which an effect found in a study can be taken to be real and caused by manipulation of the identified independent variable
Ecological	In the external validity context, the extent to which research effects can be generalised to other places and conditions. However, a term which is also a popular substitute for 'realistic' and one which has a technical meaning in perception – degree to which proximal stimulus predicts the distal stimulus for the observer. Hence a term to be careful with – watch for the author's intended meaning. Badly used if a study outside the laboratory is automatically assumed to be 'more ecologically valid'

External	Extent to which results of research can be generalised across people, places and times
Population	Extent to which research effect can be generalised to rest of the population or other populations
Threat to	Any aspect of the design or method of a study that weakens the likelihood that a real effect has been demonstrated or that might obscure the existence of a real effect

5 Quasi-experiments and non-experiments

- *Quasi-experiments* occur when participants are not randomly allocated by the experimenter into conditions of the manipulated independent variable (a non-equivalent groups design) or where the researcher does not control the independent variable. A common case of the latter is a *natural experiment*. Some natural experiments can be analysed as a *time series* design.
- *Threats to internal and external validity* have been emphasised in the literature promoting the value and pitfalls of *quasi-experimental* and non-experimental work in field research.
- The *laboratory experiment* is compared for validity with *field experiments* and studies.
- *Non-experimental methods* investigate variables that exist among people irrespective of any researcher intervention, often by *correlation* of variables or by the investigation of existing *group differences*. In these studies no independent variable is manipulated.
- Any of these study designs may be used to eliminate hypotheses and therefore support theories; each is vulnerable to different kinds of *threat to validity*.

The field and the laboratory

In the last chapter we saw that the misused term 'ecological validity' had something to do with a comparison of the laboratory and the field in psychological research. Remember that the laboratory is used for the scientific purpose of controlling extraneous variables. The psychology laboratory does not usually contain the stereotypical lab equipment of retort stands and bubbling bottles. The psychological researcher's laboratory may include interview rooms, group discussion rooms, a soundproof room or even a toddlers' nursery, though some psychological laboratories often do contain technical equipment and computers. The term 'laboratory' is used, however, where the research participants come to the premises of the psychologist in a controlled environment.

FIELD STUDIES are those conducted outside the laboratory and very often in the natural environment of the people studied. The major advantage of a field study is the opportunity to capture natural behaviour as it occurs in everyday life – in which case the design can be called NATURALISTIC. Many field studies assess participants on their home turf, even though the testing or observation itself would not be a part of everyday activity. To the extent that participants are *aware* of the measures, observations or research aims, then, all the appropriate 'threats' described in Chapter 4 would still apply. However, it is likely there will be far less evaluation apprehension, and fewer effects associated with the artificial surroundings of a laboratory. In addition, the laboratory can force researchers to use highly limited variables and measures. For instance, Bandura (1977) measured children's aggression rather narrowly in terms of the hitting of the now notorious Bobo Doll and other imitations of an adult. The researcher observing playground behaviour can record naturally produced aggression (so long as the coding system is broad enough) even if the design is still basically experimental, for instance by observing children who have or have not experienced an anti-bullying programme.

Pause for thought

You might now like to consider this dilemma. Participants are asked to attend for a psychology experiment. As they sit in the waiting room, another 'participant' (actually a confederate), who is either attractive or unattractive, obtains through conversation their views on a popular film. The attractive confederate is expected to extract a more positive response. The issue to debate here, though, is whether or not this counts as a laboratory or a 'field' setting. Correctness of your answer is not crucial but discussion should highlight the central differences between laboratory and field and why we should consider them carefully. (Thanks to Cara Flanagan for this exercise.)

True experiments and field experiments

So far, we have worked with the simplistic notion of a 'pure' or TRUE EXPERIMENT. In a true experiment, the experimenter maintains complete control over all variables, holds most of these constant, and manipulates one or more independent variables, hence observing their effect on the uncontrolled but measured dependent variable. If the design of a field study is experimental then it is termed a FIELD EXPERIMENT and, though true field experiments are possible – see p. 120 for examples – this kind of design can run into difficulties in trying to conform to the rigid criteria of a true experiment.

Field experiments and increased validity threats

For the advantage of studying behaviour in a naturalistic setting field experimenters incur greater threats to the validity of their findings. Field studies inherently involve a problem of loss of control over extraneous variables. In particular, very often the researcher is unable to create *equivalent groups*. In the study conducted by Cialdini, Reno and Kallgren (1990) briefly described in Chapter 3, the researchers used as experimental conditions different numbers of pieces of litter lying on the ground as people walked along a path to an amusement park. The dependent variable in the study was whether the passers-by dropped a leaflet they had just been handed by researchers pretending to advertise that night's show. In this setting the researchers are completely unable to determine who goes into which condition. They had to use in their experimental conditions those people that happened along their path when each condition was being run. For all we know, more litterers may have come along for the 16-piece condition and hence it might appear that more litter created greater littering when, in fact, the cause was the type of person in the condition, an internal validity threat. The researchers, in short, may be suffering the problem of non-equivalent groups in an independent samples design – see p. 67. Because participants in this study cannot be randomly allocated to conditions the design is known as a *quasi-experiment*.

The quasi-experiment

We have now encountered a major fork in the road regarding experiments. The design problem of comparing NON-EQUIVALENT GROUPS led researchers in educational psychology field research to introduce the concept of a *quasi-experiment*. Cook and Campbell (1979) produced the classic text on quasi-experiments but have revised this in Shadish, Cook and Campbell (2002). Both texts give a thorough grounding in the issues of quasi-experimentation and in the associated concepts of *validity* introduced earlier. Social and applied psychologists (for instance, working in health, education, sport and so on) face the dilemma of wishing to research in realistic everyday settings but recognise the lack of control this can involve.

Nowadays plenty of research is non-experimental, but back in the 1950s and 1960s the psychology establishment suffered from an almost unswerving and extreme faith in the superiority of the experiment over all other research approaches. It was then often hard to get good but 'flawed' experimental research taken seriously or published. Cook and Campbell argued that plenty of good field research in educational and health psychology was therefore not properly accepted and its value was overlooked. While admitting, via the general arguments about validity, that very many field designs are not truly experimental, they also argued that, with sufficient attention paid to compensating controls, such work could nevertheless be presented as possessing a high degree of validity. They promoted the term QUASI-EXPERIMENT to refer to well-controlled research designs that were 'almost' experiments but lacked one or more of the essential features of a true experiment, the two most central of these being:

1 Random allocation of participants to conditions, without which we have *non-equivalent groups*

2 Full experimenter control over the independent variable.

Non-equivalent groups

The very nature of social or applied psychological research in the field often entails not being able to allocate participants to conditions of an experiment *at random*. Whenever we do not allocate at random we can usually imagine a way in which initial differences *between the groups* might be responsible for any difference found. For instance, we may wish to study the effectiveness of new drivers displaying a green 'P' on their car for the first year after full qualification. Samples of those who do and do not choose to display a green 'P' would be *self-selecting*, since the researcher cannot randomly allocate them to their 'conditions'. If it turns out that green 'P'-plate wearers have fewer accidents we cannot be sure that this is a result of their 'P'-plate wearing, or of their general conscientiousness, demonstrated by their decision to wear the plate in the first place.

As another example, if health psychologists wish to study the effects of fitness training sessions on recuperation patterns, they may have to compare those who attend the sessions with those who do not. Unfortunately, the comparison may well be between the more committed and the less committed. *This* variable may be responsible for later differences between groups, not the content of the sessions themselves. We can, of course, attempt to extract from all possible participants two representative samples that are similar on several variables that we could intuitively isolate beforehand. However, there is always the possibility that some difference between attenders and non-attenders, not identified for matching, *could* be responsible for differences found in recuperation.

Applied researchers in the field might typically wish to assess the effects of:

- a stress-reduction training programme on employees' sickness records and productivity
- a radical new rehabilitation programme for ex-drug addicts on readjustment
- an educational intervention programme on children's attainments.

In each case we often cannot allocate randomly and we may not be able to match up equivalent groups. We may have to use the ex-addicts attending a Thursday session for the new programme and compare these with the Tuesday group staying on the conventional programme. Here, we often cannot ensure that the two groups are roughly equivalent. If the programme is intended to improve self-esteem, among other things, then we *can* employ a pre-test and final test of participants on self-esteem. The dependent variable would then become each participant's *change* in self-esteem over the period, not their final score. This way we control, to some extent, for pre-existing differences between the two groups.

No control of the independent variable including the 'natural experiment'

Psychologists often have to exploit naturally occurring conditions rather than a programme they have set up themselves. Again, this is often the case in applied field research. In the examples given above it might well be the case that the researcher investigates the effects of 'compensatory' education programmes on children where the conditions and administration have all been set up by education professionals rather than by the researcher. The trouble here is that conditions will not necessarily have been organised with research interests in mind but in a way that will be ethically and professionally acceptable, and of greatest educational benefit to the children involved. Hence, the educational organisers will not always have been thinking about threats to validity and rigid adherence to a standardised procedure, closely comparable control groups and so on. The researchers may have to utilise skills of persuasion and tact in their negotiations with personnel (nurses, teachers, administrators) in order to maintain as much control as possible over key variables. It also may not be possible to use equipment as sophisticated as that employed in the laboratory. Altogether these conditions throw up a host of validity threats.

In some cases life just throws up convenient sets of conditions that no one has programmed to occur, psychologist or otherwise. Such events, if exploited by researchers, can be called NATURAL EXPERIMENTS. The introduction of the breathalyser produced such conditions in the UK in 1967 and a study based on it is described under the 'time series' heading below. A dramatic example is given in Box 6.2, where the researchers involved had the opportunity to observe the effects of television, introduced to the island of St Helena for the first time in the mid-1990s, on children's pro-social behaviour, which was observed before and after the event. In each case the researchers identify natural independent variables and dependent variables; in the breathalyser example we have absence of breathalyser tests and presence as the IV and traffic casualties as a DV. In the St Helena example, before and after television are levels of the IV with pro-social behaviour measures as DV.

A rather elegant and subtle design used by Wardle and Watters (2004) provided evidence that exposure of younger girls to much older girls in school is a factor which increases negative attitudes to weight and eating – see Table 5.1.

		Type of school	Oldest pupils
'Exposed' girls	9 years	Middle school	13 years
	11 years	Secondary school	18 years
'Non-exposed' girls	9 years	Junior school	11 years
	11 years	Middle school	13 years

Table 5.1 Categories of girls, and results in the Wardle and Watters (2004) eating attitudes study

In general, 'exposed' girls had a thinner ideal, felt more overweight, had more friends who had dieted, scored higher on the Child Eating Attitudes Test and had lower self-esteem. This is a neat arrangement since the two samples of girls, 'exposed' and 'non-exposed', are exactly the same age yet are in different conditions. 'Exposed' girls have peer models at school four to seven years older than themselves whereas 'non-exposed' girls have models only up to two years older.

Interrupted time series designs

Some quasi-experiments do not study specific individuals but use publicly recorded data on large numbers of people – often referred to as *archival data* (see Chapter 6) – in a TIME-SERIES design often used on single individuals or small samples. A time-series design tracks performance over several measurements; in the interrupted design this leads up to the introduction of a 'treatment' (a level of the independent variable) and several measurements occur *after* the intervention. An effect is then highlighted by a detectable change in the dependent variable of interest, and by no change in other variables *not* expected to be affected. Ross, Campbell and Glass (1973) studied driver and accident behaviour before and after the introduction of the breathalyser test to the UK. They wanted to show that traffic casualties reduced as a result of the new measure. Their data (see p. 292) showed that accidents dropped particularly during drinking hours (disputing the view that there was a *general* accident decrease). Further public data statistics were elegantly employed to eliminate several other alternative hypotheses:

- the reduced accident rate was not simply a result of people generally driving less (British Road Research Laboratory data showed a reduction in *number of accidents per mile driven*)
- people were *not* drinking less after the measure (there was no reduction in alcohol sales)
- people were *not* just driving more carefully after drinking (a survey showed more people reported walking home after drinking and post-mortem data showed that fewer post-breathalyser fatalities had alcohol in their blood).

Non-experimental research

Group difference studies

The dividing line between quasi-experiment and non-experiment is very hard to define. Many texts on experimental designs do not include, in their description of various experimental and quasi-experimental approaches, any title for the simple test of difference between two or more groups, a design which is, though dangerously flawed, extremely common in practical work for the new learner in psychology. In this design members of one group, defined by personality, biology or demographic characteristic, are compared with members of another group or with non-members. Very many studies, for instance, attempt to demonstrate some personality or behavioural difference between the sexes, an interesting example being the fairly regular finding that a sample of females will often rate their own IQ (in the absence of any specific knowledge about IQ tests and scores) lower than does an equivalent sample of males (e.g. Beloff, 1992). Other common studies are differences between samples of introverts and extroverts, between occupations (e.g. nurses vs non-nurses), between economic classes, and between members of different cultures or ethnic groups (see the section on cross-cultural research in Chapter 9).

The trouble with fitting these sorts of studies into the quasi-experimental category is that they lack a central feature of experimental and quasi-experimental designs. Take a look back at Figure 3.3. The classic experiment has some participants in two groups and then a 'treatment' is applied to one of the groups. The treatment is almost always fairly time specific, although it can include, for instance, a therapy programme lasting a year or two. In more sophisticated designs there are several different 'treatments'. In repeated measures designs participants are often tested with and without the treatment. By contrast, in what I prefer to call GROUP DIFFERENCE STUDIES, it is difficult to see how we can talk of a treatment being applied to previously 'untreated' individuals at all. One can argue that foetuses had maleness and femaleness (plus the entire lifetime experience of being one sex or the other) 'applied' to them, but this is a bit far-fetched and hardly 'controlled' in any way. The situation is even more blurred for characteristics like 'extroversion' and 'introversion'. When, exactly, is this 'treatment' applied? For occupations, over a relatively short period of time, it *is* possible to see the experience of being a nurse, say, as a 'treatment', especially if we can obtain before and after measures.

Correlational, observational and ex post facto studies

Some texts use the term 'correlational' for studies where we simply investigate whether there is a relationship between one variable and another 'out there' in the field. The trouble with this term is that 'correlation', which we shall meet in Chapter 17, is a specific statistical technique and is *not* what we use to investigate a difference between two groups, for instance, yet it is generically applied to this sort of study as well. In other words, to the confusion of students, a 'correlational study' can be one in which a statistical test of *difference* is used to investigate differences between existing groups.

Where 'correlational' is contrasted with experimental, what is meant is that we can only know there is some sort of *relationship* between two variables and that our evidence does *not* permit us to make inferences about cause *or* its *direction*. For instance, if we find that graduates have greater career motivation than non-graduates, we may *not* conclude that experience of the degree course *created* greater motivation. We may *only* say that the motivational difference is *related* to graduate status. University experience *might* cause increased motivation but, equally, having good motivation in the first place might have influenced the decision to attend the university course *and* might carry through to career motivation.

We have lost that special strength of the experiment, that is, the opportunity to manipulate one variable and observe its effect on the other. We also cannot manipulate sex or gender to observe its effect on, say, IQ self-estimation. We can only ask males and females to estimate their own IQ and observe the differences. From simply observing this difference there is no way we can begin to isolate the true causal variable. There will be myriad variables related to living as one sex/gender that are possible (and confounding) causal variables. There is a vast array of 'threats to validity' in this study if it is being claimed that 'being male causes people to rate themselves more highly on IQ'.

Some writers refer to most non-experimental studies as 'observational'. The trouble with this is that observation can be used as a technique for assessing the dependent variable in *true experiments* – see Bandura's work (e.g. 1965) and see Chapter 6. However, an 'observational study' again *usually* refers to one that is not an experiment and in which researchers record freely produced behaviour in a relatively natural setting. It will also cover 'observations' on existing groups, as in group difference studies

Cook and Campbell (1979) refer to such studies as being 'passive observational'. Sprinthall (2003) makes the useful distinction between experimental and 'post facto' research, 'post facto' meaning 'after the fact' and referring to all studies where we simply observe what has already happened – we can look at the difference between groups or the correlation between variables. We can of course simply divide all studies into three classifications: true experimental, quasi-experimental and non-experimental. Non-experimental studies would include all descriptive studies. It may be noted that the original Milgram situation and Asch's conformity condition are simply descriptive demonstrations and would not count as an experiment. They only show what happens when people are asked to obey or asked to give an answer when others have already answered. They become experiments when comparative conditions are introduced – in the case of Milgram various versions were compared (e.g. victim behind wall, in room, participant holding his hand on shock plate) while Asch compared participants' answers with those obtained when no conforming majority was present.

Non-experimental studies that test hypotheses tend to be correlational – they use correlations or tests of association in their analysis – see Chapters 16 and 17 – or they tend to measure group differences. There seems to be no common agreement on what to call the latter type of study so we'll continue to use the term of obvious description 'group difference'. The most important point about non-experimental studies of these kinds is that, if we are trying to identify cause and effect, they are associated with a far greater number of threats to validity than is the much more controlled true experiment. The situation is further complicated when we come to look at more complex 'factorial' experimental designs as described in Chapter 19. Here, a person variable is very often used as one independent variable (or factor) when a second independent variable is a more typical 'treatment'. For instance, we might be interested in whether feedback can improve problem-solving. Hence one independent variable will be the manipulation of feedback – given to one group of participants and not to another. We may also be interested in how the effect of feedback differs across genders so our second independent variable is gender. Overall this is not a true experiment since the IV of gender does not have participants randomly allocated to its levels.

I think the safest thing the student can do is to just *not* treat group difference designs as true experiments, nor even quasi-experiments, and to be aware of just how little a sex difference study (or extrovert/introvert comparison) tells us if it is not related to predictions from a general theory

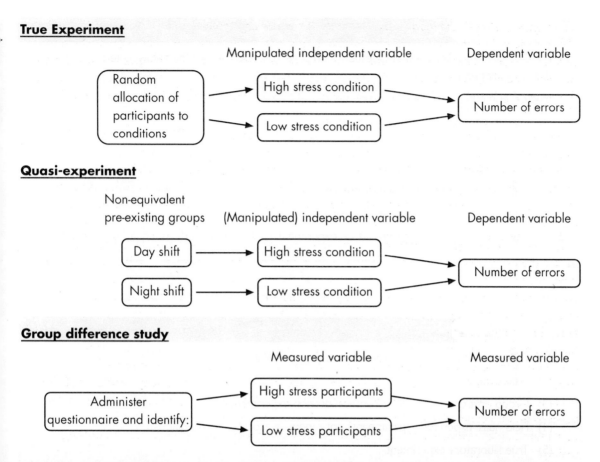

Figure 5.1 Design and variables in a true experiment, quasi-experiment and group difference study. The top design shows a classic true experiment where participants (in a factory) are randomly allocated to 'low stress' or 'high stress' conditions by controlling the speed of a production line; number of errors is the dependent variable. In the quasi-experimental design, management might deny the research psychologist the option of allocating participants at random, so the second best option might be to run the high- and low-stress conditions on two different groups: the day and night shifts. Trouble here is that the day workers might *already* be more error prone and/or might contain an abnormally high number of workers who respond adversely to stress. In the group difference study, the researcher has not manipulated conditions to produce stress at all but has directly identified higher- and lower-stressed workers. All are observed for error rate and the analysis looks at the differences between the two stress-level groups.

and, even then, just how ambiguous any result will be in terms of leading us to any cause–effect relationship. Sex-difference studies are certainly not true experiments. The most important thing of all, however, is to demonstrate awareness of the features of true experiments, to understand what definitely *would* be termed a quasi-experiment, and always to discuss possible 'threats' and weaknesses when interpreting the results of any type of study at all.

1 For each of the studies listed in Question 1 on page 104, select any of the following terms to describe the design appropriately:

true experiment   field experiment

quasi-experiment   field investigation

non-experimental   natural experiment

laboratory experiment   correlational

laboratory investigation   group difference

More than one term can be chosen for each study.

2 What two conditions, missing from a true experiment, qualify a field study as a quasi-experiment?

Answers

1 (1) Group difference; field investigation; non-experimental

(2) True experiment

(3) Group difference; laboratory investigation; non-experimental

(4) Field quasi-experiment (participants not randomly allocated to conditions).

(5) True laboratory experiment.

(6) Laboratory investigation; group difference; if the experience of being an addict is counted as a 'treatment', then this is arguably a natural quasi-experiment.

(7) Correlational; field investigation.

(8) Natural quasi-experiment (researcher doesn't control independent variable).

(9) Field quasi-experiment (no random allocation).

(10) Natural quasi-experiment.

2 1 No random allocation of participants to conditions.

2 Experimenter does not have full control of the independent variable.

Control and validity in the laboratory and in the field

The laboratory – advantages

Most studies carried out in laboratories are experiments, but not all. The true experiment demands careful control of all variables and, disregarding any other objections to the experiment, this aim is best achieved in a laboratory setting, particularly where highly accurate recordings of human cognitive functions (such as memory, perception and selective attention) are required. In the field, certain variables – such as noise, interruption and distraction – may not be in the control of the experimenter. For instance, Bandura's (1965) experimental procedure permitted him to control strictly the conditions of his experiment (children saw a film of a rewarded, non-rewarded or punished adult). He could then carefully assess, through a one-way mirror, the children's consequent play behaviour with the Bobo Doll. However, an equivalent attempt to observe play behaviour in the playground would involve such lack of control as children moving off, being obscured by others or simply lacking energy in cold weather. The children may also wish to play with the observer if he or she isn't hidden.

A further advantage of the laboratory is the fact that complex equipment, requiring careful setting and maintenance, can be used, which might be too cumbersome to transport to a field setting.

The laboratory – disadvantages

There are many critics of the use of the laboratory method in psychological research, however, several arguing that behaviour studied out of context in an artificial setting is meaningless. Many experimental psychologists were rather taken aback in 1978 when Ulric Neisser, a leading research psychologist who had been very much associated with the laboratory investigation of human cognitive processes, said publicly:

The results of a hundred years of the psychological study of memory are somewhat discouraging. We have established firm empirical generalisations but most of them are so obvious that every ten-year-old knows them anyway . . . If X is an interesting or socially significant aspect of memory, then psychologists have hardly ever studied X. (1978: 4–5)

This was pretty strong stuff and came from within the ranks! Psychologists were already used to the criticism of experimental laboratory procedures made by those who did not use them but here was a dedicated experimentalist, Ulric Neisser, calling for memory researchers to move towards studying 'real' memory in normal life. (In this speech he was also responsible for creating early confusion in the ecological validity debate – see Hammond, 1998). Partly as a result of Neisser's appeal, mainstream memory research now includes a great number of 'everyday memory' studies and a whole new approach has developed around this theme, including the use of qualitative data recording (for instance, the diary method of Wagenaar (1986) in Chapter 6 and the memory work of Haug, 1987 in Chapter 10).

Some of the regular criticisms of laboratory work were as follows:

Narrowness of the independent variable and dependent variable

As we said earlier, although Bandura exerted strict control over variables, the kinds of aggression he measured were a very narrow range of what children are capable of in the way of destructive or hostile behaviour. It could be argued that at least this fraction of aggressive behaviour, we are now aware, could be modelled but, in general, the unrealistic and narrow nature of many operational measures made in the laboratory are a major threat to construct validity. Some time ago, Heather argued:

Psychologists have attempted to squeeze the study of human life into a laboratory situation where it becomes unrecognisably different from its naturally occurring form. (1976: 31)

Inability to generalise

A reliable effect in the laboratory may bear little relationship to life outside it. The popular late 1960s concept of an 'iconic memory' or very short-term 'visual information store', holding 'raw' sensory data from which we rapidly process information, has been considered by later psychologists (e.g. Haber, 1983) to be an artefact of the particular experiments that produced evidence for it, though not all agree (Eysenck and Keane, 1995).

Remember, studies performed outside the laboratory do not automatically possess greater external validity. However, many laboratory psychological experiments have been criticised because the effects they demonstrate probably would not be replicated in everyday settings. Asch's famous demonstrations of conformity (e.g. 1956), for example, were conducted among relative strangers, who had to judge the length of lines with no discussion. Everyday conformity almost always concerns familiarity and social interaction with one's peers, or at least with local social norms. Asch's findings would increase their external validity if we could reproduce the effect, say, among friends in a school classroom setting.

A very strong contender for the claim of laboratory artefact is the supposed phenomenon of 'social loafing' – the idea that individuals perform with less effort when within a group than when working individually. Several investigators showed that the *opposite* of this occurred in non-individualistic cultures (Earley, 1989; Gabrenya *et al.*, 1985) such that individuals worked *harder* in a group than when alone. Holt (1987, in Brown, 1988) showed that the original effect disappeared even in a Western experimental setting when participants were given very minimal interaction with their colleagues prior to the experimental trial. Hence, Holt argued for the term 'social labouring' and saw social loafing as an odd phenomenon occurring only under very artificial conditions where participants are isolated from a normal sense of social responsibility.

On the other hand it is sometimes possible to argue that if an effect occurs in a narrow laboratory setting how much *stronger* must that effect be in everyday life. If Asch's participants would conform to such obviously wrong answers as those given by confederates then how much more likely would they be to conform to more ambiguous and complex 'real world' issues? Similarly, if Milgram's participants obeyed in the laboratory setting, where they could simply walk away with no sanctions, how much more likely would they be to obey when there were, as there would be in everyday life, real threats of social disapproval, sacking, imprisonment or court martial for disobedience?

Artificiality

To continue with this theme, a laboratory is an intimidating, possibly even frightening, place. People may well be unduly meek and over-impressed by their surroundings. If the experimenter compounds this feeling by sticking rigidly to a standardised procedure, reciting a formal set of instructions without normal interactive gestures such as smiles and helpful comments, a participant (until recently known as a 'subject') is hardly likely to feel 'at home' and behave in a manner representative of normal everyday behaviour.

In defence of the laboratory

In the study of brain processes, or of skilled human performance, stimulus detection and so on, not only does the artificiality of the laboratory hardly matter, it is the only place where highly technical and accurate measurements can be made, with random error reduced to a minimum. If we study human vigilance in detecting targets, for instance, does it matter whether this is done in the technical and artificial surroundings of a laboratory when results may be usefully applied to the almost equally technical and artificial environment of a radar monitoring centre? If we wish to discover how fine newborn babies' perceptual discriminations are, this can be done with special equipment and the control of a laboratory. The infant, at two weeks, is hardly likely to know, or care, whether it is at home or not.

Without a laboratory, physicists would not have been able to split atoms. Psychologists have discovered effects in the laboratory which, as well as being interesting in themselves, have produced practical applications. Without the laboratory we would be unaware of differences in hemispheric function, the phenomenon of perceptual defence or the extreme levels of obedience to authority that are possible. In each case, the appropriate interpretation of results has been much debated, but the phenomena themselves have been valuable in terms of human insight and further research.

The artificiality of scientific experiments is deliberate. It is a direct consequence of the attempt to eliminate explanations by separating out the correlating and confounding variables that normally determine events in the real world. Without the artificiality of experimental conditions we would not know that feathers and lead fall with exactly the same acceleration under the influence of gravity alone. Following Figure 5.2, we hypothesise from a theory in order to test it. Let's say we are Newton trying to show that gravity has the same effect on all matter; any object falls to earth at the same rate, even a feather or a piece of coal. We can't show this is in 'real life' because of the confounding factors of wind resistance, air flow etc. We therefore construct an experiment in a laboratory – in this case we make a vacuum and drop a piece of coal and a feather in it. They fall at the same rate. We have tested the theory and supported a hypothesis. We can *now* transport the theory, but *not* the actual effect, outside the laboratory and into practical applications in real life. A highly artificial laboratory demonstration has practical use and helps us develop more theory.

Develop hypothesis
from theory

Theory can be applied in practical
settings outside laboratory; more
success, more hypotheses to propose

Test hypothesis in
artificial but
controlled laboratory
setting

Test results
confirm theory

Figure 5.2 The role of the artificial laboratory experiment in theory development

In this context it can be argued that we should not *want* to generalise results of laboratory studies directly to 'real life' at all, nor even demonstrated effects. In the laboratory we test out specific hypotheses that follow from the *theory* under investigation. If these are successful, it is the *theory* that we might then attempt to generalise to more realistic contexts (Leary, 1995: 202).

The attempt to mimic real life inside the laboratory is often termed MUNDANE REALISM (Carlsmith *et al.*, 1976), whereas researchers are more likely to be interested in EXPERIMENTAL REALISM. This refers to a compelling context, perhaps quite unlike real life, but one in which participants fully engage because they are caught up in the reality of the experiment. In these circumstances we can be more confident that demand characteristics and expectancies are less likely to operate. The participant does not have the opportunity or inclination to work out 'What should happen here?'

Research conducted under laboratory conditions is generally far easier to replicate, a feature valued very highly by advocates of the experimental method and an important factor in determining the generalisability of our effects. What counts as a 'naturalistic environment' is also sometimes hard to gauge, as you may have discovered in debating the issue in the Pause for thought box on page 107. Human behaviour often occurs in what is not, to the individuals concerned, a 'natural' or at least an everyday environment. Examples might be the doctor's surgery, a visit to the police station or the inside of an aeroplane. For some participants the laboratory can be no less natural than many other places. In Ainsworth, Beli and Stayton's (1971) study of infant attachments, behaviour was observed when the mother was present, when she was absent, when a stranger was present and when the mother returned. From the infant's point of view it probably wasn't of great consequence where this study was carried out – the local nursery, a park or the laboratory (which looked something like a nursery anyway). The infant is very often in situations just as strange, and what mattered overwhelmingly was whether the mother was there or not. External validity is high if the infant behaves here as she would at the doctor's.

Studies in the field

Having defended the use of the laboratory, it must also be accepted that if we wish to broaden the effects that psychology can study to more than just what can be 'trapped' in a laboratory, we must accept and deal with the problems of studying human behaviour in a natural context. Referring back to the Cialdini *et al.* littering study described in Chapter 3, it would be difficult to invent within a laboratory setting a situation in which people might genuinely drop or not drop litter as they would in a public street. The organisational, clinical or health psychologist simply must work in the everyday world for much, if not all, of the time. The price paid, however, for studying behaviour in everyday settings with real and complex variables is, according to the conventional scientific model, a certain loss of precision because critical variables have not been, and cannot be, controlled. This in turn leads to a certain loss of confidence in the validity of any effect we might hope we are demonstrating.

For instance, Bowlby (1953) claimed (infamously) that institutionalised children displayed a significant amount of psychological distress because they lacked a single maternal bond. This explanation, based on field observations of children's behaviour in orphanages and the like, compared with the behaviour of two-parent children, was seriously confounded by the parallel presence of several other variables – regimented care, lack of social and sensory stimulation, reduced educational opportunity, rapid staff turnover and so on – all of which could potentially contribute towards an explanation of the children's behaviour. Lacking a single maternal bond *might* be a contributing factor to the children's psychological problems, or it might not contribute at all – it might simply co-exist with the real causes, some of which might be those just listed. The research and explanation are flawed because there are too many uncontrolled, possibly confounding, variables.

Many confounding problems could be associated with a field study by Kraut *et al.* (1998). This produced evidence of an association of internet use with depression and loneliness, along with a loss of immediate social contacts. This is a good example of the media misrepresenting the generalisations possible from exploratory psychological field research. In an article in which this work was reported, the *Guardian* (31 August 1998) stated that 'One hour a week on the internet *led to* an average increase of 1% on the depression scale . . .' (my italics). The words 'led to' make the claim that internet use *caused* the increased depression. There is, of course, the possibility that those participants who used the internet more often were those that had reached that stage of adolescence where introverted activities, social withdrawal and experience of greater 'angst' often seem to coincide. There again, people who are depressed, or who are only going through a 'rough patch', might be more likely to turn to lone interests such as using the internet.

In this case, however, it would be feasible to run a true experiment that could eliminate all these typical interpretive problems from a correlational study. Student volunteers could have been randomly allocated to groups and either asked to use the internet for certain periods (at the university's expense, of course) or to refrain from doing so, over a certain period of time. (In the Bowlby example, it would of course be totally unethical to have children randomly allocated to parent-rearing and institution-rearing experimental groups!) To do useful realistic research, psychologists cannot rely solely on the true, well-controlled experiment. They must use alternative methods, which have both advantages and disadvantages over the true experiment (see Table 5.2).

Field experiment	Factor	Laboratory experiment
Natural	Environment	Artificial
Controlled (partially)	Independent variable	Controlled
Random	Allocation of participants to conditions	Random
Weaker	Control of extraneous variables	Tighter
Participants may be unaware of study (if so, can't guess design, try to look good, etc.)	Awareness of aims by participants	Participants (except very young children) must be aware of being in experiment (though not what the design really is)
Harder	Replication	Easier
Higher	Mundane realism	Lower
To similar settings – good; to *other* practical settings – probably weaker	Generalisation (external validity)	To everyday settings – often very weak
Usually higher	Expense and time	Usually lower
Perhaps can't be brought to field situation	Equipment	Can be complex and only usable in the laboratory
Other disadvantages More confounding possible because of greater number of uncontrolled variables; researcher has to negotiate with field setting personnel – conditions may not end up well controlled.		Narrow independent variable and dependent variable can lead to low construct validity; setting more likely to create apprehension, wariness of strange surroundings, etc.

Table 5.2 A comparison of field and laboratory experiments on several factors

Field experiments

This is not to say that well-designed experiments cannot be run in the field. Here are two examples where the independent variable was experimenter-controlled and where random allocation was employed.

Regan and Llamas (2002) conducted a field experiment in which a woman confederate of the researchers wore either formal clothes (skirt and blouse) or gym clothes (leggings and T-shirt). She entered randomly selected shops in a large shopping mall and the time taken for an assistant to recognise her was recorded. In formal clothes, recognition times were significantly shorter.

Chapman and Rowe (2001) randomly allocated real job applicants to one of two interview procedures: face-to-face or videoconference. Among other results a significant bias was found in favour of videoconference applicants. In addition, it was found that female interviewers rated applicants more highly when the interview was unstructured than did all interviewers when the interview was structured.

A major disadvantage with field experiments is the lack of control the investigator can exert over extraneous variables, over strict manipulation of the independent variable and over careful, accurate measurement of the dependent variable. All these are vulnerable to more fluctuation in the field setting than might occur in the laboratory. Note that in the Regan and Llamas study, although shops were randomly allocated to conditions, the researchers had no control over the selection of assistants who responded. (A comparison of field and laboratory experiments is given in Table 5.2.)

Exercises

1 Without looking at Table 5.2, try to think of two advantages and two disadvantages of laboratory experiments and the same for field experiments.

2 You are discussing with a colleague two methods of measuring 'conformity'. One involves recording how often people will answer a simple question wrongly when several other people in the room have already answered wrongly (laboratory study). The other involves stopping people in the street who have infringed a traffic light or litter regulation, and taking those who agree to do so through a short questionnaire (field study). Find arguments for and against each proposal, concentrating on the suggested location of and method for the study. I hope you can think of at least three points for and three against each one.

Answers

1 Check your answers against Table 5.2.

2 Open answer.

Glossary

Correlational study	Study of the extent to which one variable is related to another, often referring to non-manipulated variables measured outside the laboratory
Experimental realism	Effect of attention-grabbing, interesting experiment in compensating for artificiality or demand characteristics.
Field study	Study carried out outside the laboratory and usually in the participants' normal environment
Field experiment	Experimentally designed field study
Group difference study	A post facto study that compares the measurement of an existing variable in two contrasting groups, e.g. male/female or introvert/extrovert

Mundane realism	Feature of design where experiment resembles everyday life but is not necessarily engaging
Naturalistic design	Design in which experimenters investigate participants in their everyday environment
Natural experiment	Events beyond researcher's direct control but where an IV and DV can be identified
Non-equivalent groups	Possible feature of groups of participants who have not been randomly allocated
Observational study	Research which gathers data by watching and recording behaviour
Post facto research	Research where pre-existing and non-manipulated variables among people are measured for difference or correlation
Quasi-experiment	Experiment in which experimenter does not have complete control over all central variables
Time-series design	Design in which behaviour is recorded for a certain period before and after a treatment point in order to look for relatively sudden change
True experiment	Experiment in which the experimenter has complete control over the manipulation of the independent variable and control of all other relevant variables

Observational methods – watching and being with people

This chapter covers most methods that are generally classed as observation. In a sense, all data from people are gathered through some form of observation, but the techniques described here mostly involve direct records of participant behaviour as it occurs, rather than methods of requesting information (interview, questionnaire) or of manipulation (experiment). Distinctions are made between the following:

- Observational *technique* and *design*; observations can be simply the *technique* for measuring the dependent variable in an experiment but *observational designs* rely primarily on observational records of relatively unconstrained, natural behaviour.
- *Participant observation* (where the observer acts in the observed group) and *non-participant observation*; so-called 'participant observation' studies often use interview techniques more than they use pure observation.
- *Disclosed* (people know what the observer is doing) and *undisclosed* observations.
- *Structured* (where some kind of coding is used) and *non-structured* observations.
- *Controlled* observation (often in the laboratory) and *naturalistic* observation (in the observed person's own environment).

Issues raised are the relative strengths and weaknesses of the various techniques and approaches, the objections of some qualitative researchers to structure and control in observational studies, *reliability* of observations, degrees of participation and specific ethical issues of undisclosed participant observation.

Advantages and disadvantages of the individual or group *case study* are considered along with some research examples; the case study provides unique information, unavailable by any other method, which may trigger more general and structured research.

Further topics covered are: *role-play* and *simulation*, *diary studies*, indirect observation via *archival data* (public and statistical records, media) and *verbal protocols*.

Observation in general

In the last few chapters we have seen that there can be fairly serious problems with the use of the experimental method in psychology, particularly in the laboratory, where a very narrow, and perhaps artificial, selection of behaviour may be studied, where 'demand characteristics' may distort the procedure and where persons studied are 'dehumanised'. A set of methods that can avoid some, but not always all, of these hazards is that known generally as 'observational methods'.

In a sense, behaviour is observed in almost all psychological studies. A researcher makes observations of the participants' reaction times, answers to a questionnaire, memory performance and so on. The emphasis, in using the term 'observational', however, is on the researcher observing a relatively unconstrained segment of a person's freely chosen behaviour.

'Observational' carries broad meaning in research literature. In a narrow sense it can refer simply to the technique of making observations and this can be used within an experimental design as a measure of a dependent variable, as well as being used in a variety of other settings. Used as a general description it can refer to all non-experimental studies where researchers simply take data from naturally occurring situations. If the basic design of a study is referred to as 'observational', however, then the emphasis is on observation as the main procedure for data gathering, a non-experiment in which records are made of relatively unconstrained behaviour as it occurs. This will be the main focus of the present chapter, though it should be noted that a quite common form of applied and often qualitative study – 'participant observation' – very often consists largely of interviews and notes on forms of social organisation, and perhaps little pure observation at all.

Observation as a technique or as an overall design

As technique

Observation may be used as a *technique* within a traditional experimental design, as in Milgram's (1963) work on obedience where, in addition to mechanical recordings of participants' responses, film record was made in order to observe changes in emotional reactions. Bandura (1965) studied children's imitation of adults in an experimental setting. Children observed an adult on film exhibiting various specific aggressive responses. One dependent variable was the number of responses specifically copied by the child. This was measured by observing the children (one at a time) let loose on the equipment, including the famous Bobo Doll, and recording the child's responses on camera through a one-way mirror.

The two examples above employ observational *techniques* in a laboratory setting. Field experiments also often use observation as a technique to measure the dependent variable. Rabinowitz *et al.* (1993) observed the behaviour of store cashiers in Salzburg who made transactions with confederates of the researchers who either underpaid or overpaid for their souvenirs. Observers recorded on a checklist, unobtrusively, besides various store and cashier details: whether the cashier returned or retained the overpayment or requested money for an underpayment, the speed of the exchange, occurrence of eye contact and a written description of the exchange among other variables. In 26% of overpayment cases where the money was counted the surplus was retained. Female cashiers were more likely to keep overpayments made by female confederates than by male customers.

Although, in the interests of sticking to human psychology, I generally refrain from using animal behaviour studies as examples, I couldn't resist giving one further case of a field experiment with observation used to measure the dependent variable. Uetake, Hurnik and Johnson (1997) played music to cows at milking time. They fluctuated between music and non-music days on a random basis and it was found that on music days more cows were near the milking area. Observations showed that these cows were more behaviourally ready to access the automatic milking system.

As overall design

If an investigation is given the title 'observational', this is usually in order to contrast it with other designs, particularly the experimental. In this case, the researcher has chosen to observe naturally occurring behaviour and not to experiment with it, i.e. no independent variable is manipulated.

Strengths and weaknesses of observational studies

Strengths	Weaknesses
Produces immediate data on real behaviour rather than possibly distorted self-reports.	People's behaviour can be affected by the awareness of being observed; reactivity effects.
Can gather data on behaviour which is not amenable to experimentation, e.g. real playground aggression; many kinds of infant behaviour.	As with other non-experimental studies it may not be possible to identify cause and effect. Children who watch more violent TV programmes may display greater playground aggression but this aggression could be a cause of the programme selection.
If conducted in field settings can gather data on completely genuine behaviour unconstrained by laboratory or other artificial setting.	Can be very time-consuming (especially participant observation) compared with the experiment or questionnaire study.

Participant and non-participant observation

A participant observer is to some extent a part of the group of individuals being observed, whereas a non-participant observer observes from a distance and ideally has no effect on the behaviour being observed. This is a 'dimension', since there are varying degrees of participation; these are described later. There is also a dimension of *disclosure* in that researchers may or may not inform the people studied that they are being observed and the information given can be partial or can involve a certain amount of deception in order to obtain more genuine behaviour or at least behaviour that is not affected by knowledge of the research hypothesis.

The discussion of indirect, structured and controlled observation that follows is related entirely to non-participant studies. Participant observation is largely a qualitative approach and will be discussed later in the chapter.

Structured (or 'systematic') observations

The main features of a structured or systematic approach to observation are:

- defining behaviour categories to be recorded prior to commencing the main observational sessions[1]

- sampling of behaviour in a consistent manner using one of the sampling devices described below

- training of observers in the use of a coding system and to a good level of agreement prior to main data-gathering sessions (i.e. a high level of *inter-observer reliability* is established – see p. 129).

Data-gathering devices

Records of behaviour can be made using any or a mixture of the following devices:

- visual recording

- still camera

- audio (to record spoken observations)

- hand-written notes, ratings or coding 'on the spot'.

Visual recording has the advantages that behaviour can be analysed ('rated' or 'coded') after the event at the researcher's own pace, and repeated viewing is possible. Any of the methods above might be used discreetly such that the participant is either completely unaware of the recording process (in which case ethical issues arise) or at least unable to see or hear the equipment during the observation session. This can be achieved with the use of screens or Big Brother style 'one-way' mirrors, which act as a mirror for the participant but a window for observers or camera.

Coding behaviour

Observers need to code behaviour either as it occurs or as they view a visual recording. Depending on the research question it might be that short-term *events* are of interest – e.g. 'takes mother's hand' – or longer-term *states*, such as 'watching other children'. *Event coding* (or *event sampling*) is driven by the occurrence of events or changes of event. If something changes the observer records the new event. *Interval coding* is driven by time – the observer records what happens during set time intervals. If these intervals are not consecutive, then the procedure is known as *time sampling*. An observer might, for instance, be asked to record behaviour during five-minute intervals interspersed with ten-minute 'off' intervals for elaborating what happened in the observation interval. Alternatively, time intervals might be selected at random in order to ensure a representative picture of behaviour during a whole day.

[1] In fact, Bakeman and Gottman (1997) argue that the early stages of an observational study need not be highly structured nor be testing specific hypotheses. In this sense, the approach sounds much like many of the qualitative approaches (see Chapters 10 and 22). However, in the latter stages of an observational study they would expect a structured and reliable system of gathering data to test hypotheses that have now been made specific, if not prior to the study, at least prior to final data-gathering sessions. Their text is a good guide to these latter, more structured, stages.

Event coding

Pause for thought

Before reading further, suppose you were interested in how children play with others and you record the activities of several three-year-old children in a nursery. Try to make a list of the events that you would want to record and try to define each so that an observer could go and record these events reliably for you.

In the chart shown in Figure 6.1 observers could simply tally every event as they watch a child in the nursery, in which case only one of the lines below the headed columns would be needed for recording the tally. However, a popular treatment of data is *sequential analysis* (Bakeman and Gottman, 1997) where observers record the *sequence* of a child's activity. In this case observers could enter a number below each heading using extra rows as needed. In Figure 6.1, the child moves from reading to looking on to parallel play with other children, back to solo play and back again to parallel play. This records the sequence of the child's activities but does not record how long the child spent on each one. It would be possible to enter time periods on the sheet but a slightly different approach is to use *Mutually Exclusive and Exhaustive* categories. For instance, if the four left-hand categories were simply reduced to 'solo activity', and if 'with member of staff' were added, then observers should *always* be able to select a column no matter what the child was doing so long as defining boundaries are agreed during observer training. Now, instead of entering codes or tally marks, the observers can simply enter the time at which each activity begins because when the *next* activity begins, by definition, the previous one ends so we know the duration of each one. Recording the sequence of activity can be important where a research hypothesis concerns the events that certain kinds of activity tend to follow or precede.

Solo activity				Playing with others			
Inactive	Reading	Playing alone	Looking on	Different activity	Same activity – parallel	Cooperative activity	Directed by adult
	1	4	2		3		
					5		

Figure 6.1 Observation sheet for event coding

Interval coding

In this form of observational data gathering observers note what activity occurred during successive time intervals. If the interval chosen is too large there might be several changes of state or event during it and selecting a single code will be difficult. Sometimes observers are asked to select the most representative activity or state for that period. Looking at Figure 6.1, it would be easy to adapt this sheet for interval coding by adding a left-hand column which puts, say, a five-minute time interval onto each row. Observers could record *all* the activities that occur in that period by ticking under the appropriate column or they could record what happened *mostly* during that five-minute period.

To exemplify interval coding and the complexity of observational studies we can look at a study by Halliday and Leslie (1986) in which acts of communication between mother and child (both ways) were coded from video recordings made over a period of six months' data gathering. The researchers sought to extend Bruner's ideas and show that children do more than just make requests or references in their interactions. They were interested in how these other actions might contribute to language acquisition as the child increasingly finds non-verbal methods inadequate. The researchers identified a set of 42 different actions, shown in Table 6.1, during pilot sessions with a couple of mother/child pairs. In the main study, an average of 12 half-hour sessions were recorded with 12 mother/child pairs. Each of these video sessions was coded using the 42 categories. There could be as many as five actions from the mother, and five from the child, in any five-second interval. The success of standardisation was estimated by finding the number of occasions on which two observers agreed for a sample of 15% of the tapes. They agreed 76.7% of the time.

Verbal categories

A	Demands attention		O	Orders, gives positive commands
D	Describes, gives information		ON	Orders not to
ET	Gives detailed label		PR	Praises
F	Corrects		PT	Prompts
I	Imitates completely		Q	Questions
IP	Imitates partially		QT	Questions about a label
IQ	Imitates as question		S	Tells story or recites rhyme
IS	Imitates as sentence		T	Labels, names
N	Says 'no'		TH	Says 'thank you' or 'ta'
NU	Count		Y	Says 'yes'
			Z	Adds tag

Non-verbal categories

a) Vocal | | **b) Non-vocal**

B	Babbles (with intonation)		GO	Gives object
G	Laughs, giggles		H	Holds, takes hold of
QN	Makes questioning noise		L	Looks around
V	Makes monosyllabic vocalisation		LO	Looks at object
V2	Makes two-syllable vocalisation		LP	Looks at mother
VE	Makes an emotional noise		LI	Lifts child
VN	Makes an object-specific noise		OB	Obeys
VS	Vocalises one syllable continuously		P	Points
	PL		Plays	
W	Cries		R	Reaches
YN	Makes affirmative noise		TO	Touches

Source: From Halliday and Leslie (1986)

Table 6.1 List of codes and definitions

Reliability of observational techniques

We need to know that the observations from several observers have *reliability*. We saw in the Halliday and Leslie (1986) study that observers agreed on 76.7% of occasions that were sampled for a reliability check and this is known as a measure of INTER-OBSERVER RELIABILITY. Ways to assess this agreement numerically are shown in Box 6.1. If there is good agreement between observers we do not know that they are observing and categorising *correctly* but we do at least know that they are *consistent* as a group. Reliability is enhanced by specifying in advance precisely what behavioural acts are to count in particular categories. Observers have to decide, for instance, when a push counts as 'aggressive' or when a child is being 'demanding'. Observers are usually trained to a high enough standard of reliability and accuracy before the observational study proper begins.

Info Box 6.1　Calculating inter-observer reliability

Let's suppose that for every observation point (e.g. each child in a nursery) two observers must choose one of four categories. They might for instance have to categorise each child as behaving according to codes 1, 2, 3 or 4, each code describing a different type of behaviour.

We add up all the occasions on which the two observers select the *same* category for the same child. Let's suppose this total is 42 out of a total of 50 (*N*) observations. This means that the observers agree on 84% of observation occasions and disagree on 16%. We can say their agreement rate is 84% *or* we can calculate a statistic known as Cohen's Kappa or *K*.

For Kappa multiply the total number of times observer A chose category 1 by the total number of times observer B chose category 1. Divide the result by the total number of observations. Do the same for categories 2, 3 and 4 and add the results. Call this value *E* and let's say this is 15.5

Call the number of cases of agreement *O* (i.e. 42 in this example).

$$K = \frac{O - E}{N - E} = \frac{42 - 15.5}{50 - 15.5} = \frac{26.5}{34.5} = .768$$

Values of *K* from .4 to .6 are considered 'fair', .6 to .75 'good' and above this 'excellent', so in this example we would have excellent inter-observer reliability. Notice that .75 is not as high as the .84 (or 84%) we obtained when only looking at how often the observers agreed. This is because we have now also taken into account how much they differ from one another when they do disagree.

Correlation (see Chapter 17) can also be used where, for instance, observers are counting occurrences of behaviour in successive intervals. As an example, see Table 6.2.

Controlled observation

Observations can be controlled through structure, as outlined above. Control can also be exercised over the environment in which observations take place. A high degree of environmental control can be exercised in the laboratory, though the participant need not be acutely aware that the environment is a 'laboratory'. Discussion groups may be observed in a comfortable 'seminar room', for instance. Ainsworth, Beli and Stayton's (1971) study of separation anxiety, briefly introduced in Chapter 5, used a carefully organised playroom where the floor was marked into squares and trained observers recorded on film (and by speaking on to audio tape) the movements of a child when its mother left and a stranger entered the room. The infants' behaviour was also filmed and the results were related to events of sensitivity in mothers' interactions with their children.

Problems with control – naturalistic observation

Observation studies in the laboratory do not escape many of the criticisms of laboratory experiments made in Chapter 5, in the sense that the laboratory can provide a highly artificial, possibly inhibiting atmosphere. Behaviour in the normal social context cannot be observed here. Some researchers, in search of realism, go out into the field and engage in NATURALISTIC OBSERVATION in, say, the home, the nursery or the workplace. For example, Steelman *et al.* (2002) conducted naturalistic observations of mothers to investigate the effect of early maternal warm responsiveness on the development of their children's social skills. Data were collected four times between the child's ages of one year and four and a half years and, each time, methods included questionnaires for the mothers and various psychological tests on the children, as well as one hour's observation in the home environment. Through a statistical technique known as *structural equation modelling* the researchers were able to make a strong claim for a direct positive effect of maternal warm responsiveness on the child's later social skills level. Naturalistic observation can be carried out with the same degree of structure as described above using a coding system and reliability checks. The difference may only be in the setting for the observations. However, many studies may use a more qualitative approach.

The 'baby biographers', whom we shall encounter below, were carrying out naturalistic observations, as did Piaget on his own children (e.g. Piaget, 1936). However, perhaps these studies also incorporated a certain amount of participative involvement on the part of the observers! Because much of the behaviour observed in these studies, so long as the observer is discreet, would have occurred anyway, realism is high and behaviour observed is entirely genuine. In some studies, however, people are aware that they are being observed. This can mean a video camera following them around the house. In this case we still have the problem of so-called 'Hawthorne effects' or participant *reactivity*. As Shaffer records:

Consider the experiences of one graduate student who attempted to take pictures of children's playground antics. What he recorded in many of his photos was somewhat less than spontaneous play. For example, one child who was playing alone with a doll jumped up when the student approached with the camera and informed him that he should take a picture of her 'new trick' on the monkey bars. Another child . . . said 'Get this' as he broke away from the kickball game and laid a blindside tackle on an unsuspecting onlooker. (1985: 16)

Reactivity effects

Reactions to knowledge of observation can be more subtle. Zegoib, Arnold and Forehand (1975) showed mothers under observation interacting more with their children, becoming more engaged in their activities and being more warm and patient than when not observed. Brody, Stoneman and Wheatley (1984) showed that siblings tended to reduce teasing, to quarrel less and to use less threatening behaviour under observation. The issue has become ambiguous, however. Jacob, Tennenbaum, Seilhamer and Bargiel (1994) found very few reactivity effects either in high- or low-obtrusive observation at family mealtimes. However, Gittelsohn *et al.* (1997) found higher observation reactivity on the first day of their structured observations in Nepalese households. They also found that, on days when reactivity was higher, there were also increases in positive health behaviour towards an observed child and decreases in socially negative behaviour. Their recommendation is that reactivity be controlled for (e.g. as in their case, by repeat observations) in order to enhance internal validity.

Reactive effects could, of course, be eliminated by the use of hidden and secret cameras, but this introduces ethical problems and is anyway impossible where the researcher wants to investigate behaviour within the home setting, unless, say, parents collude so that only the children are unaware that their behaviour is being observed. One way to reduce reactivity effects is to become a predictable and familiar part of the environment. Charlesworth and Hartup (1967) made several visits to a nursery school, interacted with the children, learned their names and so on. This also gave them the opportunity to test out and improve the reliability of the observation scheme they were going to employ.

| Info Box 6.2 | Turn that telly off! It's ruining the kids' behaviour |

People often blame television for decline in the quality of young people's behaviour. Researchers led by Charlton (Charlton *et al.*, 2000) had the rare opportunity to study the effects of television on children's behaviour when it was introduced for the first time to the community on the island of St Helena in the mid-1990s. The researchers focused specifically on pro- and anti-social behaviour. Using video recordings, they found that, compared with playground observations on three- to eight-year-olds made four months before television started, five years *after* its introduction there were 5 out of 64 measures showing a decrease in pro-social behaviour. However for boys, only, there were significant increases on two pro-social measures and significant decreases on two anti-social measures. In other words, for boys at least, there was almost as much positive as negative effect.

Problems with structured observation

Because systematic observation can be so structured and rigid, it would be considered inadequate by groups of qualitative researchers, who argue against the reduction of behaviour to artificially isolated units. What is the smallest unit we can work with? To describe a person as 'lifting an arm' may be objective physically but is stripped of social meaning compared with 'she waved', 'he made a bid' or 'she threatened the child'. Reduction to the simplest units of behaviour (the 'molecular' level) can create observations that are numerous, separated and meaningless.

The attempt to categorise interactions or assess responses by number can produce data at the 'reliable but not rich' end of the data-gathering spectrum. This positivist approach would be criticised by, for instance, humanists and phenomenologists, who promote a 'holistic' view of the person in psychology. Diesing (1972) states that the holist (psychologist) studies a 'whole human system in its natural setting', and says:

The holist standpoint includes the belief that human systems tend to develop a characteristic wholeness or integrity. They are not simply a loose collection of traits or wants or reflexes or variables of any sort . . . they have a unity that manifests itself in nearly every part . . . This means that the characteristics of a part are largely determined by the whole to which it belongs and by its particular location in the whole system. (1972: 137–8)

Something is lost, it would be argued, by categorising responses and simply counting them, or by giving them a rating-scale value. It is more important to record events observed such that the social meaning of actions is preserved for analysis. This may mean recording as much as possible of the social context in which actions occur. It may also mean making a comprehensive record of an individual's behaviour, such that specific actions are understood and perceived within the pattern of that person's unique experiences and motivation. It is not possible to do this using a highly constraining 'grid' or other pre-constructed framework for observation. We now turn to methods that attempt to generate a richer account of human behaviour in initially unquantified, descriptive form – that is, qualitative data (see also Chapters 10 and 22).

Qualitative non-participant observation

In Ainsworth *et al.*'s (1971) study mentioned earlier, some of the observers produced a running commentary on each child's behaviour by speaking into a tape recorder as they watched. The same technique has been used by observers following the interactions of mothers and children in their own homes. This generates a lot of raw data in qualitative form. These studies, however, are not usually conducted under the holistic or qualitative research banner. Rigid structure may be imposed on the data, during analysis, by independent raters trained in a specific coding scheme that reduces qualitative data to frequencies of occurrence.

Some studies of this sort, though, do go further along the qualitative route. The unquantified, descriptive data may not be simply categorised or coded. The data may also be analysed for illuminative insights leading to fresh research topics, as occurred when Milgram's post-experimental interviews were analysed. Or they may be presented alongside quantitative analysis in order to illustrate qualitative differences and issues that numerical reports cannot portray. Such is the cross-cultural psychological work of Edgerton (1971, cited in Lonner and Berry, 1986), who compared eight communities in East Africa. He produced a broad 'portrait' of the personality type in each community prior to analysis of psychometric test data. The impressionistic descriptions were apparently in good accord with the subsequent test findings.

It is also possible, in *grounded theory* approaches, for example (see Chapter 10), that the sorts of observation made might change as the study progresses as a result of formative revision of method, where feedback from early observations informs the researcher on optimum ways to proceed. The more the aim of the study tends away from purely positivist analysis, the more the data gathered become susceptible to the qualitative methods outlined in Chapters 10 and 22.

Problems with open descriptions of behaviour

Where observers make open descriptions of behaviour, that is they do not use any form of coding or classification system, there can be problems of omission or distortion. One is reminded of the 'blind' soccer referee or ice-skating judge. In the study of animals it is easy to 'see' human characteristics in animal behaviour. In child development studies, it could be falsely assumed that Jason 'follows' an adult (and is perhaps insecure) when he happens to be walking in the same direction. Or Jenny might be mistakenly described as 'copying' when she looks into a box to see what it was Sarah was looking at. From the psychology of social perception we know that each person's view of a situation is unique and that our perceptions can be biased by innumerable factors. An under-trained observer might readily add personal evaluation where the researcher wants *only* an objective, factual report. Where the trained observer reports a hard blow, the novice might describe this as 'vicious'.

Role-play and simulation

Discussion of role-play and simulation methods is situated here because, although some observations of role-play have been relatively pre-structured, the tendency has been to develop categories and models from fairly free-flowing, unrestricted participant behaviour and speech. In some cases, participants observe role-plays (non-active role) but, by and large, it is participants' role-playing that is observed (active role). The techniques have been used for a long time in psychological research, particularly in social psychology, but their use became highlighted when they were advocated as an alternative to the use of gross experimental deception during the 1970s.

Active role

A study might require *active* role-playing within a simulated social setting, such as being asked to get to know a stranger. Participants may take on a specific role – e.g. being chairperson of a group making risky decisions. In each case observations may be made at the time, or behaviour might be filmed for subsequent detailed analysis. Participants have been asked to simulate various emotional feelings and accompanying behavioural expressions, to take on specific roles (such as prisoner or guard; see the section on Zimbardo's (1972) study on p. 593 or to role-play in juries of various sizes, under varying pressures and especially where majority and minority influences are investigated (e.g. Wolf, 1985).

Non-active role

Participants may be asked to watch a role-play or simulated performance and then be asked to report feelings, reactions or suggestions as to how the depicted scene might continue. They may be asked how they would behave in the continuing situation. In this case, the simulation simply serves as material for what is basically a question-asking method. An example of a closely related research style is worth mentioning here, partly because it figured strongly in the controversy over experimental deception. Mixon (1979) analysed Milgram's famous studies (1974) on 'destructive obedience' and, along with ethical objections, argued that the true social situation, for Milgram's participants, had not been understood thoroughly. Milgram described the experiment to a group of psychiatrists, who predicted that less than one in a thousand people would continue obeying the experimenter in giving electric shocks to an obviously suffering 'learner'. Mixon argued that Milgram made it obvious to the participants that the experiment was really about 'destructive obedience'. Mixon gave his participants scripts of the experiment to read, with no clue given to the real experimental aims. He asked them to describe how they thought the experiment would continue. He then altered the scripts with different groups. Only when the script included the experimenter seeming a little concerned for the victim did all participants say that they expected Milgram's participants to discontinue obedience. Mixon argued that the social context of Milgram's experiment gives strong messages that the norms of scientific professionalism are in place and that no harm can come to the victim (though, obviously, pain is occurring). He also argued that this kind of role-play can be revealing when creating the real situation for unsuspecting participants is unethical.

In a few cases the participant can be actor and audience. Storms (1973) had people engage in a two-person interaction, which was filmed. They then viewed the film, either seeing only their partner or only themselves. A major effect shown in this study was that actors were more likely to emphasise external influences on their behaviour (events for which they are not responsible) after engaging in the role-play, as people often do when asked to explain their own behaviour – part of the 'self-serving bias'. However, when they observed a *recording* of their own behaviour, they acted more like observers usually do in this situation and made more dispositional attributions. That is, they were more ready to explain their behaviour as being a product of their personality and internal motives.

Weaknesses of role-play and simulation

Critics have argued that role-play can be non-spontaneous and passive, that people would act in socially desirable and superficial ways, and that what people *say* they would do and what they *actually* would do are very different matters. Proponents argued back that experiments, too, can produce artificial, superficial behaviour and that deception itself, of the Milgram variety, introduces unreal conflict for participants between what seems to be happening and what could be expected to happen in a humane, scientific establishment.

On the issue of spontaneity, several studies are cited as producing very great personal commitment and lack of pretence (a form of *experimental realism*), perhaps the most dramatic being the simulated prison role play of Zimbardo (1972) described briefly on p. 593.

The diary method

Towards the end of the nineteenth century, some academics began to realise that they could not argue endlessly about whether children were born with innate tendencies – 'inherently good' as Rousseau would have claimed – or with a mind more similar to Locke's empty-headed 'tabula rasa'. They realised that a scientific approach was necessary. The first steps towards this were taken by the 'baby biographers', of whom Charles Darwin (1877) is probably the most notable. Data were in the form of a diary of daily observations on the growth and development of his own son. Most diaries were developmental records of the observers' own children. The studies were therefore 'longitudinal' (see Chapter 9). The diary method has the great advantage that the observed persons are acting quite naturally, particularly so in the case of babies, since they are at home with their own parents. This must be a source of some of the richest, most genuine and intimate data in the business!

A problem with these diary accounts was that each biographer had his or her own particular perspective to support and tended to concentrate on quite different aspects of their child's behaviour from other diarists. They also tended not to standardise the intervals between their recordings.

Later, as child development study became a well-established discipline, Piaget (e.g. 1936) kept diaries of the development of his children. He had a thorough model of cognitive development and his observations were used to exemplify aspects of the theory (not to serve as hypothesis tests). He developed procedures to demonstrate certain characteristics of children's thought at various ages – such as egocentricity – which he then used with other children, employing the *clinical method* (see Chapter 7).

Diaries are also kept during most participant observation studies. Where observation is covert these will be constructed, where possible, at the end of each day, either completely from memory or from any discreetly jotted notes recorded where opportunities have arisen.

As an example of a quantitative diary approach, Jones and Fletcher (1992) asked couples to keep a daily diary of mood, stress and sleep variation over a period of three weeks. Comparing one partner with the other on these three variables, they found significant correlations overall, supporting the view that occupational stress is transmitted from one partner to the other, although individual couples varied very much in the extent to which their stress levels were comparable.

A further use of diaries has occurred in participative research (see Chapter 10) where participants keep diaries of their activities and perceptions throughout a study. The researcher then subjects the diary records to some form of *content analysis* (see Chapter 22). Tandon (1981) did this in a study aimed at improving peer-group organisation and initiative taking in a rural agricultural training and modernisation programme. He found that questionnaire data gathered were often at odds with the diary records, the latter being far more congruent with the researcher's own field notes.

Diary studies can occur in that heartland of quantitative research, cognitive psychology. Wagenaar (1986), for instance, recorded some 2000 events in his life over a period of six years along with cues to help him recall the events later. The cues were in the form of 'what', 'who', 'where' and 'when' information about the event. He found that 'what' cues were most effective and 'when' cues almost not at all if taken alone. Giving himself three cues was more effective than fewer but even with three he could not recall almost half the events over a five-year interval. If another person was involved in and provided information on the event, Wagenaar almost always recalled it, suggesting that most of our long-term event memories are never completely lost.

1 Outline a research study that would use observation to investigate the following hypotheses.

   (a) During exploratory play, mothers allow their sons to venture a further distance away from them than they do their daughters.

   (b) When asked personal or slightly embarrassing questions, people are likely to avert their gaze.

   (c) Women are safer drivers than men.

   (d) In groups asked to produce volunteers for an unpopular task it is possible to observe common patterns of behaviour among the group members.

Ensure that variables are operationalised and that the exact method of data gathering is described, including the location, sample selection, data collection method and equipment used.

2 A researcher is concerned that a rating scale is not producing good inter-rater reliability. The observations of two observers are given in Table 6.2 below.

Would you say this represents good reliability or not? What statistical procedure could tell us the degree of reliability? (See Table 6.2 and Chapters 8 and 17.)

	0–5	6–10	11–15	16–20	21–25	26–30	31–35	36–40	41–45
Observer A	1	3	4	2	5	12	9	4	8
Observer B	2	10	8	7	1	3	5	5	6

Table 6.2 Observation for child X: altruistic acts in five-minute intervals

3 Describe ways in which Bandura's hypotheses, including those that investigate the influence of different types of child and adult model, could have been investigated using naturalistic observation rather than the laboratory.

4 Work with a colleague and decide on a variable to observe in children or adults. Make the variable something that is likely to occur quite frequently in a short observation period (ten minutes), such as one person smiling in a two-person conversation in the college refectory. Decide on a structure for data gathering including people, intervals, behaviour codes. Use your observation system for a short interval on the same set of people being careful to follow ethical principles. Compare your results to see whether you tend to agree fairly well or not.

5 Without consulting Table 6.3 (which appears later) try to list the advantages and disadvantages of naturalistic and controlled observation as you understand them so far.

Participant observation

Where researchers are involved in taking notes on people's behaviour in their natural surroundings on a day-to-day basis, it is difficult to see how they can remain clinically detached from the context. Many researchers decide that more authentic PARTICIPANT OBSERVATION of people can be made by being involved in their day-to-day interactions within their normal network of human group relationships. By coming round from behind the camera and into the social setting as an interacting person, the observer can experience life from the perspective of the individual, group or organisation of interest. The meaning of their behaviour should then be more accessible than with the passive approach and there should be less scope for the gross misrepresentations that can occur with 'snapshot' observations. Whether these objectives can be achieved in a manner that would still count as 'scientific' is a matter of debate and one that will be evaluated later on. What should be noted is that in many so-called 'participant observation' studies the methods used are not observation at all in the strict sense, but a combination of semi-structured interviews, open questionnaires and perhaps some data on roles and interactions within an organisation.

Degrees of participation

The degree to which an observer can participate in the group being studied is, according to Patton (2002), a continuum. We can distinguish between a few possible points on that continuum.

Full participant

The true research role is hidden ('undisclosed') and the observer is taken as an authentic member of the group. In this case private information may well be disclosed that would not be given to a known researcher. However, Douglas (1972) argued that even known researchers, who are respected and trusted, may be handed secrets that other genuine group members might not receive, simply because genuine members might misuse the information, whereas a researcher is a professional who will one day leave the group.

Participant as observer

The participant's observational role is not hidden but 'kept under wraps'. It is not seen to be the main reason for the participant's presence. Members relate to the participant mainly through roles and activities central to the group. An example here might be that of a researcher who effectively becomes a temporary member of a school's teaching staff in order to conduct research of which other staff are aware in general terms. Alternatively, a teacher might conduct research for a further qualification and use her work setting as the subject of her study.

Observer as participant

Here, the observer role is uppermost and members of the group accept the observer in their midst as researcher. If valued, the researcher may be given quite intimate information, but they may be constrained in reporting it if such information is offered in confidence.

Full observer

This is the role of uninvolved observer. We have already discussed this as 'non-participant observation'.

Info Box 6.3   Classic examples of (largely) undisclosed participant observation

Festinger, Riecken and Schachter (1956) joined a religious sect that believed the world would end on a certain date. They followed developments up to and just past the fateful moment, observing reactions during the 'last moments of life' and the subsequent 'reprieve', explained later by the leader as caused by the members' great faith in their god.

Rosenhan (1973) participated with confederates in a still controversial study, which promoted criticism of the (US) medical establishment's handling, labelling and diagnosis of psychiatric conditions. Researchers presented themselves at hospital out-patients' departments complaining of hearing voices making certain noises in their heads. Apart from this they behaved in their normal way. During their subsequent voluntary stays in a psychiatric ward, they made observations on staff and patient behaviour, and attitudes towards them. Patients often detected the 'normality' of the researchers well before the staff. An excellent example of seeing behaviour as pathological because of its producer's 'label' was the fact that a nurse recorded a researcher's note-taking as 'excessive writing behaviour'. To be fair, the nurse was dutifully carrying out strict instructions to observe and record anything unusual in patients' behaviour.

Both the studies above are examples of completely undisclosed participant observation whereas Whyte's (1943) project was slightly different and more like the participant as observer role described above. Whyte studied an Italian street gang in Boston by joining it and living in the gang's community for four years. However, it was obvious he was not a normal gang member. His 'cover' was that he was writing a book about the area. He made the famous statement that 'I began as a non-participating observer. As I became accepted into the community, I found myself becoming almost a non-observing participant' (1943: 321). He also took on the role of secretary to the Italian Community Club in order to be able to take field notes unobtrusively.

Ethical issues in undisclosed participant observation

One of the reasons humanists, for instance, object to many psychological experiments is that they involve deception of participants. Participant observation that is undisclosed obviously suffers from this criticism too. The researcher has also to decide what, if anything, can be published without the group's or any individual's consent. A particular hazard is that, when the observer 'comes clean' and declares the research role, any one individual studied may not be able to recall what they have divulged, or how they have behaved, since the research began. The individual should be allowed to view material for publication and to veto material they object to where anonymity does not protect against the nature of the material identifying them. Lack of consent-seeking leads to a greater mistrust of the distant and elite research body. An answer to the problem of deception is, of course, to disclose one's research role and objectives. These ethical issues are discussed more fully in Chapter 23.

Disclosed participant observation

Contemporary participant observation studies are found very frequently in various areas of applied psychological research in a practitioner field such as health or sport and, in particular, disability research; see, for instance, Box 6.4. These are usually conducted on the basis that participants *know* that someone with whom they are in close and possibly professional contact is also making observations as part of an ongoing research project. Many such studies are conducted in organisations, such as that by Rachel (1996) who tracked radical organisational change in a computer systems design office partly by concentrating on the relationships between two groups: the 'Systems' and the 'Change Management' teams. Rachel's study, like many in the field, employed an *ethnographic* approach, which descends from a long history in anthropological research, such as the work of Malinowski (1929) in the Trobriand islands (summarised in Hammersley and Atkinson, 1994). Rachel made the point that worries the advocates of detached

---

Info Box 6.4 — **Give up smoking – not while I'm in here. An example of disclosed participant observation**

Lawn (2004) conducted a participant observation study in a psychiatric hospital with the aim of investigating suspected institutional barriers to patients giving up smoking. She conducted an intensive programme of observations in two separate Australian locations, the second serving as a follow-up in order to attempt to generalise findings from the first institution. Random visits to wards were made lasting several hours from which extensive notes were recorded on the spot or soon after. Discussions were held with staff and patients. Observers' own reflective notes were also recorded and several other sources of information added to the overall data collection. The study was largely qualitative but quantitative observations were also made of the interactions between participants which involved smoking matters.

Using a qualitative *grounded theory* approach (see p. 231), Lawn produced a set of fascinating findings, too detailed to outline fully here, but which highlight the central role of smoking in the lives of the clients and in the job roles of the psychiatric staff. Smoking breaks were seen as times for staff and clients to talk more closely and become better acquainted. Cigarettes were often used as instruments to help control difficult behaviour (for the staff) by taking clients for a smoke. Cigarettes were also used as a central form of currency by clients to exchange for food and even sex.

It is difficult to imagine how Lawn could have painted such a complete picture of the role of smoking on a psychiatric ward simply by using a pre-conceived questionnaire or even through interviewing alone. Rather than a fixed interview, Lawn used her participation on the wards to engage in detailed discussions with staff and clients as part of being there, as things happened, rather than simply dropping in for a pre-arranged meeting.

experimental, 'positivist' approaches, when she argued for the use of a conscious strategy not to impose a structure on the likely outcomes of the study before gathering any data, stating:

The skill then becomes that of finding a way to . . . maintain oneself as a member of an academic community while opening oneself up to the possibilities that would follow from belonging to the community that one wants to study. (1996: 115)

Pause for thought

1 Considering this radical difference from the aims and principles of laboratory experiments, try now to list and describe the strengths and weaknesses of participant observation. When you have done this, have a look at Table 6.3.

2 Try to list the advantages and disadvantages of disclosure to participants. For some answers see the following section on strengths of and difficulties with participant observations.

Strengths of participant observation

Flexibility

A pre-set structure for observation, interview or survey questionnaire imposes the researcher's framework, assumptions and priorities on those who are to be studied. What is relevant in the target group's social world has already been decided. Participant observation is flexible. What is to be covered in the study is not set in stone at the outset. Indeed, the extent to which the observer will participate may not be the same throughout the study, as Whyte's famous statement in Box 6.3 makes clear. Whyte also found that, through participant observation, 'I learned the answers to questions I would not have had the sense to ask if I had been getting my information solely on an interviewing basis' (1943: 303).

Relationship with observed group

Specific groups in the local environment, such as gangs or strongly identifying cultural groups, are likely to see an establishment researcher as an authority figure and, consequently, to be suspicious. Methods for research, other than participant observation, such as interviewing or survey by questionnaire, do not give the researcher long enough to establish trust and to dissipate such suspicions. The research encounter is too brief to ensure genuine cooperation. Participant observation may sometimes be the only way to discover what truly makes such groups 'tick', and to find out which expressed attitudes stem from prior and perhaps deeper values and beliefs.

Kidder (1981) argued that the longer the participant observer spends in a research setting where their aims and purpose are disclosed to group members, the less likely it is that their presence will influence or distort the behaviour of the observed persons. This seeming paradox is explained by pointing out that, although group members may wish to appear in a certain light to the observer, if this behaviour is unnatural for them they will not be able to sustain it for long among friends or relatives. Even if the observer does not recognise artificiality, friends and co-workers will, and the observer is likely to hear about it. Kidder adds that it is much easier for experimental, one-day participants, whose identities remain anonymous, to distort reality by behaving quite uncharacteristically.

	Advantages	Disadvantages
Controlled	Compared with many experiments, behaviour studied can be more flexible and continuous. If used in an experiment, then cause–effect relationships are less ambiguous than in non-experimental settings. Less intrusion from extraneous variables than in natural settings.	Often conducted in an artificial environment which might seriously distort natural behaviour patterns. Participants might guess research aim and can act in a socially desirable manner. Reactive context.
Naturalistic	Reactivity not a problem where participants unaware of being in research context and, if so, genuine behaviour produced. Even if target is aware of being observed, natural setting ensures that behaviour observed is usually more representative than it could be in the laboratory. An important and useful approach where: • intervention is unethical (e.g. unacceptable experimentation on children or animals) • cooperation from targets is unlikely • the full social context for behaviour is required.	Greater ambiguity from extraneous variables and unpredictable behaviour gives greater potential for observer bias than in more structured/laboratory studies. Extraneous variables poorly controlled and pose much greater threats to validity than in the laboratory. Difficulty of remaining undiscovered by targets. Replication may be more difficult. Cannot employ the sophisticated equipment used to make quality recordings in the laboratory (though new technology has greatly improved things).
Participant	Behaviour is usually genuine and natural, unless participants are aware of researcher's presence and aims. Meanings and context of participants' behaviour more readily available than in non-participative studies. Trust and informality give information and insights unavailable in other methods.	Researcher may have to rely on memory for data collection. Replication often more difficult than in structured approaches, but this may be irrelevant (see discussion of reliability in qualitative studies, p. 574). Problem of 'blowing cover'. Public checks on data difficult. Researcher's interactions with participants may alter normal relations.

Table 6.3 Advantages and disadvantages of controlled, naturalistic and participant observation designs

Difficulties with participant observation

The presence of a participant observer must change group behaviour to some degree, if only marginally, since, unless the researcher remains mute and passive (and therefore doesn't participate), interactions must occur that wouldn't have occurred otherwise. Here is a statement from one of the members of Whyte's gang:

You've slowed me down plenty since you've been down here. Now, when I do something, I have to think what Bill Whyte would want to know about it and how I can explain it. Before I used to do these things by instinct. (Whyte, 1943: 301)

This is pretty damning for the researcher who claims their presence to be unobtrusive and non-influential. However, researchers like Whyte argue that they blended into and became a part of the activities of the group, rather than changing what happened substantially, a position which supports Kidder's view above.

As Whyte's earlier statement testifies, the researcher obviously becomes socially and emotionally involved in the group and this must cast doubt on their eventual objectivity in reporting. The participant observation supporter would argue, however, that the attempt to be totally 'objective' leads to the artificiality and rigidity we discussed earlier.

The participant researcher can't usually make notes at the time of observation. Most have to rely on diary-keeping after the day's events (or by taking on a role that permits unobtrusive note-taking). Necessarily, then, most participant observers are prey to the psychological factors of memory loss and distortion. Also, since the researcher is the only observer present, and since events observed are unique, there is no opportunity to verify results with a second observer. Conclusions can only be loosely generalised to similar situations and groups.

Table 6.3 shows the advantages and disadvantages of controlled, naturalistic and participant observation designs

Case studies

A case study involves gathering detailed information about one individual or group. Participant observation studies, such as Rachel's, above, are often better termed case studies on organisations. Festinger *et al.*'s study (1956), described above, would count as a case study of a group. Typically, *individual* case studies would include a comprehensive case history, usually, but not exclusively, gathered by interview. This would be the person's record to date in employment, education, family details, socio-economic status, relationships and so on, and might include a detailed account of experiences relevant to the issue, which makes the person of particular research interest. The interest might be in a rare medical condition that has psychological implications, in cases of severe deprivation, in an extraordinary ability (e.g. astonishing memory) or in a person's particular social position – single parent, manager, psychiatric patient, criminal.

The person would be interviewed regularly, mostly in an unstructured manner, and may be asked to take psychological tests. There might also be a role for naturalistic observation, particularly where the person is a young child, as when, for instance, a severely deprived child's play activities and developing social interactions are monitored for change.

In some instances, the individual is selected for a forward-looking case study because they are about to undergo a particularly interesting and possibly unique experience. Gregory and Wallace (1963) studied the case of SB, blind almost from birth, who received sight as the result of a surgical operation at the age of 52. The researchers were able not only to study in depth his visual abilities and development, but also gathered qualitative data on his emotional reactions to his new experiences and progress. This included his initial euphoria and his later depressions, caused partly by loss of daylight and his disillusionment with impure surfaces (flaky paint, old chalk marks on blackboards). A case study, such as this one, though intrinsically valuable, can also shed light on general psychological issues such as the nature-nurture debate in perception. However, since SB had spent a lifetime specialising senses other than vision, his perceptual learning experiences cannot directly be compared with those of a young infant.

Freud developed his comprehensive psychoanalytic theory of human development using, as fuel and illustration, his records from dozens of patients' case histories. Much work in clinical psychology, by its nature, is based on case study work. In the area of developmental psychology, the research of Koluchová (1976) studied the effects of severe deprivation on a pair of identical twins, discovered in dreadful conditions at the age of five. They made impressive gains over the next two years. The value of such studies is to demonstrate not only just what the human organism can survive, but the extent to which it can still develop relatively normally.

The value of case studies

Being a somewhat unstructured, probably unreplicable, study on just one individual or group, the case study design would seem to be of the rich but not generalisable type. Bromley (1986) has argued, however, that case studies are the 'bedrock of scientific investigation'. Many psychological studies, he argues, are difficult to replicate in principle and it is the interesting, unpredictable case that has traditionally spurred scientists towards changes in paradigm or theoretical innovation. Bromley feels that a preoccupation with the experiment and psychometrics has led to a serious neglect of the case-study approach by most psychologists. He points out that psychological evidence can be valid and effective, yet remain unquantifiable.

Advantages of the case study

Outstanding cases

A phenomenon may occur that is unique or so dramatic it could not have been predicted or studied in any pre-planned way. Thigpen and Cleckley (1954) reported on 'Eve White', a patient exhibiting three distinct personalities emerging through psychotherapy. Rather stern and 'prim', she was unaware of her other self, 'Eve Black', a gregarious life-lover who rejected Eve White. Finally, stable, contemplative 'Jane' emerged, aware of both the others. The Eves underwent the usual therapeutic interviews but were also given psychological tests and had EEG measures taken on their brainwave patterns. These distinguished Eve Black from the other two. Much controversy has surrounded Dr Thigpen's treatment of 'Eve' – see Box 6.5.

Luria (1969) studied a Russian journalist, Sherishevski, who had amazed his boss by not taking notes at briefing meetings, and who amazed Luria by being able to recall long word lists accurately over periods of 20 years or more. Such cases may bring to attention possibilities in the human condition that were not previously considered realistic, and may prompt investigation into quite new, challenging areas.

Info Box 6.5   Out of interest . . . What happened to Eve?

In 1977 the real Eve revealed herself as Christine Costner-Sizemore through her book *I'm Eve*'. She claimed to have had many other personalities and to have suffered for 18 years after her therapy with Thigpen. She claimed that Thigpen's portrayal of her in the film *Three Faces of Eve* was exploitative; he made something like $1 million out of the film whereas she had received $7000. Thigpen himself had tried to stop her writing *I'm Eve* because he claimed the rights to her life story. She later found that the film company Twentieth Century Fox had a contract she had signed which, they claimed, gave *them* sole rights to her life story and that therefore she could not work with Sissy Spacek on a film version of her second book, *A Mind of My Own*. In 1988, she won a case against Fox and the contract became void. After her publications she became a public speaker on mental disorder and an advocate of rights for those designated mentally ill. She was still giving talks in June 2006, see www.stetson.edu/marcom/articles/view.php?type=stories&id=198

Contradicting a theory

One contrary case is enough to challenge seriously an assumed trend or theoretical cause—effect relationship. It has been assumed that humans go through a 'critical period' where language must be heard to be learned, or where attachments must be formed and maintained in order to avoid later psychological problems. One case of an isolated child learning language, or of a maternally deprived child developing normal adult social skills, after deprivation during much of the critical period, is enough to undermine the critical period hypothesis quite seriously and to promote vigorous research seeking the crucial variables. The Koluchová (1976) study above served this purpose well.

Data pool

In an effort to identify common factors or experiences, a mass of information from many case studies may be pooled, sorted and analysed. The focus may be, for instance, psychiatric patients or children with a particular reading disability. As a result, quantitative studies may be carried out, once related variables have appeared or are suspected. Yin (1994) points out, however (and in the spirit of 'negative case analysis' to be covered in Chapter 22), that multiple case studies can be seen as similar to a series of experiments (not the gathering of a 'sample'). Multiple case studies serve as replications or as extensions of a prior study in order to refine an initially broad hypothesis or to check up on anomalies.

Insight

Whether or not case studies of special circumstances lead to later, more formal, structured and quantitative studies, the richness they provide is their unique strength. Very often we could not possibly imagine the special experiences of the person studied, and we could not ask the appropriate questions to find out. These experiences may cause us to restructure completely our thoughts on a particular condition, allowing us to empathise more fully, for example, with the AIDS sufferer or to understand the full impact of unemployment on a family. This adds to our overall knowledge pool and comprehension of human psychology, though it may not test any specific hypothesis.

Disadvantages of the case study

Reliability and validity

There is an obviously high degree of unreliability involved in individual case studies. No two cases are the same. Many studies are quite unreplicable; indeed their uniqueness is usually the reason for their being carried out in the first place. Their strength is in richness, their weakness in lack of generalisability, but only if one views them from a traditional hypothesis-testing perspective.

Some check on reliability can sometimes be made, however, by comparing information gained from different sources for instance, the person themselves in interview, close relatives' accounts, documentary sources such as diaries and court reports. This is similar to the notion of 'triangulation' described in Chapter 22.

Realism is high. The experiences recorded by the researcher are usually genuine and complex. Historical material, however, often depends on just the person's own memory, which is notoriously error-prone and subject to distortion. Experiences we claim to recall from childhood are often our original reconstruction from relatives' stories told to us about our life before our own detailed memory was possible. Contrary to popular imagination, one cannot, in fact, remember being born!

Observer interaction

Information collection is prone to the interpersonal variables discussed in the following chapter. The case study necessitates a very close relationship between researcher and participant over an extended period and many intimate observation or interview sessions. Though the very depth of this relationship may promote an extremely rich information source, it may also interfere seriously with the researcher's objectivity.

Subjective selection

There is another possible element of subjectivity. Rather than present everything recorded during a case study, which might take as long as the study itself, the researcher must be selective in what information enters the final report. This may well depend on the points of background theory, or issues that the researcher wishes to raise or emphasise. It would be easy to conveniently ignore contradictory information. Further, for every illustrative case study, we do not know how many cases did *not* deliver the kind of information the researcher wished to present.

How does psychology compare here with 'real' sciences?

In Chapter 10, we shall meet the argument that psychologists probably worry about the rigidity of scientific method more than do conventional scientists in physics, chemistry and the like. Case studies have been viewed with extreme suspicion or hostility by many psychologists because they are a 'sample of only one', often qualitative, and subject to conventional criticisms of subjectivity and lack of reliability. However, 'real' science contains very many case studies, and Robson (2002) argues that, anyway, experiments, surveys and the like should themselves be seen as types of case study in each instance. Hayes (1997) points out that case studies such as those of Penfield and Rasmussen (1950), who stimulated the cortex and recorded patients' consequent vivid memories, have not been queried as unscientific, probably because they are safely within the 'hard' science of medical research – 'scientific by association, and [were] therefore beyond suspicion' (1997: 2). The notorious study of 'Little Albert' by Watson and Rayner (1920) (Watson being an archetypal experimentalist) is written up very much as a diary-cum-case-study with qualitative observation throughout. You can read the original article at: http://psychclassics.yorku.ca/Watson/emotion.htm

Indirect observation

Archives

Some events have already occurred but can serve as empirical evidence for social science theories. Durkheim, a sociologist, made groundbreaking studies of relative rates of suicide, comparing these with varying social conditions. Many events, like suicide, are of interest to psychologists and are either unpredictable or do not occur often enough for thorough scientific research. Examples are the infrequency of governmental elections, which makes the study of voting behaviour somewhat inconvenient, and the almost complete unpredictability of earthquakes and terrorist attacks. All these events have the potential for analysis as *natural experiments*.

Because such events are so unpredictable, researchers might, instead, use observed social statistics as data. These can be drawn from historical sources (ARCHIVAL DATA), government information or the media. Television programmes might, for example, be observed for rates and types of human aggression (see, for example, Cumberbatch *et al.*, 1988a). To provide evidence on the positive effects of not smacking children, Durrant (1999; 2000) used police, health service and social services records, among others, following 20 years of a ban on physical punishment of children in Sweden. Far from the pessimistic prediction often made that lawlessness and delinquency would increase, she showed that rates of youth involvement in crime, alcohol and drug use, rape and suicide had *decreased* beyond any decline predicted by other related factors; public support for corporal punishment had also declined; identification of children at risk had increased; rates of prosecution had remained at the same level; social service intervention had become more supportive and preventative. On occasion, a study such as this might be referred to as a *survey* of social statistics; the common use of 'survey' is discussed in Chapter 7.

Note that, although indirect, these studies do make observations on the behaviour of people and, through some interpretation, constitute evidence on prevailing attitudes and behaviour. This is a perfectly legitimate way to test and eliminate hypotheses about causal factors in social phenomena. The observation of electronic or printed media coverage could be subjected to *content analysis*, which we shall look at when discussing qualitative data analysis in Chapter 22.

Verbal protocols

A further way to gather observations indirectly is through the use of VERBAL PROTOCOLS. These are the recorded product of asking participants to talk or think aloud during an activity. They may report on the thoughts they have while trying to solve a mental arithmetic problem, or 'talk through' the reasons for their decisions while operating a complex piece of machinery, such as the control-room instruments in a nuclear power installation. The method is closely linked with the practice of *knowledge elicitation*.

Following Ulric Neisser's plea (see p. 115) for more realistic and socially appropriate memory research, the use of verbal protocols, generating qualitative data, was an interesting development in the strongly experimental area of cognitive psychology. Ericsson and Simon (1984) made a powerful case for the use of verbal reports as data. Good theories of problem-solving should produce rules from which problem-solving by humans can be simulated. Verbal protocols can then be compared with the simulation in order to verify the theory. Ericsson and Simon argued that asking participants to talk while they work does not necessarily impair their performance. It depends on what the verbalising instructions are. These could be:

1 verbalise your silent speech – what you would say to yourself anyway while solving this problem (doing this task) – known as a 'talk aloud' instruction

2 verbalise whatever thoughts occur to you while doing this task – a 'think aloud' instruction

3 verbalise your thoughts and decisions, and give reasons for these.

In analysing the results of many studies they found that only type 3 instructions seriously affected performance – not surprising really, since the participant is being asked to do so much in addition to the task. Type 2 instructions did not seriously affect accuracy but did slow down solution times. Type 1 instructions had little effect on time or accuracy. In addition, Ericsson and Simon found that concurrent verbal reports (produced as a task is performed) were more accurate than retrospective ones.

Knowledge elicitation work has generated 'expert systems' – bodies of knowledge about procedures, for instance in medical diagnosis, derived from the verbal protocols of experts. In addition, the difference between experts and novices has been the subject of research, either for practical uses, in the reduction of life-threatening work errors for instance, or as pure academic research on expertise in problem-solving. A further academic use is in the investigation of people's 'mental models' of everyday systems (e.g. your central heating system) or laboratory-produced simulations (e.g. launching a spaceship).

Martin and Klimowski (1990) used verbal protocols to investigate the mental processes employed by managers as they evaluated their own and their subordinates' performance. It was found that they used more *internal attributions* when evaluating others than when evaluating themselves. An internal attribution occurs when we see behaviour as largely caused by a person's enduring characteristics, rather than being caused mainly by the surrounding situation.

Leahy and Sweller (2004) showed that instructing children to imagine the steps in certain kinds of problem produced fewer errors and shorter completion times than simply asking a different group of children to 'study' the problem. There was explicit training in how to imagine the steps and the finding supported earlier evidence for the 'imagination effect' in learning. In a further experiment they asked the children to 'think aloud' while solving the problems. There was strong evidence from the transcripts that the 'imagination' children really were following the imagination instruction whereas the 'study' children were not. Hence, by using verbal protocols the researchers were able to investigate the cognitive mechanisms that are associated with the imagination effect.

Exercises

1 A student decides to carry out participant observation on her own student group. She is interested in the different ways her classmates cope with study demands and social commitments. Discuss the ways she might go about this work, the problems she might face and the ways in which she might surmount difficulties.

2 Write out a list of advantages and disadvantages of participant and non-participant observation. Use Table 6.3 to check your answers.

3 How could you use archival data to provide evidence that the weather has an effect on our moods? Outline strengths and weaknesses of the case study approach.

Answers

1 Open answer

2 See Table 6.3.

3 See if prescriptions for anti-depressants increase in winter months. See if people hire more 'feel good' films in summer months, etc.

4 Advantages: rich, detailed information, probably genuine if interviews and in-depth study well conducted. Disadvantages: information may remain unique to case and cannot be generalised; intense involvement of researcher with participant; information published dependent on researcher's subjective selection from large body of data.

Glossary

Archival data	Data obtained from public records and used as evidence
Code (coding)	Quantifying by giving similar observed instances of behaviour a symbol
Diary method	Data-gathering method where participant makes regular (often daily) record of relevant events
Disclosure	Letting people know that they are the object of observation
Ethnographic approach/ethnography	Methodological approach deriving from social anthropology; involves 'immersion' in a setting and an attempt to reflect that context from the perspective of group/culture members
Event coding	Recording pre-specified behavioural events as they occur

Inter-observer reliability	Extent to which observers agree in their rating or coding
Interval coding	Recording what behaviour is occurring, or the typical behaviour, in specified time intervals

Observation types

Controlled	Observation in controlled setting often a laboratory or observation room
Indirect/archival	Observations not made on people directly but using available records
Naturalistic	Observation without intervention in observed people's own environment
Participant	Observation in which observer takes part or plays a role in the group observed
Structured/systematic	Observation that uses an explicitly defined coding framework for data recording
Observational technique	Procedure using observation in some way and that may or may not be part of an experiment
Observational design	Study that is solely observational and does not include any experimentation
Observer bias	Threat to validity of observational recordings caused solely by characteristics of the observer
Role-play	Study in which participants act out given parts
Simulation	Study in which participants re-create and play through, to some extent, a social interaction
Time sampling	Interval coding but where observations are taken only during specified non-continuous time intervals.
Verbal protocol	Recording of participant's speech when they have been asked to talk or think aloud during a task.

Interview methods – asking people direct questions

This chapter introduces general principles concerning the asking of questions.

- The dimension of interview techniques across the structured–unstructured dimension is introduced, from non-directive, through semi-structured to fully structured (survey type) interviews. The clinical method is included in these. Strengths and weaknesses of structure are discussed. In general, less structured studies generate more rich and genuine, but more local and less generalisable, data.

- The general possible effects of *interpersonal variables* (gender, ethnicity, roles, personality, cues to interviewer's aims) in the face-to-face questioning situation are discussed.

- Advice on interviewing is presented, mainly oriented towards a qualitative approach.

- Techniques to *achieve and maintain rapport* are introduced, with the underlying assumption that good rapport produces more useful and valid data from interviewees. Other aspects of good interview practice and recording methods are discussed.

- Types and sequencing of questions are covered, along with a short discussion of *recording techniques*.

- Finally, *surveys* are introduced as fully structured interviews. Surveys can be used purely to gather descriptive data and/or to test hypotheses. Surveys can be conducted face to face, by post, telephone or electronically, e.g. by e-mail.

- Panels and focus groups are briefly described as methods of assessing opinion on an issue.

Introduction – Self-report methods

So far we have seen that psychologists can gather data by setting up experiments to see what people do under different conditions, or they can use observation techniques to record segments of behaviour in more or less natural circumstances. Perhaps the reader has asked by now 'Why don't psychologists just go and ask people directly about themselves?' There are in fact many ways in which psychology researchers ask questions of individuals. They can and often do this after carrying out experiments. The interviews conducted by Asch and Milgram after their celebrated demonstrations of seemingly bizarre human behaviour give some of the most revealing, fascinating and rich data one can imagine and certainly formed the springboard for a huge volume of further illuminating and productive research.

In general, any method that asks participants to report upon themselves is a SELF-REPORT METHOD and these methods include questionnaires, psychological assessment scales, interviews and also the use of verbal protocols discussed in the last chapter. Self-report *measures* however usually refer to psychological scales measuring personality and attitudes and are discussed in the next chapter.

In this chapter we are concentrating on studies where the gathering of information through direct questioning, usually face to face (but often by telephone, post or e-mail), is the *primary* data gathering mode. First, we look at the central issue of *structure*. FACE-TO-FACE personal interviews, where the interviewee sits and talks with the interviewer, tend to be less structured situations than those where a questionnaire is formally administered.

Structured interviews

In a more STRUCTURED design, every RESPONDENT (person who answers questions) receives exactly the same questions, usually in much the same or exactly the same order. More unstructured approaches, using a 'conversational' style with open-ended questions, tend to produce richer, fuller and perhaps more genuine responses. This is similar to the observational dimension of structure covered in the last chapter. According to the positivist perspective, an unstructured approach would suffer in reliability and the technical comparison of cases; generalisability would also be weak. However, the researcher has the advantage of flexibility towards the respondent and of asking questions in a more informal, relaxed and natural atmosphere in which complete and meaningful answers, kept in context, may be more forthcoming. The more unstructured the approach, the more the outcomes rely on the skills of the interviewer and may be distorted through the potential effects of interviewer influence and selectivity. In the most highly structured approaches the influence of the interviewer is minimal but perhaps not insignificant.

This issue of structured vs unstructured (or 'loose') designs really takes us to the heart of the quantitative–qualitative debate again. A positivist view of interviews is that they are used to get facts from respondents and that, using various technical guards against sampling and procedural bias, interview data should provide a close match with an objective reality waiting to be discovered and described. The interviewer is simply a utility to pose questions methodically.

An alternative view, fairly common to qualitative approaches (and described more fully on p. 575), is that interviewees construct their unique reality in the interview session, which is a social interaction in which the interviewer is a human participant. Hence, interviewers should provide the most flexible and naturally humanlike circumstances in which interviewees can express themselves fully and can uniquely define their world. De Waele and Harré say:

By taking the participants' interpretations seriously we avoid the falsification of reality which occurs when self-reports are confined to the replies to questionnaires etc. which have been designed in advance by the investigator. (1979: 182)

The common advantages and disadvantages of loose and structured interview techniques are outlined in Table 7.1.

	Advantages	Disadvantages
Loose (non-directive, informal, semi-structured)	Interview questions can be adapted to context, interviewee characteristics and the general flow of answers. Respondent more relaxed, informed and involved. Relatively natural conversation produces richer, fuller, more genuine, more realistic information on interviewee's own terms; enables capture of respondent's construction or unique perspective.	Length and depth of process may limit numbers it is possible to interview, and some people may not want to commit the time and energy. Problems with reliability and generalisation. Important topics could be missed if no schedule or questionnaire to check. Thorough training of interviewers may be costly and time consuming. Limits data analysis to qualitative.
Structured (closed question survey; standardised interview)	Ease of data comparison and analysis. Can be replicated and data reviewed by other researchers. Reduction of interpersonal bias factors. Results more generalisable. Interviewers need not have all the skills and experience required for loosely structured procedures. High reliability from 'positivistic' view. Speedy administration; respondents may feel more ready to participate given low time/effort commitment.	Data obtained can be trivial. Narrow range and quality of information gathered. Respondent constrained and cannot express complexities and subtleties of an issue or experience. Does not capture meaning in respondent's own terms or respondent's unique perspective. Question wordings cannot be adapted to levels of understanding of the respondent. Suffers general questionnaire weaknesses – see Chapter 8. Limits data analysis to quantitative

Table 7.1 Advantages and disadvantages of loose and structured interview techniques

Effects of interpersonal variables in interviews

This section is about asking people questions mostly to gather information. We have seen that some research designs, particularly the laboratory experiment, have been criticised for their artificiality and for being threatened by demand characteristics. However, questioning approaches, no matter how informal and so long as participants are aware that there is a research aim, may also contain an element of artificiality, distortion and reaction to the research context. There is an interaction of roles: interviewer and interviewee. Characteristics of the interviewer's style and presentation may affect the quality of information obtained. Cues from the interviewer or questionnaire may serve as demand characteristics and the interviewee might try to behave according to perceived research aims. Researcher expectancies may also bias proceedings where the interviewer is aware of expected or desired results.

Gender

Several studies demonstrate differential effects of female and male interviewers. Rubin and Greene (1991) found that more negative attitudes towards gender-exclusive language were produced by interviewees when the interviewer was female than when male. Young men interviewed by males reported using the least gender-inclusive language while older females with female interviewers reported using the most. Wilson *et al.* (2002) reported that, for a sample of Californian Latino couples, the men interviewed by women reported fewer sexual partners and fewer sexual encounters with strangers than men interviewed by men. Age of interviewer had an effect too: men were more likely to report sex with prostitutes to an older interviewer, where women were less likely to report oral sex.

Sex-of-interviewer effects in interviews where the topic is not related directly to sex or gender are harder to find, though for senior citizens in the US, Stephenson *et al.* (1999) found that in cross-sex interviews women talked almost twice as much about their career, education and Second World War experience than in same-sex interviews while, in the same comparison, men emphasised their family more as part of their identity.

Ethnicity

That race or ethnic group creates differential interviewing behaviour was shown by Word, Zanna and Cooper (1974). They found that white students acting as interviewers showed significantly lower 'immediacy' (interpersonal distance, eye contact, forward leaning and so on) to black 'job applicants' than to white. Subsequently they trained interviewers to give the low-immediacy feedback seen in the first study to naïve students acting as applicants. These participants performed less adequately and were more nervous than participants treated like the white interviewees in the first study. They also perceived the interviewers to be less friendly and tended to produce less immediacy in their own interview behaviour. Hence we can assume that when a white interviewer increases distance, decreases eye contact etc. with a black interviewee, even if they are not aware of doing this, the effect will be detrimental to the black interviewee's performance. We can perhaps assume too that this effect will generalise to any interview situation in which the interviewer lowers immediacy towards members of a specific social group.

In a simulation study Awosunle and Doyle (2001) exposed black and white participants acting as job selectors to just one of three identical tape recordings of an interview, with the only variation being the accent of the interviewee between African-Caribbean (black) and East London (black and white). The black East London condition was included to ensure that only the cue of accent was signalling 'race'. A combined performance and suitability score was derived for each interview. A 'same race' effect was demonstrated in that white ratings of the owners of the East London accents were higher than those for the African-Caribbean accent, and vice versa for black raters (see p. 505).

Formal roles

Sex and ethnic difference may have greater effect if the interviewee also views the researcher as an authority figure. This perception will partly depend on the style the researcher adopts, but even a highly informal style may not deter the interviewee from seeing her or him as very important. Interviewees' answers, then, may lack fluency because they are constrained by a search for 'correct' language or content. Because interviews may have always been associated with authority or failure (e.g. the young offender, the unemployed) they may be interpreted differently by some interviewees and the interviewer may need to understand this perspective in order to interpret the data provided fairly.

Personal qualities

Interacting with these major differences will be other personal qualities and characteristics of both people. The interviewer, instructed to be informal, may find this quite difficult with some people and may therefore behave rather artificially, this being detected by the interviewee. There may be something else about the interviewer that the interviewee just doesn't feel comfortable with.

Social desirability

A common problem in asking questions is that of social desirability (see p. 183). Faced with an esteemed researcher, people may well 'manage' their attitudes and behaviour to a misleading extent. It is notoriously difficult, for instance, to measure prejudice openly. When asked, many people will make statements like 'I believe we're all equal' and 'Everybody should be treated the same', whereas, in their everyday life and in conversations with friends, other more negative attitudes and behaviour towards some groups may well emerge. On issues like child-rearing practice, careful driving or safe sex, people usually know what they ought to say to an interviewer and may keep their real views and behaviour well hidden.

Evaluative cues

It is unusual to be asked for one's opinion in a situation where no criticism or argument can be expected. The interviewer has to be careful not to display behaviour inadvertently, however subtle, that might be interpreted as either disagreement or encouragement, since the interviewee may well be searching for an acceptable or desired position. Not all researchers agree with this passive role for the interviewer (see Box 7.1).

Info Box 7.1   The discourse analytic view of interview bias

Conventional research lore holds that interviewers should not engage or lead the respondent as one would in normal conversation. However, there is a contemporary research view quite the reverse of this. It is bound up with the discourse analysis approach, which is discussed in more detail in Chapters 10 and 22. Potter and Wetherell (1987) explain that the entire focus of discourse analysis is on the ways in which people use language, in conversation, to construct and 'negotiate' a view of the world. They argue that traditional research is wrong in assuming that there is some 'pure' truth in people's heads which we can get at if only we remove all possible bias and distorting influences. Their interest is in the ways people use discourse to promote certain versions of events, often those that serve their interests, put them in a good light or at least make their position coherent and reasonable. Hence, for the discourse analytic interviewer, the interview should be naturalistic to the extent of promoting this everyday discursive use of language.

The diversity which traditionally structured interviews try to minimise, in order to get 'consistent' responses from interviewees, is positively encouraged by the discourse approach. Consistency, for Potter and Wetherell, is a sign that respondents are producing only limited, probably compatible, interpretations. They see the interview as 'an active site where the respondent's interpretive resources are explored and engaged to the full' (1987: 164) and as a 'conversational encounter'. The discourse analytic interview can therefore be conducted on an 'interventionist and confrontative' basis – not as a dispute but as a situation in which the interviewer is prepared to come back to areas obviously difficult or ambiguous for the interviewee in order, perhaps, to elicit some alternative construction. The interviewer will also be prepared to use probes and follow-up questions in fruitful areas.

This makes the interview something similar to the *informal but guided* type below, with elements also of the *clinical method*, discussed later.

Types of interview

Face-to-face interviews vary in style across the range of structure already described, using the whole range from closed to open-ended questions. Answers to open-ended questions will often be coded by placing them into categories, such as 'left wing' or 'right wing' for political questions, or, for example, by rating them on a scale of one to ten for computer anxiety. In some surveys, interviewers code answers on the spot as they are received. In the less structured type of interview, response analysis is a long, complicated and relatively interpretive process.

In qualitative research studies there may be no interest in quantifying responses at all beyond basic categorising. The emphasis will be on collating, prioritising and summarising all information acquired (see Chapter 22), analysing for themes and perhaps suggesting areas and strategies for action. The setting and procedure for interviewing may also be more or less structured and we will consider five categories of interview, starting at the relatively unstructured end of the continuum.

1. Non-directive

Some psychology practitioners use interviews in which the interviewee can talk about anything they like and in which the psychologist gives no directing influence to the topics but provides reflective support throughout the session. The main aim would be to help the 'client' increase self-awareness and deal with personal problems. This method would be used by psychotherapists and counsellors, and the main aim would not be academic research data gathering. However, clients do, in a sense, research their own perhaps troubled experiences and the psychologist may need the information in order to proceed with helping the client. The approach may be used in collecting data that form part of a case study, as discussed in Chapter 6.

The insights derived from such studies often get drawn together into an overall psychological theory, model or approach that adds, in time, to the pool of knowledge and ideas. These may become a stimulus for further research by other means. Freud's insights, for instance, influenced Bandura in his development of social learning theory, which he supported mainly by controlled observation experiments.

2. Informal

An informal interview has an overall research data-gathering aim. It is directive only to the extent of keeping the interviewee on the topic and perhaps adding prompts when they 'dry up'. At the non-structured extreme the session is similar to the non-directive approach just described.

Though the fact is obscured by the more celebrated aspects of the Hawthorne studies described in Chapter 4, the researchers at Hawthorne were also responsible for an early use of the almost non-directive interview in industrial relations research work. Early structured interviews were not successful, not least because many were conducted by the worker's supervisor and the relationship was necessarily lop-sided in power. Employees were reluctant to get marked out as complainers. The 'indirect approach', which the researchers then developed, involved non-judgemental, neutral interviewers listening patiently, making intelligent comments, displaying no authority, giving no advice or argument, and only asking questions when necessary, e.g. to prompt further talking, to relieve anxiety, to praise, to cover an omitted topic and to discuss implicit assumptions if thought helpful. 'Rules of orientation' for the interviewer took into account many of the points made strongly today by qualitative researchers (see Chapters 10 and 22). They found employees became far more articulate than in the structured meetings and, as an overall outcome of the study, management realised that seemingly trivial complaints were only the external symptoms of much deeper personal and social problems, requiring more than the superficial response to employee complaints they had originally envisaged. One man, for instance, exclaimed 'I tell you, it does a fellow good to get rid of that stuff' (Roethlisberger and Dickson, 1939: 258; see also Hollway, 1991).

Interviewees can talk in their own terms in the relaxed atmosphere of the informal interview. They don't have to answer pre-set questions which they might find confusing or which they just don't wish to answer. They are not constrained by fixed-answer questions that produce rather narrow information. The approach has been used in social science research for some time and has more recently become popular in areas of applied research, particularly by the proponents of qualitative approaches who would argue that the attempt at objectivity, through being a cool, distant and impersonal interviewer, is only likely to instil anxiety. Interviewees grasp at clues to what is really expected from them and how their information will promote or hinder 'success'. I have been interviewed for research and remember feeling anxious to know what the context was so I could manage my answers more effectively, and perhaps recall more relevant ideas and experiences. I also remember interviewer comments like '. . . well, I shouldn't strictly say this now but . . .' and similar, straying from the structure at several points. Realistically, most formally structured interviews run like this. Dropped comments and asides may well form some of the most memorable and insight-producing information.

3. The semi-structured interview (informal but guided)

This extremely popular form of interviewing retains the main advantages of the previous approach by keeping the procedure informal, by not asking pre-set questions in exactly the same order each time. However, interviewers are provided with a guiding outline of topics to be covered and information required. The guide usually leaves the interviewer to decide, on the day, how to work in and phrase questions on the various topics. Questions need not be put if respondents spontaneously produce the required answers in response to earlier interview enquiries, but if they do not these questions will be returned to until they have been answered as fully as possible. In other words, the interviewer 'plays it by ear' but covers all central topics.

The semi-structured interview is the interview style of choice in much qualitative work. Interview content can also be subjected to content analysis (Chapter 22) and therefore partially quantified. Advantages are a natural conversation flow, freedom for the respondent to explore unpredicted avenues of thought, and flexibility of the interviewer in selecting aspects of the discourse to follow up. These are finely balanced against the disadvantages, from the positivist point of view, of weak reliability or comparison across respondents. However, this begs the question of what kind of scientific research model proponents are following and is the starting point for Chapter 10.

4. Structured but open-ended

To avoid the looseness and inconsistency that accompany informally gathered interview data, the interview session can use a standardised procedure. The interviewer gives pre-set questions in a predetermined order to every interviewee. This keeps the multiplicity of interpersonal variables involved in a two-way conversation to a minimum and ensures greater consistency in the data gathered. The respondent is still free to answer, however, in any way chosen. Questions are open ended and not leading. For instance, 'Tell me what you think about physically punishing children' might be asked, rather than 'Do you approve of physically punishing children?'

5. Fully structured

In this type of interview, as with the last, questions are pre-set and ordered, but here they are also fixed-answer items of the type that can be found on p. 174. In fact, this approach is hardly an interview worth the name at all. It is a face-to-face data-gathering technique, but could be conducted by telephone, post or computer (which might reduce bias from interpersonal variables still further). The fully structured method is usually in use when you're stopped on the street as part of a survey by someone with a clipboard. Responses can be counted and analysed numerically but can often be difficult to make because the respondent wants to say 'yes' (for this reason) but 'no' (for that reason) or 'I think so' or 'sometimes'. A sensitive structured system has a list for choosing responses including alternatives such as 'sometimes', 'hardly ever' or 'certain', 'fairly confident', and so on (to be outlined in Chapter 8).

In contemporary psychological investigation, the last two methods have been rejected by many researchers because they lack the fundamental aspects of normal human conversation that are likely to produce the most natural, complete and realistic discourse from the interviewee. In normal conversation we constantly check that the other has understood what we mean, is on the same wavelength and is comfortable in telling us all that they would wish on a particular topic. Semi-structured and looser approaches permit a process of doubling back and altering one's wording in order to permit the respondent the fullest opportunity to express what they might have to say. As Smith reminds us:

You may need to ask yourself how engaged the respondent is. Are you really entering the personal/social life world of the participant or are you forcing him or her, perhaps reluctantly, to enter yours? (1995b: 15)

The clinical method (or 'clinical interview')

The CLINICAL METHOD is used where there is a clear data-gathering or hypothesis-testing goal, where quite specific answers to specific questions are sought, yet where there is felt to be a need to rephrase questions and probe further where the interviewee is suspected of not fully understanding the point or has further knowledge to display. Piaget typically used this approach in trying to determine exactly what a child thought about the quantities involved in his conservation tasks, for instance. In giving children these problems it is very easy to extract an apparently 'wrong' (i.e. non-conserving) answer with an injudicious choice of question wording or with 'clumsy' conversation. The question 'Is there more liquid in this glass?' is a leading one (see p. 186), which may well prompt the child into saying 'yes' in order to please. In any case, after the typical conservation change, the column of liquid *is* 'more' – it's taller (though narrower). The question 'Is there more in this glass, more in this other one, or are they both the same?' is rather demanding on the child's short-term memory!

The clinical method has standardised aims but uses a non-standardised procedure in order to avoid the artificiality that can occur even for adults when given a rigid set of questions. Children are probably more vulnerable to rigid questioning and may well appear to 'fail' when they don't understand the questions properly, whereas a simple but natural alteration in question form might reveal that the child does, after all, have the concept. Piaget believed that he could get the most accurate information about a child's thinking by varying the questioning in what seemed to the child a fairly natural conversation, though of course the method is open to the usual alleged validity threats of non-standardised procedures. Freud's methods, too, have been said to involve the clinical method, since the aim of some sessions was to test a specific hypothesis about the client's unconscious network of fears and ideas.

Semi-structured or open interviewing – gathering qualitative data

If the interview is *completely* structured, the interviewer will be using a questionnaire; the construction of these is outlined in Chapter 8. Some of the techniques and procedures described in the following pages could apply to structured interviews but mostly they apply to any other form of interview, particularly the semi-structured and those in which open-ended, qualitative data are sought. For a fuller account of the semi-structured interview, and how to analyse associated data, see Smith (2008, Chapter 4) and Patton (2002, Chapter 7), the latter for a particularly full, in-depth account of qualitative interviewing.

Principles of the open interview – an easy option?

Open interviewing, like qualitative research in general, should never be seen as a soft option by students or researchers who see it as a way to avoid formal testing of participants and perhaps any involvement in quantitative methods. It seems easy to just go and ask some respondents a few questions in an informal manner. However, one of the major principles of qualitative research is the notion that data analysis does not occur *after* data gathering, as in quantitative research. *Data analysis occurs as the data are gathered form the participants.* That is, it occurs *during* the interview process. What this means is that the interviewer is not *just* listening and recording. They are or should be attempting to establish the full meaning of the respondent's account from their point of view. For this reason the qualitative interviewer is not a passive recipient of information but needs to be active in checking what the interviewee is saying, watching for inconsistencies, encouraging fuller detail where a story is incomplete and generally keeping the research aims in mind throughout the process. During an interview there may be a need to return to certain points in order to fill in detail or to investigate why points occurring in previous interviews have not occurred in this one.

This last point raises another important principle of most qualitative interviewing. Not only might points arising from previous interviews be missing form the current one, but the current interview might throw up issues which have not occurred previously. In several of the approaches to qualitative research described in Chapter 10, it is seen as desirable to return to earlier participants for further interviewing, where possible, in order to obtain their perspective on these later emerging points *or* to alter the questioning of later participants in the light of new emerging issues.

Semi-structured interviewing then, as a research method, is very demanding on the interviewer/researcher and is certainly not just a series of friendly conversational meetings in which answers to a few questions are sought. I have encountered many students who have started off with this idea and, of those who continued to take this approach, most have found themselves raising far more questions than answers during their analysis and have wished they could have answered at least some of these by checking during the interview and using early analysis to inform their later interviews.

In the interests of research flexibility, a fundamental aspect of qualitative research, there can be no set of rigid instructions on how to conduct qualitative or open interviews. What follows here then are some guiding characteristics of open interviewing.

Giving information

Interviewees are at their most curious and probably their most nervous levels at the very start of the session. The interviewer can ease the atmosphere by giving give full information at this point about the purpose of the research, for whom it is conducted, what sorts of topics will be covered and, in particular, how confidentiality or anonymity will be maintained.

Anonymity and confidentiality

Interviewees will feel a lot easier, and will probably divulge more, if it is guaranteed that there is not the slightest possible chance that their comments, if published, will be attributable to them. This is particularly so in an applied setting with relatively small numbers – for instance, where a researcher conducts *action research* inside a company. This kind of research is intended to produce positive change as well as to provide research information (see, as an example, Hayes, 1991).

Since interviewees are usually quoted verbatim in the research article – a central principle of most qualitative research – then *confidentiality* cannot be offered in most qualitative studies. However, what therefore must be offered and rigorously enforced is the principle of *anonymity*. If there is only one female Asian middle manager on the staff and her comments make reference to her gender and ethnicity, then clearly the researcher must effectively disguise this in any published report or exclude the comments from it.

As Hayes (1997) points out, many employers or managers may claim that they are open to any comments from the workforce but the reality is that individuals making negative comments become vulnerable. Breaking the anonymity rule can ruin reputations. In the 1950s, the people of Springdale village in the USA vilified researchers (Vidich and Bensman, 1958) who, though using pseudonyms, made identification of individuals possible because their problems were analysed in the research report. The villagers held an effigy of 'the author' over a manure spreader in their 4th of July parade!

In order to ensure that published comments are acceptable to the interviewees, participants should be reminded of their right to veto comments made throughout the project and should, if possible, be shown any draft report in order to exercise discretion over personal information divulged.

Achieving and maintaining rapport

In an unstructured interview, the quality and characteristics of the interviewer's behaviour are of utmost importance and not just the interesting 'extraneous variables' they are often considered to be in the structured interview or survey study. People reveal a lot more about themselves when they are feeling comfortable and 'chatty' than in a strained, formal atmosphere where suspicions are not allayed. An awkward, 'stiff' or aggressive interviewer may produce little cooperation, and even hostility from the interviewee. How then may rapport be established?

Language

It is valuable to spend some time discovering terminology used by the group under study. They may have nicknames and use their own jargon. At the time of writing my children's school vernacular has started using 'sick' to mean 'really good'. Not knowing this, I seriously misunderstood their comments on items of family news or food they were served. Interviewees will be most comfortable and fluent using their normal language mode (dialect, accent, normal conversational style) and must be made to feel that its use is not only legitimate but welcome and valued. Without patronising, the interviewer can attempt to explain things in the most appropriate register and to give plenty of concrete examples where appropriate.

Neutrality

Accepting the language style and any non-verbal behaviour of the interviewee will help to assure her/him that the interview is entirely non-judgemental. Interviewees must feel that no moral assessment of what they say is, or will be, involved otherwise the researcher is simply not going to obtain the fullest possible genuine account. To this end, especially when the topic is sensitive, the interviewer needs to develop a repertoire of responses like 'I see' and 'uhuh' in order not to sound judgemental when an interviewee says something like, 'Yeah, well, I'm a pretty jealous guy. I hate people looking at my wife and I have been known to go over and smack them one.'

Listening skills

The interviewer needs to learn when not to speak, how to show attention and interest and generally to get the most out of the interviewee by careful listening. There are various listening skills, too numerous to detail here, which include:

- not trivialising statements by saying 'How interesting, but we must get on'
- hearing that a 'yes' is qualified and asking whether the interviewee wants to add anything – what follows may well amount to a 'no'
- not being too quick or dominant in offering an interpretation of what the interviewee was trying to say.

Interest

It is essential that the interviewer remains interested and believes that their respondents' information and sacrificed time are valuable. Patton (2002, Chapter 7) urges that the concept of the bad interviewee should be ignored, arguing that it is easy to summon up stereotypes – of the hostile or withdrawn interviewee, for instance. He suggests that it is the sensitive interviewer's task to unlock the internal perspective of each interviewee by being adaptable in finding the style and format that will work in each case.

Non-verbal communication

The interviewer needs to be sensitive to non-verbal cues, though not to the point of awkwardness. A literature review by Vrij (1991) suggested that, in Western majority cultures at least, a more favourable perception is given to a conversational partner by looking at them, giving supportive head-nods and gestures, limiting one's body movements (e.g. few trunk movements or changes of position), responding directly and having a fluent conversational style. Interviewers should avoid assuming what could be interpreted as a dominating position or tone of voice and should also be sensitive to the interviewee's non-verbal behaviour which might signal discomfort, embarrassment and so on.

Natural questioning

This is a central factor and involves the interviewer in trying to make the discussion feel as natural as is possible, and therefore more likely to produce authentic answers, whilst getting through a set of major questions. The context is one in which the interviewee will do most of the talking and the interviewer will mainly be asking questions. Hence it is not a natural 'conversation' and the interviewer will be revealing little about their life or attitudes. However, if the interviewer has only four or five target questions, then it is possible to make at least some of the interview session feel more like a 'chat'.

An advantage in the semi-structured interview is that, unlike the case with formal questionnaires, the interviewer can explain the purpose of any particular question. A natural questioning environment should encourage the interviewee to ask what the interviewer has in mind but offering this information is courteous and keeps the participant involved.

Info Box 7.2 — Developing the questions and order for your interview guide

Only ask what is needed

We'll start with a what-not-to-do item. Many students create a questionnaire around a topic but when asked why certain questions have been asked say 'Because I thought it might be useful'. Don't just throw in questions because you *think* they might be useful *and if you haven't already carefully considered how you are going to analyse them*. Your questions should all be developed from a consideration of your research aims. Don't use a shotgun approach and ask everything you can think of. A respondent's time is precious so why ask for information you are probably not going to use?

Biographical details (age, sex, marital status) *can* serve as ice-breakers or can be obtained through a written pre-interview questionnaire or even from school or company records.

Make sure questions *can* be answered.

'How many times have you been to a supermarket this year?' may be quite difficult for most people to answer at all accurately.

Make sure questions will be answered truthfully.

Questions related to strong social norms are unlikely to be answered truthfully if the truth is in fact rather incriminating. In this case the interviewee may well simply answer with well-known public opinion not their own actual behaviour or beliefs. Questions on child rearing, for instance, if not phrased very explicitly, are well known for producing answers more in accord with prevailing 'expert' views on good practice than with the parent's *actual* practice.

Make sure questions will not be refused.

Some sensitive topics will obviously produce more refusals. Most respondents will continue on a sensitive topic, once started, but may balk at a sensitive question turning up suddenly in an otherwise innocuous context – for instance, a sex-life question among items about shopping habits. The interviewer has to provide a context in order to justify sensitive points, or else avoid them.

Problem items

It is deceptively simple to ask poor or problematic questions. Some of the common mistakes to avoid are outlined in the principles of questionnaire design described on pages 185 to 187. Questions to avoid are those that are double-barrelled, complex, ambiguous, leading or emotive. In addition, the following points might be noted:

1 It is easy to ask two or more questions at once if the interviewer gets enthusiastic. For instance, the sequence: 'So tell me about it. What was it like? How did you feel? Did you regret it?' would put a memory strain, at least, on the interviewee.

2 CLOSED QUESTIONS have only a few, fixed answer options. For instance, 'Are you enjoying the course?' may well receive a monosyllabic answer. OPEN-ENDED QUESTIONS like 'Please can you tell me what you are enjoying about the course?' will be more likely to produce rich information and at least let the interviewee know that an extended answer would be appreciated.

3 'Why?' questions can be wasteful in time. Asking a student 'Why did you join the course?' will produce a variety of replies in quite different categories. For instance:

- 'It'll get me a decent qualification'
- 'To meet new people'
- 'It was nearer than London'
- 'My mother thought it was a good idea'

are all possible answers. We can decide, during the planning stage, what *category* of reply we would like, and design questions accordingly, e.g. 'What led you to be interested in Psychology?'. What should certainly be avoided is an implication that the answer that has actually been offered is not valued by saying, for instance, 'No, I didn't mean that . . .'.

Although a certain amount of biographical detail helps to break the ice without representing difficult questions for the interviewee to answer, interest may not be maintained if too many personal background details are requested. We will see that this point is valid for surveys, too, below.

Probes and prompts

PROMPTS are supplementary questions given to each interviewee unless they make these redundant by offering the exact information the interviewer was looking for. For instance, asked about reasons for joining a course, a respondent's answer of 'Because it interested me' might be followed by 'In what ways did the course interest you?', which would have been asked whatever the interviewee's response unless they happened to state spontaneously what interested them about the course. PROBES are more general requests for further information, such as 'Could you tell me a little more about that?', 'How did you feel about that?', which interviewers use as needed.

Feelings and reactions

As with more formal questioning methods, the interviewee will feel more comfortable if the session does not kick off with emotionally charged or controversial items. Even if not traumatic, it will be hard to discuss feelings about, or reactions towards, an issue or event until the interviewee has had a chance to acclimatise by describing it. Early questions can be aimed at eliciting a description, and later questions can prompt feelings about, or reactions towards, events described.

Helpful feedback

An interview will run more smoothly if the interviewee is aware of the position reached and the future direction of questioning. In particular, it might be useful to let the interviewee know . . .

1. . . . when the interviewer is about to change topic; for instance, 'Now let's talk about the students on the course'

2. . . . that the next question is particularly important, complex, controversial or sensitive; for instance, 'You've been telling me what you like about the course. Now, in particular, I'd like to find out about what you *don't* like. Can you tell me . . .'

3. . . . about what the interviewer thinks the interviewee has just said, or said earlier, without, of course, reinterpretations that depart far from the actual words used. This feedback and summary of what the interviewee is understood to have said is central to semi-structured interviewing and most qualitative approaches. It permits the interviewee to realise they are making sense and being productive; also, that they are not being misrepresented. They can alter or qualify what they have said. The process also keeps the interviewee actively involved and confident. However, it is important, of course, not to summarise interviewees' statements in a manner that might seem patronising.

Recording the interview

Interviewers have three common ways of saving data: note taking, audio-recording or visual-recording.

Note taking

Taking handwritten notes will obviously slow down the procedure, will constantly remind the interviewee that their words are being recorded and will generally run counter to the great advantage of semi-structured interviewing – the feel of a natural conversational encounter. It could be useful to develop some form of personal shorthand – at least, short forms of commonly used terms and phrases. One handy advantage of the notebook is that it can be a place to store discreetly the interview questions or outline. If used, the interviewer needs to be careful not to give the impression that what the interviewee is saying at any particular moment is not important because it is not being recorded. Mostly, though, it will be far better to record the interview electronically so that the interviewer is free to engage in conversation and to take the emphasis off the recording process.

Audio recording

Many people feel inhibited in the presence of a recoding microphone. The interviewer needs to justify its use in terms of catching the exact terms and richness of the interviewee's experiences. Confidentiality must again be assured. The interviewee has to be free to have the recording switched off at any time. The recorder has the advantage of leaving the interviewer free to converse naturally and encourage the greatest flow of information. Though this may sound obvious, it is worth making sure before each interview the distance from which the microphone works best, that the batteries are new and that the tape is fully rewound to the start or that discs are compatible. Any interruption (and one may be inevitable in order to turn over or change the tape or disc) serves to remind the interviewee that they are being recorded, may interfere with established rapport and relaxation of tension, and may inhibit responses.

Video recording

A 'live' video camera in the room may dominate and can hardly help retain the informal atmosphere that a loosely structured, open-ended interview is supposed to create. It is possible to acclimatise interviewees to its presence over quite a number of sessions, but this is costly in time. The great value, of course, is in the recording of non-verbal communication at a detailed level and the chance to analyse this at a comfortable pace. If this information is not required, however, then video is an unnecessary, intrusive gimmick.

Both video and audio recordings could be conducted unobtrusively by simply not revealing their presence to the interviewee, but, in this case, serious ethical issues must be addressed. Two answers to possible dilemmas here are as follows.

1 Inform the interviewee of the recording process but keep equipment completely hidden.

2 Give information about the recording only after the interview has taken place, but emphasise that recordings can be heard or viewed, sections omitted or the whole recording destroyed at the interviewee's request. This second option is of course potentially wasteful and time-consuming.

The danger of both audio and video recording is of taking too much information if the intention is to covert to the written word everything that a respondent says – a process known as TRANSCRIPTION. Pidgeon and Henwood (1997) estimate that it takes eight to ten times the duration of recorded speech to transcribe it into written form, and Potter (1996) puts this ratio at 20 to 1. Transcription is discussed further in Chapter 22.

Surveys

A survey consists of asking a relatively large number of people for information. In the informal, loosely structured interview, each interviewee's answers form a small case study. A survey can consist of a set of such small case studies. Much more often, though, it would involve the use of a structured questionnaire (see Chapter 8), with answers open or closed, as described in interview types 4 and 5 above. Each set of responses forms an equivalent unit in a large sample. The sampling strategy would be strict and often quite complex, using the procedures described in Chapter 2. Interviewers usually work as a team and procedures are therefore fully standardised. Each will be briefed on the exact introductory statement and steps to be followed with each respondent. A survey may be used for two major research purposes: descriptive or analytical.

Info Box 7.3   Examples of research surveys – descriptive

Here the researcher wants an accurate description of what people, in some target population, do and think, and with what frequency or to what extent. Quine (2002) conducted a questionnaire survey on 594 junior doctors in the UK about the subject of workplace bullying. She found that 37% reported being bullied in the past year and that 84% had experienced at least one of 21 listed bullying behaviours from peers. Black and Asian doctors were more likely to be bullied than others, and women were more likely to be bullied than men. An extremely comprehensive survey (Jowell and Topf, 1988) gathered information on then current British social attitudes – including AIDS, the countryside, industry's and unions' influences on political parties, the government's current economic policies, education, the north/south divide and which household jobs should be shared – according to married and single persons' opinions. Selwyn (2008) investigated undergraduates' use of the Internet for study and assignments and found that this use was the most common ('some' or 'all of the time') after e-mailing, closely followed by social uses such as blogging and Facebook, etc. Females used the internet for study purposes significantly more than did males, as did those with their own computers compared to those forced to use public access machines. Finally, students in medicine and social science made significantly more use of the internet for assignments than did those in architecture, planning and the creative arts.

Survey design

In survey work there are three major areas of decision-making necessary before initiating contact with respondents. These are the sample, mode of questioning and the questions themselves. The first two areas will be dealt with now, and the content of questions will be covered in Chapter 8, which is on questionnaires and tests in general.

Info Box 7.4 | **Examples of research surveys – analytic**

Survey data can be used to test hypotheses. Sears, Maccoby and Levin (1957) conducted a wide-ranging survey of child-rearing practices, using mothers from two suburbs of Boston, USA. Many hypotheses were tested by correlating rearing techniques with children's characteristic behaviour – that is, seeing which discipline techniques were associated with which behaviours in children. Raters assessed answers to open-ended questions without meeting the mothers who provided them. The analysis showed that greater use of physical punishment was associated with higher levels of aggression in children; mothers who were rated as warm and mainly used 'withdrawal of love' as a disciplinary technique had children with stronger consciences. Both these variables, withdrawal of love and strength of conscience, were assessed indirectly from the interview data and are examples of constructs, operationally defined by the coding system.

The findings square with those of Durrant (1999; 2000; see Chapter 5) whose survey of public records found a decrease in various forms or effects of aggression consequent upon the banning of corporal punishment in Sweden. Hence the hypothesis that physical punishment is a cause of aggression was supported.

Oswald and Blanchflower (2008) used survey data from several countries to support their hypothesis developed from earlier studies, that our feeling of well-being is a U-shaped distribution through life. That is, feeling good about ourselves and our lives starts to decline from our early adult years onwards then takes an upturn again from around our late 40s onwards. The researchers report empirical data to support this well-being life curve in 72 developed or developing nations throughout the world.

The sample

Of all methods, the survey places particular emphasis on the sample, since the aim, very often, is to make generalisations about a relatively large section of the population, if not all of it. If the coverage *is* the whole population then the survey is known as a CENSUS. We dealt with the main methods and issues of representative sampling in Chapter 2. Survey work has been particularly responsible for the development of two sample types mentioned there: the panel and the focus group.

Panels

This is a specially selected group of people who can be asked for information on a repetitive basis. They are much used by market research companies, government survey units and audience research in broadcasting. It is easier and more efficient to rely on the same, well-stratified group to provide information each time it is required. However, panel members can become too sophisticated in their reviewing and may become unrepresentative because, for instance, they feel they must watch all the programmes mentioned in their questionnaire.

Focus groups

The idea of a FOCUS GROUP is to bring together a group of individuals with a common interest and to conduct a form of collective interview. Though not providing much in the way of quantifiable data, such groups can provide valuable insights into a topic and may also provide a starting point for research into a specific area. They are encountered again briefly in Chapter 22 and have become increasingly popular in applied research. Advantages of focus groups are that much more data can be gathered in a session than in the one-to-one interview. Some people indeed refer to them as 'group interviews'. Discussion among members may provoke an exchange of views and points raised might prompt others to contribute ideas that they otherwise might not have thought of, providing information and insights less likely to surface during a one-to-one interview. Disadvantages are that focus groups can be hard to facilitate, one or two people may dominate discussion and others may feel more intimidated than in the on-to-one situation.

Olson, Kutner and Warner (2008) ran focus groups with 12- to 14-year-old boys on the subject of violent video games. Each session involved four to five boys for between 75 and 90 minutes and went through ten major questions. The researcher found boys were attracted to violent games for five clusters of reasons including power and fame fantasies, challenge and exploration, coping with anger and sociability factors (e.g. achieving status). Some salient points relevant to the popular media scares linking violent games and youth crime were that the boys constantly and clearly distinguished between game and reality stating that games were fun because you could do what you certainly would not do in real life. They were concerned that children younger and more vulnerable than themselves might encounter such games and learn bad behaviour from them. They saw positive factors in the games in that they could safely teach others about real life and also helped develop creativity and problem solving skills. The theory of catharsis was supported in that several boys said that games helped them to relieve pent-up anger caused by previous real life encounters (e.g. with bullies).

The interview medium

The medium through which respondents are questioned can, these days, be one of many: face-to-face, telephone, post, e-mail, internet and even by texting. A telephone interview approach might recruit interviewees who are otherwise too busy or too intimidated to be interviewed in person though 'cold-calling' may make it hard to convince people that there is not ultimately a selling motive. However, research has suggested that the telephone has several other advantages such as the lack of visual clues from the interviewer, greater anonymity, greater economy and even safety for the interviewer! (see Sturges and Hanrahan, 2004; Musselwhite et al., 2007). The research also suggests that data quality can be just as high from telephone interviews as from face-to-face ones and that there are several other minor advantages to weigh against the disadvantages of it being harder to interpret interviewee mood or intention (e.g. cynical humour) and of it being much easier to conclude a telephone interview prematurely. The method would also produce biased samples in countries where telephones are not common in all households.

The privacy of the postal method could be a factor that will produce less social desirability and more honest answers. This can also depend upon the topic. McEwan, Harrington and Bhopal (1992) found that, compared with face-to-face interviews, more information on sexual behaviour and more socially unacceptable responses were obtained through a postal approach when studying HIV/AIDS; the postal response rate was also no lower. In a postal approach, interpersonal variables, discussed earlier, are reduced to a minimum and the method is also less time consuming.

The disadvantages of postal surveys are, first, that the questionnaire must be exceptionally clear, and unambiguous instructions for its completion must be written carefully. Even so, respondents may answer in an inappropriate way that a 'live' interviewer could have corrected. Second, though McEwan et al. (1992) did not find this, the proportion of non-returners is often likely to be higher than the number of refusals by other approaches (e.g. Cartwright, 1988). This matters a lot when, for instance, it is reported that 75% of respondents (300) agreed that government should continue to finance higher education substantially, if it is also true that only 400 out of 1000 persons contacted bothered to complete and return the form. Do we count the missing 600 as neutral or not bothered, or do we assume that 75% of them also agree?

Electronic surveys

A recent development is the growing use of e-mail or the Internet to conduct survey studies. A criticism raised about Internet surveys has been that the sample gathered may be severely skewed in terms of representing the general population since only around 57% of the population have access to the Internet at home,[1] whereas 95% of all households have a telephone. One might expect that Internet users would be better off; Baker, Curtice and Sparrow (2003) claim that Internet users are more likely than the general population to be below retirement age, working full-time, with a mortgaged property, to own two or more cars, and to have taken a foreign holiday in the last three years. Hence we might expect a problem in using an Internet sample in order to generalise results to the population as a whole, especially where the psychological topic in any way concerns social issues and attitudes.

Baker *et al.* argued that the problem was even more acute when one considers that researchers do not use a random sample of Internet users but only those willing to complete a questionnaire or to join an 'Internet panel'. They compared the demographics of such a panel with those of traditional telephone samples fairly representative of the general population. They found that those with access to the Internet differed significantly from telephone samples on several issues and attitudes. In addition, willing Internet panel members, compared with telephone samples, were far more sure about their political actions, more likely to vote, more certain how they would vote and far less likely to refuse to give a voting intention. They were generally more left-wing in outlook and somewhat more likely to support the Liberal Democrats. They were more willing than Internet users in general to try new things, though both groups were much higher on this than telephone

Advantages	Disadvantages
Many respondents can be questioned fairly quickly – lower costs	Large-scale surveys can be expensive in terms of employing assistants – higher costs
With sensitive issues more likely to elicit genuine socially undesirable responses	Structured questions miss more rich and informative data
Less influence from dynamics of interpersonal variables; effects of social desirability probably lower	More influenced by superficial interpersonal variables if face-to-face; respondent has no time to trust and confide in interviewer
Less reliance on interpretation in the analysis of answers, since questions are structured	If not face-to-face respondent cannot ask for guidance and interviewer cannot spot hesitations or possible confusion.

Table 7.2 Advantages and disadvantages of the survey compared with the in-depth interview

[1] 2006 UK government figures obtained from National Statistics at www.statistics.gov.uk/pdfdir/inta0806.pdf

samples. Internet users, compared with telephone samples, were much less in favour of the death penalty, more opposed to the tightening of asylum laws, more favourable to the Euro, and more politically knowledgeable, with willing panellists even stronger on the last three of these items.

Hence if psychologists are to increase their reliance on the Internet both for surveys and for other information-gathering exercises, and even for experiments, they need to recognise that, at present though perhaps not in the future, willing Internet participants are not likely to represent the characteristics of the population as a whole.

Table 7.2 shows the advantages and disadvantages of the survey compared with the in-depth interview.

Exercises

1 Without looking back at the text, or at Table 7.2, try to think of several advantages and disadvantages the survey has compared with the informal or in-depth interview.

2 A researcher interviews participants and then goes through each interview transcript rating each respondent on scales of 'warmth' and 'openness'. What flaw is there in this procedure?

3 Suppose you decide to conduct a survey in your area on attitudes towards genetically modified crops. Outline the steps you would take in planning and conducting the survey, paying particular attention to:

   1 the sample and means of obtaining it

   2 the exact approach to respondents you would use

   3 the types of question you would ask.

   To answer this last point in detail, you will need to read pages 184 to 187 in Chapter 8 on questionnaires, at least briefly.

4 A researcher wishes to investigate specific instances of racism (abuse, physical harassment, discrimination) that members of minority ethnic groups have experienced. Four assistants are employed to conduct informal, guided interviews starting with individuals recommended by local community leaders. They also ask the community leaders to recommend others who would be likely to have experiences relevant to the research aims.

   (a) What kind of sample is drawn?

   (b) One interviewer records far fewer instances than the other three. Can you give at least five reasons why this might be?

   (c) Another interviewer argues that the study should follow up with a structured questionnaire over a far wider sample. Why might this be?

5 You are about to conduct an interview with the manager of a local, large supermarket. He is 43 years old, quite active in local politics and is known to be fairly friendly. Make a list of all the variables, especially those concerning his and your own personality and characteristics, which might influence the production of information in the interview.

6 Construct (and, if you have time, administer) a semi-structured interview schedule that would investigate people's reactions to an event such as the death of Princess Diana in August 1997 or the London tube bombings of July 2005. Try to include questions that would elicit evidence of 'flashbulb' memory phenomena (where people tend to recall vividly and visually exactly what they were doing, down to trivial specifics, when they first heard the news). If you do interview several people as part of this exercise, try to adapt your schedule in the light of this experience, rephrasing, adding and deleting items.

Answers

There are no set answers to questions 3, 5 and 6.

1 See page 168.

2 The researcher might be biased through expectancy factors since she has already had an interview session with each participant. Answer is to employ a 'blind' rater to assess the transcripts.

4 (a) This is the start of a snowball sample.

(b) Initial interviewee unwilling to admit problem; initial interviewee gives fewer further contacts; interviewer doesn't see some incidents as serious; interviewer doesn't want to record the incidents for personal, political reasons; interviewer is a poor questioner, is aggressive, shows prejudice, etc.

(c) Structured questionnaire more reliable; results more comparable; larger sample more representative; quantitative hypotheses can be tested.

Glossary

Census	Survey of whole population
Clinical method	Interview method using structured questions but may be tailored in response to interviewee's answers; seeks to test specific hypothesis
Closed questions	Question with only a specified set of responses that the respondent can choose from, e.g. 'yes/no'
Face-to-face	Interview in which researcher and interviewee talk together in each other's presence
Focus group	Group, often with common interest, who meet to discuss an issue in a collective interview
Non-directive interview	Interview in which interviewer does not direct discussion and remains non-judgemental
Open-ended questions	Type of interview/questionnaire item to which interviewees respond at length
Panel	Stratified group who are consulted in order for opinion to be assessed

Probe	General request for further information used in semi-structured interview
Prompt	Pre-set request for further information used in semi-structured interview if the information is not offered spontaneously by interviewee on a particular item
Respondent	Person who is questioned in an interview or survey
Self-report method	A general term for methods in which people knowingly provide information about themselves
Semi-structured interview	Interview with pre-set list of topics but in which 'natural' conversation is attempted and the interviewer 'plays it by ear' as to whether sufficient information has been provided by the interviewee
Structure	Dimension of design which is the extent to which questions and procedure are identical for everyone
Survey	Relatively structured questioning of large sample
Transcription	Written recording of directly recorded speech as exactly as possible; often includes pauses, intonation, etc.

8 Psychological tests and measurement scales

This chapter looks at a variety of procedures for gathering data using some form of *questionnaire, scale* or *test*. There is some overlap with the last chapter since some interviews consist of going through a structured questionnaire with the respondent.

- Psychological scales, tests and questionnaires are introduced along with the area of psychological measurement known as *psychometrics*.
- Questions can be *fixed* or *open-ended* (in the latter the respondent has freedom in type and length of response). Fixed items need careful consideration if data gathered are not to be distorted by the task the respondent faces in selection of a response.
- Types of *disguised* questioning are introduced, including the *bogus pipeline* technique.
- Features of good questionnaires are outlined: they should be *reliable, valid, standardised* and they should *discriminate.*
- The attitude scales of *Thurstone* and *Likert* are described, along with *Osgood's semantic differential* and the *Visual Analogue Scale*. Likert's is probably the most popular and, with this, decisions must be made about how many points on the response set to use (often five) and how the 'neutral' mid-point will be interpreted.
- Methodological issues of *response bias*, respondents' interpretations of scales and *social desirability* are discussed.
- Steps in the construction of an attitude scale are outlined including common problems in the writing of scale items and how to score the scale.
- *Projective* tests are described as assuming that unconscious mental processes can be assessed from the way people respond to ambiguous stimuli such as the *Rorschach* and *Thematic Apperception Tests.*
- The use of *factor analysis* is briefly described as an important statistical procedure for providing evidence for the constructs that psychological scales measure.
- *Reliability* is consistency within a test (*internal*) or between repeated uses of it (*external*). Measures of a test's internal reliability are *Cronbach's alpha* and *split-half reliability*. A test can be made reliable using several kinds of *item analysis*, and SPSS procedures are included for performing these tasks as well as for finding Cronbach and split-half values. *Validity* concerns whether a test measures what it was created to measure. Concepts of *face, content, criterion, predictive* and *concurrent validity* are described. *Construct validity* is described as the wide scale provision of evidence for psychological constructs through hypothesis testing and theory development.
- *Standardisation* involves creating norms for tests so that comparisons between groups or within populations are possible. The value of creating tests where scores form a normal distribution is emphasised but it is pointed out that normal distributions for constructs such as human intelligence are convenient human constructions not biological realities.

Introduction

Psychological tests are both very much enjoyed and very much feared or even scorned. Many people like filling out a questionnaire in a popular magazine and then turning to the 'scoring key' to see what kind of lover they are, how well they treat their friends or how sociable they are – as if they didn't already know! Oddly, people seem quite kindly disposed towards simple-minded horoscopes yet hostile towards psychologists' personality tests. Yet, whereas the quiz or horoscope is probably devised in five minutes on a journalist's desk, the psychological scale will often have taken months, if not years, to devise, pilot, standardise and implement, to say nothing of periodic revision in order to keep the scale reliable and valid for each population on which it is used. In this chapter we will look at the features and types of questionnaires and scales which attempt to measure psychological characteristics, as well as some of the major steps in their development.

Measurement vs. information gathering: scales, tests, inventories and questionnaires

Psychologists developed psychological tests and scales as *measuring instruments*. Though these can be in the form of questionnaires very often they are not. In an attitude or personality scale (or *personality inventory*) very often the items in the scale are *statements* (e.g. 'I am often in a hurry to get things done') to which the respondent answers on a RESPONSE SCALE (typically 'Strongly agree, Agree . . .', etc. see p. 179). Each item is seen as measuring a small aspect of the whole construct (attitude or personality characteristic) and hence the respondent's *single* score is the sum of all responses on the scale and this depends on how much they veer towards one end or the other of a *dimension* – for example, extroversion – introversion. Very often this is forgotten when psychologists talk of 'extroverts' or 'introverts' when what they mean is 'people who scored towards the extroversion end of the dimension'.

Whereas questionnaires often simply gather information, tests and scales are seen as scientific *measuring instruments*. Questionnaires used in surveys are usually constructed for the specific research topic and tend to test for current opinion or patterns of behaviour. Attitude scales, ability tests and measures of intellectual reasoning or personality are usually intended to be more permanent measures and are seen by the PSYCHOMETRICIAN or PSYCHOMETRIST (a psychologist who practises PSYCHOMETRICS) as technical tools, equivalent to the pressure gauge or voltmeter of 'hard' science.

PSYCHOMETRIC TESTS require a significant degree of expertise in their development. The test constructor must pay rigorous attention to sampling methods since the ways in which sample members differ on the test will be taken as indicative of how the population that they represent will differ. For this reason, the constructor must specify appropriate populations and will often provide *test norms* for different sub-sections of the general population so that test administrators will know how the scores of, for instance, social workers, maintenance staff or 18–25-year-old men would be distributed around their group's average. Establishing these norms is achieved through a process known as STANDARDISATION. In addition, tests and scales must be *reliable* and *valid* (dealt with later in this chapter).

A psychologist might use a psychological scale for a variety of reasons, including:

- selecting personnel in applied work in occupational psychology
- measuring clients' levels of 'depression' in clinical psychology work
- measuring a cognitive or personality variable in theoretical research (e.g. 'self-esteem').

In the last case, the psychometric measure may be used as a dependent variable; experimental participants might be assessed for 'self-esteem' before and after a 'treatment' in which they are made to feel successful and scores compared with those of a control group not given success feedback. On the other hand, the psychological measure might be used to identify a group difference (a non-manipulated 'independent variable'; see Chapter 5) and then both groups might be measured on a dependent variable. For instance, DeBono and Packer (1991) used a measure of *self-monitoring* (how much we are aware of our own image in a social setting) to identify high and low self-monitors. They then asked all participants to rate image-oriented (IO) and quality-oriented (QO) advertisements (adverts appealing to the way the product would enhance one's image and those appealing more to the quality of the product). They found, as predicted, that high self-monitors preferred the IO ads, whereas low self-monitors preferred the QO ads.

Open and closed questions

We saw in the last chapter that interview questions tend to be *open* such as 'Please tell me about your feelings for your parents'. Questions used in psychological scales tend almost always to be *closed*. This makes the gathered data amenable to quantitative analysis. Examples are:

---

1 I voted in the last election   Yes/No

2 [Select one option only] I would describe my present dwelling as:
   (a) fully owned by me
   (b) owned by me with a mortgage
   (c) owned by me as part of a housing association
   (d) rented from the local council
   (e) rented from a private landlord
   (f) provided by employer
   (g) other (please state)

3 My age is:
   (a) under 16
   (b) 16–21
   (c) 22–35
   (d) over 35

4 I feel confident when introduced to strangers:
   Strongly agree   Agree   Undecided   Disagree   Strongly disagree

5 At what age did your baby start crawling? .... months

---

Pause for thought

Is it possible to check more than one answer in any of the items given above? If so, which one(s) and why?

Some questions will permit the respondent to tick or check more than one item, but if a single response is required then possible overlap must be carefully avoided. I would think there might be confusion if I were 35 and answering item 3. In item 2, (e) and (f) might overlap. Although the fault is very obvious in item 3, it is common for draft versions of student project questionnaires to contain this kind of overlap.

Note that items 1, 2 and 4 are typical *statements* rather than questions. We can see here that there is a world of difference between fixed-choice 'questions' of the form 'Which of the following do you agree with?' or 'Are you nervous at meetings? (Yes/No)' and normal conversational questions of the 'Why . . .?' and 'What do you think . . .?' variety, which produce *qualitative* data.

Problems with closed questions – the Kalamazoo study

Closed items have the great advantage that they can form part of a scale which produces a quantified measure of a psychological construct. However they have certain disadvantages which a qualitative researcher would be quick to point out:

1 Respondents can be frustrated by the constraint imposed by the possible responses.

2 Respondents can misinterpret the meaning of the item or simply not understand it.

3 Closed items deliver very limited numerical information; there is no rich information and it is not possible to tell *why* a respondent chose a specific response (unless it is a factual item).

4 Closed items can be unrealistic. We rarely have simply to agree or disagree, or say how strongly, without giving our reasons.

The importance of giving respondents the freedom to say what they really think is demonstrated by the results of a piece of applied psychological research conducted by Peronne, Patton and French (1976), who were evaluating a new accountability system set up by the Kalamazoo Education Association (USA) in its schools. The system had been heavily criticised. Teachers were asked to complete a questionnaire with fixed-choice questions: 'agree' or 'disagree'. The researchers also set a couple of open-ended questions to which staff could respond in their own words at any length.

School board members (equivalent to our school governors) were prepared to dismiss the quantitative results from the fixed-choice questions as biased. It was in their interests to assume that the rather artificial and perfunctory questioning method had produced unrealistically negative responses from teachers. However, on publication of the qualitative results they could hardly ignore the clear statements of fear, concern and frustration that dominated replies to the open-ended questions and they were influenced strongly enough to make substantial changes (Patton, 2002). Most course evaluation questionnaires worth their salt will include an opportunity for students to write out specific comments on their learning experience as well as answer fixed questions.

Open-ended interview questions can be used to generate information that is later organised into a structured questionnaire; this was done, for instance, by Niles (1998), who obtained from Australian and Sri Lankan interviewees open lists of achievement goals (what people most wanted in life) and means of satisfying these; she then organised these into a structured questionnaire, which was administered to many more participants.

Disguise

In order to avoid social desirability effects and to facilitate honest, genuine answers psychologists in some theoretical areas have used a certain degree of DISGUISE to keep the respondent from knowing the true nature of the measuring instrument at least while they are answering it. Disguising the researcher's true aim may help to obtain valid information where issues are highly sensitive, potentially embarrassing or otherwise felt as a threat to the respondent if disclosed.

Psychoanalytic researchers have developed 'projective' tests (see page 187) that, they claim, uncover aspects of personality or of unconscious anxieties hidden even to the respondent. Levin (1978) used the Rorschach ink blot test to assess women's degree of the Freudian construct of 'penis envy'. The responses were rated by 'blind' raters and she apparently found that career women had greater unconscious penis envy than 'homemakers'.

Hammond (1948) used a rather cunning strategy known as the 'error choice technique'. Respondents were asked factual questions about days lost through strikes, say, and had to tick an answer from two, one of which was far too high and one far too low. Without it being obvious to the respondent, attitude to trades unions was said to be measured on the assumption that selecting the answer unfavourable to unions was related to an internally negative attitude towards them and vice versa.

Bishop and Slevin (2004) used an error choice measure (The Knowledge about Epilepsy scale) to assess teachers' attitudes towards epilepsy. Their scale contained items with four multiple choice answers all of which were wrong but which veered either towards a position *more* positive than the truth or to one *less* positive than the truth. They found that almost 30% of the teachers had negative scores, a position indicating more negative than positive choices and therefore taken as representing a more negative than positive attitude towards epilepsy. This is a large number considering that in an equal opportunity environment, probably very few teachers would utter negative comments about epileptic students in public.

A further fairly common way to disguise research aims is to ask questions about the topic of interest and simultaneously record a physiological response, such as the respondent's galvanic skin response (GSR) which is an indication of anxiety.

The bogus pipeline technique

In a cunning but deceitful exploitation of the GSR indicator, and as a way of dealing with interviewees who hide their true attitudes and wish to 'look good', Jones and Sigall (1971) introduced the 'bogus pipeline' technique. Participants are hooked up to a machine which, they are assured, can detect signs of anxiety – a form of 'lie detector'. The researcher already has some attitude information about each participant obtained by clandestine means. The participant is asked to lie unpredictably to some of a set of personal questions. However, unknown to the participant, of course, the researcher has already obtained the correct answers. Hence, when the participant lies as instructed the researcher is able to report a detected lie. Apparently, people tend to be more embarrassed at being found to be a liar than they are about revealing unpopular attitudes. Hence, when the participant is subsequently asked the questions of genuine interest to the researcher, they tend not to lie! Although the method appears successful it has, as might be imagined, come in for some ethical criticism.

The technique is still used in controversial or sensitive areas where people are most likely to distort their views to remain socially acceptable, for instance in studies attempting to detect real racial prejudice where people tend to present superficially acceptable views. Gannon *et al.* (2007) used the technique in the highly sensitive area of child abuse where it is known that child abusers often hold attitudes that cognitively justify their actions against children; they are subject to cognitive distortions. Naturally child abusers themselves are able to identify which beliefs are deemed to be cognitive distortions and therefore pathological and are able to 'fake good' on questionnaires designed to expose them. However, having been hooked up to a convincing lie detector a group of child molesters increased the number of incriminating cognitive distortions they agreed with compared with their own performance previously without the detector and compared with a control group.

Features of good psychological measurement scales

Where scales and tests attempt to measure psychological characteristics, the following points are extremely important:

1 They should *discriminate* as widely as possible across the variety of human response. They shouldn't identify a few extreme individuals while showing no difference between individuals clustered at the centre of the scale. This is referred to as DISCRIMINATORY POWER and it is dependent on the sensitivity of items and the response system.

2 They should be highly RELIABLE (they should measure *consistently*).

3 They should be supported by tests of VALIDITY (they should measure the construct *intended*).

4 They should be STANDARDISED if they are to be used as general, practical measures of human characteristics. (Similar scores should mean similar things within the same population and we should know the typical scores of identifiable populations).

A questionnaire, scale or test will normally be piloted, perhaps several times, before the researcher is satisfied that it meets these criteria. Even a limited scale, constructed by students as part of course practical work, should be piloted at least once to highlight pitfalls and possible misinterpretations. Tests for the criteria above are dealt with later in this chapter.

Attitude scales

Attitudes are relatively enduring positions that we take in terms of our behaviour towards and beliefs about certain things or issues in the world. We can have an *opinion* about the latest city scandal or a new type of music. Opinions tend to be short lived or superficial and psychologists would see them as being created or driven by our longer-standing attitudes which are more or less our typical ways of responding. Along with the components of behaviour and beliefs, attitudes include an emotional response which is probably the hardest component to shift and the most strongly conditioned. We can know that a certain position is rational but can find it hard to behave accordingly. Central attitudes would be, for instance, how authoritarian we are, our political stance, our attitude towards child discipline and so on. Psychologists believe that we cannot simply ask people what their political attitude is or how authoritarian they are. We can instead present a series of items which each assess a small area of the attitude object. An authoritarianism scale for instance would contain items like:

- People should learn to respect those who are older and wiser than them.
- The best decisions are made though negotiation and peaceful resolution.

Each item on a scale measuring attitude to parental discipline, for instance, would sample the areas of physical punishment, psychological methods, the effects of weak discipline on children and society and so on. The scores of each respondent on *all* the items are totalled and the scale therefore delivers just a *single score*, which is treated as a measure of attitude strength and direction. Strictly speaking, though, since an attitude is defined as an *enduring* response to the attitude object, attitude scales should be administered *twice*, at either end of a substantial interval, in order to establish that the views assessed are not simply transient opinion. However, this is rarely done in attitude measurement. We will now consider several popular types of scale.

Equal appearing intervals (Thurstone, 1931)

The central idea of a Thurstone scale is that, for each statement on the scale, if a person agrees with it, they are given a score equivalent to the *strength* of that statement (or 'item'). For instance, part of an equal opportunities for women attitude scale might appear like this:

Please tick any of the following statements with which you agree:

Companies should pay full salary for maternity leave	(9.8)
Companies should provide more toilets for women	(6.2)
Women are less reliable employees because they are likely to leave through pregnancy	(2.1)

The scores in brackets would not appear to the respondent. They indicate the *strength* of the item (its SCALE VALUE), which is derived through a scaling process described below.

The first step in creating a Thurstone type attitude scope is to decide, from your study of theory, prior research and overall rationale, exactly what is the construct you are trying to measure. Constructs like 'prejudice' are extremely broad and it might pay to consider just what aspect of prejudice you are after. This could be prejudice towards a specific group or it could be prejudice towards authority, a political party, drug addicts and so on.

1 Produce a large number of statements (say 70–100), like the examples above, *both positive and negative,* towards the attitude object.

2 Ask a panel of judges to rate each statement on a scale of 1 (extremely unfavourable attitude) to 11 (extremely favourable attitude). It is important that the judges use the whole scale; they should not express their own attitude but simply decide how favourable or unfavourable towards the attitude object each statement is. Edwards (1957, in Kline, 2000) recommends that at least 100 judges are used, a rather tall order in most situations.

3 Take the mean value, for each statement, of all the judges' ratings. Our first item above has been given an average rating of 9.8, for instance, while the second one scores only just positive at 6.2. The third item is very negative towards female employees. These average ratings become the items' *scale values*.

4 In the interests of reliability, reject statements where the judges' individual values have a high *variance* (see Chapter 11), indicating wide disagreement between judges on that item.

5 In the finished scale, a respondent now scores the total of all scale values on *items they agreed with*. Hence, people favourable to equal opportunities measures will tend to score only on items *above* the average value and thus end up with a high overall score. Misogynists will score on the low-value items.

Info Box 8.1   **Difficulties with the Thurstone scaling method**

1 The judges themselves cannot be completely neutral, although they are asked to be objective. In an early debate on this issue, Hinckley (1932) was severely criticised for rejecting judges as 'careless' because they sorted a majority of items into a few extreme categories, against the exhortation mentioned in item 2 of the construction process above. It turned out that most of these judges were black (or pro-black whites), who rated as fairly hostile certain statements seen as relatively neutral by white judges unaware of, or unconcerned by, black issues.

2 Edwards (1957, in Kline, 2000) persuasively argued that for a scale to be reliable around 100 judges would be necessary. This makes the cost of creating a Thurstone scale rather prohibitive.

3 There is a difficulty in choosing the most discriminating items from among those with the same scale value.

Summated ratings (Likert, 1932)

A Likert-type scale consists of a set of statements which are responded to using a fixed scale of choices such as:

5	4	3	2	1
Strongly agree	Agree	Undecided	Disagree	Strongly disagree

To avoid response set (see below) around half the items are favourable and the other half unfavourable, for instance:

- Capital punishment should be re-introduced for the crime of murder (*for* capital punishment)
- Under any circumstances capital punishment is a barbaric sentence (*against* capital punishment)

If we want a high score to represent an attitude which strongly supports capital punishment then the respondent would score 5 if they agree with the first statement. However, because it is in the opposite direction, we would *reverse* all scores on the second item so someone who disagrees with it (scoring a raw 1 and obviously agreeing with capital punishment to some extent) would be given 5 when the score has been reversed. The final scores on each item are summed to give the respondent's overall attitude score.

Unlike the Thurstone scale, the Likert scale can contain items that are not obviously measuring the attitude directly. Such items are called *diagnostic*; they are included because they are known from previous research to correlate well with other items that clearly do relate to the attitude object. For instance, we might find that respondents fairly hostile to equal opportunities issues also tend to agree with the item '*Women have an instinctive need to be near their child for the first two to three years of its life.*' This item then might predict fairly well a negative attitude to equal opportunities. That such items do correlate with the rest of the scale items can be checked through a process of *item analysis*, a check for reliability of the scale, which is described on p. 195. Each item in a scale is useful in that it *contributes* a small part to the overall measurement of an attitude and item analysis tells us which items are out of synch with the rest and are probably not contributing usefully to the measurement of the attitude.

Info Box 8.2 Difficulties with the Likert scaling method

1 Thurstone considered the intervals on his scale to be truly equal, thus creating a powerful *interval* level of measurement (see Chapter 11). In a Likert scale, each respondent's score only has meaning relative to the scores in the distribution obtained from other respondents. Data produced might be better treated as *ordinal*.

2 The 'undecided' score, 3, is ambiguous. Does it imply a neutral position (no opinion) or an on-the-fence position with the respondent torn between feelings in both directions?

3 Partly as a consequence of difficulty 2, overall scores central to the distribution (say 30 out of 60) are quite ambiguous. Central scores could reflect a lot of 'undecided' answers, or they could comprise a collection of 'strongly for' and 'strongly against' answers, in which case perhaps the scale measured two different attitudes.

The semantic differential (Osgood, Suci and Tannenbaum, 1957)

The original intention behind this scale was to use it for measuring the *connotative* meaning of an object for an individual – roughly speaking, the term's *associations* for us. Thus, we can all give a denotative meaning for 'nurse' – we have to define what a nurse is, as in a dictionary. The *connotation* of a nurse may, however, differ for each of us. For me, a nurse is associated with caring, strength and independence. For others, by popular stereotype, he or she may be seen as deferential and practical.

On a semantic differential scale the respondent is invited to select a point between bi-polar adjectives according to the position they feel the object holds on that scale for them. For 'nurse' on the following bi-polar opposites, I might mark as shown:

Honest	<u>x</u>	_	_	_	_	_	_	Dishonest
Tough	_	_	_	_	_	<u>x</u>	_	Tender
Energetic	_	<u>x</u>	_	_	_	_	_	Lazy

Osgood *et al* claimed that *factor analysis* (see later in this chapter) of all scales gave rise to three general meaning factors, to one of which all bi-polar pairs could be attached:

- 'energetic–lazy' (or 'slow–fast', 'hot–cold', etc.) would be an example of the *activity* factor
- 'tough–tender' (or 'rugged–delicate', 'thick–thin', etc.) would be is an example of the *potency* factor
- 'honest–dishonest' (or 'clean–dirty', 'pleasant–unpleasant', etc.) would be an example of the *evaluative* factor.

Adapted to attitude measurement, the semantic differential apparently produces good reliability values and correlates well with other attitude scales, thus producing high *concurrent validity* (see later in this chapter).

Info Box 8.3 **Difficulties with the semantic differential**

1 Respondents may have a tendency towards a 'position response bias' where they habitually mark at the extreme end of the scale (or won't use the extreme at all) without considering possible weaker or stronger responses. This can occur with a Likert scale too, but is more likely here since the scale points lack the Likert verbal designations (of 'strongly agree', etc.)

2 Here, too, to some extent, we have the problem of interpretation of the middle point on the scale.

The visual analogue scale

As we shall see on p. 187, asking people to respond in just one of two categories can produce quite a distortion in assessing human characteristics. For instance, suppose for the purposes of an investigation I asked you:

'How is your mood today?' (a) high (b) low

Not only might you find this difficult to answer, as you may be somewhere in between, the data gathered will produce just two groups, high and low participants, rather than a score for each person that we can compare with scores on another variable (e.g. a problem-solving task). One popular way to get around the need for a category measure is to use a VISUAL ANALOGUE SCALE e.g.:

> Please indicate with a cross on the dotted line the level of your mood today.
>
> Low |- -| High

Participants are asked to mark a point along the scale to indicate their position. This is then measured off and the variable is expressed as a distance. Some VIS examples have wording at the mid-point or even at several points along the line. Of course you're going to say 'Well how do we know that *your* two cm. along the scale is the same as *my* two cm.?' and you have a point – the scale is *subjective* – but at least we do have a measure which is not a category in a form of words *forced* onto the respondent. We can at least use a VIS to indicate improvement or change within the same individual before and after treatment (e.g. after reading about different kinds of crime).

Central issues in the use of psychological scales

Response acquiescence set (or response bias)

People seem to find it harder to disagree than to agree with a statement put to them. This effect is known as RESPONSE ACQUIESCENCE SET and often occurs when participants respond to questionnaires. This tendency has been termed 'Yeah saying' (see Figure 8.1). To avoid confounding from this effect, items need to be an unpredictable mixture of positive and negative statements about the attitude object. This has the effect of keeping the respondent thinking about each item. If someone *were* to simply say 'yes' to every item then they would obtain a score right in the middle of the range because, remember, half the items are in one direction and half in the other. We will talk more about scoring Likert type scales in a moment. There is also some evidence of a smaller bias towards *disagreeing* with items.

Figure 8.1 'Yeah saying' – the effect of response set

Respondent's interpretation

Respondents often act as if the interviewer actually believes the items on the scale and may become hostile where some of these are extreme and contrary to what the respondent believes. Therefore it is a good idea to explain to respondents that both positive and negative items will appear on the scale for reasons of balance. This is a further reason for including both positive and negative items since a set of statements all contrary to what the respondent thinks might well set up strong emotional defences. For the same reason it would be best to start with less extreme statements.

There are also *demand characteristics* (see Chapter 4) associated with responding to a questionnaire. The respondent may well try to interpret the aim of the questioning and this may not be useful at this stage of the investigation. Again, if all initial items are in the same direction the respondent may form an impression of the interviewer's aims or attitudes that might distort the respondent's later answers.

Social desirability

Defined in Chapter 4, this factor involves respondents guessing at what is counted as a socially acceptable or favourable answer, and giving it in order to 'look good'. The bogus pipeline technique was described earlier and is a method for diminishing the effects of respondents attempting to 'look good'. A further reason for guessing might be to 'please the researcher' by giving the results it is assumed are required. Some questionnaires attempt to deal with this problem by including items that only an angel would agree or disagree with. If too many such items are answered in this 'saintly' manner, the respondent's results are excluded from the research. Eysenck and Eysenck (1975) called their set of items a *lie scale*, though an excluded respondent is not necessarily lying. They may be angelic or they may be distorting the truth just a bit.

Info Box 8.4 **Constructing a Likert-type attitude scale**

The steps below can be used by students to construct a simple Likert-type attitude scale, though they are also largely those for constructing more sophisticated scales such as measures of theoretical aspects of human personality. However, personality tests, and certainly those to be used in psychological practice, would be given far more thorough development and trialling than can be achieved by students on the average research methods course.

1 Produce roughly twice the number of items finally required, balanced for:

   (a) strength (some 'weak' statements, some 'hard')

   (b) breadth (is the whole attitude area covered?)

   (c) direction (to avoid *response set*, half the items should be favourable to the issue and half unfavourable. Half of each of these sets should be weak and the other half strong).

The number of items to start with depends to some extent on the focus of the proposed attitude topic. In general, the larger the number of items in a scale, the higher will be its *reliability* (see p. 194). With a larger number of items, random errors – from respondents' individual interpretations and misunderstandings – should cancel each other out. However, fewer items would be needed to achieve acceptable reliability where the topic is unambiguous and highly focused, such as attitude to fox hunting. Broader-attitude topics might be attitude to child discipline or general political attitude. With a narrower focus, the reliability-testing procedure mentioned in step 8, and described fully in Box 8.5 on page 196, will probably produce high reliability from a set of 20 items, which will reduce to 15 or even 10 as a consequence. For broader topics, 40–60 items, reducing to say 25 or 30, might be required. However, the final number of items used in a scale needs to be kept manageable in terms of time and the respondent's patience.

2 Check these items with a few people for ambiguity, misunderstanding, etc. – see pp. 185–6

3 Replace deleted items by new ones, still keeping a balance.

4 Repeat 2 and 3 until all items appear to be unproblematic.

5 Arrange positive and negative items in a random or alternating order (to discourage response bias).

6 Decide on a response scale, e.g. whether to use a central position or not. Don't be tempted to use 1 'for strongly agree' since it is the first number of the set. You will easily get confused later on when high scores do not represent favourable attitudes but unfavourable ones.

7 Pilot the draft scale on a good-sized sample (100 would be good but certainly more than 30).

8 Test for *reliability* by conducting a form of *item analysis* (see p. 195) until the reliability correlation, or Cronbach's alpha, is at least about .75, preferably higher.

9 Inspect or test final version for *validity*. After the reliability achieving process, do items still cover main issues? Do some topics now dominate? Some form of *criterion validity* procedure can be performed. For a scale measuring, for instance, attitude to youth crime punishment we might predict that police officers would score higher (*for* strict punishment) than would social workers (*against* strict punishment; *for* rehabilitation). The scale should *discriminate* between these two criterion groups (though for various reasons it might not). If validity is unsatisfactory, go through all steps again!

Scoring the scale

Give each respondent a score according to the point on the response scale they checked, 5 for 'strongly agree', 4 for 'Agree', and so on. As explained earlier one set of items (favourable or unfavourable) must have their raw scores *reversed*. For instance, an anti-hunt respondent might score as follows:

(a) Hunting should be banned completely   5

(b) Hunting is a necessary part of country life   1

. . . and though they are strictly against hunting, their score for the two items would even out at an average of 3. To avoid unnecessary cognitive strain it is always sensible to make *high* overall scores represent a *pro* view (here, high scores mean pro-hunting; low scores anti-), otherwise, when analysing and discussing results, it is easy to get muddled and make mistakes. So think this through carefully before reversing one set of scores. In this case, then, we would reverse the scores on all *anti* items so that the person above would score only 1 on item (a). Item (b) stays as it is, so our anti-hunt person scores just 2 overall. A solid redcoat, though, strongly disagreeing with a ban, would obtain 5 on item (a) because their raw score would be 1 reversed up to 5, while their response to item (b) would be a straight 5, so they would score 10 altogether on these two items. A procedure for reversing all appropriate item scores using SPSS is given on p. 196. In general, you should reverse scores according to the following system:

1→5   2→4   3→3   4→2   5→1

Scale items – what to avoid in statement construction

The scale constructor has to be careful to phrase questions clearly and unambiguously, such that the respondent is in no doubt which answer to give. The ideal is that all respondents will interpret an item in the same way. However, this is another of those unrealistic ideals, possible to *approach* in simple arithmetic tests perhaps, but completely contrary to what we know about how people vary in their interpretation of the world, including the interpretation of language. What we can aspire to is clarity, avoiding obvious ambiguities and biasing factors for *most* of the population for whom the test or scale is intended.

Pause for thought

What do you think is unsatisfactory about the following statements, intended for an attitude scale? Explanations are given in the following sections.

1 We should begin to take compensatory action in areas of employment and training where, in the past, members of one ethnic group, sex or disability type have suffered discrimination or experienced disadvantages as a direct result of being a member of that category.

2 Society should attempt to undo the effects of institutional racism wherever possible.

3 Immigrants should not be allowed to settle in areas of high unemployment.

4 Abortion is purely a woman's choice and should be made freely available.

5 It should not be possible to ask a woman about her spouse's support, when husbands are not asked the same questions.

6 The Labour government has deceived and betrayed its traditional voters.

7 Don't you agree that student grants should be increased?

8 Do you have a criminal record?

What can you see as problems with the following sorts of item and scale?

1 State to what degree you enjoyed the lecture course:

Very much indeed   Quite a lot   A lot   A little   Not much   Didn't like it

2 Who did you think was more responsible for the attack? (Referring to a description of a fictitious sex attack by a man on a woman where the woman, in one condition of the study, was said to have worn 'provocative' clothing.)

The man   The woman

1. Complexity

Not many respondents will take this in, all in one go. The statement is far too complex. It could possibly be broken up into logical components.

2. Technical terms

Many respondents will not have a clear idea of what 'institutional racism' is. Either find another term or include a preamble to the item that explains the special term.

3. Ambiguity

Some students I taught used this item and found almost everyone in general agreement, whether they were generally hostile to immigrants or not. Hence, it was not at all *discriminating*. This was probably because those positive towards immigrants considered the plight of immigrants new to the country *and* unemployed. Others were probably producing a knee-jerk stereotype to the term 'immigrant'.

4. Double-barrelled items

This quite simple item is asking two questions at once. A person might well agree with free availability – to avoid the dangers of the back-street abortionist – yet may not feel that only the woman concerned should choose.

5. Double negatives

The item in the exercise box has two negatives in it and this can easily be confusing.

In the interests of avoiding *response set* (see below), about half the items in a scale should be positive towards the object and about half negative. However, it is *not* a good idea to produce negative statements simply by negating positive ones. It can be confusing to answer a question with a double negative, even where one of the negatives is camouflaged, as in: '*It should not be possible to reject a candidate's application on the grounds of disability.*' This could be rephrased as: 'A candidate's disability should be completely ignored when considering an application.'

6. Emotive language

A statement such as this may not get an attitude test off to a good start, particularly in 'New Labour' constituencies. If there are emotive items at all, it might be best to leave these until the respondent is feeling more relaxed with the interviewer or with the test itself.

7. Leading questions

Most scale items are statements not questions. However, some do use bi-polar responses. This wording here carries with it an implication that the respondent should say 'yes'. If you don't feel this is so, just try to imagine a friend or colleague opening the day's conversation with such a question. To the respondent it can seem hard to disagree, something that people would usually rather not do anyway. They might begin with 'Weeell . . .' or 'Yes, but . . .', where the 'but' amounts to disagreement, even though the response is recorded as agreement.

8. Invasion of privacy

This is private information, along with sex life and other obvious areas. The student conducting a practical exercise should avoid any such intrusion. If in doubt about what you can ethically ask, consult your tutor.

9. Balance of scale items

Here the student respondent cannot state just how *much* they disliked the lectures. The final data here could be 'massaged' with the claim that X% of students 'enjoyed' the lectures if the first four categories are collated together.

10. Sensitivity of scale items to level of measurement

This item was presented by a student who wanted to assess the degree to which people felt a female victim was *partly* responsible for an attack by wearing revealing clothes on a street late at night. Of course, no participant blamed the woman *more*. The student had unfortunately chosen a *dichotomous variable* for the response – only two bi-polar opposites. The item was too insensitive to capture the increased victim responsibility some men may have assumed in the 'provocative' condition (a hypothesis in the experiment). The student needed to use a *scale* instead, such as the visual analogue scale described earlier or the following:

On a scale from 1 = not at all responsible to 10 = entirely responsible, how responsible for the attack do you feel was:

The man   The woman

Projective tests

PROJECTIVE TESTS have been developed out of the psychoanalytic tradition of research and therapy. They are based on the Freudian notion that we project our inner conflicts and anxieties onto the external world, but disguised as a defence mechanism. When situations are ambiguous, and we try to interpret them, our ego, which normally acts as a censor, is particularly likely to be caught off guard. Psychoanalytic researchers have developed sets of abstract and/or ambiguous pictures which are presented to respondents who are asked to respond. These are *open* and *disguised* questions. The Rorschach ink blot test is a set of designs rather like those that children produce with 'butterfly' paintings (see Figure 8.2). The respondent reports what he or she feels they can see in the picture. Similarly, the *Thematic Apperception Test* (TAT) is a set of pictures, often of people with their

Figure 8.2 Rorschach ink-blot – a projective measure

emotional expressions ambiguous or hidden, about which the test-taker is asked 'What is happening?' Responses are analysed according to generally agreed associations with psychoanalytic concepts; events concerning attacks, loss or harmful intentions towards oneself, for instance, may be interpreted as symbolic of castration.

It is argued that the projective tests can be used to measure such factors as the affective, usually hidden, component of attitudes and that their open-endedness produces richer information. Their disguised nature provides genuine data, unbiased by people guessing the researcher's (or therapist's) intent. Grossman, Wasyliw, Benn and Gyoerkoe (2002) produced evidence that sex offenders who 'minimised' their psychological problems using a conventional personality scale (the MMPI) were nevertheless analysed as exhibiting pathological traits to a significant degree when their Rorschach responses were analysed. If you recall, this is similar to what Gannon *et al.*'s (2007) error choice technique was also designed to expose (p. 177).

Validity and reliability of projective tests

Of course, studies such as that just described require that those who rate the Rorschach responses are unaware of the level of the independent variable applicable to the participant. Raters can be provided with a comprehensive coding scheme and simply score according to this, ignorant of the overall aims of the research. This procedure is followed in most cases where Rorschach tests are used to assess concealed aggression, hostility, anxiety, sexual fantasy and so on, in hypothesis-testing work like that of Levin (1978) described earlier. In this way, no matter how subjective some Rorschach concepts may appear, we can eliminate researcher knowledge of the desired result as a factor in producing the differences in Rorschach scores.

A further aspect of reliability is that we require inter-rater reliability to be high. That is, whatever the raters are actually assessing, we want them to agree independently in their assessments of the same responses. In Levin's study the agreement was reported as being between 84% and 91%. Following broad criticism of Rorschach methodology, more recent and specific studies of inter-rater reliability for the popular Rorschach Comprehensive System (Exner, 1993), report 'acceptable' to 'excellent' levels of inter-rater reliability (Acklin *et al.*, 2000; Meyer *et al.*, 2002).

Intelligence and personality tests

Although some attitude scales have become highly refined, and even projective tests are sometimes called 'psychometric' if well standardised, it is intelligence, ability and personality tests that have undergone a high degree of standardisation and scrutiny for validity and reliability. This is partly because such tests are used in professional practice where people's life chances may be affected by results. They are used, for example, in job selection, clinical diagnosis and educational assessment. They are seen as technically *standardised* measurement instruments and the British Psychological Society provides verification of assessors who can award you a certificate of competence in test administration. The tradition of psychological test assessment goes back to Galton, who began the measurement of mental abilities in the late 1800s by testing thousands of people on many sensory and cognitive tasks. At the Great Exhibition of 1884 many people queued up to be tested and paid Galton a three pence fee for the privilege of knowing where they were relative to the average!

Figure 8.3 Sir Francis Galton.© Mary Evans Picture Library/Alamy

Intelligence tests in particular need periodic revision, since they are highly sensitive to bias from cultural, class and other social factors. It is on these grounds that their validity has been most seriously challenged and thoroughly investigated. For instance, to the question 'What should you do if you find a stamped addressed envelope in the street?', it might be 'intelligent', in a very poor area, where petty crime is unremarkable, to steam off the stamp – a response that gained no mark in one famous test. A picture depicting a boy holding an umbrella at the wrong angle to falling rain was said by Puerto Ricans to be incorrect, not because of the angle but because the boy was holding the umbrella *at all*. This is apparently considered highly effeminate in Puerto Rican society.

It is beyond the scope of this book to cover intelligence and personality testing in depth, along with all the weaknesses and criticisms of the tests. This is covered very well in other available texts, in particular Kline (2000) and Loewenthal (2001, for a briefer introduction). The examples given above simply demonstrate the need for standardisation and constant revision from a research methods point of view. They also exemplify, I hope, what is meant by class and cultural bias in tests.

As with interviews and questionnaires, data from psychometric tests can be used as the dependent variable in experimental work, though it is more common to find them being used in correlational and group difference type studies, and in practical applications of psychology in the professional

189

field. Most tests will be beyond the scope of student use, since they are closely guarded as technical instruments of the psychological profession. It can be extremely expensive both to qualify in the use of some tests and to purchase copies for administration to participants. Many come with user restrictions and are often subject to copyright laws. Most may not be copied or adapted without the supplier's permission. They also usually have quite complex scoring manuals, which are even more closely monitored. There are some, however, that can be found in published articles and textbooks and on the internet (such as Rotter's, 1966, Locus of Control scale) and are therefore open to general use, though you will of course require the scoring scheme.

Factor analysis

Researchers often support the development and use of psychometric tests by employing a form of *construct validity* (see Chapter 2; this is also explained later in this chapter), which involves a complex statistical procedure known as FACTOR ANALYSIS. The aim is to find 'factors' (hidden or 'intervening' variables) that might explain the observed relationships between people's scores on several tests or sub-tests.

Let's start with a completely imaginary but 'concrete' example that might make understanding somewhat easier than launching straight in with psychological factors. Imagine that we select a few hundred people of average fitness and subject them to various athletic events. We *correlate* the results of every event with every other, producing a table, part of which might look like Table 8.2.

	200 Metres	3000 Metres	5000 Metres	Shot	Discus	Long Jump
100 Metres	.87	.24	.31	−.65	−.32	.47
200 Metres		.19	.28	−.61	−.29	.39
3000 Metres			.91	−.16	.03	.13
5000 Metres				−.08	.11	.09
Shot					.65	.14
Discus						−.02

Table 8.2 Correlation matrix for performances in various athletic events

As we'll see in Chapter 17, if people tend to score at roughly the same level on two variables we expect a *correlation* value close to +1 between the two variables. If there is a tendency to be high on one variable while being low on the other, and vice versa, we'd expect a value approaching − (negative) 1. No relationship at all between the two variables is signified by a value close to zero. As we might expect from common-sense prediction, in our fictitious example there is a strong correlation between individual performances at 100 and 200 metres, and between 3000 and 5000 metres. There is a moderate correlation between discus and shot-put, and between 100 metres and long jump, whereas the correlation between 100 metres and shot-put is moderately negative.

Intuition might suggest that the underlying factors that explain these relationships are *sprinting ability*, *stamina* and *strength*. Researchers use the results of factor analysis to support this kind of interpretation. Now let's just look in a little more detail at the steps involved in factor analysis:

1 A large sample of people is measured on several tests or sub-tests.

2 Correlations (see Chapter 17) are calculated between every possible pair of tests or sub-tests, and arranged in a matrix as in Table 8.2.

3 The matrix of correlations is fed into the factor analysis program, which looks for 'clusters' – groups of tests or sub-tests that all correlate well together.

4 The researcher sets the program to solve the matrix for a particular number of 'factors'. Factors, at this point, are nothing real, just mathematical concepts that will 'account for' as much as possible of the correlation found. The program then gives the best configuration of this number of factors to account for all the variation in correlations.

5 Alternatively, the program will offer a solution in the best possible number of factors, with the least amount of variation unaccounted for. The whole 'explanation' is purely statistical, accounting for the numerical relationships.

6 The researcher might ask the program to solve for a higher number of factors if the amount of 'unexplained' variation is too high.

7 When the statistical procedure has produced the most economical or elegant explanation of the data, the factors that emerge are recognised and named intuitively by the researchers or they are picked out as being in parallel with psychological explanations that were expected from theory or prior research. For instance, a factor that is closely related to items like 'I worry a lot about the future' and 'New places terrify me' and that correlates with the behaviour of sleeplessness might be recognised as 'anxiety'. In our athletics example (Table 8.2) we would probably identify strength, stamina and speed by looking at which results relate most closely to the factors produced by the analysis.

Roughly speaking, this is what factor analysts do with the scores of large samples on personality and intelligence tests and sub-tests. The factors emerging are identified, explained where possible and validated against existing tests and other known factor arrangements. The factors are seen as explanations of participants' variations in performance across the tests. In our athletics example, if we asked a factor analysis program to solve for just two factors it would probably tell us that, no matter which way the matrix was solved, a lot of relationship between variables was left unaccounted for. For three variables it might well give us a good solution with little variation unexplained. However, it is important to note that it would be up to us to name the factors and to debate what real processes might be indicated by them. The model for this kind of attempt to explain inter-test correlations and to look for deeper psychological constructs is shown in Figure 8.4.

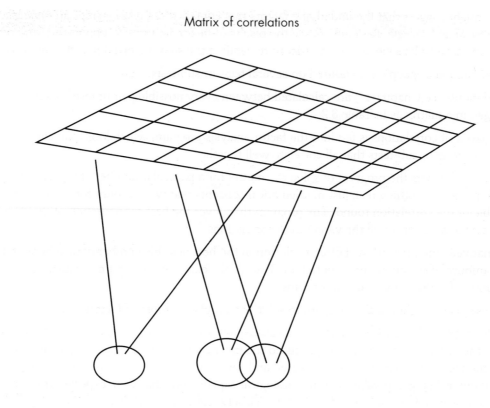

Matrix of correlations

Underlying factors

Figure 8.4 Model of factor analysis – underlying factors 'explain' observed relationships between test performances

Factor analysis does not 'prove' that a real psychological construct exists corresponding to each factor identified in the statistical analysis. It simply provides *supporting evidence* that allows the researcher to claim that intelligence or personality *could* be organised in a particular way and that the factor analysis results don't refute this. As an example, Niles (1998), mentioned earlier, was able to identify four major achievement goal factors: family and social responsibility, material prosperity, personal fulfilment and personal development. Sri Lankans scored more heavily on the first social- and duty-oriented factor, whereas Australians were more oriented towards the individualist goals of the last three factors. Factor analysis is a purely statistical process which supports theoretical speculation. It can be performed and interpreted in many different ways by theorists with different models of psychological functioning to defend. For a fairly comprehensive introduction, see Kline (2000, Chapter 7) and, for a relatively simple statistical explanation with SPSS instructions, see Pallant (2007). An extensive and severe criticism of the use of factor analysis to support models of intellectual structure was provided by Block and Dworkin (1974).

Exercises

1 Comment on any flaws in the following potential attitude scale or questionnaire items.

   (a) Don't you think that the government has moved too far towards Europe?

   (b) What do you think is the best way to punish children?

   (c) How many times were you late for work in the last two years?

   (d) People from other countries are the same as us and should be treated with respect.

   (e) It should not be possible to avoid taxation and not be punished for it.

   (f) Women are taking a lot of management posts in traditionally male occupational areas (in a scale to measure attitude to women's rights).

   (g) Tomorrow's sex role models should be more androgynous.

2 Imagine the items below are a small part of a scale to measure 'assertiveness' developed by some students. What problem can you see?

   (a) ....

   (b) Do you take things straight back to the shop when you find a fault?

   (c) On a scale of 1 to 10, how loudly would you say you speak to shop assistants compared with other people?

   (d) ....

3 A researcher administers a Rorschach test to a control and experimental group of psychiatric patients. She then rates each response according to a very well-standardised scale for detecting anxiety. How can she avoid the criticism that her ratings are biased and subjective, given she knows the expected result?

Answers

1 (a) Leading: Question invites agreement.

   (b) Leading: Assumes children *should* be punished.

   (c) Difficult for most people to make an accurate response.

   (d) Double-barrelled – 'people *aren't* the same, but should be treated with respect' is a possible response.

   (e) Double negative.

   (f) Ambiguous response. Extreme sexist *and* feminist might well agree but for quite different reasons. Item may not discriminate.

   (g) Technical term. Will this be understood?

2 Items in a scale measuring one psychological construct must be of the same type; we cannot mix and match items like this because there would be no sensible way to add up the person's score on the scale.

3 Use blind assessment using a different naïve researcher to rate the test and analyse results.

Reliability, validity and standardisation

Psychology is not an exact science. There are no truly universally agreed measures of psychological constructs. 'Anxiety', 'motivation', 'intelligence', 'self-esteem' etc. are all measured with a variety of scales, most of which agree quite well with one another but all of which have some unique aspects not included in the others. Some variables appear as constructs invented solely within psychology, examples being: 'extroversion' and 'introversion', 'figure dependence' or 'ego-strength'. The tests psychologists construct in order to measure such constructs often serve as *operational definitions* of the concept under research. That is, our measure of, say, anxiety, is also our definition of it for the purposes of a study designed to show anxiety reduction. Here, our only evidence would be a reduction in anxiety test scores. That being so, we would expect to have confidence in such a measure by seeing that it produces consistent measures where we expect them (RELIABILITY) and that it somehow measures *real* anxiety, rather than mere nail-biting (VALIDITY). We would also expect such a measure to be applicable to a population of people and not just the few students participating in our study (STANDARDISATION). We will discuss each of these checks in turn.

Reliability

We introduced the idea of reliability of measures back in Chapter 2. Reliability has to do with the *consistency* of a measure either across different testings (external) or within itself (internal). We are not here considering whether a test measures what it is intended to measure – this is a test's *validity*, which we will consider after dealing with reliability.

External reliability – stability across time

Any measure, but especially one we have just invented, must be queried as to the stability of its results on different occasions. A reliable measuring instrument is one that consistently produces the same reading for the same amount. Consider a practical example. If you have kitchen scales that stick, you won't get the same reading for the same amount of flour each time you weigh it. The measure given by your scales is unreliable. The scales have poor reliability.

If we want to check the external reliability of a scale we want to see whether it produces the same scores each time we use it on the *same people*. If we do not test it on the same people we have no anchor point for comparison. The method used is known as TEST–RETEST RELIABILITY and to use it we test the *same* group of people once, then again some time later. The two sets of scores are *correlated* to see whether people tend to get the same sort of score on the second occasion (see Figure 8.6 and Chapter 17). If they do, the test has high external reliability. Correlations achieved here would be expected to be at least around .75–.8. Rather than testing at two different times, it is also possible to test the same group of people on two PARALLEL FORMS of the same test, though these are rare and expensive to create as well as raising doubts as to whether two 'versions' of the same test really can be entirely equivalent.

Internal reliability – internal consistency of the test

A difference between kitchen scales and instruments used for human characteristic measurement is that psychologists often use tests with many items, whereas weight is measured by just one indicator: the dial reading. Psychological tests of, for instance, political attitude can be queried as to their INTERNAL RELIABILITY, meaning 'Is the test consistent within itself?' High internal consistency generally implies that respondents answer related items in similar ways – a person with a high *total* score on 'conservatism' tends to score in the conservative direction *on each item*. If internal consistency is not high then the test must be measuring more than one construct (but see Kline (2000) for the dissenting argument of Cattell, who says that a test with high internal consistency will be an extremely narrow measure of anything). Despite Cattel's technical arguments, however, it is generally agreed by test constructors that internal consistency should be high for a test to be of any practical use.

The difference between internal reliability (internal consistency) and external reliability (stability) might be pictured as follows. Imagine you were giving a statement to the police. Your statement might be found to be unreliable in two distinct ways:

1 *internal consistency* – you may contradict yourself *within* the statement

2 *stability* – you may alter important details when asked to repeat the statement some time later.

Methods for checking internal reliability

Split-half method

A psychological scale that consists of several items or questions can be split so that items are divided randomly into two halves, or by putting odd numbered items in one set and even numbered ones in the other. If the test is reliable then people's scores on each half should be similar. The extent of similarity is assessed using correlation (Chapter 17). Positive correlations of .75 upwards, from the possible positive range of zero to one, would be expected. A small problem here is that the reliability estimate is based on a test half the length of the actual test. To provide an estimate for the *whole* scale the *Spearman-Brown formula* can be applied and this is simply where *r* is the split half correlation coefficient. If you calculate a split half correlation in SPSS it will supply you with this Spearman-Brown value. In Box 8.5 make sure you select 'Split half' instead of 'Alpha' in step 10.

Cronbach's alpha

CRONBACH'S ALPHA is probably the most commonly used statistic for estimating a test's reliability. It depends largely on how people vary on individual items. If they tend to vary a lot on the individual items relative to how much they vary overall on the test, then the test is assessed as unreliable and a low value for alpha is achieved. Alpha is equivalent to the average of all possible split-half reliability values that could be calculated on the data set. Good reliability, therefore, is represented with alpha values from around .75 up to 1. If the items in the scale are *dichotomous* (answers are bi-polar, e.g. 'yes' or 'no' only), then a simpler version is used, known as the KUDER–RICHARDSON measure.

Increasing the reliability of a test through item analysis

1. Reliability coefficients

If we want to increase the reliability of a scale then we want to *remove* items that are causing the reliability to be lower than it could be; that is those items that are keeping alpha low. The most common method is to compute alpha for the scale and then, for each item in turn, ask our program

Info Box 8.5 — Reliability analysis with Cronbach's alpha using SPSS

For general instructions on entering data into SPSS, see Chapter 11

1 First, each item of the scale is entered as a variable (column) in SPSS and each person's score on each item is entered (see Figure 8.5). Each person is a *row* in the SPSS spreadsheet. The score will probably be 1 to 5 (for 'strongly agree', 'agree' etc.).

Reversing the scoring by recoding variables

2 The next step is to reverse the scoring on all the appropriate items. If you are measuring attitude to corporal punishment and have decided that a high overall score will indicate a pro-smacking stance, then all items with a statement *against* smacking will have to be reversed. This needs thinking about carefully. If '5' means 'strongly agree' then this response to an anti-smacking item will give the respondent 5 points. However, we want such participants to score *low*; we *reverse* anti-smacking items.

3 Click **Transform/Recode into different variables**.

4 Select the items you wish to reverse from the left-hand box and click the right-facing arrow to move them over to the box entitled **Numeric Variable › Output Variable**. Highlight each of these in turn and give it a new name in the Name box on the right-hand side. A sensible name for reversed item 7 might be **item7r** (**Label** can be used to give a longer and more understandable name to the variable and this name will appear in results tables). Click change.

5 Click **Old and New Values.**

6 Enter '1' into the **Value** box (top left) and, on the right-hand (**New Value**) side, enter the value that '1' will become when reversed; in our example above, '5' goes into the right-hand **Value** box.

7 Click **Add**. *Don't forget* this move, otherwise clicking **OK** will bring up an error and changes not added will not be made.

8 Carry on for each of the other values, 2 to 5 becoming transformed into 4 to 1.

9 Click **Continue** and then **OK**. The new variables will appear on the data sheet.

Conducting the reliability analysis using Cronbach's alpha

10 Click **Analyze/Scale/Reliability Analysis**. Check the **Model** selected is 'Alpha'.

11 The items now to be used are all the original scale items unless an item has been reversed, in which case use the **itemXr** version. Move these across from the left-hand box to the right-hand box labelled Items.

12 Click **Statistics** and then check **Scale if item deleted** at the top left. If you want the mean and standard deviation for each item then check the two items above this too.

13 Click **Continue** and **OK**.

14 The output screen will show you three tables. The first is a 'Case processing summary' and just tells you how many respondents have been included in the analysis. The second gives you the value of Cronbach's alpha as the scale stands at the moment. Below this is a table showing, for each item, four columns of what would happen to scale statistics if that item were deleted. If alpha is acceptably high at .75 or above you may not want to proceed further. If it is not, or if you want in any case to reduce the number of items, then continue. We are interested here in the extreme right-hand column. This tells us what alpha would become if each item were deleted. Look for the highest alpha value and that is the item to delete for the next round. Let's say this is item number 8.

15 Go back to the reliability analysis box (Step 11) and move item 8 back to the left-hand box and out of the analysis. Now click **Continue** and **OK**. You will be presented with another sheet of data just like the last except that item 8 will be missing, alpha will be the value that SPSS said it would be if you deleted item 8, and you can now look at the right-hand column for the next offending item to remove, and so on.

	item1	item2	item3	item4	item5
1	2.00	1.00	3.00	4.00	4.00
2	5.00	4.00	3.00	1.00	2.00
3	1.00	1.00	1.00	3.00	4.00
4	3.00	3.00	3.00	2.00	4.00
5	2.00	2.00	3.00	4.00	4.00
6	1.00	1.00	1.00	1.00	5.00
7	3.00	1.00	5.00	1.00	5.00
8	1.00	3.00	1.00	2.00	1.00
9	1.00	1.00	2.00	1.00	1.00
10	4.00	3.00	2.00	1.00	3.00
11	1.00	1.00	3.00	2.00	3.00

Figure 8.5 Scale item scores entered for analysis

to give us the value that alpha would become *if that item were deleted from the scale*. This would be laborious by hand (though people used to do it frequently) but a computer program will do this in a flash. Instructions for conducting a reliability analysis using SPSS are given in Box 8.5. Basically, for each item in the scale we ask the programme to tell us what value alpha would become if that particular item were deleted. We then select the item that would most increase alpha if it were deleted and then go ahead and delete it. We calculate alpha (whose value we already know from the previous exercise) and again ask for the values of alpha if each item were deleted, and so on. We stop when we either reach a satisfactory alpha value (above .8 if possible), or when we are running out of items (e.g. down to 10) with alpha reasonably high (say, .65), or when we have reduced our original set of items to a useful number (so long as alpha has remained high).

This procedure does not follow rigid rules but is a matter of pragmatics, given that the scale is adequately reliable and validity is not compromised. Note also that the same procedure could be used for calculating the split-half reliability on each turn rather than alpha. Finally, if alpha remains stubbornly unsatisfactory, it's back to the drawing board with a revised set of items after inspection of the present ones for clues as to why respondents were so unpredictable and variable in their answers. The answer probably lies in item ambiguity, vagueness or irrelevance of items to the intended construct.

2. Item–total correlations

The SPSS procedure described in Box 8.5 will also produce all item–total correlations. These are the correlations of participants' scores on each item with their score overall. If people tend to score low or average on an individual item, while scoring high overall (and vice versa), the correlation will be low, and this in turn will lower reliability. The item is inconsistent with the general trend and it is best to discard items with the lowest item-total correlations as far as possible.

3. Item discrimination between extreme groups

This method of establishing reliability depends on removing those items in which there is *low discrimination* between people scoring high on the test *as a whole* and those scoring low. Even if we are not sure that all the items in our test are good measures of, say, attitude to physical punishment, we can assume that those scoring very high overall on the draft set of items (i.e. pro-smacking) differ in attitude to those scoring very low overall. Hence, we can use these as criterion groups and see how far these two extreme groups differ *on each item*.

Info Box 8.6   **Using item discrimination to improve reliability**

1   Calculate individuals' scores overall on the draft test

2   Identify the highest 10% and the lowest 10% of scores (this 10% is not fixed and could be 15% or 20% if desired).

3   Find the total sum of scores for these two groups on each separate item of the test.

4   Where the two extreme groups scored *very differently* the item is discriminating. Where the two groups scored very similarly it is not.

5   Discard the least discriminating items e.g. the worst 20 out of 40.

6   Technically better is to discard the worst, re-do all the calculations on the remaining 39 items, find the worst, discard and so on.

Circularity of reliability analyses

All these reliability testing methods may be accused of *circularity*, in a kind of bootstrap process, since we are using overall *draft* totals to decide for each item, *contributing to that total*, how much it affects overall reliability. The totals themselves will change as each poor item is removed. That is, the test for reliability uses as a criterion scores on an as yet probably unreliable test! At the end of all this item removal we may well have a highly reliable test that now contains nothing like the range of content that was originally envisaged. High *reliability* may well come at the cost of a severe reduction in *validity*.

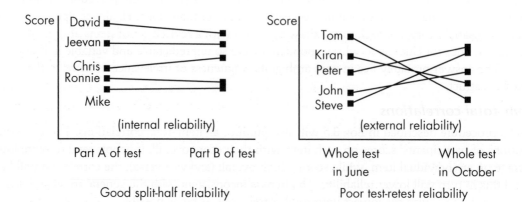

Figure 8.6 Split-half and test–retest reliability

Validity

As we saw above, a test may well have high reliability but may not be measuring what was originally intended – that is, it may lack VALIDITY. This criticism is often levelled at tests of intelligence which, though quite reliable, measure only a narrow range of intellectual ability, missing out, for instance, the whole range of creative thought that the public language definition would include. Raters can be highly reliable on projective tests but the validity of what they are claimed to assess can be very much in dispute. There are various recognised means by which the validity of tests can be assessed.

Face validity

Simply, a test has FACE VALIDITY if it is obvious what it is measuring. This would be true of, for instance, a typing speed test. For many tests, although they appear to be testing something connected with personality, it will not always be obvious to the test-taker what is going on. This can be a disadvantage where people are applying for jobs that seem unrelated to the test content. Kline (2000) argues that a strength of face validity, then, is its potential for motivating test-takers who can clearly see that the test is worthwhile, but its weakness is that the test also then becomes easier to fake. On its own face validity just refers to the test 'making sense' and is in no way a technically adequate measure of test validity.

Content validity

A researcher may ask colleagues to evaluate the content of a test to ensure that it is representative of the area it is intended to cover. They will carry out this task using their expertise in the topic area to judge whether the collection of items has failed to test certain skills or is unduly weighted towards some aspects of the domain compared with others. In some ways this is a more sophisticated version of face validity. For specific attainment or ability tests we can be fairly certain of real validity because our experts know what it takes to be good in a specific skill (e.g. a music test). For personality measures, however (e.g. a depression test item such as 'Do you often just feel down?'), no expert can tell us that this *is* a valid item, even though it appears to have face validity.

Criterion validity

The validity of a test of neuroticism might reasonably be established by using it on a group of people who have suffered from a neurotic condition and comparing scores with a control group. Use of the neurotic group would be an example of what is called a KNOWN GROUPS CRITERION. A test such as this could form part of a research programme aimed at establishing construct validity and is really just a part of that process. In general, with criterion validity procedures, we are looking for criteria on which scale scores successfully relate to other known data in ways that could be predicted, given the theoretical nature of the measure. Two specific forms of criterion validity are:

Concurrent validity

If the new test is validated by comparison with a currently existing measure of the construct, we have CONCURRENT VALIDITY. Very often, a new IQ or personality test might be compared with an older but similar test known to have good validity already, or simply with an existing competitor. An issue here might be that if we are developing a test for a new theoretical construct, or are challenging the validity of an existing one, then we may well want to show that the new test does *not* correlate very well with previous relevant tests.

Predictive validity

A prediction may be made, on the basis of a new intelligence test for instance, that high scorers at age 12 will be more likely to obtain university degrees or enter the professions several years later. If the prediction is borne out then the test has PREDICTIVE VALIDITY. *Both* these methods are in fact predictive since, in science, the term 'predict' does not only mean 'forecast'. A social scientist may well predict a relationship between *past* events. Used in this sense, then, there is virtually no difference between the concepts of predictive and concurrent validity except for the point of time involved in the prediction. However, 'concurrent validity' tends to be reserved in the literature for those occasions where performance on a new test is compared with performance on a similar test or older version of the same test.

Construct validity

CONSTRUCT VALIDITY is a much wider concept than the previous ones which are all mainly attempts to show that a scale is a good measure of a relatively familiar construct. In another sense they can all be *part of* the process of construct validity. What we are discussing with construct validity is the whole scientific process of establishing that a psychological construct, such as extroversion or achievement motivation, in fact exists or at least is a theoretically sound concept that fits into surrounding theory.

We met the ideas in Chapter 2 when discussion hypothetical constructs and again in Chapter 4 on p. 88. In something like the same way that physicists propose the existence of a particle, then set about establishing the validity of the concept by conducting many different kinds of experiments providing confirmatory evidence, so the psychologist develops theory and establishes constructs through various directions of research: comparisons with other scales, experiments, non experimental investigations and so on.

This is not a quirk of psychology but the way in which all science works. Physicists, for instance, do not directly see the latest sub-atomic particle and never will be able to do so. What happens is that they postulate the existence of a particle then carry out experiments that should produce one kind of result if the particle does exist and another if it doesn't. The existence of the particle is never 'proved' but established as very likely because of the number of different scientific outcomes it can explain. So it is with the psychological construct. An example of the development of such a concept through large scale construct validity research is outlined in Box 8.7.

Construct validity then is not a simple one-off procedure that will give us a numerical value for validity of a scale. It is the development of evidence for a hypothetical psychological construct through the rigours of hypothesis testing and scientific method.

Info Box 8.7	Establishing construct validity for a need for approval construct

Rosnow and Rosenthal (1999: 148) describe in detail work by Crowne and Marlowe in the 1950s who were researching in the area of socially desirable responding to personality tests and turned their attention to a wider concept, need for social approval, for which they developed a scale – the Marlowe-Crowne Social Desirability scale (MCSD). The scale consisted of items which reflected social desirability but which, if answered in one direction, would make the person just too good to be true (e.g. 'No' to 'I sometimes feel resentful then I don't get my own way'). First of all it was shown that the new scale had predicted correlations with other paper and pencil measures – high MCSD scorers favoured low risk behaviours and avoided evaluations of others. The scale did *not* correlate, again as predicted, with tests of psychopathology (the scale was developed so as to be independent of this factor).

The researchers then embarked on a series of experimental demonstrations that would further support the construct of social desirability in that persons high on this factor should be conforming, vulnerable to social influence and should find it hard to assert independence. They showed that, compared with low scorers, higher scorers on the MCSD who carried out a repetitive packing and unpacking task for 25 minutes reported the task as more interesting, more instructive and more important to science and were more eager to participate again in similar studies.

In further studies it was shown that those scoring high on the MCSD went along with majority judgements in an Asch-type conformity study significantly more often than did low scorers. Plenty of other research followed and most of it supported the construct of a need for approval. Not all of the research was supportive and, as with any good research programme, further studies and attempted replications had the effect of somewhat altering the accepted status of the original construct within the research community.

Standardisation

A test is standardised by developing norms for it. Why do we need norms? Well, if I tell you that you scored 112 on an IQ test whereas your friend only scored 108, what do you know? Only that you did better than her. You don't know whether you both did well or badly. You don't know if four points is a large or only a very trivial difference. Basically you don't know how everyone else like you did. This is what norms would tell you. We need to be able to compare individuals fairly and with confidence because psychological scales, unlike scales for measuring height or weight, are not interval scales (see p. 254). To make norm comparisons, the test must be administered to a large sample of the target population, from whom means and standard scores (see Chapter 13) are established. This will tell us the overall average and the extent to which people vary around this average. IQ scales for instance are adjusted until their mean is 100 and the average variation around them (the *standard deviation* – see p. 272) is 15 points. On this scale then, using the system of z scores which we will meet in Chapter 13, we can say that your friend scores better than about 70% of the population whereas you score better than 78%. Norms for large samples allow us to estimate in this way how the population is spread out along the points of the scale.

Psychometric tests are used in research but also on an applied basis in decisions about people's life chances and opportunities with respect to education, job selection and so on. Therefore, it is of the utmost importance that these tests do not discriminate, in a particular way, against some groups of people, a property that, anyway, would reduce their scientific value. Standardisation has, therefore, both ethical and scientific importance.

Standardisation and the normal distribution

Many tests are developed and adjusted until testing of a large sample produces a score distribution that approximates very closely to the normal distribution (see Chapter 13). One reason for doing this is that the properties of the normal distribution allow us to perform some extremely powerful statistical estimates. The fact that IQ tests do produce normal distributions of scores for large groups has been used as 'evidence' by some researchers (e.g. Eysenck, 1970) that the test therefore measures a largely innate quality, since many biological characteristics are indeed normally distributed through the working of many random genetic processes together.

Critics (e.g. Kamin, 1977) have argued that the adjustment of the test to a normal distribution is an artificial procedure – which it most certainly is – and that, far from showing that intelligence *is* normally distributed through the population, it merely shows that a measure can be constructed that *produces* a normal distribution. Furthermore, many biological characteristics are *not* normal in distribution. Certainly, some psychological phenomena need not be normally distributed. Attitudes to some issues on which people are somewhat polarised in position (for instance, on switching to the Euro as a currency or the morality of abortion) will be spread, as measured by questionnaire, in a *bi-modal* (two-hump) fashion.

An extremely important point here is that a test standardised on a particular population can obviously not be used with confidence on a quite different population. This criticism has been levelled at those who claimed a difference existed between white and black populations in the USA on intelligence. There was a difference in IQ score but, until 1973, the Stanford-Binet test had not included black persons in its sample for standardisation. Hence, the test was only applicable, with any confidence, to the white population. In addition, this is a particular issue for cross-cultural psychology researchers who attempt to transport 'western'-based measures to 'non-western' cultures and societies. Ben-Porath *et al.* (1995) discuss three major reasons why a researcher might wish to use a personality measure developed in one culture with respondents of a different culture, while Paunonen and Ashton (1998) ask what criteria would establish that a personality measure is applicable to a culture other than that in which it was devised and standardised.

Exercises

1 A scale measuring attitude towards nuclear energy is given a test/re-test reliability check. It is found that correlation is .85. However, it is also found that scores for the sample as a whole have decreased significantly.

(a) Should the test be used as it is?

(b) What might explain the drop in sample scores?

2 A student friend has devised a test of 'Attitude towards the British' which she wants to administer to a group of international students just about to leave the country.

(a) How could the test be validated?

(b) How could the test be checked for reliability?

3 A friend says 'My dog loves Beethoven. Every time I play some he comes and curls up on my lap.' Is this a reliable test, a valid test or neither?

4 Another friend says 'I did a test while I was visiting that college in the States and I came out very low on 'individualism' and 'sociability'. I wonder what that means.' Comment on the friend's thoughts.

5 Match the term to the definitions in the table below. In the blank column enter the number of the left-hand validity type that corresponds to the right-hand definition. Note: none of the right-hand descriptions corresponds to the left-hand term in the same row.

		Enter matching number here	
Face validity	1		Extent to which test scores can predict current or future behaviour or attitude scores.
Concurrent validity	2		Extent to which test scores predict future related performance or human characteristic
Predictive validity	3		Extent to which a test's purpose in measurement is clear to both researcher and test-taker.
Construct validity	4		Extent to which a test predicts scores on another older or similar test
Content validity	5		Validity established through programme of hypothesis testing and coherent psychological research.
Criterion	6		Validity established by expert evaluation of the tests' coverage of all relevant areas and aspects of the construct or skills under measurement.

Answers

1 (a) It has been found reliable since the correlation is high, hence should be all right to use in this respect.

(b) Recent nuclear accident?

2 (a) Compare results with interview data?

(b) Can't test the students again under similar circumstances so reliability will have to be checked only *internally*.

3 Reliable but not necessarily valid!

4 She is comparing herself with norms for an American student population. These two constructs are ones on which we might well, given previous research, expect US students to have a higher mean. She is forgetting the issue of test standardisation and cultural equivalence.

5 Matching numbers going down column: 6, 3, 1, 2, 4, 5

Glossary

Attitude scales

Likert	Scale using a response format where respondents select from an ordered range, e.g. 'strongly disagree' (1), 'disagree' (2) etc. and a ranked score is given to the response as shown in the brackets
Semantic differential	Scale measuring meaning of an object for the respondent by having them place it between the extremes of several bi-polar adjectives
Thurstone	Scale in which raters assess the relative strength of each item and respondents agreeing with that item receive the average 'scale value' for it
Visual analogue	Scale where respondents mark their position on a line between two polar opposites and the distance of their mark from one extreme is measured as a score
Diagnostic item	Item not obviously or directly connected to the attitude object, yet which correlates well with overall scores and therefore has *discriminatory power* and predictive power
Discriminatory power	Extent to which item, or the test as a whole, separates people along the scoring dimension
Disguise	Feature of questioning approach that keeps interviewees ignorant of the aims of the questioning
Factor analysis	Statistical technique, using patterns of test or sub-test correlations, that provides support for theoretical constructs by locating correlational 'clusters'
Psychometric test	Test that attempts to quantify psychological constructs: skills, abilities, character, etc.
Psychometry	The technology of test creation for the quantification of psychological constructs
Psychometrist/psychometrician	Person that creates and works with psychometric tests
Reliability	Consistency of a psychological scale
Cronbach's alpha	A measure of scale reliability using the variance of respondents' scores on each item in relation to overall variance on the scale
External (or stability or test–retest method)	Stability of a test: its tendency to produce the same results when tested on the same people at two different times
Internal	Consistency of a test within itself. Tendency for people to score at the same strength on similar items
Item analysis	Checking each item in a scale by comparing its relationship with total scores on the scale
Kuder–Richardson	A special form of Cronbach's alpha performed on a test with dichotomous items (e.g. with answers 'yes'/'no')
Split-half	Correlation between scores on two equal parts of a test
Response acquiescence	Tendency for people to agree with test items as a habitual response
Scale value	On a Thurstone scale, the average of judges' ratings of an item; respondent is given this score if they agree with it

Standardisation	Setting up of measurement norms for the populations for whom a psychometric test is intended
Validity	Extent to which a test measures the construct that it was intended to measure
Concurrent	Extent to which test results conform with those on another test assumed to measure the same construct and taken at the same time
Construct	Extent to which the existence of a construct is established through an interlinked set of diverse research findings. The theoretical establishment of a psychological construct through concerted and logically related psychological research
Content	Extent to which test covers the whole of the relevant topic area, as assessed by experts
Criterion	Extent to which test scores can predict scores on predictive future behaviour or attitude
Face	Extent to which the validity of a test is self-evident
Known groups	Test of criterion validity involving groups between whom scores on the test should differentiate
Predictive	Extent to which test scores can be used to make a specific prediction on some other variable

Comparison studies –
9 cross-sectional, longitudinal and cross-cultural studies

This chapter looks at studies that are comparisons, either of the same people as they mature over longish periods, or of several sub-group samples (e.g. ages, class, sex, occupation) studied at the same time. It also includes studies that compare samples from more than one culture.

- *Cross-sectional* studies capture several groups, usually of different ages, at one specific point. The general goals are to map developmental stages or to compare differences across groups on a psychological variable.

- *Longitudinal* studies follow a group (*cohort*, if a large group) through a longish period of time, possibly comparing with a control group if the first group is receiving some 'treatment'.

- There are several types of longitudinal study: *time lag, panel studies, cross-sectional short term design*.

- Cross-sectional and longitudinal studies are compared. Both suffer from problems of interpretation because they are non-experiments.

- A cross-cultural study compares psychological variables or effects across different cultures or ethnic groups. Cross-cultural psychology aims to create a more universal psychology.

- Some studies of cultures or cultural sub-groups have been highly controversial especially in the area of IQ and 'race'.

- Psychologists have exhibited ethnocentrism in the past but cross-cultural studies try to broaden the scope of psychology across cultures without value judgement.

- Most cross-cultural studies are non-experimental and suffer the usual increased threats to validity over tightly controlled experiments.

- The *constructs* of individualism and collectivism are introduced along with research examples which support the importance of the dimension and show that researchers need to be aware of the effect of quite different cultural norms when conducting cross-cultural research.

- The *emic-etic distinction* is discussed in terms of attempts to merge findings from two or more cultures into 'derived etics' (general dimensions of behaviour) rather than work, as in the past, with 'imposed etics'.

- The pitfalls of conducting a 'race' project as student coursework are briefly discussed. Preparation needs to be thorough in order to avoid giving offence. Attention to one's own stereotypes, received views and language is important.

What are comparison studies?

In the design of many of the studies we have considered so far, the objective has not been to compare different categories of people but to investigate some general feature of behaviour or mental life. The exception has been our glance at 'group difference' studies where comparison of groups was the aim. In this chapter, I have collected cross-sectional and longitudinal research designs because they focus on groups within the population, either across time (longitudinal studies) or across sections of society, very often age groups (cross-sectional). Cross-cultural studies look at differences between groups in different societies. One of the main purposes of both cross-sectional and longitudinal studies is to provide information on changes in a psychological variable over time. This may well in turn provide evidence for a developmental theory – for instance, that television affects the emergence of children's aggression or that girls develop language faster or in a different way compared with boys. Cross-cultural studies can be used in exactly the same way, but they can also be used specifically to strengthen or weaken theories that certain psychological characteristics are universal to humans and possibly innate, or are socially constructed.

Cross-sectional studies

A cross-sectional study compares samples drawn from separate distinguishable sub-groups within a population – very often, different age groups. A cross-sectional study can do this by taking groups of children or adults from different age bands and comparing them at the same moment in time. Although age groups are a common focus for cross-sectional studies, gender difference studies, too, are cross-sectional since they compare representative samples of females and males drawn from their respective populations (perhaps not all males and females, but often from a limited population such as students or patients). Likewise, one could compare across occupations, types of educational institution, disability groups, and so on.

Cross-sectional data are often used to support developmental theories such as those of Piaget or Freud. Some examples of cross-sectional studies are:

1 Kohlberg (1981) developed his theory of changes in the style of children's moral reasoning from a study of 10-, 13- and 16-year-olds' attempts to solve several moral dilemmas. Kohlberg and his colleagues also extended this to a cross-cultural comparison in later work.

2 Csapo (1997) investigated the development of inductive reasoning in 2424 Hungarian schoolchildren through the 3rd, 5th, 7th, 9th and 11th grades (roughly 9 to 17 years old). Tests were of number and verbal series completion, number and verbal analogies (e.g. 'cat is to kitten as dog is to . . .'), and so on. The greatest development took place between 11 and 15 years old. Interestingly, results on inductive reasoning tests predicted performance on applied science tests twice as well as did the children's general school grades.

3 Weich *et al.* (2002) surveyed 1887 residents in North London to establish an association between measured depression and type of residence independent of socio-economic status, floor of residence or housing problem. A large sample like this, carefully selected across age, economic and other relevant sections, enables researchers to draw reasonable conclusions about relationships as the authors did here about the links between depression and the built environment.

Longitudinal studies

The big disadvantage of cross-sectional studies is that of group equivalence, a problem encountered in any study using independent samples. No matter how well we sample, we can't ever be sure that our two or more groups are similar enough for fair comparison. The longitudinal approach surmounts this difficulty since it employs repeated measures on the same group of people over a substantial period, often a number of years. In this way we can observe genuine changes in psychological characteristics over time or we may establish that certain characteristics remain stable. If we check at short intervals we may be able to observe major points of change, such as the shift from pre-operational to operational thinking in children around five years old.

In some longitudinal studies, a control group is used for comparison where the 'treatment' group is receiving some form of intervention programme. This happened in several ways during the 1970s when there was a strong programme of intervention research in 'Educational Priority Areas'. Smith (1975) followed children through pre-school nursery projects, where children given special language training experiences tended to gain in mental age over a control group. Such gains were monitored into school in a further programme where carefully matched samples acted as controls or experimental participants, the latter receiving language tuition each school day.

Info Box 9.1   Is television bad for your weight?

Longitudinal studies are common where research concerns children or adolescents. Henderson (2007) analysed data from a very large US national survey of health behaviours related to obesity risk. In the study 9–10-year-old US black and white girls were visited annually over a period of up to ten years. Henderson found that, for white girls only, Body Mass Index (BMI) rose significantly more over the first four years for those who started with a higher level of TV viewing than for those who were viewing less TV when the study began. Thereafter there was no relationship between BMI changes and TV viewing and none in any period for black girls. Henderson suggested a relationship between TV viewing and obesity.

We might assume that the girls put on weight because watching more TV means doing less physical activity. However, in an interesting demonstration of how a study can come up with completely null results yet be an important contribution to knowledge, Smith, Rhodes and Naylor (2008) followed up the behaviour of another group of 9–11-year-olds but this time in Canada. They found that, irrespective of gender, ethnicity and a few other variables, there was no correlation between degree of physical activity and amount of TV viewing whereas previous research had suggested possibly a negative correlation – more TV, less activity. The authors argued that intervention programmes (see Chapter 23) aimed at reducing TV viewing by increasing physical activity may not be worth the cost of running them.

Studies such as those described in Box 9.1 which consider changes in people over time are sometimes known as PANEL DESIGNS. What is worth mentioning is the general size of the panels which are followed through in longitudinal studies of this kind. Henderson's study took data from a US national survey which visited some 2,379 girls over the ten-year period, though a portion of those would of course drop out of the study over time. Smith, Rhodes and Naylor studied a more modest 344 participants but theirs was a single study they conducted themselves.

Cross-sectional	Longitudinal
Advantages	
Support for stage and other developmental theories can be achieved rapidly, at one instant in time	Can follow changes in same individuals; therefore stage-type theories are better supported – we know the differences between seven- and nine-year-olds, for instance, are not the result of non-equivalent samples
Relatively inexpensive and less time consuming	
Few people lost during study (low 'attrition')	No *cohort effect* (see below)
Participants cannot become 'wise' to the tests which, in a longitudinal study, they may take more than once	Useful where following through the effect of a 'treatment' (e.g. educational intervention) and comparing with a control group
Cross-generational problem avoided (see below)	Usually better knowledge of individuals and only way to observe changes over time within one individual or same individuals
Disadvantages	
Non-equivalent groups may confound the differences observed, e.g. a sample of seven-year-olds may have weaker verbal abilities than did a group of nine-year-olds when they were seven, thus making reading improvement from seven to nine look greater than it actually is	**Attrition** risk much higher (i.e. loss of participants through the course of the study)
	Decisions made at the start often cannot be reversed. Modification mid-way might ruin the potential for objective comparison
Can't observe or detect maturational changes that confound results. For instance, difficult questions will be more easily answered by nine-year-olds than by seven-year-olds. We might falsely conclude that the younger children don't have the knowledge or concept that certain questions ask about. Older children might just be more capable of guessing what a researcher is after	Participants may become wise to the tests used and/or too familiar with researchers so that they can learn to give what the researchers want to find
	Time-consuming and expensive. A long wait for results
	Replication very difficult
Cannot observe changes in same individuals	**Cross-generational problem** – Comparison of one developmental study with another may be confounded by different general conditions (e.g. war) for one of the generations
Cohort effect – if age difference between the groups studied is large then any difference found might be the result of different experiences (e.g. change in educational practice) and not of e.g. maturation or stage development	

Table 9.1 Advantages and disadvantages of cross-sectional and longitudinal designs

Occasionally, longitudinal studies even larger than those above are carried out on samples from the whole population, often children, in order to give some idea of national trends. In such cases the large sample of children is known as a COHORT. An example would be Davie, Butler and Goldstein (1972), who followed almost 16,000 children from birth (one week in 1958) to the age of 11. This project, which became known as the National Child Development Study, is still continuing and is managed by the Institute of Education, part of the University of London. The children have been questioned, where tracing them has been successful, at the ages of 7, 11, 16, 23, 33 and 41 (in 1999). There are several other such large-scale national surveys, the latest being the Millenium Cohort Study (MCS) following up 18,818 children born over a 12-month period starting September 2000 (December for Scotland and Northern Ireland). There are already over 100 published journal articles, books, chapters, reports or conference presentations based on MCS findings.

Evaluation of longitudinal and cross-sectional studies

Clearly there are strengths and weaknesses of purely cross-sectional or purely longitudinal designs. Perhaps you would like to make a list of these, as you see it, before checking against the contrasts made in Table 9.1.

Lagged designs

The cohort effects mentioned in Table 9.1 can be made the object of research by selecting a group of 16-year-olds, for instance, in the years 1995, 2000 and 2005. This is known as a TIME-LAG STUDY. Here we obviously cannot make longitudinal comparisons (we have different people) or cross-sectional comparisons (same age but different time), but we can see whether attitudes have altered or abilities improved in the population studied, so long as we have confidence that the samples are all equally representative of 16-year-olds in that year.

Figure 9.1 shows the design for a panel study where measures of amount of violent TV viewing and aggression are taken on the same group of children at times 1 and 2, known as 'waves'. Here we have a time lag study with the same group and we can strengthen certain hypotheses using the CROSS-LAGGED CORRELATIONS indicated by the diagonal arrows in the diagram.

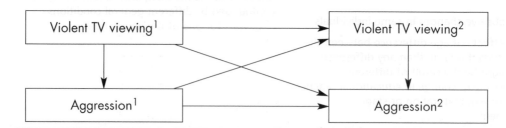

Figure 9.1 Two-wave longitudinal study conducted on the same panel at time 1 (^{1}) and time 2 (^{2})

'Violent' TV would include cartoons which include destruction and apparent physical harm as well as 'real life' violence. Time 1 could be an age for the children when there is little correlation between violent TV viewing and aggression, a time when they are only just beginning to understand the full implications of what they see. If we find at time 2 that there is a significant positive correlation between violent TV viewing^1 and aggression^2 then this finding supports the hypothesis that violent TV causes aggression. However, as with all such correlations there is an alternative interpretation –

that more aggressive children choose to watch more violent TV. In other words the aggression causes the TV viewing rather than the TV viewing causing the aggression. What would provide better support for the TV causes aggression hypothesis then would be the finding that the correlation between aggression[1] and violent TV viewing[2] is much lower than that between violent TV viewing[1] and aggression[2]. This finding would in effect be telling us that the more you watch violent, TV the more aggressive you become but *not that* the more aggressive you are, the more violent TV you will watch.

Cross-sectional, short-term longitudinal study

This is a compromise design for the study of age comparison. Figure 9.2 represents a study in which four groups of children aged 6, 7, 8 and 9 are selected in 2009 and studied over three years so that we effectively study the age range 6 to 11 in just three years. An example comes from Halliday and Leslie (1986), who studied mother–child communications with children ranging from 9–29 months at the start of the study, to 15–36 months at the end, so the age range of 9–36 months was covered in six months' recording. The design is similar to what Fife-Schaw (1995) terms a *longitudinal cohort sequential design*. Breakwell and Fife-Schaw (1992), for instance, studied attitudes to AIDS/HIV and sexual activity preferences among 16–21-year-olds. They drew a sample of each age group (16, 17, 18, 19) in 1989, following these through to 1991 but adding an extra sample of 16-year-olds each year to 1991 (this would be like adding to the groups shown in Figure 9.2 an extra 6-year-old group in 2010 and another in 2011). Here they could compare longitudinal effects for the same samples but, also, they could check whether changes in one group of 16-year-olds would also occur for a later group of 16-year-olds. Yet again, they could see whether an external event (say, a hard-hitting AIDS warning publicity campaign) had a similar effect on 19-year-olds' sexual behaviour as on that of 17-year-olds.

Figure 9.2 Design of a cross-sectional, short-term longitudinal study

Cross-cultural studies

Problems with generalisation

Psychologists who discover reliable effects or demonstrate strong developmental trends within one culture may well be interested in whether these may be found in other cultures too – they will want to extend their study's *population validity* (see Chapter 4). If the trends appear elsewhere, the case for universal psychological factors is strengthened. Aspects of grammar development, for instance, seem to occur in stages recognisable in all cultures so far studied, though debates arise about more specific details.

Unfortunately, there are often problems of ethnocentrism, and even racism, involved in attempting to generalise findings and theories from one culture to another. Fortunately, not many psychologists have been as overtly racist as C.G. Jung (1930) who claimed:

'The inferior (African) man exercises a tremendous pull upon civilised beings who are forced to live with him, because he fascinates the inferior layers of our psyche, which has lived through untold ages of similar conditions' and 'the famous American naïveté . . . invites comparison with the childlikeness of the Negro'. (Jung, 1930)

No one can talk sensibly of the 'African mind' or the 'Indian character', as if hundreds of millions of people could share the same psychological characteristics with each other and not with the rest of the world. Even talk of the 'Irish temperament' seems, to me, to be spoken from the wrong end of the telescope. Psychological researchers are human and will inevitably carry some of the baggage of history that has left Westerners with distorted views of 'other' cultures. Hence they have to be extremely vigilant in checking that their unquestioned preconceptions about 'races' and cultures do not influence, if not dominate, their attempts to objectify the study of cultural differences. Jung's comments above demonstrate the frightening effect of having no objective method for comparison at all.

However, also questionable is the impression of objectivity lent by the scientific aura of psychological instruments and methods when these are exported unquestioningly to cultures they were not developed with or standardised upon. In an astonishing example that is worth explaining at length in order to outline the serious dangers, beyond academic psychology, that some researchers can create, Lynn (1991a) estimated the black African IQ to be around 75 points. Africa is rather a large place so this would be a truly outstanding feat! In fact, the data came from 11 studies ranging from 1929 to 1991 and conducted in just half a dozen countries, using a variety of non-equivalent samples (sometimes children, sometimes adults) and a number of non-equivalent assessments that were not IQ tests. Lynn 'converts' non-IQ scores into 'potential scores' using a dubious and unpublished formula (Kamin, 1995). It is interesting that two-thirds of the tests were carried out in South Africa under Apartheid, since Herrnstein and Murray, in their controversial 1994 text, *The Bell Curve*, use these very data as evidence that black people, other than in the USA, also get low IQ scores. This, in turn, is intended to explain why the US phenomenon then can't be the result of general discrimination and racism! There is a noticeable silence over what Apartheid meant in South Africa up to 1994. This kind of pseudo-science with a purpose really must be actively resisted and this has a bearing on the ethical issues concerning professional scientific publication described in Chapter 23 (and see the debate in the May and July issues of *The Psychologist*, 1990) over the British Psychological Society's publication of virulently racist 'research' by Rushton.

The aims of cross-cultural studies

Cross-cultural studies usually compare samples from two or more cultures on some psychological construct(s). An experimental effect found in one culture, often in the West, may be tested for in a different culture by replication. Although the study in one culture is an experiment, the comparison of the two sets of results does *not* count as a true or even a quasi-experiment (see Chapter 5) since we are simply comparing two different groups (a group difference study) and will incur all the usual threats to validity of such a comparison. The main aims of such comparisons are:

- *To try to make psychology more universal*

- *To see if some constructs occur in the same way in all cultures (e.g. language development stages)*

- *To extend knowledge of an effect by looking at how it is moderated by culture.* For instance, social loafing was an effect demonstrated in Western laboratories. It was found that people tended to work less hard in a group than when alone. When the experiment was carried out in some non-Western societies it was found that people actually worked harder in a group. Hence social loafing became a broader construct which varied with culture – a dimension from social loafing to *social labouring* (Karau and Williams, 1993, and see p. 116). Psychology is very seriously limited to Western cultures, particularly to the USA. It needs to 'get out more' – see Box 9.2.

- *To test hypotheses developed from theory.* Some psychologists have used the fact that conditions in some societies are different from others *solely* to test a hypothesis using a from of natural experiment. For instance, an explanation for the effect found in the famous Muller-Lyer illusion was that we live in a 'carpentered' environment full of angles and corners (Gregory, 1966). We (Westerners) therefore are susceptible to 'depth cues' occurring in two-dimensional drawings and, in particular, the geometrical illusions. To test this theory there was an obvious need to find people who did *not* live in a carpentered environment. When this happened it was found that such people are not as affected as Westerners by the illusion, if at all (Segall *et al.*, 1968). This therefore supports the carpentered theory. Note that the interest in another culture here is *only* related to the theory test. That is, the non-Westerners are not here being tested out of intrinsic interest in that particular culture but as part of an ongoing research programme.

As a matter of interest, Gregor and McPherson (1965) found no differences between rural and urban Australian aboriginals in susceptibility to illusions and according to the carpentered world hypothesis they should have since urban living is carpentered and rural living, in the Australian outback, generally is not. They *did* find a difference between schooled and unschooled aboriginal people. They suggested the carpentered world effects could mostly be explained, not by the carpentered/non-carpentered environment variable, but by the confounding variable of general exposure to western-style education and culture, which includes an emphasis on the interpretation of printed, two-dimensional graphic materials as representing three-dimensional scenes. This is a very clear example of confounding emphasising the serious threats to validity incurred by the mostly non-experimental nature of cross-cultural investigations.

Info Box 9.2 — Just who is psychology all about?

When you read in a glossy psychology textbook something like 'So we find that people are likely to do . . .', always remember that the people being referred to are almost exclusively Western and probably American. Narrower still, as we saw in Chapter 2, they may well mostly be students, probably of psychology! There is a desperate need for cross-cultural psychology, but also for psychology done solely outside the West, simply because so much psychological research is pretty low on population validity, a concept described in Chapter 4. Where is the evidence for these dramatic claims?

Smith and Bond (1998) began with an analysis of the citations contained in standard psychology textbooks. They showed that in Myers' (1996)* text, *Social Psychology*, one of the best on cross-cultural issues, only 228 of the 2700 studies cited came from outside North America. Of the nearly 2000 citations in Hogg and Vaughan's (1995)* *Social Psychology* text, where the authors are from Australia and New Zealand, 500 were studies conducted outside North America but, of these, most came from western Europe (most of these in the UK) with only a handful of studies beyond these areas of the world. Baron and Byrne's (1994)* *Social Psychology* contained about 1700 citations, of which just over 100 were of non-North American studies. However, in 44 of these 100 the reader was not told the study's location. On average, psychology in major social psychology textbooks concerns around 10% of the world's population in about 5% of the world's nations. Rosenzweig (1992)* reported that 64% of the world's psychological researchers were American. It's true that these surveys are now a little dated but probably not much will have changed in the interim.

*All references are cited in Smith and Bond (1998).

'Race' – not a useful scientific concept

An emphasis on biological 'race' differences has diminished (except in the work of a few researchers such as Lynn) as biologists have impressed upon us, for 80-odd years, the scientific worthlessness of the concept of 'race'. The idea of large-scale, isolated breeding pools, with clear, genetically based behavioural or psychological differences is contrary to contemporary biological knowledge. There is vastly more genetic variation within 'races' than there is between them. The clear visual distinction between people of African-Caribbean origin and North Europeans leads some people to believe, superstitiously it turns out, that there must be some distinct genetic separation between them. One may as well distinguish between people with blonde and brown hair. There is, on average, about the same amount of genetic variation between any two members of neighbouring populations (e.g. England and Scotland) as there is between any two members of different so-called 'races' (Gould, 1997; Jones, 1981; Montagu, 1975; Richards, 1997). In any case, the lay person often confuses 'race' with appearance, ethnicity, culture, country of origin or even religion.

Ethnocentrism in early cross-cultural studies

In early cross-cultural studies, psychologists often tested members of a tribal community on, say, visual illusions or counting tasks. The emphasis was often on what tribes 'lacked', and the studies tended to be ethnocentric. Ethnocentrism is the tendency to judge the behaviour and values of another culture by those of one's own. An example would be to assume that infants in all cultures should be in their own room or bed by age two. North Europeans, who generally greet with a firm handshake and full eye contact, tend to describe many Asian cultures' greetings, which involve a bowed head and no eye contact, as 'deferential' or as exhibiting a 'shy' cultural personality. This is an ethnocentric description which ignores Asian norms of greeting. It carries the unspoken implication that the interpretation is somehow true, and that North European greetings are the neutral basis from which to assess others. Such value judgements are culturally bound and have no universal validity.

Ethnocentrism very easily leads to false interpretations of behaviour. In Mozambique, I was told of an educational psychologist who got children to do the 'draw a man' test – a projective test (see Chapter 8) where the drawn man is interpreted in psychodynamic terms. The children's very tiny drawings were interpreted by the educational psychologist as demonstrating the poor self-image of Mozambican children resulting from centuries of Portuguese colonialism. It was pointed out to her that Mozambican school children at that time were under strict instructions not to waste paper in times of great shortage and a weak economy!

Working against ethnocentrism

Campbell (1970) argued that some protection against ethnocentrism could be gained by carrying out a design in which a researcher from culture A studies cultures A and B (the usual cross-cultural design), while a second researcher from culture B also studies cultures A and B. This should distinguish differences that emerge because of ethnocentric bias from true differences between the two cultures. This procedure is rarely carried out. However there is a common procedure for trying to de-Westernise a psychological scale known as BACK TRANSLATION. In this process a scale in language A is translated into language B then back again into language A. If the meaning is still as intended, then the scale is said to have *translation equivalence*. This procedure was followed in research by Green, Deschamps and Páez (2005), who translated their revised measure of individualism and collectivism from English into French, Spanish, Mandarin, Russian, Portuguese, Turkish, Greek and Italian.

Some lessons in non-ethnocentric work have been taken from social anthropologists, who tend to conduct intense participant observation studies as a member of a village community for many months, if not years. These researchers have studied the community in its own right, not as a comparison with the West. They use qualitative methods to record the interrelationship of local customs, norms, taboos and social interactions such as marriage and trade. Ruth Benedict (1934) used the term *cultural relativity* to underline her view that an individual's behaviour and thinking must be viewed through, and can only be understood using, that person's own cultural environment.

Research examples

Cross-cultural studies in psychology have increased markedly since the late 1960s. The cross-cultural psychology research movement has been led particularly by Triandis, Berry, Poortinga, Dasen, Segall, Brislin, Herskovits and Campbell, the last of whom we also encountered leading the debate on quasi-experimentation and internal/external validity. Research examples, along with discussion of many methods and issues, can be found in the *Journal of Cross-Cultural Psychology*. Ironically, the movement is led by mainly US psychologists, but the studies now conducted have lost a lot of their early ethnocentrism. Nevertheless, Nisbet (1971) argued that the cross-cultural method is just another way, seemingly scientific and respectable, of placing European and US cultures at the top of a graded hierarchy.

One clear dimension has emerged from cross-cultural research and that is the difference between INDIVIDUALISTIC societies (where people tend to be more person-centred when answering questions about social norms and moral dilemmas) and COLLECTIVIST societies (where social rules and relationships take precedence over one's own personal needs), see Hofstede (1980). Even within a single country or society there are usually ethnic groups which differ from the mainstream on these variables. The lesson is that, if researchers blissfully ignore this distinction, they will run into great difficulties when trying to transport Western-based tests or to replicate Western findings in other societies. For instance, reading a US 'glossy' social psychology textbook section, one might conclude that certain attribution effects, such as the 'fundamental attribution error' or the 'self-serving bias' were universal aspects of human behaviour.

This is far from the case. In fact, in several so-called 'non-western' societies, people tend to perform in the opposite direction. Shikanai (1978) found that Japanese college students who succeeded on a task tended to make external attributions ('it was an easy task') whereas they blamed lack of ability and effort (an internal attribution) to explain their failures. US students tend to do the opposite – using a 'self-serving bias' – if I do well, I can take credit for ability; if I do badly, I can blame the exam, the teachers, the lack of textbooks etc. Hess *et al.* (1986) found that Japanese mothers often explained their own children's poor performance as due to lack of effort (internal attribution – it was the children's 'fault'). US mothers were more likely to blame external factors, such as quality of school training. Again the reverse of the self-serving bias was found in a less individualistic society.

Stipek (1998), in a comparison of US and Chinese college students, found Chinese students preferring to express pride in others' achievements (e.g. those of their child, a good friend or colleague) rather than the US preference for expressing pride in one's *own* achievements. Here is a good example of the dangers for the inexperienced researcher. It would be easy for the naïve British researcher to assume that people everywhere 'naturally' express pride in their achievements and see no harm in that. For many cultures, particularly in Asia, this just is not the done thing. One is modest and one waits to be praised.

It should be stressed here that labelling a society as 'collectivist' does not in any way imply that all members of that society behave in a collectivist manner, any more than all males behave in a masculine way all the time. The same goes for individualism. We are talking of statistical tendencies only and collectivism-individualism is a *dimension* upon which Hofstede (1980) was able to place 53 countries based on questionnaire responses from large samples.

The emic-etic distinction and psychological constructs

Pike's (1967) notion of emic and etic constructs was elaborated by Berry (1989) and is now generally associated with his work. An emic psychological construct is one that is peculiar to one culture, whereas an etic construct is thought to apply to all human behaviour or thought – a universal. Berry argues that, because researchers so often cannot shake off the influence of their own culture in their usage and understanding of relevant psychological constructs (perhaps it is impossible ever to transcend one's original culture in this respect), they generally work with imposed etics – they assume a construct is universal and impose it on new cultures. For instance, they might assume that the self-serving bias occurs everywhere. A major goal for cross-cultural psychological researchers, according to Berry, is to change these imposed etics progressively, by becoming submerged within a new culture and working from an emic viewpoint, eventually modifying imposed etics to produce *derived etics* – universal psychological dimensions that are valid cross-culturally, or at least can be used to compare several cultures. An example would be the individualism-collectivism dimension or the development of the social loafing construct into the social loafing-labouring dimension described earlier.

Ethnicity and culture within one society – doing a 'race' project

Research projects on differing cultures within one society are referred to as *intra-cultural studies*. Students conducting a third-year dissertation or other project very often choose to do such a study on 'prejudice' or 'race', mostly for the best of possible reasons: they are concerned about racism and injustice or, more positively, fascinated by a different social perspective from their own. Such studies, however, are fraught with the dangers of ethnocentrism, stereotyping and misunderstanding. I feel it is not possible to be reared in the UK (white or black) without subtly absorbing the 'race' images and themes that existed in our past. Up to the 1960s, many people in this country would not have thought twice about Jung's statement (p. 212).

I would recommend that students *do* concern themselves with 'race' issues but, in choosing to do what might seem a simple project, there would need to be a lot of preparation and groundwork on cultural perspectives and the language of 'race'. The researcher needs to investigate his or her own sense of ethnicity first – white people often don't think of themselves as 'ethnic'. This is partly because the term 'ethnic' has come to mean 'noticeably different (or exotic) minority' with 'white' being the assumed norm. When we use the term 'ethnicity', however, we refer to the culture by which people feel most strongly defined. Hence, though the term 'ethnic food/clothes/dance' is often bandied about, with the real intention being 'exotically different', I would argue that fish and chips, bowler hats and ballroom dancing are all 'ethnic'!

The issue of language is crucial, since it is the conveyor of subtle, historically interwoven and politically tangled concepts. Objections cannot be laughed away with the argument that they are attempts to be 'politically correct'. In order not to alienate participants and to treat them with dignity, the student/researcher should seek advice on all the terms to be used in, say, a questionnaire or vignette. They can consult tutors or, better still, some people representative of the groups who are to be the subject of the study. Deeper still, students/researchers should study thoroughly their own politics on the relationship between their own ethnic group and another.

It is important that the researcher conveys an attitude of valuing difference while validating equal rights and status. British culture is not homogenous and never was (see bottom of Table 9.2). If the researcher's approach is open and receptive, ready to listen and appreciate the richness of cultural diversity, then participants will sense a positive approach and will forgive innocent gaffes, such as assuming that English is a 'second language' for most Indians. If they are, however, 'colour blind', assuming that 'we are all the same really' (i.e. White and English), then this too will be sensed and the research relationship will be strained.

Advantages	Disadvantages
Can demonstrate universal development trends, psychological characteristics and effects	Can support disguised ethnocentric assumptions
Can help to make psychology as a whole less Anglo-centric	Costly and time-consuming (though not if researchers in two or more different cultures simply share data)
Can show that a psychological effect is limited to the culture it was first demonstrated in, or that the effect occurs in different directions in different cultures	Variables may not be culturally comparable
	Difficulties of communication. Subtle differences between 'equivalent' terms may make large difference
Gives insight into quite different cultural systems, beliefs and practices. Increases knowledge of the world and can contribute to lowering of ethnocentric bias and prejudice in general	May present some societies as exotic and different rather than different but normal
Can provide reassessment of 'home' society's norms in culturally relative terms	Can ignore the fact that the 'home' culture is not homogeneous. British society comprises many identifiable cultures, which include African-Caribbean, Indian (several separable cultures), Pakistani, Scots (highland and lowland), Irish, Welsh (north and south), Geordie, Scousers and Cornish, to name but a few
Provides rich data unavailable by any other method	

Table 9.2 Advantages and disadvantages of cross-cultural designs

Readings on 'race', culture and psychology

Berry, J.W., Poortinga, Y.H., Segall, M.H. and Dasen, P.R. (2002) *Cross-cultural psychology: Research and applications* (2nd edn). Cambridge: Cambridge University Press.

Gould, S.J. (1999) *The mis-measure of man*. London: Penguin.

Howitt, D. and Owusu-Bempah, J. (1994) *The racism of psychology*. Hemel Hempstead: Harvester Wheatsheaf.

Laungani, P.D. (2006) *Understanding cross-cultural psychology: Eastern and Western perspectives*. London: Sage.

Littlewood, R. and Lipsedge, M. (1997) *Aliens and alienists: ethnic minorities and psychiatry* (3rd edn). London: Routledge.

Matsumoto, D. and Juang, L. (2007) *Culture and psychology*. Belmont, CA: Wadsworth.

Price, W. and Crapo, R. (2002) *Cross-cultural perspectives in introductory psychology*. Pacific Grove, CA: Wadsworth.

Richards, G. (1997) *'Race', racism and psychology*. London: Routledge.

Saraswathi, T.S. (ed.) (2003) *Cross-cultural perspectives in human development*. New Delhi: Sage.

Segall, M.H., Dasen, P.R., Berry, J.W. and Poortinga, Y.H. (1990) *Human behavior in global perspective: an introduction to cross-cultural psychology*. New York: Pergamon.

Shiraev, E. and Levy, D. (2006) *Cross-cultural psychology: Critical thinking and contemporary applications* (3rd edn). Boston: Allyn and Bacon.

Smith, P.B., Bond, M.H. and Kagitcibasi, C. (2006) *Understanding social psychology across cultures: living and working in a changing world.* London: Sage.

Triandis, H.C. (1994) *Culture and social behavior.* New York: McGraw-Hill.

Tucker, W.H. (1994) *The science and politics of racial research.* Chicago: University of Illinois Press.

Exercises

1 Without looking back at the text (to start with anyway!) decide, for the following research projects, whether the design is longitudinal (panel, time lag or cross-sectional short-term longitudinal), cross-sectional or cross-cultural.

   (a) Samples of children aged four, six and eight are given various Piaget-type problems to solve.

   (b) A sample of children is tested on Piaget-type problems when the children are four, six and eight years old.

   (c) UK and Iranian five-year-old children are compared on several Piaget-type tasks.

   (d) UK and Iraqi children are compared at four, six and eight years old on their development of story-telling ability.

   (e) Samples of 18-year-old school leavers are tested on school attitudes in 2004, 2008 and 2012.

   (f) People of 54, 56 and 58 years old are studied for a period of six years as they approach retirement in order to assess changing attitudes towards the world of work.

   (g) A large group of children is assessed on the number of hours they spend per week on video games and on literacy skills in two waves two years apart.

2 A researcher decides to investigate how people from a newly discovered rainforest tribe will compete against each other in an individual problem-solving contest. Is the researcher making emic or etic assumptions about the research topic? In what way? Can you suggest a better way to go about investigating this topic with this community?

Answers

I (a) Cross-sectional

(b) Longitudinal (panel)

(c) Cross-cultural

(d) Cross-cultural and longitudinal (panel)

(e) Longitudinal (time lag)

(f) Longitudinal (cross-sectional, short tem)

(g) Longitudinal (Two wave cross-lagged panel).

2 Researcher is making an imposed etic assumption about competition; not all societies value individual competition; better, perhaps, to make an in-depth, ethnographic or participant observation study of the tribe members' everyday and collective behaviour in order to determine where, if at all, and in what ways, competition occurs between individuals or groups.

Glossary

Attrition	Loss of participants from a research study
Back translation	System of translating a psychological scale from language A into language B and then back to language A again to ensure equivalence.
Cohort	Large sample of people, often children of the same age, identified for longitudinal or cross-sectional study
Cohort effect	Confounding in cross-sectional study when two different age groups have had quite different experiences
Collectivist	System of social norms and beliefs in which the individual's needs and aspirations are subsidiary to those of the group, often the family. Duty and responsibility to others rule over independence and self-seeking goals
Cross-cultural study	Comparative study of two or more different societies, or social/ethnic sub-groups
Cross-generational problem	Confounding occurring when one longitudinally studied group is compared with another that has generally had quite different social experiences
Cross-lagged correlation	Correlation of variable A at time 1 with variable B at time 2, or vice versa, in a time lag study where more than one variable is measure on the same group at two different times
Cross-sectional short-term, longitudinal study	Comparative study of several cross-sectional groups taken at intervals over a relatively short period (say, two or three years)
Cross-sectional study	Comparative study of several sub-groups captured for measurement at a single time

Cultural relativity	View that a person's behaviour and characteristics can only be understood through that person's own cultural environment
Derived etic	General/universal psychological construct modified from its origin in one culture after researcher's immersion in one or more new cultures
Emic	Psychological construct applicable within one or only a few cultures
Ethnocentrism	Bias of viewing and valuing another's culture from one's own cultural perspective
Etic	Universal psychological construct, applicable to all cultures
Imposed etic	Psychological construct from researcher's own culture, applied to a new culture without modification
Individualistic	System of social norms and beliefs where individual needs and goals dominate over responsibility to others. The self is paramount and independence from others is a primary value
Longitudinal study	Comparative study of one individual or group over a relatively long period (possibly including a control group)
Panel design	Design in which the same group of participants is tested at the beginning and end of one interval or more
Time-lag study	Comparative study where measures are repeated at long intervals on an equivalent sample each time (say, new sample of five-year-olds each year)

10 Qualitative approaches in psychology

This chapter presents a summary of qualitative researchers' objections to the mainstream research model (empiricist, hypothetico-deductive and quantitative) and summarises a variety of methods now commonly used in mainstream psychological research. Methods here, however, are usually not just an alternative set of procedures but incorporate a fundamental philosophical critique of the mainstream approach and a specific epistemological position.

- Traditional *quantitative methods* have often produced relatively artificial and sterile results, inapplicable to the realities of everyday human life.
- The alternative approaches presented here emphasise rich meaningful data, closeness to participants' reality and analysis by theme and theory emerging from the data rather than by statistical measurement and testing. Qualitative methods encourage free and natural responses from participants, often in the form of unrestricted talk.
- *Grounded theory* requires saturated analysis of data to extract the fullest 'local' explanatory framework (i.e. not generalised, but peculiar to these specific data).
- *Interpretive Phenomenological Analysis* attempts to describe an individual's perspective on, and understanding of, the world, while recognising the constructive role of the researcher in the interpretation of that individual's experience.
- *Discursive psychology* (a version of discourse analysis) focuses on the ways people construct individual versions of events, and perform 'speech acts', through their conversation.
- *Thematic analysis* gathers qualitative data and recognises most qualitative objections to the quantitative paradigm, but is not dependent on a specific epistemology and can be used in a variety of ways including theory construction and qualitative models but also the testing of hypotheses.
- *Ethnography* hails from sociology and is the basis for participant observation.
- *Participative research* involves participants in the research process and validates findings against their recognition. In *collaborative research*, participants largely conduct their own research under the guidance of the researcher, who acts more as consultant.
- *Action research* involves intervention in human systems, and recognises the researcher's power to effect beneficial change.
- *Reflexivity* involves the researcher in reflection on the role of their own prior assumptions and biases in the development and writing up of the research project and requires the author to reflect on ways in which the construction of the research findings may have been influenced by the methodology and analysis adopted.
- *Feminist psychological research* emphasises and has substantially promoted qualitative and participative research methods, arguing that these were relatively neglected by the male establishment that had dominated psychological research development until feminist psychology started to have influence.

Psychology and the positivist paradigm

In Chapter 2, we encountered a controversy. The start of that chapter took the conventional view that methods in psychology have a lot to do with finding appropriate measures of psychological constructs so that we can test our hypotheses in a quantitative manner. The approach is modelled on the successful 'natural' sciences, which largely incorporate a philosophical view of science known as POSITIVISM. This view holds that the only things worthy of scientific study are those that can be observed and measured. It also incorporates a fundamental assumption of REALISM, the view that there is a single concrete reality out there and all we have to do as scientists is to be as objective and unbiased in our investigative methods as possible and we will find it as the truth.

Some thinkers, however, take a CONSTRUCTIVIST view of knowledge, including the scientific. They point out that everybody has a slightly different perceptual construction of, say, a concrete bollard. To most of us it is a concrete pillar, although our personal pictures of it will all be slightly different. To some (rare people) it might be a phallic monster, to a child, a ship's funnel. However, even to the relatively sober, it differs: to me it's an object to be avoided by my car's bumper; to another it's a blight, an eyesore and only made necessary by the curse of the car. In the same way scientists are human and each has a different construction of their research area. One might study gender expecting to find differences whereas another looks for similarities. To constructivists, this position on perception of the world leads to a conclusion that all knowledge is relative and a uniquely different construction for each person – a position close to the idealism of Berkeley in the eighteenth century. From this perspective, all scientific activity would need reassessment. Scientists, as everyone else, construct meanings from experience; GM crops can be presented as the solution to starvation or a serious ecological threat. However, some take the view that the problem of relative knowledge is only acute in the social sciences. This view then does not object to hard positivistic science as such, but more specifically to the attempted application of methods and concepts developed in the natural sciences to the world of psychology and social science. To be specific: one can measure a concrete bollard publicly to most people's satisfaction; however, the idea of similarly measuring 'extroversion', or of agreeing about observations of 'dependency', is a completely different ball game.

The constructivist theory of knowledge production is intended to apply to the physical sciences as much as any other area. However, whereas there can be fairly close agreement about the qualities of a piece of metal, the world of human affairs is awash with social judgements, differing values and competing systems of moral thought. Nevertheless, the highly scientific and complex statistical nature of mainstream psychology can camouflage the fact that culturally specific norms and dominant values are integrated into what appears to be a 'neutral', objective set of theoretical concepts and systems. The scientific aura of quantitative psychology can fool the unsuspecting public into accepting what are only speculative and specific findings on limited samples as generalised 'facts' about the world.

A now well-accepted demonstration of this built-in conservatism masquerading as factual enquiry was the feminist critique by Gilligan (1982) of Kohlberg's (1976) once much respected and supported work on moral development. Kohlberg had found, by asking participants to respond to moral dilemmas, that children develop through several stages towards what he termed a justice orientation. As it happened, more males than females appeared to reach this stage by a certain age.

Gilligan argued, however, that the stages were slanted towards the kind of thinking that boys were socialised to use. Girls favoured one of Kohlberg's 'earlier' stages, which leant more towards an individual care orientation. She argued that the justice orientation was no more mature than a care one; it was just that Kohlberg, being male and working with male participants, had taken the justice stage to be naturally more advanced. Gilligan argued that female moral thinking was not less advanced, but different.

The quantitative-qualitative debate

The debate within psychology is not new. It existed as far back as 1894 when Dilthey criticised the experimental psychology of the time for copying the natural science model and for consequent reductionism in explaining mental process. It sometimes dies down but has been particularly potent during the last 20 years. Psychology's extreme concern to be thoroughly scientific is often contrasted with traditional science's lack of concern over similar matters. It seems, sometimes, as though psychology has over-reacted in its pressing desire to be recognised as a 'true' science, and has worried about things even 'hard' scientists are not so rigid about. Woolgar (1996) discusses this issue and argues that psychology has been guilty of pushing an idealised account of what scientists actually do in their daily research work. Scientists are pragmatic in their progress of knowledge, rather than following the rigid code that is often presented as the ideal to work towards in psychology methods courses.

Qualitative and quantitative researchers use each other's approaches

It somewhat over-polarises the debate to talk of 'qualitative' researchers opposed to quantitative researchers. Many qualitative researchers have no particular objection to quantification in its appropriate place, and many of the arguments raised against the conventional scientific model in psychological research have been used by traditional quantitative researchers within their own paradigm (for instance, see Neisser's comment on p. 115). Qualitative researchers often make tacit quantitative statements, perhaps without realising it, when they compare the strengths of categories or give an idea of how often participants mentioned a certain concept. For example. In a qualitative article on the causes, maintenance and effects of dental phobia, Abrahamsson *et al.* (2002: 662) say: 'In our study, those informants reporting strong social support for their families reported *fewer* negative emotions' (my italics). This statement just cries out for empirical quantitative evidence. We need to know the numbers with and without strong social support and then how many negative emotions each reported. If the difference is tiny then we might take this claim by the authors with a pinch of salt.

As qualitative researchers stray easily into the quantitative arena, so quantitative researchers, by contrast, almost always summarise their work, discussing its worth, relevance and contribution in a largely qualitative manner. As mentioned in Chapter 7, both Milgram and Asch, though squarely in the quantitative camp, conducted intensive qualitative interviews after their experiments in order to discover just why their participants behaved as they did and the results of these led to rich new veins of research in their areas. However, for the sake of ease of communication I will generally use the term 'qualitative researcher' to refer to a strong proponent of qualitative methods and one who generally rejects the conventional scientific paradigm as restrictive on progress within psychology. A 'quantitative' researcher will be one who generally accepts the status quo and sees no great advantage in qualitative approaches, possibly remaining rather sceptical about their worth, and concerned about how reliability and validity of findings can be checked. These are idealised extremes. Most psychologists accept both approaches but differ over the extent and the areas to which either should be applied.

The problem with quantification in psychological research

A major objection to the use of the quantitative paradigm in psychology is this. If we carry out research using the highly controlled procedures and exact quantification of operationalised variables recommended by 'traditional' science, will we not be gaining only very narrow, perhaps sometimes useless knowledge of human behaviour and experience? Allport (1963), often quoted as a strong promoter of psychology as a conventional science, says: 'We should adapt our methods so far as we can to the object, and not define the object in terms of our faulty methods' (cited in Smith *et al.* 1995: 2).

Consider an experiment where the independent variable is 20 common and uncommon words in a mixed list, presented one per second via computer screen. The final results table will be two sets of numbers, a pair for each participant, representing the number of words they correctly recalled during the 60 seconds after exposure of the last item. This provides us with the not unsurprising information that infrequently met words are harder to recall. The quantitative researcher argues that, nevertheless (and in the spirit of the points made in Chapter 1 about common-sense claims), the research is required to back up what is otherwise only an unsupported, casual observation.

A critic might argue as follows: only in psychology experiments and party games do people have to learn a list of 20 unrelated words. How can this relate to the normal use of human memory that operates in a social, meaningful context? The data difference may be significant but it tells us little of relevance. The study gives us no information at all about the participants' experiences. They all, no doubt, used personally devised methods and found their own unique meanings in the combination of words presented. This information is powerful and 'belongs' to the participants, yet is unused and is not asked for, which could even constitute something of an insult to 'subjects', who participated in what, for them, was to be 'an interesting experiment'.

Examples of narrowness and artificiality in the establishment paradigm

Measures in psychology can be very narrow indeed. For instance, many studies measure attitude using a scale of the kind we looked at in Chapter 8. On this, each participant ends up with a single numerical value. On political attitude, for instance, a person's position may be represented as 34, where 40 is the highest value a 'conservative' person could score, the other end of the scale being 'radical' (left-wing). Using this system, we are assuming political attitudes to lie along a unitary dimension, whereas, in fact, if we asked people in depth about their ideas and principles, we would uncover various unique combinations of left- and right-wing views that couldn't, meaningfully, be averaged down to a mid-point on a bi-polar scale.

Pidgeon and Henwood (1997) argued that such narrowness is very much an inevitable product of the conventional paradigm, tending to narrow down the research focus and limit the potential for new perspectives by always testing hypotheses from established prior theory, rather than generating hypotheses through new work. This is not strictly true, otherwise psychology could never have developed new ideas. However, it certainly is true that, having established the definitive topic areas for psychological research, it has been very difficult to diverge and investigate entirely new phenomena. It is also true that the quantitative paradigm forces the narrowing of constructs such that an original proposed research topic becomes unrecognisably different from and intrinsically less interesting than its original form. Students are often understandably and intensely interested in researching meaningful everyday constructs. They may be fascinated by the teenage self-concept, yet they might well find that course requirements urge them towards quantification – for instance, counting how many more times girls use social terms to describe themselves compared with boys – because this measure can be used in a verifiable test of a hypothesis, even though the result might be immensely uninteresting.

It is essential to be clear about what one wants to observe, otherwise communication suffers and researchers can be accused of engaging in quackery and a journalistic style. However, we can distinguish between being clear and being unrealistic. The requisite clarity of thought is achievable without an automatic knee-jerk reduction to numbers. Astronomers, chemists and biologists don't always count – they look for patterns. So did Freud, Piaget, Bartlett and many other psychologists whose insights do not fundamentally depend on strictly quantified data. Although today we would almost certainly consider the term 'qualitative experiment' to be an oxymoron, Titchener, the leading introspectionist psychologist in the early twentieth century, published his *Experimental Psychology: A Manual of Laboratory Practice:* Volume I, *Qualitative Experiments* in 1901 and only four years later did the accompanying Volume II, *Quantitative Experiments* appear. Titchener asked his participants to report their direct mental and phenomenological experiences when performing simple laboratory tasks.

The major objections to the traditional paradigm

Some of the objections to quantitative approaches have already been touched upon in covering the more qualitative aspects of interviewing and observing, as well as in the case study section, and in the argument above. However, let's put together the general case 'against'.

- Traditional research treats people as isolatable from their social contexts. It even treats 'parts' of people (e.g. their memory or attitude) as separable. 'Subjects' are to be treated as identical units for purposes of demonstrating the researcher's preconceived notions about humans, which the 'subjects' cannot challenge. They are manipulated in and out of the research context.

- Whereas we all realise that to know and understand people one has to stay close, the researcher, in the interests of objectivity, strains to remain distant. The researcher's attitudes and motives are not recognised, revealed or seen as relevant to the research process. This cool distancing, however, is nevertheless a kind of social relationship, responded to by participants in experiments but not often recognised by quantitative researchers, who are concerned with variable control and reduction of 'error variance'.

- The objectivity just described is seen as mythical. The attempt to stay coolly distant blinds the researcher to his/her own influence and active role in the research process, which is a social context. When students administer structured questionnaires to peers, for instance, the respondents usually want to know what the student thinks and whether they believe all those statements the respondent had to check.

- The experimental situation or survey interview can only permit the gathering of superficial information. In the study of person perception and interpersonal attraction, for instance, mainly first or early impressions have been researched with traditional methods. Most research designs do not permit an analysis of longer-term changes in attraction.

- Experimental procedures restrict the normal powers of 'subjects' to plan, react and express appropriate social behaviour in the context of the research topic, yet the investigator uses the results to make generalised statements about human behaviour. The resulting model of the person is simplistic and mechanistic. Heather claimed that 'human beings continue to be regarded by psychologists as some kind of helpless clockwork puppet, jerked into life only when something happens to it' (1976: 20).

- Deception develops an untrustworthy and one-sided relationship between researcher and researched.

- The relationship between experimenter and researched is like that of employer and employee. It is dominating and elitist. Hence, behaviour exhibited will mirror this particular kind of social interaction.

- Highly structured research methods predetermine the nature of resulting information. Psychological scales, for example, do not usually ask what people know or think; they request only a limited response to unexpected and sometimes odd statements about a topic. Information obtained is therefore narrow, rarefied and unrealistic. Qualitative researchers argue that the use of predetermined variables imposes theoretical frameworks on participants and precludes the possibility of participants giving up information on how they themselves make sense of and interpret the world. Participants themselves can feel frustrated by not being able to provide sufficient data to truly express their view. They can lose faith in the research process knowing that they have contributed in a trivial if not meaningless way to the programme.

So what do qualitative approaches propose?

Thomas Kuhn (1962) made the term PARADIGM popular when he discussed ways in which science goes through radical changes in its overall conception of appropriate models and methodology. A 'paradigm shift' occurred when Einsteinian physics replaced Newtonian. The paradigm that qualitative researchers are seeking to replace is the positivist, quantitative one, which embraces the traditional scientific (hypothetico-deductive) model. But there is not just one new methodology. The call for change crops up in several contexts. It occurs among groups with a variety of backgrounds, principles and aims, but with most of the objections above in common. Feminist psychologists were particularly influential in the development of the critique of traditionally scientific psychology; the call for change was then joined by many working in applied fields such as health and disability. Although there are wide divisions among the range of qualitative approaches in existence today, these approaches are probably agreed on the following points.

- Psychological research should concentrate on the meanings of actions in a social context, not on isolated, 'objective' units of behaviour – a 'holistic', not an 'atomistic' approach.

- Research is a relationship between researcher and participant, not an objective look through a microscope. The research output is a construction out of the interaction and negotiation between the researcher and researched.

- Qualitative researchers generally recognise the central role of the researcher in the research process as a direct influence on the participant and on the interpretation of data. Data are not 'facts' but are translated to create a particular construction influenced by the researcher's own perspectives and biases. Therefore, to the extent this is true, REFLEXIVITY is overtly addressed – that is, research articles often include a reflection by the author on their role and influence during the research process and on the final analysis and conclusions.

- Qualitative researchers are not generally interested in the discovery of cause–effect relationships. They are concerned with people and their perceptions and experiences of the world. They ask how people make sense of their world, how they manage relationships within it and what it feels like to do all this.

- To capture life as it is, and to permit participants the greatest liberty to act as normal, research needs to be conducted in naturalistic settings. However, Hammersley and Atkinson point out that to distinguish the 'artificial laboratory' from 'naturalistic' settings is 'to take the positivists' rhetoric for reality, to treat them as if they really had succeeded in becoming Martians, viewing society from outside' (1983: 11). In other words, laboratory experimenters cannot really investigate uncontaminated human behaviour in a vacuum filled only by the independent variable and devoid of 'nuisance' variables. The laboratory itself is a social setting: it is within society. Participants are not inert non-reactive beings to be experimented *on*.

- Research is conducted as closely as possible *with* the person(s) studied. A quotation from Hall makes this point:

Social science research often appears to produce a situation in which a medical doctor tries to diagnose a patient's symptoms from around the corner and out of sight. The social scientist uses his 'instruments' to measure the response of the patient as though they were a kind of long stethoscope. The focus of the researcher has been on developing a better and better stethoscope for going around corners and into houses when the real need is for the researcher to walk around the corner, into the house and begin talking with the people who live there. (1975: 30)

- Participants' own terms and interpretations are the most central data or at least the most important starting point. This avoids the 'falsification of reality' mentioned by De Waele and Harré (1979) (see p. 151).

- Induction is preferred to the hypothetico-deductive approach. The latter starts with a hypothesis that is to be supported, confirmed or challenged. Deductive logic is involved in saying 'if this hypothesis is true then this should happen ', as was explained in Chapter 1. It has been argued

Pause for thought

In the table below tick either the qualitative or quantitative box beside each item according to whether you think the wording describes a qualitative or quantitative approach. Answers at the end of the chapter.

	Qual	Quant			Qual	Quant
1 Participant free to express themselves in context in fullest terms	☐	☐	15 Researcher-participant in unequal power relationship		☐	☐
2 Participant as passive respondent	☐	☐	16 Local theories		☐	☐
3 Researcher respectful of participant's integrity and mindful not to intimidate	☐	☐	17 Researcher as distant and neutral		☐	☐
4 Positivistic	☐	☐	18 Reflexive		☐	☐
5 Generates rich meaning	☐	☐	19 Replication an important goal		☐	☐
6 Universal theories	☐	☐	20 Naturalistic research settings		☐	☐
7 Structured research settings, usually	☐	☐	21 Inductive		☐	☐
8 Emphasis on people's constructions of their world	☐	☐	22 Narrow measurement		☐	☐
9 Emphasis on genuineness	☐	☐	23 Researcher and participants in social interaction		☐	☐
10 Aspects of self can be treated in isolation	☐	☐	24 Main aim is search for truth		☐	☐
11 Emphasis on reliability and validity	☐	☐	25 Participant as active being, interacting with research context		☐	☐
12 Generalisation of findings	☐	☐	26 Person's behaviour can be analysed separately from their normal active selves		☐	☐
13 Participant constrained by test situation and variables	☐	☐	27 Person treated at holistic level; irreducible to parts		☐	☐
14 Emphasis on cause–effect relationships	☐	☐	28 Deductive		☐	☐

(e.g. by Henwood and Pidgeon, 1992) that this leads to research concentrating on the disconfirmation of existing theories rather than the generation of new ones. Most qualitative research seeks new information in its own right. It mostly uses induction to move from individual cases to a wider understanding of human phenomena. Hence, the findings and theories that it develops start out very 'local' – that is, relevant to the context of those who have just contributed to the research project. Qualitative researchers do not (or should not) make massive generalisations about the nature of human thought or personality. They can offer guidelines for those going further with the same concepts in their own research. That is not to say that quantitative research can go much further. Article authors very often conclude a study, involving say as few as 40 participants, with universal sounding statement even though they have entirely failed to indicate to whom the findings might tentatively be generalised.

- In some more radical versions of qualitative work there is a high degree of participation by those researched in some or all of the development, running and analysis of the research project. It can even be that the target group acts as a group of *collaborative* researchers themselves. The main researcher can then become more of a consultant and data organiser/analyst. Any findings or interpretations are discussed and modified by the group as a whole in its own terms. Reality is 'negotiated'. The reason for this emphasis on participants' perspectives is not politeness or sheer humanism. Hammersley and Atkinson make this distinction here between the positivist and what they term the 'naturalist' (loosely, the qualitative proponent):

Positivism treats the researcher – by virtue of scientific method – as having access to superior knowledge. The radical naturalist, on the other hand, views the social scientist as incapable of producing valid accounts of events that compete with any provided by the people being studied. (1983: 234)

Qualitative data gathering

Qualitative approaches make use of a number of qualitative data-gathering techniques. The use of any of these does not guarantee that the approach in use is a fully qualitative one; the techniques themselves do not belong to any one approach, and each approach could use several. Some of the more technical issues involving these techniques have already been encountered as we progressed through the previous chapters on different data-gathering techniques. Those that could count as qualitative include:

- open-ended questionnaires
- unstructured and semi-structured interviews
- qualitative observation
- participant observation
- the diary method
- the clinical method (to some extent)
- role-play and simulation (depending on particular research)
- individual case studies.

All researchers using these techniques are not necessarily 'qualitative' in their outlook. Some traditional methods of analysis have accepted qualitative data as a legitimate product of research investigation but have then reduced these to quantitative values in order to conduct statistical analyses. Content analysis is an example and is dealt with briefly in Chapter 22. However, we will now consider thorough-going qualitative approaches in which research aim is to use data in their qualitative form and not extract from them just that which can somehow be represented numerically. In qualitative approaches, the data are retained in their original form of meanings; they are not quantified in any way.

Getting started – types of qualitative method

Although the principles outlined earlier are generally accepted across the board, it would be as wrong to see qualitative approaches as a unified movement as it would to see the Christian religion as a harmonious and united front. There have been bitter divisions and schisms among original founders and there are pleasant surprises when researchers from quite disparate areas, several outside psychology, come to realise that they have been saying much the same thing. One would expect that all the approaches would hold dear a respect for openness and honesty with one's participants. Again one would be wrong. The subterfuge and secrecy of some participant observation studies run counter to several of the principles outlined above. The people studied are often not participants in the research, and are kept in the dark to the extent that they can feel quite betrayed when the researcher finally comes clean. The presentation of results can sometimes sound patronising and as distant from the people studied as any quantitative study. Hence, there is no great homogeneity among qualitative approaches. As early as 1990, Tesch was able to identify at least 26 varieties. However, though there can be serious political differences among these, there are near universally binding principles such as the emphasis on meaning, on people's own experiences and on the researcher's own position in the research context.

The purpose of this next section, then, is simply to introduce the main features of several of the more popular qualitative approaches currently used in psychological research. I could not include everything. I have omitted for instance, narrative analysis (e.g. Murray, 2008) apart from the section on memory work, general case studies, Foucauldian discourse analysis (see Willig, 2008) and a few others. Should one of the approaches introduced below seem attractive or appropriate to you, then you would be advised to seek further comprehensive detail from some of the recommended further reading at the end of this chapter and in Chapter 22 which deals with the more hands-on issues of data gathering and analysis, but which will also refer back to the principles outlined here.

What is really crucial is that you do not start gathering any data before you have made a decision on which approach you are going to use. This is similar to the principle in quantitative studies that you know the type of analysis you are heading for before gathering data, since the type of analysis you use may demand a specific kind of data-gathering approach. You simply do not want a pile of data you cannot use for the purpose you had intended.

Grounded theory

Grounded theory (GT) is popular and has been imported from sociology where Glaser and Strauss (1967) first introduced it in an attempt to counter the effect of dominance, under the mainstream hypothesis-testing model, of just a few overarching theories. They argued that new, more local theories would emerge if they were 'grounded' in the qualitative data from which they were developed. Grounded theory is both a method for developing categories that summarise central features of the data and also an analysis that presents, at the end of the research, a theory or a model. This theory is in essence the explanatory framework provided by the categories that have emerged from the data, and these categories are more than just labels (such as 'happiness'). They are analytic in that they explain groupings of more descriptive categories (e.g. 'self-esteem' as a grouping for 'happiness, 'success', and 'improvement'). CONSTANT COMPARATIVE ANALYSIS is used to keep checking the groupings of categories, perhaps undoing and rebuilding the emerging network as analysis proceeds. Comparisons can be made between participants' accounts, between one participant's several accounts, between data and category formed from it and between different categories. EMERGENT THEORY is what develops as the data are analysed and as further data gathering proceeds as a consequence. It is important to note that in this approach analysis proceeds *along with data gathering*. That is, unlike quantitative studies, where data are gathered *then* analysed, here the researcher can analyse data after each interview and then alter questions in future interviews to take account of new ideas and categories which are emerging but which weren't originally predicted. Also, where quantitative studies often force data into pre-ordained categories which they do not comfortably fit, grounded theory alters and reforms categories according to the data until *they* fit the data.

Grounded theory can be performed on data gathered through any of the techniques listed above, but the full version of GT requires that the researcher move from category analysis back to data gathering as part of the overall research process. Because later data gathering is used to check on emerging categories, *purposive sampling* is employed (see p. 46) – the researcher looks only for certain kinds of data from certain kinds of people in a process known as THEORETICAL SAMPLING; this process might also be used in the cause of NEGATIVE CASE ANALYSIS, which is the search for cases with a poor fit to the category system, so that it can be further amended and refined. This analysis is performed up to a point of SATURATION, which is where no new categories emerge, further modification is trivial, yet a large part of the data has been accounted for. Where GT is used on a previously gathered data set (e.g. old interview transcriptions, political speeches, participant observation notes) then the abbreviated version is used where the researcher cannot go back and gather more data from the same types of sources, or change questions, in order to check the emergent theory. A further feature of the full version is that the research question is not set in stone; if comparative analysis and theoretical sampling throw up new directions or show that the original question was too broad, too limited or off-beam, then GT permits the reforming of the question based on the emergent theory developed from the earlier interviews.

A final point to be borne in mind by the student interested in GT as a prospective method is that GT has had its own internal schism. In the late 1980s, Strauss produced a 'hands-on' guide to conducting the process of GT (Strauss and Corbin, 1990), which incorporated advice to look for certain kinds of pattern in the data. Categories could be linked by using higher-order codes (especially 'process' and 'change') to organise categories into a structure. Glaser (1992) objected to this, arguing that the original version permitted patterns of categories to be recognised only if they emerged through the analysis. With Strauss's *a priori* criteria for analytic procedure, Glaser argued that the method had been compromised and now limited (or 'forced') the ways in which data could be analysed. In addition, Glaser objected to the use of pre-structured interview guides and other recommended preparations for data gathering, preferring to leave the researcher completely free to obtain the most genuine interactive data possible. However, Smith (2008) disagrees and argues that such guides are useful especially for the novice, and encourage open questioning and help to balance the interview process, also avoiding loaded or leading questions. For his side of the story, see Glaser (1992, 1998).

Interpretive phenomenological analysis (IPA)

This approach (whose initials need not be confused with a type of beer) depends very heavily on the philosophical principles of *phenomenology*. A phenomenological stance views a person's own perception of the world as primary. This view influenced Carl Rogers' Client Centred Therapy, for instance, by asserting that, whatever the client in a therapeutic session reports as their experience, however bizarre or paranoid from a rational person's point of view, this view was to be validated by the therapist as the client's genuine current view and investigated with them as such. IPA attempts to preserve fully that validation of people's perceptions of the world by attempting to get inside their heads and reflect that unique view as far as is possible. At the same time, the principles of phenomenology themselves dictate that any attempt to report on another individual's experience will necessarily be distorted by the phenomenology of the reporter. Hence, the reflexive role (see below) of the researcher in the interpretation of their participant's perception and experience is to the fore in IPA research.

The raw data for IPA is usually the content of interview transcripts. IPA favours the use of semi-structured interview techniques (see Chapter 7), although participants' diaries and autobiographies are also sometimes used. The founder of IPA, Jonathan Smith, provides an excellent and detailed guide to the conduct of such interviews (Smith, 1995a; 2008). Unlike discourse analysis, IPA is interested in mental processes and tries to record what is real in participants' minds, but strictly from participants' own phenomenological perspectives (Smith, 2008). It takes a relativist view that knowledge is uniquely constructed by the individual (researcher). Hence, analysis of transcripts involves identifying themes that recur and that make sense together but always in a consciously reflexive manner.

The following steps in analysis are largely taken from Smith (2008). The IPA researcher initially reads the transcript several times, making notes that are descriptive, a record of the researcher's associations or an early interpretation. The second stage consists of identifying emergent themes from the transcript and early notes. At a later stage, these themes are re-ordered and organised into those that cluster together or those that are at a higher level and incorporate more primary themes. Through each of these latter two stages there should be a constant referring back to the transcript and, preferably, themes should be given titles using the participant's actual words. Finally a table of organised themes is drawn up, with the best clustering and hierarchy that can be achieved and, unlike in GT, allowing some earlier themes that prove weak or unconnected to the final structure to be dropped.

IPA methodology often involves interviews with several participants, and these are chosen with some form of purposive sampling. The participants will all have the research topic of interest in common in some way. For instance, all might have been seriously bullied or have been recently diagnosed with diabetes. The research topic here might be the participants' perspectives on their self-image in either case or in their picture of how their life is about to change. The themes that emerge from each participant can be integrated with each other in order to gain further understanding of the phenomenon, or those from the first participant may be used to analyse the transcripts from later participants.

Discourse analysis (DA)

Qualitative researchers are interested in meanings, and human meaning is transmitted largely through language. Conversation Analysis (CA) is a method developed within sociology specifically for the purpose of analysing what Hutchby and Wooffitt (1998) call *talk-in-interaction*. The emphasis followed philosophers' arguments that conversation could often be analysed as consisting of *speech acts* (Austin, 1962, cited in Hutchby and Wooffitt, 1998). For instance, when we promise to do something, we make a contract with our speech. The person who starts a statement with the phrase, 'I'm not a racist, but . . .' is probably about to say something precisely racist but is putting in a disclaimer beforehand in order to distance himself from the negative interpretations of what he is about to say. Another ploy is 'Now don't get me wrong, but . . .'. CA is not covered here, but the reader might consult the text mentioned above, Sacks (1992), Have (1999) or Drew (in Smith, 2008) for full accounts.

Discourse analysis (DA) is to some extent a descendant of CA but has developed its own independent existence and, as with grounded theory, has two distinct strands (Willig, 2008). The older strand is the discourse analysis of Foucault, while the later approach, inspired by CA and ethno-methodology, also goes by the title of *Discursive Psychology* (see Edwards and Potter, 1992). It is this latter approach that will be dealt with here, though both approaches share many of the major principles.

DA, like most qualitative approaches, is grounded in a larger philosophical outlook. It takes a strong constructionist position, arguing that language is a constructor of versions of truth as it occurs. For instance, there is an infinite number of ways in which I can describe to you my (negative) views on, say, privatisation of welfare services. DA's view is not that these are all versions of some ultimate reality inside my head but that I would redefine and negotiate my view each time I attempted to explain it, dependent on the challenges I receive, my listeners' views, who else can hear, how formal we are, and so on. Above all, my production is *social action*. DA talks of speakers having a *stake* and using language to promote that stake within social discourse. This is not to say that people are constantly devious, but simply that it is in the nature of language use to create a 'version' each time we speak. In some ways this is reminiscent of Bartlett's view on memory. Each time we recount an event, say, the office party, it is different and will depend intimately on the status and role of the people with whom we construct the account and on our motives whilst doing so.

This notion of language as social construction is extended by DA to some of the heartlands of mainstream psychology, including cognitive and social psychology. This is another difference from CA, which can in places be seen as content neutral. The major DA proponents (e.g. Edwards and Potter, 1992; Potter and Wetherell, 1987) mounted what amounts to a frontal assault on mainstream cognitive and social psychology. Topics such as memory and attribution theory are treated as processes of discourse between people, not events that occur inside people's heads. Memories are not seen as close attempts to recall 'the facts' (the view of mainstream cognitive psychology) but are reconstructions in a social context. Memories are motivated constructions by people with a stake in producing an account that suits circumstances. These are not necessarily conscious constructions but they may, for instance, suit defences against blame or accountability, or may promote one perspective of a situation. What people say, when memorising, cannot be taken as a rather opaque window on to actual cognitive memory processes within the organism. DA sees memorising as a construction in a social context; when I tell you about my weekend I construct it with you and in the context of how we relate together, our shared cultural assumptions, our roles and status, etc.

Much of the controversial debate around DA is beyond the scope of this book. The debate, at times, carries the image of David (DA) and Goliath. A flavour of the heated debate DA (the discursive branch) caused in its early days can be gained from a reading of *The Psychologist* (October 1992). The specialist texts cited here and in Chapter 22 will give ample detail. What is important here is to appreciate some of the typical principles of research using DA so that you can decide whether this sounds like an appropriate method for you to use.

Principles of DA research

DA is better performed on naturally occurring talk or text that has been gathered without the speaker's knowledge of observation, i.e. natural discourse. However, studies are often now performed on interview and focus-group transcripts, but it needs to be kept in mind that the analysis might to some extent disclose participants' ways of managing their stake in the specific research context. Silverman (1993) has argued that DA often deals with 'exotic' or institutionalised exchanges, not with everyday conversation. Much of Edwards and Potter (1992), for instance, deals with interchanges between Margaret Thatcher, Nigel Lawson (then Chancellor of the Exchequer) and the media. By 'institutionalised exchanges', Silverman means exchanges strongly governed by social norms such as teacher–pupil or doctor–patient, and he recommends looking at less social rule-driven exchanges in everyday conversations between people of equal status.

In DA the transcript (see p. 565) of the social interaction under study is 'interrogated'. The emphasis is not on what the script is saying but on what it is *doing*. This is an absolutely central principle to be established if you want to 'do DA'. You are not, for instance, so interested in what new mothers say about their experience, how it felt, what their fears and joys were; you are interested, for instance, in how they construct the new role of mother, how they downplay problems and talk up the positive side (their stake). In DA, tone and emphasis are important. When a new mother says, cynically, 'I just so *lurve* meeting the milkman at 5 am', we consider how she is constructing her new way of life.

One important criterion for doing DA is that the researcher needs to get fully inside the philosophy that DA espouses. Attempts by students to do a 'discourse practical' after just two or three weeks of lectures would be greeted with horror by DA specialists, rather like boy scouts being let loose on your car. We discuss this point further in Chapter 22 but the focus here is a matter of DA research principle; the researcher must see the data and the procedure from a fully DA perspective, preferably by immersing themselves in the literature. At present, much of the research literature starts with a denunciation of the mainstream history of tackling a psychological area, such as the limitations of cognitive models of attribution. However, Willig (2008) suggests that DA has matured enough for research writers to begin including, in the introduction to their articles, a review of topic-relevant DA studies.

Thematic analysis

Thematic analysis is a poorly demarcated, rarely acknowledged, yet widely used qualitative analytic method within psychology.

So begins a seminal paper by Braun and Clarke (2006: 77), which goes on to give a full account of this approach, along with a step-by-step project guide, and is highly recommended as further reading for any student considering a qualitative project who has not attempted one before. Thematic analysis (TA) is pretty much the basic procedure used in several other qualitative approaches but without the requirement to progress from text analysis to satisfying the theoretical or ideological principles of any specific approach (for instance as is the case in GT, IPA or DA). Most qualitative methods search for central themes immersed in the text of interviews or other textual material. TA does this too. However, the approach is highly versatile and can be adapted to several kinds of research aim. It most often analyses texts from several individuals or groups.

Data-driven (or *inductive* or *bottom-up*) TA is very close to GT in that the idea is to let theory emerge from the analysis of data and not to start out with preconceived notions of what the final themes should look like. The emergent themes, however, may well be related back to other relevant literature (see, for instance, Harcourt and Frith, 2008). *Theoretical* (or *theory-led* or *top-down*) TA uses previous theory and the researcher's already declared interest to search for categories and themes which have been identified before the analysis commences. From a previous quantitative study on changes in self-esteem in people who have just failed exams one might investigate, through intensive interview, themes of self-worth, success and failure in the respondents' narratives. Used this way the approach is not far off content analysis. It is also possible for TA research to incorporate a certain degree of quantitative analysis, as when the researcher counts the number of occurrences of a theme or category or compares occurrences in one respondent with those of another.

It is even possible for TA research to be hypothesis-testing. Hayes (1991) conducted research into two software companies. Using background theory, including social identity theory and aspects of organisational culture research, she was able to analyse interview data in a theory-led manner and this enabled her to organise the causal attributions that employees made about their working environment and their employers to support hypotheses from the theory. This study (see Hayes, 1997, for an account) clearly demonstrates the way in which meaningful statements, not significance tests, can collectively support theoretical predictions.

However, returning to the quotation provided above, why do Braun and Clarke say that TA is 'poorly demarcated' and 'rarely acknowledged'? Basically TA is a methodological process pure and simple and is not allied to specific philosophical positions (e.g. as IPA is wedded to phenomenology). Anyone can use it and need not espouse particular methodological principles apart from the fact that it is usually used in a thorough going qualitative context. The poor demarcation of TA alludes partly to the fact that TA researchers rarely express in detail the exact method they used to generate themes; the lack of acknowledgement stems partly from the fact that researchers (and students) often use the method but perhaps dress it up as, for instance, 'grounded theory' (Braun and Clarke, 2006).

TA's lack of allegiance to a specific epistemological position and freedom from specific analytic format means that it is really the most common and certainly the most accessible approach for students, new to qualitative analysis. It contains the core elements of the data analysis procedure in many other, named qualitative approaches and as such is an ideal way for students to start analysing qualitative data. The student should not feel obliged to give their approach a label beyond its borders. TA can stand alone as a method but it is particularly important for you to give in exact detail the method used to develop themes in order to make it clear to your reader that your method was thorough and exhaustive (though many published TA reports fail to do this). Perhaps the main drawback of TA is that it does not inevitably lead on to theory production. It has the distinct disadvantage that it might end up declaring the obvious and failing to rise far above the mundane. However, students can add a lot of substance to a TA project by relating findings carefully back to previous theory and research and expanding wherever possible in the light of the developed themes.

TA involves the analysis of text for themes. These themes are often explicit in the text and exemplified directly by quotations, in which case the analysis uses what Braun and Clarke call a *semantic* approach. The analytic aim here will be to organise content to demonstrate patterns in the data which can then be related back to existing theory or may serve to develop new concepts. In contrast, a *latent* approach seeks to identify underlying ideas and constructs that produced or influenced the overt content of the data. Thus a latent approach automatically takes the analyst into the realms of theoretical conjecture.

The derivation of themes follows pretty much the same procedures as are outlined in Chapter 22 for GT or IPA. The outcome of the research, as published in a report, can be of various kinds depending on the original research aim. The themes might be treated in any or several of the following ways:

- simply listed and described
- organised under more generic themes and (perhaps theoretical) headings
- related back to previous theory
- subjected to latent analysis for explanations underlying the themes
- used to support hypotheses
- counted (as in content analysis but this approach is rare.

Braun and Clarke (2006) address the potential student project designer directly and usefully divide the process of analysis of data into six stages:

1 Familiarising yourself with the data.

2 Generating initial codes.

3 Searching for themes.

4 Reviewing themes.

5 Defining and naming themes.

6 Producing the report.

The stages are not all sequential. In particular, stage 4 requires a check back to see whether generated themes fit the rest of the data or perhaps are contradictory; themes may be found to be in need of revision, splitting, combination, and so on. Though there are no set rules for TA it is certainly necessary in one's report to support each generated theme with adequate direct quotation from the analysed text, using original line numbers.

Ethnography

This is an import from sociology and particularly anthropology, the originators of participant observation on an extended scale. Ethnography as a recognised research method stems from the social anthropologists' attempts to generate an understanding of a society from substantial experience of living within it, perhaps for several years. The method was taken up by various sociologists as a way to counter stereotypical assumptions about groups under study. Going among them might help curb preconceptions and develop empathy with the community from their own perspective. The approach was seen at one time to sociology as qualitative work often is to contemporary psychology – a kind of 'palace rebellion'. From this, psychology has largely inherited the tradition of participant observation. The specific methods involved are very close to those of grounded theory and, indeed, Glaser and Strauss's model can be seen as a direct offshoot.

Action research

This is not another approach to data gathering and analysis but a theme within much qualitative work, initially promoted by Kurt Lewin in the mid-1940s. He called for research to be applied to practical issues occurring in the everyday social world. The idea was to enter a social situation, attempt change, and monitor results. This might be setting up or contributing to a programme designed, for example, to raise awareness about dietary needs or the dangers of smoking. The approach has been used extensively in the area of occupational psychology concerned with organisational change. Associated examples come from the work of the Tavistock Institute and its concentration on *socio-technical systems* where there is an emphasis on facilitation of a work group in developing human systems that counteract the otherwise dehumanising influence of machinery and technology. A guiding principle is that the researcher involves the work group, or representatives of it, in the process of change, so the project is *collaborative* (see below). There are examples as far back as Trist and Bamforth (1951), who reorganised workers in the Durham coalfields, and Rice (1958), who did the same in Ahmedabad, India. Obviously, here is an approach where the research aim and area lend themselves to a qualitative and participative approach. We are most likely to see it in action in areas of applied psychology, such as education, work and health.

Recent examples include the work of Dineen and Niu (2008) who delivered part of a Chinese design curriculum to Chinese students either using the traditional Chinese method or a typical UK creative teaching approach. The UK approach was found to be effective in enhancing learner creativity and also had effects on confidence, motivation and enjoyment. Interestingly this conclusion was supported by both qualitative and quantitative data. Stewart *et al.* (2008) ran a series of participatory workshops involving Indigenous Canadian young school students (i.e. those belonging to a pre-European ethnic culture). The aim was to enhance students' learning about conceptions of health and wellness in their own community context. The students researched and then produced their own educational videos which were presented at a community event.

Following 35 qualitative interviews asking students about their experiences in the research project, it was possible to identify themes of *community* (e.g. recognising the value of older people's wisdom), *culture* (e.g. exploring the relevance of traditional healing methods and herbal remedies), *confidence* (e.g. students gained in confidence through their project achievements and mastering new technology) and *control* (e.g. students developed control of their diet and were able to gain new control over alcohol and tobacco).

Participative research and collaborative research

Many qualitative research projects, like the Stewart *et al.* example, incorporate the notion of people participating or even collaborating in the research process, the latter term meaning that participants actually part-run the project. The idea is not so new. Madge, as far back as 1953, argued that, with collaboration, the distinction between researcher and participant becomes a small matter of degree – the researcher is more experienced with more complex aims but all are collaborating in the project.

In participative research, participants know what the research project is all about, help to conduct it and have some kind of stake in its outcomes. It is a descendant of the anthropological concept of *endogenous research*, in which a researcher, rather than living with a community for a year or so, coming away, then publishing a report, involves members of the community in a research project on their own customs, norms and organisation, in their own terms. The approach has often been combined with action research to become what is sometimes termed *collaborative research* and is very similar to cooperative inquiry (see, for instance, Reason and Riley, 2008). Here, participants are involved as fully as possible in research on their own organisation or group. The researcher, acting more in the role of an expert consultant, may have to lead at the beginning, but as participants realise the nature of the game they become more centrally involved in the progress of the research. In some cases the research is initiated by an already existing member of the organisation or group.

This approach is particularly suitable where the group is planning or undergoing change and requires evaluation. Participants take up data-gathering ideas, develop their own, consider the researcher's findings or analyse their own, and debate progress, directions and results in group meetings. Collaborative research is not without confrontations, but the idea is to build on these natural differences constructively. A major goal is for participants to direct their own change, rather than be told by an outside expert what is wrong and what might be changed, after that expert has conducted research on those participants. Sims (1981) set out to study 'problem generation' in health service teams and found that, as the participants became interested in the issues, they took on their own lines of investigation. This created an atmosphere of awareness-raising and constructive change, which additionally generated a perspective on problem-solving that could be transferred, with modification, to other group situations.

Memories as narratives

A clear example of collaborative research occurs in the work of Haug and her colleagues (Haug, 1987, in Willig, 2008). *Narrative psychology* is the study of the ways in which people construct narratives about their lives. Telling a story about some aspect of our life inevitably involves a construction or reconstruction of events or experiences out of a set of disorganised fragments and 'memories' distorted by time and perhaps several retellings. It is the way in which stories are constructed and the attempts people make to define themselves through them which is of interest to the narrative researcher, see Langdridge (2007).

Haug and her colleagues used a version of the narrative approach to explore 'how they themselves had played an active part in the construction of their identities as women' (Willig, 2008: 135). They used memories on the argument that the ways in which we reconstruct memories is an indication of the ways in which we construct our self-identity. What makes Haug's approach entirely collaborative is the fact that the participants are co-researchers, not people whom the researcher tries unfeasibly to work alongside as equals. Crawford *et al.* (1992, in Willig, 2008) present guidelines for carrying out a memory research project which were essentially those that Haug *et al.* used.

First, a group is formed in which all feel trusting and comfortable and in which status differences are minimised. The group decides on a trigger for memories of specific situations such as 'danger' or 'saying no' and, at best, avoiding common topics (such as 'first love') which prompt over-rehearsed stories; the emphasis is on the *process* of constructing a self, not confirming a stereotyped identity.

The individuals in the group (usually between four and eight individuals) then write their memories over a period of time and usually alone. They then reconvene and go through each memory narrative and subject each one to a textual analysis similar to those used in grounded theory or discourse analysis. Themes are noted, role descriptions and contradictions highlighted, and omissions suggested. Then the group compares all the memories and their analyses with one another to generate contrasts, recurring themes and aspects in common. Both these two sessions are recorded and transcribed so that the discussions made by the group at this stage *also* become part of the final data analysis.

At this stage group members might return to re-write their memories in the light of their growing understanding of the social context which produces them. Finally memories to different triggers are compared and here is where the group discussion data are also analysed in the light of existing psychological theory and in the context of modifying and creating new theory to encompass the overall findings. The writing up of a memory work research is of course also a completely collaborative effort.

Reflexivity

One of the strong currents within most qualitative approaches, which to some extent protects research findings from claims that they lack validity or credibility, is a strong relationship and commitment to the self-critical theme of REFLEXIVITY. This is a term developed within modern sociology in the area of studies of scientific knowledge (Woolgar, 1988), but it is now a central plank of qualitative work in psychology. A reflexive account is the researcher's reflection upon how their own position may have impacted their research procedures, data interpretation and conclusions. By 'position' is meant the researcher's own values, ideas, beliefs, experiences, political leaning, social identity and wider aims in life (Willig, 2008). The need for reflexivity in research followed from Woolgar's arguments that scientists don't discover pure, cold, unarguable facts at a distance; rather, they construct versions of the facts according to schemata, stereotypes, pressures, socially accepted values, and so on. Scientists, in constructing their accounts of the world, call on available models (e.g. atoms are or were 'little balls'; the brain as a computer) and these are culturally determined. Scientists too are required to demonstrate how well they have used sponsors' money. According to Woolgar, then, scientific facts are constructions and the scientist's position, far from being removed from the situation as in the 'hard', neutral fact-finding model of science, is integral to the scientific constructions that are presented to the world.

A general principle, then, is to take 'methodological precautions' which ensure somehow that readers are aware of your own role in constructing what they are reading, of your own possible 'stake', and so on. Challenging the conventional researcher's pose of neutrality, Reinharz (1983) argued that researchers' attitudes should be fully discussed, and their values revealed and clearly located. This reflexive philosophy is a strong theme in feminist psychological research. Some texts include commentaries by the authors or peers after each section. As we shall see in Chapter 22, grounded theory and similar approaches recommend that researchers submit a diary of their thoughts as they gather data, analyse them and construct theory during their research project. They comment on their own attitudes and possible biases in coming to this or that conclusion or in proceeding in this or that way in the research process. Rather than footnotes, or doubts admitted to trusted colleagues in the pub, this material is seen as equivalent in importance to the raw, summarised and analysed data.

Some writers, as we shall also see in Chapter 22, also use the term 'reflexivity' to refer to a process of self-appraisal on the part of participants in research – for instance, those keeping long-term diaries or those engaged in forms of participative or collaborative research. Willig (2008) refers to both *personal reflexivity* – how our views and attitudes may have influenced the research and how conducting it may have changed us – and *epistemological reflexivity* – the ways in which the research question, design and analysis have constructed the findings, that is, ways in which the study could have been conducted differently and the implications of assumptions made during the research that bear upon the final interpretation and presentation of knowledge.

A feminist perspective

A powerful force within psychological research methods from at least the late 1970s onwards was the mounting of serious challenges to the traditional research paradigm from the point of view of the politics and ideology of the women's movement. Some would argue that a large part of the driving force behind the rapid 'normalisation' of qualitative research methods has been the appropriateness of them for feminist researchers in their particular areas of investigation and analysis.

It is now hard to believe that women did not until fairly recently, 'own' research into themselves. It is about as stunningly inappropriate that a male should author research on *The Psychology of Women* (I still have the Penguin paperback!) as that white psychologists should conduct studies on 'the Negro' (as, until fairly recently, did Richard Lynn; see Chapter 9). The early stages of women's research involved studies, under a conventional paradigm, which attacked traditional stereotypes of women's nature or deficits relative to men. Research literature now contains a fair amount of stereotype challenging and consciousness-raising work. This 'content-oriented' period also challenged the lack of female authorship and visible presence within the research community. There was a parallel with racism in that, where women had produced good scholarship, this had somehow become marginalised or obscured. The overwhelmingly male-oriented and male-dominated research community had edged such work to the periphery.

However, the content-oriented period just described, though continuing, led on to a realisation by women involved in the research process that the conventional methods they had been using to develop the content were themselves largely the product of a male research perspective and thought base. This is not to say that women would think, reason and conduct their research utterly differently, given the opportunity. It would fall back on old stereotypes to suggest that women didn't tend to use quantification or feel happy testing hypotheses statistically. The logic underlying chess, computer programming and the statistical tests in this book are in a major sense neutral. But they were 'owned' and promoted for so long by men that it is hardly surprising that when women came to assess their values in the research process they were alerted to methods and research relationships neglected or rejected as 'soft' up by male researchers, and felt by many female researchers to be more valid and more authentic in representing women's experience. The position is exemplified in Sue Wilkinson's *Feminist Social Psychology* (1986).

Masculinist research

Recognised as characteristic of a male approach to research and understanding the world are: preoccupation with quantifying variables; an emphasis on control, mastery and manipulation; a tendency to remain distant rather than be involved with the subjects of research; a preference for gadget-oriented research over naturalistic enquiry; competition; ego building. The contemporary recognition of power relations in the research context is very much a product of feminist psychology – see Paludi (2001), whose title is *The Psychology of Women*, but this time by a woman! She argues that the terms 'control', 'manipulate' and 'subject' are symptomatic of the 'masculinist' nature of the cool, distant, white-coated image of science that the main body of psychological research tried to project, particularly in the middle period of the twentieth century.

Keller (1986) argued persuasively that being objective has been associated with being male and that to be objective one must take up a distant, uninvolved position. Feminist researchers challenge this assumption, as do qualitative researchers in general, arguing that this stance projects a deceptive image of neutrality; it cashes in on the socially accepted view of science as a world of expert 'truth', where challenges to this method are somehow 'biased'. Hence, to get involved, to listen, to treat interaction with the research participant as an everyday social encounter, will 'contaminate' the research process and findings. Women will be very familiar with being told that their judgements are unsound because they permit emotion to cloud their perception of the situation!

As qualitative research often has to define itself against quantitative methods as the norm, so feminist researchers describe having to define their position against the norm of maleness (aggression is normal – females just happen to have 'less' of it). A background norm in sex and gender research has been to find differences. Hence, absent from the literature are the many studies actually carried out that don't find differences, plus those not attempted because it is not even suspected there might *be* differences (Tavris, 1993). The unwary psychology student will be aware only of 'sex-difference' research, not of sex-similarity findings.

A further related conceptual trap formed by this perspective is that by testing for significant difference, an impression of group difference is created. This is inherent in the decision to conduct research in this significance-testing manner. In Chapter 5, I tried to highlight in a technical way the grossly misleading ideas that can be generated by conducting a group difference study, particularly if such a study is given 'scientific' endorsement by being termed an 'experiment'. Even with a highly significant difference there can be a very large overlap of two populations (see Chapters 12 and 13). What is more important, the overlap or the difference? If we leave casual psychology users and readers with the impression that women do worse on X than men, simply because there is a small mean difference, will they then, in some future position of power, act upon the incorrect assumption that nearly all women are poor at X? It is not just feminist and anti-racist psychologists who should be aware of the biases inherent in different methodological approaches – we all have this duty and we should be particularly wary of apparently 'value-free', 'neutral' and 'universally applicable' methods and systems.

Contemporary qualitative methods

It was only in 1992 that Henwood and Pidgeon produced a seminal review paper 'Qualitative research and psychological theorising' in the *British Journal of Psychology*, which Richardson (1996: 5) described as 'one of the first papers on qualitative research methods to be published in a mainstream psychology journal in the UK'. Smith is now able to report 'an explosion of interest in qualitative psychology' (2008: 1) and how right this is. Since Henwood and Pidgeon's article was published, qualitative research has pretty well 'normalised' itself within psychology; public examination boards now include questions on qualitative methods, most psychology degree students will experience at least a module's worth, there is an increasing number of PhD theses using qualitative methods, and there is now a pretty wide range of qualitative articles in peer-reviewed journals to give guidance to students on how to approach their use. There is an imbalance in that the majority of these articles will be found in journals of applied psychology or in the more specialist series. However, 2004 saw the first volume of a new journal in the UK: *Qualitative Research in Psychology* (Hodder & Stoughton). In 1989, qualitative work in psychology was 'radical'; now degrees that qualify students for the Graduate Basis for Registration with the British Psychological Society are *required* to include some qualitative methods content.

It is of interest to see how the once more radical qualitative researchers cope with being normalised. As qualitative methods become part of standard university research methods, courses and public examination syllabuses, so tutors have to become competent in marking work and agreeing on standards. This issue has already caused some debate and several workshops and conferences. It brings into play the whole issue of reliability and validity in research, and we will look at this in more detail in Chapter 22. Whereas it is easy to see whether a 2 x 3 between subjects design has been appropriately implemented, variables well defined and results accurately and fairly analysed, it is relatively difficult to compare alternative interpretations of qualitative data (but see Madill *et al.* (2000) for comparisons of grounded theory accounts on the same data).

The very principles of those constructionist and reflexive approaches not based on scientific realism would predict different analyses by different researchers. How are we to know, then, that this is a good and valid piece of work? How are we to distinguish between good work and something that any non-psychologically trained journalist might produce? What, indeed, are the criteria for validity if the conventional concept of validity is discarded? Yardley (2008) describes the mayhem encountered at a qualitative conference where apparently, because the constructionist perspective sees every view as equally valid, every paper was accepted and researchers were giving talks in corridors. She describes the impossibility of knowing which talk was worth going to. She then presents a sound chapter on ways of establishing qualitative research validity. A problem is that all the methods she presents are by no means generally accepted as *the* paradigm for validity. We return to this issue in Chapter 22.

The issue of acceptable validity is important for students wishing to conduct a qualitative project because they want to be confident that they will know what to do, and will be fairly assessed, before starting out. It is disconcerting for them to discover that there is not one qualitative approach or paradigm but several, most differing from the rest on their particular take on relevant and valid research. The perspective from some of the approaches is that it would be contrary to their philosophy of research to draw up criteria for quality and validity or even for marking and deciding upon 'good' work. I think it would be sound advice to the student contemplating a qualitative research project to enquire which sorts of qualitative method their supervisor specialises in, to thoroughly discuss the main elements of the approach and even to ask for some kind of checklist that runs through the favoured criteria for validity and good quality associated with this approach as far as the supervisor is concerned.

The debate about qualitative and quantitative methods will probably intensify and move on to new territories before qualitative methods are fully integrated into mainstream psychological research methodology, but they have come a long way fast. It is to be hoped that the climate in which the issues are debated, especially (for the student's sake) those concerning the validity and integrity of qualitative research reports, will be less adversarial than it has often been over the past two decades. Cooperation and mutual understanding may just lead us all on to a constructive and profitable synthesis.

Recommended further reading

There is a comprehensive list of more practically oriented texts at the end of Chapter 22. The texts listed below are those that do not appear there and are largely theoretical.

Banister, P., Burman, E., Parker, I., Taylor, M. and Tindall, C. (2002) *Qualitative methods in psychology: a research guide.* Buckingham: Open University Press.

Corbin, J. and Strauss, A. (2008) *Basics of qualitative research: techniques and procedures for developing grounded theory.* London: Sage.

Edwards, D. and Potter, J. (1992) *Discursive psychology.* London: Sage.

Forshaw, M.J. (2007) Free qualitative research from the shackles of method. *The Psychologist, 20,* 8, 478–9.

Henwood, K. and Pidgeon, N. (1992) Qualitative research and psychological theorising. *British Journal of Psychology, 83,* 97–111.

Morris, P.E. and Sykes, R.N. (eds) *Practical aspects of memory*. London: Academic Press.

Parker, I. (2002) *Critical discursive psychology*. Basingstoke: Palgrave Macmillan.

Smith, J.A., Harré, R. and Van Langenhove, L. (eds) (1995) *Rethinking methods in psychology*. London: Sage.

Tavris, C. (1999) *The mis-measure of woman*. Gloucester, MA: Peter Smith.

The Psychologist (1995) Special Issue on Qualitative Methods, *8*, 3, 115–18.

Unger, R. and Crawford, M. (2003) *Women and gender: a feminist psychology*. New York: McGraw-Hill.

Ussher, J.M. (1991) *Women's madness: misogyny or mental illness?* London: Harvester Wheatsheaf.

Wilkinson, S. (1986) *Feminist social psychology*. Milton Keynes: Open University Press.

Answer to exercise on p. 229

qt = quantitative   ql = qualitative

1	2	3	4	5	6	7	8	9	10	11	12	13	14	15	16	17	18	19	20	21	22	23	24	25	26	27	28
ql	qt	ql	qt	ql	qt	qt	ql	ql	qt	qt	qt	qt	qt	qt	qt	ql	qt	ql	qt	ql	ql	qt	ql	qt	ql	ql	qt

Glossary

Action research	Practical intervention in everyday situations, often organisations, using applied psychology to produce change and monitor results
Collaborative research	Research in which participants are fully involved to the extent of organising their own processes of research and change. Researcher as consultant
Constant comparative analysis	Regular checking of the emergent category system (in GT) with raw data and sub-categories in order to rearrange and produce the tightest fit
Constructivism	Theory holding knowledge to be relative and 'facts' to be social constructions, not permanent realities
Conversation analysis	Approach that views talk between people as a system of speech acts; talk is analysed in terms of the techniques people use in interaction
Cooperative enquiry	Investigation involving researcher and participants working together
Discourse analysis	Qualitative analysis of interactive speech, which assumes people use language to construct the world as they see it, and according to context and interests; talk is not evidence of internal psychological processes
Emergent theory	Theory that emerges from data as they are analysed; not based on prior research literature

Endogenous research	Research involving group members in researching their own customs and organisational norms
Ethnography	Intense study of a culture from within
Feminist psychology	Emphasis on women's perspectives and on research methods appropriate to investigations that integrate gender politics
Grounded theory	Theory driving the analysis of qualitative data in which patterns emerge from the data and are not imposed on them before they are gathered
Interpretive phenomenological analysis	Approach that attempts to describe an individual's experiences from their own perspective as closely as possible, but recognises the interpretive influence of the researcher on the research product
Negative case analysis	Process of seeking contradictions to emergent categories or theory in order to adjust category system to incorporate and explain more of the data
Paradigm	A prevailing agreed system of scientific thinking and behaviour within which research is conducted
Participative research	Research in which participants are substantially involved in the investigative process as active enquirers
Purposive sampling	Non-random sampling of individuals likely to be able to make a significant contribution to the data collection for a qualitative project
Realism	Theory of knowledge holding that there is a unitary reality in the world that can be discovered using the appropriate investigative methods
Reflexivity	Researchers' recognition that their personal perspective constructs the research interpretation. Researchers' position and potential influence may be discussed in qualitative articles, along with possible alternative constructions of findings
Relativism	Theory of knowledge holding that objective facts are an illusion and that knowledge is constructed by each individual through a unique personal framework
Saturation	Point in GT work where additional data make only trivial contributions and cannot alter the emerged framework of categories and themes
Thematic analysis	General analysis of qualitative data into themes. Not allied to any epistemological position and may also be used in qualitative or hypothesis testing work
Theoretical sampling	Use of purposive sampling (see above) to find data that might support or contradict an emergent explanatory framework

Statistics – organising the data

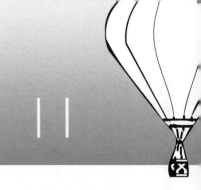

- Precision in research requires quantitative measurement, which is carried out at various *levels of measurement*.
- A distinction is made between *categorical* variables, where data points are placed into qualitatively different categories, and *measured* variables, where data points appear along a scale, are separated from one another and where the scale can be *discrete* or *continuous*. The traditional measurement levels of *nominal*, *ordinal*, *interval* and *ratio* are defined.
- *Nominal* level is simple classification. At *ordinal* level, cases are ranked or ordered. *Interval* scales should use equal intervals. *Ratio* scales are interval but include a real zero and relative proportions on the scale map to physical reality.
- Attempts are made to convert many psychological scales to interval level using *standardisation*. Many scales used in psychology can be called *plastic* or *quasi-interval scales* because numerically equal appearing intervals on the scale do not measure equal amounts of a construct.
- Higher levels of measurement give more information about the original data or phenomenon measured. Level of measurement limits choice in treatment of data, especially in terms of the statistical significance tests that may legitimately be carried out.
- *Descriptive* statistics are summaries of gathered data. *Sample* statistics usually include a measure of *central tendency* (*mean*, *median* or *mode*) and a measure of *dispersion* (*variation ratio*, *range*, *semi-interquartile range*, *mean deviation*, *standard deviation* or *variance*, the last two being common for interval-level data; variance is simply the square of the standard deviation). The appropriateness of the statistical description selected depends upon the *level of measurement* of the data.
- *SPSS* is introduced and instructions given for entering data. Procedures are then outlined for finding descriptive statistics.

Measuring things

How data arrive

In this chapter we move carefully into the world of numbers and describing measurements and findings in numerical terms – that is, using *statistics*. As with other concepts in this book, many of the ideas here will be known to you or, at least, you will find that you have used the concepts in your life already many times but perhaps not in a formal way. I will attempt throughout to stick closely to the everyday experience of statistical things (for instance, working out your average shopping bill or estimating whether we've had a particularly rainy month).

The reason you need to be familiar with statistics in psychology is that it is, qualitative objections aside, broadly an empirical science. In studying psychology you will encounter many studies that compare sets of data. You will probably have to work on data you have gathered yourself in practical investigations. You will need to be able to present your findings to a reader in a clear but economical style. You also need to make decisions about whether you have results that support your claims. For instance, we have already seen (in Chapter 3) that more people dropped their litter when others had already done so. How do we know whether the extra amounts dropped are sufficient to rule out simple chance variation? People are apparently more worried after being exposed to negative news bulletins (Chapter 4). How should we measure 'worry' numerically? Without some sort of measurement of such states it is difficult to see how we could ever verify these typical psychological claims. To progress with this notion we need to show that 'worry' scores after negative news are a lot higher than the scores after a positive bulletin.

In this first section of the chapter, before we deal with organising and analysing quantitative data, we start out by simply looking at the different ways in which we can gather data. That is, the different *scales* that might have been used to acquire the raw data with which we start assessing results. RAW DATA are the unprocessed data gathered directly from participants (e.g. 'yes' or 'no'; words recalled; number of them) before they are organised or treated statistically. These data do not appear in a research report but summaries of them must. For instance, you might report the average number of words recalled by participants in an experimental group. You might report the frequencies of people saying 'yes' and 'no'. Before we can decide how the raw data are best summarised we need to decide what *kind* of data we have.

Starting out on measures

The previous chapter looked at ways in which quantitative methods can fall short of giving realistic or 'rich' information. We also looked at theoretical objections to basing psychology on numerical measurement. The case *for* numerical measurement, as a part of psychological research, is simply that many things *can* be measured and people (who may be vehemently opposed to counting and measuring, who may hate maths) actually do use quantitative judgements in their everyday conversations. Take for instance:

- Helen is more artistic than Clare.

- George is a contemplative type, whereas Rick is practical, energetic and impulsive.

It may appear that a difference of *quality*, such as that expressed about George, does not need numerical values to confirm it, but how exactly do we know Rick is 'energetic' or 'impulsive'? We must be comparing some things he does (how strongly and how often) with their occurrence in others. We must define what *counts* as energetic and impulsive, and show that Rick is like this more often or to a greater degree than is George. Hence, to demonstrate a difference, we would need some numerical measure or at least a *count* of similar behaviour patterns displayed by Rick and George. What many people feel uncomfortable about in psychological measurement is the *crudity* of the measures and the *transparency* of the attempt. Nevertheless, it is hard to see how someone could claim that Rick is more energetic or more impulsive, or even that George falls into a 'contemplative' category, without some *description* that would come close to measurement, or at least to *categorising*.

Categorical and measured variables

Let's follow up that last point and introduce two major types of variable that can produce two different forms of data – *categorical* and *measured*. Suppose your friend Karen says:

Lucy is a Pisces, extremely extroverted and six foot tall.

Karen has introduced three variables on which she has assessed Lucy. The first is a *category system* – people fall into one category or another and they can't be placed in between (forgetting, for now, all that stuff about 'cusps'!). You can't be half a Pisces or 2.7 Aries, in the same way as you can't have voted 0.7 Labour. You may not fully agree with the government's policies but the voting system forces you to choose either them or another party. In these cases, the set of star signs or political parties would be called a CATEGORICAL VARIABLE. It is useful to call any other sort of variable that operates above the level of mere categorising a MEASURED VARIABLE. This is the sort of scale Karen used for her second two measures. She has not measured extroversion on a quantified scale but she has placed Lucy as 'more extreme' than many other people. She must therefore have some crude concept of *degree* of extroversion by which people can be separated. On the last measure, of course, there is no argument (apart from the issue of going metric!). Feet and inches are divisions on a measured variable which is a publicly agreed, standardised and therefore checkable scale of measurement.

In very many experimental studies the independent variable is categorical and the dependent variable is a measured variable. Have a look at Table 11.1 which shows this distinction for several of the experiments we have discussed so far in this book. Cover up columns 2 and 4 if you wish to test yourself. Notice that the only categorical dependent variable in the table is the dropping or not of the leaflet in the Cialdini *et al.* study and that, in this study, the independent variable was *measured*. However, for data analysis purposes, as will be explained, we can *treat it* as categorical, as did Cialdini *et al.*

Independent variable	Categorical/ measured	Dependent variable	Categorical/ measured
Good or bad news bulletin	categorical	Worry score	measured
Complex or simple visual pattern	categorical	Number of seconds gazed at	measured
Perform in front of audience or alone	categorical	Number of errors made	measured
Number of pieces of litter already on ground	measured (but see text)	Dropped leaflet or not	categorical

Table 11.1 Level of measurement of several independent variables and dependent variables

A quick introduction to different levels of measurement

When we measure a psychological construct, such as extroversion or self-esteem, and when we measure physical variables such as time, speed or weight, we need to consider the *level* at which the measurement is made. This is usually a tricky area for students to grasp, so, before going into details, let's introduce the levels through an imaginary but simple classroom scenario. Suppose it's a snowy day and only eight people have turned up for your psychology class. Your tutor decides to abandon plans for a 20-participant experiment and decides on a quick demonstration of *levels of measurement* instead. She instructs you to divide into two groups, one 'short people' and the other 'tall people'. After some shuffling around, two groups are formed (see the bottom of Figure 11.1). Suppose you are in the tall group. If this is all the information I have about you then I can't

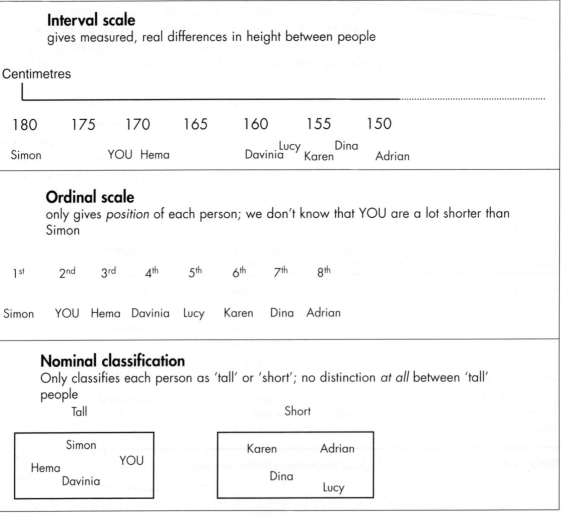

Figure 11.1 Levels of measurement and information obtained

separate you from the other three people in your group. All four get the *equal* value 'tall'. We have used a simple categorical variable. The categorisation into 'short' and 'tall' uses a form of measurement scale known as NOMINAL; we will investigate that term further in a few moments. Some people think that the 'nominal scale' is not a scale at all since it involves categorising rather than 'measuring' *along* a scale. We shall absorb that point and move on, recognising that 'nominal scale' can be short for 'use of a categorical classification system'.

Your tutor now asks you to get into a line in *order* of height. This causes some more shuffling and a couple of back-to-back contests before the line is finally formed (see the middle of Figure 11.1). Your position in this line is second, next to the tallest person. When we put things in order we use *ranks* (first, second, etc.) and when we do this we are using an ORDINAL level of measurement. When we were using only the nominal scale for information we had no way to separate members of the 'tall' group from one another. However, now we know what position or rank you occupy in the group, relative to the rest. We are now measuring along a scale, in that there is one, and only one, order in which the students' heights can be arranged. We are using a *measured variable* – height – but the scale is rather crude. It does not take into account the fact that you are *way* below the first person in the line (Simon) but only a smidgin above the third (Hema). The ordinal scale gives us more information than the nominal, but not the most we *could* have.

To get the most subtle measure of class height we need a tape measure or wall chart. Of course the tutor has these and we now produce the familiar measurement of height in feet and inches (or centimetres), which is an example of an INTERVAL scale (and also a *ratio* scale – to be explained later). Now we can say, accurately, whether the tallest person is a little above you or tends to gather snow on top (see the top of Figure 11.1). We can also compare you to the *general* measure of height used everywhere else. We can tell whether you are tall relative to the general population. That is, the measurement scale is *standardised*.

The nominal level of measurement

The nominal level of measurement refers to data that are categorical. For some differences of quality we do not need numbers in order to distinguish one item from another. For instance:

- male and female
- red, green and blue objects
- straight hair, wavy hair, curly hair.

Here we simply compare each item with some learned concept – what counts as green, fully straight hair or a male. On occasion we may count number of features present before categorising, for instance when deciding whether to categorise a car as 'luxury' – how many luxury features does it need to have? In psychological research, participants might be categorised into 'figure dependent' or 'figure independent' categories, based on the number of 'embedded figures' they can detect in five minutes.

What matters with categorisation, however, is that we must be able to place each item or person in just one category, for purposes of comparison. We might decide to categorise people as 'energetic', 'average' and 'slow', for instance. A person is either male or female and can't, when we use a nominal system, be included in both categories because he/she is a bit of both. Difficulties may arise in categorising a person as smoker or non-smoker, extrovert or introvert, optimist or pessimist, but nominal categories are *separated groups*. People and things are bunched together on the basis of a common feature – Jason is not the same as Jonathan but they have curly hair in common. All irrelevant differences are ignored for the measurement purpose at hand.

If we conducted a survey that investigated use of the college refectory, we might count the number of people using it and categorise these according to their role (student, teacher, non-teaching staff etc.). Table 11.2 shows the frequencies we might obtain if we recorded the role of several hundred people. Note that we can *code* (e.g. 'student' = 1; 'teacher' = 2) and that we *have* to do this if we are entering data into SPSS (see p. 275). The coding of these roles shows us the origin of the term 'nominal' (i.e. relating to names) – the numbers or codes given to the categories here are only *names*. Code '1' (students) is not half of code '2' (teaching staff) or in any way prior to or less than the others in quantity. The numbers are simply convenient but arbitrary *labels* for identifying each category of person. In the same way, numbers on football players' backs denote the player, not quantities. Likewise, your student number or exam number is also just a 'name' made up of numbers, which computers adore.

Code	Role	Frequency
1	Student	245
2	Teacher	18
3	Non-teaching staff	33
4	Visitor	9
5	Other	3
Total		308

Table 11.2 Frequencies of roles of people using a college refectory

Data such as those in column 3 of Table 11.2 are known as FREQUENCIES or FREQUENCY DATA. They represent the number of times an event in each category occurred, e.g. the number of events given code 1. These numbers are being used to count, they *do* stand for quantities and are known as *cardinal numbers*. Some typical examples of data gathered in categories at a nominal level are given in Table 11.3.

Variable	Categories
Type of children's play	Non-play Solitary Associative Parallel Cooperative
Type of pet owned	Dog Cat Guinea pig Rabbit Horse Bird Other
Ethnicity	Black White Asian Other
Marital status	Single Married Cohabiting Separated Divorced

Table 11.3 Typical categorical variables

Ordinal level of measurement

Ordinal numbers do not represent quantities or counts; they represent *rank position* in a group. They are the positions: first, second, third and so on, in a race or test. They do not tell us how far ahead the winner was from the second placed. They tell us nothing at all about distances between positions. It may be annoying to be beaten by one-tenth of a second in a cycle race when you and the leader were ten kilometres ahead of the rest of the bunch, but what goes on your record is just 'second'. To the horserace punter it doesn't matter by what margin Golden Girl won – it won! In Figure 11.1 we can see that Simon is a lot taller than YOU but the ordinal scale hides this fact.

How to rank data

Giving ranks to scores or values obtained in research is very easy but must be done in a precise, conventional manner, otherwise the various significance tests based on ranks will give misleading results should you calculate them by hand. Suppose we have to rank the scores of eight people on a general knowledge test, as shown in Table 11.4.

Person	Score	Rank of Score
1	18	5.5
2	25	7
3	14	1
4	18	5.5
5	15	3
6	15	3
7	15	3
8	29	8

Table 11.4 An example of ranking – interval-level data changed to ordinal-level data

The score of 14 is lowest and gets the rank 1. In competitions we usually give the winner rank '1' but in statistics it is less confusing to give low ranks to low values. Persons five, six and seven 'share' the next three ranks (of 2nd, 3rd and 4th). In sport we might say 'equal second', but in statistical ranking we take the *median* value (see p. 265) of the ranks they share. If the number is odd, this is just the *middle* value. From 2 3 4 the middle value is 3. If the number is even we take the number midway between the two middle ranks shared. Persons one and four share the ranks 5 and 6. The point midway between these is 5.5. If four people shared 6 7 8 9, the rank given to each would be 7.5.

In this example we have converted data that were at a higher, more informative level (interval data, which we will discuss below), into *ordinal-level* data. The *scores* are interval level; the *ranks* are ordinal.

Interval level of measurement

An interval scale uses *equal units*. Time is measured in equal units, so if you came second in a bicycle race by a whisker and were a good ten minutes ahead of the bunch, this scale will deliver that information to your friends, whereas the ordinal scale would not. Interval scales measure the same amounts for the same scale units. The distance between three feet and four feet is the same as that between five feet and six feet. However, will this apply to *psychological* scales? If these were interval scales then it ought to be true that:

- two children scoring 5 and 8 respectively on an achievement scale are as far apart in motivation to achieve as two children scoring 9 and 12

- Jane, whose IQ is 100, is as far ahead of John (IQ 80) in intelligence as Jackie (IQ 120) is ahead of Jane.

In practice, it is hard to believe that most psychological measures operate in this seemingly accurate and scientific manner. However, it is the job of psychometrists to ensure that scales approach this criterion as closely as possible. It should be that intervals on a good test operate like intervals on the publicly accurate measures we are used to in everyday life – rulers, scales, air pumps, thermometers – where equal intervals represent equal changes in the phenomenon that is measured. Test creators attempt to design scales that produce a *normal distribution* (see p. 308) of scores when administered to a large sample of the population, so that the test produces the same *proportions* of people along the points of a scale as would any human physical measure.

Numbers used as measures can give an impression of what is in fact spurious accuracy. Suppose you receive 60 for your essay while Tim gets 50 and Sean gets 40. This does not mean that the difference between Tim's and Sean's essays is equal to the difference between yours and Tim's. In UK higher education establishments, essays are very often graded on a time-honoured but actually rather peculiar scale that has a wider area for failed work – 0–40 – than it does for the whole range from barely passable to the start of the first-class category, that is: 40–70. On this sort of scale, even where tutors standardise very carefully, it would be safer to assume that the grades are really on an *ordinal* scale. It would probably be uncontroversial to claim that your essay is *better* than Tim's and that Tim's is better than Sean's but *not* by the same 'amount'.

In the same way, although the temperature scale certainly uses equal intervals (based on expansion of mercury, for instance), the *experience* of heat changes would be better treated as an ordinal measure. An increase of 3° in a room originally at 14° will be noticed as more of a change than the same increase from 33°. Many psychological measures behave in a way that prompted Wright (1976) to call them 'plastic interval' scales and some people call them QUASI-INTERVAL SCALES. For instance, on an attitude item, it might well take a bigger shift for someone to move from 'agree' to 'strongly agree' than from 'undecided' to 'agree'. Intervals along the scale are not equal, yet the familiarity of numbers can induce us to treat them as such. A further example is those quickly invented measures that ask you: 'On a scale of 0 to 10, please state how anxious you tend to feel before exams; 0 is not anxious and 10 is extremely anxious.'

So what sort of scale were my questionnaire data on then?

As a general rule of thumb, if you are using a published psychological scale then you can treat the data it produces as being at interval level. However, wherever data are gathered on an unstandardised, invented scale of human judgement – such as rating an observed aggressive act on a scale of 1 to 10, or adding up response codes to several Likert-type items where you have invented these yourself and have not tested for reliability – it would be safer to treat the data as ordinal, that is, convert the scores to ranks. This means that you use different *descriptive statistics* to summarise your data (see pp. 261–74) and different significance tests to analyse your data for differences or correlations – see Chapter 14. Your data are treated as ranked but you will not usually have to calculate the ranks – a computer programme such as SPSS will do this for you.

Ratio level of measurement

30°C is not twice as hot as 15°C, even though these are values on a truly interval scale. Although the *number* 30 is twice 15, on a Fahrenheit scale the temperatures represented by these numbers would be 86°F and 59°F, and the second is now no longer half of the first. This is simply because both these temperature scales do not start from an *absolute zero* point. Similarly, it makes no sense to say that a person with an IQ of 120 is twice as intelligent as a person with 60, since IQ scales are not calibrated from a true zero point, though they are treated as interval measures. RATIO SCALES are interval-type scales that *do* start from a real zero point and on these scales ratios of values *do* make sense – six pounds is twice three pounds in the absolute sense, otherwise we couldn't argue with a shopkeeper over short weight. Typical ratio scales are all the measures of physical quantities we are familiar with, including weight, length, time, pressure and so on. In practice, as a student of psychology, you can ignore, unless raised in your syllabus content, the concept of ratio data. For the purposes of choosing an appropriate statistical test (Chapter 21), you need only be able to decide that your data are *at least* at an interval scale of measurement.

Comparison of the different levels

The interval/ratio levels in Table 11.5 give us the greatest amount of information about people's positions in a population or sample. On a nominal (or categorical) level, each person simply gets a category name or code, and we only know how many people were in each category. On an ordinal level of measurement each person gets a rank, and we only know who was ahead of or behind whom. On interval and ratio scales we know the number of scale points between each position and we can compare these *distances* between points meaningfully. Some typical measures at each level are given in Table 11.6.

Nominal	*Only* tells us that you are in one category, not another
Ordinal	Tells us your position in a group but *not* the distance between you and any other person in the group
Interval	Tells us how many intervals on the scale each person is from anyone else
Ratio	Same as interval but we can treat *ratios* of values meaningfully

Table 11.5 Comparison of different levels of measurement

Overall type	Level	Examples
Categorical	Nominal	Gender: male/female
		Stopped at amber/stopped at red/jumped red
Measured	Ordinal	Position in race
		Foods placed in order of preference
	Interval	Gender orientation scale (score on 'masculinity' and/or 'femininity')
		Number of words recalled correctly
		Verbal intelligence score

Table 11.6 Typical measures at each level

How important is it to know about different levels of measurement?

At this point the reader may start to feel 'Are we fussing over obscure academic concepts here?' I assure you we're not, otherwise we certainly wouldn't bother. You will need to think about levels of measurement before selecting an appropriate significance test for analysis – see Chapter 21. However, if you do not pay attention to data levels when *setting up* your measures for an investigation you may find yourself in all sorts of trouble when you come to attempt that analysis.

Why? Let's go back to the salutary tale concerning a student's project – the case of the questionnaire item about responsibility for an attack on a woman (p. 187). Here, the student chose a *dichotomous* categorical variable measure (i.e. one with only two fixed alternatives). Participants had to decide whether the man or the woman 'was more responsible for the attack'. Because the question was set in this way, the form of the data was already determined as categorical – the response was 'man' or 'woman' – and the student could do nothing with the rather useless data gathered. All of the participants, of course, saw the man as *more* responsible so she could not show that participants held the woman more responsible if she wore revealing clothing than if she didn't. No increase in score was possible. Had the question been altered to asking for *degree* of responsibility along a 1–10-point scale, or on a visual analogue scale (see p. 181), the variable would then have become a *measured* one and the gathered data would be treated as ordinal or even interval. This, in turn, would have led to an analysis where a subtle *increase* in attribution of responsibility could have been revealed under statistical analysis. As it was, the scale chosen completely prevented this possibility. (In fact, the student was lucky enough to be able to go back later and ask most of her participants again – but this was not really the most unbiased way to obtain her measures!)

Changing data from one level to another – you can only go downwards!

The basic problem just discussed was that data originally collected at one level *cannot* be elevated to a higher level. Nominal-level data cannot be made, after collection, into ordinal or interval-level data so you must be careful about the measure you use if your goal is, for instance, to demonstrate a correlation or look at average score differences between groups. However, the reverse process of *reducing* data from a higher level in order to treat them at a lower level is very common. In Table

11.4, scores for general knowledge were reduced from interval-level data to ordinal level. We can also reduce data all the way from interval level to nominal level, that is into categories. Suppose we assess people for anxiety by counting the number of anxiety indicators they display. This anxiety indicators score (let's call it AI) is on an interval scale. However, we may only want to identify two groups of people – high anxiety and low anxiety – in order to test a hypothesis that those with higher anxiety have lower self-esteem. We can divide the anxiety scores into two groups by taking the median or central value (see below) and then we would have, for each individual, only a category label (high or low) rather than the AI score we started out with (see Figure 11.2).

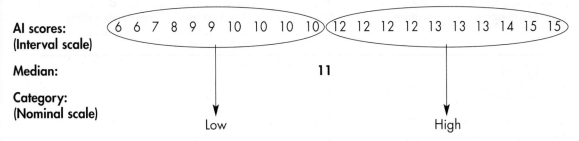

AI scores:
(Interval scale)

Median: 11

Category:
(Nominal scale)

Low   High

Figure 11.2 Values on interval scale reduced to nominal by median split method

Continuous and discrete scales of measurement

A further division of scales is possible, into DISCRETE or CONTINUOUS. On *discrete* scales each point is entirely separate from the next; there are no real points in between. It is not possible to have two and a half children, for instance. The *average* of 2.4 children does not imply that anyone could ever have two and a bit children! In a memory experiment you can only recall a discrete number of words, perhaps 13 out of 20. On *continuous* scales there is no limit to the sub-divisions of points that are possible and meaningful, though there will be limits in practice, depending on the type of measuring instrument used, e.g. down to millimetres on a household ruler for measuring the length of a piece of wood. It is theoretically possible to measure your height to the nearest thousandth of a millimetre; technically this might be difficult and, in practice, is hardly likely to be useful. Interval and ratio scales can be either continuous or discrete. Nominal categories can only be discrete. Ordinal scales generally have .5 as the smallest division.

We measure to intervals, not points

It is important to note that with a truly interval scale we avoid the issue of measuring to the nearest thousandth of a millimetre or whatever by using *intervals*. In practice, when we use a tape measure and say someone is 175cm tall we can only truthfully assert that they are in a certain interval and the limits of this are determined by our tape measure or by convenience. If we have *decided* not to include half centimetres then we are actually claiming that the person is between 174.5 and 175.5cm tall. If we *do* use half-centimetres then we can claim that they are between 174.75 and 175.25cm and so on, depending on the accuracy we choose or are limited to.

1 When judges give their marks in an ice-skating contest for style and presentation, at what level of measurement is it safest to treat their data?

2 A set of surgical records classifies patients as 'chronic', 'acute' or 'not yet classified'. What level of measurement is being used?

3 At what level are the measurements in Table 11.7 (a, b, c and d) below being made? Choose from nominal, ordinal, interval or ratio.

Premiership	a Position	b Pts	Area c 1 = London 2 = Northern 3 = Southern	d Popularity rating (fictitious)
Arsenal	1	56	1	1
Manchester	2	50	2	8
Newcastle	3	48	2	3
Chelsea	4	45	1	4
Everton	5	45	2	5
Liverpool	6	42	2	2
Southampton	7	39	3	6
Charlton	8	39	1	7

Table 11.7 Premiership table (top)

4 Your sister argues that, since she came top in each of the three maths tests held in her class this year, she must be *far* better than all the other pupils. What might you point out to her? (Would you dare?)

5 Think of three ways to measure driving ability, one using nominal-level data, one ordinal and one interval/ratio.

6 Can you change the data in Table 11.8 first to ordinal level, then to nominal level? The blank tables are for you to fill in. Hint: for ordinal level, treat all the values as *one* group. For nominal, try a median split – see p. 257.

a) Time taken to read (seconds)		b) Ordinal level		c) Nominal level
Consistent story	Inconsistent story	Consistent story	Inconsistent story	
127	138			
136	154			
104	138			
111	117			
152	167			
111	117			
127	135			
138	149			
145	151			
Median of all times = 137				

Table 11.8 Reading times for exercise 6

7 Below are several methods for measuring dependent variables. For each measure decide what level of measurement is being used. Choose from *Nominal, Ordinal, Interval* or *Ratio*. Remember that human judgements used as measures are better treated as ordinal level data.

   (a) People are interviewed in the street and, on the basis of their replies, are recorded as: pro-hanging, undecided, or anti-hanging.

   (b) Stress questionnaire for which various occupational norms have been established.

   (c) Participants' estimates of various line lengths.

   (d) Time taken to sort cards into categories.

   (e) People's choice of: the *Sun*, *The Times* or the *Guardian*.

   (f) Participants' sense of self-worth, estimated on a scale of 1–10.

   (g) Critical life events given positions 1–10 according to their perceived importance to each participant.

Answers

1 Ordinal.

2 Nominal.

3 (a) Ordinal.

   (b) Ratio.

   (c) Nominal.

   (d) Interval-like but safer treated as ordinal.

4 'Top' is a measure on an ordinal scale. We don't know how far ahead of the others she was.

5 Examples: nominal – did/didn't hit kerb; ordinal – positions after exercise on smoothness; interval/ratio – measure speed in race.

6

Ordinal level			Nominal level	
Consistent	Inconsistent		Consistent	Inconsistent
6.5	11	**Above median** 3		6
9	17	**Below median** 6		3
1	11			
2.5	4.5			
16	18			
2.5	4.5			
6.5	8			
11	14			
13	15			

7 (a) Nominal.

   (b) Interval (because standardised).

   (c) Interval-like but unstandardised human judgement.

   (d) Ratio.

   (e) Nominal.

   (f) Interval-like but unstandardised human judgement.

   (g) Ordinal.

Summarising data – statistics are a selection

In this section, and in Chapter 12, we are looking simply at the ways in which statistical information can be summarised and presented to a reader. Most research studies gather far too much information for every item to be presented, so statistical procedures start by organising the data into a reasonable *summary*. 'Reasonable' here means fair, useful and not misleading. When a survey of political attitude is conducted or an experiment is run on 35 participants, we end up with a DATA SET. This is the collection of individual scores on each item of the attitude questionnaire or the scores of the experimental participants on the dependent variable(s). These are the *raw data* gathered in the study, which need to be summarised and analysed. Tables 11.2, 11.9, 11.10 and 11.11 show *data sets*, though the *raw data* for Table 11.2 and Table 11.11 would *originally* have been the tallies taken as cases were counted.

When we summarise a data set it must be noted immediately that the very act of summarising inevitably introduces distortions. If we present only averages, for instance, we immediately camouflage any *range* or variation among people's scores. It is a well-known statistical joke that the average person has one testicle! Politicians and companies, among others, are renowned for presenting data in the best possible light *for them* rather than for the reader to make their own judgements. However, *a psychologist should be looking at the best way to present data only in terms of what gives the clearest, least ambiguous summary of what was found in a research study.* What is more, the raw data set should be kept available for any other researchers to query and perhaps look at in a different, selective way in order to argue against some of the original researcher's initial conclusions. This is what companies very often do *not* do, and politicians would very often be *reluctant* to do!

But I can't do sums!

As with many ideas in this book, the things we will study are based on everyday common-sense notions you have undoubtedly used before. Even if you hate maths, dread statistics and have never done any formal work in this area, you have undoubtedly made statistical descriptions many times in your life without necessarily being aware of it. You may believe that only clever, numerically minded people do this sort of thing, but consider this. Imagine you have just come home from your first session at a large evening lecture and I ask you what sort of age are your class colleagues. You would not proceed to tell me the exact age of each class member. This could take far too long. You'd be likely to say something like 'Well, most people in the class are around 25 years old but there are a couple of teenagers and one or two are over 40.' You have in fact summarised the class ages statistically, albeit rather loosely. First, you gave me a rough *average*, the *typical* age in the group, then you gave me an idea of the actual *variation* from this typical age present in the group. These two concepts are absolutely *fundamental* to statistical description of measured data. Here we have an example of going from concepts that *naturally* occur to you in everyday life to a more formalised version of the same thing for statistical purposes, using the following terms.

- CENTRAL TENDENCY – This in some way refers to the most central or typical value of a data set with different interpretations of the sense of 'central'. In the example above you gave me the value 25 for this. In normal language, central tendency is better and more loosely known as 'the average'. In statistical description, though, we have to be more precise about just what sort of average we mean.

- DISPERSION – This is a measure of the extent to which all the values in a set tend to vary around the central or typical value. This is a vital concept in statistics and appears in many other operations. It can be exemplified by considering the following situation.

Table 11.9 shows scores on an attitude to fox-hunting scale for seven people from Dunton Parva, a rural community with a history of fox hunting, and seven from Slumditch, a deprived area of a large city. The *average* for each group is identical but look at the *variation* within each group. It looks like the people of Dunton Parva are quite divided whereas the people of Slumditch don't seem to have strong opinions either way – why should they, you don't get many fox hunts in Slumditch! Figure 11.3 shows the relative size of the two variations or dispersions.

	Respondents' attitude scores							Mean
Dunton Parva	38	12	36	8	25	34	9	23.1
Slumditch	19	27	23	24	21	22	26	23.1

Table 11.9 Attitude to fox-hunting scores in Dunton Parva and Slumditch

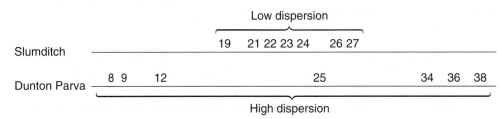

Figure 11.3 Different sizes of dispersion for the fox hunting scores

As a further example of dispersion differences, have a look at the data in Table 11.10. Overall, the girls speak just about twice the amount that boys do. We would see this if we calculated the *average* for each group. Not only this, the boys' times *vary* widely compared with the girls' times, from as little as five seconds to nearly the highest girl's time.

Girls	Boys
332	132
345	34
289	5
503	237
367	450

Table 11.10 Girls' and boys' talking times (in seconds) during 10 minutes' observation

Measures of central tendency

Millions of Brits have more than the average number of legs!!

This shock-horror headline is in fact true! Not everyone is fortunate enough to have two legs. A few people have one or none. Hence the overall *mean* average would be around 1.999. . . each. The conclusion is daft only because the wrong type of central tendency measure has been used. The *mode* would be far more appropriate and to find out why read on.

The mean

In normal language we use the term 'average' for what is technically known as the ARITHMETIC MEAN. There are other means, but this term is usually shortened to just 'the mean'. It is what we get when we add up all the values in a data set and then divide by the total *number* of values. Hence, if five people took 5, 2, 12, 1 and 10 seconds to solve an anagram, the mean time taken is:

$$\frac{5+2+12+1+10}{5} = \frac{30}{5} = 6 \text{ seconds}$$

The mean has the particular property of being the exact mid-point of all the combined values. It acts rather like the fulcrum of a balance as I hope Figure 11.4 will demonstrate. If you balance equal weights on a pivoted 12-inch ruler at the points marked 1, 2, 5, 10 and 12 (our set of data points above) you will find that the ruler balances at the point designated by our mean, i.e. 6.

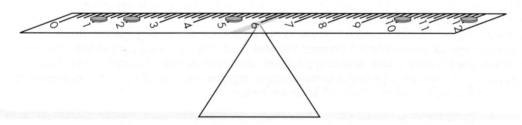

Figure 11.4 The mean as a central, balancing point among values

Finding the mean

The formula for calculating the mean is: $\bar{x} = \dfrac{\sum x}{N}$

The symbol for the mean of a sample is: $\bar{x}$ (you can call this 'x bar')

The symbol used to denote the mean of a *population* is μ (but you will rarely, if ever, use this). Usually in psychological studies we treat the data we have as a *sample* drawn from a *population* (see Chapter 2 and p. 274.)

The expression for the mean, above, is our first encounter with a *formula*. A formula is only a short-hand set of instructions, rather like following a recipe or instructions for Dr Jekyll's magic potion. In the example above we are told to:

1 add up all values in the data set – this is $\sum x$

2 divide by the *total number* of values – always represented as *N (for the entire group)*

Σ is a symbol that simply means 'add up each of what follows' and in the formula for the mean above what follows is *x*. For *x* you can read 'each value'. So we simply add up all the values and divide the result by *N* – but you probably knew this, at least in an informal way. There is a section at the end of this chapter on notation and the rules for following a formula. I hope this will help you if it's some time since you did any 'sums' or if you hated them (or thought they were pointless). Rest assured that the *only* mathematical operations you need to perform in going through this book are the four junior school operations ('+' '–' 'x' '÷') and squares (which are multiplication anyway) and square roots (which are always found at the touch of a button). All work *can* be done on the simplest of calculators but, of course, and certainly towards the end of the book, computer programs such as SPSS can make life a lot easier.

Info Box 11.1	**A note on decimals and spurious accuracy – before we go any further: DON'T USE 7.34959!**

Very often, in a student report, and sometimes because unformatted computer programs are to blame, the mean of 9, 8, 7, 5, 4, 3 and 2 might be reported as '5.4285'. The last three decimal figures add *nothing at all* to the accuracy of this calculation since the original numbers were *whole numbers*. They represented *intervals* like 6.5 to 7.5, so the answer just *cannot* be that accurate, i.e. to ten-thousandths of a whole! A general rule of thumb is to round to *one place below* the original intervals. Hence, here the appropriate mean value would be 5.4. At times this book breaks this rule, usually just to show that two calculations give the same answer. Rounding processes can sometimes make this appear not to be so. When you use SPSS you must be careful to round figures appropriately since SPSS often gives answers to four or even five decimal places – it doesn't know any better!

Advantages and disadvantages of the mean

Advantages

- The mean is a powerful statistic used in estimating *population parameters* (see p. 274) and this estimation is the basis for the more powerful *parametric* tests we can use to look for significant differences or correlations.

- It is the most sensitive and accurate of the three measures described here because it works at an *interval* level of measurement and takes account of the exact distances between values in the data set.

Disadvantages

- Because the mean *is* so sensitive there is also a problem that it is easily distorted by one, or a few, 'rogue' and unrepresentative values. For instance, if we had six people doing our anagram task (p. 263) and the sixth person took 60 seconds to find the solution, then the total would now be 90 seconds and our mean would become 15 seconds. This value for the mean is quite unrepresentative of the group as a whole. No one from the original five people actually scored even as high as this new mean. Single 'rogues' or 'outlier' values can distort the mean; *equal* rogues, but in opposite directions, tend to cancel one another out.

- A further small disadvantage of the mean is that with *discrete* variables we get 'silly' values for the mean and this is sometimes misleading or at least distracting – for instance, the notorious case of parents with 2.4 children.

The median

Using the MEDIAN gets us around the main disadvantage of the mean – that extreme values give a distorted value. The median is the *central* value of a set. If we have an odd number of values in a small data set then this couldn't be easier to find. The central value of our first five anagram solution times above is the third one. To find this we must first put all five in numerical order. This gives 1, 2, 5, 10, 12 and the median is 5. Here are the formal rules for finding a median.

If there is an odd number of values in the data set

1 Find the MEDIAN POSITION or LOCATION. This is the place where we will find the MEDIAN VALUE. This is at $\dfrac{N+1}{2}$. Call this position 'k'.

2 k will be a whole number. The median is the value at the kth position. In the set of five values above we would get: $\dfrac{5+1}{2} = 3$. The median is the value in the *third* (k^{th}) position when the data are ordered, so the median is 5.

If there is an even number of values in the data set

1 Find the *median position*, as above. It will be midway between two whole numbers. For a six-digit set we get: $k = \dfrac{6+1}{2} = 3.5$ so 3.5 tells us that the median is between the 3rd and 4th members of the set; that is, if the set is 1, 2, 5, 10, 12, 60, between 5 and 10.

2 We take the *mean* of these two values, so we get: $\dfrac{5+10}{2} = 7.5$

Notice that the median of 7.5, as an average, is reasonably representative of the group of values, unlike the mean we found above, which was 15.

If there are several tied values in the data set

Suppose we have the data set: 7, 7, 7, 8, 8, 8, 9, 9, 10, 10

Here, there are two possible approaches: the rough and ready, and the fastidiously correct. Which you use depends on the purpose at hand and also on the collection of values in your data set. The rough and ready approach says use the usual formula. Here we have an even set of numbers, ten in all, so the median is midway between the fifth and sixth values, i.e. 8 and 8. Hence it would be 8. This will do for many purposes and even the statistical program SPSS goes no further. After all, 8 is pretty representative of the set.

However, technically, what we require for the median is a position, *within the interval* 7.5 to 8.5, where the median would fall, based on the proportions of values either side of it. To be absolutely accurate then we would use the procedure below. However, this procedure, though complicated, is also very useful (in fact necessary, unless you're doing computerised statistics) where you have a very large data set and the results are organised into frequency categories as in Table 11.11.

$N =$	0	1–5	6–10	11–20	21–30	31–40	41+
	65	45	78	32	11	4	3

Table 11.11 Large frequency table – number of people smoking N cigarettes per day

The formula to find the median here is:

$$\text{Median} = L + \frac{N/2 - F}{f_m} \times h \text{ where:}$$

L = exact lower limit of interval containing median

F = total number of values below L

f_m = number of values in interval containing median

h = size of class interval

N = total number of values in data set.

So, for the cigarette-smoking data in Table 11.11, we would need to substitute values. The categories 1–5, 6–10, 11–20, etc. in Table 11.11 are called CLASS INTERVALS. Notice that in this example they are not all the same size. Here, it is difficult to see where the median could be. There are 238 cases altogether so the median is the value above and below which 119 of all cases fall. This must be somewhere in the 6–10 category. The formula assumes that values in this category are evenly spread throughout it. Therefore L is 5.5; this is the exact start of the 6–10 interval (see p. 257). F is 110, f_m is 78, h is 5 and N is 238. Putting these values into the formula we get:

$$\text{Median} = 5.5 + \frac{238/2 - 110}{78} \times 5 = \mathbf{6.08}$$

I'll leave you to calculate the median for the small set of tied values above. You should get 8.16.

Advantages and disadvantages of the median

Advantages

- Unaffected by extreme or 'rogue' values in one direction. Hence, better for use with '*skewed*' distributions (see p. 317).

- Easier to calculate than the mean (as long as there are small groups and no ties, or if tied values are overlooked).

- Can be obtained when the *value* of extreme data points is unknown.

Disadvantages

- Doesn't take into account the exact distances between values.
- Can't be used in estimates of population parameters – see p. 274.
- In a small data set, can be unrepresentative; for instance, with 2, 3, 5, 98, 112 the median would be 5.

The mode

If we have data on a nominal scale, as people's roles in Table 11.2, we cannot calculate a mean or a median. We can, however, say which role occurred most often, i.e. which category had the highest frequency count. This is what is known as the MODE or MODAL VALUE. It is the most frequently occurring category and therefore even easier to find than the mean or median. The mode of the set of numbers:

1, 2, 3, 3, 3, 4, 4, 4, 5, 5, 5, 5, 5, 5, 6, 6, 7, 7, 7, 8

is therefore 5 since this value occurs most often. In the set of values 5, 2, 12, 1, 10 there is no single modal value since each value occurs once only. For the set of numbers 7, 7, 7, 8, 8, 9, 9, 9, 10, 10 there are *two* modes, 7 and 9, and the set is said to be BI-MODAL.

In Table 11.2 the modal value is 'student'. Be careful here to note that the mode is *not the number of times* the most frequent value occurs, but that value itself. 'Student' occurs most frequently.

The mode is the typical measure of central tendency for nominal-level data but is also often a more comfortable alternative with *discrete* measurement scales, avoiding the unrealistic 'average' of 1.999 legs and giving us the *typical* statistic of 2.

Advantages and disadvantages of the mode

Advantages

- Shows the most frequent or 'typical' value of a data set.
- Unaffected by extreme values in one direction.
- Can be obtained when extreme values are unknown.
- Often more informative than mean when scale is discrete.

Disadvantages

- Doesn't take into account the exact distances between values.
- Can't be used in estimates of population parameters.
- Not at all useful for relatively small sets of data where several values occur equally frequently (e.g. 1, 2, 3, 4).
- For bi-modal distributions two modal values need to be reported.
- Can't be estimated accurately when data are grouped into class intervals. We can have a modal interval – like 6–10 cigarettes in Table 11.11 – but this will change if different intervals are used.

Central tendency measures and levels of measurement

Interval/ratio

The mean is the most sensitive measure but should only be used where data are at least at the interval level of measurement. Otherwise, the mean is calculated on intervals that are unequal and is misleading.

Ordinal

If data are not at interval or ratio level but can be ranked, then the median is the appropriate measure of central tendency. The median *may* also be used on interval/ratio data.

Nominal

If data are in discretely separate categories, then only the mode can be used. The mode *may* also be used on ordinal and interval/ratio data.

Measures of dispersion

Think back to the description of new evening classmates. The central tendency was given as 25, but some 'guesstimate' was also given of the way people *spread* around this central point. Without knowledge of spread (or, more technically, DISPERSION), a mean can be very misleading. Take a look at the bowling performance of two cricketers shown in Figure 11.5. Both bowlers average around the middle stump but (a) varies much more than (b). The attempts of (a) are far more widely *dispersed*. Average wages in two companies may be the same but distribution of wages may be very different.

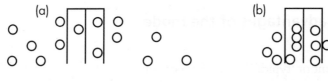

(a) high variability   (b) low variability

Figure 11.5 Two bowlers' deliveries – same mean, different variation

The range

Remember that we said that the talking times of girls in Table 11.10 tended to vary far less than did those of the boys. The simplest way to measure the variation among a set of values is to use what is called the RANGE. This is simply the distance between the top and bottom values of a set.

Finding the range

1 Find top value of the set.

2 Find bottom value of the set.

3 Subtract bottom value from top value and add 1.

For Table 11.10 this gives:

Girls (503 – 289) + 1 = 215 Boys (450 – 5) + 1 = 446

Why do we add the 1? This might seem a little strange. Surely the distance for boys between 5 and 450 is, straightforwardly, 445? As we said on p. 257, we measure to *intervals*, not points. When we say that a child spoke for 5 seconds, if our lowest unit of measurement is 1 second, then we can only genuinely claim that the child spoke for something between 4.5 and 5.5 seconds, the limits of our basic measurement interval. Hence, the range is measured from the lowest possible limit of the lowest value to the highest limit of the highest value. The boys' talking times range between possible values of 4.5 and 450.5. Many statistics books do not recognise this picky point and nor does SPSS.

Advantages and disadvantages of the range

Advantages

- Includes extreme values.
- Easy to calculate.

Disadvantages

- Distorted by extreme values and can therefore be misleading.
- Unrepresentative of any features of the distribution of values between the extremes. For instance, the range doesn't tell us whether or not the values are closely grouped around the mean or generally spaced out across the entire range.

The interquartile range and semi-interquartile range

The INTERQUARTILE RANGE avoids the second weakness of the range and focuses specifically on the *central* grouping of values in a set. It represents the distance between the two values that cut off the bottom and top 25% of values, i.e. the bottom and top quarters. These two values are known as the first and third *quartiles* or the twenty-fifth and seventy-fifth *percentiles*. We shall deal with these terms more precisely in chapter 13. The SEMI-INTERQUARTILE RANGE is *half* of the interquartile range.

In the following data set:

	Q1				M			Q3		
3	3	4	5	6	8	10	13	14	16	19

4 is the first quartile and 14 the third quartile. The distance between these is 10 (the interquartile range) and half this (the semi-interquartile range) is 5. Note that M is the median and the second quartile

Finding the interquartile and semi-interquartile range

The inter-quartile range is: $Q_3 - Q_1$

The semi-interquartile range is half of this value, that is: $\dfrac{Q_3 - Q_1}{2}$

For most purposes (as with the rough and ready median) you can take the first quartile (Q_1) and the third quartile (Q_3) to be the value cutting off the bottom and top 25% of values respectively. These are the 25th and 75th percentiles; a formula for finding exact percentiles is given later.

Advantages and disadvantages of the semi-interquartile range

Advantages

- It is representative of the central grouping of values in the data set.
- It is a useful measure for ordinal level data.

Disadvantages

- Takes no account of extreme values.
- Inaccurate where there are large class intervals (i.e. where first and third quartiles cannot be identified accurately).

The mean deviation

An important way of looking at the spread of values in a set is to use the concept of DEVIATION. A DEVIATION VALUE/SCORE is simply *the amount by which a particular value deviates from the mean*. For instance, if the mean average shoe size in your class is 6 and you take a 4, your *deviation value* is –2. Note the *negative value* as you are *below* the mean. We always take $x - \bar{x}$. In this case that's $4 - 6 = -2$.

Look back to the fox-hunting attitude scores in Table 11.9. We saw that the Dunton Parva scores were much more widely spread out than the Slumditch scores. We can represent all these scores as deviations as shown in Figure 11.6.

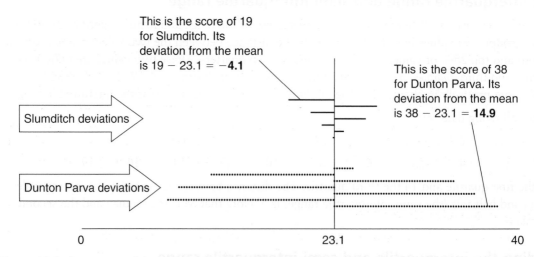

Figure 11.6 Comparison of deviations of Slumditch and Dunton Parva fox hunting attitude scores

The MEAN DEVIATION is the mean of all the deviation values in a data set. The mean of the values depicted in Table 11.9 for Slumditch would obviously be a lot smaller than the mean for Dunton Parva. However, let's go through an example that will be somewhat easier to calculate. Suppose you and five others took an IQ test with the following results:

Stacey	Hema	Lee	Chirag	You
85	90	100	110	115

The mean is 100 and your personal deviation score is $115 - 100 = 15$.

If we are going to *summarise* dispersion in terms of people's deviations from the mean, it seems sensible to report the *average* of all the deviations in the set. The set of deviations for the IQ scores above is shown in Table 11.12. Ignore the column headed 'squared deviation' for now.

Score (x)	Mean ($\bar{x}$)	Deviation (d) ($x - \bar{x}$)	Squared deviation (d^2) ($x - \bar{x}$)²
85	100	−15	225
90	100	−10	100
100	100	0	0
110	100	10	100
115	100	15	225
		$\Sigma d = 0$	$\Sigma d^2 = 650$

Table 11.12 Deviation of IQ scores from their mean

The sum of the deviations (Σd) is zero and therefore the mean of the deviations would also be zero. This isn't what we wanted. If you look back to Figure 11.4 you can see why this has happened. The mean sits precisely in the centre of all the deviations around it. Values above the mean have a positive (+) deviation and those below have a negative (−) value. When added together, all these will exactly cancel each other out. The deviations shown in Figure 11.4, where the mean is 6, are, from left to right: −5, −4, −1, +4 and +6; both the negative and positive sets add to 10 and cancel each other out. What we want is the average of those deviations, *ignoring their sign*. This value is known as their *absolute value*. This is represented mathematically by two vertical bars either side of a number, e.g. |−10| = 10. So, for the absolute value of a deviation score, we would write $|x - \bar{x}|$ or just $|d|$.

Finding the mean deviation

The formula for the mean deviation is $MD = \dfrac{\Sigma|x - \bar{x}|}{N}$ or more simply $MD = \dfrac{\Sigma|d|}{N}$

To step through this equation, calculate as follows.

1 Find the mean $\bar{x}$.

2 Subtract the mean from each value in the data set $(x - \bar{x})$ to obtain a set of *deviations* (d).

3 Add up all these deviations taking no notice of any minus signs, i.e. find $\Sigma|d|$.

4 Divide result of step three by N.

Using this on our IQ data we get: $\Sigma|d| = 15 + 10 + 0 + 10 + 15 = 50$

$MD = \dfrac{50}{5} = 10$

Advantage and disadvantage of the mean deviation

Advantage

- Takes account of all values in the data set.

Disadvantage

- Not possible to use in making estimates of *population parameters* (see the section on *standard deviation*, below).

The standard deviation and variance

The standard deviation and variance play a central and extremely important role in statistics, particularly in the estimation of *population parameters* – that is, estimating from a sample how the values of a population are distributed. This is what we look at on p. 274. The standard deviation also deals, like the mean deviation, with *deviation values* but instead of *ignoring* their negative signs, in the standard deviation we *square* them.

Finding the standard deviation

The usual formula for standard deviation is: $s = \sqrt{\dfrac{\Sigma d^2}{N-1}}$ (but see below for some alternatives)

The usual formula for variance is: $s^2 = \dfrac{\Sigma d^2}{N-1}$

Note that the *variance* is simply the square of the standard deviation and is denoted as s^2 while the standard deviation is just s.

What the formula for STANDARD DEVIATION says is:

- *take each deviation value*
- *square it*
- *add all the squared deviations up*
- *divide by N–1*
- *finally, take the square root.*

Step by step we work as shown in Table 11.13.

Procedure	Calculation on data in Table 11.12
1. Find the mean of the data set	$\bar{x} = 100$ see Table 11.12
2. Subtract the mean from each value in the data set obtaining the deviation values $(x - \bar{x})$ in each case but use d as shorthand	See Table 11.12, column 3
3. Square each d	See Table 11.12, column 4
4. Find the sum of the squared deviations $(= \Sigma d^2)$	$\Sigma d^2 = 650$ (See Table 11.12, bottom of column 4)
5. Divide the result of step 4 by $N-1$	$s^2 = 162.5$ (NOTE: this is the VARIANCE)
6. Find the square root of step 5	$s = 12.75$

Table 11.13 Procedure for calculating standard deviation

Variance calculation without finding deviations

There is a version of the formula for sample variance that avoids the calculation of deviations and for which you only need the set of values and their total:

$$s^2 = \frac{\Sigma x^2 - (\Sigma x)^2/N}{N - 1}$$

The standard deviation would be the square root of this value. In more advanced work this is a highly important equation, especially in the whole area of significance testing using *analysis of variance* (Chapters 18–20). *If you do use this formula, beware of the difference between Σx^2 and $(\Sigma x)^2$* which is explained at the end of this chapter.

The 'whole group' or 'uncorrected' version of standard deviation and variance

If you are finding the standard deviation *just* for the group of values you have (i.e. treating them as the entire population) and you are *not* using the standard deviation to make estimates of the underlying population from which your sample was drawn, then you could use the so-called 'UNCORRECTED' version of the formulae, which simply uses N instead of $N - 1$. Call this standard deviation S (big, not little s). However in most cases, and if you are uncertain about this, it is usual to use the so-called 'UNBIASED ESTIMATE' versions used above, which contain a small correction factor that is explained further on p. 275. If you are conducting significance tests on your data, then you should certainly use the unbiased versions above.

The 'uncorrected' formula for standard deviation is: $S = \sqrt{\dfrac{\Sigma d^2}{N}}$

Degrees of freedom

The value $N-1$ used in the variance equation when we are estimating the population variance is known as the DEGREES OF FREEDOM of the sample. It is argued that, if we know the mean of a sample, then all the values that make up that sample are free to vary *except one*. For instance, if a sample mean is five and there are four values in the sample, then, if we know that three of the values are 5,8,4, the final value must be 3 in order that the total is 20 and the mean is 20/4 = 5. The concept of degrees of freedom is rather obscure but all you need know is that they are associated with any statistical value in which an estimate is made of population parameters from sample statistics, and that they are always the number in the appropriate sample minus one.

Advantages and disadvantages of the standard deviation or variance

Advantages
- Can be used in population parameter estimates.
- Takes exact account of all values.
- Is the most sensitive of measures covered.
- Can be calculated directly on many calculators.

Disadvantages
- Distorted by extreme values.
- Somewhat more complicated to calculate (if you don't have an appropriate calculator).

Appropriate dispersion measures for different levels of measurement

The *variance* and *standard deviation* are most appropriate for *interval level* data and above, and are associated with the mean. Where populations are particularly *skewed* (see p. 317) an *ordinal level* measure might be preferred, such as the interquartile range and semi-interquartile range, which depend upon ranked positions and are not affected by extreme values. They are associated with the median. For *categorical data* dispersion is not an appropriate concept since categories are usually not related to each other in a linear manner – i.e. categories do not increase in related value. However, to give some idea of how cases spread *across* categories we can calculate something called the VARIATION RATIO. This is the number of non-modal values divided by the total number of values. In Table 11.2 this would be 63/308 = .2.

Population parameters, sample statistics and sampling error

The idea of an uncorrected and unbiased estimate version of the standard deviation, referred to just above, introduces a central notion in statistical work. When we assess a group of people on some experimental variable or psychological scale we are usually not interested in that sample as such but in *the underlying population from which they were drawn*. This is why accurate and unbiased sampling methods (see Chapter 2) are so important. Measures of a *sample*, known as SAMPLE STATISTICS, are very frequently taken as an *estimate* of the same measures of a *population*, known as POPULATION PARAMETERS. The measures concerned are most often the mean and variance. We are not usually able to assess *directly* whether two populations differ on a certain variable. Either populations are too large or they may be infinite (such as all the scores we could ever gather on a memory task). What we do (and this is what psychological experiments are all about) is *draw samples* and assume that the sample statistics reflect the populations as a whole. We assume that the mean of the sample is the same as the population mean, though we will usually be a little bit out in this (see the concept of *sampling error* on p. 315). The 'little bit out' will vary from sample to sample, sometimes too high, equally often too low.

The sample variance, too, will be different from the population variance but, unlike the mean, the sample variance will almost always be smaller than the population variance. This is because the sample is *most likely* to draw individual values from nearer the centre of the distribution (there are more values here) whereas the population variance, of course, is based on the entire range of values (see Figure 11.7). If we always assume that the sample and population variances are the same, we would *consistently* underestimate the population variance. Hence, to make some correction for this we divide by N–1 in the variance equation, rather than just N. Since we are now dividing by a smaller number, the resulting estimate of variance will be *larger* and this, to some extent, compensates for the 'error' in estimating the population variance from the sample variance. When N is very large, the subtraction of 1 will make very little difference at all.

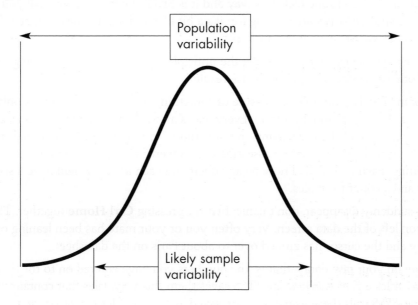

Figure 11.7 Sample variance is usually smaller than the population variance

Population estimates are used in conducting certain kinds of *parametric test* that are very powerful and most likely to give us an accurate assessment of whether or not we should accept sample differences as *significant* – that is, accept it as a likely real difference between the underlying populations. We shall discuss the role of these estimates further when we encounter '*t* tests' in Chapter 15.

Using SPSS to calculate statistics

Getting started

SPSS is a very powerful statistical package which is nevertheless quite easy to use once you have got to grips with a few guiding principles. It is the package of choice for most university psychology departments. It is also used in many other subject areas. The procedures outlined here and in following chapters, limited by space, cannot hope to replace the several good manuals on the market but the inclusion of SPSS procedures here is aimed at relieving you of the necessity of carrying two books to class, once you have learned the basics from your methods tutor or from your specialist SPSS manual. The advantage is that you can learn about the theory and rationale behind a test, in depth, in this book then go straight to using the test in SPSS.

There is a new version of SPSS about every two years. The instructions given here apply to SPSS versions 15 and 16 (v.15 and v.16) but are mostly applicable to several earlier versions. The graphics are from v. 16.

There are a few golden rules and points to appreciate before getting stuck in.

1 SPSS *always* gives you far more than you asked for! Students often panic about this, thinking they should understand every bit of information that SPSS has given them on a results sheet. *Don't worry about this!* Everyone feels this way and it is SPSS's fault, not yours. All you need to learn is how to spot what *you* are looking for; it's a bit like looking in a newspaper *only* for the things that are relevant to you at this moment.

2 Before entering any data you *must* consider the principles laid out below concerning the *design* of your study, otherwise you may get nonsense results.

3 Every *column* in SPSS is a variable (a measure of something, even if the measure is only categorical, e.g. 1 for 'yes' and 2 for 'no'). Every *row* is a *case*. What we mean by a case is almost always a person – one of the participants in your study. However, suppose you had studied gender stereotyping in TV adverts by assessing each advert for technical content and number of males appearing. Each case would now be an advert and each advert would have a score for technicality and a count for males.

4 If your data suddenly disappear, don't panic; first try pressing **Ctrl Home** together. This takes you to the top left of the data screen. Very often you or your mate has been leaning on the enter or arrow key and the cursor has zipped over to about Paris on the datasheet.

5 Files that contain your raw data – that is, the numbers you have entered on to the datasheet – have *****.sav titles e.g. *memoryprac.sav*. SPSS saves them this way. Files that contain the *results* of your analyses (SPSS calls these *output* files) are saved as ****.spo files e.g. *memoryprac.spo* in v.15 and earlier. For v. 16 this changes to an .spv extension and, sadly, spo files from earlier versions are not viewable in v. 16. If you are using v.16 and want to view an earlier output file then you need to install SPSS Smartviewer 15 ('Legacy Viewer').

If you can't find a file on your disk, it may be that you are looking at the wrong screen. When looking at the data sheet and asking to open a file you will only see .sav files. When looking at the output screen (where results are displayed) you will only see .spv files (or .spo in v.15). You can change the file types visible by selecting an alternative from the box marked **Files of Type** in the open file box. I always think it's safest to select **All Files** so that you can see everything that is there.

When you start SPSS, you'll be confronted by an awkward box asking you what you'd like to do. Cancel this if you are starting afresh and even if you're loading a file, it's usually easier to use the more familiar **open file** button to the top left. Now let's get started on how to enter your variables.

Entering variables

Let's say we wish to enter the male and female infant talking times in Table 11.10. We need to tell SPSS that we have values on two variables for each child, first their sex and then their talking time in seconds. In SPSS every variable has its own column. Remember a variable is just a measure we have taken for each person in our sample.

Let's create our first variable, the talking times. Double-click on the faint '**var**' at the top of the left-hand column on the datasheet (or click **Variable View** at bottom left). At the top of the column to the left of your screen (titled 'name') you now enter a variable name, which must not contain spaces or other symbols – just letters or numbers and not numbers first. Let's use *talktime*. To give a fuller and more friendly title we can enter 'Talking times in seconds' in the column headed '**Label**' and this title will appear in the results output later on – see Figure11.8.

Name	Type	Width	Decimals	Label	Values	Missing	Columns	Align	Measure
talktime	Numeric	8	2	Talking times in seconds	None	None	8	▆ Right	⬚ Scale

Figure 11.8 Defining a variable in SPSS

If you now go back to the datasheet by clicking **Data View** at the bottom left of the screen. You'll see *talktime* at the top of the leftmost column.

Now we need to create a second variable which will denote the child's sex. This is slightly more complicated because we have a categorical variable and we have to use numbered codes to represent category names. Here we will use 1 for female and 2 for male. These codes are also known as 'dummy' values. They are nominal values as explained on p. 251 Usually they cannot be used in mathematical calculations. For instance, if we had one male and one female and took the average of their sex codes we would get 1.5 which would be a meaningless value. We would be saying, on average their sex code was 1.5 which is a bit daft. It is best to keep in mind that the codes are used as *names* for categories. In fact, in Figure 11.8 you can see that the far right column of this variable says 'scale'. You can tell SPSS that your variable is scaled (measured), ordinal or nominal. This doesn't always matter but can help when SPSS is drawing graphs for instance.

Coding a variable

To create our variable for sex and allocate codes, go to the **variable view** screen again. On the row below our talktime variable type *genderchild* under 'Name' then click the cell under **Values**. You should now see three grey dots to the right of this cell. Click on these and the box shown in Figure 11.9 should appear. Enter the first code (1) in the **Value** slot and the name of the level it stands for (*female*) in the **Label** box. You must not forget to click on **Add**. When you have entered your codes click **OK**, and your variable should appear as in Figure 11.10.

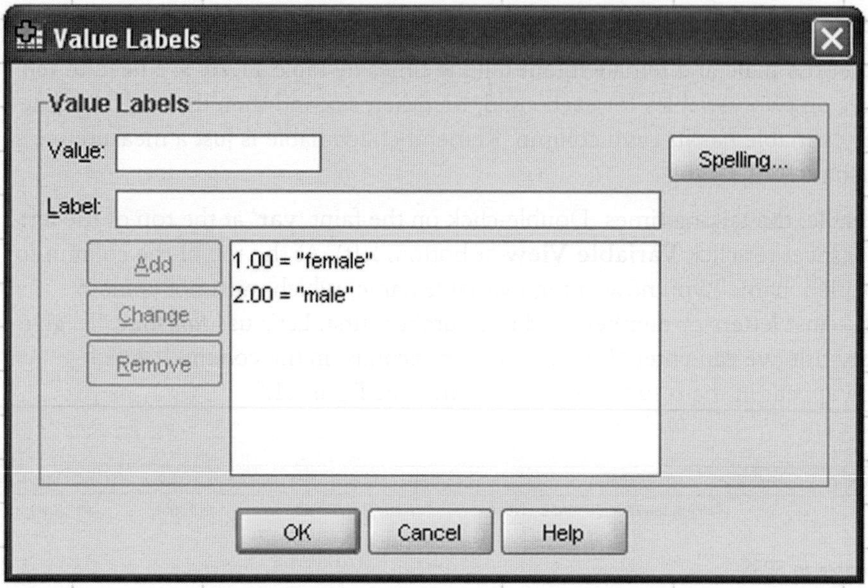

Figure 11.9 Giving labels to coded value

Name	Type	Width	Decimals	Label	Values	Missir
talktime	Numeric	8	2	Talking times in seconds	None	None
genchild	Numeric	8	2		{1.00, femal...	None

Figure 11.10 Variables for the data in Table 11.10 entered into SPSS

Entering data

Now switch to **data view**. Use navigation keys or the mouse to highlight different cells and start with the top left hand cell highlighted. Enter values by typing in the value then pressing enter or the down or across arrow. If you make a mistake, simply type over it with the correct value. Beware! SPSS lets you type over with no warning and it even lets you delete entire variables without warning you that this is what you are about to do!

The value to go in the top left cell then is 332, the first female child's score in Table 11.10. This first child, represented by the top row in SPSS, also has a gender which we wish to enter in the second column. Enter a '1'. Carry on and enter the rest of your data. If you click **view** on the top menu bar and then **value labels**, you will see the 1s and 2s change to the labels 'female' and 'male' which is a lot friendlier. It is easier to do this after entering your data as otherwise entering the codes is more fiddly – SPSS presents an annoying choice box. Your data sheet should now look like Figure 11.11.

	talktime	genderchild
1	332.00	female
2	345.00	female
3	289.00	female
4	503.00	female
5	367.00	female
6	132.00	male
7	34.00	male
8	5.00	male
9	237.00	male
10	450.00	male

Figure 11.11 Layout of data for an unrelated design in SPSS (gender and talking times)

Unrelated and related designs

Unrelated designs

One of the most basic difficulties learners encounter with SPSS is the temptation always to enter data in columns side by side as we would on paper. If you enter the data from Table 11.10 as it is shown you are telling SPSS that, in the top row, the same child scored 332 and 132. This just isn't so. The first female child at the top of the left-hand column has nothing whatever to do with the first male child at the top of the right-hand column. This is an *unrelated design* with two separate groups of people. The way to think is that each child has two scores, one for gender and one for talking time and then lay out your data as in Figure 11.11.

Related designs

Suppose you have asked participants to learn and recall a word list in a hot room and then to do the same with a new list in a cold room. This is a *repeated measures* (*related*) design and we have a pair of scores for each participant. In this case we *do* need two columns in SPSS – one for each level (**hot** and **cold**) of the independent variable **temperature**. Participant 5, for instance, will have *two* scores, one on **hot** and one on **cold** and these two scores *must* appear on the same row (for the same 'case'). We need to create two variables as shown in Figure 11.12.

	Hot	Cold
1	14.00	10.00
2	7.00	6.00
3	9.00	8.00
4	12.00	10.00
5	7.00	9.00
6	13.00	11.00
7	6.00	6.00
8	15.00	12.00
9	12.00	10.00
10	13.00	11.00

Figure 11.12 Layout for repeated measures in SPSS

Here the participants are numbered 1 to 10 on the left and then columns for our two measures follow, one for participants' **hot** scores and one for their **cold** scores. Note that the independent variable here is **temperature** but we do not enter this name anywhere at this level of analysis.

Figure 11.13 shows the layout for a *matched pairs* design where children have been paired (Child A and Child B), one group ('ChildAreadingscore') has undergone a reading enhancement programme and now both groups have been given a reading test with these (not very impressive) results. Remember you can make the variable name more friendly on your results sheet by entering a name in to the **Label** cell when defining the variables in **Variable view**.

	ChildAreadingscore	ChildBreadingscore
1	14.00	10.00
2	7.00	6.00
3	9.00	8.00
4	12.00	10.00
5	7.00	9.00
6	13.00	11.00
7	6.00	6.00
8	15.00	12.00
9	12.00	10.00
10	13.00	11.00

Figure 11.13 Layout for matched pairs design in SPSS

Descriptive statistics using SPSS

Interval measures – means, standard deviations and normality checks

If your variable measure is at least at interval level, you will usually want the mean and the standard deviation or variance. In addition, you may wish to check for skewness and kurtosis in order to check that your data do not depart far from what would be expected if the sample is drawn from a normal distribution (see p. 317). This assumption of normality for your data is *central* to the decision as to whether a *parametric* test (see p. 364) is legitimate for your data or not.

To find interval level statistics for each variable

There are two main ways to obtain descriptives statistics such as the mean and standard deviation. I have used **Descriptives** here as it is the norm. However, if you want the median or mode you can use **Frequencies** as described on p. 319.

1 From the top menu select **Analyse/Descriptive Statistics/Descriptives**.

2 Select your variable(s) on the left and put these over to the right-hand box marked **Variables**.

Info Box 11.2   **Selecting variables (in all similar SPSS operations)**

In all similar SPSS dialogue boxes, where you want to shift specific variables, select your variable(s) by clicking on them, then click on the central right-pointing arrow. In V.16 you can also do this by dragging and dropping or just double click. If you have several variables to move, in V.15 you can select them all by clicking and holding on the top one and dragging your cursor down through all the required variables. In V.16 you have to highlight the first, hold down shift, then highlight the last in the list. If you want to select only specific variables, and not others appearing in between, hold down Ctrl and click each one. When the correct variables are selected click the central arrow. *Remove* a variable from the Variables box by selecting it and clicking the now left-pointing arrow or, in V.16, double clicking or dragging.

---

3 Click **Options** and decide which boxes to check. By default SPSS will give you mean, standard deviation, minimum and maximum values. Other choices can be the **Variance** (the square of the standard deviation), **Range**, **Sum** (of all values), **Standard error (se) of the mean** (used in the *t* tests – see p. 316), **Skew** and **Kurtosis** – see pp. 317–19.

4 Click **Continue** and return to the main dialogue box.

5 **Save standardized values as variables** will provide, if you need them, *z* scores for all the values of a variable (see p. 312).

6 Click **OK**.

7 SPSS now produces a new screen called **Output** and displays a table of results that should be self-explanatory. Remember to round up appropriately the long decimal parts of numbers before reporting these in your work – see p. 264!

The screen at which you enter data is known as the **Data Editor**. If you want to save your raw data then this must be the screen you are in when you save. To save your *results* (the **Output**) you must be in the output screen when you save. That's the screen that appears with the results of your statistical operations. Output files have the extension '.spo' (V.15) or '.spv' (V.16) while data files have the extension '.sav'.

If you want the means for two or more groups (independent samples)

Very often we will be dealing with a between groups design (independent samples) where we have a score for two or more separate groups. For example, we may want the means for female and male children's talking times from Table 11.10. To obtain statistics for both groups proceed as follows.

1   Click **Analyze/Compare Means/Means**.

2   Enter the grouping variable (that's the variable that identifies groups – the 'independent variable' – *genderchild* in Figure 11.11) into the box headed **Independent list**. Enter the dependent variable (the variable that is a measure or a 'score' e.g. in this case *talktime*) into the **Dependent list** box.

Mean, standard deviation and *N* (number of cases) are given by default. Click **Options** to select several other statistics on the left-hand side, using the arrow or dragging to transfer them to the right-hand side. Click **Continue** to proceed. Click **OK** unless you want to enter more sub-groups (see immediately below).

Sub-categories of categorical variables

Sometimes you may want to find means for males and females (***gender***) on a variable such as ***reading score*** but also arranged by another categorical variable, e.g. ***ethnicity*** (e.g. Black, Asian and White). In the main dialogue box you will notice a heading in the middle, **Layer 1 of 1**. First enter ***gender*** into this box. Then click **next**. Then enter ***ethnicity*** into the box. This will provide ***reading score*** statistics for all levels of ***ethnicity*** on the first level of ***gender***, then statistics for the second level. You will also get the total of ***ethnicity*** regardless of ***gender***. For ***gender*** statistics regardless of ***ethnicity*** you need to enter the variables the other way around, first ***ethnicity***, then ***gender***.

Exercises

1 Find the mean and median and standard deviation of the two sets of talking times in Table 11.10.

2 You are told that a set of seven scores includes one score that is 0.8. The standard deviation for the set is 0. Can you give the mean of the set and say anything else about the six other scores in the set?

3 The following times were recorded (in seconds) to solve an anagram:

12, 8, 23, 13, 17, 15, 18, 21, 18, 14, 18, 29, 55, 12.

(a) Decide which would be the most appropriate measure of central tendency.

(b) Calculate the mean median and mode for the data.

(c) Can you suggest why the mean is a bit higher than the median?

(d) Calculate the range, interquartile range and standard deviation.

Answers

1 Males: mean = 171.6; median = 132; sd = 180.31. Females: mean = 367.2; median = 345; sd = 81.07.

2 Since there is absolutely no variation, all scores must be the same; all scores are therefore 0.8 and the mean is 0.8.

3 (a) The measure is at interval level, so the mean would be appropriate, but you might have noticed that the mean will be affected by the extreme score of 55 so perhaps the median is a better bet.

(b) mean = 19.5; median = 17.5; mode = 18

(c) as we said above the mean will be affected by the score of 55; the median isn't.

(d) range = 48; iq range = 21 − 13 = 8; standard deviation = 11.49

Glossary

Bi-modal distribution	Data set with two modes
Categorical variable	Variable where cases are merely placed into independent, separate categories
Central tendency	Formal term for any measure of the typical or middle value in a group
Class intervals	Categories into which a continuous data scale can be divided in order to summarise frequencies
Coding	Giving 'dummy' numbers to levels of an independent variable in an unrelated design

Continuous scale/variable	Scale where there are no discrete steps; theoretically, all points along the scale are meaningful
Data set	Group of data points or values which can be summarised or analysed
Degrees of freedom	Common term in statistical analysis having to do with the number of individual data points that are free to vary given that overall summary values are known
Deviation score/value	Amount by which a particular score differs from the mean of its set
Discrete scale/ variable	Scale on which not all subdivisions are meaningful; often one where the underlying construct to be measured can only come in whole units (e.g. no. of children)
Dispersion	Technical and general term for any measure of the spread of scores in a sample of data or population
Frequency data/ Frequencies	Numbers of cases in specific categories
Interquartile range	Distance between first and third quartile in a distribution
Levels of measurement	Levels at which data are categorised or measured
Interval	Level of measurement at which each unit on a scale represents an equal change in the variable measured
Nominal	Level of measurement at which numbers are only labels for categories
Ordinal	Level of measurement at which cases are arranged in rank positions
Quasi-interval	Scale that appears to be interval but where equal intervals do not necessarily measure equal amounts of the construct
Ratio	Interval-type scale where proportions on the scale are meaningful because an absolute zero exists
Mean (arithmetic)	Average of scores found by adding them all and dividing by the number of scores in the set
Mean deviation	Measure of dispersion – mean of all absolute deviations
Measured variable	Variable where cases measured on it are placed on some sort of *scale* that has direction
Median (value)	Measure of central tendency; middle value of data set
Median position/location	Position where median is to be found in an ordered data set
Mode/modal value	Measure of central tendency – most frequent value in a data set
Range	Measure of dispersion – top to bottom value
Raw data/scores	Untreated, unconverted values obtained directly from measuring process used in a study
Semi-interquartile range	Half the distance between first and third quartile in a distribution
Standard deviation	Measure of dispersion – the square root of: the sum of all squared deviations divided by N or $N - 1$
Unbiased estimate (of SD)	Version of standard deviation or variance that is used for population estimates (uses $N - 1$ as denominator)

Uncorrected (SD)	Version of standard deviation or variance that is used if *only* wanting summary statistics for the group and *not* making population estimates (uses N as denominator)
Variance	Measure of dispersion – square of standard deviation
Variation ratio	Measure of dispersion – proportion of non-modal values to all values

Appendix – Statistical notation and symbols

N is the number in a sample

N_a is the number in sample a

X is a value from the sample, such as Jane's score (can be lower case: x)

Y is also a value where there are two measured variables (or lower case: y)

Σ Greek letter S ('sigma') – means 'add up each of what follows'. For instance, where these are scores: 1 3 7 2 5, and each score is denoted by 'x', $\Sigma x = 1 + 3 + 7 + 2 + 5 =$ **18**

$\sqrt{}$ Square root. The square root of number X is the number which when multiplied by itself becomes X. Hard to say, easier to demonstrate. The square root of 9 (or $\sqrt{9}$) is 3 because 3 x 3 = 9.

S^2 Square the number S. e.g. $4^2 = 4 \times 4 = 16$

Statistical symbols

Sample			Population		
Mean	Standard deviation	Variance	Mean	Standard deviation	Variance
$\bar{x}$	s *(unbiased)*	s^2	μ	σ	σ^2
	S *(uncorrected)*	S^2			

Some rules

1 In mathematical formulae it is confusing, especially in statistics, to use the multiplication sign ('x') because there are so many x's dotted around anyway. 'x' refers to a particular score or value. In formulae the multiplication sign for multiplication is omitted so when one value is next to another we know we have to multiply them together. For instance, rN means 'multiply r by N'.

2 Always complete what is *inside* a bracket, or after a Σ or $\sqrt{}$ symbol, before going on to do the operation *outside*. Here are some examples of the rules in action:

ΣXY means 'multiply all the Xs by their paired Ys and add up all the results'. Notice that XY means 'multiply X by Y' and we add up the results only after doing the multiplications on all Xs and Ys

ΣX^2 means 'square all the Xs, *then* add them all up'. *Be careful* to distinguish this from:

$(\Sigma X)^2$ means 'find the total of all the Xs and square the result'

$\Sigma X \Sigma Y$ means 'multiply the sum of all the Xs by the sum of all the Ys'

$\Sigma(x-\bar{x})^2$ means 'subtract the mean from each score (x), square each result, then add up all these results'

$(N-1)(N-2)$ means 'find $N-1$, find $N-2$ and then multiply these two results'.

$r\sqrt{\left(\dfrac{N-2}{(1-r^2)}\right)}$ means:

1. Find r^2
2. Find $1-r^2$
3. Find $N-2$
4. Divide step 3 by step 2
5. Find the square root of step 4
6. Multiply the result of step 5 by r

Graphical representation
of data

This chapter deals with the representation of data sets in charts or graphs.

- In a *bar chart* only discrete categories of data are presented for comparison and this must be done fairly, without visual distortion.
- *Line charts* are useful for visually demonstrating, as a *time series*, changes over time in a measure of a person or group.
- Interval data points, grouped into categories, can be represented graphically as a *histogram* or as a *frequency polygon*.
- Tukey (1977) promoted techniques of *exploratory data analysis* with an emphasis on thorough examination of patterns *before* submitting data sets to tests of statistical significance. Two methods are included here: *stem* and *leaf* diagrams, and *box-plots*.

Graphs in general

Students often like drawing graphs and are prone to putting far too many of them into a report to make it look more interesting. But it's worth stopping to think, just what is a graph or chart for? Basically it transmits useful information to your reader. It should be a way of summing up at a glance the main features of your data or some important aspect of it. If it doesn't do that, if it isn't easy to understand completely (without referring to the text in your report) *or* if it presents the absolutely obvious, then it isn't a good or useful chart. Before you rush to produce what many students find to be the most interesting part of a psychological research report, do take note of some cautionary advice.

- *Over-production and decoration* – don't scatter charts around your report showing every conceivable arrangement of data and in a profusion of pretty colours and patterns. You should be very parsimonious (economical with the information) and *only* produce what will be helpful, not distracting, to your reader. Unless asked to produce more by your tutor, just one well-conceived chart will usually be sufficient (if any). You will not gain extra marks for artistic abundance.

- *Charts are summaries* – *do not draw the raw data!* Many students like to draw a chart of their results with a single column representing each participant's score, as in Figure 12.1. *Please don't be tempted to do this.* The resulting chart has no order – participants could be arranged in *any* order along the *x*-axis – their position is arbitrary and the chart resembles an unruly set of mountain peaks and valleys. Worse, the chart tells us nothing we don't already see from the raw data set. It shows us everything in a way that tells us nothing general. What we want from a chart is an overall picture of any *pattern* in our data.

- *Chart information is specific* – notice the titles in the charts in this chapter. They all say *precisely* what is represented. A bar is not labelled 'Group 1' (or worse still 'gp1') but '11-year-olds' for instance, or 'caffeine-deprived condition'. The Y axis cannot have an ambiguous title like 'score' or 'time' but should state specifically what measure it represents – which is how you would define a dependent variable. For instance, we might see 'Time (seconds) to recall list' telling us what units the variable is measured in.

The last point applies also to tables of data.

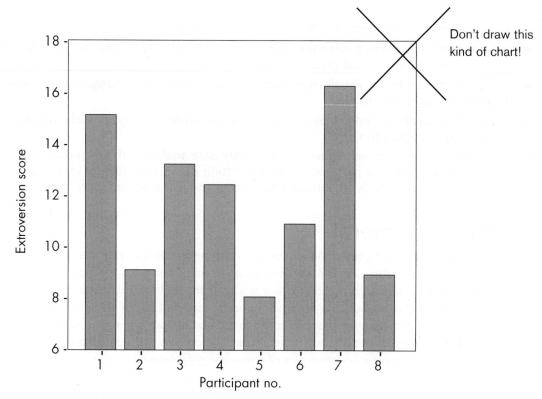

Figure 12.1 Inappropriate bar chart of each participant's score in a data set

The bar chart

A bar chart displays some kind of summary statistic for a categorical variable, such as the mean score of several groups. The summary statistic might also be totals, percentage values, ratios, proportions, ranks, and so on. The categorical variable is usually placed on the *x*-axis (horizontal) while the value for each category is placed on the *y*-axis (see, for example, Figure 12.2).

- Because the **x**-axis variable has categorical values the columns of a bar chart should be separated (no matter what your computer does!).

- Not all the values of the categorical variable need be shown on the **x**-axis. For instance, we might only show, by way of contrast, the number of psychological articles published on climate control beliefs in 2004 and 2009.

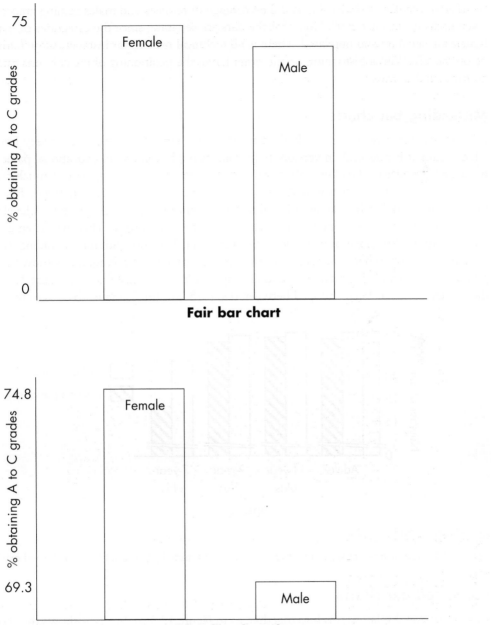

Source: *Guardian* at http://education.guardian.co.uk/alevels2001/tables/0,10951,774597,00.html

Figure 12.2 Percentage of female and male students obtaining grades A to C in A level mathematics, summer 2002 (all boards)

As an example, Figure 12.2a shows the percentage of females and males gaining grades A to C in A level maths in summer 2002. Note that the bars are separate, since the categories of male and female are separate and unrelated. There is no technical reason, for instance, why 'female' should be on the left. With a histogram, on the other hand, the positioning of the columns cannot be arbitrary in this way.

Misleading bar charts

It is very easy to mislead with unfairly displayed bar charts. Newspapers do it very frequently. Take a look again at Figure 12.2. In version (b) journalists might foment an educational panic with the headline 'Girls streak ahead in maths', whereas the correct version, (a), gives a much fairer impression of the true situation (still interesting since it was only in 1995 that girls first passed boys in maths at GCSE level). The fairer headline here might be 'Girls edge ahead in A level maths'. The cheating journalist has chopped off the scale from 0 to around 69%. This chart is an unfair representation of the facts and shouldn't be used at all. The convention for avoiding this possible misrepresentation, when you need to economise on space in your diagram, is shown in the chart produced by David, Chapman, Foot and Sheehy (1986), reproduced here as Figure 12.3. Notice that the vertical scale has been chopped between 0 and 15, but this is made obvious to the reader.

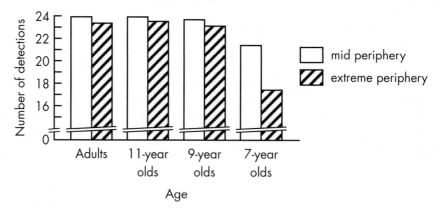

Source: From David *et al.*, 1986

Figure 12.3 Mean number of apparent movement detections made by four age groups in mid and extreme periphery

Combined bar charts

A bar chart can display two values together, as in Figure 12.3. Figure 12.4 shows the results of an experiment by Gordon, Bindrim, McNicholas and Walden (1988) in which participants were asked to give a jail sentence to a fictitious person who had either committed burglary or embezzlement and who was either black or white, giving four conditions in all under which different participants were tested. Mean sentences are shown in Figure 12.4 and note that the chart requires a 'legend' to identify the different columns.

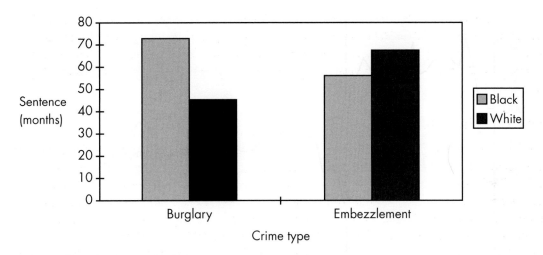

Source: Data from Gordon *et al.* (1988)

Figure 12.4 Mock sentences given to a fictitious black or white burglar and embezzler

Line charts

LINE CHARTS are useful for plotting the progress of groups over several measurement intervals. For instance, the chart in Figure 12.5 is very useful as a visual description of the comparison between regular progress for two groups of children who received different training-to-read programmes. Here, measures have been taken each month, though the data points could represent a month's average of weekly or daily test results. Such charts are also known as TIME-SERIES plots. Figure 12.6, as a good example, shows the clear change in road accident casualties following intense and well-publicised use of the breathalyser in the UK in October 1967. These data were referred to in discussing natural quasi-experiments in Chapter 5.

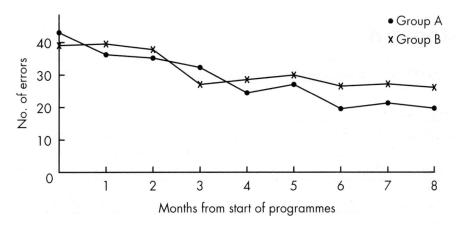

Figure 12.5 Line chart – reading error scores for two groups of children progressing through two different training-to-read programmes

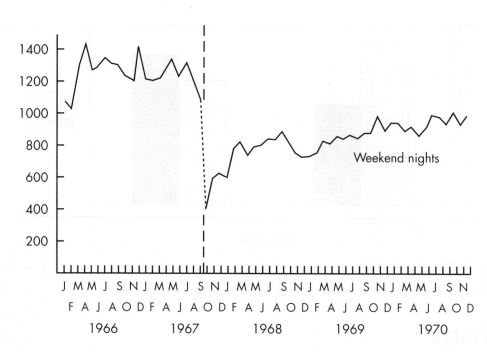

Source: From Ross *et al.* (1973)

Figure 12.6 Time-series chart – casualties (UK) before and after the 1967 breathalyser crackdown

Line charts can also be drawn where the horizontal scale is *not* continuous. The horizontal axis might carry the values of several trials in an experiment. Line charts are conventionally used to demonstrate the *interaction effect* in a two-way ANOVA analysis (see Figure 19.2 as an example). Here we can clearly see the way that one independent variable (accent) varies in different ways for the two levels of the other independent variable (rater's perceived ethnicity).

The histogram

A histogram is a way of showing the pattern of the *whole* data set to a reader. It communicates information about the *shape* of the distribution of values found. The extroversion scores data from Table 12.1 are depicted in a histogram in Figure 12.7.

Note that each category (or 'bin') of the frequency table is represented by one vertical bar. Frequency is usually shown on the *y* (vertical) axis. The scale or class intervals are shown on the

Data set of extroversion scores:

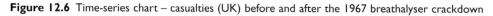

8	9	9	10	10	10	10	11	11	11	11	11	11	12	12
12	12	12	13	13	13	14	14	15	15	16	16	16	18	18

Table 12.1 Extroversion data set for histogram in Figure 12.7

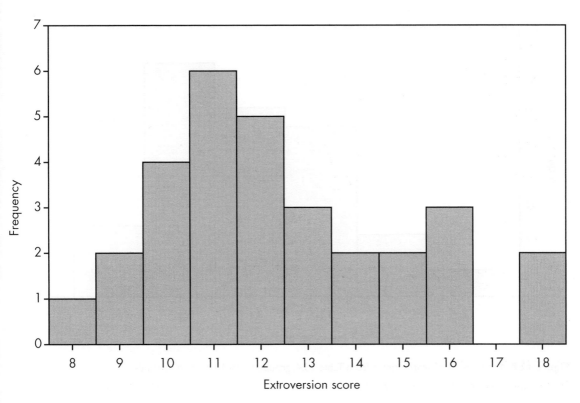

Figure 12.7 Histogram of extroversion scores

x-axis. All the bars are joined because the chart represents a continuous and whole group of scores, and therefore a gap must be left where a category is empty (see the column for 17) to show there are no scores in that class interval, except at the ends of the distribution. Each column is the same width, and since the height of each column represents the number of values found in that category, it follows that the *area* of each column is proportional to the number of cases it represents throughout the histogram. It also follows that the total of all column areas represents the whole sample. Conventionally we call the whole area *one unit*. The column for 16 in our histogram represents 3 of the 30 people in the entire group so the column for 16 is 10% of the whole in area, that is, .1 units if the whole area is 1. This is also true for the column representing people scoring 13, whereas the column for scores of 11, being 6 of the 30 scores, is 20% or .2 of the whole area 'under the curve'. Statisticians like to talk of a 'curve' even where a chart has jagged edges like this one. Most charts of large distributions *are* more curved than jagged, as we shall soon see.

A histogram of the distribution of search time scores in Table 13.4 is shown in Figure 12.8. Notice here that the *centre* of each column is marked by the mid-point of that category, since here each category does not represent a single value but a *range* of values. Hence, 14.5 is the mid-point of the category 9.5 to 19.5 and these are the extremes of the interval, as explained in Chapter 11.

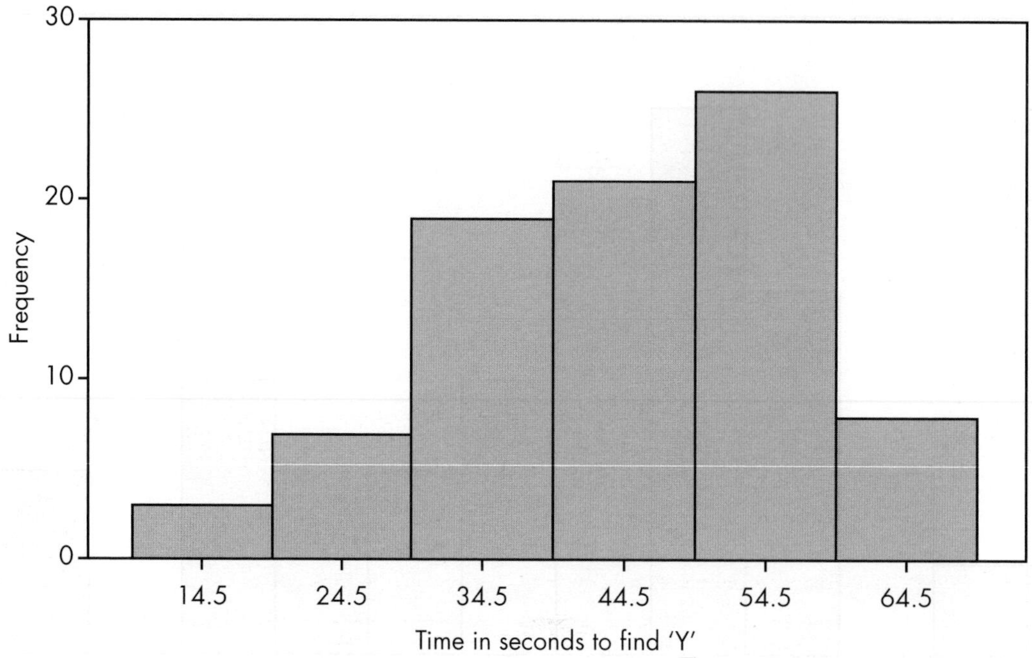

Figure 12.8 Frequencies of search times from Table 13.4, grouped into 10-second intervals

Features of the histogram

- Columns are equal width per equal category interval.
- Column areas are proportional to the frequency they represent and they sum to the total area. The entire area of the histogram is considered as *one* unit.
- Columns can *only* represent frequencies.
- No space between columns (they are not separated bars as would appear in a regular bar chart).
- All categories are represented *even if empty*, except at the two extremes of the distribution.

Frequency polygon

If we redraw our histogram of search times (Figure 12.8) with only a dot at the centre of the top of each column we would get what is known as a FREQUENCY POLYGON when we joined up the dots, as in Figure 12.9.

Exploratory data analysis

Within the last few decades the emphasis on good, informative display of data has increased, largely due to the work of Tukey (1977), who introduced the term EXPLORATORY DATA ANALYSIS. Tukey argued that researchers had tended to rush towards testing their data for significant differences and the like, whereas they should try to spend more time and effort than previously in

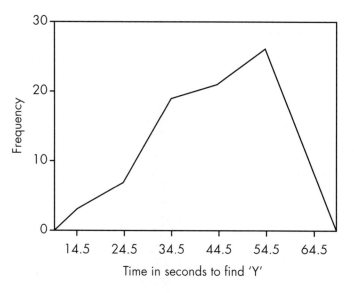

Figure 12.9 Frequency polygon of search times in Table 13.4

exploring the patterns within the data gathered. He introduced a number of techniques, and we shall cover two of the most common graphical ones here. The main aim here is to present data in visually meaningful ways while retaining as much as possible of the original information.

The stem and leaf display

This cunning, horticultural-sounding type of diagram manages to display the pattern in a data set while still also showing every value in the set. Figure 12.1 shows all the raw scores in a data set but completely fails to show any useful pattern among them. In contrast to this, have a look at Figure 12.10. Here we see that:

- the *stem* is the tens digit of each value, e.g. 3 is the 30 part of a score like 34
- the *leaves* are the units of each value – hence, if you look to the right of stem '2', you can see that there was a 21 (20 + 1), a 22 and a 29 in the set
- the diagram takes up the shape of a sideways histogram with the same intervals
- note that we obtain this general histogram-like shape but retain each of the original individual values, which would be lost in a traditional histogram
- the column headed 'cumulative', which is not always included, gives the CUMULATIVE FREQUENCY of cases (see p. 306) – e.g. there are 25 people with 49 or less
- if there are too many data for each stem we can use a symbol to show a sub-division of the usual 10 units; In Figure 12.10, * represents the 5 to 9 leaves of the 50 and 60 stems.

Cumulative	Stem	Leaf
1	0	5
1	1	
4	2	129
11	3	3445569
25	4	00122235667778
51	5	000001112223333333344444444
78	5*	5555566666667777777888899999
107	6	000011111111222222222233334444
123	6*	5666666777788899
131	7	13445788
133	8	03

> Data for the 30–39 stem:
> 33 34 34 35 35 36 39

Figure 12.10 Stem and leaf display of exam results for 133 students

Box-plots

These are based on *ordinal* measurements of the set of data. They give us a graphical display of the interquartile range – the spread of the middle section of the data – while also giving us a view of the extremities. The following values have been calculated from the data in Figure 12.10 and produced the box-plot shown in Figure 12.11.

Median position	$(N+1)/2 = (133+1)/2 = $ **67**
Median	67th value = **57** (we needn't worry about being accurate *within* the set of 6 values of 57. This is a chart, not a fine calculation)
Hinge position	(Median position$+1)/2 = (67+1)/2 = $ **34**
Lower hinge	34th lowest value = **52**
Upper hinge	34th highest value = **63**
Hinge spread	upper hinge – lower hinge = **11**
Outer fences	low: lower hinge – (1.5×hinge spread) = 52 – (1.5×11) = **35.5** high: upper hinge + (1.5×hinge spread) = 63 + (1.5×11) = **79.5**
Adjacent values	lower (= first *inside* low outer fence, nearer to median) = **35** upper (= first *inside* high outer fence, nearer to median) = **78**

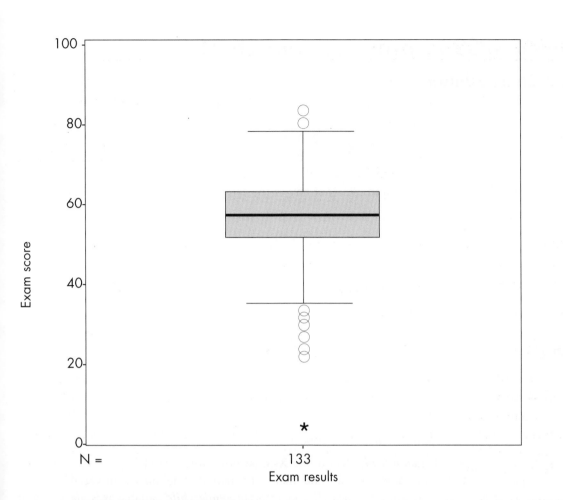

Figure 12.11 Box-plot of exam scores from Figure 12.10

Explanatory notes

The box has a bar showing the median and is bounded by two 'hinges', which are the first and third quartiles. The 'hinge spread' is therefore the interquartile range (see p. 269). The 'fences' are 1.5 times the hinge spread away from the hinges. The 'adjacent values' are those scores furthest from the median yet still inside the fences. These are shown on the plot by the 'whiskers' – the horizontal lines at the ends of the thin lines coming away from the hinges. Finally, any extreme values are shown where they fall or, when showing them would make the plot awkwardly squashed because of a huge scale, they are simply given at the edges with their actual values. Extreme values are defined by SPSS as being more than three box lengths from either edge of the box. The box length is 11 here and 3 times this is 33. Hence, scores below 19 (being 52–33) would be 'extreme' here and this is why the value 5 is shown as such (with a star). Perhaps this is the score of a student who was sick at the start of the exam or who had 'spotted' the wrong questions in advance – a very dangerous practice!

Using SPSS to produce your charts

The Chart Builder

Recent versions of SPSS have included a very friendly and easy to use Chart Builder. Earlier versions used a set of menu items and dialogue boxes to achieve the same results. These procedures are still available in v.16 by clicking **Graphs/Legacy Dialogs.** However, here we will use the Chart Builder as it appears in v.16. There are slight differences from v.15 in the overall layout but the same essential items are all available in that version. If you are using an even older version, then you could get the 'Dialogs' from Coolican (2004) or any of the earlier dedicated texts such as Pallant (2004).

Creating a bar chart

We'll create a bar chart of the means for girls' and boys' talking times in Table 11.10.

> Click on **Graphs/ Chart Builder** and you see the screen shown in Figure 12.12.
>
> Click on **Bar** in the **Choose from** list.
>
> Click and hold on the type of bar chart you would like and drag it into the main **Chart Preview** box.
>
> A box entitled **Element Properties** will appear. Close this, although you may need to come back to it later. If so you click the **Element Properties** button to the lower right of the **Chart Preview** box.

We want our categories ('*female*', '*male*') to appear on the horizontal x-axis so:

Click and drag the variable *genderchild* over to the **X-axis?** box. Note that SPSS picks up and correctly places the two value labels 'female' and 'male'. It is here that defining your variable originally as *nominal, ordinal* or *scale* is crucial. If you left your *genderchild* variable as '*scale*' you will get an odd-looking chart with a numerical scale along the bottom. We don't want that. However, all is not lost. You can right-click on the *genderchild* variable while it is in the left hand variables box and temporarily change it to nominal.

Now drag *Talking time..* over to **Count** box. Note that SPSS has picked up the precisely defined label for this variable, not its short form from the data sheet. You can edit all labels and titles later. SPSS will by default graph the mean value of this variable but if you want some other value click on the choice bar in the **Statistics** area of the **Element Properties** box.

That really is all there is to it! Before finally seeing the chart, note that the chart you see in the preview is not the exact shape that your actual chart will take with your data. The **Chart preview** box, as it says, uses only fictitious data just to show you what elements your chart will have, that is, what it will look like in general. Before clicking **OK,** just check you have all the right parts in the right places and that the preview is how you wish your final chart to appear.

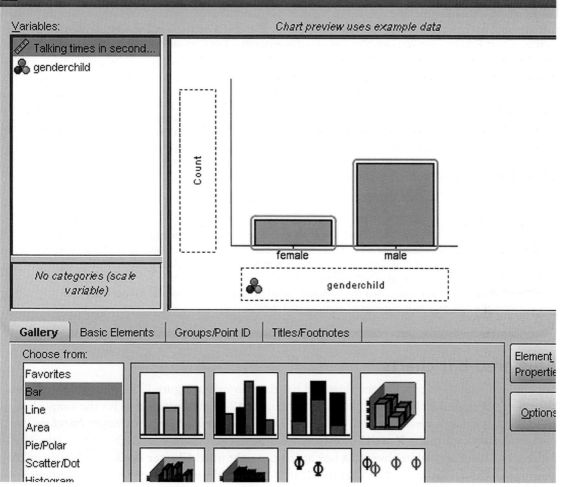

Figure 12.12 The Chart Builder in SPSS

Click **OK**.

There may be a little wait depending on the capacity of your computer but the chart will next appear in an output screen along with any other results you have so far produced.

Info Box 12.1 Editing charts with the Chart Editor

When your bar chart first appears you can double-click on it and a new screen will appear called the **SPSS Chart Editor**. Here you can alter just about everything – titles, headings, labels, colours, patterns, scales (on the axes) and styles.

Editing labels and titles

To add a title select the **Titles/Footnotes** tab, make a selection and enter your text in the **Element Properties** box. SPSS will pick up your variable names or labels (if you've used them) and also the value labels given to variable codes. If you have used a term like 'audpres' for an experimental condition this will need to be edited into a label that makes sense to your reader. Never present your charts with these shortened and meaningless labels such as 'Gp1' or 'Intgce'. Also make sure that your title is fully informative as described earlier. Your reader should be able to see what the chart is all about *without* having to refer to your main text.

Pretty charts

When the technical aspects of your chart are satisfactory, you can entertain yourself playing with the various colour, pattern, shading and bar styles that are available in the chart editing window. However, be aware that your tutors will howl at over-fancy charts and really a simple, clear black and white version is always preferable whatever your artistic tendencies! No marks are awarded by any assessment system for pretty charts while they *are* awarded for sufficient detail in headings and labels, for accuracy and presenting the appropriate groupings of summarised data.

Clustered bar charts

Suppose we wanted to produce the clustered bar chart shown in Figure 12.4. We would select and drag over the clustered chart style (second left in Figure 12.12) and proceed as for the simple bar chart. First, we drag a variable which we might have named *crimetype* (with values *burglary* and *embezzlement*) over to the **X-axis?** box. Next we drag the second independent variable *ethnicity* (with levels black and white) over to a box at the top right titled **Cluster on X** which appears for this type of chart. Finally we drag over the dependent variable, which might be called *sentence length (in months)*, to the **Count** box. For a clustered bar chart where one variable is a repeat measure, see the next section.

Repeated measures

If you want a bar for each repeated measurement of a variable on the same people (e.g. errors at *time1*, *time2* and *time3*), then select the simple bar chart and drag your first variable (e.g. *time1*) over to the **Y-axis?** box. Now where to put the other two variables? Well, they are also going to be measured on the Y-axis scale so why not drag them all there? Yes, you can do this! Drag over *time2* and when your cursor is over the **Y-axis?** box you should see a smaller red box with a cross light up. When this happens, drop *time2* in and then do the same with *time3*. That's it! If you had measures on these three variables for a second category variable (e.g. *trained* and *untrained*), then drag this to the **X-axis?** box and you will produce a *clustered bar chart with a repeated measure*.

Histograms

Select **Histogram** from the **Choose from** list and select the simplest (top left) design. Drag this into the **Preview box**. Drag the required variable into the **X-axis?** box. Done! If you want a normal curve with the same mean and variance to be superimposed on your columns check the **Display normal curve** option in the **Element Properties** box.

Line charts

Select **Line** from the **Choose from** list and select the simplest (left-hand) form.

Enter your variables in exactly the same way as you did for the bar chart above.

For repeated measures from the same people, follow the same procedures for the repeated measures bar chart.

Interaction charts – line charts for two categorical variables

Interaction effects (see p. 503) can occur when *two* independent variables are manipulated together, e.g. the effects of heat *and* noise on memory performance. If you have this kind of data set you *can* use the line chart function to produce a typical interaction chart following exactly the same procedure as that described above for the clustered bar chart by selecting the **Multiple** option. However, a much easier option is to use the **Plots** option in the two-way ANOVA procedures described on pp. 513 and 514 since you will probably be using this analysis in any case.

For an interaction where one independent variable is repeated measures, enter the variables in the same way as described under *repeated measures* above.

Stem and leaf displays and box-plots

Select **Analyze/Descriptive statistics/Explore**

Move your variable(s) to the right-hand side.

Check **Plots** – the third radio button from the left at the bottom under the heading **Display.**

To speed things up, if you want only stem and leaf plots, click the **Plots** button to the right-hand side and check the **None** button for box-plots. These, but not stem and leaf charts, can also be obtained from the **Graphs** menu.

Click **Continue** and then **OK**.

1 Consider the following set of times, measured in 1/100ths of a second:

62 65 71 72 73 75 76 77 79 80 82 83 92 100 106 117 127

65 70 72 72 74 75 76 77 79 80 82 88 93 102 110 121 128

65 70 72 73 74 76 76 78 80 81 83 90 95 103 112 122 135

For this data set: (a) Produce a histogram

(b) Design a stem and leaf chart

(c) Draw a box plot

2 Suppose that the children in Table 11.10 are again observed for talking time but on this occasion they are told that some adults are observing them. Let's say that the following data are obtained for the same children in the same order as in Table 12.2:

Girls	224	156	101	333	203	Times spent talking in seconds
Boys	145	123	85	198	434	

Table 12.2 Children's talking times when observed

Draw a clustered bar chart showing the mean talking times for boys and girls when unaware and aware of being observed.

Answers

1 (a) Histograms can be drawn in different ways depending on the size of the intervals you choose to be represented by columns. However, please save your attempt until we reach the exercises in the next chapter on p. 320.

(b) Stem and leaf diagram:

Stem	Leaf
6	2555
7	0012222334455666677899
8	000122338
9	0235
10	0236
11	027
12	1278
13	5

(c) Box plot details:

Median position: 26   Median: 79

Hinge position: 13   Lower hinge: 73   Upper hinge: 95

Hinge spread: 22   Low outer fence: 40   High outer fence: 128

Outlier: 135   Adjacent value: 62   Adjacent value: 128

2

Talk times (secs.) of female and male children when aware/unaware of observation

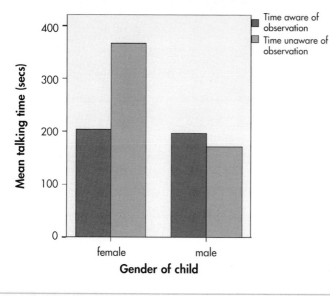

Glossary

Bar chart	Chart in which (usually) the x-axis represents a categorical variable and the *y*-axis can represent frequency, average, percentage etc.
Box-plot	*Exploratory data* chart showing median, central spread of data and position of relative extremes
Cumulative frequency	Distribution (table or chart) that shows the number of cases that have occurred up to and including the current category
Exploratory data analysis	Close examination of data by a variety of means, including visual display, before submitting them to significance testing; recommended by Tukey
Frequency polygon	*Histogram* showing only the peaks of class intervals
Histogram	Chart containing whole of continuous data set divided into proportional class intervals
Line chart	Chart joining continuous data points in a single line
Stem and leaf chart	*Exploratory data* analysis tool showing every value in a data set but organised into class intervals to give a histogram shape
Time series	*Line chart* showing measures of variable at progressive time intervals

Frequencies and distributions

13

This chapter looks at how we deal with frequencies and with larger sets of data and, in particular, with the properties and use of the *normal distribution*. Subsequent work on statistical significance all leans heavily on the assumption of an underlying normal distribution for our variables so that we can make use of known properties to estimate the likelihood of differences and correlations occurring.

- Large sets of data form a *distribution* and these may be represented in several ways. They may be divided into *categories* and presented as a *frequency table*.

- Statistics of distributions include *percentiles*, *quartiles* and *deciles* and we can describe distributions in terms of *cumulative frequencies*.

- The *normal distribution* is an extremely important distribution shape. Data approximating to this shape can be tested with the most powerful significance techniques; techniques to estimate underlying population *parameters* from sample statistics are readily available.

- z values are the *deviation* of a value measured in the number of standard deviations it is from the mean and on the normal distribution they cut off known percentages of area under the curve.

- The concept of *sampling* from underlying *populations* is examined and the concept of a *sampling distribution* is introduced; this concept is central to the *inferential* statistical analyses later in the book, especially *parametric tests,* which make estimates of *population parameters* from *sample statistics*.

- Distributions with substantially more values at the high end of the measurement scale are said to be *positively skewed*. More values at the lower end produce a *negatively skewed* distribution. If a skewed distribution shows bunching at the top end because too many people score the maximum or very near it, then the variable measure shows a *ceiling effect*. Bunching near the bottom is a *floor effect*. Distributions with two distinct 'humps' (higher frequencies) are known as *bi-modal*.

- *Kurtosis* refers to the overall shape of the distribution in terms of height and width; *platykurtic*, normal and *leptokurtic* distributions are described. Calculations are provided for skew and kurtosis.

Dealing with larger data sets

So far we have looked at samples and distributions of data only in terms of their numerical central tendency and dispersion. This is usually all that is necessary for a small data set – for example, scores on a memory task for ten experimental participants, though we might like to inspect the set for extreme values that are distorting the mean. However, where a large data set has been gathered we would often like to look more closely at the overall DISTRIBUTION formed by our data. We can pick out patterns here that cannot be seen in a small sample simply because there are not enough repetitions of the same or similar values for us to be able to consider the *frequency* with which these occur. With a large enough sample, we can estimate the shape of the distribution for the whole population from which the sample was drawn and this is central to the development of psychological and educational tests.

Table 13.1 shows some extroversion scores for 30 participants. Table 13.2 shows the frequency table that SPSS produces for these data. The left-hand column shows each score value. The next column shows the number of these scores that occurred (the FREQUENCY for that value). This column is a FREQUENCY DISTRIBUTION. The third column shows the percentages at each score value and the fourth column shows the *cumulative percentage*. This is the percentage of cases that have occurred up to and including the value shown. Such a table could also show *cumulative frequency*, which is the *number* of cases that have occurred up to and including the given value. Table 13.3 shows cumulative frequency for children making different numbers of observed utterances in a single day. Here the range of possible values is high – from 0 to 79. Hence it makes sense to group the measured variable into broad categories (0–9, etc.). These score categories are called '*bins*'.

8	9	9	10	10	10	10	11	11	11	11
11	11	12	12	12	12	12	13	13	13	14
14	15	15	16	16	16	18	18			

Table 13.1 Extroversion – raw scores for 30 participants

Extroversion			
	Frequency	**Percent**	**Cumulative Percent**
8.00	1	3.3	3.3
9.00	2	6.7	10.0
10.00	4	13.3	23.3
11.00	6	20.0	43.3
12.00	5	16.7	60.0
13.00	3	10.0	70.0
14.00	2	6.7	76.7
15.00	2	6.7	83.3
16.00	3	10.0	93.3
18.00	2	6.7	100.0
Total	30	100.0	

Table 13.2 Frequency table of extroversion scores

No. of utterances	Frequency (No. of children)	Cumulative frequency
0–9	3	3
10–19	0	3
20–29	15	18
30–39	43	61
40–49	69	130
50–59	17	147
60–69	24	171
70–79	4	175
Total	175	

Table 13.3 Frequencies of telegraphic utterances made in one day

Notice here that, technically, each class interval has limits half an interval *beyond* the range of values given for each category. That is, the 10–19 interval, strictly speaking, runs from 9.5 to 19.5, so that if we had a value somewhere *between* 9 and 10 we would know how to decide into which category interval it fell. However, since 'number of utterances' is measured on a *discrete* scale (we can only have a whole number of utterances), this is not a problem here, and calling the intervals 10–19 presents no decision difficulties. However, where we use a *continuous* scale we must be very careful to recognise class interval limits. In Table 13.4, we see a summary of participants' times taken for a visual search for a 'Y' hidden among a page of 'X's. Times are measured on a continuous scale so a value of 19.4 falls into the '10–19' category, whereas 19.7 falls into '20–29'. For the very rare value that falls right on the division (e.g. 19.5), we simply toss a coin to decide in which category it should be counted or decide on the basis of the pre-rounded decimal.

Time interval (secs)	Frequency (participants)	Cumulative frequency	Class interval limits
10–19	3	3	9.5 to 19.5
20–29	7	10	19.5 to 29.5
30–39	19	29	29.5 to 39.5
40–49	21	50	39.5 to 49.5
50–59	26	76	49.5 to 59.5
60–69	8	84	59.5 to 69.5

Table 13.4 Frequencies of search times

Percentiles, deciles and quartiles

When tests are *standardised* they are piloted on very large samples of the intended population and various estimated norms for the population are calculated. These are similar to those you encounter when taking a baby to the health clinic. The nurse will have a chart showing average heights and weights at various ages and she can tell at a glance where the baby is relative to these norms. She will use the term PERCENTILE. This is a point that cuts off a certain percentage of the population.

The 'tenth percentile' is the point on a scale that cuts off the bottom 10% of cases. In Table 13.5 you can see that the bottom 10% (34 out of 340 cases) are contained in the categories from 13 to 16 months. Assuming we are measuring to the nearest half month then 16.5 is the tenth percentile. The median (19.5) is the fiftieth percentile; it cuts off the lower 170 cases or 50%. It is also the fifth DECILE, because deciles cut off the distribution in 10% units; the third decile cuts off the bottom 30%, for instance. The median is also the second quartile because quartiles cut off in 25% (or quarter) units.

Age (months)	13	14	15	16	17	18	19	20	21	22	23	24	25	26	TOTAL
Frequency	3	0	8	23	37	64	35	83	21	37	20	0	4	5	340

Table 13.5 Age in months at which parents report first telegraphic utterance

As with the median, if we want to calculate a percentile that is somewhere *within* a class interval, we need a formula:

$$Percentile = L + \frac{(Np/100 - F)}{f_m}(h)$$

where p is the percentile required and the other symbols are the same as for the median calculation on p. 266.

The normal distribution

Having introduced distributions we now move to one of the most important ones in statistical work – the *normal distribution*. On p. 257 I pointed out that a measurement value, such as a person's height of, say, 163cm, is really a statement that the value falls within a *class interval*. We are saying that the person, for instance, is closer to 163cm than 162cm or 164cm, rather than that they measure 163cm exactly. They are in the *interval* between 162.5 and 163.5cm. In effect, if we measure to the nearest centimetre, we are placing individuals in *class intervals* 1cm wide. It happens that if we take a large enough random sample of individuals from a population and measure physical qualities such as height (or weight, or length of finger), especially if we use a fine scale of measurement (such as to the nearest millimetre), we get a distribution looking like Figure 13.1.

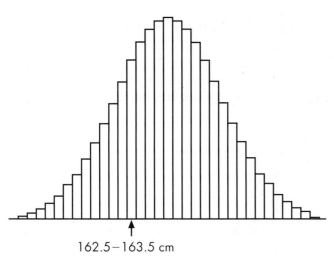

162.5−163.5 cm

Figure 13.1 Frequency distribution of heights measured to nearest centimetre

The curve that typically results from such measurements *closely approximates* to a very well-known 'bell-shaped' mathematical curve, produced from a shockingly complicated formula (which you or I need not bother with) devised by Gauss. The curve is therefore known as 'Gaussian' but in statistical work we more commonly refer to it as a NORMAL DISTRIBUTION CURVE (see Figure 13.2), i.e. it plots a NORMAL DISTRIBUTION.

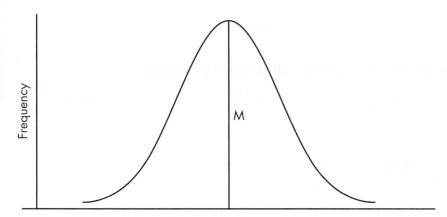

Figure 13.2 A normal distribution curve

Characteristics of a normal distribution curve

1 It is symmetrical about the mid-point of the horizontal axis.

2 The point about which it is symmetrical (the line marked 'M' in Figure 13.2) is the point at which the mean, median and mode all fall.

309

3 The 'asymptotes' (tail ends) of the perfect curve never quite meet the horizontal axis. Although for distributions of real large samples there are existing real limits, we can always hypothesise a more extreme value in a theoretical population.

4 It is known what area under the curve is contained between the central point (mean) and the point where one standard deviation falls – see Figure 13.3. In fact, working in units of one standard deviation, we can calculate *any* area under the curve.

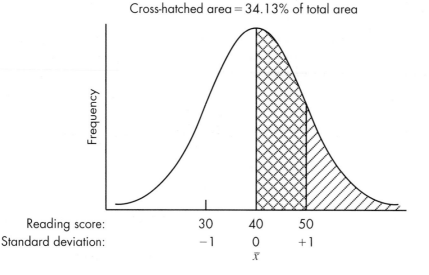

Cross-hatched area = 34.13% of total area

Reading score:	30	40	50
Standard deviation:	−1	0	+1
		$\bar{x}$	

Figure 13.3 Distribution of reading scores for eight-year-old children

Approximations to the normal curve – and normal people

It is very important to remember, in all that follows, that when psychological variables are said to be 'normally distributed', or 'standardised to fit a normal distribution', we are always talking about *approximations* to a pure normal curve. People *en masse* always differ a bit from the ideal. This matters, because, when we come on to testing significance, the statistical theory often assumes a normal distribution for the population from which samples were drawn. If population values on the variable form nothing like a normal distribution, then the conclusions from the significance test may be seriously in error. It's also important not to be morally outraged by the use of the term 'normal' apparently to describe people. The curve is called 'normal' for purely *mathematical* reasons (you may remember the use of the term 'normal' as meaning 'perpendicular' in geometry).

Area under the normal distribution curve

Suppose we devise a reading test for eight-year-olds and the maximum score possible on the test is 80. The test is standardised to a normal distribution such that the mean score for a large representative sample of eight-year-olds is 40 and the standard deviation is 10. I hope it is obvious, for starters, that 50% of eight-year-olds will therefore be above 40 and 50% below. The area for the top 50% is *all* the shaded area in Figure 13.3.

What we know, from the theory underlying the normal curve, is that one standard deviation, *on any normal distribution curve*, falls at the position shown by the line above 50 on Figure 13.3. What is also known from mathematical tables (see Appendix Table 2) is that 34% of values fall between the mean and one standard deviation above the mean (34.13% if being more precise). Treating the entire area under the curve as one unit, this means that the area between the mean and one standard deviation above it is .34 of the whole, shown cross-hatched. Hence we know that 34% of children score between 40 and 50 points on this test, since the standard deviation is 10 points. Also, since 50% of all values lie above the mean, the proportion *above* 1 standard deviation must be 16% (50% − 34%).

Table 13.6 shows (in more precise values) the areas cut off by 1, 2 and 3 standard deviations. The positions of these standard deviations are shown in Figure 13.4. Note that you can add the values

Section	z values	% of area under curve	Area as proportion of whole	
$\bar{x}$ to 1 standard deviation above $\bar{x}$	$z = 0$ to $z = 1$	34.13	.3413	
$\bar{x}$ to 2 standard deviations above $\bar{x}$	$z = 0$ to $z = 2$	47.72	.4772	
$\bar{x}$ to 1.65 standard deviations above $\bar{x}$	$z = 0$ to $z = 1.65$	45	.45	5% limit, one-tailed
$\bar{x}$ to 1.96 standard deviations above $\bar{x}$	$z = 0$ to $z = 1.96$	47.5	.475	5% limit, two-tailed

Table 13.6 Proportions and areas under the normal curve

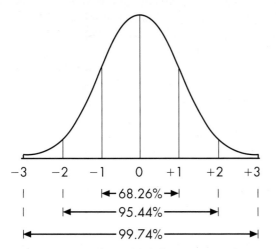

Area between $-n$ and $+n$ standard deviations on the normal curve.

Figure 13.4 Positions of standard deviations and the areas they enclose on the normal distribution

above together to get different areas. For instance, the area from the mean to one standard deviation *below* the mean is also 34.13%. Hence we know that the number of children scoring within 1 standard deviation of the mean (either way) must be 68.26% and the number below a score of 30 must be nearly 16%.

The two lower rows in Table 13.6 will become important when we discuss significance testing over the next few chapters. A *z* score (see below) of 1.96 cuts off the most extreme 5% of the distribution, 2.5% at either end.

z scores (or 'standard scores')

In the reading test example (see Figure 13.3) a child with a score of 50 lies one standard deviation above the mean. We could say that the number of standard deviations she is from the mean is +1 (the '+' signifying 'above'). If we measure number of standard deviations from the mean in this way we are using *z* SCORES, which are a particular type of STANDARD SCORE. It is very often useful, especially in work involving measures on psychological scales, to convert all raw scores to *standard* measures that tell us how far each person is, on any scale, from the mean. For instance, you could be told that your child is 1.2 standard deviations above the mean on height but only 0.3 standard deviations above the mean on weight. We would not need to work with the raw measures of height (cm) and weight (kilos). You would know that your child was taller than at least 84% of children his age. Similarly, SATs scores for children on writing, spelling, maths, etc. are given only in standard units that assess your child relative to all other children tested.

There is a formula for *z* scores but it is always worth repeating to yourself that *a z score is the number of standard deviations a score is from the* mean. The formula is:

$z = \dfrac{x - \bar{x}}{s}$ where *s* is the standard deviation and $x - \bar{x}$, I hope you'll see, is the *deviation score*.

Dividing the deviation score by the standard deviation answers the question 'How many standard deviations is this score from the mean?' Let's say the mean for shoe size in your class is 8, with a standard deviation of 1.5. If your shoe size is 5 and I ask you how many standard deviations your size is from the mean you would probably have no difficulty in saying that your size is 2 standard deviations below the mean. You have a *z* score of –2 for shoe size. You actually followed the formula above. The only reason we need it is for when calculations involve numbers that aren't so friendly. Let's check using the formula:

$z = \dfrac{5 - 8}{1.5} = \dfrac{-3}{1.5} = -2$

z scores and the normal distribution

We saw above that standard deviations cut off various known proportions of the area under the normal curve. Since *z* scores are just numbers of standard deviations, they too cut off the same proportions. Therefore we know the percentage of the population enclosed between the mean and any *z* score. For instance, Table 13.6 shows that the area between $z = 0$ and $z = +1$ is 34.13%. That is, it is the same as the area between the mean and one standard deviation above the mean.

There are tables for intermediate areas cut off by z values all along the x axis. For instance, let's consider the percentage of values between the mean and z of 1.5. We go to Table 2 in the Appendix. Notice that the table is made up of three columns which are repeated across the page, the first of these being the required z value. So we need to find the value 1.5 in the z column. On the right of this value in the next column you should find the value .4332 which is 43.32% of the area and this can be seen in the diagram at the head of this column. A larger version appears shaded on the right in Figure 13.5. The final right-hand column of Appendix Table 2 contains the percentage between the z value and the *extreme right* of the distribution. Values for *negative z* scores are calculated using a mirror image. A z score of −2.2 traps .486 of the area between it and the mean on the left-hand side of the curve. Since the *whole* of the left-hand side of the mean is .5 of the area, then by subtracting 486 from .5, we find that only .014 is left at the left hand extreme beyond −2.2 standard deviations. This is shown by the cross-hatching in Figure 13.5, and by consulting the right-hand column of the z score table entry for $z = 2.2$.

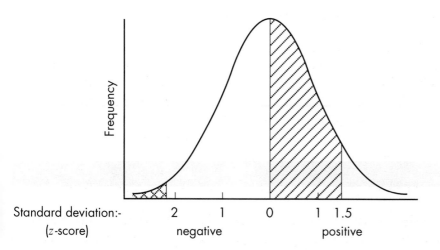

Figure 13.5 Areas between the mean and z value of +1.5 (shaded) and below a z value of −2.2 (cross-hatched)

1 Try to use the formula to check what z score a child with a score of 25 on the reading test discussed above would have.

2 In an IQ distribution, where the mean is 100 and standard deviation 15:

(a) what IQ score are 95% of people above?

(b) what percentage of people would score less than 90?

(c) what z score does a person have who scores 120?

3 In Table 13.7 complete all the blank spaces indicated by letters.

Mean	SD	Raw score	Deviation	z score	% above	% below
40	10	a	−15	−1.5	93.3	6.7
100	15	135	35	b	c	d
17.5	2.5	e	f	2	g	h
i	4	57	j	−1.75	k	l
21	m	25	4	n	30.85	o
15.6	3.47	p	q	r	s	55.96

Table 13.7 Scores and statistics for exercise 3

1 −1.5

2 (a) 75.31 (b) 25.14% (c) 1.33

3 a: 25; b: 2.33; c: 0.99; d: 99.01; e: 22.5; f: 5; g: 2.28; h: 97.72; i: 64; j: -7; k: 95.99;

l: 4.01; m: 8; n: 0.5; o: 69.15; p: 16.12; q: 0.52; r: 0.15; s: 44.04

Standardisation of psychological measurements

The relationship between z scores and area under the normal curve is of crucial importance in the world of testing. *If* (and it is a big if) a variable can be assumed to distribute normally among the population, *and* we have a test standardised on large samples, then we can quickly assess the relative position of people by using their raw test score converted to a z score. This is valuable when assessing, for instance, children's reading ability, general intellectual or language development, adult stress, anxiety, aptitude for certain occupations (at interview) and so on. However, always recall that the 'if' is big and much work must go into the justification of treating a test result as normally distributed (see the points made on p. 202). Note that psychologists have not *discovered* that intelligence has a normal distribution in the population. The tests were purposely created to *fit* a normal distribution, basically for research purposes and practical convenience in test comparisons. Usually an IQ test is *standardised* (raw scores are adjusted) to produce a mean of 100 and a standard deviation of around 15 points.

Sampling distributions

Now that we have introduced the properties of the normal distribution and the idea of sections of a distribution it will be useful to introduce the notion of SAMPLING DISTRIBUTIONS in order to prepare the ground for significance tests in the next chapter and beyond. Sampling distributions are (usually) distributions of means of samples rather than of individual values. We said earlier that a sample mean will always be a little bit out from the true population mean. This 'bit' is known as *sampling error*. On a box of matches you will often see the words 'average contents 40', which means that the overall average number of matches in a box is 40. Obviously this varies a little from box to box. Suppose we were at the match-making factory and took a random sample of ten boxes from stock. We take the average content of all the boxes and find it is 41.3 across our ten boxes. We take another ten boxes at random and this time the mean content is 38.9. This difference between samples is the result of SAMPLING ERROR and could also be called *sampling variation*. What might we guess is the true mean of the entire population of match boxes? Obviously there is no finite population as the factory keeps on producing more and more boxes. However, we might guess from the couple we have tested so far that the ideal population mean is 40. This is what the machines are set at and is the average we would get if we measured every box ever manufactured with these settings. What match box quality inspectors need to know is: are the match box contents varying *too far* from 40? They cannot be expected to measure every box. They have to take samples and they need to know whether their sample mean is acceptably far from 40 or just too far. How is this done?

As a more psychology-based example, let's return to our reading test for eight-year-olds for which the population mean is 40. Let's say we sample 20 eight-year-olds at random (don't quibble over how this might be done) and obtain a mean of 37.3. We find 20 more eight-year-olds and obtain 43.2 and so on. Now suppose we did this many hundreds of times (don't worry; no one ever does; statisticians have ways of making figures talk; they use formulae to make reasonable estimations). We can plot all these sample means on a chart and we would usually obtain a distribution looking like that on the left of Figure 13.6. Note that this shape approaches that of a *normal distribution* as

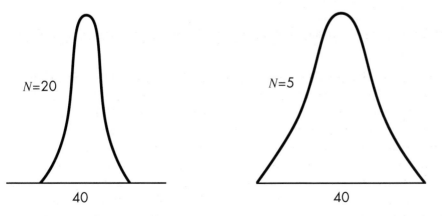

Figure 13.6 Sampling distribution of means for $N = 20$ and $N = 5$ with population mean of 40

sample size increases. The distribution we have here is a SAMPLING DISTRIBUTION OF MEANS. Here are some important points about sampling distributions.

For the same population the sampling distribution of means becomes narrower as the size of N increases; Figure 13.6 also shows a distribution when $N = 5$.

- We assume that the sampling distribution has the same mean as the population (and this is estimated as our sample mean).

- The distribution has a standard deviation but in this special case we call it the STANDARD ERROR. The idea is that each point on the distribution represents an 'error' in estimating the true population mean (of 40). That is, most sample means are a little bit out.

- From a sample of values we can estimate the standard error using the CENTRAL LIMIT THEOREM. This says that if the sample size is N then we can find the standard error of the sampling distribution using:

$$se = \frac{s}{\sqrt{N}}$$ where s is the standard deviation of the sample and N the number in it.

To summarise: a sampling distribution of means is the collection of the means of all possible random samples, size N, from a population. The mean of this sampling distribution is estimated as the sample mean and the standard error is estimated by the formula given just above.

Confidence intervals

We will use the concept of sampling distributions when we are discussing significance tests. However, there is one use we can make of them straight away. In statistics we can use sampling distributions to estimate CONFIDENCE LIMITS for the mean of a sample. This means that we state a range of values within which we are 95% confident that the true population mean lies. When we take the mean of a sample we can use that as an estimate of the *population* mean. We estimate *population parameters* from *sample statistics*. When you read about the state of the parties in the run-up to an election the pollsters will tell you that their estimate is accurate to within +/− 3%. This is something like what we do with confidence intervals. Using an observed sample mean and our knowledge of standard errors and the normal distribution, we can estimate the *range* of mean values within which we are 95% confident that the real population mean must fall. That is, we say we are 95% confident that the true population mean falls within a certain range, which we are now about to calculate.

Suppose, for 20 people, we have a mean of 35 and a standard deviation of 9.6. The bottom row of Table 13.6 tells us that 47.5% of values fall between the mean and a z of 1.96, hence 95% of values fall between a z of −1.96 and 1.96. On a sampling distribution, a z value is the number of standard errors a sample mean is from the true population mean. So we know that on a sampling distribution 95% of means lie between −1.96 and + 1.96 standard errors from the mean. How do we find the standard error? Well we did this just a little while ago. We use:

$$se = \frac{s}{\sqrt{N}} = \frac{9.6}{\sqrt{20}} = 2.147$$

For the upper limit of our confidence range then we need $z \times se = 1.96 \times 2.147 = 4.208$.

For the lower limit of our confidence range we need $z \times se = -1.96 \times 2.147 = -4.208$.

Hence we can be 95% confident that the true population mean falls between $35 + 4.208$ and $35 - 4.208$ which is between 30.792 and 39.208. If someone had estimated that the true population mean was below 30, we would have a strong case against this view.

Confidence limits have been put forward as an alternative to traditional significance testing which we are going to encounter in the next chapter. In fact, they both rest on exactly the same logic but can be more appropriate for one situation than another. We will calculate and report both as we progress through the significance tests in Chapters 15 to 20. Your psychology course methods tutors might require you to present confidence ranges (or limits – the values at the ends of the range) in your research project reports when reporting the results of your significance tests.

Skewed distributions

Some distributions obtained from psychological measures that might be expected to be normal in fact turn out SKEWED. That is, they are 'lop-sided', having their peak (mode) to one side and a distinctive tail on the side where more extreme values occur. Have a look at Figure 13.7.

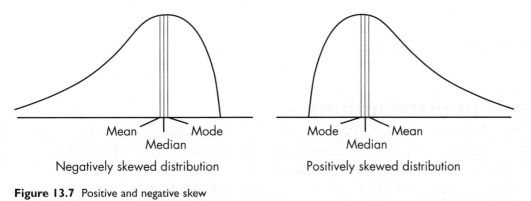

Figure 13.7 Positive and negative skew

Pause for thought

How would you construct a test that produced a negative skew – make it very hard or very easy?

Positive and negative skew

A negatively skewed distribution can be produced where a test is relatively *easy*. Most values are clustered around the top end of the distribution. Such a test produces what are known as CEILING EFFECTS. People can't score much *higher* than the mean if the mean is, say, about 17 out of 20, but a substantial number of people can still score a lot *lower* than the mean. The greater number of extreme values below the median has the effect of shifting the mean towards the tail. The mean, you may recall, is said to be most sensitive to extreme values. This is why the median or mode would be preferred here as a more appropriate and useful measure of central tendency. The opposite phenomenon, a hard test producing mostly low values and a positively skewed distribution, is said to have a FLOOR EFFECT.

Pause for thought

Suppose we were measuring reaction time for responding to words displayed one at a time on a computer screen. Participants have to decide as quickly as possible whether the word is English or non-English. The typical reaction time is around 0.7 seconds. Over many trials, what type of skewed distribution might develop?

It is possible to be very much slower than the majority of values, but is it possible to be very much faster, when the majority of values are around 0.7 seconds? This is like the situation in athletics where times can be quite a bit slower than the current good standard but not a lot faster. We would get a positively skewed distribution then. Notice that a positive skew has its *tail* up the *positive end* (higher values) of the horizontal axis.

Central tendency of skewed distributions

Notice in Figure 13.7 where the mean, median and mode fall on each type of skewed distribution. The mode obviously still falls at the top, where the majority of values are. In each case the mean is furthest from the mode – not surprising really, since we said that it was the most affected by extreme values in one direction. The median is in between.

Kurtosis in distributions

Distributions can also show KURTOSIS. This term refers to the overall shape of the curve in terms of its peak and the bunching of values. In comparison with the normal distribution, Figure 13.8 (a) shows a PLATYKURTIC DISTRIBUTION, where the data are spread out and not very peaked in the centre, whereas Figure 13.8 (b) shows a high peak and narrow bunching of data – a LEPTOKURTIC DISTRIBUTION. If you need to remember these terms, then think of the curve 'leaping up' in the latter case and being rather a 'plateau' in the former.

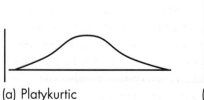

(a) Platykurtic

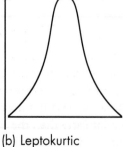

(b) Leptokurtic

Figure 13.8 Leptokurtic and platykurtic distributions

Normality checks on your data – overdoing the skew

When we encounter the *parametric* tests of significance in forthcoming chapters (*t* tests, all ANOVA designs and Pearson's correlation and regression) you will find that a condition of running these tests and being able to have confidence in their results will include the assumption that the data population from which samples have been drawn is a normal distribution (though quite a bit of tolerance is usually allowed in this). This is because we want to be able to make fair assumptions about the nature of underlying sampling distributions. To find the values of skew and kurtosis using SPSS, follow the procedure for descriptives on p. 281.

A common rule of thumb for deciding whether a distribution departs seriously from normal is to consider this so when the value of the skewness or kurtosis *statistic* is greater than twice the value of its *standard error*. SPSS provides these figures side by side for checking. Skewness is a more important consideration than kurtosis when deciding whether or not to conduct a parametric test. Where skew is indeed more than twice the standard error then you should either change to a non-parametric test or follow the procedures outlined in Chapter 15.

If you do not have access to SPSS, then another rule of thumb is to look at the difference between the mean and the median. If they are far apart, say half a standard deviation, then there is a lot of skew.

Calculating skew and kurtosis by hand

You can calculate the skewness of your data with the following, rather daunting, formula. Don't cringe. It is in fact only more of the same stuff:

$$Skewness = \frac{\left(\sum d^3\right) N}{s^3 \, (N-1) \, (N-2)}$$

Here you *cube* each deviation value (that's $d \times d \times d$) and you also cube the standard deviation of the sample. So the top line is 'add up all the cubed deviations and multiply by N'. The lower line is 'cube the standard deviation and multiply by $(N-1)$ then by $(N-2)$'.

The formula for kurtosis is:

$$Kurtosis = \frac{\sum d^4}{s^4 N} - 3 \text{ where } d^4 = d \times d \times d \times d \text{ and likewise for } s^4$$

Frequencies, percentiles and other things in SPSS

The **Frequencies** function will also give all the statistics that **Descriptives** gives except *z* values. To find *z* values follow the procedure on p. 281. The frequency table you are given will show you the number of cases obtaining each score value for the variable concerned (e.g. how many got one word right, two words right, and so on, if the variable is 'number of words recalled'). You also get that frequency as a percentage of the whole group and the **cumulative percentage** (see Table 13.2). This last (right-hand) column is very useful if you want to split your group evenly into, say, two categories ('high' and 'low') on the variable.

Click **Analyze/Descriptive Statistics/Frequencies**.

Just frequencies are given by default. If you want other statistics, such as the median or quartiles and percentiles, click **Statistics** and make your selections. The **Format** box gives various sorting and organising options.

Exercises

I Look back to Exercise I on p. 302. Have a look at the sketch you drew (I hope!) of the distribution.

(a) Decide what would be the most appropriate measure of central tendency.

(b) Calculate this measure.

(c) Calculate an appropriate measure of dispersion.

2 Sketch two roughly normal distributions that have the same mean but quite different standard deviations. Also sketch two normal distributions with the same standard deviation but different means.

3 What sort of skew is present in a distribution that has the following characteristics?

Mean = 50	Median = 60	Mode = 70

Answers

I (a) Data are skewed, therefore use median.

(b) Median = 79 (or 79.25 if the precise formula is used).

(c) Semi-interquartile range: 11 (1st quartile 73; 2nd quartile 95).

3 Negative skew.

Glossary

Ceiling effect	Occurs where measure produces most values near the top end of a scale
Central limit theorem	Used in the theoretical estimation of standard error of sampling distribution from standard deviation of a sample
Confidence limits/intervals	Limits to the likely range (interval) within which a population mean lies, based on an estimate (e.g. 'with 95% confidence') from a sample mean and standard error
Deciles	Points on a measured scale that mark off each 10% of the data set or population
Distribution	Shape and spread of data sets/populations
Floor effect	Phenomenon where measure produces very many low scores
Frequency	How often a certain event (e.g. score) occurs

Frequency distribution	Distribution showing how often certain values occurred in categories
Kurtosis	Overall shape of a distribution in terms of height and width compared with normal distribution
Leptokurtic distribution	Non-normal distribution that is closely bunched in the centre and tall
Negatively skewed	Description of distribution that has a longer tail of lower values
Normal distribution	Continuous distribution, bell-shaped, symmetrical about its mid-point
Percentile	Point on a measured scale that marks off certain percentage of cases in a data set
Platykurtic distribution	Non-normal distribution that is widely spaced out and low in the centre
Population parameter	Statistical measure of a population (e.g. mean)
Positively skewed	Description of distribution that contains a longer tail of higher values
Quartiles	Points on a measured scale that mark the 1st, 2nd and 3rd 25% of the data set
Sample statistic	Statistical measure of a sample (e.g. mean)
Sampling distribution (of means)	Theoretical distribution that would be obtained by taking the same statistic from many same size samples (e.g. the mean)
Sampling error	Difference between a sample statistic and the true population statistic, usually assumed to be random in origin
Skew/skewed distributions	Non-normal distributions that have a lot more scores on one side of the mode than on the other
Standard error	Standard deviation of a sampling distribution
Standard score	Number of standard deviations a particular score is from its sample mean
z score/value	Alternative term for standard score

14 Significance testing – was it a real effect?

When data differ under two conditions we suspect we have detected a real effect. However, the data *might* differ simply because of random and/or sampling errors. *Significance tests* are used to help us decide between the *null* and the *alternative hypotheses*. The first of these says there is no effect in the population, while the other says there is and is usually what we would like to support with our evidence. This chapter is about the principles of significance testing.

- Significance decisions involve rejecting or retaining a null hypothesis (H_0). A null hypothesis usually claims that underlying populations are identical or that population means are equal or the population correlation is zero. A version of this is that two or more samples have been randomly drawn from the same population. If the probability of a result occurring under H_0 is low, then H_0 is rejected in favour of the alternative hypothesis (H_1).

- Probability of events occurring is measured on a *probability* scale of 0 (not possible) to 1 (must happen). Calculated probability is represented by p. A *probability distribution* is a histogram with columns measuring the likelihood of occurrence of the events they represent.

- Social scientists reject the null hypothesis when the probability of a result occurring under it is less than .05 (the conventional set level of '*alpha*'; alpha is the level of probability acceptable for rejection). This is often called the '*5% significance level*'. The area of the probability distribution for a particular statistical test cut off by the set level of alpha is known as a *rejection region*. If a result falls into this area we may reject H_0.

- If the null hypothesis is true but has been rejected because $p \leq .05$, it is said that a *Type I error* has been made. *Replication* is a safeguard against the acceptance of such 'fluke' significant results. A *Type II error* occurs when the null hypothesis is retained, because $p > .05$, yet there is a real underlying effect.

- The concepts of *power* and *effect size* are introduced and it is stressed that different values of p cannot be compared sensibly without considering the size of the effect being investigated, the sample sizes and the type of statistical test used.

- Differing levels of significance are introduced. When the hypothesis tested is controversial, either theoretically or ethically, it is usual to seek significance with $p \leq .01$ or still better. A result with $p \leq .1$ might warrant further investigation, tightening of procedures, altering of design and so on.

- If the hypothesis investigated was *directional* then a *one-tailed test* of probability may be used, but there is controversy surrounding this issue. For *non-directional hypotheses* the test *must* be *two-tailed*. Results tested with a one-tailed test are more likely to reach significance than with a two-tailed test for the same sample size, but if the direction of results is opposite to that predicted, even if the difference is past the significant critical value, the null hypothesis must be retained.

- The general procedure for using a statistical test of significance is introduced.

Pause for thought . . . Guy or Doll – Which do you want?

A few years ago there was a news report about a private clinic that claimed to be able to assist couples in producing a baby of the sex they would prefer. At the end of an interview, both technical and self-promotional, the director was asked how successful the clinic had been so far. 'Well,' he said, 'we've had six couples through and four of these have left with the result they wanted.'

Suppose you had to advise a couple whether to spend a lot of money using this clinic to try to get a baby of the sex they desire. Would you be convinced from the data above that the clinic's work is effective?

Although the exercise above does not involve an everyday decision, people do use the logic of significance testing many times over in their everyday lives, usually without realising it and often despite the fact that, as psychology students, they find the concept impenetrable. The clinic example does not provide us with too much difficulty. We know that if its staff have no power whatsoever to affect the outcome of boy or girl then there is a 50–50 chance that any couple will get the sex of baby they desire. Hence, we would expect three out of six couples to be happy merely by chance alone. How much better than that then is four out of six? This question, which you might like to return to later, encapsulates the absolute heart of significance testing. In a SIGNIFICANCE TEST we find the probability that a result would have occurred if there is, in fact, no real effect.

Significance decisions

What potential clients have to do with the Guy or Doll clinic is to decide whether they will use it or not. They cannot say something like 'Well, it's performing a little bit above chance level so maybe we'll use it', or 'we'll use it a little'. In practice, we have to say, 'Either it's doing well above chance level – in which case we'll use it – or it's performing too close to chance level – in which case we're not convinced and we won't use it.' The same thing happens in significance testing – we either claim that we have a significant difference between groups or conditions or we dismiss the data as quite likely to have occurred even if there's nothing going on with the variables concerned.

Take a look at the data in Table 14.1 (a) and (b). Assume that both sets were gathered as part of an independent group project on social facilitation/inhibition in a psychology methods class. Participants were asked to perform a 'wiggly-wire' task (attempting to pass a loop of metal along a wiggly wire without touching it) either alone or in front of an audience. Your group (b) obtained the data shown on the right of the table. Using a different method, another group (a) in the class obtained the data on the left of the table. Typically, both groups were only able to use small samples of people. 'Eyeballing' the data we can see that group (a) appear to have produced no effect, whereas your group has produced a sizeable difference between the two conditions. In your group's case, it would be tempting to say 'It worked!' But beware! Differences may appear large but you should always submit your data to a significance test in order to be able to claim confidently that you have supported the hypothesis you set out to test. There will *always* be a difference between two groups using these sorts of measures but where do we make the decision that there *really was* an effect rather than explaining the difference as simply the result of random sampling error (see Chapter 13)? What we do is carry out a test of significance (also known as an INFERENTIAL TEST).

(a) Student practical Group A

Experimental conditions	
With audience	Alone
9.9	5.2
15.1	3.3
16.2	9.1
11.7	6.1
11.1	16.2
9.1	2.7
10	7.8
8.5	18.2
1.3	10.3
2.4	9
Mean 9.53	Mean 8.79

(b) Student practical Group B

Experimental conditions	
With audience	Alone
14.8	4.1
13.5	3.2
9.6	5.7
8.7	9
12.2	11.3
15.3	2.8
18.6	5.1
12.1	6.1
15.8	3.3
17.1	7.2
Mean 13.77	Mean 5.78

Table 14.1 Time (seconds) spent in touching wire while performing alone and in front of an audience

Significance testing tends to baffle students, yet it is the kind of intuitive process we use all the time in order to judge whether a mere coincidence has occurred or not; whether to get back to the shopkeeper and complain or to accept your underweight tomatoes are only a bit under; whether to believe Hayley in the office really can tell people's birth signs or to put her recent run of success down to chance guessing; whether to assume that someone is really clumsy or that we're just remembering the last couple of unfortunate incidents.

Here's a practical example of using common-sense significance:

Pause for thought

Suppose you are in a pub and have complained about the amount of time it has taken to get served. Subsequently you are sold a 'pint' of beer that turns out, you feel, to be well short of the pint mark on the glass. Rather than topping it up, as friendly bar staff normally would, the barman argues as follows. 'You can't fill a pint glass exactly to the line every time. They're always a bit out. That's a bit of quite acceptable error.' How might you argue back?

In the situation just described you might well argue that your 'pint' is a lot shorter than what might be expected as 'acceptable error'. Note this concept of 'error' here. We already encountered it in Chapter 13 where we said that any sample of scores taken from a population will be a little bit out. Exactly the same thing happens when you try to cut shelves to an exact size or even when you buy shelves that are supposed to be identical. The barman, in the course of a busy evening, will probably pull a distribution of pints that would look pretty much like Figure 13.2 in Chapter 13, with 'one pint' at the position of the mean. What needs to be decided in the pub example is whether the barman is right, and his shortfall is sheer random variation among all the pints he draws in a day, or whether *you* are right and it is 'significantly' below the mean. Of course you have an underlying theory that he did this because you complained; you have a *rationale* for suggesting significant variation.

What you have just done, in using this kind of 'everyday' reasoning, is to incorporate all the central features of a significance test. You have:

1 assumed a normal range of error around an average pull of one pint

2 assessed the likelihood of a pint being drawn as short as yours is, taking into account this normal range of error

3 decided that the likelihood of your pint being drawn under these circumstances is *far* too low and that therefore your explanation of barman revenge is supported.

Shortly we will define these stages in more formal terms, but always come back to the simple situations described here in order to keep making sense of them.

The null and alternative hypotheses – working in the glove department

I now want to introduce two crucial and central concepts in the process of significance testing. These are concepts that are almost universally misunderstood and yet they are the simplest of notions. I continue using non-psychological but concrete and 'everyday' situations (well, sort of) and in this next instance I'd like you to imagine that you are working in a department store and specifically in the glove department.

Imagine you are at work and have gone down to the stockroom in search of a particular pair of gloves. You know, or at least you think you know, that the drawer you are at contains many left- and right-hand gloves in equal numbers. Suddenly the lights fuse and you are left in the dark. 'No problem,' you think, 'If I pull out several I'm bound to get a match.' You pull out five, assuming that should be enough to get a left- and a right-hand glove in your sample. However, on returning to the light, you find that they are all right-hand gloves. You could pass this off as remarkable coincidence, which it must be if no one has tampered with the drawer. On the other hand, if one of your colleagues tends to play practical jokes or is just awfully forgetful, then you might suspect that they have indeed messed about with the glove drawer. Why? Because five gloves of the same hand is a very unlikely outcome if only 50% of the gloves really are right-handed.

The null hypothesis

The assumption that the frequency of right-hand and left-hand gloves is equal in the drawer is known as a NULL HYPOTHESIS (symbolised as H_0). It is what you *assume* is true in order to estimate the degree of coincidence. You also assumed a null hypothesis when thinking about the error involved in pulling pints all night and in the clinic example. The null hypothesis was that the mean of the population of pints poured by the barman in an evening was indeed one pint.

The null hypothesis is *an assumption about the population(s)* from which samples are drawn. When we say 'Blimey, what's the odds of that happening then?' we assume the null hypothesis is true and then think about how unlikely our result was, if so. It is easier in the following work to talk of *'the probability of the result under H_0'* – always remember this means 'the probability of our result occurring *if the null hypothesis is true'*. When we said the glove outcome was a bit of an unlikely coincidence, then, we assumed that the two populations of left- and right-hand gloves were the same. This is very often what a null hypothesis does; it assumes that two populations from which two different samples are drawn *do not differ.* We would write the glove null hypothesis symbolically as follows:

$$H_0 : f_r = f_l$$

meaning that the frequency of right-hand gloves is equal to the frequency of left-hand gloves. Having made this assumption we can proceed to work out the probability of obtaining five consecutive right-hand gloves when selecting them at random from the population of all gloves (in the drawer). If this probability is very low we might reject our null hypothesis and have more faith in what is known as the ALTERNATIVE HYPOTHESIS, written as H_1. This is everything that the null hypothesis is not, so in this case we would be claiming that the frequency of left-hand gloves is different from the frequency of right-hand gloves or:

$$H_1 : f_r \neq f_l$$

The meaning of inferential in 'inferential testing'

Significance testing is *always* about choosing one of these two alternatives; either we go with the alternative hypothesis or stick with the null hypothesis. When we calculate the probability of our result occurring *if* the null hypothesis is true, we go on to *infer* that it either is or it isn't. We use the statistics of our sample to *infer* something about the whole population.

Currently, however, we are stuck with the problem of working out the probability of obtaining our unusual string of right-hand gloves. We need to detour for a short while into the world of probability but do keep in mind that we will return to this glove problem soon.

Probability

Probability is an eerie phenomenon and is always lurking around ready to trick us into thinking we have witnessed some unbelievably rare event or that we somehow have mystical powers. My partner is an avid supporter of India in cricket, which leads to some interesting days in our house when they play tests against England. Watching a hapless batsman get out on 98 one time she remarked, 'So many batsmen get out on 98 or 99 – they get so nervous.' In fact, a quick survey of scores showed no such evidence; as many go on to the early 100s as flounder just before it – it's only a number after all! Some things (like unlucky batsmen) stand out in our minds while we easily ignore other uninteresting facts. In the same way, my partner fervently believes that numbers in the 40s come up far more often in the lottery despite my going back nerdishly over three years to show that, on average, they don't. Perhaps that's why I think that my supermarket queue is always slower (ignoring the good times). For a description of an amusing BBC programme on "Sod's law" (the law that things *will* go wrong if they can) have a look at the Sod's law section on the companion website at www.hodderplus.com/psychology/. This will answer the question you've often wondered about – why does toast always fall butter side down?

Measuring probability

There is a conventional system for the measurement of probability and we shall move towards this using the following exercise. Have a look at the statements below. For most of them, you'll find you have some idea of how likely or not it is that these events will occur. Try to give a value between zero (not at all likely) and 100 (highly likely) to each statement, depending on how likely you think it is to occur.

1 It will rain on Wednesday of next week.

2 You will eat breakfast on the first day of next month.

3 Your psychology tutor will sneeze in the next lesson.

4 The sun will rise tomorrow morning.

5 You will think about elephants later today.

6 A coin tossed fairly will come down showing tails.

7 Two coins tossed fairly will both come down tails.

8 If there were 20 students in your class and the tutor was about to pick one of them to talk about this week's reading, what is the probability that she will choose you? What is the probability that she will (phew!) choose someone else?

In order to calculate the probability of events we need to specify the event we are talking about (let's call this event X) and then also identify all other events in the population that X comes from (call these 'all'). To make that clearer, if we are interested in the probability of throwing a one with a die then the event we are interested in is 'throwing a one' and the total of all possible events is six, using a standard six-sided die. The formula used for probability is:

$$\frac{\text{Number of events of interest}}{\text{Number of possible events}} \quad \text{or} \quad \frac{X}{\text{all}} \quad \text{which in this case gives us} \quad \frac{1}{6}$$

Probability is always denoted by *p* and is measured *in decimal* values on this scale:

0 ◄─────────────────────── to ─────────────────────► 1

NOT possible   MUST happen

If you now take the values between 1 and 100 that you produced for the probability guessing exercise just above, and divide each of them by 100, they should come out as decimal values on the scale above. For item 1 if you live in the UK, whatever the time of year, you may have answered with 50, which becomes .5 – on the scale. However, if you live in Mumbai, and the month is October, you'd end up with perhaps .05. For those who have forgotten their decimals note that .05 is ten times lower than .5 – something you'll need to be very careful with in significance testing. Item 4 in the list above cannot be given zero as there is an infinitesimal chance that the sun will not rise tomorrow (in which case your work here on methods for psychology will be rather wasted!). Item 5 has probably shot up in value now that you've read it! Item 2 depends on your own breakfast habits.

In the discussion of significance we sometimes need to switch between a percentage value (e.g. 25%) and a probability value (e.g. .25, the equivalent of 25%). If you find this equivalence of values a bit tricky then please have a look at Box 14.1 for future reference.

Info Box 14.1	**Sums for the numerically challenged – percentages and decimals**

From percentage to decimal

5% to p = .05

1 Remove the '%' sign (= 5)
2 Put decimal point after the whole number (= 5.)*
3 Move the decimal point two places to the left, inserting zeros as you go where necessary (i.e. first move .5, second move .05 – this is how we divide 5 by 100)

* If there already is a decimal point, leave it where it is and go straight to step 3, e.g.

2.5% → 2.5 → .25 → .025

From decimal to percentage

p = .05 to 5%

1 Move the decimal point two places to the right (05.)
2 Lose any zeros to the left of the first left hand whole digit (= 5.)
3 Lose the decimal point if there is nothing to the right of it (= 5)
4 Add the '%' sign (= 5%)

e.g. for .025: .025 → 0.25 → 02.5 → 2.5 → 2.5%

Logical and empirical probability

Items 3 and 6 in the list of events above demonstrate the difference between what are called *logical probability* and *empirical probability*. *Logically* for item 6 we have just two possible outcomes and one that we're interested in. Hence the probability is ½ or .5. When we want the probability of one event *and* another one, we *multiply* the probabilities of each event. Hence Item 7 is found by multiplying the odds for getting one tail (½) by the odds of another tail (½). We have ½ x ½ which gives us ¼ as our answer, or .25.

Item 3, however, presents a new kind of problem. We have no way of answering it from a purely logical point of view. We can't specify numbers of sneezing and non-sneezing events. We need *empirical evidence* to know how frequently our tutor tends to sneeze. Similarly, with other real-life events where people have a real interest in predictions, such as the chance of an earthquake, a plane crash, a horse winning or of England beating Australia in cricket, we can't make logical calculations. There are just too many variables to account for.

Instead, in these circumstances, researchers rely on 'actuarial' data – that is, data that are already available. The process is backward rather than forward looking. We say, to estimate the probability of X happening, 'How many X-type events have happened so far out of the total number of relevant events?' This is the basis for calculation of your car insurance premium. The company assesses the risk you pose based on the accidents of people with your characteristics (age, experience, residence and so on). For item 3, then, we would need, on the top of our probability equation, the number of classes in which your tutor has sneezed so far. On the bottom we require the total number of classes overall. If she has sneezed in 30 out of 100 classes so far then the probability of a sneeze, based on empirical evidence, is 30/100 or .3.

Back to the glove drawer problem

Now that we have some ideas about probability we can return to the glove problem. We ask what is the probability of obtaining five right-hand gloves *if the null hypothesis is true*? Well, if H_0 is true then the probability of selecting a right-hand glove at random is ½ – there are two possible outcomes and we are interested in the probability of one of these happening. The probability of drawing *five* consecutive right-hand gloves is therefore:

½ x ½ x ½ x ½ x ½ = 1/32 = .031[1]

What probability means in a significance test

Now we can see that the selection of five right-hand gloves was indeed an improbable event using our numerical definition of probability. The value $p = .03$ (rounded from .031), expressed as a fraction, is 3/100. In other words, this event, *carried out on a population of equal numbers of left and right hand gloves*, would happen only 3 times in 100. We can say *p is the probability of this event occurring if the null hypothesis is true*. Very often a short version of what the probability calculated in a significance test means is given as 'the probability of this event occurring by chance'. *Never* be tempted to take this short-cut – it is an ill defined claim. *Always* replace 'by chance' with the phrase 'if the null hypothesis is true', or, better still, 'under H_0'. Hence we get:

p is the probability of this event occurring under H_0

[1] For the alert mathematical sort of people among us, yes, we are selecting without replacing the glove each time so the probability of ½ actually drops a little after each selection of a right-hand glove. However, for the purposes of this example I'm assuming that there are so many gloves in all that such a tiny change makes no material difference.

To summarise so far ...

When we test a difference for significance we make two major steps:

1 assume an appropriate null hypothesis (H_0)

2 calculate the probability of our difference occurring under H_0.

The null hypothesis is *always* a claim about the underlying population(s) and assumes, in a sense, the status quo. It is what would be true about the world if the result you got were 'mere coincidence'. In order to assess the degree of coincidence we ask, in effect, *what is the probability of this happening if there really is no effect*; in our case here, *what is the probability of randomly selecting five consecutive right-hand gloves if the populations of right- and left-hand gloves are equal?*

How low is low? Rejecting the null hypothesis

In the glove example, we said that, having suffered the extreme frustration of selecting five right-hand gloves when looking for a pair, you might well suspect, at this point, that someone has messed with the drawer contents. In formal statistical terms we would say that you *reject the null hypothesis* that the left-hand and right-hand populations are equal. If H_0 *were* true, it would be highly unlikely that you would draw out five right-hand gloves in succession.

We have said that if the probability of your result occurring under H_0 is low you would reject it. In social science research and in statistical theory generally, it has been found very useful to agree upon a common level of probability for rejection that counts as a formal SIGNIFICANCE LEVEL. I have said before that I believe most people have developed from their experience with the world an informal sense of many statistical concepts. Many people, I believe, have an ability to get fairly close to the statistical level at which it is decided that events are too unlikely to have been 'mere coincidence'. That is, they select a level of probability, without actually calculating it, at which they reject a null hypothesis. They argue that, if it were true, the events they have witnessed would be highly unlikely to occur. To see where this level of unlikelihood might lie, in formal statistical practice, have a look at the scenario described in the pause for thought box.

Pause for thought

Suppose a friend said she could reliably forecast the sex of unborn babies by swinging a stone pendulum above the mother-to-be's womb. Let's assume she guesses your baby's sex correctly. Would you be impressed? Your personal involvement might well cause you to react with 'Amazing!' or at least, 'Well it is interesting; there might be something in it.' Stepping back coolly from the situation you realise she had a 50–50 chance of being correct. Nevertheless most people would begin to think she had something going if she managed to go on to predict correctly the sex of two or three more friends' babies.

Suppose we set up a scientifically controlled test of her ability and give her a sample of ten babies' sexes to guess under strictly controlled conditions. How many would you expect her to predict correctly in order for you to be impressed that she's not just guessing and being lucky? For instance, would seven out of ten convince you? Would you want more or would fewer do?

The decision of a vast majority of students to whom I have presented this scenario is that nine or ten correct out of ten would convince them and this, as we shall see, pretty well coincides with the result that social scientists would want in order to record her result as 'significant'. If she gets only eight correct the audience starts to waver and perhaps only a third of them are still convinced. A few romantic people tend to choose seven or even six as enough to satisfy them that her system works, whereas there is also always the odd cynic who claims that even ten out of ten is not strong enough evidence.

Figure 14.1 shows the probabilities for getting the sex of *n* babies correct, by chance, from a total of ten babies. It is generally the probabilities for *n* correct random yes/no guesses out of ten. It is also what we would expect to happen if we tossed ten coins and recorded the outcome, head or tail, each time. The histogram shows what would happen if we repeated our ten trials over and over. The probability of guessing four babies' sex correctly (or six) is .205. We can say that if we were to guess ten babies' sex, over and over again (i.e. lots of sets of ten), we would get four correct .2 or 20% of the time (assuming we know nothing about guessing the sex of babies).

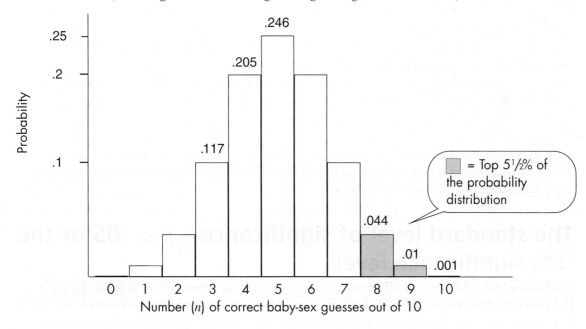

Figure 14.1 Probabilities of guessing correctly the sex of *n* babies out of 10

The central column (.246) is what we would expect to happen most frequently *if the null hypothesis is true*. The null hypothesis claims that correct and incorrect guesses occur equally frequently in the 'population' but a version of this is that the probability of a correct guess on each trial is .5. The same is true for tossing a coin; it is .5 for every toss no matter what has gone just before. The frequencies of heads or tails occurring *before* a single coin toss can have absolutely no effect on the present toss outcome. If events are random in occurrence, then they cannot affect the outcomes of further random events – a principle that lottery gamblers usually find hard to believe about lottery ball numbers.

I said that a very good majority of students are satisfied to reject coincidence if the sex-guesser achieves at least eight or more correct guesses. Notice that I said 'at least'. They are not interested in her getting *exactly* eight correct guesses. They are satisfied if she does *at least* that well, i.e. that well *or better*. From the far right-hand column in Figure 14.1 we can see that the probability of her getting *all* correct guesses (assuming she *is* just guessing, that is) comes out at just .001. In fact the result is less than one in a thousand; it is 1 in 1024. This is because the probability of the first guess being correct (assuming she *is* guessing) is ½ . The probability of the first *two* being correct is ½ x ½ = ¼; the probability of *all ten* correct then is (½)^{10} (½ times itself 10 times) and this is 1/1024. To get a sense of just how unlikely an event with a 1/1024 probability of occurrence really is, imagine that I ask a volunteer from the audience to think of, but not reveal, a number between 1 and 1000. I then ask you to pick a number from 1000 raffle tickets, already checked and shuffled in a bag. If I 'get' you to pick the same number as the volunteer is thinking of you'd think I was a pretty good conjuror, not just lucky! We can rely on the rarity of probability extremes so much that a local garage can safely offer a free new car to anyone throwing seven sixes with seven dice at a village fête (work out the odds)!

The probability of our baby-sex-guesser getting *at least* nine correct guesses is the addition of the last two columns on the right of the figure and this comes to .011 – just 11 in 1000 – so those convinced only by at least nine correct guesses might seem to be pretty demanding. If she gets eight correct sexes, then the probability of her doing this, or better, under H_0 is .055 (.001 + .01 + .044). So most people are pretty sure that the sex-guesser isn't guessing so long as she gets nine or more sexes correct but are more wary if she gets just eight correct. This is the point where p is a little above .05. That is, the probability of her getting eight out of ten right or better is .055 *if she really is just guessing.*

Most people are prepared to dismiss the idea that she's only guessing so long as p is under .05. When it rises above that figure a majority tend to think that her performance could too easily be just a fluke. What do the statisticians think?

The standard level of significance – $p \le$ .05 or the '5% significance level'

Statisticians use a standard cut-off point for making the decision about when to reject H_0: H_0 is rejected when the probability of an effect occurring under it is equal to or less than .05. Hence our audiences who accept nine guesses out of ten as convincing but are wary of only eight correct guesses are working at exactly the same level as trained researchers and statisticians in the social sciences (and elsewhere, e.g. biology). This is no coincidence. It is at around the probability level of .05 (that's 1 in 20 or 5%) that people tend to feel 'No! That's enough! That just couldn't be coincidence! It beggars belief ....' and the like. If I handed you a pack of cards and said either it's shuffled (null hypothesis) or it's fixed with the red cards on top, and you dealt out four then five consecutive red cards you would probably stop at this point and say 'I'm pretty certain it's fixed.'

The phrase 'pretty certain' in the line above is of central importance. A significant result does not *prove* anything. You need to exorcise the word 'prove' from your vocabulary when dealing with statistical tests of significance and the results of your psychology practicals in general. The result could yet turn out to be a fluke. Many dramatic results in the history of science have turned out to be just that. However, a significant result *does* give *support* to our alternative hypothesis and, in turn, to whatever psychological theory we are trying to establish as a reasonable explanation of observed phenomena. We talk of being 'reasonably confident' that we have demonstrated a real effect.

Although significance results are universally reported in *p* values (i.e. a decimal value from zero to one), statisticians also talk of the '5% significance level' because .05 as a portion of one is 5%. Later we will also encounter the 1% level and a few others. In your reports of psychological studies, however, you should always stick to the decimal *p* value version.

Rejecting and retaining the null hypothesis

The language to use in reporting results is as follows:

If the probability of our result occurring under H_0 is not greater than .05, we reject H_0

If the probability of our result occurring under H_0 is greater than .05, we retain H_0

When the probability for our result under H_0 falls above the required level of .05, we don't 'accept' the null hypothesis or say we have 'proved it true'. We simply state that, for now, we do not have the confidence from our results to reject it. The probability of a result occurring if it were true (i.e. there is no effect) was too high. On the other hand, if we do obtain a significant result, we have not 'proved H_1'. We have simply provided support for it because the probability found was too low for a reasonable assumption of coincidence.

The practical baby-sex-guessing result then ...

In the case of the baby-sex-guesser, then, if she got eight right out of ten she has just missed the level of probability at which we would reject H_0 and claim a significant result; *p* is .055 and just greater than .05. In short-hand we say '*p* > .05'. Getting nine or ten correct certainly *would* be a significant result. In either of the latter two cases we might say, more formally: 'the difference between hits and misses was significant ($p \leq .05$)', or 'the number of correct guesses, compared with incorrect, was significant ($p \leq .05$)'. On rare occasions, where *p* might be *exactly* .05 we say $p \leq .05$.

Critical values

We have just found that the baby-sexer must reach a minimum of nine sexes correct for us to count her result as significant. Hence, the value nine here is a CRITICAL VALUE for this particular test of significance – it is a cut-off point. If she equals this or does better we reject H_0. If she does not reach it we retain H_0. For significance, her performance must be in the top 5% of outcomes that could be expected under H_0; with this rather crude distribution of outcomes (because we are using only ten right/wrong nominal-level outcomes) we find that eight correct or better embraces 5.5% of the possible outcomes (see Figure 14.1) but nine correct or better embraces just 1.1% of outcomes. In this latter region for nine correct guesses we reject H_0 because we are in a region of less than 5%.

Significance testing – the basic model and a concrete example

We have now progressed to the point where we can summarise the three major steps in any significance test.

1 Express an appropriate null hypothesis for testing.

2 Calculate the probability of the statistical effect occurring under the null hypothesis.

3 If this probability is less than or equal to the set level (mostly .05) then reject the null hypothesis, otherwise retain it.

Info Box 14.2 **Some wrong things they tell you about the null hypothesis**

There is a lot of misunderstanding about what exactly a null hypothesis is and what we find the probability of in a significance test. This is true even of psychology tutors, academics and researchers, partly because they often have not had to study statistics formally, only enough to get by.

1 No matter what any tutor may tell you, the null hypothesis *cannot* be phrased like this:

The null hypothesis is that there will be no significant difference between experimental and control group scores.

The null hypothesis is not a prediction about what *will* happen; it is a claim about what the populations that the samples were drawn from are like. We *can* say that if the null hypothesis is true (or 'under H_0'), we would expect little difference between samples (only that resulting from sampling error). Saying what will happen *if* a hypothesis is true is not the same as stating that hypothesis.

2 We do *not* calculate:

The probability that the null hypothesis is true.

We calculate the probability that our result would occur *if* the null hypothesis is true. A null hypothesis is usually one of those purely imaginary assumptions that scientists often make in order to demonstrate a conclusion. A null hypothesis could rarely in fact be true. Suppose we test differences between male and female IQ. The null hypothesis would hold that the means for all males and all females were equal. This is almost certainly not the case, and an amazing coincidence would have occurred if it were. IQ is simply a measurement with a certain amount of error always involved, as with any measure. Even if we could fulfil the rather daft ambition of testing every single male and female (say in the UK) we should almost certainly find a slight but completely unimportant difference, as we would if we measured very accurately the weights of two 'one pound' bags of sweets or two performances from one skilled player on a PlayStation® game.

We do not find the probability that the null hypothesis is true. In fact, it is not worth asking whether any particular null hypothesis *is* 'really true'. Just assume it is and work out your probability. It would be very complicated to estimate the probability that a null hypothesis is true using research results. It is relatively easy to work out the probability that your results would occur *if* the null hypothesis is true, and that is your *p* in a significance test.

If there is lingering doubt about the model or any lack of clarity I hope the following industrial example will help further in grasping the significance testing idea. The example will lead on to applying the ideas directly to measurements gathered in psychology studies – in case you were wondering whether you picked up the wrong textbook this morning! It might help to keep in the back of your mind, through this example, the notion that a sample of memory scores is treated in psychological statistics just like a sample of screw lengths.

The example – checking your screws

Suppose you work in a screw-manufacturing company and are looking after the production line churning out screws into large barrels each containing around 500,000 screws. Your supervisor approaches you one day and says 'We think the machine cutters just went out of line and that barrel there, with the big yellow cross, is suspect. The screws might not be cut accurately. Can you check it for us?' At first, you think 'Bang goes my weekend,' because you imagine sitting and measuring every last screw in the barrel. However, an old hand tells you what to do – take a decent sample from the suspect barrel, take a similar-sized sample from a good barrel and compare the difference using a significance test.

This situation is depicted in Figure 14.2. What do we mean by a 'decent' sample? Well, this takes us back to the issues of sampling discussed in Chapter 2. In order to be an unbiased representation of the whole barrel of screws we should randomly select our samples, not just take some off the top where perhaps the shorter screws have congregated. We also mean a sample of a decent size – perhaps 20 or 30, even 50 and not just one or two. When we have these samples we can take the mean of each one and compare them to see if one is larger than the other. Of course, one *will* be larger if only because of regular sampling error. However, what we are looking for is a difference appreciably larger than that which we might expect for any two samples drawn at random from the same population.

Random sample *N*   Random sample *S*

Normal screws   Suspect screws

Figure 14.2 Barrels of good and suspect screws

What is the null hypothesis in this example? Well, we almost just stated it. If the two barrels contain identically manufactured screws then the means of the two barrels should be identical. The barrels are 'populations' from which we are selecting samples. We will use the statistics of these samples to test the null hypothesis that:

$$H_0 : \mu_{standard} = \mu_{suspect}$$

where μ is a population mean and the subscripts refer to the two different barrels. Our alternative hypothesis is, of course:

$$H_1 : \mu_{standard} \neq \mu_{suspect}$$

The distributions that are proposed by the null and alternative hypotheses are illustrated in Figure 14.3. The null hypothesis holds that both samples are drawn from identical populations, being that represented by the centre curve. The alternative hypothesis says that the distribution from which the suspect screws are drawn is different, with a mean either higher or lower than that of the standard barrel.

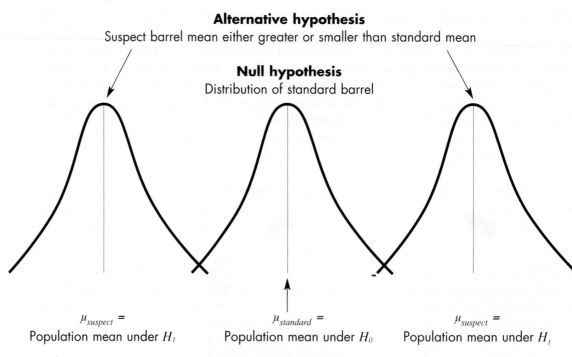

Alternative hypothesis
Suspect barrel mean either greater or smaller than standard mean

Null hypothesis
Distribution of standard barrel

$\mu_{suspect} =$
Population mean under H_1 $\mu_{standard} =$
Population mean under H_0 $\mu_{suspect} =$
Population mean under H_1

Figure 14.3 Distributions expected under null and alternative hypotheses for suspect screws

For another illustrative (and, I hope, amusing) example of the testing of the null hypothesis for a significant difference have a look at The Sociologist's Chip Shop on the companion website at: www.hodderplus.com/psychology/.

Getting back to the psychology context

Now look back to Table 14.1 (b) at the start of this chapter. In that table there are two samples of time scores for a wiggly-wire task gathered under two different conditions, with and without an audience. Statistically we treat these just as we did the two samples of screws above and we ask: *Are these two samples drawn randomly from two different populations or from the same one?*

To answer this question we assume that the two samples are from the same population; we calculate the probability of getting two means as far apart as we have, *if the null hypothesis is true*. If this probability is not greater than .05 we reject the null hypothesis. In other words we claim that we have empirical support for the hypothesis that an audience *does* affect wiggly-wire performance.

Rejection regions (and the peculiar effects of spinach)

Figure 14.3 shows that if the mean of our suspect screw sample falls either much higher *or* much lower than the mean of the standard sample we would reject H_0. This is because we were told only that the suspect barrel might be *different from,* not specifically longer than (or shorter than), the standard barrel. Such a hypothesis, where we do not predict the direction of our effect, is known as a NON-DIRECTIONAL HYPOTHESIS. It is rarely the case in science, let alone just in psychology, that our background theory, prior research and debate do not give us a sense of the direction in which we would expect our differences to fall. We shall return to this issue of direction in a moment but for the present please permit me to introduce one more unlikely scenario in order to bring out just one or two more major issues concerning significance testing and to demonstrate what a significance test actually is.

Let us suppose that a new theory has hit the news: K5, a vitamin existing abundantly in spinach, has been found to improve children's reading ability. This is pure fantasy, I must assure you; I hate spinach with a vengeance but am fine on reading. However, let's further suppose that you are interested in the theory and that you identify all the high spinach eaters in the primary schools in your area. From these you select one child at random, Natasha, who eats fields of the stuff. The theory predicts that she should have a high reading score and should appear very much to the right of the fictitious left hand distribution of reading scores shown in Figure 14.4. This distribution has

Null hypothesis
Spinach-eating child's reading score is drawn from population with mean of 40

Alternative hypothesis
Spinach-eating child's reading score is drawn from population with mean > 40

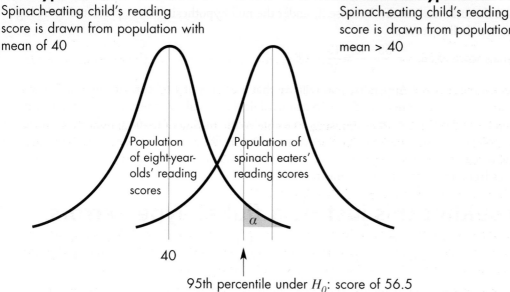

Figure 14.4 Null and alternative hypotheses for spinach-eating significance test

337

40 as its mean and a standard deviation of 10. Our girl Natasha has a reading score of 58. How can we assess this difference between her score and the normal reading population mean of 40? Effectively we have to decide whether her score is from the central or the right hand distributions shown in Figure 14.4.

Frequency distributions and probability distributions

The 95th percentile of the reading score distribution cuts off the top 5% of scores. Imagine sticking a pin at random into a register of all eight-year-old children with reading scores. What would be the probability of this randomly selected child having a reading score in the top 5% of the distribution? Well, obviously we have a 5% chance of selecting such a child and we saw earlier that a '5% chance' converts to a probability value of .05. A frequency distribution looked at this way becomes a PROBABILITY DISTRIBUTION. It shows us the probabilities of selecting at random values within certain regions of the distribution, for instance in the top 5%. Take a z value of +1; this cuts off the top 16% of scores so we have a 16% chance of selecting at random a score with a z value above +1; 16% converts to 16/100, or .16 in probability terms. We saw that the normal distribution can be seen as having an area of 1 and hence when areas under the curve are expressed as decimals this decimal value is the probability of finding a value at random in that area.

In our reading test example, then, we want to know whether Natasha's reading score falls in the top 5% of the normal distribution. If it does, we can say that there is a significant difference between her score and the mean, and we can infer that her score comes from a different population of scores (those of spinach eaters). Don't forget that the normal population is made up of children who eat little if any spinach on a daily basis. For the spinach theory to be true we would expect Natasha's score to be up there with the best of the normals. We can call this top 5% of the distribution the REJECTION REGION because if, under the null hypothesis, scores predicted to be high *do* fall here we shall reject H_0.

For Natasha's score of 58, $z = \dfrac{58-40}{s} = \dfrac{18}{10} = 1.8$

If you check Table 2 in the Appendix, you will see that a z value of 1.65 cuts off the top 5% of a normal distribution. A z score of 1.65 is 1.65 standard deviations above the mean. On the reading distribution a standard deviation is 10 points so a child with a z score of 1.65 would have a reading score 16.5 points above the mean at 56.5. Natasha's score is 58, so she is inside the rejection region; her z value of 1.8 'beats' the critical value of 1.65 and we may reject the null hypothesis that her score comes from a population with a mean of 40.

But couldn't this just be a fluke? Type I errors

Yes, of course, it could! We never 'prove' things for certain in psychology, or in any science, in this sense. What we have is simply evidence in support of H_1. The whole point of setting a significance level is that we leave only a 1 in 20 of rejecting H_0 on an extreme but random occurrence. However, any time we conduct a test and get a significant result it always *could* be a random occurrence. Such a result is known as a TYPE I ERROR – the rejection of H_0 when it is true.

If the null hypothesis is true, and spinach eaters do not differ in reading from other eight year olds, then their scores are randomly scattered throughout the normal reading score population. Trouble is, when we select a spinach/reading score at random, then we have a 5% chance of selecting it from the rejection region; that's the shaded area of the null hypothesis distribution in Figure 14.4.

The level of significance that we use in any particular analysis is given the symbol α ('alpha'). The idea is that we set this level before making our analysis, as will be explained further below. Most of the time it is set at .05. α is in fact the probability of making a Type I error *when the null hypothesis is true,* so researchers, in selecting an alpha level, are making a decision about how much probability of making a Type I error they will accept.

You may now be getting a sinking feeling about all those interesting psychological research results that you've read about in your studies of psychology so far. Couldn't 1 in 20 of all these simply be Type I errors? Well, the answer is that this is extremely unlikely for several reasons. First, as in all science, researchers do not usually test entirely random effects. That is, the 1 in 20 fluke concept only applies if data are selected entirely at random and a relationship between these is tested. In these circumstances we would indeed expect just 1 in 20 tests to show 'significance' on a chance basis. However, researchers mostly have a background of theoretical argument and previous research findings that leads them to a reasonable argument for the effect they are expecting.

Nevertheless, the history of science, including psychology, does contain a fair number of 'effects', which turned out, apparently, to be only a chance grouping of data.

Pause for thought

What steps do you think can be taken in psychological research to ensure that when a researcher finds a significant difference with $p \leq .05$, the finding is not a Type I error? In other words, what would you do if you suspected that a reported effect was not genuine but based on a fluke in the data?

Replication of studies

One of the main ways that researchers check against Type I errors is to REPLICATE studies. If another researcher confirms the results of an original study then the likelihood is far lower that the original was just a fluke. To obtain one significant result 'by chance' may be regarded as a misfortune. To obtain two such results is highly unlikely and would convince researchers that the effect, whatever it may actually be, is genuine.

If we select another spinach eater at random, then, and find that this child too has a score in the rejection region, this will strengthen our position. However, the reality here is that some spinach eaters may well not have high reading scores for all sorts of reasons. Variables such as poverty, parental encouragement and so on may counteract the effects of spinach and K5. Hence, in normal psychological research we would not rely on selecting individual children but would select a random *sample* of spinach eaters and test the *mean score* of this group against the hypothesis that their mean *should* be 40 under H_0. Such tests are introduced in the next chapter.

Levels of significance – changing the value of α

Another way of being more confident that we will not make a Type I error is to reduce our significance level to .01. That is, we will only reject H_0 when the probability of our result occurring under it falls below .01, rather than the conventional .05. Hopefully, Figure 14.5 makes clear that doing this will considerably reduce the probability of making a Type I error. The new α area is much smaller.

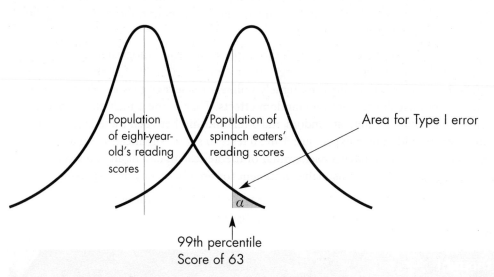

Population of eight-year-old's reading scores

Population of spinach eaters' reading scores

α

Area for Type I error

99th percentile
Score of 63

Figure 14.5 Reducing α to .01: low probability of Type I error (increased probability of Type II error)

Type II errors

However, this reduction of α to .01 comes at quite a price. Suppose the alternative hypothesis is in fact true: spinach eaters *do* have higher reading scores. When we reduce α to .01 we find that the difference between Natasha's score and 40 is no longer significant. We have become a lot more cautious and said we will only accept an apparent effect if the probability of our result occurring under the null hypothesis is less than .01. To get into the new rejection area a score would now have to exceed 63 – perhaps you would like to work out how we know this? If not, the answer is given below.[2]

By reducing the chance of making a Type I error we have automatically *increased* the probability of retaining the null hypothesis when it is false. Such an error is known as a TYPE II ERROR. Table 14.2 shows the occasions on which we make these errors or are correct in our significance decision. A Type II error occurs when the alternative hypothesis is true but we actually get a result that would be quite likely under the null hypothesis; at least more likely than .05 so we retain H_0. In Figure 14.6, you can see a shaded area to the left of the critical score of 56.5 (and remember this is the

[2] The last 1% of the normal distribution is cut off by a z value of 2.33. Hence the cut-off score is 40 (the mean) + 2.33 standard deviations of 10. This gives 40 + 23.3 and therefore 63.3.

95th percentile from Figure 14.4). If the alternative hypothesis is true, but we happen to select at random a rather poor-reading spinach eater, we may be duped into retaining the null hypothesis. This is because the shaded area falls to the left of the extreme 5% of possible results under H_0 and we have already decided that when a result falls here we do not have the confidence to reject H_0. In other words it could be true that spinach can create good readers in optimum circumstances but we might just, through sampling error, select at random one of the poorer spinach-eating readers and falsely conclude that spinach has no effect on reading (this is partly why we do not rely on taking just a sample of one; in a larger sample such a low average for the sample as a whole would be quite unlikely). The area of the alternative hypothesis distribution that is trapped by the 5% cut-off line under H_0 is known as β. It represents the probability of making a Type II error *if the alternative hypothesis is true.* In Figure 14.5, we can see that reducing the α level to .01 has the effect of greatly increasing the value of β and hence we are in greater danger of failing to find effects that are actually there. We become ultra-conservative in reporting possible effects.

Null hypothesis is:

		Retained	Rejected
Null hypothesis is actually:	True	Correct decision	Type I error
	False	Type II error	Correct decision

Table 14.2 Type I and Type II errors

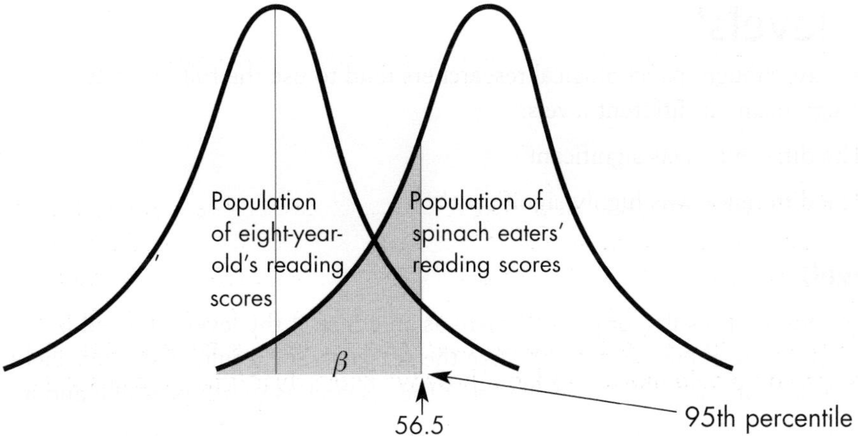

Figure 14.6 Probability of making a Type II error when H_1 is true

The question of power and effect size

Suppose we decide to stick with our significance level at 1% (i.e. keep α at .01). We can still guard against a Type II error by increasing the sample size. For reasons that we shall investigate further in Chapter 15, if there really is a difference between two populations and we stick with the same procedures and significance level, then the larger the samples we compare, the more likely we are to obtain a significant result.

Sometimes we get a result that narrowly creeps under the .05 level, whereas other times a difference is so unlikely under the circumstances that p is less than .0001. This does not automatically mean that one result is 'greater', 'better' or 'stronger' than the other. The value of p that we obtain in any test depends on several factors, including the type of test we are using, the size of the samples and the size of the effect we are investigating. The EFFECT SIZE in a study is the *real* effect in the population, for instance the difference between μ_1 and μ_2. The POWER of any particular statistical test is the probability of detecting the effect, if it is there, and of *not* making a Type II error. It is therefore the value $1 - \beta$. If the effect we are looking for is rather small, then the larger the sample sizes the greater power we will have to detect the effect (see p. 388). Without considering issues of sample size, effect size and power, it is pointless to compare different values of p from different studies. These issues are investigated more carefully in the following chapter.

Statisticians simply like to use .05 as a standard rather like the bar in a high jump. It doesn't matter how much higher than the bar you were – the only fact recorded is that you made it. This way, over time, we will accumulate mostly results that do demonstrate an effect and worry less about those that don't. However, Harcum (1990) and many others argue that the 5% significance level is conservative, and several conventions tend to favour the retention of the null hypothesis in order not to make Type I errors. This means that many actual effects are passed over and some researchers are beginning to call for changes to the conventions of significance testing. One major step that has been taken by several journals and by the British Psychological Society has been to report the *actual* value of p found rather than only stating that it was 'less than .05'.

Significance 'levels'

Whatever the statisticians say, though, psychological researchers tend to use the following terms in reporting results that are significant at different levels:

- significant at 5% – 'The difference was significant'
- significant at 1% – 'The difference was highly significant'.

$p \leq$ .1 (the 10% level)

A researcher cannot be confident of results, or publish them as an effect, if the level achieved is only $p \leq .1$. But if the probability is in fact close to .05 (like the sex-guesser's results if she gets eight predictions correct and $p = .055$), it may well be decided that the research is worth pursuing and it may even be reported, along with other findings, as a result 'approaching significance'. The procedure can be revisited, tightened or altered, the design may be slightly changed and sampling might be scrutinised, with perhaps an increase in sample size.

$p \leq$ .01 (the 1% level)

We said above that lowering α to .01 has the unfortunate effect of increasing the likelihood of Type II errors. However, sometimes it is necessary to be more certain of our results. If we are about to challenge a well-established theory or research finding by publishing results that contradict it, the convention is to achieve $p \leq .01$ before publication. A further reason for requiring this level would be when the researcher only has a one-shot chance to demonstrate an effect. Replication may be impossible in many field studies or natural experiments.

Levels lower than $p \leq .01$ (<1%)

In research that may produce applications concerning human health or life changes, such as the testing of drugs for unwanted psychological or behavioural effects, we'd want to be even more certain that no chance effects were being recorded. Hence, researchers might even seek significance with $p \leq .001$ (.1%).

When we want to support H_0 with $p > .05$

A researcher may be replicating a study that was a challenge to his or her own work. They may therefore wish to show that there is no effect using the procedures and measures of the challenging research. It may be that showing there isn't a difference is the research aim. In this case the prediction is that the null hypothesis will be supported. The probability associated with results must now fall in the less extreme 95% area under the probability curve. As just stated, Harcum (1990) finds significance testing conservative and biased towards retaining null hypotheses. Hence, obtaining a null result is not too impressive and Harcum proposes various criteria that should be met by the data where research predicts support for H_0. Scientists generally publish far fewer null results than significant ones with the effect that many important no-difference results are overlooked. Feminist psychologists (see p. 241) have argued that mainly sex *differences* get published yet there are an overwhelming number of characteristics on which the sexes do not differ at all.

Directional and non-directional hypotheses – one-tailed and two-tailed tests

We said earlier that a non-directional hypothesis (like that for the suspect screws) does not state the expected direction of differences. The spinach hypothesis we tested above was *directional*: we argued, from an underlying theoretical explanation, that spinach eaters should have *higher* scores than normal readers. We didn't just say that the population mean was *different* from the normal mean. In this case, the significance test took account of values at only one end or 'tail' of the probability distribution under H_0 – the right-hand tail of 5% (see Figure 14.4). If our child's mean came from the top 5% of that distribution, we would reject H_0. A *directional hypothesis*, then, *may* be tested with what is known as a ONE-TAILED TEST, but this can be controversial and we shall return to this point in a while.

A non-directional hypothesis, however, *requires* a TWO-TAILED TEST. If we only claim that the child's score is from a population with a *different mean* from the normal reading population, then the rejection region *must* include the possibility that the child's score came from a distribution with a *lower* mean as well as from a distribution with a *higher* mean. As before, we reject H_0 only when the child's score falls in the extreme 5% of the distribution, but, in this case, the extreme 5% is taken as being at either end of the distribution; that is, the most extreme 2.5% at each end. I hope Figure 14.7 makes this clear. We can see here that we now require a score of 60 in order to count Natasha's score as significant and, unfortunately, she is short of this. We must retain H_0. It is important to remember that a non-directional hypothesis *must* always be tested with a two-tailed test.

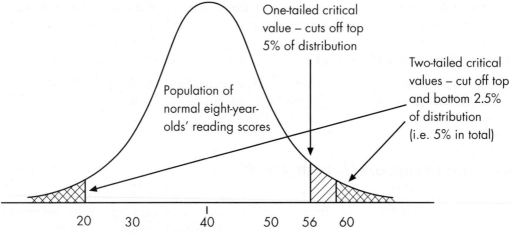

Figure 14.7 One- and two-tailed critical values

Returning to the baby-sexer for just a moment, suppose our friend had got every single prediction wrong. Would we say she was a hopeless baby-sex-guesser? Or would this be a fascinating result? After all, the probability of her doing this 'by chance' is also .001. We might suspect that she has indeed got a valid method but that she has her instrument round the wrong way or is reading it incorrectly! Since everything is symmetrical (see Figure 14.1) the probability of guessing ten sexes correctly (.001) is the same as the probability of guessing ten sexes incorrectly. The probability of getting *either* ten right *or* ten wrong is .001 + .001 = .002. Here we are *adding* the probabilities in both ends of the probability distribution. If we want the probability of getting at least nine right or wrong, we must add the two extreme probabilities at either end, that is: 10 right + 9 right + 9 wrong + 10 wrong. This is .001 + .01 + .01 + .001. Hence, the probability of getting nine or more right or wrong is .022 – still significant. Getting eight right was not significant, even using a one-tailed approach. So, a two-tailed test here produces the same result as a one-tailed test – she must get nine or more right to convince us.

Why not always do one-tailed tests?

If we use a two-tailed test on the spinach-eating score, we cannot report a significant difference between Natasha's score and the general mean. If we use a one-tailed test we can. Why not always do a one-tailed test then? Well, if we use a one-tailed test we cannot have our cake and eat it too. We must put all our eggs in the one basket – all the 5% at one end – and accept that if the result were extreme in the *opposite* direction, we'd still have to treat this as just a chance occurrence, support for H_0.

If your result for a one-tailed test is extreme in the opposite direction from that predicted by the hypothesis, you cannot report a significant result. You cannot suddenly switch and say 'Ah it's significant but the other way!' This is because you would then really be working with a significance level of .1, being the .05 you first chose to work with and then the new .05 you've just included *post hoc*.

MacRae (1995) argues that there is very rarely a situation with psychological data where a directional test is appropriate. If we predict that children viewing a violent video will be more aggressive afterwards than a group viewing a nature video, and it turns out that the nature video children are more aggressive, with the difference in the rejection zone, then this *must* be a result of interest. We can't say we are not interested in results that go that way. An example where this *can* be said occurs in economics where a government agency is checking on a company to see that it meets its claim to include a *minimum* amount of (costly) vitamin X in its product. It predicts and tests for variations *below* the minimum. Variations above are not of interest and almost certainly are relatively small and rare, given the industry's economic interests. There are very few if any situations like this in psychology.

Other psychologists (e.g. Rodgers, 1986, in Howell, 1992) have argued that it is odd ('scientifically dumb' according to Rodgers) to construct a case for an effect in one direction after a thorough review of literature and development of theory and then to put half the rejection region in the other tail. The point is though that if we get a result in the extreme 2.5% of the distribution but in the opposite direction to what we expected this counts as a significant effect and we can immediately start speculation on why this might have happened. If we carried out a directional test, then we cannot. What we would do, of course, is say 'That's interesting; it's worth following that up perhaps.'

The critical value for a one-tailed test is always less extreme than the value for a two-tailed test. In crude terms, 'it is easier to obtain'. I say 'crude' because it is easy to slip into the habit of thinking something like 'Oh, let's get a result, whatever. Surely there's some way this result is significant? It *is* for a one-tailed test.' This is kind of dangerous because what we want is confidence that we really do have an effect, not 'something concrete to report in our assignment'. Students would not usually be expected to carry out a simple one-tailed test in their research work. However they worry about not 'getting a result'. In fact, nowhere should students lose marks solely because they do not obtain a significant result. The important thing to do on such 'failure' is to analyse critically both the design of the study and the theory that led to it. A failure to produce a significant difference may well be a very important outcome, especially if prior research predicted a difference. You might be pleased to hear that the issue of two-tailed tests mostly disappears once we leave simple two-condition tests behind; that is, after the next three chapters.

For an extended account of the one-tailed/two-tailed debate, see the companion website at: www.hodderplus.com/psychology/

So, to summarise the 'rules' outlined above:

- if you use a one-tailed test and the result is extreme in the opposite direction from that predicted you may not claim a significant effect
- a one-tailed test is only appropriate with a directional hypothesis (but even then the use is controversial)
- if you test a non-directional hypothesis you must use a two-tailed test
- *generally* use a two-tailed test but ensure you take large enough samples to get significance if it's there.

It is safer then, overall, to always use two-tailed tests. No one can then accuse you of switching sides. The disadvantage of two-tailed tests is that we need to obtain a larger difference in order to make it into the rejection region. However, you will still obtain significance, assuming there is an effect to be found, if you use a large enough sample.

Conducting a significance test – the general procedure for all tests

The next few chapters take you through several of the commonly used statistical tests of significance. In all cases you will have some data and will want to analyse it. In most cases you will want to know whether the relationship you predicted does indeed exist to a significant degree in your data. You will want to know if it is legitimate to reject H_0 for each test on your data that you conduct. The steps listed in Table 14.3 apply to *all* significance tests but there may be extra steps to follow for specific tests.

---

1 Choose an appropriate test. Appropriateness will depend on the design of your study, what you want to show, the level of data measurement you decide upon and in some cases various preliminary tests on the data to see whether they are suitable for the test you have in mind. Chapter 21 gives a guide to all the tests and the data for which they are suitable.

In the spinach eating example we used a z value. This is because we had only one child to test against a population Usually we would have a *sample* of scores and we would select one of the tests covered in the following chapters.

2 Calculate a test statistic. All tests have a variable associated with them that is calculated from your raw data. This will be explained further in each chapter.

In the spinach-eating test we conducted, we found a value for z.

3 You then find the probability associated with the occurrence of your test statistic under H_0. There are two ways of doing this.

With computer software
If you use a program like SPSS it will give you the test statistic and the *exact* probability of obtaining it under H_0.

Calculating by hand
If you calculate by hand you will need to obtain your test statistic then look up *critical value tables* for that statistic as in the back of this book. The table will tell you if your test statistic reaches the appropriate critical value for significance with $p \leq .05$ or .01 and perhaps some other values. If your statistic does reach the critical value, then you know that the probability for your result is less than or equal to .05.

In the spinach-eating test we found that the critical value for z was 1.65 with $p \leq .05$ and Natasha's z value of 1.8 exceeded this. Hence significance was below .05.

See p. 355 where consulting regular critical value tables is explained in more detail.

4 If your probability, obtained by either of the two means outlined above, is less than .05 ($p \leq .05$) then you may reject the null hypothesis (H_0) and claim provisional support for H_1. Your research prediction is correct and you have provided support for your research hypothesis.

The probability of obtaining Natasha's score, if H_0 were true, came out at < .05. Hence we rejected H_0 and claimed support for the spinach-eating hypothesis. (Don't forget: we did not '*prove*' anything.)

Table 14.3 Procedures for significance tests

Exercises

1 State whether the following values of z (on a normal distribution) are significant or not ($p \le .05$) for:

(a) one-tailed tests:

1.32 1.75 −1.9 −.78

(b) two-tailed tests:

−2.05 1.89 −1.6 1.98

2 State whether tests of the following hypotheses might permit one- or two-tailed tests.

(a) Diabetics are more health-conscious than other people.

(b) Extroverts and introverts differ in their ability to learn people's names.

(c) Job satisfaction correlates negatively with absenteeism.

(d) Self-esteem correlates with outward confidence.

3 A student sets out to show that attitude change will be greater if people are paid more to make a speech that contradicts their present attitude. Her tutor tells her that this runs directly counter to research findings on 'cognitive dissonance'.

(a) What would be the appropriate significance level for her to set?

(b) If she had originally intended to use the 5% level, is she now more or less likely to make a Type II error?

4 A z score of 2.0 is significant (two-tailed), with $p \le .05$ because it is greater than the critical value of 1.96 for $p \le .05$. This is why the first line of the table below is marked 'true'. Can you complete the rest of the table with ticks or crosses?

	z	One- or two-tailed test	$p \le$	True or false
(a)	2.0	Two	.05	True
(b)	1.78	One	.05	
(c)	2.2	Two	.025	
(d	2.88	One	.002	
(e)	3.35	Two	.001	
(f)	2.22	One	.01	

Answers

1 (a) 1.32 and − .78 are not significant. 1.75 and −1.9 are significant (critical value = ± 1.65)

   (b) 1.89 and − 1.6 are not significant. − 2.05 and 1.98 are (critical value = ±1.96)

2 (a) possibly one

   (b) only two

   (c) possibly one

   (d) only two

3 (a) α- = .01

   (b) more likely

4 (b) true

   (c) false

   (d) true

   (e) true

   (f) false

Glossary

(α) Alpha	Percentage of the probability area under H_0 that forms the 'rejection region'; level set for acceptable probability of Type I error under H_0
(β) Beta	If the null hypothesis is not true, this is the probability that a Type II error will be made
$p \leq .1$ (10%)	Significance level generally considered too high for rejection of the null hypothesis but where, if p under H_0 is this low, further investigation might be merited
$p \leq .05$ (5%)	Conventional significance level
$p \leq .01$ (1%)	Significance level preferred for greater confidence than that given by the conventional one and that should be set where research is controversial or a one-shot-only trial
Alternative hypothesis	Assumption that an effect exists (e.g. that populations differ)
Critical value	Value that the result of our test statistic (e.g. z) must reach in order for the null hypothesis to be rejected
Directional hypothesis	Hypothesis that states which way a difference or correlation is expected to occur
Effect size	The size of the effect being investigated (difference or correlation) as it exists in the population

Empirical	A measure of probability based on existing frequencies of occurrence of target events
Inferential test/statistics	Procedures for making inferences about whole populations from which samples are drawn, e.g. significance tests
Logical	A measure of probability calculated from logical first principles
Non-directional hypothesis	Hypothesis that does not state which way a difference or correlation is expected to occur
Null hypothesis	Assumption of no effect in the population from which samples are drawn (e.g. no mean population difference)
One-tailed test	Test referring to only one tail of the distribution under H_0; may be used if alternative hypothesis is directional (but controversial)
Power	The probability of not making a Type II error if a real effect exists; the probability of selecting a case or sample above the level cut off by β in the population defined by the alternative hypothesis
Probability	A numerical measure of pure 'chance' (randomly based) occurrence of events
Probability distribution	A histogram of the probabilities associated with a complete range of possible events
Rejection region	Area of (sampling) distribution where, if a result falls within it, H_0 is rejected; the area cut off by the critical value
Significance levels	Levels of probability at which it is agreed to reject H_0. If the probability of obtained results under H_0 is less than the set level, H_0 is rejected
Significance test/decision	Test performed in order to decide whether the null hypothesis should be retained or rejected
Two-tailed test	Test referring to both tails of the probability distribution under H_0; must be used if alternative hypothesis is non-directional
Type I error	Mistake made in rejecting the null hypothesis when it is true
Type II error	Mistake made in retaining the null hypothesis when it is false

Testing for differences
between two samples

This chapter introduces statistical significance tests for assessing the significance of differences between two samples and also introduces calculation of *effect size* and *power*.

- The *related* t test is used where data are in pairs, from a repeated measures or matched pairs design. H_0 is that the mean of the population of *difference means* (mean of differences between each pair of values) is zero.

- The t test for *unrelated data* (from independent samples) tests H_0 that the population of differences between two means has a mean of zero; that is, it assumes that the two populations from which the two samples are drawn have identical means.

- The *single sample* t is used to test the hypothesis that a single sample was drawn from a population with a certain mean; we usually want to show that this is unlikely and therefore that the sample is from a different population.

- t tests are a type of *parametric* or *distribution dependent* test that depend on certain data assumptions for their results to be reliable – *homogeneity of variance*, *interval level data* and a *normally shaped sampling distribution*.

- These tests are considered *robust* and more *power efficient* than their *non-parametric* equivalents, which are also dealt with here – the *Mann-Whitney* for unrelated data and the *Wilcoxon matched pairs* for related data. These *non-parametric tests* use ranks of the data and are considered to have on average 95.5% of the power of their parametric equivalents.

- The *sign test* for related categorical data is described.

- SPSS procedures for all tests in the chapter are provided.

- *Effect size* is introduced as a concept concerned with the size of the effect that the study was investigating whether or not a significant effect was found; if significance was not found, and there *is* an effect, a Type II error has occurred and it is stated that many researchers find the traditional structure of reliance on the significance test too conservative with the fear that many effects are missed through Type II error.

- The likelihood of missing an effect, if it is there, is the probability β and *power* of a specific test is defined as $1 - \beta$. This is the probability of demonstrating a significant effect if an effect really exists. Ways to increase power are discussed.

- Calculations are provided for effect size and power of t tests.

Tests of difference between two conditions or groups

This chapter deals with significance tests on typical data from a two-condition investigation such as those depicted in Table 15.1. We first deal with so-called PARAMETRIC TESTS, or DISTRIBUTION DEPENDENT TESTS, which are the various kinds of *t* test. These are conducted on data that are at least at *interval level*. We then look at non-parametric equivalents – the Mann-Whitney and the Wilcoxon tests – which are used on data that have been ranked (that is, they are at *ordinal level*). We usually only use these when the data have qualities that make a conclusion from a *t* test unsafe. The sign test is used on categorical related data.

In all cases we are dealing with the situation where you have two sets of data, typically scores for two conditions of an experiment or scores for two different groups of people. In order to select the appropriate test for your data you also need to decide whether they are *related* or *unrelated* (see Chapter 3). Data from *matched pairs* designs or from two measures of the same participant (*repeated measures* design) are *related*. *Unrelated* data occur where the two groups of participants providing scores consist of entirely different people; in other words, the two sets of scores to be tested come from two completely different (independent) sources – an *independent samples* design. (See also Chapter 21 and pp. 279–80.) Though it will seem odd, data produced where a single participant provides scores in two conditions of an experiment, several trials in each condition, are treated as unrelated – see p. 76.

Parametric tests

The *t* test for related data

When to use the related *t* test

Type of relationship tested	Type of data required	Design of study
Difference between two conditions	At least interval	Within groups: repeated measures matched pairs

Data assumptions: see required data assumptions on p. 363. The data in the example below do not violate any of these assumptions.

Note: If your data do not approximately meet the data assumptions for the test explained on p. 363. you will need to transform your data or use a non-parametric or distribution free test such as the Wilcoxon matched pairs signed ranks test (see p. 368).

Data for a related t test

Take a look at the data in Table 15.1, which displays results from an experiment on the improvement in memory recall produced by using imagery. Each participant has been tested in *both* the control condition (no specific instruction) *and* the imagery condition (where they were asked to form vivid images of each item). Hence it is a *repeated measures* or *related* design. The data come in pairs. Let's just think step-by-step through what we expect to happen here, if there is an 'effect' from imagery. Because we argue that imagery should be a memory aid we would expect the imagery scores to be higher than the control condition scores. Note that, in general, they are, but we cannot just say 'it worked'; we need a significance test to demonstrate to the research world that the probability of these differences occurring, if the null hypothesis is true, is less than .05.

	Number of words recalled in:			
Participant number	Imagery condition (*I*)	Control condition (*C*)	Difference	
			d	d^2
1	6	6	0	0
2	15	10	5	25
3	13	7	6	36
4	14	8	6	36
5	12	8	4	16
6	16	12	4	16
7	14	10	4	16
8	15	10	5	25
9	18	11	7	49
10	17	9	8	64
15	12	8	4	16
12	7	8	−1	1
13	15	8	7	49
	$\bar{x}_i = 13.38$	$\bar{x}_c$ 58.85	$\Sigma d = 59$	$\Sigma d^2 = 349$
	$s_i = 3.52$	s_c 51.68	$(\Sigma d)^2 = 3481$	
	Mean of differences ('difference mean') $\bar{d} = 4.54$			
	Standard deviation of differences $s_d = 2.60$			

Table 15.1 Number of words correctly recalled under imagery and control recall conditions (columns *I* and *C*) and statistics required to calculate related *t*

Calculating statistical significance tests

Note that, although we will go through the derivation of the *t* test in detail, in order for you to be able to understand what is going on, I will also with each significance test, provide a standard formula so that you can just submit your data to a test by simply following the steps of the calculation. These steps are given in special boxes after the explanation of each test. It is also likely, if you are at a university, that you will use SPSS to do the analysis.

Starting out on the related *t* test

Remember that every inferential statistical test is a test of a null hypothesis. We want to calculate the probability of our result occurring if nothing is really going on. It might help here, then, to think about what kind of results we'd expect if there is no effect – imagery does not help memory.

If we look at the *difference between each person's two scores* we will see whether they improved in the imagery condition or got worse. If the null hypothesis is true then people don't generally improve and all these differences should be close to zero. However, our research argument is that most people should *improve*. In turn this means that differences (imagery score minus control score, shown as *d* in Table 15.1 should generally be *positive*. The larger they are, if positive, the better for our research hypothesis. This is a *directional* approach. In a *non-directional* approach we would simply be saying that the differences should go in one direction, without specifying which.

The null hypothesis in the related *t* test

The null hypothesis here is that the two samples of scores come from populations with the same mean. However, since this is a related design, we can state the null hypothesis in terms of the *difference values*. If there is no imagery effect then the differences should all centre round zero and be relatively small – only the result of random error. Our null hypothesis, then, can be re-stated: the population of differences has a mean of zero (Figure 15.1). We can write this as:

$H_0 : \mu_d = 0$

where μ_d is the mean of the population of differences.

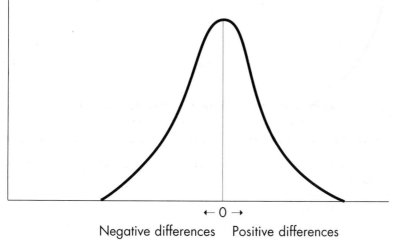

Negative differences   Positive differences

Figure 15.1 Hypothetical distribution of differences under H_0

353

Testing the null hypothesis

Think of the population of difference values as like the barrel of screws from the last chapter. The set of differences shown in the '*d*' column of Table 15.1 is a *sample* of score differences drawn randomly from this population and it has a mean of 4.54 (see the bottom of the *d* column). This mean of differences is known as a DIFFERENCE MEAN. Hence to test for significance we need to know the probability that a sample of 13 differences with a difference mean as large as, or larger than, 4.54 would be drawn at random from the population in Figure 15.1, which has a mean of zero.

What would be handy would be to know how *other* samples of difference values would be arranged. If, under H_0, the underlying population of differences has a mean of zero then samples taken randomly from it should all *also* have means close to zero. They would differ a bit from zero through *sampling error*, sometimes positive, sometimes negative, sometimes large, mostly small. What would happen if we kept on taking samples of 13 differences from this population? What kind of distribution of difference means would we get? If we knew this, then we could compare *our* difference mean of 4.54 with this distribution and see how unlikely ours would be to occur. Funnily enough, we have already encountered this concept of sampling over and over again in a previous chapter. In Chapter 13 we met the concept of a *sampling distribution*. You might like to re-read the appropriate section of that chapter in order to refamiliarise yourself with the idea.

Figure 15.2 shows the kind of distribution we might obtain if we were to dip into the population of close-to-zero differences taking samples of 13 many times over and recording the difference mean each time. It is called a *sampling distribution of difference means*. Note that it is much narrower than the distribution of differences because it is composed of *samples* of differences taken 13 at a time. The means will not vary as much around zero as the individual differences do.

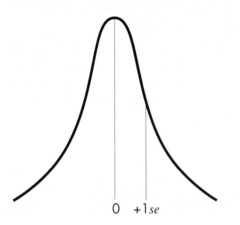

Figure 15.2 Sampling distribution of difference means under H_0

If we knew the statistical properties of this distribution we would be able to say whether our difference mean was a much-to-be-expected one or an extreme one. Trouble is, we don't have those properties ... or don't we? We need the mean and standard deviation of the sampling distribution because we just need to know how many standard deviations our difference mean is from the mean. Well we know the mean. We have already said that if the null hypothesis is true, the difference means will centre around zero. But what about the standard deviation? Well, on p. 316 we saw that statisticians have a formula for *estimating* the standard deviation of a sampling distribution using the sample that you have drawn. Don't forget, though, that the standard deviation is called the *standard error* here. This is because each sample, drawn randomly under H_0, differs from the mean of zero only because of sampling error. Each deviation of a sample from the population mean is an 'error'.

To estimate the standard error of the sampling distribution shown in Figure 15.2 then, we use the *central limit theorem* using standard deviation of the differences (s_d), which gives us

$$se = \frac{s}{\sqrt{N}} = \frac{2.6}{\sqrt{13}} = 0.721$$

Now we can just ask 'How many standard errors is *our* difference mean away from the hypothetical difference mean of zero?' We can get this by dividing our difference mean by the standard error: 4.54/0.721 which gives us 6.297. This value is known as a *t* value.

So our difference mean, if it was sampled at random from all difference means, would be 6.297 standard errors away from the population mean of zero. Is this a long way, making it a very unlikely occurrence? In Chapter 13, we learned that the number of standard deviations a score is from the mean is a *z* value (see p. 312 and a *z* value of over 6 is ever such a long way from the mean on a normal distribution. We might be tempted just to look up our *z* table as we did in Chapter xx and find the probability of a *z* that large occurring. There is just one little snag with this. The distribution of *t* is not normal in shape unless *N* is very large (e.g. 120 or more) when *t* can indeed be treated as a normal *z* value. The lower the value of *N*, though, the more the distribution of *t* would be broader than a normal distribution.

For the theory and mathematical tables associated with *t* distributions, and the *t* tests, we are indebted to William Gossett, who worked for the Guinness organisation. Guinness, at the time he did his stuff, did not permit its workers to publish findings connected with company work. Hence he published under the pseudonym of 'Student' and the distribution statistic is known, therefore, as Student's *t*. As a result of his work, however, we can consult *t* tables and find out whether our obtained value for *t* exceeds the critical value contained in the table.

Consulting critical value tables

We want to know if the probability of obtaining a *t* value of 6.297 is less than α in order to be able to claim our difference between means as significant. We therefore go to the Appendix where we find Table 3 containing critical values for *t*. In order to use this table we need to know a few things.

- First, we need to decide what level of α is appropriate. Usually this is .05 and you should always use this value to start with.

- Next, we have to decide whether we are conducting a one- or two-tailed test. As explained at the end of Chapter 14 it is best to use two-tailed tests and hope that your effect is large enough to show significance with the design you are using.

- Finally, we need to know our *degrees of freedom (df)*. This term was introduced in Chapter xx. It is the number of items in our sample that are free to vary, given that we know their mean. If we knew the mean of the differences but no individual values for *d*, we could enter any values we liked up to the 12th value but the 13th would then be fixed in order to make the mean what it actually is. Here we have 13 differences so 12 are free to vary and *df* = 12. The **Procedure** for each significance test will provide a simple formula for calculating *df* where needed.

Analysis of our result for *t* – effect size and power

Now we are ready to enter Table x appropriately. We see that for a two-tailed test with α at .05 and with 12 *df*, the critical value for *t* is 2.179 and our value of 6.297 easily beats that. In fact it also beats the value for $p \leq .01$ over to the right. We said in the last chapter that a result significant with $p \leq .01$ is not automatically 'better' than one where *p* is $\leq .05$. It all depends on sample size, *effect size* and *power*. *Effect size* is an estimate of the size of effect we appear to have demonstrated. *Power* is the probability of not making a Type II error. If we have low power, then a real existing effect might not show as significant. This issue is discussed more fully later on in this chapter but do be aware that nowadays reports of effect size, along with significance, are becoming more common and may be expected.

Whatever the objections of the statisticians, psychological researchers would tend to report this difference as 'highly significant' and to give the $p < .01$ value. Certainly, based on our sample results, we can confidently reject the null hypothesis (that there is no population difference) and argue that the use of imagery in this experiment appears to improve memory recall for words. However, we should also report on the estimated size of the effect (see p. 385).

Formula for calculation of related *t*

(1) $t = \dfrac{\bar{d}\sqrt{N}}{s}$ or   (2) $t = \dfrac{\sum d}{\sqrt{\dfrac{N\sum d^2 - \left(\sum d\right)^2}{N-1}}}$

Equation (1) is just a slight rearrangement of what we did just above when we divided the difference mean by the estimated standard error of its sampling distribution. This one is the easier calculation if you have a simple statistical calculator that will give you standard deviations. Here are the calculation steps for equation (2) where you only need the differences themselves and *N*. SPSS procedures are given on p. 379.

Hand calculation of related t

Procedure	Calculation/result of steps
1 Find the mean for each condition	From Table 15.1 $\bar{x}_i = 13.38$ $\bar{x}_c = 8.85$
2 Arrange columns so that condition with higher mean is to the left of the other condition; this is to make subtraction easier.	Column I before column C in Table 15.1
3 Subtract each score C from score I	See 'd' column in Table 15.1
4 Square each d	See 'd^2' column in Table 15.1
5 Total all d (Σd) and all d^2 (Σd^2)	$\Sigma d = 59$ $\Sigma d^2 = 349$ (see Table 15.1)
6 Square Σd to get $(\Sigma d)^2$ Note: This is not the same as Σd^2 – be careful to distinguish between these two terms. $(\Sigma d)^2$ says add the ds then square the result. Σd^2 says square each d then add the results.	$(\Sigma d)^2 = 59 \times 59 = \mathbf{3481}$
7 Find $N \times \Sigma d^2$	$13 \times 349 = \mathbf{4537}$
8 Subtract $(\Sigma d)^2$ from the result of step 7	$4537 - 3481 = \mathbf{1056}$
9 Divide the result of step 8 by $N-1$	$1056/12 = \mathbf{88}$
10 Find the square root of step 9	$\sqrt{88} = \mathbf{9.38}$
11 Divide Σd by the result of step 10 to give t	$t = 59/9.38 = \mathbf{6.29}$
12 Find df * In a related design $df = N-1$	$N-1 = \mathbf{12}$
13 Check t for significance in critical value table, finding the *highest* table value of t that our obtained t is greater than, and make significance decision.	For 12 df t must be ≥ 3.055 (two-tailed) for significance with $p \leq .01$ our obtained t is greater than 3.055, hence the difference is highly significant and we reject H_0.

* Degrees of freedom: see explanation of this concept on p. 273.

Reporting results of significance tests – what you should actually write

Research psychologists generally employ the conventions laid down by the American Psychological Association (APA) in reporting the results of statistical analysis. You will probably be asked to follow this format in presenting your results section where your assignment is a scientific report of a quantitative psychological investigation. Consequently, after we have looked at the analysis of each test from now on, the APA format for reporting will be given. Most courses will not ask you to report the estimated size of your effect (see p. 385) or confidence limits (see p. 316) but some do, so this information has been included. If you are not asked to report these values then just ignore the last sentence below (before the note) and in future results report examples.

Reporting results of a related t test

The mean number of words recalled in the imagery condition ($M = 13.38$, $SD = 3.52$) was higher than the mean for the control condition ($M = 8.85$, $SD = 1.68$) resulting in a mean increase ($M = 4.54$, $SD = 2.6$) in the number of words recalled per participant. This increase was statistically significant, $t (12) = 6.29$, $p < .001$, two-tailed. The mean difference (mean difference = 4.54, 95% CI:2.97 to 6.11) was large (Cohen's $d = 2.638$).

Note: If this result were not significant do NOT say it was 'insignificant'. Write:

' ... This increase was not significant, $t (12) = 1.477$, $p = .165$'

(or you could write 'ns' or '$p > .05$')

The t test for unrelated data

When to use the unrelated t test

Type of relationship tested	Type of data required	Design of study
Difference between two conditions or groups	At least interval	Between groups; Independent samples

Data assumptions: see required data assumptions on p. 363. The data in the example below do not violate any of these assumptions.
Note: if your data do not approximately meet the data assumptions for the test explained on p. 363. you will need to transform your data (if skewed) or select the appropriate line in SPSS. The alternative is to use a non-parametric or distribution free test such as the MANN-WHITNEY U TEST – see p. 371.

The reasoning for the unrelated t test is similar to that for the related t, the difference being only that the two samples of data have come from independent sources; that is, they are not pairs of scores from the same person or from matched participants. Typically we might have scores in two experimental conditions where each participant has been tested *in one condition only*. Another common source of data for the unrelated t test would be scores on a psychological measure from two different groups of people, e.g. reading scores for dyslexic and non-dyslexic students. Differences between groups of males and females would be unrelated (unless they are brothers and sisters!).

Data for an unrelated t test

Take a look at the data in Table 15.2 where participants have been divided into two groups, those above the median on a measure of disturbed sleep and those below this median. It was proposed that participants with a higher level of disturbed sleep would have higher anxiety levels than participants whose sleep was less disturbed. This does appear to be the case; the mean anxiety score for the higher sleep disturbance group is 12.4 (h = high disturbed sleep) whereas the mean for the lower sleep disturbance (*l*) group is 10.1 However, we need to know whether this difference between means is significant or not.

Anxiety scores for:

participants above median on disturbed sleep (*h*)		participants below median on disturbed sleep (*l*)	
Score x_h (*N* = 10)	x_h^2	**Score** x_l (*N* = 11)	x_l^2
14	196	8	64
11	121	10	100
9	81	9	81
12	144	11	121
13	169	9	81
15	225	11	121
13	169	8	64
11	121	12	144
17	289	11	121
9	81	13	169
		9	81
$\Sigma x_h = 124$		$\Sigma x_l = 111$	
$(\Sigma x_h)^2 = 15376$	$\Sigma x_h^2 = 1596$	$(\Sigma x_l)^2 = 12321$	$\Sigma x_l^2 = 1147$
$\bar{x}_h = 12.4$		$\bar{x}_l = 10.1$	
$s_h = 2.55$		$s_l = 1.64$	

Table 15.2 Anxiety scores for high and low sleep-disturbed participants

The null hypothesis for the unrelated *t* test

The null hypothesis here is that the two populations from which our two samples have been randomly drawn have equal means. We can write this as:

$H_0 : \mu_h = \mu_l$

Testing the null hypothesis

We can think of our two samples of anxiety scores here as like the two samples of screws taken from the two different barrels we encountered in Chapter 14. Because the two samples of scores are independent (from two *different* sets of people) we cannot, as in the related *t* test, look at pairs of scores and find the difference for each participant. However, what we *can* do is consider what would happen if we took two samples from two identical barrels at random, many times over, and each time recorded the difference between the two sample means. What we would obtain, if we plotted these differences each time, is a distribution looking much like that in Figure 15.3.

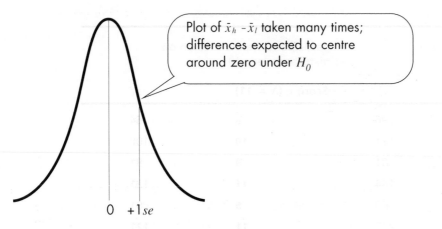

Plot of $\bar{x}_h - \bar{x}_l$ taken many times; differences expected to centre around zero under H_0

$0 \quad +1\,se$

Figure 15.3 Sampling distribution of differences between two sample means

Under H_0, if the two underlying population means are identical, then the mean of this sampling distribution will be zero. That is, if we take two samples from the same population many times over, sometimes the difference between these two means will be positive and sometimes negative; sometimes it will be large but mostly it will be small. Under the laws of random selection the distribution of differences will look like that in Figure 15.3. What we want to know, then, is how far away from zero on this distribution does our *obtained* difference between two means fall? If we know this we can easily find the probability of our difference occurring under H_0.

Again, we need the properties of the sampling distribution of differences between two means. We know its mean is zero so what will be its standard error? Well, unfortunately this is not as easy a question to answer as it was for the related *t* test. In keeping with the philosophy that psychology students need only understand the basic principles of statistics rather than appreciate the finer points of derivation, I will simply explain what the equation *does* rather than produce a comprehensive explanation. Remember that all we want to do is to estimate where our obtained difference between two means falls on the distribution expected under H_0 and shown in Figure 15.3. To do this, as for a *z* value, we divide the difference by the standard error of the distribution. This answers the question 'How many standard errors is our obtained difference from zero?' In the related *t* test we used the central limit theorem to estimate easily the population variance from the sample variance. Trouble is, on this occasion we have *two* variances from two samples. What we do in the unrelated *t* test is estimate the variance of the distribution shown in Figure 15.3 from the POOLED VARIANCE of the two samples. Now, if you can bear it, take a peek at equation 3 below, but please do not panic! Yes, it is nasty, but it involves no more arithmetic than can be done on the simplest of calculators – there's just a lot of it!

The nasty bit on the bottom is the pooled variance used in the estimate of standard error of the sampling distribution of differences between two means (i.e. the standard deviation in Figure 15.3).

On top of the nasty equation below, then, is our obtained difference between two means. Below is the estimated standard error. The equation will give us t, which will be the number of standard errors we estimate our difference to be from the difference of zero expected under the null hypothesis. This estimate takes into account the fact that sample sizes may be different.

$$\frac{|\bar{x}_a - \bar{x}_b|}{\sqrt{\frac{\left(\sum x_a^2 - \frac{(\sum x_a)^2}{N_a}\right) + \left(\sum x_b^2 - \frac{(\sum x_b)^2}{N_b}\right)}{(N_a + N_b - 2)}\left[\frac{N_a + N_b}{N_a N_b}\right]}}$$

By-hand calculation of unrelated t

Obviously, equation (3) looks pretty complex but in fact it just involves a lot of basic steps with the emphasis on *a lot*! If you want to calculate t by hand, the following procedure box will take you through these steps. Computer packages like SPSS will of course whisk you through it in a jiffy … but you won't have the satisfaction of cracking this monster! SPSS procedures appear on p. 381.

Please note that, from the general equation above, in this example a has been substituted by the h or *high sleep deprivation* scores, whereas b is substituted by the l or *low sleep deprivation* scores.

Procedure	Calculation/result of steps See Table 15.2 for all summary statistics
1 Add the scores in the first group	$\Sigma x_h = 124$
2 Add all the *squares* of scores in the first group	$\Sigma x_h^2 = 1596$
3 Square the result of step 1; always be careful here to distinguish between Σx_h^2 and $(\Sigma x_h)^2$	$(\Sigma x_h)^2 = 15376$
4 Divide the result of step 3 by N_h	$15376 \div 10 = 1537.6$
5 Subtract result of step 4 from result of step 2	$1596 - 1537.6 = 58.4$
6 Steps 6–8: Repeat steps 1 to 3 on the scores in the second group	Step 6: $\Sigma x_l = 111$
	Step 7: $\Sigma x_l^2 = 1147$
	Step 8: $(\Sigma x_l)^2 = 12321$
9 Divide the result of step 8 by N_l	$12321 \div 11 = 1120.1$
10 Subtract result of step 9 from result of step 7	$1147 - 1120.1 = 26.9$
11 Add the results of steps 5 and 10	$58.4 + 26.9 = 85.3$
12 Divide the result of step 11 by $N_h + N_l - 2$	$85.3 (10 + 11 - 2) = 4.49$
13 Multiply the result of step 12 by: $\dfrac{N_h + N_l}{N_h N_l}$	$4.49 \div 21/110 = 0.85$
14 Find the square root of the result in step 13	$\sqrt{0.85} = 0.92$
15 Find the difference between the two means	$(x_h - x_l)$ $12.4 - 10.1 = 2.3$

16	Divide the result of step 15 by the result of step 14 to give t	$t = 2.3 \div 0.92 = \mathbf{2.5}$
17	Find degrees of freedom (df) where $df = N_h + N_l - 2$	$10 + 11 - 2 = \mathbf{19}$
18	Consult Appendix Table 3 and decide upon significance	For a two-tailed test with $df = 19$, t must be $\geq$ 2.093 for significance with $p \leq .05$; hence the difference between means here is significant.

We can reject the null hypothesis that people with high sleep disturbance do not differ from people with low sleep disturbance on anxiety. It remains open to question, since this was *not* an *experiment*, whether disturbed sleep is a cause of anxiety or whether anxiety causes sleep disturbance. The issues of effect size and power should also be considered in reporting this result (p. 385).

Reporting results of an unrelated t test

> High sleep-disturbance participants produced higher anxiety scores ($M = 12.4$, $SD = 2.55$) than did the low sleep-disturbance participants ($M = 10.1$, $SD = 1.64$). The difference between means was significant, $t(19) = 2.5$, $p < .05$, two-tailed.
> The difference between means (difference = 2.3, 95% CI: 0.37 to 4.25) was large (Cohen's d = 1.08)

The single sample t test

Data requirements: Interval level data and normal distribution

The tests so far covered are the most common type of t tests, those where we do not know the features of the appropriate underlying population and where we are testing the difference between two samples. Usually we have a second sample, which is a *control* group, because we need to make a comparison with what would happen if no treatment were applied. In some cases, however, we *do* know the features of a population, in which case our significance testing is made easier. In this case we do not need a control group because we already know the population mean for the condition in which no specific treatment is applied.

Let's return to the spinach-eating example in Chapter 13. There we found that the mean reading score for a population of eight-year-olds was 40, with a standard deviation of 10. We said there that significance tests would normally be carried out on a *sample* of children's scores, not just one. Suppose we identified a sample of 20 spinach-eating children whose combined average reading score was 43 with a standard deviation of 6. This is in favour of our hypothesis that spinach eating enhances reading. However, we need to test our difference for significance.

The null hypothesis for a single sample t test

In a single sample t test we know (or can argue for) the population mean for the variable under investigation. In the spinach case we assume: H_0: $\mu = 40$

What we don't know is what the sampling distribution for samples of 20 children at a time would look like, so we can again use the central limit theorem to estimate this for us. The standard error of the sampling distribution will be

$$se = \frac{s}{\sqrt{N}} = \frac{6}{\sqrt{20}} = 1.34$$

Our sample mean is 3 points away from the assumed mean of 40 under H_0 (which assumes that our spinach-eating kids have been randomly sampled from the normal reading population). How many standard errors is this from 40? We must divide the difference between our mean and 40 by the standard error. This will be our obtained value for t, so let's find it:

$$t = \frac{3}{1.34} = 2.23$$

df here, as usual, are one fewer than the number of data points we have, so $df = 19$. From Appendix Table 3, t must be ≥ 2.093 for significance with $p \leq .05$ (two-tailed). Hence this difference is significant and we may reject the null hypothesis that spinach-eating children do not differ from other children on reading (I do stress this is fictitious; don't rush to the greengrocer's!). The issue of effect size should also be considered in reporting this result (see p. 385).

Reporting the result of a single sample t test

The spinach-eating group produced higher reading scores ($M = 43$, $SD = 6$) than the known mean for the normal population ($M = 40$, $SD = 10$). This difference was significant, $t (19) = 2.23$, $p < .05$.

The difference between the sample mean and the population mean (3) was medium (95% CI: 0.188 to 5.812. Cohen's $d = 0.5$).

(**Note:** The data set for these calculations is provided on the companion website at: www.hodderplus.com/psychology/

Data assumptions for t tests

The t tests are often referred to as being in a class known as *parametric tests*. Actually, they are more appropriately known as *distribution dependent tests* and this is because, as we saw above, they make estimations of underlying distributions. These estimations will be seriously distorted if the data we have gathered do not conform to certain criteria. In turn, any inference we make from our data may be suspect and we may need to rethink the analysis of our data in order to be more confident of the decision we make about them. There are three basic considerations about the data for our dependent variable that we must make, and these are described below.

1 The level of measurement must be at interval level

This is a much-debated point but there is an easy rule of thumb. As we saw in Chapter 11, interval-level data have equal amounts for equal measures on the scale. Hence, distance (which is also a ratio measure) increases in equal amounts for every increase in unit. We know that this can hardly be true for many psychological measures such as intelligence, extroversion, and so on, although it is the psychometrist's dream to create such scales. However, if a scale has been *standardised* (see p. 201) it is usually safe to treat its scores as interval-level data. Scores on a memory test or errors on some other cognitive task represent sensible ratios – six words recalled is twice as good as three words recalled – but we would not claim therefore that Harry with six has twice as good a memory overall as Ron. We are only measuring performance on an isolated task. Hence one need not get into this kind of metaphysical argument in order to be satisfied that these kinds of measures produce data we can safely treat as being at interval level.

Where we run into difficulty is with invented scales that rely on human judgement. Typically, we might ask people to 'rate your level of confidence on a scale of 1 (= not at all confident) to 10 (= highly confident)'. Here we know that your 8 might be my 6 and we have no independent way of knowing that people using this scale are separating themselves from others by equal amounts. When using this kind of scale to produce data which we then want to test for significance there are two main options: (1) subject the data to normality checks as described below and in more advanced textbooks, transforming the data if necessary, or (2) choose one of the *non-parametric tests* to be described in the next section.

2 Data from a normal distribution

Our data should have been drawn from an underlying normal distribution. For a standardised psychological measure this should be true since this is what is created when the test is first developed. However, you may be drawing data from a somewhat different population from that on which the test was standardised. For any data set it is worth checking that there is not too large a skew and that the data are distributed as would be expected if drawn from a normal distribution (see p. 308). Your data are not normally distributed if they do not fit the criteria outlined on p. 319. In addition you can inspect several kinds of plot using SPSS, especially the Normal Q-Q plots, as described in Pallant (2007).

What do you do if you find the data really are a long way out from normal? Chapter 13 tells us that skew is too much when the value for skew is twice its standard error. There are two common solutions, the first of which is simply to use a non-parametric test (see below). The other is to stay with the *t* test and use, instead of actual scores, a TRANSFORMATION of these scores. This sounds like a glorious cheat but in fact we can 'normalise' our data this way and then legitimately carry on with the *t* test, so long as the skew is now acceptable. Among the transformations you can perform are:

- square
- square root
- log (to base 10 or other bases).

Be careful if you use square root since the square root of zero is an impossible calculation and SPSS will exclude all scores of zero from the analysis. The answer is to first add 1 to every score. Getting the log of each score can be done quite easily using a computer spreadsheet (such as Microsoft Excel or SPSS) or using a simple scientific calculator. You can use log10, $\log_e$ (as **LN** does in the SPSS instructions below), or any other log base, so long as it has the effect of normalising your data (reducing the skew).

In SPSS the commands are: **transform/compute**. You see a box, top left, labelled **Target Variable** which asks you to name a new variable that will be the log of your raw scores (e.g. *loghits*). You then select **Sqrt LOG10** or **LN** after clicking **Arithmetic** on the right-hand side (scroll down alphabetically) and click that upwards into the box labelled **Numeric Expression**. Place the cursor between the two brackets in the new expression and double-click the variable to be logged (e.g. *hits*). It should now appear between the two bracket signs (e.g. you should see **LN(*hits*)**, and you're ready. Click **OK** and a new logged variable will appear in your datasheet; check that its skew is not more than twice its standard error and use this instead of *hits* as the dependent variable in conducting your *t* test. If this doesn't work try another transformation. Note that, although you use this transformed variable in your analysis (e.g. the *t* test), having explained to your reader that this is what you have done, you should from then on refer to *hits* and not *loghits* when discussing your findings.

3 Homogeneity of variance

For two condition tests, this check need only be made where the design is unrelated and the sizes of N_a and N_b are very different, e.g. 7 and 23. Homogeneity of variance requires that the variances in the two populations are equal and we check this by showing that the two sample variances are *not* significantly different. The reason for this lies in the estimation of pooled variance in the formula on p. 360. The null hypothesis assumes that both samples are drawn from similar distributions. Each individual sample variance is an estimate of the underlying population variance and we average these two to get a better estimate. This averaging makes no sense if the variances are very different.

To test for homogeneity of variance you can do the following:

1 If using SPSS, you will automatically be given the result of a Levene's test when you conduct an independent samples *t* test. You just need to note that the significance value for this is *not* under .05; if it is, the variances are not homogenous. If this happens then you just have to consult the line '*Equal variances not assumed*' in the *t* test results table.

2 Use a rough guide – if you cannot use these methods you can at least decide that a *t* test is unsafe if one variance is more than four times the value of the other (for small *N*, i.e. 10 or fewer) or more than twice the value for larger *N*.

3 Consult more advanced texts – such as Howell (2001) – for Levene's and O'Brien's tests, calculated by hand.

If you do not think that the homogeneity of variance assumption is satisfied you can decide to use a non-parametric test, probably the Mann-Whitney, which is described later in this chapter. Alternatively you can add participants to the condition with lower *N* until numbers in each condition are equal (of course, you don't then have random allocation).

Why not wing it? – The robustness of *t* tests – the alternatives and their power efficiency

A certain amount of leeway is tolerated with these assumptions. If you are in a position where you wish to use a *t* test but have violated one of the conditions a bit, then you can draw your reader's attention to this but also hope that the significance level is so high (i.e. *p* is so low) that it is likely that you are still making the correct decision about the existence of the effect you are investigating. For this reason the *t* tests are called 'robust' (you can violate the assumptions a bit and still trust your result). However, if you really are in doubt there is simply no big problem with switching to one of the NON-PARAMETRIC or DISTRIBUTION-FREE equivalent tests, which we will move on to below (and they are a *lot* easier to calculate by hand). These tests (usually the Mann-Whitney U and the Wilcoxon T tests) will give you the same significance decision as the t test on the large majority of occasions. The reason they don't always do so is because they deal with less of the information in the data than do interval-level tests. The non-parametric tests reduce data to ordinal level thus losing the distance between individual positions of scores (see p. 255).

Because rank tests do not always detect significance when a t test would, they are sometimes described as being less POWER EFFICIENT. Power efficiency is determined by comparing one type of test with another in terms of their ability to avoid Type II errors. With rank tests, then, we are somewhat more likely to retain H_0 when it is false than with the t tests. However, if the research study is well designed, with appropriate and large enough samples, an effect should be detected with either test. The issue of statistical power is dealt with later in this chapter.

Exercises

1 What precautions need to be taken before carrying out a t test on each of the following two sets of data:

(a)	17	23		(b)	17	23	
	18	9			18	11	
	18	31			18	24	
	16	45	(unrelated data)		16	29	(related data)
	16				12	19	
	18				15	16	
	17						
	6						

2 Brushing caution aside, calculate the t values for the data in 1a and 1b above any way you like.

3 A report claims that a t-value of 2.85 is significant ($p < .01$) when the number of people in a repeated measures design was 11. Could the hypothesis tested have been non-directional?

4 At what level, if any, are the following values of t significant? The last two columns are for you to fill in. Don't forget to think about degrees of freedom.

	$t =$	N	Design of study	One- or two-tailed	$p \leq$	Reject null hypothesis?
a)	1.750	16	related	2		
b)	2.88	20	unrelated	2		
c)	1.70	26	unrelated	2		
d)	5.1	10	unrelated	1		
e)	2.09	16	related	2		
f)	2.76	30	related	2		

5 Two groups of children are observed for the number of times they make a generous response during one day. The researcher wishes to conduct a *t* test for differences between the two groups on their 'generosity response score'. A rough grouping of the data shows this distribution of scores:

Number of generous responses

Group	0–3	4–6	7–9	10–12	13–15	16–19	20–22
A	2	16	24	3	1	0	1
B	5	18	19	4	5	1	3

(a) Why does the researcher's colleague advise that a *t* test on the raw data might be inappropriate?

(b) What are the options for the researcher?

Answers

1 (a) Variances not at all similar, unrelated design and very different sample numbers. If using SPSS use 'unequal variances line' (see p. 382) or carry out the non-parametric equivalent.

(b) Lack of homogeneity of variance but related design. Therefore, safe to carry on with *t*.

2 (a) $t(10) = 2.06$; (b) $t(5) = 1.57$

3 No. $df = 10$. Critical value (two-tailed) at $p \le .01 = 3.169$

4 (a) NS, keep NH
   (b) .01, reject NH
   (c) NS, keep NH
   (d) .005, reject NH
   (e) NS, keep NH
   (f) .01, reject NH

5 (a) Distributions are skewed. As samples are large, the whole population may well be skewed too, and this is contrary to normal distribution assumption.

(b) Try to get rid of skew by transformation of the data or switch to a Mann-Whitney.

Non-parametric tests of difference

We have seen that there are some restrictions on the type of data that are suitable for a safe significance assessment using *t* tests. Sometimes your data just won't be suitable. You may have a scale that certainly isn't interval – it does not have equal intervals for equal amounts of the variable measured. Typical here are those invented assessment scales that ask you to 'Assess … on a scale from 1 to 10…'. You may have severely skewed data that won't go away with a transformation. This isn't as big a problem as it might seem. You can use a non-parametric test (usually easier to calculate if doing it by hand) and still get the significant result that a *t* test would give. Non-parametric tests are estimated to be 95% power efficient as compared with *t* tests. That is, on 95 occasions out of 100 they will give you significance if the *t* test does.

The Wilcoxon (*T*) matched pairs signed ranks test

When to use the Wilcoxon

Type of relationship tested	Type of data required	Design of study
Difference between two conditions	At least ordinal	Within groups: Repeated measures Matched pairs

Data assumptions: Data at least at ordinal level.
Note: When *N* is > 20 and/or if the Wilcoxon critical values table does not include your size of *N*, please see p. 375

The Wilcoxon is one of two major tests used at the ordinal level for testing differences. It is used with related data (from a repeated measures or matched pairs design). One initial word of warning: the Wilcoxon statistic is *T* and this is very easy to confuse with the (little) '*t*' test we met in the previous section. SPSS does not help by referring to *t* as *T*! Just be aware of which test you are in fact using. There is also a rarely encountered Wilcoxon's rank sum test for unrelated samples.

Data for Wilcoxon's *T*

Suppose we ask students to rate two methods of learning which they have experienced on two different modules. Method A is a traditional lecture-based approach while method B is an active assignment-based method. We might hypothesise that students would be very likely to prefer a more active, involved approach. If you look at the data in Table 15.3 you'll see that, for each student, we know which they preferred by looking at the sign of the difference between their two ratings (column C). If the sign is positive then their rating for Method B was higher than their rating for Method A. In column D, the sizes of the differences have been ranked, ignoring the sign of the difference. This converts the differences in column C into *ordinal data*. Just three students prefer the lecture method to the assignment method, and this is shown by the fact that their differences are negative.

	Rating of traditional lecture	Rating of assignment-based method	Difference (B–A)	Rank of difference
Student (N = 15)	A	B	C	D
Griffiths	23	33	+10	12
Ashford	14	22	+8	9.5
Woodlock	35	38	+3	3
Jamalzadeh	26	30	+4	5
Manku	28	31	+3	3
Masih	19	17	—2	1
Salisbury	42	42	0	
Maman	30	25	—5	6
Quinliven	26	34	+8	9.5
Blay	31	24	—7	8
Harrison	18	21	+3	3
Ramakrishnan	25	46	+21	14
Apostolou	23	29	+6	7
Dingley	31	40	+9	11
Milloy	30	41	+11	13

Table 15.3 Student ratings of a lecture-based and an assignment-based module

If we are to convince ourselves and others that the preference for an assignment approach is real, and that we can dismiss the idea that the ratings fluctuate only randomly, we need more positive than negative differences. However, it would also be much more convincing if those negative differences (i.e. the 'unwanted' ones) were small compared with the others. In a sense, if we were arguing for the assessment-based method, we could say 'Sure, there were a couple of people who voted in the opposite direction, *but not by much.*' The way we show that the unwanted differences are not large is by looking not at the actual difference (as we did in the t test) but at the *ranks* of the differences. We want the negative ranks to be small. T is simply the smaller of the two sums of ranks – the sum for the positive differences and the sum for the negative differences. If we have a significant difference then T will be very small because differences that went in one of the two possible directions are also very small.

For any fixed value of N there is a fixed sum of ranks for the differences. In Table 15.3 there are 15 people. One of these does not have a difference since they rated both methods the same. For the purposes of the Wilcoxon analysis we ignore any ties like this. Hence, the 14 remaining participants must receive the ranks 1 to 14. These ranks add up to 105 (that's $1 + 2 + 3 + 4 + 5 + 6 + 7 + 8 + 9 + 10 + 11 + 12 + 13 + 14$). We will have two sums of ranks, one for negative and one for positive differences. Hence, these two sums must add to 105. This will be true *whenever* there are 14 data pairs no matter what was measured on whatever scale. Ordinal data are just the ranks – the raw scores are not used in calculations. If there is no difference between ratings of the two teaching methods (for the 'population') then every time we sample 14 people's pairs of ratings we should get a T close to 52.5. T is the smaller sum of ranks but if there is no difference between the methods then most of the time the two sums of ranks will be equal and T will be half of the total sum of 105. In other words, if we obtained a sampling distribution of Ts by taking 14 pairs of scores over and over again, the mid-point of this distribution would be where $T = 52.5$.

The null hypothesis for the Wilcoxon matched pairs signed ranks tests

It is conventional to state the null hypothesis as the claim that the two populations from which scores are sampled are identical. Most of the time this is more specifically that the two medians are equal (not *means* because we are working at the ordinal level).

Testing the null hypothesis

T values of around 52 and 53 will occur most frequently, then, if we persist with the drawing of 14 random score pairs. Values for T will range either side of this but very few will be close to zero or to 105. In other words, we are sampling under H_0 and we could work out how likely it is to get any value for T. Fortunately, those who have gone before us have developed tables of critical values. These will tell us what value of T will occur less than 5% of the time if the null hypothesis is true. If our T is lower than or equal to the critical value, then the probability of our T occurring under H_0 is $\leq .05$.

By-hand calculation of Wilcoxon's (related) T

Procedure	Calculation/result of steps
1 Find the difference between each pair of scores; it makes things easier to subtract in the direction that differences were expected to go or, anyway, smaller from larger	See Table 15.3 column C
2 Rank the differences, *ignoring their sign*; see p. 253 for ranking method; omit any zero differences from the analysis*	See Table 15.3 column D
	Note we drop Salisbury from the analysis
3 Find the sum of ranks of positive differences and the sum of ranks of negative differences; the smaller of these is T	Since the sum of ranks for negative differences will obviously be smaller we need only add these, so: $T = 1+6+8 = 15$

4 Consult Appendix Table 5 to find the critical value required; use N, which doesn't include any zero difference scores already discarded	Relevant line is $N = 14$
5 Using two-tailed test values, for significance T must be less than or equal to the table value for α i.e. usually $p \leq .05$	Critical value of T when $p \leq .05$ is 21; our obtained T is less than this, so the difference is significant; we may reject H_0
NOTE: In the t test our value for t had to be greater than the crucial value; here T must be *lower*	Note that the obtained T also equals the critical value for $p \leq .02$ so we know that p was in fact as low as .02

Note: *Almost all writers tell you to ignore zero differences so you'll be in safe company if you do, and you can certainly ignore them when there are only two or three. However, with larger numbers, a small bias is incurred and Hays (1973) advises the following: with even numbers of zero differences, give each the average rank that all the zeros would get – they get the lowest ranks, before you move on to values of 1 and 2 so four zeros would get the ranks 1, 2, 3 and 4, and each would receive the average of these which is 2.5. Arbitrarily give half of the zero score ranks a negative sign. Do the same if there is an odd number of zeros, but randomly discard one of them first. This might make some results significant that wouldn't otherwise be. Notice, this has no effect on our calculation above because, with one zero difference, the methods are the same.

It appears that there is a real overall preference among students for the assignment-based teaching method. Effect size and power should be considered (see p. 385).

Reporting the results of a Wilcoxon matched pairs signed ranks test

One student showed no preference for either method and this result was discarded from the analysis. The remaining 14 students were rank ordered by the size of their preference for one teaching form over the other. A Wilcoxon T was used to evaluate these differences. A significant preference was shown for the assignment-based method, $T = 15$, $p \leq .05$; the total of the ranks where students were in favour of the assignment-based method was 90 and the total for the traditional method was 15.

The effect size was medium to large, $r = .43$ (see p. 393 for effect size calculation)

The Mann-Whitney U test

When to use the Mann-Whitney

Type of relationship tested	Type of data required	Design of study
Difference between two conditions	At least ordinal	Between groups: Independent samples

Data assumptions: Data at least at ordinal level.

Note: When N is > 20 and/or the Mann-Whitney critical values table does not include your size of N, please see p. 375.

Data for the Mann-Whitney U test

In order to understand how the Mann-Whitney test works have a look at the data in Table 15.4. Imagine that children's tendency to stereotype according to traditional sex roles has been observed. The children have been asked questions about several stories. The maximum score was 100, indicating extreme stereotyping. Two groups were observed, one with mothers who had full-time paid employment and one whose mothers did not work outside the home.

Stereotype scores for children whose mothers had:

Full-time jobs		No job outside home	
Score	Points	Score	Points
17	9	19	6
32	7	63	0
39	6.5	78	0
27	8	29	4
58	6	39	1.5
25	8	59	0
31	7	77	0
		81	0
		68	0
Totals:	**51.5** U_1		**11.5** U_2

U is the lower of 51.5 and 11.5, so U is 11.5

Table 15.4 Stereotyping scores for children with employed and unemployed mothers

It looks as though the stereotyping scores for children of employed mothers are far lower than those for the other group. It is true that there are two fewer employed than non-employed mothers. However, this doesn't matter and the statistical test will take this into account. Never worry about slight disparities between participant numbers in two conditions (though it is a good idea to plan on getting even numbers if you can). Certainly never use this as a critical point when discussing a research study unless the disparity is very large. The statistical procedures reported in this book all take into account such disparities and nevertheless calculate the value of p under H_0 in all cases.

The Mann-Whitney test, like the Wilcoxon, is based on rank order, though you will not need to do any ranking in order to perform the test. Imagine that the values in columns 1 and 3 of Table 15.4 were the scores obtained by members of team A and team B respectively, each throwing three darts at a dartboard. Because we are only working at ordinal level the information that 81 in the B team is far higher than the highest score of 58 in the A group is not used. All we use is the information that 81 is better than the highest team A score; we don't take into account *how much* better it is. What we do, in fact, is to find out, for each person in a group, how many people in the other group beat that person's score. We do this by allotting points according to the following simple system:

- each time a score X is beaten by one in the other group award a point to score X
- each time a score X equals a score in the other group award ½ a point to score X.

If you look at columns 2 and 4 of Table 15.4 this has been done. The first score in the first group is 17. This is beaten by every score in the other group so 17 is awarded 9 points. You'll see that in this (rather odd) scoring system the higher your points total the more people have beaten your score. The third score in the first group is 39. This is beaten only by the scores of 63, 78, 59, 77, 81 and 68 in the other group, so 6 points are awarded. However 39 is also equalled by the fifth score in the second group so a half point is awarded here also, giving 39 a total of 6.5 points altogether. We proceed in this way through both groups, although if it is obvious which group has the higher scores you need only award points for that group. The total of points for each group is found and the lower of these two totals is the statistic U.

There is a simple rationale to this. Suppose each person in each group has played each person in the other group just once, each throwing the three darts. There will be 7 x 9 contests altogether, giving 63. For each of these contests a point is awarded, either one to the winner or a ½ each in the case of a draw. This is precisely what we just did in awarding our points. Hence we must have awarded 63 points altogether, and you can tell this by adding the two values of U. We know, then, that:

$$N_1 N_2 = U_1 + U_2$$

and you can use this in future just to check you haven't made an error.

The null hypothesis for the Mann-Whitney U test

In general, H_0 is that the populations from which the two samples have been randomly selected are identical. In most cases it is specifically that the two population medians are equal.

Testing the null hypothesis

Remembering that points awarded here are like penalty points, if the members of team B are really brilliant at darts they'll have very few points awarded against them and team A will amass a large score. If, on the other hand, the two teams are equally matched, then each time they play it is like drawing samples under the null hypothesis. The most either team can get is 63 and the least zero. Under H_0 we would expect 31 or 32 to occur most frequently (with equal team numbers) and smaller values of U to occur relatively less frequently. For each combination of N_1 and N_2 there will be a value of U where, if our obtained value of U falls below this, the probability of the difference occurring (under H_0) is $\leq .05$. This will be our critical value, then, and our statistical train spotters have of course devised tables for us to consult (see the Appendix, Table 6).

By-hand calculation of Mann-Whitney U

Procedure	Calculation/result of steps
1 For each score in each group give a point each time it is beaten by a score in the other group and a ½ point for a tie; if one group obviously has higher scores you need only do this for that group	See columns 2 and 4 of Table 15.4
2 Add up the points for each group and find the lower of two values; this value is U	In Table 15.4 we have $U_1 = 51.5$ and $U_2 = 11.5$ (Check: $N_1 N_2 = U_1 + U_2$: $7 \times 9 = 51.5 + 11.5 = 63$ so we have not made an error) $U = \mathbf{11.5}$
3 Consult Table 6 for critical values with a two-tailed test and α at .05	Critical value for $N_1 = 9$ and $N_2 = 7$ is 12 11.5 is less than 12 so we have a significant result (just!) and may reject H_0.

We have support for the hypothesis that children of working mothers are less likely to use sex-role stereotypes. Effect size and power should be considered (see p. 393).

Reporting the results of a Mann-Whitney U test

The children's stereotyping scores were each allocated points when they were exceeded by or equalled each score in the other group. The lower points total was taken as a Mann-Whitney U value for $N_1 = 7$ and $N_2 = 9$. The results indicated lower stereotyping scores for the children of full-time employed mothers than for the other children. This difference was significant, $U = 11.5$, $p < .05$, with 51.5 points for the employed mother group and 11.5 for the non-employed mother group. The effect size was large, $r = .53$.

Note: Where the formula approach is used (see below), and scores are rank ordered, you would include the rank totals for each group rather than the points total.

Formula for U

Most texts ask you to rank all the scores *as one group* then apply two formulae to find U_1 and U_2. The original procedure is that just described but statisticians like to encapsulate procedures in a formula. Some argue that the points method is unwieldy for large N but my view would be that the ranking method is even more frustrating and error prone for large numbers, where many ties occur and where the student inevitably finds they have to restart at least once. Even with large samples, if I had to calculate by hand, I would always choose the points method. To calculate with formulae, first, rank all 16 scores as one group. Then use the ranks in the following formulae:

$$U_a = N_a N_b + \frac{N_a(N_a + 1)}{2} - R_a \qquad U_b = N_a N_b + \frac{N_b(N_b + 1)}{2} - R_b$$

where R_a is the sum of ranks for group A and R_b is the sum for group B. Again you select the lower value of U_a and U_b as your observed U.

Non-parametric tests and z values – Effect size and large N

Both U and T can be converted to a z value. This is particularly useful in calculating effect sizes and we will do this on p. 395.

It is also useful when N is large and the critical values only go up to a modest sample size of 20 or 25. The value of z has to be large enough to cut off less than the final 5% of the normal distribution at the predicted end (one-tailed tests) or less than 2.5% at either end (two-tailed tests). From the normal distribution table in the Appendix, Table 2 I hope you'll agree that a z score of 1.96 is the critical value for a two-tailed test and that 1.65 is the critical value for a one-tailed test, where α is .05. The relevant formulae are:

Mann-Whitney

$$z = \frac{U - \dfrac{N_a N_b}{2}}{\sqrt{\left(\dfrac{N_a N_b}{N\,(N-1)}\right)\left(\dfrac{N^3-N}{12} - \sum \dfrac{t^3-t}{12}\right)}}$$ where N is $N_a + N_b$

t accounts for tied scores. Each time you find a tied value in your data set you count up how many times the value occurs and this value is t. Remember though that you have to do this for each value that is tied and add up the results. For instance, for the data in Table 15.2 the score 11 appears five times so $t = 5$ and you then put this into the $\dfrac{t^3-t}{12}$ formula and record your result. Then you do the same again for 9, which also occurs five times, 12 which appears twice, 13 which appears three times and 8 which appears twice. Finally you add the results of these five calculations. If there are no ties then $\dfrac{t^3-t}{12}$ is just ignored.

Wilcoxon signed ranks T

$$z = \frac{N\,(N+1) - 4T}{\sqrt{\dfrac{2N\,(N+1)\,(2N+1)}{3}}}$$ where the T is the observed Wilcoxon's T

The (binomial) sign test for related data (S)

When to use the binomial sign test		
Type of relationship tested	Type of data required	Design of study
Difference between two conditions	In categorical form – may be reduced from interval or ordinal level	Within groups: Repeated measures Matched pairs
Data assumptions: Measures of the dependent variable have two equally likely values under H_0, e.g. negative or positive, correct or incorrect and so on.		

Data for the sign test

The sign test works on a very simple kind of categorical data. When we have interval-like data on each participant taken under two related conditions we may feel that the *difference* between the two values cannot be taken as a meaningful interval measure. For instance, if you rate two modules on a scale of 1 to 10, giving one 8 and the other 4, we cannot claim that the difference of 4 is an interval measure. However, what we can say pretty confidently is that you preferred the first module to the second. We can take as data the *sign* of the difference. Often, all we *have* is one of two possible outcomes.

Suppose that, in order to assess the effectiveness of therapy, a psychotherapist investigates whether or not, after three months of involvement, clients feel better about themselves or worse. If therapy improves people's evaluation of themselves then we would expect clients' self-image ratings to be higher after three months' therapy than they were before.

Take a look at the data in Table 15.5 showing clients' self-image ratings before and after three months' therapy on a scale of 1–20, where a high value signifies a positive self-image. Here we would expect the scores to be higher in column C than they are in column B as we do in the related *t* and Wilcoxon tests. Therefore we would expect positive differences in column D. Unlike the *t* and Wilcoxon tests, here we ignore the *size* or *rank* of each difference, and simply put the *sign* (or direction) of each difference into column E. If the therapy is working, we would hope to obtain a large number of positive signs and a small number of negative signs, if any. The SIGN TEST gives us the probability of finding this number of negative signs (or fewer), given that the null hypothesis is true. That is, it tells us how likely it is that such a large (or even larger) split between positive and negative signs would be drawn 'by chance' under the null hypothesis where even splits are expected. This is just what we looked at with the glove drawer problem in Chapter 14.

DATA

A	B	C	D	E
Client	Self-image rating before therapy	Self-image rating after 3 months' therapy	Difference (C–B)	Sign of difference
a	3	7	4	+
b	12	18	6	+
c	9	5	−4	−
d	7	7	0	
e	8	12	4	+
f	1	5	4	+
g	15	16	1	+
h	10	12	2	+
i	11	15	4	+
j	10	17	7	+

Table 15.5 Self-image scores before and after three months' therapy

The null hypothesis in the binomial sign test

We assume that there are equal numbers of positive and negative signs in the 'population' we have sampled from – and we assume we have sampled from that population at random. This is exactly the position we were in with the baby-sexing result on p. 331 and, in effect, we went through the details of a sign test there. Here, we simply present the 'cookbook' method of conducting a sign test on a set of this kind of paired data.

Procedure	Calculation on our data
1 Calculate the difference between columns B and C, always subtracting in the same direction. If a directional prediction has been made, it makes sense to take the expected smaller score from the expected larger one. Enter difference in column D.	Find difference between scores in columns B and C of Table 15.5. We expect column C scores to be higher. Hence we take C–B in each case.
2 Enter the sign of the difference in column E. Leave a blank where the difference is zero and ignore these in the analysis.	See column E of Table 15.5. N becomes 9 because the difference for client d is zero. This case is dropped from any further analysis.
3 Count the number of times the less frequent sign occurs. Call this S.	Negative signs occur less frequently, so $S = 1$
4 Consult Table 7 in the Appendix. a) Find the line for N (the total number of signs not including zeros). b) Consult one- or two-tailed values.	a) $N=9$ (see step 2, above). b) We would be interested if the therapy made people worse so stick with two-tailed test.
5 Compare S with the critical value for the significance level set. For significance, S must be equal to or less than the critical value.	Our S is 1. The critical value under the column headed $p \le .05$ (two-tailed) is 1. Therefore, our result is not greater than the appropriate critical value and meets the criteria for significance.
6 Make statement of significance	Our result is significant with $p \le .05$. We may reject the null hypothesis.

Reporting the result of a sign test

For each client an improvement in self-image score after three months' therapy was recorded as a positive, whereas a deterioration was recorded as a negative. One client's self-image score did not change and this result was omitted from the analysis. The remaining nine results were submitted to a binomial sign test and the rate of improvement over deterioration was found to be significant, $S = 1, p \le .05$.

Exercises

1 Find out whether the test statistics in examples a, b, c and d in the table below are significant and give the lowest value for p that can be assumed from tables, for the one- or two-tailed tests indicated. You are given the numbers in groups and the appropriate test. You can put the *lowest* probability value (p) in the blank columns under 'significant'.

	Number in each group		Mann-Whitney	Significant				Wilcoxon		Significant	
	N_a	N_b	U	1-tailed	2-tailed		N	T	1-tailed	2-tailed	
a	15	14	49			c	18	35			
b	8	12	5			d	30	48			

2 For each of (a) and (b) in question 1 in the last exercise on p. 366, what is an equivalent non-parametric test?

3 Nine people are sent on an interpersonal skills training course. They are asked to rate their opinion of the need for this type of course both before and after attendance. Having attended, seven people rated the need lower than previously, one rated it higher and one didn't change in opinion.

(a) What test could be used to test for significance between the 'higher' and 'lower' ratings?

(b) Use the test you chose to decide whether this apparent negative effect of the course is significant.

4 Carry out the appropriate test (either Mann-Whitney or Wilcoxon signed ranks but try to choose without checking the text) on the data in Table 15.1 and Table 15.2 stating the result of the analysis in formal terms.

Answers

1 (a) .01 (one-tail), .02 (two-tail); b. .005 (one-tail), .01 (two-tail)

(c) .025 (one-tail), .05 (two-tail); d. .001 (one-tail), .002 (two-tail)

2 a. Mann-Whitney; b. Wilcoxon.

3 (a) Sign test; (b) S ($N = 8$) = 1 (NS if two-tailed; significant with $p \leq .05$ if one-tailed)

4 Table 15.1: Wilcoxon's $T = 1, z = 2.996, p = .0028$ (two-tailed); Table 15.2: Mann-Whitney $U = 24.5$, $z = 2.181, p = .029$ (two-tailed)

SPSS procedures for two condition difference tests

The related *t* test

On page 279, it is explained why data from a *related* design must be entered as two variables side by side. This is what you would do with the data in Table 15.1 so that they would finally appear as in Figure 15.4 showing the first eight participants' scores.

	Imagery	Control
1	6.00	6.00
2	15.00	10.00
3	13.00	7.00
4	14.00	8.00
5	12.00	8.00
6	16.00	12.00
7	14.00	10.00
8	15.00	10.00

Figure 15.4 Data entered for related *t* test

To conduct the related *t* test:

1 Select **Analyze/CompareMeans/Paired-Samples T test** (unfortunately SPSS uses the symbol 'T' when it should use '*t*' to distinguish this test from Wilcoxon's *T*).

2 You simply need to select *both* the variables to be tested (*imagery* and *control*) and shift these over to the **Paired Variables** box; in version 15 and earlier the arrow won't highlight until you have selected two variables. If you have more than two variables you can shift as many over as you like but this must be done in pairs-to-be-tested. In v.16 one variable goes into the left box and one into the right.

3 Click **OK**.

Output

The first table you see will give you descriptive statistics for each variable including the mean. The second gives the correlation (see Chapter 17) between the two variables. The table of interest here is shown in Figure 15.5.

Paired samples test

Pairs	Paired differences					t	df	Sig. (2-tailed)
	Mean	Std. deviation	Std. error mean	95% confidence interval of the difference				
				Lower	Upper			
Pair 1 IMAGERY-CONTROL	4.5385	2.6018	.7216	2.9662	6.1107	6.289	12	.000

Figure 15.5 SPSS output for a paired samples *t* test

The mean given is for the differences and *t* is 6.289, which agrees with our by-hand result earlier. The rest is either self-explanatory or not needed at this moment. Note that significance is given as '.000'. Actually the heading should really be '*p*' since the probability value given is the probability that a *t* this high would occur if the null hypothesis is true. It is on this value that we make our decision as to whether the difference is significant or not. If we have conventionally set alpha at .05 then this result is highly significant but we cannot report '*p* = .000' – see just below.

Note also that SPSS gives the 95% confidence limits around the estimated mean. We are 95% confident that the population mean difference lies in the range 2.9662 to 6.1107 (with apologies for the spurious accuracy in using four decimal places! – see p. 264).

When SPSS says '*p* = .000'

SPSS never gives a non-zero significance value lower than .001. If *p* is, in fact, .0005 or above you'll be given .001. Below this you'll be given .000. *Never* be tempted to write in your result '*p* = .000'. This is in fact impossible! It would mean that such a low result could never possibly happen and of course it always *could*. You *can* report a result like this as 'significant with *p* < .001' but traditionally statisticians say you should only report whether or not your *p* was lower than your set level of alpha. Most researchers, though, cannot resist the temptation to draw readers' attention to the fact that the chances of this being a fluke result under H_0 are pretty slim!

6	high	15.00
7	high	13.00
8	high	11.00
9	high	17.00
10	high	9.00
11	low	8.00
12	low	10.00
13	low	9.00
14	low	11.00
15	low	9.00

Figure 15.6 Data entered for unrelated *t* test – sleep disturbance (IV) on left and anxiety (DV) on right

The unrelated *t* test

As we said on p. 279, when a design is unrelated you *must* focus on the independent and dependent variables. The data from Table 15.2 have been entered and coded in SPSS (see p. 277) and are *partly* shown in Figure 15.6. The independent variable (***sleepdis***) has been entered into the left hand column as a *categorical* variable with a code for each value. If **Value Labels** on the **View** menu were not ticked we would see '1' instead of *high* and '2' instead of *low*.

To conduct the unrelated *t* test

1 Select **Analyze/Compare Means/Independent-Samples T test**.
2 Move ***sleepdis*** over to the **Grouping Variable** box because it is the independent variable (or variable that identifies separate groups).
3 Immediately after doing this, *while the grouping variable name is still highlighted*, click **Define Groups**. SPSS wants to know the codes you used for the levels of this variable. It seems this should be obvious but it wouldn't be if your independent variable had five levels and you only wanted, say, to test levels 1 and 4. Enter 1 into **Group 1** and 2 into **Group 2** (assuming you have used 1 for *high* and 2 for *low* or vice versa).
4 Click **Continue**.
5 The dependent variable, ***anxiety***, goes over into the **Test variable(s)** box. Your dialogue box should now look like the completed one in Figure 15.7.
6 Click **OK**.

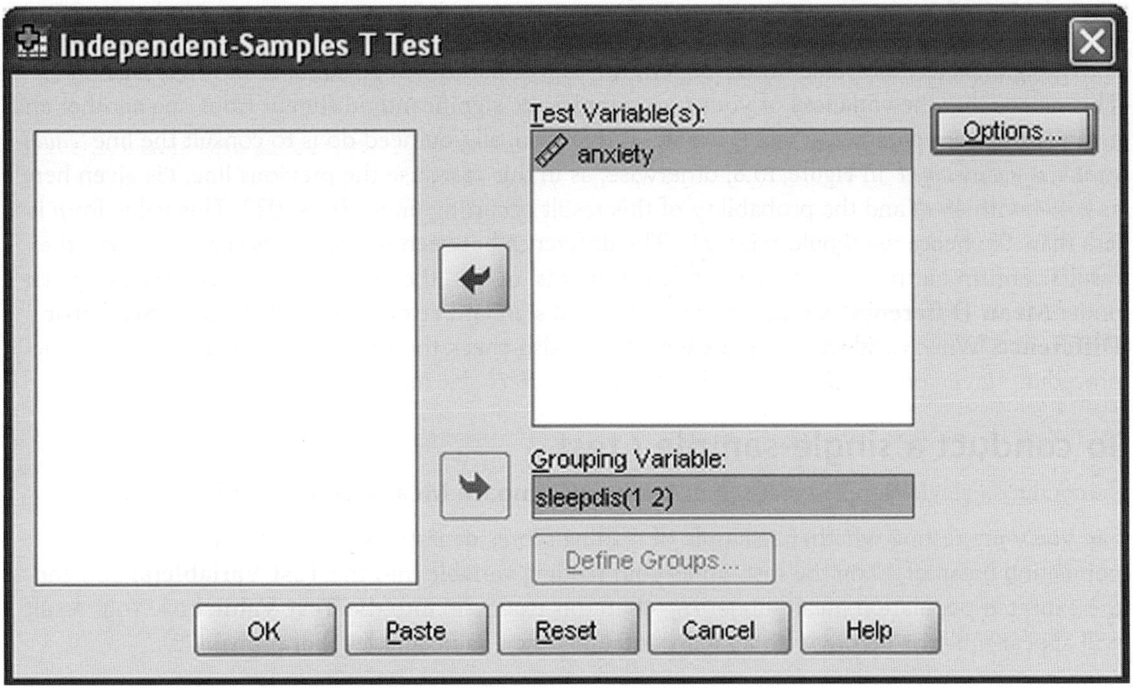

Figure 15.7 Dialogue box ready for an independent *t* test in SPSS

Note: if SPSS won't let you click '**OK**' at this point, then check the **Grouping Variable** slot; if **sleepdis[? ?]** appears, then SPSS is waiting for you to **Define Groups** as described in step 3. You need to click on **sleepdis** in the **Grouping Variable** box first, then define your groups.

Output

SPSS provides descriptive statistics for each group first, then the results table shown below.

Independent samples test

		Levene's test for equality of variances		t-test for equality of means					95% confidence interval of the difference	
		F	Sig.	t	df	Sig. (2-tailed)	Mean difference	Std. error difference	Lower	Upper
ANXIETY	Equal variances assumed	1.596	.222	2.494	19	.022	2.30909	.92584	.37129	4.24689
	Equal variances not assumed			2.443	15.130	.027	2.30909	.94526	.29582	4.32236

Figure 15.8 Output for SPSS Independent *t* test

Interpreting the results table

SPSS automatically conducts Levene's test for homogeneity of variance (see p. 365). If this test shows significance, the value under 'Sig', in the third column will be equal to or lower than .05. This means that the variances of your two samples are significantly different from one another and a straightforward parametric test is unsafe. If this is so, all you need do is to consult the line '*equal variances not assumed*' in Figure 15.8; otherwise, as in this case, use the previous line. *t* is given here as 2.494 with 19 *df* and the probability of this result occurring under H_0 is .022. This value for *p* is less than .05, hence we would reject H_0. The difference between the means is significant and the results confirm our previous by-hand calculation. *t* is, in fact, the difference between means, given under **Mean Difference**, divided by the estimated standard error of the differences – **Std Error Difference**. When conducting a *t* test you should also check the normality of your data using the procedures given on p. 364 and you should look at effect size and power (p. 385).

To conduct a single-sample *t* test

To conduct a single-sample *t* test select **Analyze/Compare Means/One-Sample T Test**.

Say you were testing whether a sample of reading scores departed significantly from a known population mean of 40 on the test. Enter your reading variable into the **Test Variable(s)** box and the expected population mean, under H_0 (40 in this example) into the **Test Value** box. Your result will appear much as before with a table containing the *t* value and level of probability.

Wilcoxon's signed ranks test – T

A small preparation tip

In v.15 if you think scores on variable X will be larger than those on variable Y, it is handy to place the predicted larger variable (X) *after* variable Y in the datasheet. In v.16 this is the opposite way around. This is not a big problem but it makes sense to have as 'positive ranks' those that apply to the differences that are positive.

To conduct the Wilcoxon signed ranks test

1 Select **Analyze/Nonparametric Tests/2 Related samples;** note that the Wilcoxon test is selected by default.

2 Move your two variables over to the **Test Pair(s) List** box. As with the related *t*, in V.15 and earlier you need to highlight variables in pairs before the right-pointing arrow will darken and permit you to move pairs over. Note that **Options** will give you descriptives, median and quartiles. Click **Continue**.

3 Click **OK**.

Output

The two tables in Figure 15.9 will appear if you test the data in Table 15.3. The first tells you that, if traditional scores are subtracted from assignment scores, the sum of the ranks of participants who scored more on traditional than assignment is 15. This our Wilcoxon's T from our by hand calculation on p. 370, though SPSS doesn't tell you this!

Ranks

		N	Mean rank	Sum of ranks
assignment – traditional				
	Negative ranks	3ᵃ	5.00	15.00
	Positive ranks	11ᵇ	8.18	90.00
	Ties	1ᶜ		
	Total	15		

a. assignment < traditional
b. assignment > traditional
c. assignment = traditional

Test statisticsᵇ

	assignment – traditional
Z	–2.357ᵃ
Asymp. sig. (2-tailed)	.018

a. Based on negative ranks.
b. Wilcoxon Signed Ranks Test

Figure 15.9 Output from SPSS Wilcoxon test

There was one tie, so the result is based only on the 14 results where a difference occurred. The right-hand table (which will appear below the first in SPSS output) tells us that the *z* value associated with this difference in ranks is 2.357 (ignore the negative sign) and that the probability of this happening under H_0 is .018. The *z* value is used in calculating effect size – see p. 395.

Mann-Whitney U test

For this example we will analyse the data in Table 15.4 and again remind you that you must enter data for an *unrelated* design as described on pp. 277–9. Your data should appear in the same format as the data in as shown in Figure 15.6 but with e.g. 'home' and 'work' replacing 'high' and 'low' as levels of the IV – perhaps called *'jobstatus'*.

To conduct the Mann-Whitney test

1 Select **Analyze/Nonparametric Tests/2 Independent samples;** note that Mann-Whitney is selected by default.

2 **Grouping variable** is the independent variable so put *jobstatus* over to this box. Immediately after doing this, *while the variable name is still highlighted*, click **Define Groups** (see note about the rationale for this box in the unrelated *t* test procedure above). Enter the code numbers you used, usually '1' in **Group 1** and '2' in **Group 2**. Click **Continue**.

3 **Test Variable** is the dependent variable so click *stereotypescore variable* over to the right-hand side.

4 **Options** will give you descriptives and quartiles. Click **Continue**.

5 Click **OK**.

If you find SPSS won't let you click **OK** at this point then you might need to highlight the grouping variable by clicking on it first (see Figure 15.7) and then selecting **'define groups'** and proceeding as described in step 2.

Interpreting the results table

SPSS gives some descriptives first. We can see from the left-hand box of Figure 15.10 that the children of mothers at home had a higher mean rank (96.5) on stereotype score than those employed full time (39.5). The U analysis appears in the right-hand box.

Ranks

Mother's occupation	N	Mean rank	Sum of ranks
stereotypescore			
Full-time employed	7	5.64	39.50
Home child care	9	10.72	96.50
Total	16		

Test statistics[b]

	stereotypescore
Mann-Whitney U	11.500
Wilcoxon W	39.500
Z	–2.119
Asymp. sig. (2-tailed)	.034
Exact sig. [2*(1-tailed Sig.)]	.031[a]

a. Not corrected for ties.
b. Grouping variable: mother's occupation

15.10 SPSS output for Mann-Whitney test

The value for U is given as 11.5 and the probability of this value occurring under H_0 is .034 (always use the Asymp. Sig. Value which is corrected for ties). The two groups differ significantly on stereotype scores. Note that SPSS also provides a z value, which is used in calculating effect size – see p. 395.

The sign test

Proceed exactly as for the Wilcoxon test but select **Sign Test** in the dialogue box and deselect **Wilcoxon** (to avoid confusion). You will be given the number of positive and negative differences and the probability value under H_0.

Effect size and power: when 'significant' is not significant

Very often we would like to have some idea of the size of an *effect* in psychological research. For instance, we might want to know *by how much* does imagery improve memory recall. It is particularly useful to consider this when planning a research project and wondering what size sample you should take in order to show that an effect does indeed exist. Students frequently badger their tutors with this very question: 'What's a decent-size sample?' (hoping to hear the smallest number possible!). In a sense what the student is asking is 'How many is the least I can use and still get a significant result?' Now the trouble with the word 'significant' is that when we use it in normal speech we are referring to something *important* or *interesting*. However, many statistically significant results can be not the least bit interesting and are quite unimportant. In statistical language 'significant' simply means that there was a less than 5% chance of getting our result under H_0. Suppose, after testing 1000 12-year-old boys and girls, we find a statistically significant difference, with girls 1.1 points higher than boys on an IQ test. Of what earthly use could this discovery be? What would we want to do about it? Often people assume that the effect they have found must be huge simply because p is so low (e.g. $p <$ .001), or they assume that there is nothing to be found when they fail to reach significance. In fact p may be > .05 only because too few participants were included in samples and an effect with $p < .001$ may be puny because thousands of participants were used to get it.

What worries many researchers about the conventional significance test is not so much that trivial effects will be found significant but that important existing effects will be *not* be found. That is, the greater worry is about the number of Type II errors that researchers are probably committing a lot of the time and thereby failing to demonstrate effects that are genuine. The reason for the built-in conservatism of the significance test, as many statisticians argue it, is that samples are often quite small in psychological studies and this will make it especially difficult to detect small but real differences between treatments as we are about to see ('treatment' is a generic term for the conditions of a psychological experiment or intervention).

Effect size

In an experiment we are trying to show that the application of an independent variable creates a sizeable difference between samples on some measure of a dependent variable. We assume that there is a difference between the two theoretical *populations* of scores that we would obtain if we could test exhaustively. Figure 15.11 shows a smaller and a larger *effect size* which is a measure of the difference between the two population means. Usually, of course, we don't know what the effect size is, certainly not before we have taken any measures. However, on other occasions researchers have a pretty shrewd idea of what size effect to expect, because they have read previous literature, because they have done some pilot trials or simply from the general literature and their thinking around the topic of investigation. For instance, in research which looks at people's estimation of their own IQ it is typical to find that male estimates of their own IQ, on average, are five points higher than female estimates of their own IQ when samples are 30 or more of each gender (e.g. Beloff, 1992). In an experiment, if the independent variable has a very strong effect on the dependent variable (e.g. effect of a lot of alcohol on a simulated driving task) then this effect is going to be quite easy to demonstrate and we would not need a large sample in order to so. However, where effects are quite subtle or weak, there are several things we might need to consider in our design, of which the simplest is usually to increase the intended sample size, the reasons for which we shall see in a moment.

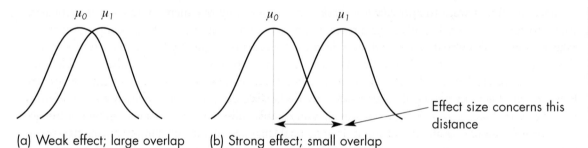

(a) Weak effect; large overlap (b) Strong effect; small overlap

Figure 15.11 Small and large effect sizes

Effect size is a very important concept and is central to the use of *meta-analysis* (p. 100) where effect sizes for a variety of essentially equivalent studies into the same phenomenon are compared in order to increase validity and to sort out consistent from unreliable results across a confusing set of findings from the literature on a research topic.

Power

As we said earlier, the power of a statistical test can be defined as the probability of not making a Type II error $(1-\beta)$. If we retain a null hypothesis when the alternative hypothesis is true (i.e. there *is* a real effect) then we are said to have made a Type II error. The probability of not making a Type I error, if H_0 is true, is always controlled in a significance test; it is α and this is usually set at .05. The probability of not making a Type II error cannot be set in this way because, of course, we do not know to start with whether or not H_1 is true. The probability of making a Type II error is illustrated in Figure 15.12. The distribution under H_0 is shown to the left with the rejection regions set on it (in dark shading). We know that if our difference falls in the dark region then we will reject H_0 and assume that there is an effect. Now let's assume that there *is* an effect and that the difference between means of the two underlying populations is as shown (the distance between μ_0 and μ_1). Note that what are shown in Figure 15.12 are sampling distributions of differences.

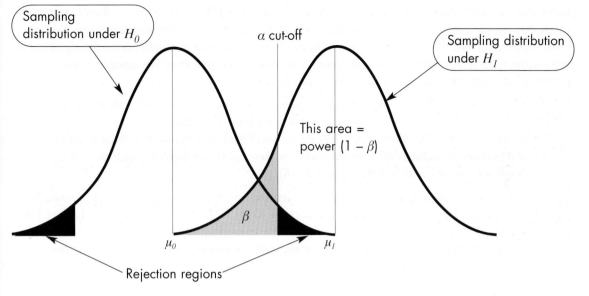

Figure 15.12 Likelihood of Type II errors

What we need to concentrate on now is where α cuts off the right-hand rejection region. Note here that this line also cuts off a good area to the left of the distribution for H_1. What would occur if H_1 is true but we happen to have drawn a rather low sample difference that falls a little to the left of the a cut-off line on the H_1 distribution? This could happen in an experiment on caffeine and reaction times if, say, our control group contained too many 'larks' (those who are sharp in the mornings) and perhaps several in the caffeine group attended a late night party the evening before. We happen to have sampled one of the rather lower mean differences that can occur under H_1. We just fail to reach significance and we would, by the rules, retain the null hypothesis and assume there is no effect when, in fact, there is.

The independent variable of caffeine then *did* have an effect; it is just that the conventional structure of significance testing is, on this occasion, too insensitive to detect the effect. Because α is set where it is, because of the sample size (N) and the effect size, all the results that fall in the shaded area marked β will lead to an incorrect significance decision that the null hypothesis should be retained, i.e. that there is no effect. This is a Type II error. Let's say that β represents about 20% of the H_1 distribution. Whenever this experiment is run with this value of N there will be a 20% chance of a Type II error. That is, there is only an 80% chance of demonstrating a genuine effect. This 80% chance is the *power* of the significance test on this occasion. Power is defined as $1 - \beta$ and is the probability that an existing effect will be detected; here, $\beta = .2$ and power = .8.

As I hope you can see, unless effects are really strong, in which case the H_1 distribution will be way to the right of the H_0 one, there will be very many occasions where genuine but modest effects are missed; H_0 will be retained when it is in fact false. It is this built-in conservatism of the significance-testing procedure that many theorists have been complaining about over the past few decades; these theorists also complain that researchers have been failing to report or pay attention to effect sizes and power in the analysis of their data (e.g. Sedlmeier and Gigerenzer, 1989;

Clark-Carter, 1997; Murphy and Myors, 1998; and most especially Cohen, 1962, 1988) Many still think that a high level of significance is automatically a guarantee that the effect they are dealing with is powerful. On the other hand, many do not realise that slavish adherence to the significance test, without analysis of effect size and power, may well mean that they are ignoring many perfectly valid effects. As Murphy and Myors put it:

It is typical for studies in these areas [including psychology] to have a 20% to 50% chance of rejecting the null hypothesis. If it is to be believed that the null hypothesis is virtually always wrong (i.e. that treatments have at least some effect, even if it is a very small one), this means that at least half of the studies, and perhaps as many as 80% of the studies in these areas, are likely to reach the wrong conclusion when testing the null hypothesis. (1998: 14)

Murphy and Myors discuss what they see as the depressingly typical design of studies in which power is as low as .2 even when small effect sizes are likely. This means that such studies are four times as likely to fail as to show an effect under the traditional significance criterion. They argue that studies producing anything under .5 power are really not worth conducting and that the conventional acceptable level for power is .8.

What can we do to increase power?

There are several approaches that can be taken to increase power.

1 Increase the sample size: this is by far the easiest and most common way to increase power. Take a look at Figure 15.13. When we increase the sample size, the mean of each sample we draw will on the whole be much closer to the actual population mean – see p. 315. Hence the sampling distribution will be much narrower because all our estimates (the samples we draw at random from the population) are much closer together. A narrower distribution means lower variance and therefore standard deviation. In the calculation of effect size just below, you'll see that the lower the standard deviation the greater is the calculated effect size. In practical terms this means that with a larger number of participants we are more likely to swamp any random errors with the actual effect, as would have happened if we'd taken far more participants in the caffeine experiment mentioned earlier. Want more power? Increase your sample size (and your research supervisor will smile more broadly!).

2 Increase α: we can make α .1 instead of .05; the obvious problem with this is that it simultaneously increases our chances of *Type I* errors (falsely rejecting H_0 when there is no effect); in addition, our research findings would not be taken seriously in the present report-publishing culture which requires p to be lower than .05 for a significant finding.

3 Increase the size of the effect: this sounds odd since usually we don't know if there *is* any effect, and certainly we usually don't know its size. However, we may glean some idea of expected effects from the theoretical literature on the subject, from the results of studies specifically similar to our proposed study or from the results of pilot trials. We can, very simply, increase the likely size of an effect by increasing the difference between levels of the independent variable. We might, for instance, use 10 mgs of caffeine rather than 5, lower illumination or increase the rate of delivery of to-be-recalled words. In the more 'hard science' areas of psychology (e.g. cognitive and physiological) it is quite common to be aware of specific effect sizes for specific

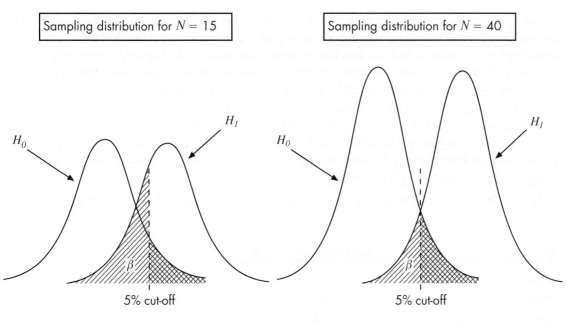

Figure 15.13 Increasing sample size to increase power by lowering β

treatments. In applied areas too though, where large numbers are involved, an effect size can be specified at a minimum level in order to justify the implementation of an intervention study – see Box 15.1. (The calculation aspect of this example will make sense only after you have read about the quantitative estimation of effect sizes and power below.)

4 Decrease the population variance: decreasing variance in the dependent variable will have the effect of *narrowing* the distributions shown in Figure 15.11 as you can see from Figure 15.13. If distributions are narrower then there is less overlap; consequently β decreases and hence power $(1 - \beta)$ increases. We could decrease variance on a motor task (e.g. threading needles) by giving participants plenty of practice beforehand; we could decrease the amount by which participants vary in estimating their own IQ by setting limits to their suggestions (e.g. it must be between 70 and 130); we can decrease variance in memory recall by ensuring that words to be recalled are of equal familiarity to all participants. Larger samples decrease variance in sampling distributions.

Calculating effect size

Two of the most popular measures of effect size are Cohen's d and η^2, spoken as 'eta squared'. The latter is more often found in psychological reports and is the statistic given by SPSS in the more complex tests to be encountered in Chapter 18 and beyond. However, in order to calculate power by hand for the simpler tests we have used already it is simpler to use d. The definition of effect size for d is:

$$d = \frac{\mu_1 - \mu_2}{\sigma}$$

where μ_1 and μ_2 are the means of the two populations from which the control and experimental groups have been sampled and σ is the common population standard deviation. This is what we would use in conjunction with an **unrelated** t **test**; recall that this test assumes *homogeneity of variance*, therefore the standard deviation of either sample *should* be an adequate estimate of the underlying population standard deviation. As a better estimate, however, where sample sizes are equal, an average can be taken. The population means are estimated as the sample means if we are calculating effect size after an experiment has been carried out. Suppose sample IQ means of trained and untrained groups are 110.3 and 104.2 respectively. The difference here is 6.1 points and, in this case, we know the population standard deviation is 15 points (this is the standardised value for IQ). Hence we have an effect size here of 6.1/15 = 0.407.

Cohen (1988) (rather arbitrarily) produced a definition of effect sizes which has become general currency. This is:

Effect size	d	Percentage of overlap
Small	.2	85
Medium	.5	67
Large	.8	53

The percentage of overlap is the % area overlap of the H_0 population with the H_1 population (e.g. control group's population and experimental group's population) – see Figure 15.11.

The calculation of effect size where there are unequal sample sizes requires finding the *pooled variance* mentioned earlier. If we took an average but there were more participants in sample 1 than sample 2, then the standard deviation for sample 2 would have undue influence on the result. We find the pooled variance using:

$$\text{Estimated } \sigma^2 = \frac{df_1}{df_{total}} S_1{}^2 + \frac{df_2}{df_{total}} S_2{}^2$$

For the data in Table 15.2 we would calculate: $\sigma^2 = \dfrac{9}{19} 6.5025 + \dfrac{10}{19} 2.6896 = 4.4957$

(remembering that df are one fewer than N in each group).

To get standard deviation we need the square root of σ^2 which is 2.1203. To get our effect size we divide the difference between our two means (12.4 – 10.1) by this figure to get an effect size of 1.08.

The calculation of effect size for a **one-sample** t **test** is the same as that given above but μ_2 will be the population mean for the null hypothesis against which the sample is being tested (e.g. 40 in the example on p. 362; we take the mean under H_0 from the estimated mean of the single sample's population). The standard deviation will also be that of the control population but can be estimated as the sample standard deviation if the true population standard deviation (under H_0) is not known or is unavailable.

The calculation of effect size for a **related _t_ test** uses the standard deviation of the score differences on the bottom of the effect size equation. We have this value (2.6) in Table 15.1, but Howell (1992) advises a better estimate of the population standard deviation of differences using:

$$\sigma_d = \sigma\sqrt{2(1-p)}$$

To estimate σ we use the average standard deviation from the two samples (an estimate of the population standard deviation for scores) and p is Spearman's rho correlation between the two variables (see Chapter 17). From the data in Table 15.1 this would mean:

$$\sigma_d = (3.52 + 1.68)/2\sqrt{2(1-0.782)} = \mathbf{1.717}$$

We now enter this value into the equation for effect size, along with our mean difference, and obtain $(13.38-8.85)/1.717 = 2.638$. You should note this is a massive effect size. Usually they are somewhere under 1 as Cohen's table of values above would indicate.

Calculations of power – the long way

We have now seen how effect sizes can be estimated. Using this knowledge, it is possible to estimate the power involved in our significance test. Let's just look graphically at what power is. Imagine that 80 children with attention difficulties have been given a training programme and that one of the outcome measures is change in IQ. Originally the group had an average IQ level between them of 100 points. Now their joint average is 105 points. Since the standard deviation for IQ scores is set at 15 points we can say that the effect size occurring here is $(105-100)/15 = 0.33$. The children have improved by 0.33 standard deviations on the scale. We need now to look at the sampling distributions for samples of size 80, i.e. the distribution we would expect to get if we sampled 80 children at random from the normal population and from the 'treated' population. On p. 316 we learned that we can estimate the standard error of a sampling distribution using $s/\sqrt{N}$ so this is $15/\sqrt{80} = 1.68$. We wish to find the point that cuts off the 2.5% right-hand rejection region. We know (from p. 311) that 1.96 standard errors (or deviations) cuts off this region so we want $100+ 1.96 \times 1.68$, which is 103.29. So, a score of 103.29 marks the point where 2.5% of sample means remain to the right. That is, 2.5% of sample means are higher than 103.29. Hence, any outcome for these measures where the mean of a sample of 80 comes above 103.29 we will call significant. This is depicted in Figure 15.14 and we can look at what this means for the sampling distribution if H_1 is true (remember this is the hypothesis that the treatment *does* work or, more technically, that the treated population has a mean of 105 and to calculate power we are assuming this is true).

A sample mean of 103.29 falls 1.71 points below the assumed treated population mean of 105. We have to work backwards now and find out where this point would fall on the treatment sampling distribution. How many standard errors is 1.71? Well, the standard error for this distribution should be the same as for the normal one since the standard deviation remains 15 points. So, with a standard error of 1.68 on the new scale, a value of 103.29 falls where z is $1.71/1.68$ below the mean. That's 1.02 below, so $z = -1.02$. Finally we consult our z table to see what percentage of the area lies above $z = -1.02$ and up to the mean. We find the area is about 34.6%. We add this to the 50% *above* the mean to get the complete area to the right of $z = -1.02$. We get 84.6%. This is our

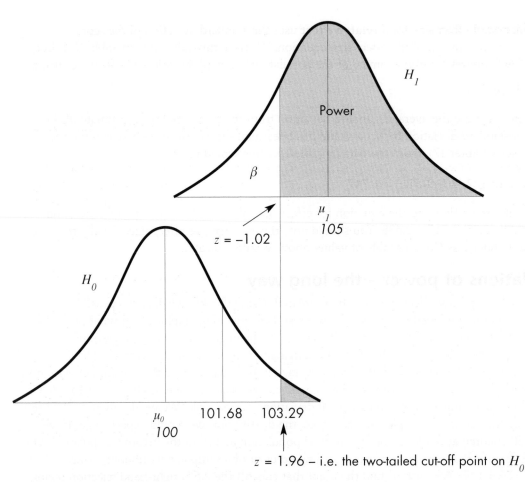

Figure 15.14 Calculating power using sampling distributions for $N = 80$

value for $1 - \beta$, in other words *power*. The area β (of 15.4%) lies to the left and is the probability of making a Type II error if the effect is real. We can say that, using this size sample, the probability of *not* making a Type II error is .846, assuming H_1. That is, if the treatment programme really does have this effect then any researcher using this sample size has an 84.6% chance of showing it does using this significance test.

Formulae for power for the different t tests

You would not be able to make calculations as we just did every time you conduct a significance test. Fortunately there are several methods for estimating the power of a test. Howell (1992) provides a solution which first involves calculating statistic δ (delta) from your effect and sample size.

For a **related t test** and the **single sample t test** we calculate δ as $d\sqrt{N}$.

For our example above, then, we get $\delta = 0.33 \times \sqrt{80} = 2.95$. To find our estimate of power we need to consult Appendix Table 4. We find (halfway between 2.9 and 3.0 and using α at the $p \leq .05$ level) that our value for power is .84 – a very close match with what we calculated long-hand above.

For an **unrelated** t **test** $\delta = d\sqrt{N/2}$

Note that with unequal samples we need to adjust so that $N_{adj} = \dfrac{2n_1 n_2}{n_1 + n_2}$ and we use N_{adj} instead of N in the equation for δ.

Uses of power and effect size – finding an appropriate sample size for a study

We can use power calculations after a significance test, as we just did, to qualify the significant result. However, an equally important role for power calculations is in checking, *before conducting a study*, the size of sample that will be required in order to demonstrate an effect. Box 15.1 gives an example of a practical situation in which, before a full study is conducted, a researcher checks out the minimum sample size she will need in order to be fairly sure of demonstrating an effect that she strongly believes does exist.

One of the most popular questions to tutors who supervise research projects conducted by their students (typically for a third year independent project) is, as we have seen, 'How many participants do you think I'll need?' to which most tutors answer – 'Well, you just go away and think about it.' For typical experiments you may be advised that fewer than ten participants per condition of a between subjects design is inadequate and perhaps 25 in each would be a good idea. However, if you know the kind of level of power you require (and you should always have .8 in your mind as a target) you can work backwards to find the value of δ required. If you have an idea of the effect size (d) then you can estimate your required number of participants by putting the δ and d values into the equations for δ above (and for later significance tests in other chapters) and moving terms around until you have a solution for N. Expected effect sizes can be estimated, as we said earlier, from prior research and/or from your pilot studies.

Cohen (1992) has provided an extremely useful short paper and table that will give you the minimum N required for power at .8 for a variety of significance tests (t tests, sign test, correlation, χ^2, ANOVA and multiple regression) with small, medium and large effect sizes at $\alpha = .01$, .05 and .1. This really is a paper worth getting hold of if you want to take adequate sample sizes in your projects.

Finally, do note that power and effect size estimates are not an exact science and different methods will lead to different estimations; statisticians all have their personal favourites, so some versions used in this book may not square with those in other texts.

A much used computer programme that will calculate power or, more usefully, calculate the sample size required to reach a specified level of power given an assumed effect size, is G-Power. This is available to download free of charge (genuine altruism does exist!) from: www.psycho.uni-duesseldorf.de/abteilungen/aap/gpower3/download-and-register

Effect size and power for non-parametric tests

Effect sizes for the non-parametric rank difference tests so far encountered are given in Box 15.2. Power calculations are not as straightforward as those given above (for details see Lehmann, 1998).

If you need to calculate for adequate sample sizes you can use the knowledge that a non-parametric test has around 95.5% of the power of the equivalent parametric test. If you want power of .8 with your non-parametric test then .8 would be 95.5% of what you would need with the parametric test. Find this higher level for power, and enter it, along with your estimated effect size, into the appropriate *t* test equation for power. Switch terms around and you can find the somewhat higher level of *N* that you need for your non-parametric test. In other words, you'll need a few more participants for the same level of power using *T* rather than related *t*.

Info Box 15.1   Using power to check the required sample size

Suppose an applied educational psychologist is keen to demonstrate that a teaching programme can increase students' grades on tests taken at 14 years old and that the overall achievement is measured in points. Let's say the county average is 40 and that the psychologist will receive funding from the local education authority only if an increase of about 3 points could be made by one class of students ($N = 30$). She wonders what size sample she needs to be fairly sure of demonstrating this effect. We know, from the consideration of power above, that the larger the sample the better will be the power and the lower will be the risk of a Type II error, if the effect 'works'. In this case, the psychologist knows the effect does work but needs to be sure of selecting a sample large enough, given her estimate of the effect size, to avoid a Type II error. She knows that the general standard deviation on the tests is 8 points. Her effect size of interest then is: $d = (43-40)/8 = 0.375$. Now she needs to relate this to sample size.

For the one-sample *t* test δ is $d\sqrt{N}$. So δ here is $0.375 \times \sqrt{30} = 2.05$. Checking Appendix Table 4 for a two-tailed test at $p \le .05$, power is .54. This means that, if the teaching programme works, the psychologist has only a .54 probability of demonstrating the 3 point increase using 30 students. This is too much of a risk. She has only just over 50% chance of success. She therefore may not get her research grant. She needs to increase the sample size, but to what? Well, let's say she wants power around .8, reducing her probability (β) of making a Type II error to .2. δ then needs to be 2.8, so $d\sqrt{N}$ needs to be 2.8 from Appendix Table 4 and $\sqrt{N}$ therefore needs to be $2.8/0.375 = 7.47$. N therefore needs to be $7.47^2 = 55.8$ which we must round up to 56 to get whole students. She needs nearly twice the number of students she was going to use to be that much surer of demonstrating her effect satisfactorily.

Info Box 15.2 Calculating eta-squared (η^2) for two condition tests

Although η^2 is often dismissed as a rather unsatisfactory measure of effect size, you may well be asked to use this measure in your course report writing. Cohen's proposed guidelines for interpreting η^2 are: 0.01 small effect; 0.06 moderate effect; 0.14 large effect.

The general formula used for t tests is: $\eta^2 = \dfrac{t^2}{t^2 + df}$ so specific formulae are:

Independent samples t test: $\eta^2 = \dfrac{t^2}{t^2 + (N_1 + N_2 - 2)}$

Paired samples and single sample t test: $\eta^2 = \dfrac{t^2}{t^2 + (N-1)}$

For the non-parametric tests the general formula is: $r = z/\sqrt{N}$

r is yet another Cohen statistic interpreted as: 0.1 small effect; 0.3 moderate effect; 0.5 large effect. For the Wilcoxon test N is the number of observations *in total* so this is *twice* the number of cases or in other words 2 x N used in the significance test. z is calculated as on p. 375.

Exercises

1 A researcher wishes to demonstrate that a course in cognitive behavioural therapy will result in a mean decrease of 3 points on a depression scale for which 20 treated patients currently have a mean of 35. The known standard deviation for this kind of client is 7.5 points. Does she have enough participants to be likely to find a significant decrease? Give reasons. If she requires more participants, then how many?

2 What is the power involved when an unrelated t is significant with $p \le .05$ (two-tailed), $N_a = 15$, $N_b = 19$, $\overline{x}_a = 23.4$, $\overline{x}_b = 27.4$, $s_a = 4.8$, $s_b = 4.1$?

Answers

1 No. Effect size = 3/7.5 = 0.4; δ is therefore 0.4 x $\sqrt{20}$ = 1.788; from Appendix Table 4, power (using $p < .05$) is therefore .44; less than .5 probability that significant difference will be shown. Hence raise sample size; need d of 2.8 (from table where power = .8); 2.8 = 0.4 x $\sqrt{N}$ (equation for δ); $\sqrt{N}$ = 2.8/0.4 = 7; hence 7^2 participants required = 49.

2 Pooled variance = $\sigma^2 = \dfrac{14}{32}\, 4.8^2 + \dfrac{18}{32}\, 4.1^2 = 19.54$; pooled s = 4.42; d = (23.4 – 27.4)/4.42 = 9; N_{adj} = 2(15x19)(15+19) = 16.76; $\sigma = 9\sqrt{16.76/2}$ = 2.61; from Appendix Table 4, power = .74

Glossary

Binomial sign test (S)	Nominal-level test for difference between two sets of paired/related data using *direction* of each difference only
d, Cohen's	Measure of effect size; used here in calculating *power*
Delta (δ)	Statistic used to estimate power using the effect size
Difference mean	Mean of differences between pairs of scores in a related design
Distribution dependent test	Significance test making estimations of population parameters
Distribution free test	Significance test that does not depend on estimated parameters of an underlying distribution
Eta-squared $\eta 2$	Measure of effect size
Homogeneity of variance	Situation where sample variances are similar
Mann-Whitney U test	Ordinal-level significance test for differences between two sets of unrelated data
Non-parametric test	Significance test that does not make estimations of parameters of an underlying distribution; also known as a *distribution free test*
Parametric test	Relatively powerful significance test that makes estimations of population parameters; the data tested must usually therefore satisfy certain assumptions; also known as a *distribution dependent test*
Pooled variance	Combining of two sample variances into an average in order to estimate population variance
Power efficiency	Comparison of the *power* of two different tests of significance.
Related t test	Parametric difference test for related data at interval level or above.
Robustness	Tendency of test to give satisfactory probability estimates even when data assumptions are violated.
S	See binomial sign test
Sign test	See binomial sign test
t	See related and unrelated t test
T	See *Wilcoxon test*
Ties (tied ranks)	Feature of data when scores are given identical rank values.
U	See *Mann-Whitney test*
Unrelated t test	Parametric difference test for unrelated data at interval level or above
Wilcoxon's T – matched pairs signed ranks test	Ordinal-level significance test for differences between two related sets of data

Tests for categorical variables and frequency tables

The *chi-square* (χ^2) test presented in this chapter is concerned entirely with categorical variables; those producing nominal data, that is, frequencies by categories.

Chi-square is first used to analyse a simple division of one variable into two levels of frequencies.

- The concept of *expected frequencies* under the null hypothesis is introduced.
- *Cross-tabs tables* are then introduced and chi-square used to analyse for *association* between two categorical variables with two levels each (a 2 x 2 analysis).
- The generalised form of chi-square testing *r* x *c* tables (those with any number of rows and columns) is then covered, e.g. three types of training by pass/fail.
- Chi-square can also be used as a *goodness of fit* test to check whether a distribution of frequencies in categories is a close fit to a theoretical distribution (e.g. whether a college's pattern of degree classifications match the average pattern for the country).
- There are *limitations* on the use of chi-square: data must be *frequencies*, not ratios, means or proportions, and must belong exclusively to one or another category, i.e. the same case (person) must not appear in more than one 'cell' of the data table.
- There is statistical debate about *low expected cell frequencies*. It is advisable to avoid these where possible. If low expected frequencies *do* occur, sample sizes above 20 make the risk of a Type I error acceptably low.
- *Power* and *effect size* calculations for chi-square are given. SPSS procedures for chi-square analyses are described.

The chapter then moves on to the analysis of *multi-way* (i.e. not just two-way) tables using *log-linear analysis*. The *likelihood ratio chi-square* is used to investigate higher-order interactions for significance, then proceeds hierarchically downwards from the initially saturated model, to one-way effects. SPSS analysis is described.

Tests on two-way frequency tables

Very often the design of our research study entails that we gather data that are *categorical* in nature. Have a look at the data in Table 16.1 and Table 16.2 which are frequency tables for people assessed on two categorical variables. Such tables are called CROSS-TABULATION (or CROSS-TABS) TABLES. In the first of these, the (fictitious) data have been gathered by observing whether a car is new or old, and whether its driver does or does not obey the amber signal at a pedestrian crossing. The hypothesis is that drivers of newer cars conform more often to the traffic regulation of stopping on amber. The rationale might be that drivers of newer cars are likely to be older and more experienced.

The numbers in the cells of this kind of table are *frequencies* – they are just a *count* of the number of cases (people in this case) observed in each cell of the table. Notice from the table that, of those driving a new car, far more stopped at amber than drove on, whereas for the drivers of older cars, the frequencies of stopping and not stopping were almost equal. Our statistical test will tell us whether this difference in stopping proportions between the two sets of drivers can be considered significant or not. We will see whether stopping is *associated* with age of car.

We *could* of course have gathered *measured* (not categorical) data by measuring speed or obtaining the exact year of manufacture of a car and by stopping drivers and interviewing them about conformity or giving them a questionnaire. This might be possible in a shopping area car park but it would be time-consuming and our drivers would be susceptible to several of the forms of bias involved when participants know they are being studied. The observation method has the great advantage of gathering data on naturally occurring behaviour but often has the disadvantage, in this case, of having the independent variable (age of car) and the dependent variable (stopped or not) *both* assessed only at a categorical level.

| | Age category of car | | |
	New	Old	Total
Behaviour at amber light			
Stopped	90 (a)	88 (b)	178
Did not stop	56 (c)	89 (d)	145
Total	146	177	323

Table 16.1 Frequencies of drivers by age of car and whether they stopped at an amber light or not

The data in Table 16.2 are the actual results of the study by Cialdini *et al.* (1990) mentioned in Chapter 3 where people were observed on a path after they had been handed a leaflet. The researchers varied the number of pieces of litter already present and observed whether each person dropped their leaflet or not. Here the independent variable is *not* originally categorical (it had the measured values 0, 1, 2, 4, 8, 16), but since the dependent variable had to be categorical (they either dropped their leaflet or they didn't) it was simplest to treat both variables as categorical by reducing the independent variable values to three categories (0/1, 2/4, 8/16) as shown in the table.

| | Amount of existing litter | | |
Observed person	0 or 1 piece	2 or 4 pieces	8 or 16 pieces
Dropped litter	17	28	49
Didn't drop litter	102	91	71

Table 16.2 Number of pieces of existing litter and consequent littering (Cialdini *et al.*, 1990)

Cialdini, R.B., Reno, R.R. and Kallgren, C.A. (1990) A focus theory of normative conduct: Recycling the concept of norms to reduce litter in public places. *Journal of Personality and Social Psychology, 58,* 1015–26. Copyright © 1990 American Psychological Association.

A measured dependent variable in any study can always be reduced to categorical level in a similar way where this is useful. We may, for instance, split a group of extroversion scores at the median value and refer to those above the median as 'extroverts' and those below as 'introverts'. We may reduce smoking information down to the categories: 'non-smoker', '1 to 5 a day', '6–20 a day' and 'over 20 a day'. The codes 1 to 4 given to these four categories could at a stretch be treated as ordinal-level data but with the practical problem that too many people would be tied at each rank. Instead, we can treat the codes as category names and simply count the number of people in each category.

Unrelated data – the Chi-square test of association

When to use chi-square or χ^2		
Type of relationship tested	Level of data required	Design of study
Association between two variables	Nominal/categorical	Between groups: Independent samples

Data assumptions: Each observed person (or case) must appear in *one only* of the frequency cells. It must be impossible for them to appear in more than one cell.

Notes: No more than 20% of the expected frequency cell counts should be less than 5.

'chi' is pronounced 'kye' in English. It is an approximation to the name for the Greek letter χ which starts with 'ch' as in the Scottish pronunciation of 'loch' and is the symbol for the statistic in this test.

Chi-square is the test to use when we are looking for an *association*, or a difference in proportions, as in the examples above, and where the variables concerned are both categorical. The design will be *between groups*. To move towards the thinking behind chi-square I would like to start with one of those situations I like to use that demonstrate the value of statistical competence in protecting us against the outlandish claims of some advertisers. Have a look at Box 16.1.

The marketing survey results described in Box 16.1 might seem, at first sight, very impressive (one colleague I spoke to about this said, 'Never mind the stats, Hugh, where do I get hold of the stuff?'!). We learn that of 550 women provided with a free sample and using it for one month, 56% reported a loss of up to one inch from their thighs, and 52% reported the same for their hips. However, let's think what we would expect if the null hypothesis were true. H_0 would be based on the concept of the women choosing one answer or the other ('gained' or 'lost') entirely at random. On this basis, then, we would expect, from 550 choices, 275 'gains' and 275 'losses'. In chi-square terminology, these frequencies predicted under the null hypothesis are known as EXPECTED FREQUENCIES – they are what we typically expect to occur with our overall frequencies *if H_0 is true*. The frequencies we *actually* obtain from our study are referred to as OBSERVED FREQUENCIES.

Info Box 16.1   Does the magic gel really work?

Some years ago Christian Dior ran an advert in a colour supplement claiming that, of 550 women asked to use a fat-reducing gel (Svelte) for one month, 52%, in a later survey, claimed they had lost 'up to one inch' off their hips during that period, while 56% had lost the same amount off their thighs. Now this might sound very impressive indeed, except that we do not know what questions were asked in the survey. This is a perfect example of the need to know what question was asked before being able to interpret fully an apparently strong piece of evidence. It is unlikely that the women were simply asked to give open-ended responses. It is very likely indeed that they were asked to respond to multiple-choice items, such as 'Over the last month did you:

(a) lose up to one inch off your hips

(b) gain up to one inch on your hips

(c) notice no change at all on your hips?'

For simplicity's sake let's ignore the last alternative since there would always be some, perhaps very tiny, change over one month. In fact, the Dior marketing people might have only asked each woman to measure their hips at the start and at the end of the one-month trial and to take the difference. There will always be a small difference between two measures of the same thing (random error) so each woman could then have recorded either 'increased' or 'decreased'.

Here, then, let's imagine we have 52% of the sample of 550 saying 'lost' and 48% saying 'gained' in reference to their hips. That's 286 positive and 264 negative outcomes from the Dior marketing perspective. Questions for you to ponder are:

1 How many of the 550 women would respond 'positive' and how many 'negative' if they were simply tossing a coin (i.e. selecting an alternative at random)?

2 On the basis of your answer to the question above, are the 286 vs 264 results impressive (i.e. will we consider them to be a *significant* difference?) or are they within the range we might reasonably expect 'by chance' if the women are selecting their response at random?

Taking the slightly more impressive 56% losing up to one inch from their thighs, you might ponder the same questions.

Calculating expected frequencies in a one-row chi-square analysis

To make things formal (and for more complex examples) we calculate the expected frequencies for a single-row analysis using N/k where N is the total number of cases (550 in this case) and k is the number of cells to average across. Hence, here, $550/2 = 275$.

	Women reporting a loss of up to 1"	Women reporting a gain of up to 1"	Total
Observed frequencies (obs)	(a) 286	(b) 264	550
Expected frequencies (exp)	(a) 275	(b) 275	550

Table 16.3 Observed and expected frequencies for women reporting losses or gains after using gel for one month

Data for a one-row chi-square analysis

The data for our first simple chi-square test on the hip data, then, would appear as in Table 16.3.

The null hypothesis for chi-square

The null hypothesis in a chi-square analysis is always that the population is distributed in the pattern of proportions shown by the expected frequencies. Our alternative hypothesis (or rather Christian Dior's) is that more people (in the population) report a loss than report a gain after one month's use. Referring to Table 16.3, we need therefore to see whether our *observed frequencies* of 286 ('loss') and 264 ('gain') differ significantly from the *expected frequencies* of 275 and 275, which would occur under H_0.

Testing the null hypothesis

The chi-square statistic gets larger as the observed cell frequencies depart from what is expected under H_0 – that is, from the expected frequencies. We can see in Table 16.3 that we would be more convinced of the effectiveness of Svelte gel the further *cell a_{obs}* rises above *cell a_{exp}*. We calculate chi-square using:

$$\chi^2 = \sum \frac{(O - E)^2}{N}$$

To calculate, we take each set of cells in turn (in Table 16.3, *cell a* then *cell b*) and perform the calculation shown after the Σ symbol above. As in the past, the Σ symbol means 'add up the results of each of what follows'.

Calculation of chi square using the data in Table 16.3

	$O - E$	$(O - E)^2$	$\Sigma (O - E)^2/E$	Result
Cell a	286-275 = 11	$11^2 = 121$	121/275 =	0.44
Cell b	264-275 = −11	$−11^2 = 121$	121/275 =	0.44
			$\chi^2 = \Sigma (O - E)^2/E = 0.88$	

In this calculation we find that χ^2 is 0.88. We need to check this value for significance. χ^2 uses degrees of freedom. For a one-row analysis *df* are *k*–1 where *k* is the number of cells, so here *df* are 2–1 = 1.

Consulting Appendix Table 8 we find that we require a χ^2 value of at least 3.84 for $p \leq .05$ with a two-tailed test. Hence our difference is not significant. The conclusion here would be that use of Svelte gel has not resulted in a significant proportion of women reporting a loss of up to one inch from around their hips.

What about the result for thighs?

You might think we cheated a little there by dealing only with the less impressive hip data. OK. Let's look at the thigh data, then.

Pause for thought

Calculate the chi-square value for the thigh data following the example above for hips. Dior said that 56% of the sample reported a loss of up to one inch from their thighs; 56% of 550 is 308 so we have *observed frequencies* of 308 lost up to one inch and 242 gained up to one inch, by our definitions. Expected frequencies are again 275 in each cell.

You should find that χ^2 is 7.92. This value is well above the required critical value of 3.84 so we certainly have a significant result here. This appears to *support* the effect of Svelte gel.

The 2 x 2 chi-square

A 2 x 2 arrangement is the simplest of cross-tabs tables and is really what we need for a fair scientific test of the gel data. Of course I wasn't going to accept that the gel worked on thighs. What any scientist worth their salt would have immediately asked on hearing that results is 'Well where was the control group?'. We can't really assume that of 550 women, using the gel for a month, just half would report a loss and half a gain. This is what we might assume if we could know no better – if we had no chance of determining what would happen under a free choice. But we *can* find out what *would* happen. What we need is a *control group* with whom to compare our 'experimental' group, the one whose results Dior reported. On one occasion I did informally ask all the women in a lecture audience to answer the thighs-larger-or-smaller-after-a-month question 'cold' (with no prior information about the gel advert, but with assurances that the purpose was statistical demonstration); 53% reported a loss and 47% reported a gain, when forced to choose between these two alternatives, even though they had not used any gel. Let's just suppose that these same percentages would be found in a formal and well-designed study using a control group of 550 women, equal in number to the Dior survey group. If 53% chose loss and 47% chose gain, then we would obtain the (rounded) figures shown in Table 16.4.

| | Participant reports: | | |
	Lost up to one inch	Gained up to one inch	Total
Gel use group	(a) 308	(c) 242	550
Control group	(b) 292	(d) 258	550
Total	600	500	1100

Table 16.4 Fictitious observed frequencies of gel-using and control group participants reporting loss or gain of up to one inch from thighs

What we have in Table 16.4 is a classic form of data table for which we would calculate a 2 X 2 CHI-SQUARE in order to discover whether there is an association between using gel and losing fat ('2 x 2' because there are two columns and two rows). Note that we are assuming that the independent variable (gel use) is having a causal effect on a dependent variable (loss or gain of fat). Note also that these two variables are both at a categorical level because they are not measured on any sort of scale and each has just two qualitatively separate levels. It is not necessary, however, for there to be an experimental independent variable and dependent variable. We could be interested, for instance, in whether introverts are more likely to feel awkward on a nudist beach than extroverts (see Table 16.5). Introversion need not *cause* introverts to feel awkward; awkwardness may be related to or simply a part of the overall introverted personality characteristic.

	Extrovert	Introvert	Total
Would feel comfortable	(a) 40	(b) 10	50
Would not feel comfortable	(c) 10	(d) 40	50
Total	50	50	100

Table 16.5 Observed frequencies of introverts and extroverts who report that they would or would not feel comfortable on a nudist beach

Expected frequencies for the new gel data

The null hypothesis for the new (fictitious) gel study is based on the assumption that there is absolutely no association, in the population as a whole, between using gel and changes in fat. More technically, it assumes that frequencies in the population are arranged as are the frequencies in the 'total' columns in Table 16.4; that is, we assume that frequencies of people reporting a loss of up to one inch would be equally split between those using the gel and those not using the gel. In other words, whether you use gel or not, you have the same chance of appearing in the 'lost' column.

Pause for thought

In our fictitious study, 550 women used gel and 550 women did not. *If there is no association between using gel and losing fat*, how many of the 600 shown in Table 16.4 who 'lost up to one inch' would you expect to find in the 'gel use' row, that is, in *cell a*?

I hope you decided that just half the fat losers (i.e. 300) should be gel users and half should be in the control group. There were equal numbers of users and non-users and, if gel use has nothing to do with fat loss, then about half those who lose weight would be from each group. The expected frequencies are shown in Table 16.6.

	Participant reports:		
	Lost up to one inch	Gained up to one inch	Total
Gel use group	(a) 300	(c) 250	550
Control group	(b) 300	(d) 250	550
Total	600	500	1100

Table 16.6 Fictitious expected frequencies of gel-using and control group participants reporting loss or gain of up to one inch from thighs

In the frequency tables above, the cells under the title 'Total' are known as MARGINALS; that is, they are the margins of all the rows, showing how many in each row altogether, and the margins of all columns showing how many altogether in each column. All expected frequencies are calculated based on the reasoning for the gel table above. We assume that the total for each column will be divided according to the proportions of the row marginals; 600 will be divided in the ratio 550 to 550. The formula for calculating expected cell frequencies is:

$$E = \frac{RC}{T}$$

where R is the total of the *row* in which the cell is situated, and C is the total of its appropriate *column*. T is the overall total (1100 in the gel table example). However, you already did in fact use a version of this in your head in deciding that $550/1100$ (R/T) of the 600 fat losers (C) would be expected in *cell a*. The general formula is used because, in most cases, the numbers are not quite as simple as the ones I've partly invented here. It is important to remember that 'expected frequencies' are those 'expected' under the null hypothesis, not those (in fact the opposite of those) that the researcher usually expects (or would like) to occur in the research study.

Let me try to outline a visual example of what a 2 x 2 chi-square does (roughly speaking) by referring to the extrovert/introvert nudist data in Table 16.5. 50% of all participants reported feeling comfortable on a nudist beach. Hence, half the introverts and half the extroverts *should*, in turn, report feeling comfortable, *if* there is no link between feeling comfortable and extroversion. The expected frequencies for this example, then, are 25 in each cell, as shown in Table 16.7. For a significant result, indicating an association between extroversion and feeling comfortable, we would want the observed frequencies in cells *a* and *d* to be much higher than 25 and for the frequencies in cells *b* and *c* to be much lower.

	Extrovert	Introvert	Total
Would feel comfortable	(a) 25	(b) 25	50
Would not feel comfortable	(c) 25	(d) 25	50
Total	50	50	100

Table 16.7 Expected frequencies of introverts and extroverts who report that they would or would not feel comfortable on a nudist beach

In Figure 16.1 we have an imaginary box with four compartments into which we 'drop' the observations in a random manner. Imagine each one of the 100 observations is a little ball dropped on to the centre spot and bouncing randomly into one of the four equal-sized compartments. There is a limitation to the randomness here – when any row or column adds up to 50 we stop permitting balls into that row or column. If we dropped the 100 balls many many times then, roughly speaking, the results would vary around those in Table 16.7, mostly by only a little but sometimes (less frequently) by quite a lot. If we calculate chi-square for every drop of 100 balls, then through this random process we will create a distribution of chi-square values. For a significant result, what we are interested in is obtaining a chi-square value that is in the top 5% of this distribution of randomly produced values – that is, we want a chi-square value that would occur less than 5 times in 100 if the null hypothesis were true (if the balls were bouncing randomly).

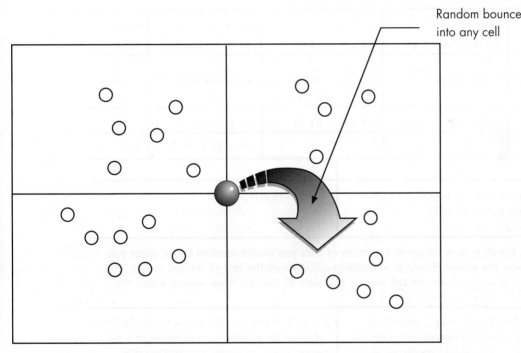

Random bounce
into any cell

Figure 16.1 Chi-square assumes random bouncing into cells up to the row and column totals

Data for regular 2 x 2 chi-square test

Now let's calculate a 2 x 2 chi-square on the data in Table 16.1. Assume these were data gathered in a psychology practical workshop and the proposal is that drivers of new cars are more law abiding, as explained at the start of this chapter. Here, then, if car age is not related to stopping at the amber light (the null hypothesis), the expected frequencies would be that just 80 of the 146 new car drivers should stop (calculated below) whereas, in fact, 90 did so. Only 50% of the drivers of old cars stopped, compared to the greater proportion of new car drivers. The observed frequencies vary quite far from the expected frequencies, so chi-square will be high and perhaps significant.

Calculation of a 2 x 2 chi-square

Procedure	Calculation/result of steps
1 Give each corresponding observed and expected cell a letter	See letters a, b, c, d in Table 16.1
2 Calculate expected frequencies using $E = \dfrac{RC}{T}$ (see p. 404)	Cell a: 146 x 178/323 = **80.46** Cell b: 177 x 178/323 = **97.54** Cell c: 146 x 145/323 = **65.54** Cell d: 177 x 145/323 = **79.46**
3 Calculate χ^2 according to the χ^2 formula given on p. 401	See the calculation table below:

	O-E	(O-E)²	(O-E)²/E	Result
Cell a	90-80.46 = **9.54**	9.54^2 = **91.01**	91.01/80.46 =	**1.13**
Cell b	88-97.54 = **–9.54**	-9.54^2 = **91.01**	91.01/97.54 =	**0.93**
Cell c	56-65.54 = **–9.54**	-9.54^2 = **91.01**	91.01/65.54 =	**1.39**
Cell d	89-79.46 = **9.54**	9.54^2 = **91.01**	91.01/79.46 =	**1.15**
			$\chi^2 = \Sigma(O\text{-}E)^2/E =$	**4.6**

Procedure	Calculation/result of steps
4 Calculate degrees of freedom (*df*) according to the formula: $df = (R{-}1)(C{-}1)$	$df = (2{-}1)(2{-}1) = 1$

Note that, for all χ^2 tests, *df* are the number of cells you would need to know, *given you already know the marginal values*, in order to calculate all the rest of the cell values; in a 2 x 2 table, once we know one cell we can calculate all the rest if we already know the column and row totals. Hence *df* = 1

Procedure	Calculation/result of steps
5 Using Table 8 in the Appendix, check that χ^2 reaches the appropriate critical value for *df* and alpha (usually set at .05) and decide upon significance.	For *df* = 1 and $p \le$ .05 and a two-tailed test, χ^2 must be greater than or equal to 3.84, hence, our χ^2 is significant and we may reject the null hypothesis.

Interpreting and reporting the result

Around half the old cars didn't stop, whereas only around a third of new cars failed to stop. Our observed frequencies differ significantly from what we'd expect if H_0 is true where the proportion stopping and not stopping would be the same for new and old cars. We have therefore provided evidence that drivers of new cars are more law-abiding at traffic lights than drivers of old cars.

Effect size

For a general introduction to the importance of estimating effect size and checking power please see p. 385. Effect size for 2 x 2 chi-square analyses can be estimated using the PHI COEFFICIENT (which we will meet again in Chapter 17 for different but related reasons). Phi is pronounced as in the English word 'fie'. The more general term is CRAMER'S PHI (also called Cramer's V) when analysing cross-tab tables where at least one variable has more than two levels or categories. The formula we require is:

$$\text{Cramer's } \Phi = \sqrt{\frac{\chi^2}{(N)\, df_{smaller}}}$$

$df_{smaller}$ means either (rows -1) or (columns -1), whichever is smaller.

For our 2 x 2 case, where (rows -1) *or* (columns -1) = 1, the expression reduces to = $\sqrt{\dfrac{\chi^2}{N}}$ which is the phi coefficient. Our Φ will be $\sqrt{4.6/323} = \sqrt{0.014} = 0.118$.

Cohen (1988) produced some effect size conventions for Cramer's Φ that depend on the df for the smaller side of the contingency table, i.e. $df_{smaller}$ (see Table 16.8).

$df_{smaller}$	Effect size		
	Small	Medium	Large
1	.10	.30	.50
2	.07	.21	.35
3	.06	.17	.29

Table 16.8 Cohen's effect size definitions for Cramer's Φ

Our effect size of 0.118 would therefore be designated as 'small' since our $df_{smaller}$ is 1.

Reporting the result of a chi-square analysis

> Some 50.3% of drivers in old cars (89/177) failed to stop at an amber traffic light, whereas only 38.4% of drivers in new cars (56/146) failed to stop. A χ^2 analysis of the difference between stop/didn't stop frequencies across drivers of new and old cars was significant, χ^2 (1, N = 323) = 4.6, $p < .05$. The effect size was small with phi = 0.118.

Quick 2 x 2 formula

This can be used only where there are two columns and two rows, as in the example above. It saves the labour of calculating expected frequencies and, if you're handy with a calculator, you'll find this can be done in one move from the observed cell totals:

$$\chi^2 = \frac{N\,(ad - bc)^2}{(a + b)\,(c + d)\,(a + c)\,(b + d)}$$

where N is the total sample size.

More complex chi-square data ($r \times c$ designs)

Each of the two variables in a cross-tabs table might have more than two values. We might for instance have introduced a placebo group to the gel study. We could give an inert cream to a third group of participants in order to account for any psychological effect that simply tending to one's body might have on one's retention of fat. We might have used the categories 'stopped', 'slowed down' and 'kept on going' in the car age and traffic light observations in Table 16.1. In addition, we might have divided cars into the categories 'new' (less than one year old), 'fairly new' (one to five years), and 'older' (over five years). In the research of Cialdini *et al.* (1990), described in Chapter 3, the researchers varied the amount of litter placed by the investigators on a path down which unwitting participants would walk after they had received a leaflet from research assistants. The design tested the proposal that more litter already present on the path would prompt a greater amount of littering by participants. Their results appear in Table 16.9.

	Amount of existing litter placed by researchers			
	0 or 1 piece *(low)*	2 or 4 pieces *(medium)*	8 or 16 pieces *(high)*	Total
Action of observed person				
Dropped litter	17 (a)	28 (b)	49 (c)	94
Did not drop litter	102 (d)	91 (e)	71 (f)	264
Total	119	119	120	358

Table 16.9 Frequency of leaflet dropping by amount of existing litter (Cialdini *et al.* (1990))

You might like to calculate the expected frequencies here using $E = \dfrac{RC}{T}$. The expected frequencies are shown in the *O-E* column below The calculation of chi-square is as follows:

	O-E	(O-E)^2	(O-E)^2/E	Result
Cell a	17–31.25 = −14.25	−14.25^2 = 203.0625	203.0625/31.25 =	6.498
Cell b	28–31.25 = −3.25	−3.25^2 = 10.5625	10.5625/31.25 =	0.338
Cell c	49–31.51 = 17.49	17.49^2 = 305.9001	305.9001/31.51 =	9.708032
Cell d	102–87.75 = 14.25	14.25^2 = 203.0625	203.0625/87.75 =	2.314103
Cell e	91–87.75 = 3.25	3.25^2 = 10.5625	10.5625/87.75 =	0.12037
Cell f	71–88.49 = −17.49	−17.49^2 = 305.9001	305.9001/88.49 =	3.456889
			$\chi^2 = \Sigma(O\text{-}E)^2/E =$	**22.44**

df here are $(3 - 1) \times (2 - 1) = 2$.

$\chi^2 (2, N = 358) = 22.44, p < .001$. Our observed χ^2 easily exceeds the required value of 13.82 for $p \leq .001$. To find effect size we take $df_{smaller}$ to be 1 so $\Phi = \sqrt{\dfrac{\chi^2}{N}}$ again and this is $\sqrt{22.44/358} = 0.25$ and close to the size for a 'medium' effect.

The 'goodness of fit' test – χ^2 on a single variable

We started this section on chi-square by considering frequencies for a single variable – numbers of people reporting a loss or gain of fat. We wanted to see how well our data fitted the theoretical distribution that would occur if people reported loss or gain on a purely random basis; we expected a distribution of 50%/50%. In general, the GOODNESS OF FIT TEST analyses whether data depart significantly from a theoretical distribution.

A single variable might have several categories, not just two. Suppose an accountancy course with 123 students was forced to close and that students had to select one (only) alternative course from those shown in Table 16.10. If we assumed that there is equal preference for each subject here (which would be a null hypothesis) then psychology and podiatry seem to depart from the trend.

(a) Philosophy	(b) Physics	(c) Plumbing science	(d) Podiatry	(e) Psychology	Total
25	28	27	8	35	123

Table 16.10 Preferred alternative subject chosen by 123 accountancy students

The χ^2 calculation for this table is performed in exactly the same way as that shown at the beginning of this section for the one-row two-category test (p. 401), except that here we must calculate for cells *a, b, c, d* and *e* (not just cells *a* and *b*). The expected frequencies, as before, follow H_0 that subjects are equally preferred. We have 123 choices and five cells. So, 123/5 gives 24.6 as the expected frequency for each cell. *df* are again (and for all one-row tests) one less than the number of cells, giving us a value of 4. You might like to calculate the result and, if so, don't look at the answer just below, which is presented in the way it would be reported.[1] This won't tell us that psychology is significantly more popular but it will tell us that the data as a whole depart significantly from the assumption of equal preference.

The null hypothesis does not always have to involve equal expected frequencies in each cell. The 'goodness of fit' test is sometimes used in the estimation of whether a large sample approximates to a normal distribution (a requirement for some significance tests; see p. 364). If so, expected frequencies would be calculated using Table 2 in the Appendix to determine the number of scores that should fall between, for example, the mean and half a standard deviation, half a standard deviation and one standard deviation and so on. Using these known proportions under the normal curve the goodness of fit test can tell us whether our observed frequencies depart from these ideal frequencies to a significant degree.

[1] $\chi^2 (4, N = 123) = 16.31, p \leq .01$

Effect size for goodness of fit

The effect size for a goodness of fit test can be found using: $w = \sqrt{\sum \frac{(prop_o - prop_e)^2}{prop_e}}$

$prop_o$ means the *proportion* of cases in one of the observed data cells; for the first cell in Table 16.10; this would be 25/123. $prop_e$ is the proportion of expected cases in each cell = 24.6/123. The formula asks us to calculate the part after the Σ for each cell and then add the results finally taking the square root of that result. According to Cohen (1988) w can be interpreted as indicting a small effect if it is between 0.1 and 0.3, moderate effect if 0.3 to 0.5 and strong effect if over 0.5. For our student choice data we get $w = 0.22$ – a small effect.

SPSS procedure for conducting a r x c chi-square test

Usually you will be wanting to conduct a chi-square test on a row by column (r x c) data table. The less common goodness of fit test is dealt with later on.

To enter the data for the Cialdini *et al.* (1990) litter-dropping test in Table 16.2 we would first need to recognise that we have two categorical variables on which each person is categorised. On the first factor (*pieces*), each person is either in the 0/1 piece condition, the 2/4 piece condition or the 8/16 piece condition. We will call these conditions *low*, *medium* and *high*, and give them the codes 1, 2 and 3 respectively. The second factor is whether or not they dropped their leaflet so this factor (*drop*) has two values: 1 = *dropped* and 2 = *nodrop*.

Weighting cases in SPSS

If we entered data in the usual way then, for each person observed in the study, we would have to enter a 1, 2 or 3 in the first column of the datasheet seen in Figure 16.2 (*pieces*) and a 1 or 2 in the second column (*drop*), and we would have to do this for all 358 participants! However, SPSS allows

	pieces	drop	count
1	low	dropped	17.00
2	low	nodrop	102.00
3	medium	dropped	28.00
4	medium	nodrop	91.00
5	high	dropped	49.00
6	high	nodrop	71.00

Chi-Square Test

	Value	df	Asymp. Sig. (2-sided)
Pearson Chi-Square	22.433[a]	2	.000
Likelihood Ratio	22.463	2	.000
Linear-by-Linear Association	21.706	1	.000
N of Valid Cases	358		

a. 0 cells (.0%) have expected count less than 5. The minimum expected count is 31.25

Figure 16.2 Datasheet and chi-square test output for the Cialdini *et al.* litter-dropping data

us to take a short-cut and just enter our cell totals by using a feature known as *weighting cases*. To do this we create a third variable called count and into this go our cell totals. For instance, on the first row we have people who were in the low pieces condition (only 0 or 1) and who dropped their leaflet. In the original table there were 17 of these, so 17 appears under count for the low/dropped row. The other 'count' values can be entered following Table 16.2.

To inform SPSS that you are weighting cases do the following:

1 **Data/Weight Cases/**

2 Click the radio button titled **Weight Cases By** and enter the variable *count* into the waiting right-hand box.

3 Click **OK**.

We are now ready to conduct the χ^2 test. Do this as follows:

4 **Analyze/Descriptives/Crosstabs**; SPSS then wants to know the name of our row variable so enter *drop* here, then enter the column variable, which is **pieces**.

5 So far, SPSS is only going to give us certain descriptive statistics concerning our table. If we want a χ^2 test conducted we have to click the **Statistics** button at the bottom of this dialogue box and check the square by **Chi-square**. To get effect size click **Phi and Cramer's V**. It might also be useful to have expected cell frequencies which you get by clicking **Cells** and then **Expected** in the top left **Counts** box. Click **Continue**.

6 Click **OK**.

The output will then appear as three tables, the first giving details of the cases included. You can make sure that weighting cases worked since you should see a total of 358 cases here. Next is the cross-tabs table of frequencies that should look just like our data table but perhaps a little more complicated if you also asked for expected frequencies. Finally comes the all-important test result box. Several statistics are given but we are only interested in the Pearson chi-square, which has a value of 22.433 (we got 22.44 by hand but this slight difference is through rounding). We are also given the *df* of 2 and the significance ($p < .001$; do not read this as '$p = .000$' since this is impossible! SPSS only works to three places of decimals for significance). Note that the result also tells us how many of the expected cell frequencies were less than five and will give a warning when the number of these is considered unacceptably high.

If you want a goodness of fit test (using a single-row analysis) then find chi-square as follows:

• **Analyze/Non-parametric Tests/Chi-Square.**

Since this use is relatively uncommon at this level I will leave the workings of this version alone for you to discover later. However, intuitively the situation is not difficult. You simply tell SPSS which single variable you want to do the goodness of fit test on and adjust the expected values box so that all values are expected to be equal, or else enter the values you expect to occur for each case in the datasheet.

Limitations on the use of chi-square

Observations must be unique to one cell

If we were to look for a relationship between social class and participation in football or cricket we might find that some participants would appear in more than one preference cell, because they participate in both sports. This would invalidate assumptions made on the chi-square findings. Each case or person must fall into *only* one of the observation cells.

Only frequencies can appear in cells

Chi-square cannot be calculated where the cell contents are: means, proportions, ratios, percentages or anything other than a frequency count of the number of instances in the data of an occurrence described by the particular cell.

Low expected frequencies

There is a problem with accepting a chi-square result where expected frequency cells are low. How low, though, is a subject of much debate among statisticians. A rule of thumb given by Cochran (1954) and used for many years was that no more than 20% of expected frequency cells should fall below 5. This would rule out any 2 x 2 calculations where a single expected frequency cell was below 5. Low expected frequencies often occur where too few data have been collected in one of the rows or one of the columns (see, for instance, Table 16.11).

Observed frequencies					Expected frequencies			
	Preferred hand					Preferred hand		
	Left	Right	Total			Left	Right	Total
Better ear					**Better ear**			
Left	2	6	8		Left	0.8	7.2	8
Right	0	12	12		Right	1.2	10.8	12
Total	2	18	20		**Total**	2.0	18.0	20

Table 16.11 Low expected frequencies – too few cases in one observed column

Some statisticians feel Cochran's rule is too 'conservative' – it leads to retention of the null hypothesis too often for a particular significance level. That is, there is a danger of too many Type II errors. Camilli and Hopkins (1978) argued that 2 x 2 chi-square tests are accurate and 'safe' even when one or two of the expected frequencies are as low as 1 or 2, so long as the total sample size is greater than 20. With both these criteria unmet, it's easy to produce an example where the chi-square calculation appears untrustworthy. Calculation on the data in Table 16.12 gives a chi-square value of 4, which is 'significant' with $p < .05$. The expected frequencies here would be 4 in each cell – the null hypothesis says there are equal numbers of seven-year-olds who conserve and don't conserve, likewise for five-year-olds. Without statistical sophistication one can see that it would be relatively easy by pure chance to obtain these results. We would predict from the null hypothesis that there should be 4 in each cell; it would surely not be remarkable to select 6 conservers and 2 non-conservers instead of 4–4 for seven-year-olds and the reverse for five-year-olds.

If you *do* have unavoidably low frequencies you can use Fisher's exact test which calculates probability straight form the frequencies and an extremely simple application for doing this can be found at: http://davidmlane.com/hyperstat/chi_square.html

Age	Conserved	Didn't conserve	Total
5 years	2	6	8
7 years	6	2	8
Total	8	8	16

Table 16.12 Data producing 'significant' but dubious evidence for age differences in conservation

Avoiding the problem – check before you gather data

In order to avoid worries about low expected frequencies there are three basic precautions you can take.

1 Avoid low samples for one category. Use a design that is unlikely to produce low frequencies in one row or column – be wary of gathering data on left-handers, conservers among younger age groups, single parents, people with a particular disorder such as dyslexia (apart from ethical considerations) and so on, unless you know in advance you can find enough of these.

2 Avoid low samples overall. As we saw, samples of at least 20 reduce the problem of low expected frequencies for 2 x 2 tables but far more is better.

3 Obtain significance at $p \leq .01$. The original worry was over too many Type I errors at the 5% level of significance. Where significance at 1% is achieved, the decision to reject the null hypothesis is far more secure.

One- and two-tailed tests

The one-tailed/two-tailed debate mentioned in Chapter 14 need not concern us very much here. Even if the hypothesis tested is directional we must *always* use two-tailed values for a chi-square square test, except for the special case with which we started this chapter – the simple one-variable, two-category test. In this special case only, the same arguments apply about one-tailed tests as were covered on p. 343.

Power

Power in a chi-square analysis can be estimated using the effect size information, total *df* and *N*. For the Cialdini *et el.* result (p. 409) we had close to a medium effect, total *df* of 2 and $N = 358$. Table 16.13 only runs to $N = 200$. However, using 200 in lieu of 358 we still find power is a very high .97 (moving down the 'Medium' column and stopping where $df = 2$ and $N = 200$). It is clear that the power here was very high indeed and certainly acceptable. It would mean that this study, assuming H_1 is true, would have approximately less than a 3% chance of failing to find an effect if repeated with the same N. Since effect size and power calculations are not an exact science, you may interpolate between the values in Table 16.13, using sensible ratios, to get a fair power estimate, *or* get hold of Cohen's (1988) more detailed tables.

Total *df*	Total N	Effect size		
		Small	Medium	Large
1	25	.08	.32	.70
	50	.11	.56	.94
	100	.17	.85	*
	200	.29	.99	*
2	25	.07	.25	.60
	50	.09	.46	.90
	100	.13	.77	*
	200	.23	.97	*
3	25	.07	.21	.54
	50	.08	.40	.86
	100	.12	.71	.99
	200	.19	.96	*
4	25	.06	.19	.50
	50	.08	.36	.82
	100	.11	.66	.99
	200	.17	.94	*

* = very close to 1

Table 16.13 Estimated power for x^2 for hypotheses tested with $\alpha = .05$

Exercises

1 Carry out a chi-square test on the data below and report results.

Politics	Pro-hanging	Anti-hanging
Left	17	48
Right	33	16

2 Should a chi-square test be carried out on the following data table? Explain your answer.

	Conserved	Failed to conserve
4 year olds	1	7
6 year olds	7	1

3 A (fictitious) survey shows that, in a sample of 100, 91 people are against the privatisation of health services, whereas 9 support the idea.

(a) What test of significance can be performed on these data?

(b) Calculate the chi-square value and check it for significance.

(c) Can this type of chi-square test be one-tailed?

(d) If, for a large sample of unknown size, we knew only that 87% of the sample were against the idea and 13% were for it, could we carry out the same test to see whether this split is significant?

4 A field study produced the following table of results with $p \leq .01$ after a χ^2 analysis.

	Observed frequencies Taste preferred			Expected frequencies Taste preferred		
	A	B	C	A	B	C
Age:						
Under 14	3	8	4	2.5	5.25	7.25
14–30	4	6	2	2	4.2	5.8
Over 30	3	7	23	5.5	11.55	15.95

(a) How many degrees of freedom are involved here?

(b) Do the data raise any concerns about interpretation of the χ^2 analysis?

Multi-way frequency tables and loglinear analysis

If you are not yet into your second year of undergraduate study you probably should not be reading this, unless of course, you just happen to be interested! The more complex statistical treatments covered in this book mostly occur towards the end but loglinear analysis (LLA) follows on so logically here that it did not seem worth creating another chapter for it. LLA is another way of dealing with frequency 'cross-tabs' tables when analysing for significance of differences across levels of an independent variable. However, it has the distinct advantage that it can deal with more complex tables than the two-way version we dealt with using standard chi-square.

A three-way frequency table

Let's look at a *three-way* table, which is an advance on Table 16.1 simply because it includes a further possibly relevant variable when looking at compliance with traffic regulations through amber traffic light behaviour – driver gender. In the previous example (p. 397) we hypothesised that drivers of new cars would be more compliant because they were likely to be older, better-off drivers. If we include gender as a variable we can see whether it too is associated with stopping at an amber light. Stereotypically we might assume that female drivers are a little more compliant, though this might be better phrased as simply being safer drivers! We might even find that for new cars there is no difference across genders in stopping but for old cars perhaps there is. In the language of multi-factor studies we would be looking at a *three-way interaction* – the effect of gender on the two-way interaction between car age and stopping.

Table 16.14 is a three-way table and is a combination of the two 2 x 2 tables that would be formed where we have, first, stopped or not by car age, and, second, stopped or not by gender. Loglinear analysis will work on four-way, five-way and basically any multi-way set of tables but the layout, calculations and analysis get mighty complicated!

To proceed further we need now to introduce the concepts of *main effects* and *interactions*. These concepts are covered more fully in Chapter 19, which you may already have read and which you might wish to revisit before moving on here. Basically, a main effect is the effect of a single independent variable, ignoring any other variable. In our driving example there are three variables

| | Age category of car | | |
	New	Old	Total
Male drivers			
Behaviour at amber light			
Stopped	**79**	**63**	142
Did not stop	**87**	**95**	182
Total	166	158	324
Female drivers			
Behaviour at amber light			
Stopped	**95**	**83**	178
Did not stop	**51**	**94**	145
Total	146	177	323
Total old/new cars:	312	335	647

Table 16.14 Stopping behaviour of male and female drivers in old and new cars

and hence three possible main effects. First there is a possible main effect for car age. This, if significant, would tell us that there are, say, more older than newer cars on the road but this is not a part of our study so we are relatively uninterested in this outcome. Depending on how we define 'new' and 'old' we can of course artificially create a major difference in frequencies but this is not relevant to the study. Neither is gender as such. It may be of passing interest here that there are as many female as male drivers overall (ignoring car age and stopping behaviour), but again this is not a part of the study aims.

In LLA we usually look selectively at the effects we predicted or that were the subject of the research hypotheses; however, the analysis may well throw up unexpected effects that may or may not be meaningful or useful. A non-meaningful main effect might simply be a matter of sampling strategy. In our extroversion and nudity example (see Table 16.5), suppose we had sampled 100 extroverts but only 50 introverts. This would show up as a main effect for extroversion/introversion (it would come out as a significant difference using the one-way, two-category analysis on p. 401) but would simply represent the fact that we sampled more extroverts than introverts.

The remaining main effect might be of some psychological interest. This is the number of people stopping at the traffic light or not *overall*. This has a general bearing on the degree of contemporary compliance with traffic rules, at least among our sample. The main point of the original study, however, was to look at an *interaction* – in that case between car age and stopping. An *interaction* occurs when the proportions of frequencies across levels of one variable are not the same for each level of a second variable. We saw this with extroversion and feeling comfortable. In Table 16.14, we can see a possible two-way interaction between gender and stopping. Although numbers of male and female drivers were almost equal, a higher proportion of females stopped (178 out of 323) than males (142 out of 324). There is another possible two-way interaction of interest in that 174 new and 156 old cars stopped whereas 138 new but 189 old cars did not stop. However, there is also a possible *three*-way interaction. Whereas there is some tendency for more older cars to stop, compared with new cars, in the male sample, for the female sample this is much more pronounced with 51 new cars but 94 old cars not stopping. Loglinear analysis is used to try to account for *all* the variation among the frequency cells of the table away from what would be expected given the margin totals. This variation is 'explained' (accounted for) by looking at the significance of main effects and interactions at different levels.

When to use loglinear analysis

Type of relationship tested	Level of data required	Design of study
Explanation of frequency differences across levels of two or more variables	Nominal/Categorical	Between groups: Independent samples

Data assumptions: Each observed person (or case) must appear in *one only* of the frequency cells.

Notes: No more than 20% of the expected frequency cell counts should be less than 5 and all should be greater than 1.

Rationale of loglinear analysis

The explanation of LLA is not simple and not very intuitive, especially because here, as elsewhere, we are avoiding full statistical theory. Hence, there will be points here where I have to present a packaged and relatively unexplained notion, leaving you, the reader, to explore further if you wish. The main aim here, as for other complex analyses in this text, is to get across the main notions involved in LLA in order for you to be able to accomplish a fair and complete analysis of your own data within legitimate statistical 'rules'.

Let's start with the analysis of the simple two-way data shown in Table 16.15 where a conventional chi-square test gives $\chi^2 (1,200) = 5.44$, $p = .02$. We can see here that the variation in cells comes from a higher proportion of smokers in the 16–24 category than would be expected from the smoker totals; a quarter of all participants smoked, yet 27 out of 80 16–24-year-olds smoked.

	Age category		
	16–24	25+	Total
Smoke	27	23	50
Don't smoke	53	97	150
Total	80	120	200

Table 16.15 Smoking by age category with interaction

The next notion to introduce here is that of a MODEL. LLA uses models to try to explain the variation across all the frequency cells in a multi-way table. You have already used a model when using simple two-way chi-square. The model tested in two-way tables is that variations within cells can be explained by the variation across columns (age categories) and the variation across rows (smoking or not). Expected frequencies are calculated on this basis and they form the basis of the null hypothesis.

We then look at the probability of our results occurring if the null hypothesis model is valid; above we say no because p is less than .05. That is, there is too much deviation of the observed cell frequencies away from the expected frequencies on this model. In other words, our data depart significantly from what we would expect, given the marginal totals. We consequently drop the model (reject our null hypothesis). This is what we did for the Cialdini *et al.* data for example.

However, in LLA, we consider *all* possible models. We start with the view that all cells are equally weighted; that an observation is as likely to fall in one cell as in any other. This would mean that in Talbe 16.15 expected frequencies would all be 200/4 = 50. This is a plainly daft suggestion, which would produce a highly significant chi-square when tested (we won't calculate this here). This model would be represented by the equation:

$$E_{ij} = e$$

where E_{ij} is the expected frequency for the cell in the ith row and jth column; e is the geometric mean of the expected cell frequencies on this model; don't worry about 'geometric mean'; for this model e is simply the average of all the cell frequencies.

This model we know won't explain all the variation in cell frequencies. We wouldn't expect 50 people in the 25+/don't smoke cell because ³⁄₄ of the 200 participants are non-smokers and ²⁄₃ are 25+. Hence, we would expect more than average in this cell. To compensate partially we *could* just take account of the fact that there were more non-smokers than smokers (a new model). The formula for expected frequencies would now become:

$$E_{ij} = ee^r_i$$

This starts to look complicated but simply means that the original e for each cell will now be multiplied by a value (e^r_i), which accounts for the row (r) the cell value is in; i stands for either the first or second row as we move down. For instance, the e value in the cell 25+/don't smoke (where $i = 2$) would be increased a bit because there were more non-smokers in the 25+ column overall. Here is one of the points where magic will apply because we will not work out exactly how the e^r_i value is calculated (but see Howell, 1992: 583, if you are curious).

To take account of the difference in overall numbers of 16–24 and 25+-year-olds we again add in a value by which e must be multiplied, so:

$$E_{ij} = ee^r_i e^c_j$$

where e^c_j is the adjustment for columns.

This is in fact the model which is tested by the standard two-way chi-square analysis you covered in the first part of this chapter. The formula just above says that the expected frequencies are proportional to row and column totals – just as we calculated on p. 404 using $E = \dfrac{RC}{T}$. We have taken account of the fact that we would expect cells to be proportional to the proportions in the sample who did and didn't smoke, and to the proportions of age categories sampled. The question remaining is 'Are there nevertheless too many smokers in the 16–24 category, and too few in the 25+ category, to be explained by mere chance fluctuation away from what is predicted by the model (i.e. the null hypothesis)?' Again that is what our χ^2 analysis tests – were the observed frequencies too far away from the expected frequencies for mere coincidence? By conventional chi-square significance testing we found that the probability of these observed frequencies occurring if true frequencies were arranged according to the expected values was < .05, so the answer to the question was 'Yes'!

What's 'log' got to do with it?

So far the expected frequencies have been found by *multiplying* together just as we did when calculating expected frequencies for the two-way examples earlier. However, this becomes cumbersome for three-way and higher-level tables and (as you might expect) statisticians have mathematical reasons for preferring an equation that only involves *addition*. You may just recall from school that if you want to *multiply* values you can take the *logs* of the values and simply *add* these logs to get the log of the answer you require. In other words, if $X \times Y = Z$ then $\log X + \log Y = \log Z$. Here, then, is the reason for the title 'loglinear'. '*ln*' is a symbol for log and to make things simpler we call *lne* 'λ'. Hence, if we substitute with log values, the equation above for expected frequencies becomes:

$\ln E_{ij} = \lambda + \lambda^r_i + \lambda^c_j$

The saturated model

As explained above, this equation produces the expected frequencies we would calculate for the conventional null hypothesis in the standard chi-square analysis performed earlier. We know it is inadequate because χ^2 is large and $p \leq .05$. This means that there is a significant remaining amount of variation among cell frequencies to explain. The observed frequencies departed significantly from the expected frequencies. What LLA does is add to the equation a *further* term that accounts for the *interaction* between smoking and age. We know from observing cells that fewer smokers were 25+ and fewer non-smokers were 16–24 than would be expected if both age and smoking were acting independently of each other. The new term includes this interaction and so the full equation becomes:

$\ln E_{ij} = \lambda + \lambda^r_i \lambda^c_j \lambda^{rc}_{ij}$

This equation denotes what is termed the SATURATED MODEL. What this means is that it accounts for *all* the variation among cell frequencies and therefore chi-square when calculated upon the data will be zero. There will be no *further* variation of cell means around these frequencies. Hence it is rather uninteresting. However, and here comes a central LLA point, the analysis *starts* with the saturated model and then proceeds to *extract* terms from the top to see whether each one makes any difference. 'From the top' means starting with the highest-level interaction (in this case two-way) and then proceeding down to simple main effects. In a three-way analysis, such as our three-way driving data above, it would mean starting with the *three-way* interaction (car age by gender by stopping), then each of the two-way interactions (car age by gender; car age by stopping; gender by stopping) and on to the three main (one-way) effects (car age, gender, stopping). For this reason, the analysis is known as HIERARCHICAL LOGLINEAR ANALYSIS (there are other kinds).

Extracting effects in hierarchical LLA

The chi-square that is calculated in LLA is not our usual statistic but another known as the LIKELIHOOD RATIO CHI-SQUARE (LR χ^2), which is more suitable when pitting one model against another – the statistic calculates the likelihood of data occurring under various hypotheses or 'models'. For our smoking data, as for any LLA analysis, we know that the chi-square for the saturated model will be zero. The next step, then, is to take out the interaction ($\lambda^r_i{}^c_j$) to see whether the model *still* adequately explains all the cell variation (we already know it doesn't). What LLA does then is calculate a CHI-SQUARE CHANGE between leaving the interaction term in and taking it out. If this change is significant then the analysis stops and all terms below the current level are 'kept in the model'. That is, λ, λ^r_i, λ^c_j and $\lambda^r_i{}^c_j$ are all required to explain the cell frequency variations.

This won't mean much in the present example but consider the data in Table 16.16. Here the 16–24-year olds are only 2 above what we'd expect on the conventional null hypothesis and all-round frequencies are close to what would be predicted when there is no interaction of age and smoking, i.e. close to the expected frequencies. The LLA analysis here would first consider the interaction and find its deletion from the equation of no consequence. In a conventional sense we would 'retain the null hypothesis'. However, LLA would then go on to consider each main (one-way) effect, the 50/150 split for smoking and the 80/120 split for age categories. It would in fact find for both of these that, if they were dropped from the equation, the change in χ^2 *would* be significant and therefore both main effect terms would be retained in the equation. Hence, for this table, the equation:

$$lnEi_j = \lambda + \lambda^r_i + \lambda^c_j$$

would be the best model to explain the cell variations. This means that although there is no interaction effect there is a main effect for smoking and a main effect for age group which explain the variations in cell frequencies.

	Age category		
	16–24	25+	Total
Smoke	22	28	50
Don't smoke	58	92	150
Total	80	120	200

Table 16.16 Smoking by age category – no interaction

The three-way analysis

So far we have not found out much that we couldn't find out with the easier versions of two-way and one-way chi-square covered earlier. However, these are pretty useless for analysing three-way tables and above, and in the past researchers just used to take variables two at a time and do several normal chi-square analyses – a rather unsatisfactory approach. We shall now look at a three-way analysis on our driving data in Table 16.14.

For a three-way table analysis the equation for expected frequencies is complex, hence we will drop the $_{ij}$ subscripts from the variable terms and refer to each variable (or factor) as: C = car age, G = gender and S = stopping. We would then find the expected frequencies with:

$$lnE_{ijk} = \lambda + \lambda^C + \lambda^G + \lambda^S + \lambda^{CG} + \lambda^{CS} + \lambda^{GS} + \lambda^{CGS}$$

The hierarchy for the analysis is that the three-way interaction (λ^{CGS}) is analysed first. If the χ^2 change with this removed is significant, then all other terms below it are retained for the equation. The two-way interactions (λ^{CG}, λ^{CS}, λ^{GS}) are analysed next; if removal of any of these produces no significant χ^2 change then it is dropped. Analysis is completed at this level on the remaining interactions with the non-significant ones dropped; if any of the interactions at this level then produce significant change in χ^2 then that term is retained along with any lower (i.e. one-way) terms which contribute to that interaction. For instance, if removal of λ^{GS} produces no significant change, it is dropped and the remaining two interactions analysed without it. If λ^{CS} also produces non-significant change it too is dropped and the equation is re-analysed with only λ^{CG} retained. If removal of λ^{CG} produces significant change it is retained and the analysis stops. However, λ^S would now also not be required in the model since it does not contribute to the significant interaction λ^{CG}. Main effects λ^C and λ^G *would* be included since they contribute to λ^{CG}.

In this way, the effects and interactions contributing to the 'explanation' of variations among cell is achieved. As with all statistical tests, no effect can be established as causal but the model provided as best-fitting, using LLA, can be used as supporting evidence for a theory which claims, for instance, that females in newer cars are at lower risk of accident.

Conducting a three-way driving analysis in SPSS

To conduct a LLA on the three-way driving table, data are entered as for weighted categorical variables as described back on p. 411. The datasheet would appear as in Figure 16.3.

To conduct the loglinear analysis, proceed as follows:

1 Select **Analyze/Loglinear/Model Selection**.

2 Move the three variables *carage*, *gender* and *stopped* over to the **Factors** box.

3 Highlight all three factors and click **Define Range**. As for two sample difference tests you need to tell SPSS which codes you have used for the levels of each categorical variable.

4 Enter 1 as **Minimum** and 2 as **Maximum** and all three variables will be defined. Note this is a short-cut. If any of your variables have three or four (etc.) levels, you will have to define these separately. SPSS allows you to define several variables at the same time with the same number of levels and codes. Click **Continue**.

carage	gender	stopped	count
old	male	yes	63.00
old	male	no	95.00
old	female	yes	83.00
old	female	no	94.00
new	male	yes	79.00
new	male	no	87.00
new	female	yes	95.00
new	female	no	51.00

Figure 16.3 Three-way driving data entered into SPSS for loglinear analysis

5 You can alter values in the lower box entitled **Model Building**; there are further choices when either the **Model** or **Options** buttons are clicked. However, until you are more skilled with this method all these values should be left at their default levels. You don't really need the **Frequencies** and **Residuals** that appear at the top of the **Options** box because these should be zero since we are using the saturated model. They are of no use here and, to save clutter, you could deselect **Frequencies** and **Residuals**. Click **Continue**.

6 Click **OK**.

SPSS output

The output for this analysis is massive but as ever you need only consult a fraction of it in order to extract the information you need. The initial information will tell you that you weighted your cases appropriately and that the codes you entered are correct. Ignore 'convergence information'. Next will be a table of **cell counts and frequencies** unless you deselected 'Frequencies and Residuals' earlier. Ignore the **goodness of fit tests** and we come to the first important table, looking like the first part of Figure 16.4 below and entitled '**K way and higher order effects**'. In the top half the line with K = 3 is showing us that the overall three-way interaction is not significant and that p is only .178 (LR χ^2 =1.811). This tells us that our hunch that there might be an interaction between gender, car age and stopping, proposed earlier, is not sound. There is not enough *extra* variation among cells over and above that which is explained by the underlying two-way interactions. Next we see that two-way interactions and the three-way interactions *taken together* are significant, p = .001. ('K-way and higher order' here means two-way and higher, i.e. two-way and three-way). Finally, one-way and above effects (i.e. all of them together) are significant ($p < .001$). This already suggests that one-way effects on their own were not significant and this is confirmed in the next section where we are given 'Tests that K-way effects are zero.' Here, one-way effects are not significant (p = .827), two-way are ($p < .001$) and of course the result for the single three-way interaction is the same as before.

Next the program starts to lop off terms from the full equation to explain cell variation, starting with the highest (three-way) interaction. As we said earlier, if the change in χ^2 caused by taking out a term is significant the analysis will stop at that point. This process of lopping off terms and checking for the χ^2 change is known as *backward elimination* and statistics for this are given in the next SPSS table in the output. Where the term 'deleted effect' occurs this says that the χ^2 given is the χ^2 change that occurs if this term is deleted from the equation. As we learned above, if the three-way interaction is deleted the change is a χ^2 of 1.811 and not significant. Now the analysis proceeds to the two-way interactions.

The next section of the table tells us what happens when each of the two-way interactions (carage*gender, carage*stopped, gender*stopped) is deleted. We can see that deletion of carage*gender does not produce a significant χ^2 change ($p = .056$) but deletion of either of the other two interactions *does* produce significant change, hence these two are retained while carage*gender is dropped. The remaining two interactions are analysed together. It is still true that removal of either of these would produce a significant change so the analysis stops here.

Interpretation of these results

There is no three-way interaction, so male and female drivers do not differ in the tendency for more stopping to occur with newer cars – the tentative hypothesis we started with. There is also no interaction between gender and age of car, so female drivers are not more associated with an age of car (old or new) than are male drivers. This was not anyway an aspect of our research question and so is irrelevant. However, there *is* a significant interaction of gender with stopping, though this was not predicted. We did however suspect it from initial inspection of our table of results. There was also a significant interaction between stopping and age of car – our original prediction. For new cars, 174 stopped and 146 did not; for old cars 138 stopped and 189 did not. As we have just seen, this effect was not associated with gender.

Reporting results of a loglinear analysis

We might report these results as follows (Figure 16.4):

A three-way backward elimination loglinear analysis was performed on the frequency data in Table 16.14 produced by combining frequencies for car age, stopping behaviour and driver gender. One-way effects were not significant, likelihood ratio χ^2 (3) = .895, $p = .827$; two-way effects were significant, likelihood ratio χ^2 (3) = 21.537, $p < .001$; the three-way effect was not significant, χ^2 (1) = 1.811, $p = .178$. The gender x age of car interaction was not significant. The final model had the generating class age of car x stopping and gender x stopping. More female drivers than male drivers stopped at the amber light as did more drivers of new cars compared with drivers of older cars. There was no evidence that the age of car and stopping relationship is different across genders.

K-way and higher-order effects

	K	df	Likelihood ratio		Pearson		Number of iterations
			Chi-square	Sig.	Chi-square	Sig.	
K-way and higher order effects[a]	1	7	24.243	.001	22.614	.002	0
	2	4	23.348	.000	21.907	.000	2
	3	1	1.811	.178	1.809	.179	3
K-way effects[b]	1	3	.895	.827	.706	.872	0
	2	3	21.537	.000	20.098	.000	0
	3	1	1.811	.178	1.809	.179	0

a. Tests that k-way and higher order effects are zero.
b. Tests that k-way effects are zero.

Step summary

Step[a]		Effects	Chi-square[c]	df	Sig.	Number of iterations
0	Generating class[b]	carage*gender*stopped	.000	0		
	Deleted effect 1	carage*gender*stopped	1.811	1	.178	3
1	Generating class[b]	carage*gender, carage*stopped, gender*stopped	1.811	1	.178	
	Deleted effect 1	carage*gender	3.663	1	.056	2
	2	carage*stopped	10.925	1	.001	2
	3	gender*stopped	9.556	1	.002	2
2	Generating class[b]	carage*stopped, gender*stopped	5.474	2	.065	
	Deleted effect 1	carage*stopped	9.622	1	.002	2
	2	gender*stopped	8.253	1	.004	2
3	Generating class[b]	carage*stopped, gender*stopped	5.474	2	.065	

a. At each step, the effect with the largest significance level for the likelihood ratio change is deleted, provided the significance level is larger than .050.
b. Statistics are displayed for the best model at each step after step 0.
c. For 'deleted effect', this is the change in the Chi-square after the effect is deleted from the model.

Figure 16.4 Output from SPSS for the loglinear analysis described

A researcher suggested that graduate extroverts/introverts should not show the divisions previously shown by *non*-graduates about feeling comfortable or not on a nudist beach. The (fictitious) data below were gathered. Analyse the data using hierarchical log-linear analysis and check whether the hypothesis is supported.

| | Graduates | | Non-graduates | |
	Comfortable	Not comfortable	Comfortable	Not comfortable
Extrovert	39	11	40	10
Introvert	24	26	10	40

The three-way interaction is significant; χ^2 (1) = 4.63, p = .031. Hence the final model had the generating class extrovert/introvert $\times$ graduation status $\times$ comfort level. Two-way interactions were also significant; χ^2 (3) = 47.234, p = .001. One-way (main) effects were not significant. The researcher appears vindicated in the proposition that graduates do not show the extremes that non-graduates show but the effect comes almost entirely from graduate introverts being less likely to feel uncomfortable than non-graduate introverts.

Glossary

Chi-square (χ^2)	Statistic used in tests of association between two unrelated categorical variables. Also used in goodness of fit test, log-linear analysis and several other tests
Chi-square change	Change in chi-square as items are removed from the saturated model in log-linear analysis
Cramer's phi or V	General statistic used to estimate effect size in chi-square analyses
Cross-tabs table	Term for table of frequencies on levels of a variable by levels of a second variable
Expected frequencies	Frequencies expected in table if no association exists between variables – i.e. if null hypothesis is true
Goodness of fit	Test of whether a distribution of frequencies differs significantly from a theoretical pattern
Hierarchical loglinear analysis	Removing items from a saturated log-linear model moving downwards towards one-way effects

Likelihood ratio chi-square | Type of chi-square statistic used in log-linear analysis

Log-linear analysis | Analysis similar to chi-square but which will deal with three-way tables or greater

Log-linear model | A theoretical and statistical structure proposed to explain cell frequency variation in a multi-way frequency table

Marginals | The total of columns and rows, and the overall total of frequencies, in a cross-tabs table

Observed frequencies | Frequencies obtained in a research study using categorical variables

Phi coefficient (Φ) | Statistic used for effect size estimate in a 2 x 2 table after χ^2 analysis

Saturated model | Model in log-linear analysis that explains all variation in a multi-way frequency table so that chi-square is zero and expected frequencies are the same as observed frequencies

Correlation – the association of measured variables

Correlation is the measurement of the extent to which pairs of related values on two variables tend to change together or 'co-vary'; it is a standardised measure of *co-variation*. If one variable tends to increase with the other, the correlation is *positive*. If the relationship is *inverse*, it is a *negative correlation*. A lack of relationship is signified by a value close to zero but a value of zero *could* occur for a *curvilinear* relationship. These relationships can be illustrated in a *scatterplot*.

Two major calculations for correlation are introduced.

- *Pearson's (r) product moment correlation* – based on variance in two sets of scores; r is high when large deviations are paired with large deviations and small with small.
- *Spearman's rho (ρ or r_s) rank correlation* – a Pearson calculation on the ranks of the values in the data set.

Important points about correlations are:

- *cause* cannot be inferred from the existence of a strong correlation between variables
- *strength* is a measure of the correlation but *significance* assesses how unlikely such a correlation was to occur under the null hypothesis (usually that the population correlation is zero). This assessment depends on the size of N. Under H_0 lower correlation values will occur with higher N
- sampling weaknesses may artificially increase or decrease a correlation coefficient – one particular phenomenon is the *restriction of range* caused by only correlating scores for certain categories of people, often only those available
- correlations for *dichotomous* variables are covered briefly (*point biserial* correlation, *biserial* correlation and the *phi coefficient*).

Common uses of correlation in psychology are:

- non-experimental studies on two measured variables
- reliability testing of scales, tests and questionnaires
- factor analysis
- twin studies
- the procedure of *regression analysis* estimates the best fit of a line through a scatter of related score pairs such that *residuals* (the differences between actual score and that predicted by the line) are minimised.

Multiple regression is used in the prediction of *criterion variable* scores from a set of *predictor variables*, particularly in practical and applied fields of psychology, such as personnel selection and educational assessments. It gives the best prediction possible of a criterion variable from this set of predictors.

The *multiple correlation coefficient* and *variance estimate* are explained, along with *partial* and *semi-partial correlation*, *regression coefficients* and *beta values*. Various data problems of multiple regression are considered – *normality, collinearity, hetero-scedasticity. Effect size* and *power* formulae are provided.

SPSS procedures for both correlation and multiple regression are included.

Simple correlation

The nature of correlation

Positive and negative correlations

Have a look at the following statements.

1 The older I get, the fewer things I remember.

2 The more you give kids, the more they expect.

3 Taller people tend to be more successful in their careers.

4 The more physical punishment children receive, the more aggressive they become when they're older.

5 Good musicians are usually good at maths.

6 People who are good at maths tend to be poor at literature.

7 The more you practise guitar-playing, the fewer mistakes you make.

These are all examples of relationships known as CORRELATION. In each statement it is proposed that two variables are related in the sense that, as one changes, so does the other in a predictable way. There are two directions in which this change might occur, producing what are known as *positive correlations* and *negative correlations*.

POSITIVE CORRELATIONS occur when one variable *increases* as the other increases. For instance:

• the further you walk, the more money you collect for charity

• the more papers you have to deliver, the longer it takes you.

Table 17.1 shows data on ten anonymised universities, which were selected from the *Guardian's* university guide for 2009 using a stratified random technique. There is a clear *positive correlation* here between the *Guardian's* teaching score and each of spend, job prospect and average A Level entry points.

University	Teaching score	Spend per student	Staff/student ratio	Job prospect score	A level entry score
A	92.9	9.1	12	86	511
B	73.4	8.5	13	73	427
C	66.4	6.7	16	75	338
D	62.7	6.4	14	72	382
E	60.1	5.6	13	68	377
F	55.6	5.5	16	60	261
G	52.8	3.8	19	61	256
H	49	4.3	20	52	257
I	44.4	4.8	20	55	232
J	34.9	3.7	19	42	197

Source: Guardian University Guide for 2009; rankings available at
http://image.guardian.co.uk/sys-files/Education/documents/2008/05/08/rankingsrevised.xls (Accessed 7.9.2008)

Table 17.1 University league table

NEGATIVE CORRELATIONS occur when one variable *decreases* as the other increases. For instance:

- as temperature increases, sales of woolly jumpers decrease
- the more papers you have to carry, the slower you walk.

In Table 17.1 we can see that, as teaching score, spend, job prospects and A level points go up so the staff /student ratio goes down – a *negative correlation* but by no means perfect in each case.

Someone once suggested the following memory 'hook' for negative correlation: 'as rain comes down so umbrellas go up', a common enough negative experience for British people! There is a more graphic example in Figure 17.1.

Figure 17.1 A perfect negative correlation between d1 and d2

Setting up a correlational study

It is fairly easy to see how we could check out the validity of statement 6 on p. 429. We could have a look at school class-test grades or exam results for people who have taken both subjects. To test statement 3 we have a straightforward measure of one variable (height) but how do we go about measuring the second variable, 'career success'? Do we measure only salary or should we include a factor of 'job satisfaction' – and with what sort of weighting? We would need to *operationalise* our variables.

The 'cases' in a correlation

Values may be paired because they belong to the same individual (for instance, maths and literature mark in class). Here the 'cases' are individuals. However, in some studies the 'cases' might be larger, more abstract units. In Table 17.1, university teaching scores are paired with other data – the 'cases' are whole universities. We can also take weeks as cases as when we pair average temperature for the week and the number of suicides in that week.

Pause for thought

The cases for the data portrayed in Figure 17.2 were residential areas in which samples of households were questioned. Each case then represents a different area sampled, from 'affluent suburban housing' to 'poorest council estates'. For each case there are two values – the number of families making 'frequent use' of red wine – and another number for their frequent use of some other household commodity. Can you guess what might be the mystery variable that decreases as consumption of red wine increases across areas? The more families use red wine, the less they use …. what? (Answer at the foot of this page.[1])

Consumption of red wine correlates negatively with what?

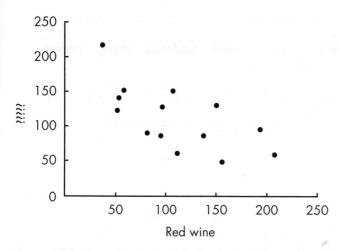

Figure 17.2 Consumption of red wine across various residential areas plotted against a mystery variable. Data from Argyle (1994)

[1] What varies negatively with red wine consumption? Consumption of brown sauce!

Measurement of a correlation

Statements like *'there is a correlation between severe punishment and later delinquency in young boys'* or *'severe punishment and delinquency in young boys tend to correlate'* are often made in theoretical literature. Actually, we would not accept these statements as valid unless the correlational relationships were at least *significant*. An important first step however is to establish the STRENGTH of a correlational relationship. There may be a *tendency* for general health to correlate with intelligence but this does not mean that every intelligent person is healthy or that all unhealthy people have low IQs. Strength refers to the degree to which this relationship holds throughout the population. It is possible for a quite weak correlation to be significant (if enough people are involved) and also possible for a strong correlation not to be significant. Hence, strength and significance are not the same thing.

We can calculate the *strength* of correlation between any two measurable variables under the sun so long as there is some way of pairing values. The calculation of correlation between two variables is a *descriptive measure*. We measure the 'togetherness' of the two variables. However, testing the correlation for significance is an *inferential* procedure. It tells us the probability of finding that level of 'togetherness' between our samples if there is no actual togetherness in the population.

The *strength* of the relationship between two variables is the degree to which one variable does tend to vary with the other. This strength is expressed on a scale ranging from –1 (perfect negative) through zero (no relationship) to +1 (perfect positive). The figure arrived at to express the relationship is known as a CORRELATION COEFFICIENT or COEFFICIENT OF CORRELATION, and is generically represented as *r*, though there are more specific symbols which we will introduce later on. It is not possible to obtain a coefficient less than –1 or greater than +1. If you do obtain such a value, there is a mistake somewhere in your calculations; the source of error can't be in your raw data, only in your processing of them. The interpretation of the correlation coefficient scale is, in general, as shown in Figure 17.3.

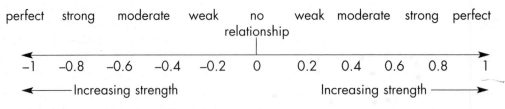

Figure 17.3 Measuring correlation from −1 to +1

Something might jar here. How can something getting more negative be described as getting stronger? Well it can. The sign simply tells us the *direction* of the relationship. The more negative the correlation, the *stronger* is the tendency for one variable to increase as the other decreases.

It is important to note here that the correlation coefficient (*r*) is not just a statistic (like *t* or x^2) that we calculate in order to see whether a relationship is significant. We *can* do this and we will discuss significance below. The correlation coefficient, however, is a descriptive statistic in its own right and is used to support theories or to help make practical decisions in applied psychology. For instance, a strong correlation between scores on an ability test and subsequent success in task learning might be used by occupational psychologists to select candidates for, say, flight training.

Warning for tests and exams!

It is very easy to call a negative correlation 'no correlation', probably because the two terms 'negative' and 'no' are sometimes equivalent, particularly among US service personnel in war films. Here, beware! *Negative* correlation means the two variables are inversely related. *Zero* correlation means there is no relationship *at all*.

Students also often write in reports something like 'There will be a positive correlation between high IQ and high self-esteem' which doesn't make sense. A correlation is a measure comparing *all* of one variable with all of another, not just parts of them. A positive correlation means that high scores will be paired with high scores *but also* low scores will be paired with low scores, so we should say *only* 'There will be a positive correlation between IQ and self-esteem'.

Scatterplots

A powerful graphical technique for demonstrating correlational relationships is the SCATTERPLOT. This plots pairs of values, one for variable A, the other for variable B, on a chart, thus demonstrating the scattering of paired values. The extent to which pairs of readings are not scattered randomly on the diagram, but do form a consistent pattern, is a sign of the strength of the relationship. I hope the scatterplots in Figure 17.4 to Figure 17.6 will demonstrate this. They represent fictitious data from one person taken after each trial on a simulated driving task. The trials represent an operational measure of practice – the greater the practice, the better the performance and the shorter the time taken. However, amount of practice is not related to amount spoken at all.

In the first example (Figure 17.4) we see that the marker for the pair of values 4 trials/105 points is placed on a vertical line up from 4 on the 'number of trials' axis and on a horizontal line from 105 on the 'points' axis. All points are plotted in this way. For number of practice trials/points we get a picture of a near-perfect positive correlation. For number of practice trials against time taken (Figure 17.5), a near-perfect negative correlation occurs. Notice that the pattern here is a mirror image of the positive correlation pattern. Negative correlation scatterplots run from top left to bottom right. For number of practice trials against number of words spoken throughout the trial (Figure 17.6) we get no correlation at all. The data here are all fictitious. However, some real data are plotted in Figure 17.7 and Figure 17.8 These are for the university data in Table 17.1. Note that each dot (or 'case') represents one university. A further negative correlation was plotted in Figure 17.2.

Regression lines

Do not be tempted to draw a 'line of best fit' on scatterplots. The 'best fit' line must be calculated mathematically and is known as a *'regression line'* (see p. 461). It has powerful properties but cannot be judged by eye. Regression is discussed later in this chapter.

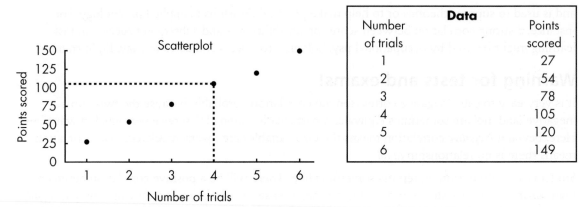

Data	
Number of trials	Points scored
1	27
2	54
3	78
4	105
5	120
6	149

Figure 17.4 Near-perfect positive correlation: number of practice trials by driving task score

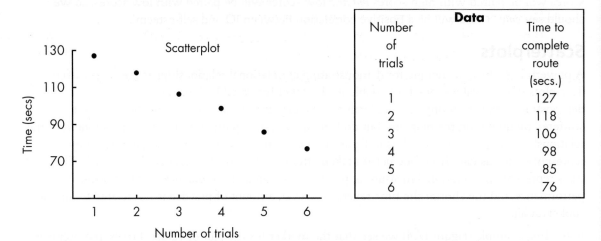

Data	
Number of trials	Time to complete route (secs.)
1	127
2	118
3	106
4	98
5	85
6	76

Figure 17.5 Near-perfect negative correlation: number of practice trials by time taken on driving task

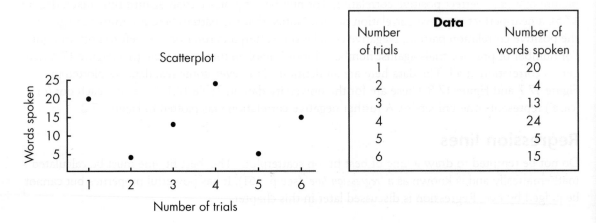

Data	
Number of trials	Number of words spoken
1	20
2	4
3	13
4	24
5	5
6	15

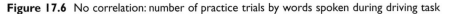

Figure 17.6 No correlation: number of practice trials by words spoken during driving task

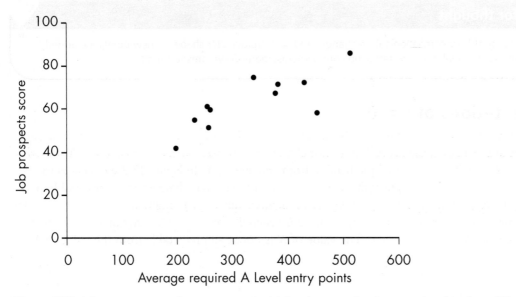

Figure 17.7 Job prospects score by average required A Level entry points for ten universities ($r_s = .89$)

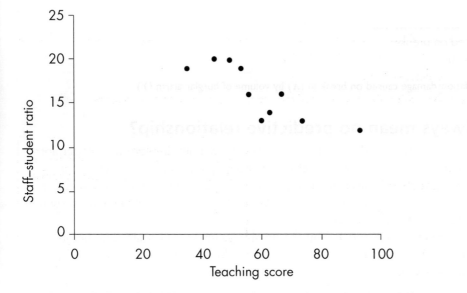

Figure 17.8 Staff/student ratio by teaching score for ten universities ($r_s = -.84$)

Interpretations of $r = 0$

Figure 17.6 shows no relationship at all between variable Y (number of words spoken) and variable X (amount of practice on the task). Y does not change in any way related to changes in X; or, we can say, changes in Y are not at all predictable from changes in X. In Figure 17.9 we have zero correlation because variable Y stays the same value no matter what changes occur in variable X. Y is predictable, but *not* from the value of X; it is predictable anyway. Y might be volume of a burglar alarm; X might be the amount of damage caused by each illegal entry. The only predictable event is that if there is an X there is also a Y. The value of X is not at all predictable from the value of Y.

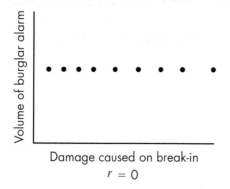

$r = 0$

Figure 17.9 No correlation: damage caused on break-in (X) by volume of burglar alarm (Y)

Does $r = 0$ always mean no predictive relationship?

If the size of r tells us the strength of the relationship, is there any point in plotting a scatterplot? Well, there are several patterned relationships that might show up on a scatterplot when our calculation of r gives us near zero. Instead of having the random relationship indicated in Figure 17.6, for instance, we might have the kind of CURVILINEAR RELATIONSHIP between variables shown in Figure 17.10. We could also obtain the reverse pattern, an upright 'U'. Here, although $r = 0$, there is a predictable relationship between X and Y. You should always inspect the scatterplot before carrying out a standard correlation analysis. If the relationship looks curvilinear then the assumption of LINEARITY between the two variables is said to be violated.

Now what might show this inverted U relationship? What about temperature and months of the year? Is there a good psychological example? An inverted U relationship usually occurs in the study of arousal and performance. When we are bored or unmotivated we do not perform so well on a task; when we are stimulated we can perform at our best, but if we are *over*-stimulated or over-anxious we may perform worse than our best.

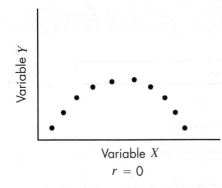

Variable X

r = 0

Figure 17.10 A curvilinear relationship between two variables

Exercises

1 Decide which of the proposed correlations (1–7) on p. 429 are positive and which are negative. Think of other examples of positive and negative correlation, in particular two of each from the psychological research you have studied so far.

2 Draw the scatterplot for the maths and music data in Table 17.5.

3 Can you think of relationships between variables (other than those mentioned above) which might be curvilinear?

4 If a student tells you she has obtained a correlation coefficient of 2.79, what might you advise her to do?

Answers

1 1 – negative; 2 – positive; 3 – positive; 4 – positive; 5 – positive; 6 – negative; 7 – negative

3 Perhaps size of audience and sports performance; no observers or very few might not stimulate a sportsperson; moderate numbers might stimulate more but large number might bring on serious 'nerves'. Think also of liking, fondness and social distance. Too close, perhaps too familiar; too far – unobtainable; but moderate distance?

4 Check her calculations – highest possible value for *r* is 1.

Correlation coefficients

The two most frequently used coefficients are:

Name	Symbol	Appropriate data level
Pearson's	*r*	Interval – a parametric test
Spearman's	*rho* or *ρ*	Ordinal – a non-parametric test

Pearson's product-moment correlation coefficient – interval level data

Pearson's correlation coefficient is the analysis of choice with simple interval level data and, like the *t* tests, needs its data to conform to parametric assumptions.

When to use Pearson's *r*		
Type of relationship tested	Level of data required	Design of study
Correlation between two variables	At least interval level	Related (pairs of data)

Note: The data should be drawn from near-normal distributions (see the check on p. 364). Data should be checked for extreme outliers (which could be errors) and for HETEROSCEDASTICTY explained on p. 471. If this latter effect is clear and extreme it would be safer to use a non-parametric equivalent – e.g. Spearman's *ρ*. The scatterplot should also be checked for *linearity*; i.e. not U-shaped (see above).

Pearson's correlation calculation is based on the idea of *dispersion*, in particular *deviations* from the mean in each group of data (check back to Chapter 11 if you need to revise these notions). Think of all scores in terms of their deviation from the group mean. If there is a strong correlation then when a person is far above the mean on one variable they should also be far above on the other. Hence they should have a large deviation score on one variable and a large deviation on the other variable also. Similarly, anyone way below the mean on one should be way below on the other, again with large deviations. The first two diagrams in Figure 17.11 show Rhiannon's deviations from the mean for tests in English comprehension and spelling. Poor old Hazel is similarly deviating *below* the mean on the same two tests. We would expect these results if there is a strong positive correlation between comprehension and spelling ability. In general, there should be a match between each person's deviation from the mean on both tests.

We now need to re-introduce a concept from Chapter 13, that of a *standard score*. What this means here is that instead of taking Rhiannon's *actual* deviation of, let's say, +10 on comprehension we take her *z* score; that's her deviation divided by the standard deviation – the number of standard

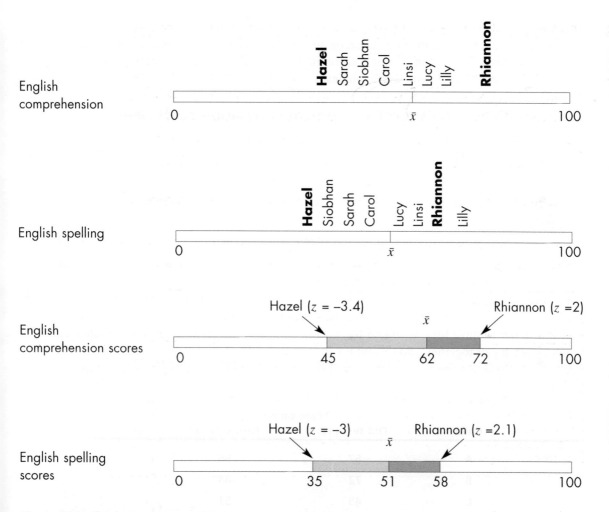

Figure 17.11 Deviations above and below the mean for English test takers

deviations she is from the mean. If the standard deviation for this test were five then Rhiannon would be 10/5 = 2 standard deviations above the mean; her z score would be +2.

The correlation coefficient is calculated by *multiplying* each person's z scores on the two variables that we are correlating, and finding the average of these results (see formula on p. 440).

With a strong positive correlation, like that shown in Figure 17.2, this multiplication will produce the highest figures; high positive deviations will be multiplied with high positives, and high negatives with high negatives. Both these multiplications produce high positive results. For Hazel on comprehension and spelling in Figure 17.11 it will be –3.4 x –3 = 10.2. For Rhiannon, we get 2 x 2.1 = 4.2. If the correlation is *not* strong then a high score on one variable might be paired with a middling score on the other and the multiplication will produce a lower result. Suppose, for instance, that we now correlate English comprehension with punctuation and there is no real connection between these two variables. Now high English scorers like Rhiannon may have an average punctuation score, so we get high positive deviation multiplied by a very small one. Hazel too might have a high negative deviation on spelling multiplied by a small z on punctuation. Hence *only* when high scorers on one variable score high on the other *and* low scorers on one variable score low on the other, do we get the highest values of r.

Calculating Pearson's product moment correlation coefficient

The grand title of this coefficient might make you feel that this could just be a little complicated … and you'd be right! There is, however, a simple way of starting out. The main formula for Pearson's r is:

$$r = \frac{\sum z_x z_y}{N-1}$$

where z_x is each person's z score on the X variable and z_y is their paired z score on the Y variable.

Here we see that for each person the two deviations (expressed as z values) are multiplied and then all the results are added. The final result is divided by degrees of freedom. The data in Table 17.2 are scores for seven children on old and new versions of a reading test. As a test of *concurrent validity* (see Chapter 8) we would expect the pairs of scores to correlate together. All we have to do, looking at our formula for r, is to find the z score for each child on each set of test scores, then multiply each pair together, add this lot up and divide by $N - 1$. If you have a statistical calculator, you can easily obtain the z values directly. If not, a version of Pearson's formula using raw scores is given further below.

Child	Score on test	
	Old test (X)	New test (Y)
A	67	65
B	72	84
C	45	51
D	58	56
E	63	67
F	39	42
G	52	50

Table 17.2 Children's scores on new and old reading tests

The calculation required for Pearson's r have been carried out in Table 17.3 where each z score on test X is multiplied by each z score on test Y and the result is seen in the far right-hand column. The sum of these (5.6) is shown at the bottom of the column and this figure is divided by $N - 1$ to give us a Pearson's correlation value of .929. From Appendix Table 9 we find that df for Pearson are $N - 2$. With 5 df an r of .929 is significant with $p \le .01$.

Score on old test (x)	Deviation from mean (d_x)	z_x $(=d_x/11.9)^*$	Score on new test (y)	Deviation from mean (d_y)	z_y $(=d_y/13.9)$	$z_x z_y$
67	10.4	0.87	65	5.7	0.41	0.36
72	14.4	1.29	84	24.7	1.78	2.29
45	−11.6	−0.97	51	−8.3	−0.6	0.58
58	1.4	0.12	56	−3.3	−0.24	−0.03
63	6.4	0.54	67	7.7	−0.55	0.3
39	−17.6	−1.48	42	−17.3	−1.24	1.84
52	−4.6	−0.39	50	−9.3	−0.67	0.26
					$\Sigma (z_x z_y) = 5.6$	

$\bar{x}$ = 56.6

s_x = 11.9

$\bar{y}$ = 59.3

s_y = 13.9

Note: *Chapter 13 tells you how to calculate z values. The formula is d/s. This is the number of standard deviations the score is from the mean – the deviation of the score divided by the standard deviation.

Table 17.3 Calculation of Pearson's r using z values* (data in Table 17.2)

Pearson's $r = \dfrac{\Sigma z_x z_y}{N-1} = \dfrac{5.6}{6} = .929$

Pearson calculation without finding z values

There is a complicated-looking formula for Pearson's r that can be used if you cannot or do not wish to calculate z scores or the standard deviations for each variable. Here it is!

$$r = \frac{N\Sigma xy - \Sigma x \Sigma y}{\sqrt{\left(N\Sigma x^2 - (\Sigma x)^2\right)\left(N\Sigma y^2 - (\Sigma y)^2\right)}}$$

With this formula you must be very careful indeed to distinguish between Σx^2 and $(\Sigma x)^2$.

Calculation of Pearson's *r* by hand using the last formula

Column: child number	A *x* (old test score)	B $(x)^2$	C *y* (new test score)	D $(y)^2$	E (xy)
A	67	4489	65	4225	4355
B	72	5184	84	7056	6048
C	45	2025	51	2601	2295
D	58	3364	56	3136	3248
E	63	3969	67	4489	4221
F	39	1521	42	1764	1638
G	52	2704	50	2500	2600
	$\Sigma x = 396$	$\Sigma x^2 = 23256$	$\Sigma y = 415$	$\Sigma y^2 = 25771$	$\Sigma xy = 24405$
	$(\Sigma x)^2 = 156816$		$(\Sigma y)^2 = 172225$		

Table 17.4 Calculation of Pearson without standard deviations (data in Table 17.2)

Calculating *r* if you have standard deviations

If you have standard deviations for each variable (simple to obtain on a statistical calculator), you can use the following alternative equation for Pearson's *r*:

$$r = \frac{\sum(x-\bar{x})(y-\bar{y})}{(N-1)s_x s_y}$$

On top are the deviations for each variable multiplied together and summed; below are the two standard deviations multiplied together and then multiplied by *N*–1.

As an exercise, now you could try calculating *r* using this equation and the data in Table 17.3. s_x and s_y are the 'unbiased estimate' versions of the standard deviations outlined in Chapter 11 – they use *N*–1 in the denominator.

Effect size and power for Pearson's *r*

The correlation coefficient is itself a measure of effect size. Cohen's (1988) interpretations for *r* were provided on p. 395 (.1 small; .3 moderate; .5 large). To obtain power estimates for Pearson's correlation coefficient *r*, Howell (1992) defines δ as $\delta = d\sqrt{(N-1)}$, hence our reading example above would give a δ of .929√6 = 2.28 and, from Appendix Table 4, power would be around .62 for α at .05. Note that, although we have a very large correlation, we only have a very small sample. With smaller samples, larger values of *r* are more likely to occur for the same two measures.

Reporting and interpreting the result

The new test scores correlate very highly with the old test scores and the degree of significance is also high. The result would be significant even with $p \leq .01$ Note also that, though we used a two-tailed value, one could argue for a one-tailed test since we would hardly be trialling a new reading test that would correlate negatively with the old one!

Reporting this correlation result

> The relationship between the old and new reading test was investigated with Pearson's product-moment correlation coefficient. There were no violations of normality or heteroscedasticity. The two sets of scores correlated strongly and positively, $r(5) = .93$, $p \leq .01$ Assuming an effect size of .93 power was estimated at only .62 due to the small sample size.

Spearman's *rho* (ρ) – non-interval data

> **When to use Spearman's ρ (also written r_s)**
>
> | Type of relationship tested | Level of data required | Design of study |
> |---|---|---|
> | Correlation between two variables | Ordinal level | Related (pairs of data) |
>
> **Note:** The Spearman formula below is a short-cut. The true Spearman's ρ or r_s is found by conducting a Pearson correlation on the ranks of the score values.
> ρ is the Greek letter r or *rho* and this is pronounced like 'row'.

As for the difference tests conducted earlier, there are times when the data we are using cannot be considered as valid interval-level data and/or one of the variables might be very skewed. In these cases we can use Spearman's ρ, a *non-parametric* measure of correlation which works with *ordinal-level data*. Spearman's ρ is the Pearson correlation coefficient that would occur if we used the *ranks* of the scores on the two paired variables as the data, rather than the scores themselves. Normally, for a strong correlation we expect that each person will score much the same value on one variable as they do on the other. It makes sense to say *also* that each person's *position* (i.e. their *rank*) on one variable will be similar to their position on the other. If your first psychology essay received the third highest mark in the class, you might expect that your second essay mark will also be close to third highest.

The rationale for the Spearman correlation coefficient is that *differences* between ranks will be small when there is a high positive correlation. If a class of psychology students took two class tests on one day, both tests based on the same material that should have been learned, then we would expect that people who have the higher ranks on one test should also have a high rank on the other test; people with a low rank on one should also receive a low rank on the other. This, then, means that the *difference* between each person's pair of ranks should be low or even zero, *if there is a strong correlation*.

Pause for thought

Before moving on, take a look at the rank differences and their squares in Table 17.5 (columns E and F). If we are expecting students to score about the same on both tests (a strong positive correlation between maths and music), what size would we expect these differences to be: large or small? What size would we expect (Σd^2) to be, then, if there is to be a strong positive correlation?

Student	A	B	C	D	E	F
	Maths mark	Music mark	Maths rank	Music rank	Difference between ranks (d)	d^2
John	58	68	4	5	−1	1
Julia	65	43	5	2	3	9
Jerry	75	64	7	3	4	16
Jean	37	65	1	4	−3	9
Jill	40	91	3	6	−3	9
Jonah	38	41	2	1	1	1
Jasmine	70	92	6	7	−1	1
						$\Sigma d^2 = 46$

Table 17.5 Class test results for maths and music

I hope you agree that, if there is to be a strong positive correlation between pairs of values, the differences between each pair of ranks (d) should all be small or zero. This will indicate that students are scoring at about the same position on both tests. Σd^2 should therefore also be small. Let's see how Spearman's approach incorporates this expectation.

Calculating Spearman's ρ

The formula for Spearman's correlation is:

$$\rho = 1 - \frac{6\sum d^2}{N(N^2-1)}$$

and we will go straight to the calculation on the data in Table 17.5.

Making sense of a formula

It should always be possible to look at a formula and see, at least in part, what it is doing – well, roughly! The right-hand part of the Spearman formula (to be subtracted from 1) has on top the value Σd^2. If the differences were all zero, then this value would also be zero; six times zero is zero so the top of the equation would have the value zero. Dividing anything *into* zero gives zero, hence the entire right-hand section to be subtracted from 1 becomes zero, and so our correlation is 1. This is the maximum value for a correlation coefficient signifying a perfect match of ranks. As the *d*s increase in value, so the right-hand side to be deducted from 1 becomes larger. If you create a set of values that make a perfect *negative* correlation, you'll find that the formula will give you the value −1. There's a little exercise for you!

Procedure	Calculation/result of steps
1 Give ranks to the set of *x* values (only)	See column C, Table 17.5
2 Give ranks to the set of *y* values (only)	See column D, Table 17.5
3 Subtract each *y* rank from its partner *x* rank	See column E, Table 17.5
4 Square each of the results of step 3	See column F, Table 17.5
5 Add the results of step 4	Total of column F $= \Sigma d^2 = 46$
6 Insert the result of step 5 into the formula for ρ given on p. 444 where N is the number of pairs of values in the data set	$\rho = 1 - \dfrac{6 \times 46}{7\,(7^2 - 1)} = 1 - \dfrac{276}{336} = .179$
7 Calculate ρ and consult Table 10 in the Appendix; ρ must be equal to or greater than the table value for significance	$\rho = \mathbf{.179}$; Critical value for $p \le .05$, two-tailed with $N = 7$ is .786; our value (.143) is not greater than the table value, hence the correlation is not significant.

Power: since Spearman is a Pearson correlation on ranks, the same procedure for power can be used as that given on p. 442.

Reporting the result

> A Spearman correlation on the maths and music scores showed no significant relationship with $\rho = .179$, $N = 7$, $p > .05$

When there are tied ranks

The Spearman formula above is technically for use only when there are no tied ranks. If ties occur, the formula is slightly inaccurate. If there are too many ties you should carry out the Pearson calculation long-hand on the ranks. In Table 17.5, for instance, we would calculate a Pearson correlation on the values in columns C and D. With ties, the resulting coefficient is a slightly more accurate Spearman's ρ. Actually, the difference between the result produced by the Spearman formula and that produced by using a Pearson on the ranks, even when there are quite a few ties, is slight. This is especially true when there are large samples.

When *N* is greater than 30

The table of critical values for ρ stops at $N = 30$. If *N* is larger than 30, ρ can be converted to a *t* value using:

$$t = \rho\sqrt{\frac{N-2}{1-p^2}}$$

t is then checked for significance with $N - 2$ degrees of freedom, as described in Chapter 15.

Pearson's *r* can also be converted with this formula.

Pearson's *r* or Spearman's ρ?

Being non-parametric, Spearman's ρ loses information from the data and sometimes may not be as sensitive in detecting significance as Pearson's *r*. This could lead to either Type I or Type II errors, depending on the data circumstances. However, it is easier to calculate and can be used on any data that can be ranked, whereas Pearson's *r* requires true interval-level data which pass normal distribution checks.

Significance and correlation coefficients

Now we turn to a familiar theme. Consider the correlation for maths and music scores in Table 15.5 (.179) and the correlation for the reading test results in Table 17.3 above (.929). I hope you'll agree that, whereas for maths and music it's pretty obvious that nothing much is going on in terms of a relationship, for the reading test scores it's equally obvious that there *is* a relationship which is not coincidental. The scatterplots in Figure 17.12 show this too.

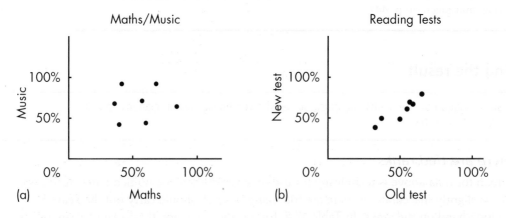

Figure 17.12 Scatterplots for maths/music data (Table 17.5) and old/new reading test scores (Table 17.2)

The theme is that we can tell when a correlation is obviously significant and we can tell when there is clearly no significance in the relationship. The big question is then: '*How do we decide when a coefficient of correlation becomes significant?*'

The null hypothesis for correlations

The discussion of significance in Chapter 14 centred mainly on differences. Here we are asking about the degree of *closeness* of a relationship between data on two variables. However, the underlying logic is basically the same. We must first assume that in the population there is *no* relationship and then see how unlikely it would be, on that basis, for our correlation value to occur.

Hence we assume the *null hypothesis* (H_0) that the population correlation is zero. The higher the value of r, the closer is the relationship and the less likely it is to occur at random under H_0.

Suppose we separated the two halves of 1000 raffle tickets and put one set of halves into a red bucket and the other halves into a blue bucket. Suppose, after completely shuffling the buckets, we then selected one ticket at random from the blue bucket and one random ticket from the red bucket. Now suppose we do this 20 times over. What we have done is to produce a random correlation for 20 pairs of values sampled from two populations whose real correlation is zero. For these buckets the null hypothesis is true, and this is what we assume when we check the correlation between 20 pairs of values for significance. We might, on one occasion, obtain a correlation coefficient of, say, .043. Now, finally, suppose we repeat the process just described many times over (or rather we let the computer do this for us while we slip off for a cup of tea). The distribution of correlation coefficients that we might then expect to obtain is shown by the unbroken line in Figure 17.13.

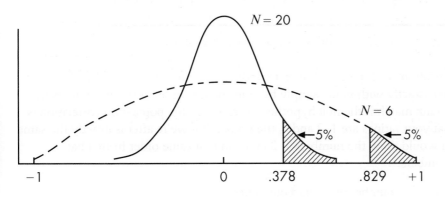

Figure 17.13 Distribution of random correlations under H_0 when $N = 6$ and $N = 20$

Following a by now familiar pattern, we find that if correlations are calculated between randomly paired data (H_0), many of them will be close to zero, either low positive or low negative, while not so many will be more extreme in value. The critical value for r will be found where the line cutting off the most extreme 5% (two-tailed) falls or where the right-hand 5% is cut off (one-tailed). Figure 17.13 shows that for $N = 20$ the top 5% is cut off where $r = .378$. For a one-tailed test, then, .378 would be the $p \leq .05$, one-tailed critical value. Remember this will *only* be for samples of size 20.

But surely a strong correlation must be significant?

It is very tempting to assume that a strong correlation is 'good' and therefore significant, whatever the circumstances. If we obtain a correlation coefficient of +1 how can this not be significant? The trouble is that we do not know the number of pairs of values the correlation is calculated from. As with the clinic that claimed 'success' when it allegedly helped four out of six couples to get the baby sex of their choice, we should not be impressed with a 'good' correlation when N is low; the odds are too high that a 'good' correlation will occur by chance alone (a Type I error). Let's demonstrate with an example.

Suppose we have obtained for some participants a piece of writing on 'Myself and my family'. You are to rate each piece for self-confidence, whereas I will rate them for warmth in the feelings expressed by each participant towards their parents and siblings. We are predicting that the two ratings will be positively correlated. We rate by placing the pieces of writing in rank order on our two variables. We rate three participants and get the results shown on the left-hand side of Table 17.6. We treat these as ordinal, ranked data.

Participant	Your ranking on self-confidence	My ranking on warmth	Rank orders I could have produced					
A	1	1	1	1	2	2	3	3
B	2	2	2	3	1	3	1	2
C	3	3	3	2	3	1	2	1

Table 17.6 Ranks of three participants on self-confidence and warmth in their writing

The strength of the correlation is +1, perfect, but is it statistically significant? How likely is it that my rankings would agree exactly with yours simply by coincidence? In other words, what is the probability of a perfect rank match if the null hypothesis is true that the population correlation is actually zero? Given that your ratings are 1, 2 and 3, the probability we're after is exactly the same as the probability that I would draw the numbers 1, 2 and 3 in that same order from a hat containing only these numbers.

Remember that probability is: $\dfrac{\text{number of desired outcomes}}{\text{number of possible outcomes}}$

We 'desire' only one specific outcome (my selection of 1, 2, 3 in that order). What is the number of *possible* outcomes? How many combinations *could* I have produced? Well there are only six possible orders that I could have produced and these are shown on the right-hand side of Table 17.6. The probability that I would produce the particular order I did (at random) is therefore 1/6. Expressed in the usual way, the probability (p) of this result occurring at random under H_0 was therefore .167. So if the null hypothesis is true and there is absolutely no relationship between warmth and self-confidence ratings, there is still a .167 chance of a 'perfect' correlation, produced at random, if I select a sample of only three, as there is *whenever* N is three. Even though the correlation is perfect in *strength*, this is not low enough to permit us to say that the correlation of +1 was *significant*. We require a p value less than .05 and therefore we must rate more participants than just three in order to have a possibility at all of a significant result.

What happens if there are four participants and our two sets of rankings match perfectly? The ranks one to four can be arranged in 24 different ways. Therefore, the probability of a perfect match under H_0 is now 1/24 and this gives $p = .042$ – a value low enough for significance, but only just!

As N increases, so the critical value for r decreases (a negative correlation in itself). The story is a familiar one. If we want to provide good evidence of a likely correlation for the population then we need to take a decent-sized sample. When N is five the critical value of correlation required for a significant r with $p \leq .05$ is .9; for $N = 6$ it is .829, as is shown in Figure 17.13 by the shaded area under the dotted line. If we had numbers 1 to 6 in two separate hats and drew one from each hat on a random basis to create six pairs, the probability of achieving a correlation between these pairs of more than .829 is .05 or less. We would a obtain a 'significant' correlation of .829 or more (by fluke) about one time in 20 that we performed this task.

Figure 17.13 also shows that if we had numbers 1 to 20 in two hats and we were perverse enough to repeat the same procedure very many times, we would obtain very much lower correlations than with $N = 6$ and would find that the value for r above which only 1 in 20 results would fall is as low as .378. Now .378 is *not* a strong correlation, though with $N = 20$ it would be significant. In fact, a glance at Table 9 in the Appendix will show you that with N above 100, correlations under .2 become significant. In fact, a correlation as low as .1 would be *highly* significant when N is as high as 2000. This is what is meant when you read in a newspaper report that there was a 'small but significant relationship' (for instance, between illnesses and the distance from transmitters or nuclear power plants).

Variance estimates – r^2

We have two problems now. One is that a rather low correlation coefficient can tell us that two variables are only weakly connected but to a significant degree. What does this weak relationship mean? What can we infer from it? The other problem is that correlation coefficients don't lie on a ratio scale. A correlation of .6 is not twice as 'good' or predictive as one of .3. One way of converting these figures to a ratio scale is to *square* the value of the coefficient, i.e. find r^2. Statisticians use this as a VARIANCE ESTIMATE, arguing as follows.

Any set of scores has variation within it – what we technically measure as *variance*. Suppose a correlation between self-esteem and peer approval ratings is .62. If r is .62 then r^2 is .384. .384 as a proportion of 1 is 38.4%. Now, the peer approval ratings have a value for variance; so do the self-esteem scores. It is argued that 38.4% of the variance in peer approval ratings is predictable from the variance in self-esteem scores. This might be a useful statistic for a job selection panel where approval of one's peers is an important criterion for success in the job being applied for. If we know a candidate's self esteem rating we can predict their peer approval rating – but only to a success level of 38%. The other 62% of variance is thought to be accounted for either by other variables (such as attractiveness, ability etc.) or by random factors.

As another example of variance estimation, suppose you heard of a study that showed a correlation of .43 between amount of physical punishment given to a child (assessed by observation and interview, say) and a measure of aggression in the child. The variance estimate would be $.43^2 = .18$ and you could assume that 18% of the variation in aggression among the children studied was linked with ('explained by') the variation in the amount of physical punishment they had received.

However, tempting though it might seem, using *only* the results of a correlation, we can't say that the punishment *causes* the aggression, only that the two are linked (it seems unfeasible but it *could* be that children who are naturally more aggressive '*cause*' more hitting by their parents). The term 'explained by' must be treated with caution. In statistical work it means merely that one set of values is predictable from another. One of the most seductive uses of statistics is to imply that a cause has been demonstrated when we *only* have a statistical relationship between two variables, an issue that we go on to consider in a later section.

SPSS procedures for correlation

Let's suppose an occupational psychologist has gathered data on 26 employees and has measures of age, health status, health attitude, ambition, work absences, anxiety and work productivity. We might assume that productivity would be negatively related to absence and possibly to anxiety too. The first step would be to check the variables for normality – see p. 319 – and for linearity and

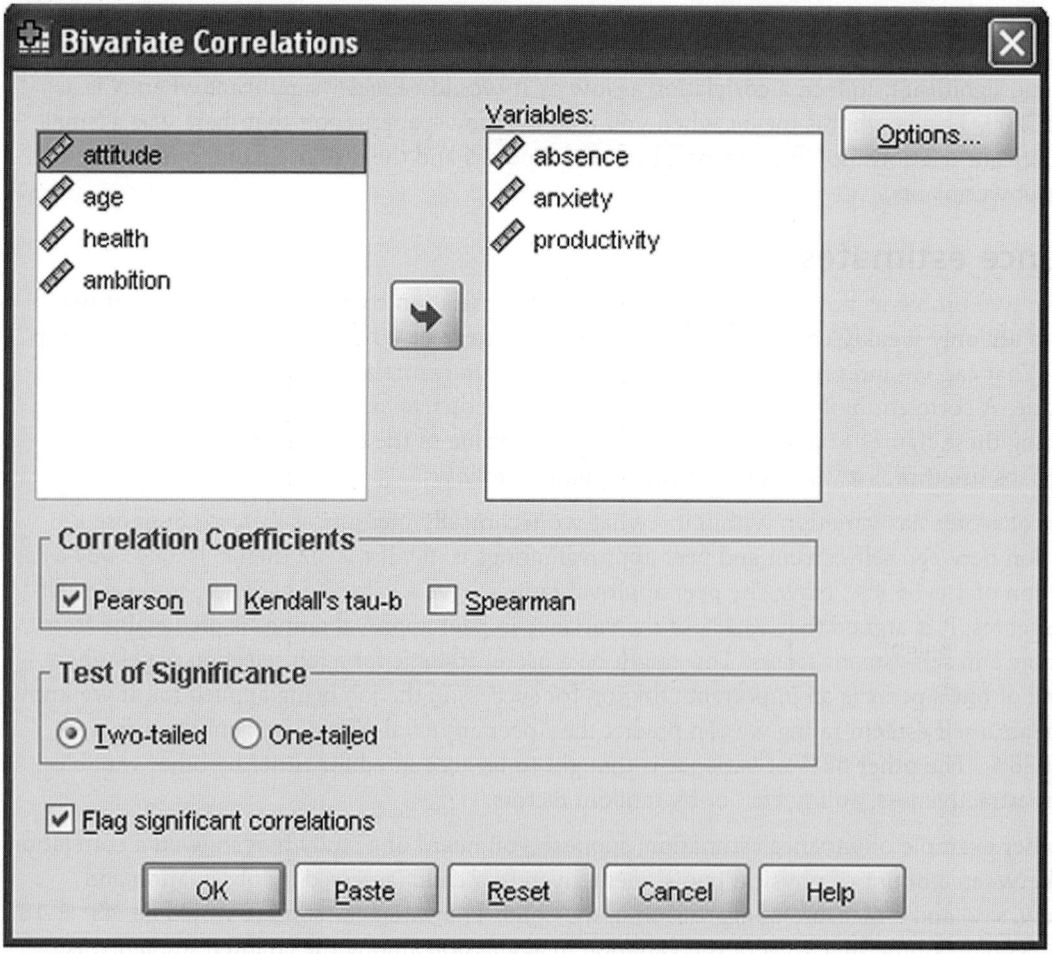

Figure 17.14 Correlation dialogue box in SPSS

heteroscedasticity as explained a little later. To conduct a correlation analysis:

1 Select **Analyze/Correlate/Bivariate**.
2 Select the variables to be correlated and move them over to the **Variables** box.
3 **Note** that you can move as many variables over as you like; in the example below we have decided to find all correlations between *absence, anxiety* and *productivity* – Figure 17.14.
4 Select **Pearson** or **Spearman** as desired and appropriate (you may select both), and use **Options** to deal with any missing values and to obtain descriptive statistics. Click **Continue**.
5 Click **OK**.

The output (without descriptives) gives a matrix of correlations…and double the information required! If you have correlated just two variables you will see a four-box display where you need only consult the top right-hand box. The output for our example is shown in Figure 17.15. The top-left box is redundant since it is the correlation of *absence* with itself which is automatically perfect at +1. In the second top row box we see that the correlation of *absence* with *anxiety* is $r = -.065$, a result extremely close to zero, and of course not significant with p at .753. The correlation of *absence* with *productivity* gives a moderate negative correlation, $r = -.471$ and SPSS has flagged this as significant with $p = .015$. In the next row we get the final combination of *anxiety* with *productivity* producing, eerily, exactly the same as its correlation with *absence* $r = -.065$; the slight difference in significance value is because the correlation figures have been rounded to three decimal places and are not *exactly* equal.

Correlations

		absence	anxiety	productivity
absence	Pearson Correlation	1.000	−.065	−.471*
	Sig, (2–tailed)		.753	.015
	N	26.000	26	26
anxiety	Pearson Correlation	−.065	1.000	−.065
	Sig, (2–tailed)	753		.751
	N	26	26.000	26
productivity	Pearson Correlation	−.471*	−.065	1.000
	Sig, (2–tailed)	.015	.751	
	N	26	26	26.000

* Correlation is significant at the 0.05 level (2-tailed)

Figure 17.15 Output in SPSS when correlating three variables: absence, anxiety and productivity

What you can't assume with a correlation

Cause and effect

Pause for thought

See if you can detect flaws in the following statements.

Research has established a strong correlation between the use of physical punishment by parents and the development of aggression in their children. Parents should not use this form of discipline, then, if they don't want their children to end up aggressive.

There is a significant correlation between early weaning and later irritability in the infant, so don't hurry weaning if you want a good-tempered child.

Poverty is correlated with crime, so if you can achieve a higher income, your children are less likely to become law-breakers.

The statements above all assume that the first variable mentioned is a cause of the second, even though *all* that has been shown is a *correlation* between the two variables. When we say that A correlates with B it is easy to assume that A is a *cause* of B. A study, mentioned on p. 119 and reported in the *Guardian* ('Loneliness of virtual living', 31 August 1998), was concerned with the relationship between Internet use and depression. The authors assumed that Internet use was a *cause* of depression but, being conscientious researchers, they reported only correlations with the *speculation* that Internet use might cause depression. The *Guardian* reporter was not so careful, however. Some way into the article the following phrase occurred: ' … one hour a week on the internet led to an average increase of 1 per cent on the depression scale, …'. The key words here are *'led to'*. It was perfectly possible that increases in depression *led to* greater use of the internet.

The ABBA gambit – for use in tests and exams

When confronted with a correlation and asked about the interpretation always remember the ABBA gambit. If it is suggested that A causes B then try the reversal – could B cause A? Does physical punishment cause aggression or does aggression in the child induce more physical punishment from parents? Does Internet use cause depression or does depression cause more internet use? Does anxiety cause more errors or do more errors increase anxiety? With any significant correlation there are several possible interpretations:

1 Variable A has a causal effect on variable B.

2 Variable B has a causal effect on variable A.

3 A and B are both related to some other linking variable(s).

4 We have a Type I error (i.e. a fluke coincidence and there is no real correlation in the population).

Interpretations 1 to 3 are presented visually in Figure 17.16. A good example of interpretation 3 would be the perfect correlation of two adjacent thermometers. The common factor causing both to vary together is, of course, heat – one thermometer cannot affect the other. Both use of physical punishment and aggression in children may be a product of the same environment. Physical punishment may not cause aggression, nor may aggression cause physical punishment; the two variables may be correlated because both tend to occur in certain environments and not in others. Where the norm is to hit children, the environment may also produce aggression; where people use reason and sanctions, children may *also* be taught to be non-aggressive. Sometimes the direction of a correlation is obvious; increasing temperatures are related to higher ice-cream sales but buying ice-creams can hardly affect the weather!

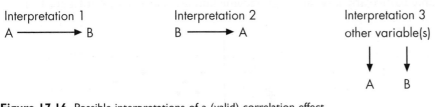

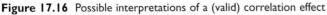

Figure 17.16 Possible interpretations of a (valid) correlation effect

When cause is more likely

1. The prior variable

One variable may be prior to the other. For instance, if tall people were found to be more successful, success could hardly have affected their height. It may, of course, make them 'walk tall' and it certainly affects others' perception of their height, as shown by US research indicating that people consistently tend to overestimate the winning candidate's height in presidential elections. However, later success can't influence the genetic blueprint for the physical development of height. Interpretation 3 is possible, however. Other genetic qualities of tall people might contribute to success in later life, not the height factor itself.

2. In experiments

In a non-experimental correlation between two measured variables it is hazardous to claim that one of the variables is the cause of the other, as with the Internet example just considered. However, in a controlled laboratory experiment we can manipulate sleep deprivation and task learning. We can then correlate number of hours since last sleep (independent variable) with errors made on a maze-learning task (dependent variable) and, if a significant correlation occurs, assume that sleep deprivation is a cause of the errors observed.

Similarly we might display words at varying brief intervals and measure the number recognised correctly each time. Here we can be more confident that A causes B, even though we've used a correlation. The correlation simply serves a statistical purpose – it demonstrates common variation between the independent variable and the dependent variable. In this example, as display period increases, so does the number of words correctly recognised. The design is still experimental. We can make the same assumptions we make in a traditional two-condition experiment about the independent variable affecting the dependent variable. Since the independent variable is altered first, the dependent variable can't be causing changes in the independent variable, though, of course, a confounding variable is still not ruled out.

The missing middle

By selecting only certain groups to be included in a correlational study (an issue known as RANGE RESTRICTION), a researcher could appear to demonstrate a strong correlational effect. For instance, a strong correlation might be announced between financial status and unwanted pregnancies – the lower the status the higher the number of unwanted pregnancies. This could be used politically, either to blame the poor for a higher birth rate (along with the sin of being poor) or for a campaign against low incomes and for better sex education. The actual facts, however, may have been obscured by biased sampling of only particularly low- and high-income families. Have a look at Figure 17.17.

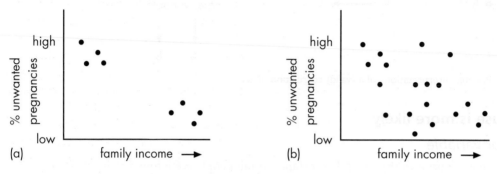

Figure 17.17 Unwanted pregnancies by financial status – two versions

The selective samples drawn in Figure 17.17 (a) may show a strong correlation, but the more representative sample in Figure 17.17 (b) may not. An opposite effect may occur when the range is restricted in a different way – the 'range' meaning the whole possible continuum of scores on either variable. Suppose a company employed an occupational psychologist to help select candidates for posts using a battery of psychometric tests, the results of which are compared with the productivity of those employed after one year in the job. For this correlation the psychologist can use *only* those who passed the entry criteria and were given employment. These would be those people represented on the right-hand side of Figure 17.18. Since there is no obviously strong

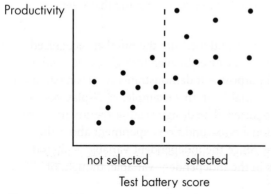
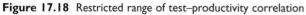

Figure 17.18 Restricted range of test–productivity correlation

correlation for these data, the psychologist might conclude that the test does not predict later productivity. However, had it been possible to measure the productivity after one year of *all* candidates, including those rejected, the correlation would have been a lot stronger.

Correlation when one variable is categorical

In general, if one variable is a purely *category*-type measure, then correlation cannot be carried out, unless the variable is DICHOTOMOUS (two exclusive values only, like male/female). We will deal with this special case later on. For now, consider the data in the first two columns of Table 17.7. The first column gives a make of car and the second a rating given in a survey of the trustworthiness of the typical owner of that kind of car. Suppose a student said that they'd like to 'correlate car type with trustworthiness ratings of their owner'. The trouble here is that the variable of car type is *categorical* or *nominal*. We can't *order* the car types meaningfully (unless cost is relevant, in which case we could rank the cost prices). The correlation of car type with average rating can't be carried out as the data stand. Often students put car type into a program like SPSS and give each car type a *code* (e.g. '1' for 'Vauxhall', '2' for 'BMW', and so on). The trouble with numbers is that they are seductive. They *look* like values but here they are not; they are just *names*. BMW is not double a Vauxhall. SPSS won't ask questions either so you *could* end up with a supposed correlation between car type code and trustworthiness rating. This 'correlation' would be absolutely meaningless. This is an extremely common error made by students trying to design their own research project. I have seen students struggling to make sense of a 'correlation' between attitude to social welfare benefits (a genuine measured variable) and the codes 1 – 'Single mother', 2 – 'Unmarried childless', 3 – 'Married mother with partner' and 4 – 'Divorced, no children'. Here '4' is not twice '2'.

Typical variables that *cannot* be correlated (unless a rational attempt to order categories is made) are: *marital status (single, married etc.), ethnicity, place of residence (town, village etc., or house, flat etc.), handedness, sexuality, degree subject* and so on.

Car owned	% rating on trustworthiness	N	Number above mean	Number below mean
			(Trustworthiness mean = 58.99)	
Vauxhall	78	12	8	4
BMW	65	15	9	6
Ford	51	14	6	8
Citroen	62	17	9	8
Porsche	49	21	7	14
Jaguar	56	16	7	9
Totals		95	46	49

Table 17.7 Type of car owned by trustworthiness rating

What *can* we do with categorical data?

Recall from Chapter 16 that χ^2 was called a test of association. As we've seen in this chapter, correlation is also a measure of association between two variables. What we can do with nominal/categorical data, such as that in Table 17.7, is reduce the measured variable to nominal level and conduct a χ^2 test on the resulting frequency table. This is only possible, however, where you have gathered several cases in each category. Imagine that 12 people assessed the Vauxhall owner with an *average* trustworthiness rating of 78%; 15 people averaged 65% on the BMW owner, and so on. We can find the overall mean trustworthiness rating (58.99 in Table 17.7) and, for each car category, record how many judgements were above and below this mean. These fictitious frequencies are shown on the right-hand side of Table 17.7. We could now proceed with a 2 x 6 χ^2 test – six rows of car types and two columns of trustworthiness, 'above mean' and 'below mean' as on the right of Table 17.7.

Correlation with a dichotomous nominal variable – the point biserial correlation

We said above that on special occasions we *can* correlate using a dichotomous variable. The special case is when one variable is categorical and has just two all-inclusive values. Examples would be male/female, car owner/non-car owner, and so on. Here, we may give an arbitrary value according to membership of the categories, e.g. '1' for car owner and '2' for non-owner. We might be attempting to correlate car ownership (either a person owns or they do not) with scores on an environmental attitude questionnaire. We would proceed with the Pearson correlation as usual. Each person has a (measured) score on the attitude questionnaire and a code (1 or 2) for car-ownership. The point biserial correlation is written as r_{pb}. This value can be turned into an ordinary *t* using the formula on p. 446, which turned correlation into a *t* value. Significance is then found using $df = N - 2$. This may sound like a cheat because we emphasised earlier that Pearson's was a parametric type of statistic and that the level of measurement should be at least interval. This is true only if you want to make certain assumptions from your result about underlying populations, which are mostly too complex for the level of this book. We will mention this again briefly, though, when looking at the assumptions underlying multiple regression.

To check this works, try calculating r_{pb} and the resulting *t* value, using columns 1 and 2 of Table 17.7. We need to reduce column 1 to an all-inclusive dichotomous variable. Give value 1 to each of the 'Luxury' cars (BMW, Porsche, Jaguar) and value 2 to the remaining 'Non-luxury' cars. Correlate the values on this variable (call it car status) with values on the trustworthiness variable. You should find that $r = .359$. Now find *t* using the formula on p. 446 (correlation conversion). Next, calculate an independent *t* test on the same two groups. You should find that the *t* values are exactly the same at 0.769.

This should not really be surprising. Looking at the extent to which luxury or non-luxury car owners are *associated* with high or low trustworthiness values is the same thing as looking at the *difference* in trustworthiness scores for luxury and non-luxury car owners. The latter analysis is in fact a more sensible analysis to perform than using correlation when you have a two-value categorical variable. The fact that this correlation *can* be performed, however, is important in the use of *multiple regression* covered later.

Truly or artificially dichotomous? – The biserial correlation coefficient

In some cases the dichotomous variable is one that has been *reduced* from what was once interval level. Here the dichotomous variable is said to be 'artificial' (rather than 'true') because there is an interval scale lying underneath. If you wish to calculate a correlation where one of the variables is formed into this sort of dichotomy, with a normally distributed variable lying underneath (but you must be relatively sure of this), then you could use the BISERIAL CORRELATION COEFFICIENT. This would occur where, for instance, you could categorise participants as *above* or *below* the population IQ mean of 100. You might correlate this division with self-esteem scores. You would calculate the r_{pb} as we did above then use this result in the following formula:

$$r_b = \frac{r_{pb}\sqrt{p_1 p_2}}{y}$$

p_1 is the proportion of people falling into the lower category of the dichotomous variable (e.g. 60% of participants below 100 would be .6) and p_2 is the proportion in the upper category. y is the height of the normal distribution (the 'ordinate') at the point where z divides the distribution into the proportions of p_1 and p_2. To get this last value you need z tables that include the ordinate. Here is an Internet site that does. http://academic.udayton.edu/gregelvers/psy216/tables/area.htm. It is safer to use r_{pb} where you are unsure of the normality of the distribution underlying the dichotomous variable.

Both truly dichotomous – the phi coefficient

If the dichotomies for two variables are both 'true', however (such as male/female and employed/not-employed), there is a correlation for these. Values for both variables can be given two arbitrary values, e.g. 1 and 2, and a Pearson calculated again. The result is called Φ, the PHI COEFFICIENT (which we met in Chapter 15), and significance is even easier to test with this one because we get $\chi^2 = N\Phi^2$ and we check in the usual way using $1df$. The resulting χ^2 is the same value we'd get from a 2 x 2 χ^2 calculation on the data.

As we said just above, the reason for using correlation in these cases, rather than the more usual difference test or chi-square analysis, is mainly to do with more advanced analyses, such as *multiple regression*, where we may want to use *several* correlations together and we may have a few categorical variables.

Common uses of correlation in psychology

Apart from the several uses already described, there are particular areas of research where a correlation is especially useful and popular.

Non-experimental studies

By far the most common use of correlation is in the sort of study where a sample is drawn and two variables are measured that already exist, i.e. the study is non-experimental. Examples have been given in this chapter but others might be: amount smoked and anxiety level; attitude on sexism and attitude on racism; locus of control and stress felt in job. This is why non-experimental studies are sometimes referred to as 'correlational' but, as I said in Chapter 5, this can be misleading because not all such studies use correlation, and correlation may be used in experiments.

Reliability

When testing for reliability, the test/re-test method (see p. 194) would involve taking a set of measurements on, say, 50 people at one time, then re-testing the same people at a later date, say six months later. Then we perform a correlation between the two sets of scores. Similarly, correlation is used in a split-half reliability test which makes a comparison between two halves of a test or between two *parallel forms* of the test (see Chapter 8). Tests between raters (people who rate) or observers for their reliability of judgement also use correlation.

Twin studies

Identical twins (and, to some extent, fraternal twins) form an ideal matched pairs design. Very often, scores for twin pairs are correlated. This is of particular use in heritability estimates and is relied on very heavily in the IQ inheritance debate, where, for instance, a strong correlation between twins reared apart provides strong evidence for a genetic contribution. The main difficulty with this approach though is that of finding separated identical twins whose environmental backgrounds are entirely *un-* correlated. Often it turns out the twins have been reared in sections of the same family or at least in environments selected by adoption agencies to be as similar as possible, thus providing similar environment as an alternative explanation of correlations between the twin pairs.

Factor analysis

This uses a matrix of all correlations possible between several tests (a 'battery') taken by the same individuals. Factors statistically derived from the analysis are said to 'account for' the relationships shown in the matrix (see p. 190).

Path analysis

Path analysis has been an increasingly popular analytic tool in recent decades of psychological research, particularly in the applied area. We have said many times that correlation, common in research outside the laboratory, has the strong disadvantage of being ambiguous in interpretation. For instance, does academic motivation influence academic success or vice versa? A mere correlation between these two variables will not give us an answer. However, in path analysis the correlations between several or even many variables are analysed *collectively* using some of the techniques we are about to encounter with *multiple regression*. In path analysis a *model* is created which gives good account of all the inter correlations between variables but which also has internal coherence. As an extremely simple example we might find that academic motivation correlates moderately with job satisfaction but also with academic success and that academic success correlates well with job satisfaction. The connections in Figure 17.19 suggest possible causal links between these variables. Path analysis might demonstrate that the .4 correlation between academic motivation and job satisfaction can be mostly explained by the indirect link of academic motivation's correlation with education achievement and this variable's correlation with job satisfaction. Path analysis is able to use correlations and partial correlations (introduced in multiple regression) to *suggest* a model to explain all relationships between variables. It cannot show the model *must* be true, only that the model is feasible and, at present, superior to any other so far suggested. Manfredi, Cho, Crittenden and Dolecek (2007) for instance, were able to present a model which accounted for quitting smoking using the variables of education, being a single mother, being African American, pregnancy and exposure to a smoking cessation programme. These background variables had effects which were more or less mediated by stress, social pressure, level of health concern, self-efficacy, confidence and motivation and by plans to quit and recent actions concerning quitting. Among many other complex relationships they were able to suggest that social pressure to quit has a direct effect on quitting whereas health concerns affect actions towards quitting which in turn increase the immediacy of plans to quit and finally plans to quit have a direct effect on quitting.

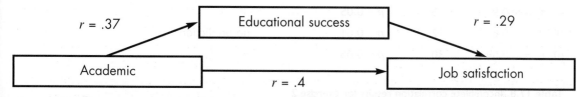

Figure 17.19 Path analysis model accounting for current salary

Exercises

1 From an article in the *Times Educational Supplement* (3 June 1988):

... teaching the sound and shape of letters can give pre-school children a head start ... children who performed best at the age of seven tended to be those who had the most knowledge and understanding of the three Rs at the age of four.

In the case of reading, the strongest predictor of ability among seven-year-olds was 'the number of letters the child could identify at the age of four-and-three-quarters' ... Tizard concludes that nursery teachers should give more emphasis to literacy and numeracy skills ...

(a) What conclusion, other than the researcher's, could be drawn from the last paragraph of the passage?

(b) Briefly describe a study that could help us decide between these alternative interpretations.

(c) What sort of correlation would the researchers have found between number of letters identified at four and number of reading errors at seven – positive or negative?

(d) Suppose the correlation between adding ability at five and mathematical ability at seven was .83. How would you describe the strength of this coefficient?

(e) What level of significance would the (Pearson) correlation of .83 be at (two-tailed) if the sample of children had numbered 33?

2 Several students in your group have carried out correlations, got their results, know what significance level they need to reach, but have sadly forgotten how to check in tables for significance. They agree to do calculations on your data if you'll just check their results and tell them whether to reject or retain their null hypotheses. The blank column in Table 17.8 is for you to fill in. Assume one-tailed tests where a direction has been predicted.

Coefficient obtained H_0?	$N =$	Significance level required	Direction predicted	Retain or reject
a) $r = 0.3$	14	$p \leq 0.01$	no prediction	
b) $r = -0.19$	112	$p \leq 0.01$	no prediction	
c) $r_s = 0.79$	7	$p \leq 0.05$	no prediction	
d) $r = 0.71$	6	$p \leq 0.05$	no prediction	
e) $r_s = 0.9$	5	$p \leq 0.05$	+	
f) $r = 0.63$	12	$p \leq 0.01$	no prediction	
g) $r = 0.54$	30	$p \leq 0.05$	−	

Table 17.8 Incomplete correlation results for exercise 2

3 Spearman's correlation may always be used instead of Pearson's. Is the reverse of this true? Please give a reason.

4 A researcher correlates participants' scores on a questionnaire concerning 'ego-strength' with measures of their anxiety level obtained by rating their verbal responses to several pictures. Which measure of correlation might it be safest to employ?

5 Another student friend has carried out a practical project in which she asked people whether they went to state school, private school, public school or some other type of school. She also asked them to fill out her attitude-to-study questionnaire. She now wishes to correlate these two sets of data. What would you advise her to do?

Answers

1 (a) Early letter recognition at four years old *correlated* with reading ability at seven years old, but may not have *caused* the superior reading. It may be the general home environment that affects both early letter recognition and seven-year-old reading ability. Encouraging the recognition of letters may not automatically lead to an increase in reading ability at seven.

(b) Could take experimental group at age four, matched with a control group, and train for letter recognition. Then follow through to seven and compare groups on reading. Could also attempt to balance out all conceivable third factors (thought possibly to cause both better letter recognition at four and better reading at seven), then follow groups from four to seven on reading.

(c) Negative.

(d) Strong/very strong.

(e) $p \leq .001$

2 (a) Retain (b) Retain (c) Reject (d) Retain (e) Reject (f) Retain (g) Retain (wrong direction).

3 No. For Pearson, data must meet parametric requirements.

4 Spearman, since human judgement ratings used. Measures not standardised. Pearson if normality of data is established.

5 Her school type variable is categorical so a correlation cannot be conducted. She can:

(a) collapse her attitude data into two groups (e.g. above/below median) and calculate chi-square. She can collapse school types if there are not enough in any category

(b) collapse the school categories into two groups (e.g. state vs private) and calculate a point biserial correlation *or* run an unrelated *t* test of difference

(c) calculate a one-way ANOVA (see Chapter 18) using the four types of schooling as the four levels of the independent variable and the attitude score as dependent variable.

Regression and multiple regression

Regression

Regression (rather than 'correlation') is the term used when we have the specific aim of predicting values on a 'criterion' (or 'target') variable from a 'predictor' variable. For instance, your psychology tutors might correlate students' numeracy scores on joining the course with their grades in examinations one year later. The tutors are conducting research in order to highlight factors that would help them raise their students' pass levels. Tutors do very many things in between the times when they are seen in a classroom! A simplified version of the scatterplot for this research is shown in Figure 17.20 which, in the terminology of regression, gives us *the regression of exam grades upon numeracy scores*.

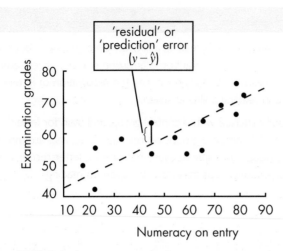

Figure 17.20 End-of-year exam grades by numeracy on enrolment

Remember that the square of the correlation coefficient gives us an estimate of the variance in y explained by variance in x. Because there is a correlation between numeracy score and exam grade we can, to a certain extent, dependent on the size of r^2, *predict* exam grades from numeracy scores. This is done by using a REGRESSION LINE, which is the line of 'best fit' placed among the points shown on our scatterplot. On this line will lie all our *predicted values* for y, symbolised as $\hat{y}$, made from our knowledge of the x values. The vertical line shown on the chart between an actual y value and its associated $\hat{y}$ value is known as a PREDICTION ERROR but is better known as a RESIDUAL because it represents how wrong we are in making the prediction for that particular case – the error 'left over'. The regression line, then, is a line that *minimises* these residuals. The calculations involved are somewhat complex and involve the use of calculus. However, for those readers with a vague memory of school algebra, you might remember that the equation of a straight line can be written as:

$$\hat{Y} = bx + c$$

$\hat{Y}$ is the *predicted* value of exam grade (whereas y is an actual value). b is known as the REGRESSION COEFFICIENT. c is a constant value. In fact, it is the value of $\hat{Y}$ when x is zero. Statistical programs and statistical calculators will kindly calculate b and c for us from a set of data pairs. In our example, b has the value 0.318 and c is 42.5 The regression coefficient has a particular message for us – it is the number of units $\hat{Y}$ increases for every unit increase in x. In this case, exam grade increases by 0.318 of a mark for every point more that is scored on numeracy. If we now put any value for x (numeracy) into the equation, we get the best prediction ($\hat{Y}$) we can for the actual value of y (exam grade), given the data set we are working with. In regression we also deal with standard scores rather than raw scores. A standard score, you may recall, is a raw score expressed as the number of standard deviations it is from the mean – see p. 312. When scores (x and y) are expressed in standard score form then the regression coefficient is known as the STANDARDISED REGRESSION COEFFICIENT or BETA. Where there is only one predictor, beta is in fact the ordinary correlation coefficient of x with y, with which we are already familiar.

Multiple predictions

Suppose our tutors have information not only on initial numeracy but also on each student's motivation, on their satisfaction with the year's teaching and so on. We have seen that values on one variable can be used to predict values on another. The tutors may think 'Well, if all these variables predict end-of-year exam grade to some extent, what a pity we can't *combine* all the regression coefficients and predict exam grade from the *combination* of predictor variables.' Well, we can. This is exactly what MULTIPLE REGRESSION is used for.

Multiple regression can be used when we have a set of variables (x_1, x_2, x_3 etc.) each of which correlates to some known extent with a criterion variable (y) for which we would like to predict values (see Figure 17.21). Although we are usually concerned with non-experimental designs in using regression, the predictor variables are sometimes called 'independent variables' and the criterion or target variable the 'dependent variable', especially in SPSS. Note also that from here on, for convenience, where we want to refer to *several* predictors we will use the symbol x_i generically to mean 'the xs' or 'any x'.

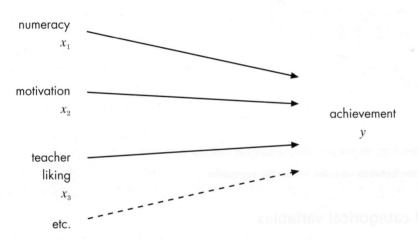

Figure 17.21 Predicting exam grades from several predictor variables in multiple regression

In Figure 17.22 (a) we see a representation of the situation when two variables vary together to some extent. The shaded portion represents the amount of variance they share in common, and this is r^2. In Figure 17.22 (b) the big shaded oval represents the variance of our students' scores on the end-of-year exam, the variance that the tutors would like to be able to 'explain' or predict. The overlap of numeracy with exam grade represents the variance in exam grade 'explained' by its correlation with numeracy. Other predictor variables, such as teaching satisfaction and motivation, will also correlate with exam grade and therefore also overlap with common variance.

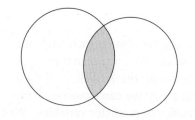

(a) Co-variation of two variables (shaded portion is the shared variance)

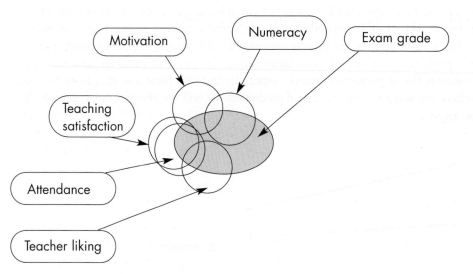

(b) Predicting exam grades from several predictor variables in multiple regression

Figure 17.22 Co-variation between variables in multiple regression

Continuous and categorical variables

Because multiple regression has so much to do with correlation it is important that the variables used are continuous – that is, they need to incorporate measures on some kind of *linear scale*. As we said with correlation (p. 445) we cannot use variables like 'marital status' where codes 1 to 4 are given for 'single', 'married', 'divorced', 'widowed', etc. The exception, as with correlation, is the dichotomous variable which is exhaustive, such as gender (see p. 456). Even with these variables, however, it does not make much sense to carry out a multiple regression analysis if almost all variables are dichotomously categorical. In this instance a better procedure would be LOGISTIC REGRESSION, which can be found in more advanced texts and on SPSS.

Collinearity

A fundamental point to grasp here is that some of these predictor variables will also correlate with one another, a feature known as COLLINEARITY. In our fictitious example, teaching satisfaction correlates highly with attendance. They share a lot of variance in common. When this happens, I hope you'll see, the value of the second predictor is greatly diminished. Suppose you ran an ice-cream van. You will of course note that there is a strong correlation between temperature and sales. Knowing the temperature in the morning helps you to predict the amount of stock you'll need for the afternoon. The number of people out on the streets is *also* a good indicator for ordering afternoon stock. However, temperature correlates well with number of people outside on the streets, so using number of people outside, *as well as temperature*, will not provide much, if any, additional help in predicting likely afternoon sales. Similarly, attendance, if it correlates highly with teaching satisfaction, will not be a helpful *additional* predictor of exam grades.

Partial and semi-partial correlation

If teaching satisfaction is to be a useful predictor of grades, independently of its relationship with attendance, we need to know its *unique* relationship with the dependent variable, exam grade. This is found using a statistic known as the SEMI-PARTIAL CORRELATION COEFFICIENT. PARTIAL CORRELATION is a way of partialling out the effect of a third variable (z) on the correlation between two variables, x and y. Suppose we believe that the number of people on the street is correlated with later ice-cream sales but we also know that both these variables correlate with temperature. We want to know the *true* correlation of people with sales, so we correlate temperature with people and look only at the residuals: we do the same with temperature and sales. If we now correlate *only* the two sets of residuals, we are conducting a partial correlation and we get a truer picture of the degree to which sales and people correlate, uncontaminated with the common correlation with temperature.

In *semi*-partial correlation we take the residuals of only one of the two variables involved. Figure 17.23 shows that both teaching satisfaction and attendance share common variance with exam grade. Semi-partial correlation gives us the common variance *only* shared between teaching satisfaction and exam grade, with attendance partialled out; we use the correlation of teaching satisfaction residuals with exam grade. In the figure, the variance that teaching satisfaction shares *uniquely* with exam grade is shown as .3. Remember that the explained variance is found by squaring the regression coefficient (which here must be √.3).

Now imagine that *for each predictor variable* a regression coefficient is found that, when squared, gives us the *unique* variance in exam grade explained by that predictor on its own with the effect of

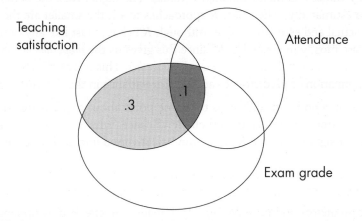

Figure 17.23 Semi-partial correlation of *teaching satisfaction* and *attendance* with *exam grade*

all other predictors partialled out. In this way we can improve our prediction of the variance in a dependent variable by adding in predictors that explain variance in y in addition to any variance already explained by the other predictors.

Regression coefficients

In multiple regression, then, a statistical prediction of one variable is made using the correlations of other known variables with it. For the set of predictor variables used, a particular combination of regression coefficients is found that maximises the amount of variance in y that can be accounted for. In multiple regression, then, there is an equation that predicts y, not just from x as in single predictor regression, but from the regression coefficients of x_1, x_2, x_3 ... and so on, where the x_i are predictor variables whose *correlations* with y are known. The equation takes the form:

$$\hat{Y} = b_0 + b_1x_1 + b_2x_2 + b_3x_3...$$

... and so on, where the b_i are the regression coefficients for each of the predictors (x_i) and b_0 is the constant (c in the simpler example above). These b values are again the number of units $\hat{Y}$ increases for each unit increase in the predictor (x_i), *if all other predictors are held constant*. However, in this multiple predictor model, when standardised values are used, the standardised regression coefficients are *not* the same value as that predictor's correlation with y on its own. What is especially important to understand is that, although a single predictor variable might have a strong *individual* correlation with the criterion variable, acting among a *set* of predictors it might have a very low regression coefficient, as we saw in the example with attendance if it correlates highly with teaching satisfaction. In this case the potential contribution of predictor x_1 to explaining variance has, as it were, already been mostly used up by another predictor, x_2, with which it shares a lot of common variance.

The multiple correlation coefficient and its significance

The multiple regression procedure produces a MULTIPLE CORRELATION COEFFICIENT, symbolised by R, which is the overall correlation of the predictors with the criterion variable. In fact, it is the simple correlation between actual y values and their estimated $\hat{y}$ values. The higher R is, the better is the fit between actual y value and estimated $\hat{y}$. The closer R approaches to +1, the smaller are the residuals – the differences between actual and estimated value. Although R behaves just like any other correlation coefficient, we are mostly interested in R^2 since this gives us the *proportion of variance in the criterion variable that has been accounted for by the predictors taken together*. This is overall what we set out to do – to find the best combination of predictors to account for variance in the criterion variable.

To find an R that is significant is no big deal. This is the same point about single correlations, that their strength is usually of greater importance than their significance, which can be misleading (see p. 447). However, to check for significance the R^2 value can be converted into an F value as follows:

$$F(v_1,v_2) = \frac{R^2v_2}{(1-R^2)v_1}$$

where v_1 is the number of predictors and v_2 is $(N - v_1 - 1)$. F values are checked in Appendix Table 11 using v_1 and v_2.

Adjusted R^2 and sample size

Computer calculations of R^2 will also provide a value for 'adjusted R^2'. R^2 has to be adjusted because with small N its value is artificially high. This is because, at the extreme, with N = number of predictor variables (p) + 1, prediction of the criterion variable values is perfect and R^2 = 1, even though, in the population, prediction cannot be that perfect. The issue boils down to one of sampling adequacy. Various rules of thumb are given for the minimum number of cases (N) to produce a meaningful estimate of the relationship between predictors and criterion in the population – remember we are still estimating population parameters from samples. Although some authors recommend very high N indeed, Harris (1985, cited in Howell, 1992) recommends that the minimum N should be $p + 50$, and most accept this as reasonable, though the more general rule is 'as many as possible'.

There are several more specific points to be made about multiple regression but these can be incorporated into the procedures to be used in SPSS, which follow.

Effect size and power

A commonly used statistic for estimating *effect size* in multiple regression is:

$$f^2 = R^2/(1-R^2)$$

and f^2 needs to be .02, .15 or .35 for a small, medium or large effect. This translates approximately into the more familiar figures of .14, .4 and .6 for f.

Example

Suppose an overall (significant) R of .38 were found for the multiple correlation when 60 exam grades are predicted from the five variables we have been considering above. This would give us R^2 = .144 Our effect size then would be f^2 = .144/(1 – .144) = .168 – a medium effect.

For *power* we need the equation:

$$\lambda = f^2 N$$

where N is the number of cases (usually people) in the sample and λ is used to enter Table 14 with alpha at .05 along with v_1 and v_2 as introduced above under 'significance'.[2] In our example, then, f^2 x 60 = 10.08 = λ. $v_2 = (N - v_1 - 1) = 60 - 5 - 1 = 54$. Entering Table 14 we can locate $v_1 = 5$ and we find just the values 20, 60, 120 and ∞ for v_2. Our value is 54. We have to interpolate. I reasoned as follows: 55 is 1/8th of the distance down from 60 to 20. The figure for power under the column headed '10' for λ when $v_2 = 60$ is .63 and the value for $v_2 = 20$ is .54. Therefore we take a value 1/8th of the way down from .63 to .54 which is roughly .62. 'Rough' is acceptable here since the distance between adjacent table values is not large and power estimations are not rocket science. The conclusion here is that, assuming the correlation of .38 was a valid and not chance outcome, the odds of finding another significant F with a sample of 60 on the same variables are just over 60%.

[2] The tables for power and multiple regression shown here are limited to the use of up to eight independent variables or predictors. Where more than these are used, please see Cohen (1988: 416–23).

Conducting and reporting a multiple regression analysis in SPSS

We will assume we are working with the variables shown in Figure 17.22 (b) and are predicting 54 exam grades (our 'dependent variable') from the other variables (our 'independent variables'). The data file for this analysis is available at www.hodderplus.com/psychology/. Proceed as follows.

1 Select: **Analyze/Regression/Linear** to obtain the multiple regression dialogue box shown in Figure 17.24.

2 Highlight *examgrad* and take it over to the **Dependent** box (Figure 17.24).

3 Highlight the rest of the variables and take them over to the **Independent(s)** variable box.

4 Leave the **Method** as 'Enter'.

Multiple regression methods are several and include **stepwise** methods, which are used to enter variables one at a time until a criterion is reached, the 'best' predictor is selected, then the next best, given that selected already, and so on. This approach is used in psychological practice where pure prediction is desired (e.g. in occupational psychology to select job applicants) but where theory is being tested it is best to stay with the **Enter** method, which will put in all predictors and give the overall solution from which you can select the more powerful predictors.

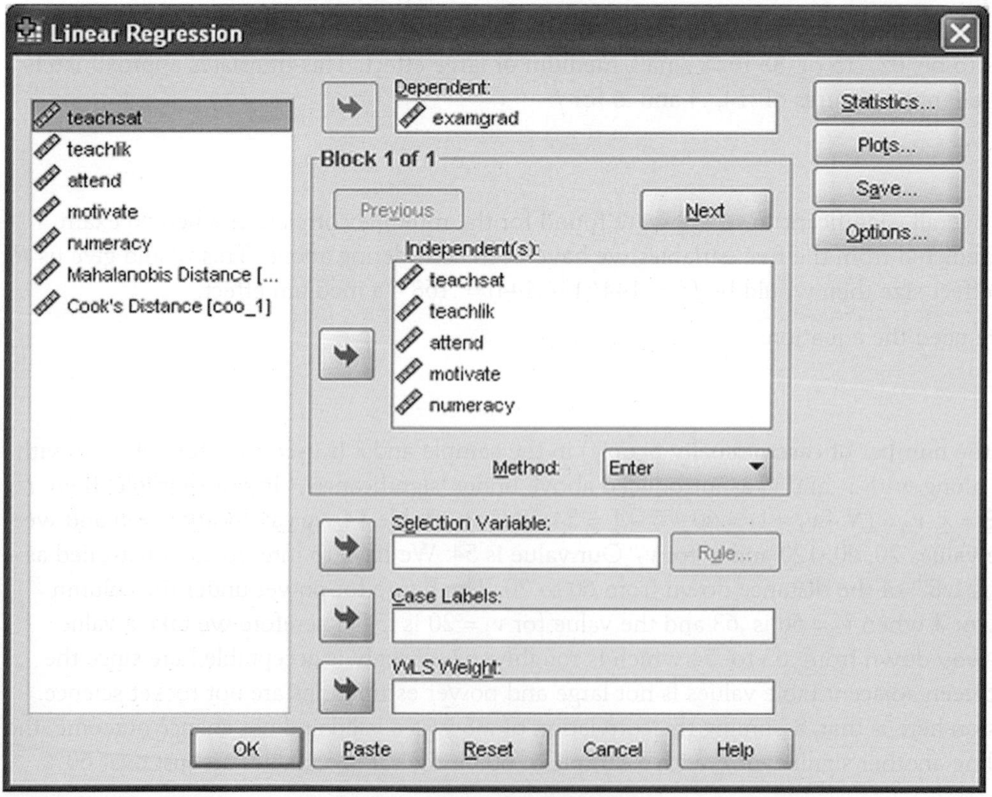

Figure 17.24 Multiple regression dialogue box in SPSS ready for using *teacher satisfaction, teacher liking, attendance, motivation* and *numeracy* to predict *exam grade*

5 Click the **Statistics** button and select **Descriptives** and **Collinearity Diagnostics** in addition to what is selected already by default. Click **Continue**.

6 Click **Plots** and put *ZPRED into the **X**: box and *ZRESID into the **Y**: box. Click **Continue**. The **Save** box takes you to a dialogue box which will give you various new variables for inspection. Especially useful are the **Distances**, which tell you how individual cases fit into the analysis, how much it would change (e.g. the residuals) if each case were removed singly, and so on. More advanced texts and courses will advise you on these, as with all the other items not mentioned here. Click **Continue**.

7 Click **Options** and select **Exclude Cases Listwise**. Click **Continue**.

8 Click **OK**.

The output tables in multiple regression analysis

If you have followed the SPSS steps given above then the first table in the Output will give the simple descriptives for each variable, the second will give the simple correlations between all variables, and the third will tell you simply which variables have been entered into the equation. The subsequent **Model summary** table, shown in Figure 17.25, gets to the heart of the matter, giving R (.743), R^2 (.553) and adjusted R^2 (.506). The next table, entitled **ANOVA**, tells us whether or not the model accounts for a significant proportion of the variance in the criterion

Model Summary[b]

Model	R	R Square	Adjusted R Square	Std. Error of the Estimate
1	.743[a]	.553	.506	.9695

a. Predictors: (Constant), NUMERACY, ATTEND, TEACHLIK, MOTIVATE, TEACHSAT

b. Dependent Variable: EXAMGRAD

Coefficients[a]

Model		Unstandardized Coefficients		Standard-ized Coefficients			Collinearity Statistics	
		B	Std. Error	Beta	t	Sig.	Tolerance	VIF
1	(Constant)	−.975	.782		−1.248	.218		
	TEACHSAT	.490	.150	.395	3.273	.002	.642	1.558
	TEACHLIK	−.11	.114	−.010	−.094	.926	.854	1.171
	ATTEND	.180	.113	.181	1.588	.119	.714	1.401
	MOTIVATE	.409	.137	.333	2.981	.004	.749	1.335
	NUMERACY	.415	.159	.296	2.612	.012	.725	1.379

a. Dependent Variable: EXAMGRAD

Figure 17.25 Tables of output from a multiple regression analysis in SPSS

variable. It is a comparison of the variance 'explained' and the variance 'unexplained' (the residuals). If there is no significance then there is no point going on to look at the contribution of individual variables. For this analysis, I have not included the table but the result was $F_{5,\ 48} = 11.855, p < .01$. ANOVA results are explained in Chapter 18.

The next table, entitled **Coefficients**, is going to be central to our analysis (along with the model summary table above) because it contains information about all the individual predictor variables. The **Unstandardized Coefficients** are the b weights that would go into the formula for multiple regression given above. For motivation, in the 'coefficients' table of Figure 17.25, we have a b value of 0.409. This tells us that for every point increase on the motivation variable there will be an increase of 0.409 marks in the exam grade, given that all other variables are held constant. Of course this is entirely theoretical since, if motivation is higher and it correlates with other predictor variables, any actual increase or decrease would also have an effect on these variables as well. Also we should resist the temptation to think of motivation as *causing* an increase in exam grade. We only know that we have predictable relationships *between* the data. It could be that motivation increases/decreases *because* students realise how they are likely to perform in their forthcoming exams.

The standardised coefficients or 'beta' values are the regression coefficients that apply for standardised scores, as explained earlier. For motivation, as an example, we see that for a one standard deviation rise in motivation there would be a 0.333 standard deviation rise in exam grade with the effect of other predictors discounted. A central part of the multiple regression analysis is to make sense of these beta coefficients. Because these are in standardised form, as explained above, we can compare one with another; *we cannot do this with the b values* since these depend on the type of scale measure being used.

Comparison of the beta values only makes sense in the context of the current analysis. As mentioned earlier, a predictor might have a strong correlation with the criterion but, because it correlates well with another predictor, its usefulness here, expressed by the size of the beta coefficient, may be limited. The beta values in the 'coefficients' table in Figure 17.25 show that *teaching satisfaction* is our strongest predictor in the context of this predictor set, while motivation is the next strongest.

The t value in the coefficients table is found by dividing the unstandardised b value by its standard error. If this t is significant, we know that the predictor is making a significant contribution to the prediction of the criterion; that is, the extra amount of variance in the criterion it accounts for is significant. We see here that teaching satisfaction, motivation and numeracy are all significant contributors, whereas teacher liking and attendance do not contribute significantly to the overall variance accounted for (R^2).

Data checking and screening

First of all, you should check all the variables to make sure they are relatively normal distributions as explained on p. 319. If not, they may have some effect on the analysis which might also be picked up from the following checks. Some of the items we selected when setting up the SPSS analysis have to do with checking that the data involved are not violating any of the other assumptions required for a multiple regression analysis, apart from normality. One of these is that there must not be too high a degree of COLLINEARITY. This is the case when the predictor variables correlate together too closely as was discussed under 'collinearity' above. If the **Tolerance** values in the **Coefficients** table are very low (e.g. under .2) then multicollinearity is present. For technical reasons, close correlations between predictors, which cause these low tolerance levels, will mess up aspects of the regression analysis, so it is best to consult the individual correlations among predictors and remove from the analysis those that correlate very closely with others, perhaps basing this decision on theoretical grounds to do with the theory under test.

There are two major assumptions concerning the residuals we should consider. One is that they should be normally distributed; the normal P-P plot[3] will tell you whether your residual values are sticking closely to the predicted straight line or not, and are therefore relatively normal in distribution. The second is that there should not be HETEROSCEDASTICITY (love the word!) among the residuals. This means that, for each value of $\hat{y}$ the variance of the residuals should be similar; there should be no obvious pattern in the scattergram we asked for between ZPRED and ZRESID; what we should see is a relatively square-shaped distribution. If you look at the plot and consider vertical 'slices' going up from the X-axis, the spread of points should be much the same across all slices, though it won't be at the extremes where only one or two points occur. It should *not* be funnel-shaped.

Finally, you should check on the scatterplot that there are not too many, if any, outliers, These would be extreme cases where the standardised residual is greater than 3 or less than –3. If this is so there may be a simple data-entry error; otherwise it is certainly worth investigating why one case is causing such a variation and also worth considering dropping it from the analysis, with good justification.

Reporting and interpreting the result

A standard multiple regression was performed between examination grade as the dependent variable and attendance, teacher satisfaction, teacher liking, numeracy and motivation as independent variables [add any information on transformation of variables here to achieve normality; report any outliers]. **Table X** (not shown) displays the correlations between variables, the unstandardised regression coefficients (B) and intercept, the standardised regression coefficients (beta), the semi-partial correlations and R (.743), R^2 (.553) and R^2 adjusted (.506). R for regression was significantly different from zero, $F_{5,\ 48} = 11.855, p < .01$.

Three independent variables contributed significantly to prediction of examination grade: teaching satisfaction (beta = 0.395), motivation (beta = 0.333) and numeracy (beta = 0.296). Altogether 50.6% of variability in examination grade was predicted by knowing scores on all five independent variables. The correlations of teacher liking and attendance with examination grade were – .094 and .057 both of which were not significant ($p > .05$). The effect size was very large with $f^2 = 1.02$

---

[3] To get the normal P-P plot select the **Plots** button in the Multiple Regression dialogue box and click on **Normal Probability Plot** in the bottom left corner.

Researchers were interested in being able to predict the length of time for which smokers will stop smoking following a programme designed to help them quit. The criterion variable is *cessation* – the number of days after the programme before participants report smoking at least one whole cigarette; 35 participants were assessed and a multiple regression analysis carried out. The predictor variables with their b weights and standardised beta coefficients are given below:

	b	Beta	Sig	Tolerance
Belief in the effectiveness of the programme	4.3	0.317	.035	.711
Internal locus of control score	2.1	0.221	.053	.622
Locus of control (health) score	0.1	0.003	.678	.113
Number of smoking-related illnesses	1.7	0.010	.328	.589
Attitude towards smoking score	4.0	0.426	.001	.872

(a) A student argues that *effectiveness belief* is clearly the most important of the predictors. Is she right or wrong? Explain why.

(b) Which predictors are significant and what does this mean?

(c) Which *is* the strongest predictor variable?

(d) One student is amazed that *health locus of control* is not a significant or strong predictor since it correlates very well with smoking-cessation measures in many other studies. What do the statistics above tell us about what has happened here?

(e) The R^2 value for this study was .542 but the adjusted R^2 value was only .329. One student is bitterly disappointed and suggests they use and report only the R^2 value since it is such a good result. What has caused the large change in value and what should you tell the student? What can be done to improve the result?

(a) Wrong; *effectiveness belief* has the largest b weight but not the largest *standardised beta coefficient*.

(b) *Effectiveness belief* and *attitude towards smoking*. It means that these two predictors account for a significant amount of the variance in *cessation* each independently of any other predictors.

(c) *Attitude towards smoking* because its standardised regression coefficient is largest (0.426).

(d) Its tolerance value is very low at .113. It shares variance with at least one other of the predictors, probably mostly with (general) *locus of control*. Hence it has little extra to contribute after its common variance with *locus of control* has been taken into account.

(e) Only 35 participants were assessed. The adjusted R^2 *must* be reported since the unadjusted value is biased by the small number of participants. The usual formula is $p + 50$, which here would mean at least 55 participants. The students could add more data to the set.

Glossary

b weight	The amount by which a criterion variable will increase for a one-unit increase in a predictor variable; a predictor's coefficient in the multiple regression equation
Beta value	Standardised b weights (i.e. as expressed in standard deviations)
Biserial (correlation coefficient)	Correlation used where one variable is artificially dichotomous, formed by categorising from an underlying continuous and normal distribution
Collinearity	Extent of correlations between predictor variables
Correlation	A (standardised) measure of relationship of co-variance between two variables
Coefficient	Number signifying strength of correlation between two variables
Curvilinear	Correlation between two variables with low r value because the relationship does not fit a straight line but a good curve
Negative	Correlation where, as values of one variable increase, related values of another variable tend to decrease
Positive	Correlation where, as values of one variable increase, related values of another variable also tend to increase
Criterion/target/dependent	Variable on which values are being predicted in regression variable
Dichotomous variable	Variable with just two exhaustive values (e.g. male/female)
Heteroscedasticity	Degree to which the variance of residuals is not similar across different values of predicted levels of the criterion in multiple repression
Linear regression	Procedure of predicting values on a criterion variable from a predictor or predictors using correlation
Linearity	Extent to which a relationship between two variables can be represented by a straight line rather than, say, a curved line
Multiple correlation coefficient	Value of the correlation between several combined predictor variables and a criterion variable
Multiple regression	Technique in which the value of one 'criterion' variable is estimated using its known correlation with several other 'predictor' variables
Partial correlation	Correlation between residuals of A after correlation with C and the residuals of B after correlation with C
Pearson's product moment correlation coefficient	Parametric measure of correlation
Phi coefficient	Measure of correlation between two truly dichotomous variables
Point biserial correlation	Measure of correlation where one variable is truly dichotomous and the other is at interval level

Predictor	Variable used in combination with others to predict values of a criterion variable in multiple regression
Range restriction	A selection of cases from a larger potential data set, which has the effect of distorting the true population correlation
Regression coefficient	Amount by which predictor variable values are multiplied in a regression equation in order to estimate criterion variable values
Regression line	Line of best fit on a scatterplot, which minimises residuals in regression
Residual ($y-\hat{y}$)	Difference between an actual score and what it would be as predicted by a predictor variable or by a set of predictor variables
Scatterplot	Diagram showing placement of paired values on a two-dimensional chart
Semi-partial correlation coefficient	Correlation between residuals of A, after correlation with C, with a criterion variable B
Spearman's rho	Non-parametric, ordinal level measure of correlation; Pearson correlation on ranks of the paired raw scores
Standardised regression coefficient	Full name for beta values in multiple regression
Variance estimate	Estimate of variance in a variable accounted for by the correlation of another variable (or other variables) with it

Multi-level analysis – differences between more than two conditions

This chapter introduces a major step into the sort of significance testing that tends to dominate experimental research. Researchers rarely use just two samples in a test of difference. ANOVA (analysis of variance) is introduced for the analysis of more than two conditions. ANOVA is a powerful parametric procedure for testing the differences between several means and (later, in Chapter 19) several independent variables. It avoids the problem of producing Type I errors that is incurred if we make multiple comparisons between pairs of means using several t tests. ANOVA allows us to compare all means as a group without raising our chance of a Type I error above .05.

- Between groups one-way ANOVA tests the null hypothesis that two or more samples were drawn from the same population by comparing the variance of the sample means (*between groups variance*) with the 'error' or *within groups variance* (the variance of all values *within* their groups). If means differ among themselves far more than scores differ within groups then the F ratio will be much higher than 1.

- Tests of specific differences between pairs of means (*pairwise comparisons*) or of specific contrasts (such as $\bar{x}_a$ against $\bar{x}_b$ and $\bar{x}_c$ together) are either *a priori* ('planned' before testing because predicted from theoretical reasoning) or *post hoc* (tested only because the difference looks significant once results are in). One or possibly two simple comparisons can be made using t tests and *linear contrasts*, which make possible the testing of combined means where a set of coefficients must be calculated.

- Making several post hoc tests on the same data raises the probability of obtaining a 'significant' result on a chance basis alone ('capitalising on chance'); the *family-wise error rate* can rise unacceptably and must be attended to. Either the significance level for each test can be lowered or several types of test, devised for multiple testing, can be used, including *Bonferroni t tests*, the *Newman–Keuls test*, *Tukey's honestly significant difference* test, and *Scheffé's test*.

- *Effect size* and *power* calculations are described.

- The *Kruskal–Wallis one-way analysis of variance*, a non-parametric version of one-way ANOVA, is described with calculation. The *Jonckheere trend test* is briefly introduced with calculation provided on the companion website.

- *SPSS procedures* for one-way ANOVA, linear contrasts, post hoc tests and the Kruskal–Wallis are provided.

Introduction to more complex tests

Having more than two conditions in your research is extremely common. Very often, researchers use two or more independent variables each with several *levels* (see Chapter 3). In this chapter we look at designs where there is one independent variable but with more than two levels. Typically there will be an experimental condition, a placebo condition and a control condition.

Pause for thought

Imagine that the students we referred to in Chapter 3 have moved on and have been asked to devise a more complex experiment which has at least three conditions. They are interested in effects on driving (having just passed their tests) and have read in the literature that, when not over tired, caffeine (in a coffee drink) can reduce number of errors made during a driving task. They decide to use a computerized hazard perception task as a performance measure. Having carefully considered and provided for central ethical issues, they decide that they should give some participants an acceptable dose of caffeine, some a placebo drink (decaffeinated coffee) which they are informed contains caffeine, some the same drink but with no information and finally a group given nothing at all. All participants perform the driving task.

- What is the dependent variable in this experiment?
- What is the independent variable?
- How many levels does the independent variable contain?

These students have done well; they've checked the literature *first,* developed a research question and are now designing the experiment accordingly. The performance task is their dependent variable. The students here are proposing to use one independent variable (caffeine) with four levels (caffeine, decaff-informed, decaff-not informed and control). They will come up against a problem when they come to compare their means. To use *t* tests they would have to conduct six tests altogether to compare means two at a time.

Capitalising on chance – increasing Type I errors

Conducting six *t* tests is time-consuming but not a big problem for a computer. The serious problem is that, if we conduct several significance tests on the same data set, we increase the probability of getting Type I errors if the null hypothesis is actually true. We saw in Chapter 14 that if we repeat 20 times the testing of randomly drawn samples under circumstances when H_0 is true (for instance, no sex difference in memory), we would expect to reach 5% significance on one of these tests just by chance. This is because that's just what our original significance estimate is based on – the critical value we have to reach is calculated as that value which only 5% of test statistics would reach *if the null hypothesis is true*. If we have several goes at testing our data then we increase the chance of hitting the 1 in 20 'fluke' result. We will discuss this issue a little further on under the heading of 'Error rates' on p. 487.

If you do a lot of tests on various aspects of a data set, each time assuming a null hypothesis and an alpha level of .05, you can be accused of 'fishing' for results or CAPITALISING ON CHANCE. You are increasing the probability of making a Type I error. To avoid this criticism you need to use a lower level of alpha *or* use tests designed for the purpose of looking for significance among several conditions, and this is where we're headed now.

Multi-level tests

All the multi-level and multi-factorial tests we will cover are designed to take into account the fact that we are comparing several groups at once. They give us the probability that groups would differ as they do given the null hypothesis is true. The tests we have already used for two samples are mostly just special cases of the more general tests introduced here. Some tests, properly called *multi-factorial tests*, deal with the situation where a researcher uses more than one independent variable simultaneously. These 'factorial approaches' will be encountered in Chapters 19 and 20. On page 546 there is a table indicating the appropriate use of multi-level and multi-factorial tests. Now we are going to introduce the simplest of these tests – the ONE-WAY ANOVA – where ANOVA stands for 'Analysis of Variance'.

One-way ANOVA – unrelated designs

When to use one-way unrelated ANOVA		
Type of relationship tested	Level of data required	Design of study
Difference Between three or more conditions of one independent variable (factor)	At least interval	Between groups Unrelated designs

Data assumptions:

- homogeneity of variance
- data on interval scale
- sampling distribution of means is normal; assumed by checking that dependent variable is normally distributed (see p. 319).

Notes: ANOVA procedures form a large family for every kind of experimental design. Here we introduce the model using the one-way unrelated design only.

The driving skill data

Through most of this section we will work with the same set of data. Let's assume the students settled on just three conditions, because the students do not want to mislead their participants. The participants will receive coffee (*c*), decaffeinated coffee (*d*) or nothing at all (*n*). The students are now using one independent variable with *three* levels. It is customary to give the independent variable a generic title so here it might be *caffeine* with the levels *coffee, decaff, none*. The dependent variable is the hazard task score, which is high when fewer errors are made. We therefore expect the coffee group to obtain the higher scores. We are not sure whether decaff will have any effect or not. The students have so far tested only four participants in each condition, which is far too few. Let's suppose they have more participants to test but are masochistic in wanting to get to grips with ANOVA by calculating an early result! The real reason for doing this is that it will be much easier to demonstrate how ANOVA works with a small set of scores on which to perform calculations. The data they have obtained are displayed in Table 18.1.

Driving skill score

	Pt	Coffee	Pt	Decaff	Pt	None	All conditions
	A	10	E	3	I	4	
	B	9	F	5	J	2	
	C	6	G	10	K	5	
	D	11	H	9	L	4	
Total (Σx)		36		27		15	78
Mean $\bar{x}$		9		6.75		3.75	6.5
$(\Sigma x)^2$		1296		729		225	6084
Σx^2		338		215		61	614

Referred to as the 'grand mean'

Table 18.1 Driving scores with coffee, decaffeinated coffee or no drink

The null hypothesis for one-way ANOVA

The null hypothesis for a one-way ANOVA test is no different from that we encountered when conducting a *t* test. It holds that the populations from which samples have been randomly drawn have equal means (see Figure 18.1).

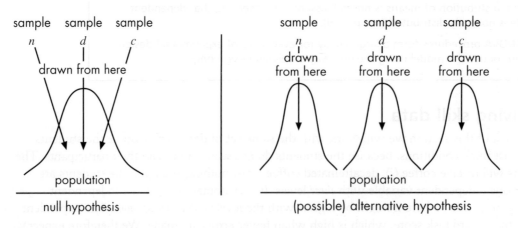

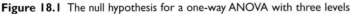

Figure 18.1 The null hypothesis for a one-way ANOVA with three levels

If we use c to refer to the coffee condition, d for decaff and n for none, then technically the null hypothesis can be written as: $\mu_c = \mu_d = \mu_n$

The alternative hypothesis is often that: $\mu_c \neq \mu_d \neq \mu_n$ but as we shall see, with more than two means we can also make specific predictions about which means differ from which.

How does ANOVA work?

Take a look back at Table 14.1(a). In this table we said there seemed to be little difference between the means of the two groups. We made that decision based on the size of the mean difference which was 9.53 – 8.79 = 0.74 but, perhaps without realising it, *we must also have considered the variation among the scores overall*. Take a look at Table 18.2.

Here we have exactly the same sample means as in Table 14.1(a). They are still only 0.74 apart but we would be much more convinced that there is a real difference between groups than for the data in Chapter 14. In fact, the difference is highly significant. Why? Because the variance *within the groups* is very low compared with the mean difference, so the differences among scores look to be caused mainly by being in one condition or the other. When we say 'the differences among scores' we are talking about the overall *variation* among *all* the scores. It is very important that you grasp this concept of overall variance as it is central to all work with ANOVA designs. You should revise it now from Chapter 11. If you look at all the 20 scores in Table 18.2 and ask the question 'what accounts for all the variation among them?', I hope it is fairly obvious that a central factor is the condition the participants were in. Almost all the scores in the alone condition are lower than those in the audience condition. The standard deviation in each group is only 0.28 so, although the difference between means is small (0.74), it is more than twice the standard deviation of either sample.

	With audience	Alone
	9.3	8.8
	9.5	8.6
	9.8	8.5
	9.7	8.8
	9.6	9.1
	9.5	8.9
	8.9	8.7
	9.9	8.5
	9.6	8.6
	9.5	9.4
Mean:	9.53	8.79

Table 18.2 Mean scores with low variance within groups

The basis of ANOVA

Put very simply, ANOVA compares the *variance between groups* with the *variance within groups*. In Table 18.2 the variation *within* groups is low (0.28) compared with the variation *between* the groups (0.74), and therefore we feel that the difference between groups is an important, not chance, one. In table 14.1(a), however, the variation within groups is large compared with the variation between groups (that is, the difference between the two means). When there is large variation *within* groups compared with low variation *between* groups, we can see that any difference between means is not convincing (see Figure 18.2 (a) where variation is represented by the spread of each shaded lollipop shape); if variation within groups is low compared with the variation between groups, however, it is clear that something is responsible for the mean differences and we suspect a real effect (see Figure 18.2 (b)).

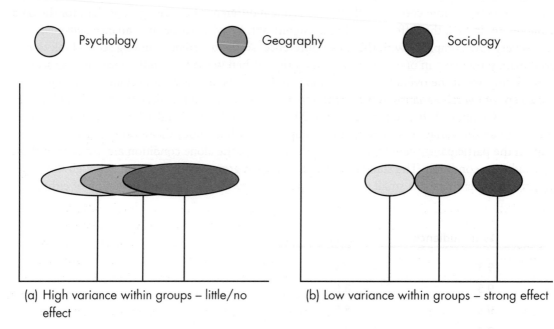

(a) High variance within groups – little/no effect

(b) Low variance within groups – strong effect

Figure 18.2 (a) High variance within groups – little or no effect; (b) low variance within groups – strong effect

Figure 18.3 shows the variation among scores in each condition of the caffeine experiment. It looks here as though the coffee condition scores might be different from the other two groups – the mean is higher and the internal variation is not great – but we now need to look more technically at what will give us a fair statistical estimate of significant difference between sample means.

The concept of 'error'

To reiterate a point: if there is a significant effect for our caffeine independent variable, we would expect the variation *within* the samples (the WITHIN GROUPS VARIANCE roughly depicted by the length of the rectangles in Figure 18.3) to be small compared with the variation of the sample means (known as BETWEEN GROUPS VARIANCE). At the extreme, if everyone within each sample scored

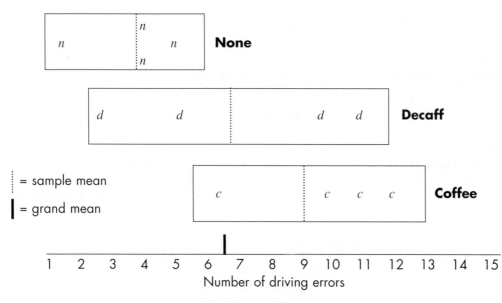

Figure 18.3 Plot of driving error scores by caffeine group

exactly the same then *all* the variation among all the scores would be attributable *only* to the independent variable. Any variation *within* groups is assumed to be attributable, not to the independent variable, but to individual differences and other random factors. Statisticians refer to this as 'error' under the argument that it is unwanted variation that clouds the effect of the independent variable. This sounds odd in psychology where we deal with people, who are fundamentally different from one another. However, we are using the language of statistics. Remember those screws in Chapter 14 where sampling at random always produces some error? The errors were minor variations around the population mean set by the machine. Technicians obviously cannot permit too much error in manufacturing two inch screws. However, individual differences in people can be quite broad and the question becomes: Is there so much 'error' (human variation) here within each group that it clouds any difference between those given caffeine and those not?

Division of deviation

The concepts of error and variance depend on the notion of *deviation scores* – go back and check in Chapter 11 if you are uncertain about this. Each score in a set deviates from the overall mean (called the GRAND MEAN) by some amount, creating dispersion. We distinguish here between the *grand mean* (6.5 for the coffee data) and the *sample means* (3.75, 6.75 and 9), indicated in Figure 18.3, which we are hoping will differ significantly among themselves. We can take each deviation and divide it into two quantities: the amount by which the score deviates from its sample mean, and the amount by which the sample mean differs from the grand mean. We can say that:

Whole deviation = Deviation from group mean + Group mean deviation from grand mean

and we can represent this visually as in Figure 18.4.

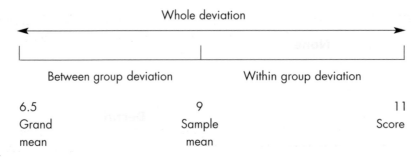

Figure 18.4 Division of participant D's score of 11 into between and within group variation

Here we see that participant D's score of 11 in the coffee condition has a deviation from the grand mean (6.5) of 4.5. When divided into within and between group deviations, however, it differs from its sample mean by 2 while the sample mean itself differs from the grand mean by 2.5. These two deviations add up to the overall deviation of 4.5.

If we treat all deviation scores like this, then I hope you can see that we want the *within group* deviations to be small while the *between group* deviations should be comparatively large, *if the independent variable has a significant effect*. What we do in an ANOVA analysis, in fact, is to find the variance for each of these three components and these are known as the *total variance*, the *between groups variance* and the *within groups variance* or ERROR VARIANCE.

The F ratio statistic

We have said several times that we need to compare the *between groups* variation with the *within groups* variation, and this comparison, using variances, is in fact the F statistic, so:

$$F = \frac{between\ groups\ variance}{within\ groups\ variance}$$

Both these variances can be seen as estimates of the true population variance. The bottom value is used to estimate population variance from the average of the variance within the groups. This is why homogeneity of variance is an assumption for this analysis (see p. 365). *Each sample* should provide an estimate of the population variance, but we use the average of all three sample variances as a better estimate. The top term in the F equation uses the *central limit theorem* (see p. 316) to estimate population variance from the *variance between groups means*. If the means are drawn randomly from the same population, which is what the null hypothesis claims, then this *between* groups estimate of population variance should be the same as that based on the *within* groups variance, and F would be equal to 1. If the means differ much more than we would expect under H_0 then the top value will exceed the bottom and F will rise to a point where we would consider it unlikely enough under H_0 to call it significant.

It will help now to recall what the equation for variance is:

$$s^2 = \frac{\sum(x-\bar{x})^2}{N-1}$$

On the top part of this equation we have the *sum of the squared deviations* – that is, take the deviation of each score from its mean, square it and then add this lot up. This value is termed the

SUM OF SQUARES OR *SS*. The denominator (lower part) of the equation is known as the 'degrees of freedom' or *df* a term already encountered. Back in Chapter 11, we introduced a computational formula for variance which is going to be easier to work with and which was:

$$s^2 = \frac{\sum x^2 - (\sum x)^2/N}{N-1}$$

This latter equation produces exactly the same result as the first. We still have the *sum of squares* on top but in a format that allows us to calculate without having to work out each separate deviation score; we need only calculate the sum of *x* and the sum of x^2.

A full calculation of ANOVA

Having said we don't need to calculate each deviation I would like now to present a full calculation of ANOVA, in order to demonstrate exactly how it works, and then to reassure you that you will not be needing to do this since the second variance equation above permits some highly economical short-cuts. Holding on to something steady, have a look at Table 18.3.

x_k	Deviation of score from the grand mean		Deviation of the group's mean from the grand mean (*between groups* variation)			Deviation of score from the group's mean (*within groups* variation or 'error')	
	D	D^2	$\bar{x}_k$	$\bar{x}_k - \bar{x}_G$	$(\bar{x}_k - \bar{x}_G)^2$	$x_i - \bar{x}_k$	$(\bar{x}_i - \bar{x}_k)^2$
10	3.5	12.25	9	2.5	6.25	1	1
9	2.5	6.25	9	2.5	6.25	0	0
6	−0.5	0.25	9	2.5	6.25	−3	9
11	4.5	20.25	9	2.5	6.25	2	4
$\bar{x}_c = 9$							$\Sigma = 14$
3	−3.5	12.25	6.75	0.25	0.0625	−3.75	14.0625
5	−1.5	2.25	6.75	0.25	0.0625	−1.75	3.0625
10	3.5	12.25	6.75	0.25	0.0625	3.25	10.5625
9	2.5	6.25	6.75	0.25	0.0625	2.25	5.0625
$\bar{x}_d = 6.75$							$\Sigma = 32.75$
4	−2.5	6.25	3.75	−2.75	7.5625	0.25	0.0625
2	−4.5	20.25	3.75	−2.75	7.5625	−1.75	3.0625
5	−1.5	2.25	3.75	−2.75	7.5625	1.25	1.5625
4	−2.5	6.25	3.75	−2.75	7.5625	0.25	0.0625
$\bar{x}_n = 3.75$							$\Sigma = 4.75$
$\bar{x}_G = 6.5$							
Total *SS* = 107			Between groups *SS*		= 55.5	Error SS	= 51.5

Table 18.3 Full calculation of sums of squares in ANOVA

In the first column of Table 18.3 are the data from our coffee experiment. The second column gives the deviation of each score from the grand mean ($\bar{x}_G$). We said above that this can be divided into the deviation of the sample mean from the grand mean (shown in column 5) and the score's deviation from its sample mean (column 7); the example in Figure 18.4 is highlighted in the table. So columns 5 and 7 give the *between groups deviations* and the *within groups deviations* respectively. In each of Columns 3, 6 and 8 the deviation has been squared so that we can then add these up to get the sum of squared deviations for the *whole*, *between group* and *within group* components respectively. In the bottom line of the whole table we find a happy outcome that is going to save you a huge amount of calculation if you are doing your ANOVAs by hand! An important point about the squared deviations is that:

Total SS = Between groups SS + Within groups (error) SS

You'll see how convenient this is as we calculate the SS using formulae, below. We would now go on to calculate total variance, between groups variance and within groups variance by dividing the totals of columns 3, 6 and 8 by appropriate df. However, we'll be doing that below with the short-hand calculation of ANOVA, which we'll now get on with. The values of Σx etc. are found from Table 18.1. An extra point of convenience is to use the source of SS as a subscript thus: total SS = SS_{total}; this makes things a lot easier to read and write later on.

Calculation of ANOVA with formulae

Procedure	Calculation/result of steps
1 Find SS_{total} using: $\sum x^2 - \dfrac{\left(\sum x\right)^2}{N}$. Note this is the top of the equation for variance i.e. the Sum of Squares as explained earlier.	$614 - 6084/12 = \mathbf{107}$
2 Find $SS_{between}$ using: $\sum n_k \bar{x}_k^2 - \dfrac{\left(\sum x\right)^2}{N}$ This first term looks a bit messy but it simply means 'square each sample mean, multiply it by the n in its group and add the results'; the reason for multiplying by n is that for each score in a group we are taking its group mean from the grand mean as in column 7 of Table 18.3. Hence we have to take the difference n times.	$(4 \times 9^2) + (4 \times 6.75^2) + (4 \times 3.75^2)$ $= 562.5$ $562.5 - 6084/12 = \mathbf{55.5}$
3 Find SS_{error}. Now here's the real labour saver! We saw that $SS_{total} = SS_{between} + SS_{error}$ so simply find $SS_{total} - SS_{between}$	$107 - 55.5 = \mathbf{51.5}$
4 To get variance we now need to divide each of these SS by their respective df; these are:	**Degrees of freedom:**
For SS_{total} $df_{total} = N - 1$	$df_{total} = 12 - 1 = \mathbf{11}$
For $SS_{between}$ $df_{between} = k - 1$ (k = number of samples)	$df_{between} = 3 - 1 = \mathbf{2}$
For SS_{error} $df_{error} = df_{total} - df_{between}$	$df_{error} = 11 - 2 = \mathbf{9}$

5 Find the variance for each component. In ANOVA this is known as the MEAN SUM OF SQUARES since this is what it is – the average of the squared deviations. We need to divide each component SS by its df.

6 Find F which $= \dfrac{MS_{between}}{MS_{error}}$

$MS_{total} = 107/11 = \mathbf{9.73}$

$MS_{between} = 55.5/2 = \mathbf{27.75}$

$MS_{error} = 51.5/9 = \mathbf{5.72}$

$F(2,9) = \dfrac{27.75}{5.72} = \mathbf{4.85}$

F is written with its df which are the $df_{between}$ followed by df_{error}

We have a value for F of 4.85 with 2 df for the numerator (between) and 9 df for the denominator (error). Checking in Appendix Table 11 tells us that this value is significant with $p \leq .05$ (critical value 4.26). (SPSS tells us that p is exactly .037.) We can reject the null hypothesis that the three means come from the same population. Coffee appears to work... or is it the decaff? For power and effect size considerations, see p. 491 and the calculation procedures below.

Effect size

Effect size in ANOVA analyses is generally taken to be the proportion of the total variation accounted for by the 'treatment' factor. In the one-way case this is the $SS_{between}$ as a proportion of the total, in other words: $SS_{between}/SS_{total}$ and in our example above this would be 55.5/107 = .519. However, we may as well give the general equation here, which will apply to *all* ANOVA terms introduced in later chapters. There are several estimates of effect size but probably the most popular, and the one calculated by SPSS (you might be relieved to know), is η^2 defined as follows:

$$\eta^2 = \frac{SS_{effect}}{SS_{effect} + SS_{error}} \quad (1)$$

SS_{effect} is what we have called $SS_{between}$ and, for the one-way situation, $SS_{between} + SS_{error}$ is all there is and together they sum to SS_{total}. However, the formula will stand for more complex terms in later chapters. If you only have F values and df (because you are, for instance, reading another's published work) you can calculate as follows:

$$\eta^2 = \frac{F_{effect}\, df_{effect}}{F_{effect}\, df_{effect} + df_{error}} \quad (2)$$

This is also a general formula, used in more complex analyses; here, F_{effect} is just our F value. Values for η^2 of .01, .06 and .14 are considered small, moderate and large effect sizes. Often your value may be much higher but if power is low (often because N is too small) then even such large effects have a low chance of being detected simply because of the weak design of the research study. Before you get bogged down with arithmetical calculations for effect size *and* power you should know that you can ask SPSS to include these in your ANOVA analysis (so long as you select the **GLM**; see below).

Reporting results of a one-way unrelated ANOVA analysis

Driving skill score means (and standard deviations) for the coffee, decaff and none conditions were 9 (2.16), 6.75(3.3) and 3.75(1.26) respectively. These means differed significantly, $F(2,9) = 4.85$, $p \le .05$. The effect size was large, $\eta^2 = .519$.

(For a way to report post hoc analyses of pairs of means see p. 491.)

Further analysis

Our F value, and the probability associated with it, tell us that there is a less than 5% chance that our three means would vary by so much *if* they were produced at random and the caffeine conditions have no effect on hazard task performance. The analysis is not yet over, however. At present, what we know from this result is *only* that *at least one of our means differs significantly from at least one of the other means.* We don't know which means these might be, but we can see from the group means that the most likely significant difference is between *coffee* and *none*, with the next likely contender being the difference between *decaff* and *none*, but we cannot tell just by eyeballing the data.

It is important to remember that *you should only proceed to consider differences between specific means if the overall F for ANOVA is significant.*

Earlier we introduced ANOVA as an alternative to conducting *t* tests between all pairs of means in order to avoid capitalising on chance (see p. 476). Nevertheless we might still wish to know if one specific mean differs from another – known as a PAIRWISE COMPARISON. We can do this, subsequent to the overall ANOVA analysis, using *a priori* and *post hoc comparisons*. These will take account of the probability of Type I errors and give us an analysis that does not run too high a risk of producing fluke differences. Remember, there is always, in all statistical work, *some* chance that a 'significant' difference is a chance occurrence.

A priori and post hoc comparisons

Have a look at the table of means (Table 18.4) from a fictitious study on memory giving the mean number of correctly recalled items from a 25-word list by different groups tested Monday to Friday.

(a) Monday	(b) Tuesday	(c) Wednesday	(d) Thursday	(e) Friday
$\bar{x}_m$	$\bar{x}_t$	$\bar{x}_w$	$\bar{x}_{th}$	$\bar{x}_f$
16.71	14.56	10.45	13.78	14.23

Table 18.4 Mean recall by day of week on which test takes place

Let's suppose that the null hypothesis is true and that, in effect, these five samples are drawn randomly from the same population; day of the week tested has absolutely no effect on memory recall. Hence: $\mu_m = \mu_t = \mu_w = \mu_{th} = \mu_f$ Suppose also that on this particular occasion of testing we had a fluke result where the sample mean for Monday *does* differ significantly from the sample mean for Wednesday, using an unrelated *t* test. On this occasion, for this specific comparison, a Type I error will occur if we reject the null hypothesis that these two samples come from populations with the same means.

Post hoc comparisons

POST HOC COMPARISONS are those we make *after* inspecting the results of our ANOVA test. Suppose, having obtained the overall results in Table 18.4, we decided to make *all* possible tests between pairs of means. Each test that comes out 'significant' we shall take as indicating that the underlying population means are different. In this case, we would be *bound* to make a Type I error since we will eventually test $\bar{x}_m$ against $\bar{x}_w$.

A priori comparisons

On the other hand, we might predict before gathering data, on theoretical grounds, that only Monday's and Friday's means would be expected to differ. We might have argued that people would be more tired at the end than at the beginning of the week. In this case, after checking the overall ANOVA result, we would only want to test one pair of means: $\bar{x}_m$ and $\bar{x}_f$. We will not now make a Type I error. Of course, we might have had a theory concerning Monday and Wednesday and we *might* have made the error. However, overall, in this situation where we are only going to make one test, our chances of hitting that fluke 'significant' result are only 1/10. This is because there are ten possible pairs that we *could* have chosen and we chose only one of these.

A PRIORI ('PLANNED') COMPARISONS, then, are comparisons we make, having made a specific prediction, based on theoretical argument, *before* conducting our ANOVA analysis. Making all possible comparisons produces a far higher probability of making a Type I error than occurs if we make selected and predetermined a priori comparisons. In fact, deciding in advance to make *all* possible comparison tests is the same thing as conducting post hoc tests.

The probability of Type I errors is often much higher with post hoc tests, mainly because they usually test all possible pairs of means. However, even where we simply select one test, post hoc, having looked at the means, the probability of Type I error is higher than if we specify beforehand. If H_0 is *true* and you look at Table 18.4 and say 'Well, let's test the two means that are furthest apart' you are giving yourself a good chance of finding a 'significantly' different pair of means that are, in fact, unusually large deviations within a random distribution.

We have mentioned 'fishing' for significant differences several times previously, but now is the time to look at the Type I error problem more technically.

Error rates and reducing α

If you make 20 tests of significance on randomly arranged data you are likely to get one 'significant' difference. That is the logic of significance testing. We look for differences that would occur less than five times in 100 under H_0 (i.e. 'at random') and count them as significant. If we set significance at $p \leq .05$, then, and make multiple tests on randomly arranged data, we know that there is a .05 probability, if the null hypothesis is true, that any comparison we make will be wrongly assumed to be significant, i.e. we will have made a Type I error. We are said to be working with an error rate per comparison of .05. If we are making several tests on our data then this error rate will increase – with two t tests on the same data it is close to .1. Hence as the number of tests increases so the chances of a type I error, assuming H_0 is true, increase sharply. If we are making several tests on our data it is possible to calculate something known as the FAMILY-WISE ERROR RATE (FW) which is the probability of making at least one Type I error when making multiple tests, if H_0 is true.

One simple and common way to deal with the increased error rate created by multiple t tests is to just lower α. We can divide α by the number of comparisons, c, we wish to make so our new α becomes α/c. With two t tests we would use $\alpha/2 = .025$. That is, we will only accept a difference as significant if p falls under .025 for the test. This may create difficulties with the t test table not giving precise probabilities (with SPSS it is no problem). If so, you could use the Bonferroni t test described below.

Tests for a priori comparisons

Howell (1992) provides a t test formula for use with planned comparisons using the MS_{error} term from our ANOVA analysis. This is not as conservative as the straightforward t test you would otherwise perform:

$$t = \frac{\bar{x}_1 - \bar{x}_2}{\sqrt{\dfrac{MS_{error}}{n_1} + \dfrac{MS_{error}}{n_2}}}$$

where n_1 and n_2 are the appropriate sample sizes. We check t using df_{error} from the ANOVA analysis.

Bonferroni t tests

If you are making no more than a few comparisons you can, instead of lowering your α level, use BONFERRONI t TESTS (which can be used a priori or post hoc, which is where they appear in SPSS). The only difference here is that, instead of lowering our level of α, we make use of tables created by Dunn (1961), which raise the critical value of t depending on the number of comparisons you perform. Use the equation above, check with df_{error} as before and use the column in Appendix Table 15, with the appropriate number of comparisons. For the coffee example, the lower half of the equation above comes to: $\sqrt{(5.72/4 + 5.72/4)} = 1.691$. Putting differences between means on top of the equation we get:

Coffee – None: $t = (9-3.75)/1.691 = 3.105$

Coffee – Decaff: $t = (9-6.75)/1.691 = 1.331$

Decaff – None: $t = (6.75-3.75)/1.691 = 1.774$

We check each of these in Dunn's table (Table 15) using $df_{error} = 9$ and the column for three comparisons. The critical t is given as 2.93 so only the coffee-none difference is significant ($p \leq .05$).

Linear contrasts – testing combinations of means

The *t* test above is a special case of making LINEAR CONTRASTS. The particular strength of these is that we can test for significance between *combinations* of means. For instance, in Table 18.4, we might wish to test between the combined mean for Monday and Tuesday and the combined mean for Thursday and Friday (so we may be testing whether significantly more is recalled on Monday and Tuesday, put together, than on Thursday and Friday together). Whether using a computer or working by hand we need, first, to devise *coefficients* – one for each mean – which are a kind of code that tell us (and the computer) which sets of means are being compared with which. The rules for these codes are as follows.

1 All coefficients must sum together to zero.

2 The sum of coefficients for one side of the comparison must equal the sum of coefficients for the other side but have the opposite sign.

3 The coefficient for any mean not tested must be zero.

To test Monday against Wednesday for instance we would give +1 to Monday, –1 to Wednesday and 0 to the other three days to show they are not involved in the contrast. The values for coefficients can be any number so long as they satisfy the criteria. However, it is easy to find suitable coefficients by following the rule that each mean is given the number of means in the group with which it is being contrasted. To test Monday and Tuesday against Wednesday, Thursday and Friday combined, we can give Monday and Tuesday 3 each and therefore the other days get –2 each in order to satisfy the rules.

The formula to use for a contrast is: $F = \dfrac{MS_{contrast}}{MS_{error}}$ where $MScontrast = \dfrac{\left(\sum\left(a_k \sum x_k\right)\right)^2}{\sum n_k a_k^2}$

OK this looks a bit forbidding but let's work though it using the example that we are contrasting, in the coffee experiment, coffee, alone, against decaff and none combined. First we give these appropriate coefficients which will be 2 for coffee and –1 for decaff and –1 for none.

Here are the calculations for $MS_{contrast}$:

Top of the equation:

1 Multiply each condition total Σx_k by its coefficient (a_k) and add results:	$36 \times 2 + 27 \times -1 + 15 \times -1 = 30$
2 Square this result	$30^2 = 900$

Bottom of the equation:

3 Square each coefficient, multiply by n for that condition and add results.

$$4 \times 2^2 + 4 \times -1^2 + 4 \times -1^2 = 24$$

4 $MS_{contrast} = \dfrac{\text{Step 2 result}}{\text{Step 3 result}} = 900/24 = \mathbf{37.5}$

To obtain F we want $MS_{contrast}/MS_{error}$. From p. 485 $MS_{error} = 5.72$ so $F = 37.5/5.72 = \mathbf{6.556}$

Linear contrasts are often tested by a t rather than an F value but the two are closely related; $t^2 = F$ so the value reported by SPSS would be $t = \sqrt{F} = \mathbf{2.56}$.

Tests for post hoc comparisons

In practice, researchers rarely make predictions about specific contrasts and by far the more common approach is to make post hoc comparisons as the results are analysed. In this case *all* possible comparisons are tested and FW is generally high. There are several tests, each with variations and complications, for carrying out post hoc comparisons. I am just going to mention three of the most popular, with their associated characteristics.

Newman–Keuls test

Also termed the *Student–Newman–Keuls* test, this alternative is generally controversial because, under certain circumstances, the error rate gets rather high. This will only happen in studies with quite a lot of conditions, and, for studies involving only three conditions, the Newman–Keuls gives a greater chance of showing real significant differences, with only slightly more risk of making Type I errors than the Tukey test, below. The calculations for the Newman–Keuls and Tukey's test are not dealt with here but the test can be automatically carried out using SPSS and similar.

Tukey's$_a$ (honestly significant difference – HSD) test

This engagingly titled test is generally considered the safest you can use if you wish to carry out all possible 'pairwise' comparisons and keep the error rate down to .05. The price you pay is that the test is 'conservative' – you might miss real differences in keeping your interpretations safe. Be careful to distinguish this test from the Tukey$_b$ test which works pretty much like the Newman–Keuls with some modification and is between that test and the Tukey$_a$ in terms of safety.

The Scheffé test

This is an even more conservative test, which keeps the error rate at .05 or less while taking into account all possible contrasts, *including combinations*.

Reporting the results of post hoc tests

The SPSS procedures later on tell you how to run post hoc tests with a one-way ANOVA analysis. However, in keeping with other treatments, the report style is given here. The wording below would usually immediately follow the report of the main one-way analysis as given earlier:

A post hoc Tukey$_b$ test showed that, with alpha at .05, means for the none and decaff conditions formed homogenous subsets, as did the means for coffee and decaff; only the means for the coffee and none conditions showed a significant difference.

Estimating power in one-way ANOVA

To estimate power there are several approaches, all producing slightly different results. Recall that power is often used in a backwards fashion where researchers, knowing something about the size of the effect they would like to demonstrate, wish to calculate the minimum number of participants they will need in order to be fairly sure of demonstrating that effect. Designs with low power have a high value for β and this is the probability of not getting a significant effect when the effect is real (a Type II error). Power is $1 - \beta$ and we want this to be high.

In order to isolate n (the minimum number of participants required per level of the independent variable for good power) we first define Φ' as $\sqrt{\dfrac{\eta^2}{1 - \eta^2}}$ (Cohen, 1988) and then calculate $\Phi = \Phi'$

$\sqrt{n}$ where n was the actual number in each condition (in each *level* of the independent variable or condition of the experiment). To convert Φ to a power estimate we need to use Appendix Table 13 armed with the value of Φ and our *df* values, df_t being the *df* for the between groups factor (i.e. number of conditions − 1) and df_e being the error *df*.

Let's consult the table with some actual values. In the coffee experiment η^2 was .519. φ' is = (.519/1 − .519) = 1.039. Φ is then 1.039$\sqrt{4}$ = 2.078. Appendix Table 13 is in four sections, each section being appropriate to the specific value of *df*. We need the second section where df_t = 2. Now we need the column for Φ that matches our value most closely. Unfortunately in this table you may have to do a bit of interpolating and this is done simply by applying ratios. Here we are lucky, though, because 2.078 is close enough to 2 so we'll use that column. Now we look down the column until we find the row that corresponds to our df_e value in the left-hand column. Our value is 9 and we are using α at the standard level of .05. There are only values for 8 or 10 so we interpolate by taking the value midway between the two values given for 8 and 10. These are .28 and .24 so we can estimate our value at .26. The next point is very easy to forget and very frustrating when you do. The values in the table are the β values; that is, the probability of making a Type II error if the alternative hypothesis is true (i.e. the probability of missing an effect if it is real). What we want of course is power and that is $1 - \beta$. Hence power in this analysis is .74. This is quite reasonable and quite close to the gold standard required of .8.

Cohen's formula above is an estimate of Φ' which is very useful if you don't want to get too complicated. However, a more accurate calculation is provided by $\Phi' = \sqrt{\dfrac{\Sigma(\bar{x}_i - \bar{x}_g)^2}{kMS_{error}}}$

This means, first, take the grand mean from each treatment mean and square the result. Then add up these results. Then divide by k times our MS_{error} value, where k is the number of treatments or levels of the independent variable. Take the square root of this final result. In our coffee example this would give for the top half of the fraction: $(3.75 - 6.5)^2 + (6.75 - 6.5)^2 + (9 - 6.5)^2 = 13.875$. There are three conditions so $k = 3$ and kMS_{error} is $3 \times 5.72 = 17.16$. Dividing 13.875 by this result gives .809 and the square root of this is .899. Now as above we have to take this value for φ' and multiply by the square root of n – the number in each condition. This won't tax us since $n = 4$, therefore $\sqrt{n} = 2$. Our final result for Φ is .899 x 2 = 1.798, which we shall call 1.8 when using Table 13. This tells us that β is around .355, hence power is $1 - .355 = .645$, a result tallying closely with the SPSS value of .647.

Estimating the n required for different levels of power

Now, suppose we want to estimate the number of participants we need in an experiment to be fairly sure of showing an effect (i.e. not making a Type II error). We might have an idea of effect size η^2 from previous studies. Alternatively we might have an idea of the general population variance of scores (for instance, IQ standard deviation is 15 so its general variance is 225); we might also know the kinds of differences between means that we could expect (e.g. from pilot studies or from logical considerations about the scales of measurement involved). We can start with a desired level of power (.8) in Table 13. We know our proposed df_1. we don't know df_2 because that depends on n which we are trying to find, but for now, a bit of trickery using $df_2 = \infty$ (the bottom row) will suffice. Now we can find a value for Φ. If we have estimates for effect size, as suggested just above, then the only unknown value left is n and we can proceed to juggle terms to find this value. Because we used ∞ for df_2 we have to go back and recalculate but, at worst, power will only be a little off .8 and we can raise n a little to compensate. See the companion website for an example.

Non-parametric ANOVA equivalent – the Kruskal–Wallis one-way analysis of variance

The ANOVA procedures using F all carry assumptions about the data gathered and these have been identified in the ANOVA test introduction box on p. 477. As with the parametric t tests in Chapter 15, if your data just do not satisfy the assumptions for an F test and you cannot transform your data (see p. 364), then there are non-parametric alternatives.

When to use the Kruskal–Wallis one-way analysis of variance test

Type of relationship tested	Level of data required	Design of study
Difference Between three or more conditions	At least ordinal	Between subjects: Unrelated designs

Data assumptions: At least ordinal level of data measurement.

Note: This is the non-parametric equivalent of one-way ANOVA; the Kruskal–Wallis is wrongly described as 'ANOVA', which tends to be reserved for the parametric approach using F; for Kruskal–Wallis the full title 'Analysis of Variance' is used.

This is the non-parametric equivalent for the one-way unrelated ANOVA analysis. The data are ranked before performing the calculations. The result tells us how likely the differences between ranks for each condition were to occur if H_0 is true. H_0 claims that the sets of ranks were drawn from identical populations. The test is calculated by ranking all scores as if they belonged to one group, then adding the separate rank totals for groups (see Table 18.5).

Driving skill scores

Pt	**Coffee**	Coffee rank	Pt	**Decaff**	Decaff rank	Pt	**None**	None rank
A	10	10.5	E	3	2	I	4	3.5
B	9	8.5	F	5	5.5	J	2	1
C	6	7	G	10	10.5	K	5	5.5
D	11	12	H	9	8.5	L	4	3.5
	ΣR_c =	38		ΣR_d =	26.5		ΣR_n =	13.5

Table 18.5 Caffeine experiment scores ranked as one group

Procedure	Calculation/result of steps
Rank all scores together irrespective of samples and add ranks for each condition	See ΣR_c ΣR_d ΣR_n in Table 18.5
Calculate the following equation: $H = \dfrac{12}{N(N+1)}\sum \dfrac{r_k^2}{n_k} - 3(N+1)$ where R_k is the sum of ranks in the kth condition and n_k the n for that condition	$H = \dfrac{12}{12(12+1)}\left(\dfrac{38^2}{4} + \dfrac{26.5^2}{4} + \dfrac{13.5^2}{4}\right) - 3(12+1)$ $= 0.077\,(1444/4 + 702.25/4 + 182.25/4) - 39$ $= 5.824$
Treat H as χ^2 with $df = k-1$ Consult Appendix Table 8	Critical value for χ^2 with $p \le .05$ and 2 df is 5.99 hence we may not reject H_0

It is interesting that this test does not give us significance, whereas the ANOVA did. This demonstrates the slightly less sensitive nature of non-parametric equivalent tests although on a very large proportion of tests, where sample sizes are adequate (e.g. ten per condition), the Kruskal–Wallis would give the same significance decision as ANOVA.

To perform *post hoc tests* you can conduct simple Mann-Whitney tests but you should reduce α to .05 divided by the number of tests you perform, as explained earlier. For *effect size* it is simplest to calculate this for the separate Mann-Whitney comparisons as described on pp. 393–5.

Reporting the results of a Kruskal–Wallis one way analysis of variance test

A Kruskal–Wallis test was performed on the skill scores under the three conditions of caffeine. The differences between the rank totals of 38 (coffee), 26.5 (decaff) and 13.5 (none) were not significant, with $H(2) = 5.824$, $p > .05$.

The Jonckheere trend test

On occasion we might predict that a dependent variable would increase in magnitude across levels of an independent variable. We might sensibly suggest that increased doses of caffeine will increase memory performance (up to a point). In this case we are predicting a *trend*. The Jonckheere trend test tells us if such a trend in scores across levels of an independent variable is significant. Space precludes a full computation here but if the reader would like to use this test then they can consult the companion website for a fully calculated example, with tables, at: www.hodderplus.com/psychology/

Multivariate Analysis of Variance (MANOVA)

Suppose you had gathered data evaluating your college course where students assessed 'usefulness', 'interest', 'enjoyment', and so on. With MANOVA it is possible to test these several dependent variables *as a combined set* across the various conditions of the independent variable, which, in this case, might be part-time, full-time and evening students. It would be possible here to conduct a one-way ANOVA for each of the assessment scores separately, adjusting α by dividing by the number of dependent variable tests involved; that is, using α/c as described above. This is generally a valid approach but in certain circumstances (when dependent variables are not correlated with each other) this approach gives a higher chance of a Type I error. MANOVA provides some 'protection' against such Type I errors. If the overall MANOVA shows no significance then you do not proceed to look at the individual ANOVAs that can be conducted on each dependent variable. If MANOVA *is* significant it is legitimate to investigate further and take as significant any of the individual ('univariate') ANOVA results which the MANOVA procedure has shown to be significant. Some statisticians argue that one should still adjust α for the number of dependent variables being tested. In a way, we are back where we were without MANOVA and it is worth consulting your supervisor here to see what they advise locally. The advantage of using MANOVA though is that, though conservative, it will be the best way to avoid Type I error. It is also possible on occasion to obtain a significant MANOVA with none of the individual univariate tests of the dependent variables producing significance. In this case, it is worth a good look at how the dependent variables are combining together, perhaps into one broad construct. Such analysis of the dependent variables can be conducted using *discriminant function analysis* a technique covered in more advanced texts.

MANOVA in SPSS

To conduct a MANOVA analysis with an unrelated design and more than one dependent variable, using SPSS, use the General Linear Model procedure given on p. 513, select Multivariate instead of Univariate in the first line of those instructions and simply enter all your dependent variables into the Dependent Variables box. In the output, if Wilkes Lambda (under Multivariate Tests) is significant then you can proceed to the next results table (**Tests of Between Subjects Effects**) and you may accept as significant any of your dependent variables that show a probability lower than the value of α. For a repeated measures design with several dependent variables treat the set of dependent variables as a second factor and conduct a two-way repeated measures ANOVA.

ANCOVA – Analysis of Co-variance

Suppose we conduct a quasi-experiment using two groups of students, one a day-time class and one a part-time evening group. This evening group is going to use a new interactive computer package for learning statistics and research methods. We want to see whether its members do as well as those in the day-time class who will be taught conventionally. The trouble is that the groups did not start off equal in competence in numeracy. We have not allocated our participant 'pool' to conditions at random. Suppose the evening group, which uses the computer package, contained more adults returning to education after several years. They are generally weaker on maths and statistics, though there is a lot of overlap between the two groups and the range within each group is wide. In addition, when we investigate end-of-year test results as a whole, we find that initial numeracy level correlates quite strongly with 'final achievement', no matter what class the student was in. We suspect that the independent learning package *did* help the evening group but the difference between groups is not significant because the test results are confounded by the initial numeracy difference, which we know will produce a systematic bias. However, unlike other extraneous variables, we have an element of control over this variable because we happen to know how it correlates with final achievement scores. ANCOVA permits us to 'partial out' the effect of the numeracy differences (known as the CO-VARIATE because it co-varies with test results). It gives us an estimate of the means of the two groups that would occur if, in a sense, both groups started from equal positions on numeracy.

It is important to note that ANCOVA does two things. First, if groups start out similar on the co-variate it only takes out the variance that is assumed to be caused by the co-variate. This reduces the error term of the standard ANOVA calculation. That is, we've reduced the 'unexplained' error in the bottom half of the F ratio calculation and we're more likely to see a significant result if there is a real population difference. Second, if the groups *differ* on the co-variate to start with, as in our example, ANCOVA is used to conduct the analysis of variance on the estimate of what the means would be if they didn't differ on the co-variate. This latter use can be controversial.

To conduct an ANCOVA analysis in SPSS select **Analyze/General Linear Model** and then conduct the regular analysis (see p. 513) but enter your co-variate(s) into the **Covariates** box.

SPSS procedures for one-way ANOVA

We will conduct the one-way ANOVA on the coffee and driving experiment data in Table 18.1. Remember that your data must be entered for a *between groups (unrelated) design* (see p. 279, 'Unrelated designs', if unsure). One column is for the dependent variable (***skill***) and one is for the independent variable (***caffeine***) with coding for three levels: *coffee* (1), *decaff* (2) and *none* (3).

1 Select **Analyze/Compare Means/One-way ANOVA**.

Note that, if you wish to obtain *effect size* and *power* estimates, then select **General Linear Model/Univariate** procedure (given on p. 513) entering your independent variable into the **Fixed Factors** box and the dependent variable into the box with that title.

2 Select ***skill*** and move it over to the **Dependent List** box.

3 Select **caffeine** and move it over to the **Factor** box. Note that you do not have to define codes; all levels will be analysed. You test specific sets of levels using contrasts or post hoc tests.

4 If you are making linear contrasts select the **Contrasts** button and enter your values into the **Coefficients** box, clicking **Add** after each one. Enter these coefficients in the order of your independent variable level codes (e.g. if **coffee** has code 1 then enter its coefficient first). Click **Continue**.

5 Select post hoc tests by using the **Post Hoc** button and selecting appropriate tests; here we will choose **Tukey**$_b$. Click **Continue**.

6 In the options box you can ask for **Descriptives** and you should select Levene's test for **Homogeneity of Variance**. Click **Continue**.

Click **OK**.

Output

If you have selected homogeneity of variance (always advisable) this box will appear first in the output. It is all right to proceed and assume homogeneity if Levene's test is *not* significant. The box of central importance is the one headed **ANOVA**. This should appear as shown in Figure 18.5. It tells us the variance **(Mean square)** for between and within groups, and the division of these producing the F value and the probability of this value occurring under H_0 – entitled **Sig.** It is a good idea to check the *df* values to make sure you've put the right variables in the right boxes.

ANOVA

	Sum of squares	df	Mean square	F	Sig.
Between groups	55.500	2	27.750	4.850	.037
Within groups	51.500	9	5.722		
Total	107.000	11			

Figure 18.5 SPSS one-way ANOVA table of results

If you have asked for contrasts these will appear next and are self-explanatory. Post hoc tests occur next. Scheffé and Tukey test each possible pair of means giving a specific result for each mean difference. Significant differences are asterisked. The result for Tukey's$_b$ appears as in Figure 18.6 and tells us that **coffee** and **decaff** form a '*homogeneous subset*', i.e. they are not significantly different from one another. The same is true for **decaff** and **none** together. Hence we can assume that **coffee** and **none** *do* differ significantly at the level shown, which is $p \le .05$. The multiple comparison tests (e.g. Scheffé, Tukey HSD, S-N-K) give the exact probability of each difference and also give homogenous subsets.

SKILL

Tukey B^a

CAFFEINE	N	Subset for alpha = .05	
		1	2
none	4	3.7500	
decaff	4	6.7500	6.7500
coffee	4		9.0000

Means for groups in homogeneous subsets are displayed
a. Uses harmonic mean sample size = 4.000

Figure 18.6 Tukey$_b$ post hoc test output in SPSS

Had we used the GLM approach and asked for effect size and power we would have obtained the main results table shown in Figure 18.7 (which has been squeezed from SPSS to fit the page).

Tests of between-subjects effects

Dependent Variable:skill

Source	Type III sum of squares	df	Mean square	F	Sig.	Partial eta squared	Noncent. parameter	Observed power^b
Corrected model	55.500^a	2	27.750	4.850	.037	.519	9.699	.647
Intercept	507.000	1	507.000	88.602	.000	.908	88.602	1.000
Caffeine	55.500	2	27.750	4.850	.037	.519	9.699	.647
Error	51.500	9	5.722					
Total	614.000	12						
Corrected total	107.000	11						

a. R Squared = .519 (Adjusted R Squared = .412)
b. Computed using alpha = .05

Figure 18.7 ANOVA results including effect size and power – using the GLM approach in SPSS

Kruskal-Wallis in SPSS

1 Select **Analyze/Nonparametric Tests/K Independent Samples**.
2 Select the *skill* dependent variable and move it over to the **Test Variable** box.
3 Select the *caffeine* independent variable and move it over to the **Grouping Variable** box.

4 Highlight *'caffeine'* in the **Grouping Variable** box (if it is not already highlighted) and click **Define Range**.

5 Enter the lowest code (1) as **Minimum** and the highest (3) as **Maximum**, unless you are limiting the number of conditions to be tested. Click **Continue**.

6 Click **OK**.

The result gives you the mean ranks for each condition, the chi-square value (*H*), *df* and the significance level (probability of this result or greater, given H_0 is true).

Exercises

1 Our coffee-testing group of students finally gets things sorted and produces results with eight participants in each condition. The data the students gathered are given below. Conduct a one-way ANOVA (by hand or with SPSS) and include *a priori* tests (use the Bonferroni *t* test described on p. 488). Give: *F*, *p*, *df*, the *SS* values and any significant pairwise comparisons.

None: 3,4,5,6,1,11,4,6; Decaff: 8,9,6,12,9,4,13,7; Coffee: 13,9,7,9,5,7,8,11

2 Produce three samples of eight values by using the random numbers in Table 1 in the Appendix (start anywhere, for each sample, and select the next eight numbers in any direction). Calculate a one-way ANOVA (unrelated) and check the *F* ratio for significance. If it is significant, tell your tutor you're a little sceptical about the 5% significance level convention!

3 If H_0 in a one-way ANOVA with five conditions has already been rejected and you now decide to test all the paired comparisons, what test would be appropriate? $Tukey_a$ or set alpha at .01 and do *t* tests?

4 Suppose, in the last example, you had predicted in your introduction that only the first and third conditions would differ. What test might it be legitimate to conduct?

5 In the same example, you wish to use a linear contrast to test for a difference between conditions one and two together against condition three. What would be the simplest set of coefficients to use?

Answers

1 $F_{2,21} = 4.29$, $p = .27$; $SS_{between} = 67.75$; $SS_{error} = 165.88$; $SS_{total} = 233.63$; From Table 15 with α at .05, 21 *df* and 3 comparisons, *t* needs to be greater than 2.6. *none – decaff, t* (21) = 2.49 NS. *none – coffee, t* (21) = 2.58, NS; *coffee – decaff t* (21) =0.089, NS). Using the Bonferroni *t* test *or* the *t* test for a priori comparisons and adjusting α gives the same result with *none – coffee* a frustrating .02 off significance and probably a signal to the students to increase their sample sizes and re-run the experiment.

3 $Tukey_a$ is safest, but is conservative. However, with five conditions there are ten possible pairwise comparisons to be made so α should be lowered to .05/10 = .005; leaving it at .01 leaves the likelihood of Type I error quite high under H_0 – double the conventional level.

4 *t* test for linear contrast p. 489.

5 1, 1, —2, 0, 0

Glossary

A priori comparisons/ tests or planned comparisons	Tests of differences between selected means, or sets of means, which, from prior theory, were predicted to differ
Analysis of co-variance (ANCOVA)	Statistical procedure that performs an ANOVA while partialling out the effect of a variable that correlates with the dependent variable (the 'co-variate')
Analysis of variance (ANOVA)	Statistical technique that compares variances within and between samples in order to estimate the significance of differences between a set of means
Between groups sum of squares	Sum of squares of deviations of sample means from the grand mean
Between groups variance	Variance of sample means around grand mean
Bonferroni t tests	Procedure for testing means pairwise, which involves raising the critical values of t
Capitalising on chance	Making too many tests with $p \le .05$ on the same data, hence increasing the likelihood of a Type I error
Co-variate	A variable that correlates with a dependent variable on which two groups differ and which can be partialled out using ANCOVA
Error rate per comparison	Given the significance level set, the likelihood of a Type I error in each test made on the data if H_0 is true
Error sum of squares	Sum of squares of deviations of each score from its own group mean
Error variance	Total variance of all scores from their group means
F test/ratio	Statistic giving ratio of between groups to within groups variance
Family-wise error rate	The probability of making at least one Type I error in all the tests made on a set of data, assuming H_0 is true
Grand mean	Mean of all scores in a data set, irrespective of conditions or groups
Jonckheere trend test	Non-parametric statistical test for the significance of a trend in the dependent variable across unrelated conditions
Kruskal–Wallis test	Non-parametric between-groups test of difference between several groups (Mann-Whitney is the two condition equivalent)
Linear coefficients	Values to be entered into an equation for calculating linear contrasts
Linear contrasts	Procedure for testing between individual pairs of means or combinations of means, a priori
MANOVA	Statistical procedure using ANOVA on more than one dependent variable.
Mean sum of squares	Sum of squares divided by df
Newman–Keuls post hoc analysis	Post hoc test of means pairwise so long as number of means is relatively low

Pairwise comparison	Comparison of just two means from a set of means
Φ (Phi)	Phi statistic for estimating power in ANOVA analyses
Post hoc comparisons/tests	Tests between means, or groups of means, conducted *after* inspection of data
Scheffé post hoc analysis	Post hoc test that takes into account all possible comparisons of combinations of means (most conservative post hoc test)
Sum of squares	Addition of the squares of deviations around a mean
Tukey$_a$ (HSD) post hoc analysis	Post hoc test of all possible pairwise comparisons; appropriate choice with a large number of means; considered conservative
Tukey$_b$ post hoc analysis	Less conservative post hoc test than Tukey$_a$
Variance ratio test	Alternative name for the F test – see above
Within groups sum of squares	Sum of squares of deviations of scores around their sample means
Within groups variance	Total variance of scores around sample means

Multi-factorial 19
designs

This chapter deals with multi-factorial ANOVA, where more than one independent variable (or 'factor') is manipulated or observed.

- A design where all factors contain independent samples is known as a *between groups*, *between subjects* or *unrelated design*. When at least one factor is repeated measures, the design is *mixed*, unless all factors are repeated measures, in which case the model is *repeated measures* or *within subjects*.

- The use of more than one factor raises the possibility that each factor may have different effects across different levels of a second factor. This effect is known as an *interaction effect*. For instance, extroverts might exhibit poorer memory in the morning than in the afternoon, whereas the reverse might be true for introverts.

- The effect of one factor over all levels of another factor taken together is known as a *main effect* (e.g. both extroverts and introverts have poorer morning memory performance). Effects of one level of one factor across the levels of another are known as *simple effects* (e.g. extroverts (only) poorer in the afternoon than in the morning).

- In a two-way unrelated ANOVA the total sum of squares (SS) is divided into the SS for the first factor (i.e. independent variable) the SS for the second factor and the SS for the interaction between these two factors. Collectively this is the *SS between groups*. The remaining SS is that for error which is the 'unexplained' variation within cells of the data table.

- The division of sums of squares is also explained for a three-way unrelated ANOVA.

- Calculations are provided for the two-way analysis and for effect and power. SPSS procedures are also provided.

Using two or more independent variables

This chapter introduces analysis of designs where more than one independent variable is manipulated or where more than one non-experimental factor is observed. In these designs independent variables are known as FACTORS and they each have several levels. As we know, the manipulation of a single independent variable with all other variables held constant is a design that has been criticised for its extreme separation from reality. In normal life, we are affected by several influences together at any one time. The two factor design moves that one step closer to reality by testing the effects of two independent variables ('factors') on a dependent variable simultaneously. The appropriate statistical analysis is termed a two-way ANOVA; three-way ANOVA is for three factors and so on. The analysis of unrelated designs, where all factors use independent samples, is commonly known as a BETWEEN GROUPS ANOVA. Where factors are related (repeated measures or matched pairs) the analysis is a WITHIN GROUPS ANOVA. Where both unrelated and related factors are involved the analysis is a MIXED DESIGN ANOVA.

In the last chapter we looked at a fictitious experiment using caffeine as an independent variable and skill as a dependent variable. Reyner and Horne (2000) in fact studied the effects of a 200 mg dose of caffeine, against a placebo dose, on driving performance (measured by lane drift in a simulation task) after five hours' sleep and after none. They also measured subjective sleepiness and EEG activity. They found, essentially, that after five hours' sleep caffeine improved driving performance compared with the placebo for a full two hours of driving whereas, after no sleep, caffeine had some effect for 30 minutes but performance deteriorated markedly thereafter.

Pause for thought

Let's suppose that our plucky students are able to partially replicate this study by asking participants to attend for the driving task *either* after exactly five hours sleep (*5hrs*) or after staying awake for the same period (*no sleep*). Of course ethical issues here are even more serious and let's assume they are satisfactorily dealt with. In each condition one-third of the students are given a strong coffee drink (*coffee*), one third are given decaffeinated coffee (*decaff*) and the remaining third are given no drink (*none*). Remind yourself of the two independent variables in this experiment, which we now call 'factors', and the dependent variable.

The students are conducting a two-way between groups factorial design. One factor is caffeine with three levels – *coffee*, *decaff* and *none*. The second factor is sleep with two levels – *five hours* or *no sleep*. The dependent variable is the score on the driving task. The statistical analysis would be a two-way (2 x 3) between groups ANOVA.

When to use two-way between groups ANOVA

Type of relationship tested	Level of data required	Design of study
Differences	At least interval	Between groups/ subjects: Unrelated design for both factors
With two between groups factors; the effects of each factor alone and of the interactions between factors are assessed		

Data assumptions: Homogeneity of variance; dependent variable normally distributed (see p. 319).

Central features of multi-factorial designs
Interaction effects

The advantage of manipulating more than one factor in an experiment is that we can get to see the ways in which one factor *interacts* with another. The use of two or more factors is often demanded by the research question itself, but is often simply convenient since, in effect, it produces two experiments in one, plus the interaction. Statistically, it is advantageous in that Type I errors are more efficiently accounted for than they would be by running several experiments each with a .05 probability of Type I error.

Godden and Baddeley (1975) conducted a neatly symmetrical 2 x 2 mixed experimental design the results of which are depicted in Figure 19.1. They asked scuba divers to learn a list of words either on dry land or under water. Half of those who learned on land were asked to recall the words on dry land; the other half had to recall while under water. Those who learned under water were similarly divided for recall. In Figure 19.1 it can be seen that learning and recalling in the same environment produces superior recall to conditions where the two environments are different. The

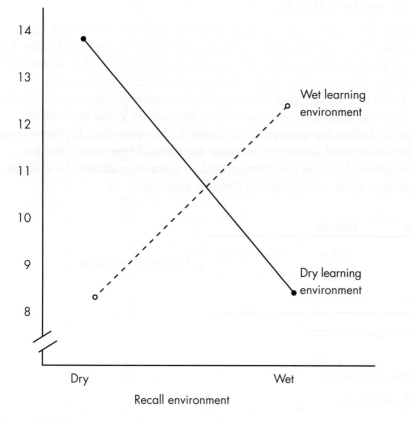

Figure 19.1 An interaction effect – mean recall scores for learning and recall either on land or under water (from Godden and Baddeley, 1975)

effect shown is known as an INTERACTION EFFECT. This is because the effect of one factor changes across the different levels of the other factor.

In this experiment, two independent variables were manipulated simultaneously: mode of learning and mode of recall. In this case the research question (can memory recall be place-specific?) demanded this 2 x 2 design. The design could be seen as comprising two separate experiments. However, had we only asked divers to learn on land then recall on land or under water we might have come to the erroneous conclusion that water interferes with learning because in this condition the divers recalled fewer words. The complementary, but odd, study would have been to have divers learn under water, then be tested 'wet' or 'dry' (the dotted line in Figure 19.1). However, by using two learning environments and two recall environments, we complete the combinations and unearth the more general principle that performance is better if both learning and recall environments are similar – a point to remind your tutors of when exams are set in the great hall! An extremely important point here is that we have *more* than simply the addition of two separate experiments. The participants here are all allocated randomly from the same participant 'pool' (no pun intended!), whereas there could be a stronger possibility of participant differences if two quite separate studies were run.

The camouflage of main effects

In the language of factorial designs a MAIN EFFECT is the effect of one factor on the dependent variable irrespective of any other factor. Suppose that in Reyner and Horne's experiment coffee had improved performance for all participants no matter whether they had no sleep or five hours' sleep. In Table 19.1 we would find that Mean a+c was higher than Mean b+d. Imagine this as an experiment on the effect of caffeine *only*, ignoring the sleep factor completely. Similarly we can also look at the main effect of sleep ignoring caffeine (Mean a+b vs. Mean c+d). When we analyse results in a two-way design we look at the main effect for factor A, the main effect for factor B and the interaction effect. In the Godden and Badeley experiment there would be a main effect for learning environment, a main effect for recall environment and an interaction effect. The analysis will tell us which, if any, of these main and interaction effects is significant.

	Caffeine	Placebo		
5 hours' sleep	Cell a	Cell b	Mean a + b	⎫ Main effect for sleep
No sleep	Cell c	Cell d	Mean c + d	⎭
	Mean a + c	Mean b + d		

These two means are the
main effect for caffeine

Table 19.1 Main effects of caffeine and sleep

The study by Awosunle and Doyle (2001) described briefly on p. 153 produced a 2 x 3 interaction effect illustrated in Figure 19.2. Here we have one two-level factor (ethnicity of participant) and a three-level factor (perceived ethnicity of candidate); both factors are between subjects.

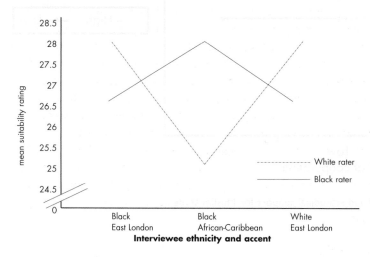

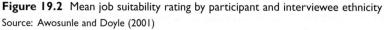

Figure 19.2 Mean job suitability rating by participant and interviewee ethnicity
Source: Awosunle and Doyle (2001)

In this experiment, if we *only* looked at the ratings of the black and white observers we might conclude that their ratings are exactly the same since the mean rating for black observers is 27.17 and the mean for white observers is also 27.17. Likewise, if we *only* consider the mean ratings of the interviewees we get 27.38 for the Black interviewee with East London accent, 26.63 for the Black interviewee with Afro-Caribbean accent and 27.5 for the White interviewee – virtually no difference. The two main effects are not significant but they camouflage a strong interaction effect.

Interaction effects do not always have to be so dramatic. Rabrenovic, Levin and Oliver (2007) used a 2 x 3 factorial design to investigate the hypothesis that greater cooperation with members of an out-group would improve attitudes towards them. They arranged for groups of students to interview other Muslim students on campus about their family lives. All the 'Muslim students' were in fact confederates of the experimenter and acted a predetermined role. In the 'high cooperation' condition the 'interviewees' were easy to contact and student participants could complete four or five interviews. In the 'low cooperation condition' phones were unanswered or busy and only one interview could be completed. In the zero contact condition no contact was involved at all. Student participants were also divided into 'high fear' and 'low fear' around the mean of a perception of threat scale which assessed how fearful students were of another 9/11 type attack on the USA. As a measure of attitude towards Muslim students, participants were asked how likely they would be to support a policy of investigation of Muslim students without 'probable cause'. Opposition to this policy was taken as support for Muslim students. Figure 19.3 shows the significant interaction effect that occurred.

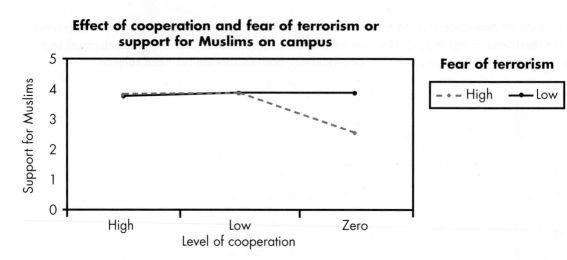

Figure 19.3 Interaction of contact level and attitudinal support for Muslim students
Source: Adapted from Rabrenovic *et al.* (2007: 299)

Contrary to the experimenters' expectations high or low cooperation had no overall effect on support for Muslim students. However, high fear students in the zero co-operation condition were lower on support than low fear students, whereas, high fear and low fear students in the high and low co-operation conditions did not differ. In the language of ANOVA, there was no main effect for co-operation, no main effect for fear but the interaction effect was significant.

Figure 19.4 shows some of the kinds of interaction effect that can occur in research using multi-factor ANOVA. The effects mentioned are significant. Of course, researchers often use three- and even four-way ANOVA analyses but, when they do, interaction effects are harder to display and even harder to interpret.

Multi-factorial designs can become quite complicated. Cook and Wilding (2001) tested participants' recognition of a voice after they had either heard it saying a short sentence once or three times, when an accompanying face was present or not, and with or without explicit instructions to attend to the voice; this gives a 2 x 2 x 2 design. David, Chapman, Foot and Sheehy (1986) used a 4 x 2 x 16 design in the investigation of road accidents, and Gulian and Thomas (1986) used a 2 x 2 x 3 x 4 design where males and females were tested in high or low noise, under three different sets of instructions about the noise across four different periods of testing! There is no limit to the complexity of designs that can be used – apart from the researchers' patience with data analysis and the size of the willing participant pool.

Simple effects

A SIMPLE EFFECT occurs when we extract part of a multi-factor ANOVA result and look at just the effect of one level of one factor across all levels of another factor. For instance, in Rabrenovic *et al.*'s

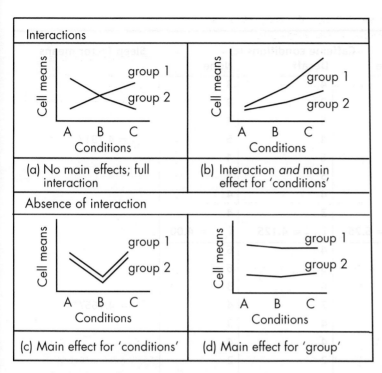

Interactions

(a) No main effects; full interaction

(b) Interaction *and* main effect for 'conditions'

Absence of interaction

(c) Main effect for 'conditions'

(d) Main effect for 'group'

Note on line charts for ANOVA results: Technically speaking the points in interaction charts such as these should not be joined up because there are no points between condition A and condition B. Here, we'll follow the standard convention, however, of graphically representing the direction of effects remembering that the lines should not be read as representing values between discrete values of the independent variables.

Figure 19.4 Two-way ANOVA possible interaction effects

study there was a simple effect in the zero co-operation condition across high and low fear students. Simple effects are like the simple experiments we have considered so far, extracted from the overall multi-factorial ANOVA results. They can be investigated for significance using *t* tests, planned contrasts or a one-way ANOVA if there are three or more levels. Like post hoc tests, the investigation of simple effects must still avoid 'capitalising on chance'.

Data in a two-way unrelated ANOVA design

Let's return now to our project students and take a look at some fictitious results they might have gathered. The hypothesis is that coffee improves skill scores after five hours' sleep but not after none. The data obtained are arranged in the 'cells' shown in Table 19.2.

Don't be put off by this table. I have had to use subscripts in order to be clear about exactly which statistic is being referred to, now that we have a more complex design. The subscript s refers to the sleep conditions, hence $\bar{x}_{s1}$ is the mean for the first sleep condition overall (the five hours' sleep participants). $\bar{x}_{s2c3}$ is the mean for the participants in the second sleep and third caffeine condition (no sleep and no drink).

Skill scores

Sleep conditions (s)	Coffee	Caffeine conditions (c) Decaff	None	Sleep factor means
	8	4	3	
	7	2	3	
	6	5	4	
5hrs	6	4	5	$\bar{x}_{s1} = 4.7917$
	3	6	4	
	5	5	5	
	9	4	4	
	6	3	4	
	$\bar{x}_{s1c1} = 6.25$	$\bar{x}_{s1c2} = 4.125$	$\bar{x}_{s1c3} = 4.00$	
	5	4	6	
	4	5	6	
	3	6	3	
Nosleep	2	7	4	$\bar{x}_{s2} = 4.1667*$
	4	4	3	
	7	4	4	
	4	2	2	
	3	3	5	
	$\bar{x}_{s2c1} = 4$	$\bar{x}_{s2c2} = 4.375$	$\bar{x}_{s2c3} = 4.125$	
Caffeine factor means	$\bar{x}_{c1} = 5.125$	$\bar{x}_{c2} = 4.25$	$\bar{x}_{c3} = 4.0625$	$\bar{x}_{sc} = 4.48$ (grand mean)

$$\Sigma x = 215$$
$$\Sigma x^2 = 1081$$
$$(\Sigma x)^2 = 46225$$
$$(\Sigma x)^2/N = 963.02 = C$$

* Overlong decimal figures are used here in order that our figures come close to those given by SPSS. With sensible rounding, our ANOVA results would be more different from the SPSS result than they are.

Table 19.2 Driving skill scores by caffeine and sleep conditions

Partitioning the sums of squares

For the one-way analysis in Chapter 18 we found that when we calculated the sums of squares for the one-way ANOVA we had three terms: SS_{total}, $SS_{between}$ and SS_{error}. For two-way unrelated ANOVA, we divide the sums of squares as shown in Figure 19.5. Here, the split is the same as for the one-way analysis – we have the same three elements. However, $SS_{between}$ becomes known as SS_{cells} and it is the variation of the six individual experimental condition means around the grand mean (the means in the six cells of Table 19.2). By 'condition' we mean the six 'cells' formed by the 2 x 3 design, five hours and coffee, five hours and decaff, and so on. The variation of these six cell means around the grand mean amounts to all the 'explained' variation in the scores overall. The 'unexplained' variation or 'error' is the amounts by which individual participants' scores vary *within* the six conditions.

TOTAL *SS*

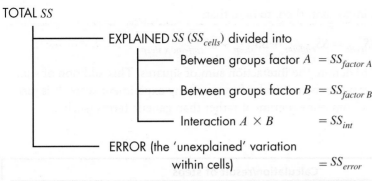

- EXPLAINED *SS* (SS_{cells}) divided into
  - Between groups factor *A* = $SS_{factor\,A}$
  - Between groups factor *B* = $SS_{factor\,B}$
  - Interaction $A \times B$ = SS_{int}
- ERROR (the 'unexplained' variation within cells) = SS_{error}

Figure 19.5 Division of sums of squares in a two-way unrelated ANOVA

The special feature to note here, however, is the fact that the 'explained' variation (SS_{cells}) can be broken up according to the factors of the experiment. We have $SS_{caffeine}$ which is the variation of the overall caffeine condition means ($\bar{x}_c$) around the grand mean. We have SS_{sleep}, which is the variation of the overall sleep condition means ($\bar{x}_s$) around the grand mean. Finally we have the new and centrally important contribution to explained variation, which is caused by the interaction effect. Interactions are significant when individual cell means across the levels of one factor do not run in the pattern occurring across the other level(s).

Although it is jumping ahead a little, have a look at the interaction from our students' fictitious experiment with coffee and sleep in Figure 19.6. Interaction occurs because the cell means for *5hrs* do not run in the same pattern as the cell means for *no sleep*. The coffee condition difference seems to be the culprit here.

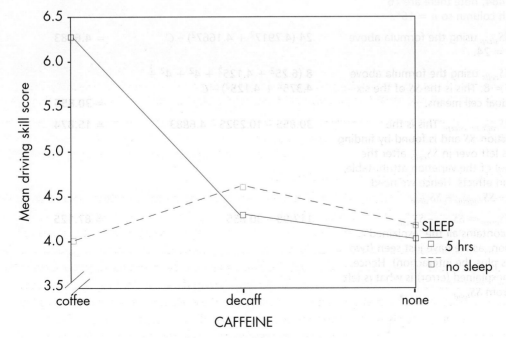

Figure 19.6 Interaction of caffeine conditions with prior sleep

In the calculations that follow it is important, then, to note that:

$$SS_{total} = SS_{cells} + SS_{error} \text{ AND } SS_{cells} = SS_{caffeine} + SS_{sleep} + SS_{caffeine \times sleep}$$

The last term here is what we use to denote the interaction sum of squares. This addition of sums of squares would be valid no matter what the particular factors of any experiment were. It is just simpler here to use the actual terms from our experiment rather than generic terms (such as $SS_{factor\,A}$).

Procedure	Calculation/result of steps
1 Find SS_{total} as on p. 484. Use all the individual scores (x) in the equation: $$\sum x^2 - \frac{(\sum x)^2}{N}$$	$\sum x - \dfrac{(\sum x)^2}{N} = 1081 - 46225/48$ $= 1081 - 963.02 = \mathbf{117.98}$ Note: from this point $\dfrac{(\sum x)^2}{N}$ (963.02) is referred to as C for simplicity.
2 Find $SS_{caffeine}$ using $\quad n\sum \bar{x}_k^2 - \dfrac{(\sum x)^2}{N}$ as we did for $SS_{between}$ on p. 484; note there are 16 in each column so $n = 16^*$.	$16\,(5.125^2 + 4.25^2 + 4.0625^2) - C \quad = \mathbf{10.2925}$
3 Find SS_{sleep} using the formula above and $n = 24$.	$24\,(4.7917^2 + 4.1667^2) - C \qquad = \mathbf{4.6883}$
4 Find SS_{cells} using the formula above and $n = 8$. This is the SS of the six individual cell means.	$8\,(6.25^2 + 4.125^2 + 4^2 + 4^2 + 4.375^2 + 4.125^2) - C$ $= \mathbf{30.855}$
5 Find $SS_{caffeine\,xsleep}$; This is the interaction SS and is found by finding what's left over in SS_{cells} after the removal of the variation attributable to main effects. Hence we need: $SS_{cells} - SS_{caffeine} - SS_{sleep}$	$30.855 - 10.2925 - 4.6883 \qquad = \mathbf{15.874}$
6 Find $SS_{error} = SS_{total} - SS_{cells}$ SS_{cells} contains all the 'explained' variation, as we have just seen (two factors plus the interaction). Hence, the unexplained (error) is what is left over from SS_{total}	$117.98 - 30.855 \qquad\qquad = \mathbf{87.125}$

7 df are $n-1$ where n is as above; for interaction df multiply together the df for each factor involved. For error subtract all df from $N-1$ (here, 48 results so $N-1 = 47$ and error $df = 47 - 2 - 1 - 2 = \mathbf{42}$

	SS	df	MS	F
Caffeine	10.293	2	5.146	2.481
Sleep	4.688	1	4.688	2.260
Caffeine x Sleep	15.874	2	7.937	3.827
Error	87.125	42	2.074	

MS are found as before by dividing the effect SS by appropriate df. F is MS_{effect}/MS_{error}

Note that we have an effect/error calculation for each effect, main$_A$, main$_B$ and interaction$_{A \times B}$.

Check for significance with the appropriate df

*Note that, so long as n is the same in each condition we can put n outside the bracket and just multiply the result inside brackets by n once; in the one-way ANOVA example earlier we multiplied each mean by n in order to emphasise the procedure.

Interpretation

Checking in the F table, only the interaction of caffeine with sleep is significant with $p \leq .05$. The shape of the interaction, shown in Figure 19.6, makes it pretty clear that the source of this interaction is the effect of coffee only in the five hours' sleep condition. This simple effect could be tested using the t test described on p. 488 and using the error term here of 2.074 and 42 df. The results in general should be considered in the light of effect size and power implications (see below).

Reporting the result of a two-way unrelated ANOVA

The general rule here is not to give details of those effects that were not significant. We might say here that 'No other effects, besides the interaction, were significant ...', or we might identify them as we have done here.

A two-way between subjects ANOVA showed that the main effects for caffeine and sleep deprivation were not significant. The interaction between caffeine and sleep deprivation was significant, $F(2,42) = 3.827$, $p \leq .05$. The effect size was large (partial $\eta^2 = .154$). Means for the interaction are shown in Table X, where it appears that coffee improved scores in the five hours' sleep condition but not in the sleep-deprivation condition. (Table X would be provided in the report.)

Because it would look cluttered to include all the means for the interaction, the reader is referred to a table of means (not shown here). If the main effect for caffeine *had* been significant it might be reported as follows, including the means: 'As expected, the mean score for the coffee conditions (M 5.63, SD 1.99) was higher than for the decaff conditions (M 4.25, SD 1.39) and the no drink conditions (M 4.06, SD 1.12). This main effect was significant, $F(2.38) = 5.67$, $p \leq .05$ ...'

Effect sizes and power

For a general introduction to the importance of estimating effect size and checking power, please see p. 385. The effect size for either main effect or the interaction can be found using formula 2 for η^2 on p. 485, just making sure that the appropriate F_{effect} is chosen along with the associated df. Note that here the effect size is referred to as 'partial eta squared' as there are several effects. The fuller calculation of Φ' in a two-way design with factors A and B is complicated but here are the procedures in brief since they do give more accurate estimations.

For factor A, $\Phi'_A = \sqrt{\dfrac{\sum \alpha_i^2}{a\sigma_e^2}}$ where α_i is the difference between the grand mean and each

mean for factor A ignoring any difference across factor B. Ideally, these means would be the true population means if known but in calculating power after an experiment we use the sample means and assume these are good estimates of the population means. For our caffeine/sleep study, then, the grand mean is 4.48 and the α values would be the differences between 4.48 and each $\bar{x}_c$ value, that is, 5.13 (*caffeine*), 4.25 (*decaff*) and 4.06 (*none*). Each of these differences is squared, the results added and this result for the top of the equation is divided by a, the number of levels of A (three in the caffeine case) multiplied by the mean square for error (MSE). To find Φ, we multiply Φ'_A by the root of the number in each condition but we must remember that 'condition' here means level of factor A. There are 16 in each level. The formula for Φ is $\Phi'_A \sqrt{bn}$. n is the number in each cell of the table and b is the number of levels in the other factor (i.e. 2 x 8 = 16 scores in each level of factor A).

For factor B we use $\varphi'_B = \sqrt{\dfrac{\sum \beta_j^2}{b\sigma_e^2}}$, b being the number of levels in factor B (2) and β being the

differences between each *sleep* level mean (4.79 and 4.17) and the grand mean (4.48).

For the interaction things really are tricky. The formula is $\Phi'_{AB} = \sqrt{\dfrac{\sum \alpha_i \beta_j^2}{ab\sigma_e^2}}$. The calculation of $\alpha\beta$

is carried out for each individual cell of the data table. The calculation is: $\bar{x}_g - \bar{x}_{Ai} - \bar{x}_{Bj} - \bar{x}_{AiBj}$, where $\bar{x}_g$ is the grand mean, $\bar{x}_{Ai}$ is the factor A level mean for that cell, $\bar{x}_{Bj}$ is the appropriate factor B level mean and $\bar{x}_{AiBj}$ is the individual cell mean. As an example, for the top left coffee/5hrs cell (i.e. *s1c1*) in Table 19.2 the calculation would be: 4.48 – 5.13 – 4.79 – 6.25. This operation has to be completed for all six cell means in our example, and the result divided by $abMSE$ to obtain Φ'_{AB} after taking the square root. We then need to multiply by $\sqrt{n}$ (n being just the number in each cell this time) to obtain Φ_{AB}. When you consult Appendix Table 13, you need to use the appropriate df as df_t, for the effect you are checking. df_e is the error df as before.

Three-way ANOVA calculation

I hope you would never be unfortunate enough to find yourself needing to calculate a three-way unrelated ANOVA by hand (not a likely event in the twenty-first century). I will list here the components that would need to be found, however, so that you can understand what a computer printout is telling you. It's important to lay out your data clearly even if you're using a computer, since otherwise you'll get in a mess wondering what all the components of the results table are.

Imagine that our dogged students used a further condition where participants either performed their driving task alone or in front of an audience. Call this factor 'observe' with the levels *alone* and *audience*. Table 19.2 might be the scores for the *'alone'* condition and there would be an identical table, but with different scores, for the *'audience'* condition. In this three-way design there would be three main effects for the three independent variables, three two-way interactions and an overall three-way interaction! $SS_{caffeine}$ and SS_{sleep} would be found as before except that in this example n for caffeine would be 32 and for sleep it would be 48 as it would also be for $SS_{observe}$. To find the interaction between caffeine and sleep you would need to calculate $SS_{cells\ caffeine\ x\ sleep}$. There would be six caffeine x sleep cells ignoring the split between alone and audience. In other words the first (top left) cell would contain the alone caffeine/5hrs results (as in Table 19.2) *plus* the audience caffeine/5hrs results – 16 in all, so you would use the SS_{cells} formula given earlier but with these means and $n = 16$. $SS_{caffeine\ x\ sleep}$ would then be $SS_{cells\ caffeine\ x\ sleep} - SS_{caffeine} - SS_{sleep}$. For $SS_{sleep\ x\ observe}$ you would ignore all caffeine divisions and find $SS_{cells\ sleep\ x\ observe}$. There would be four of these cells and as an example the first would be that for 5hrs/alone. This would be all the values at present in the top row of Table 19.2. There would be a similar set of 24 scores for 5hrs/audience, hence in these calculations $n = 24$. $SS_{sleep\ x\ observe}$ would be $SS_{cells\ sleep\ x\ observe} - SS_{sleep} - SS_{observe}$. $SS_{caffeine\ x\ observe}$ would remain to be calculated and finally there is a three-way interaction term $SS_{caffeine\ x\ sleep\ x\ observe}$. Here you would use the 12 individual experimental groups (coffee/5hrs/audience etc) as the basic cells, finding $SS_{cells\ caffeine/sleep/observe}$ ($n = 8$) and subtract all the other SS for main effects and two-way interactions from it in order to obtain the three-way interaction value. To find SS_{error} we would calculate SS_{total} using all the individual scores as in the two-way example and then subtract from this all the SS for the three main effects, the three two-way interactions and the three-way interaction.

SPSS procedure for two-way between groups ANOVA

1 Select **Analyze/General Linear Model/Univariate**.

2 Enter *skill* as the **Dependent Variable**.

3 Enter the *caffeine* and *sleep* factors into the **Fixed Factors** box to the right. (Don't worry about Random Factors; if you ever need to use these you would already know why!)

4 It is very useful to select **Plots** here to get an interaction chart. Usually it is less confusing to have fewer lines on your chart, as in Figure 19.6, so put *sleep* into the **Separate Lines** slot and *caffeine* into the **Horizontal axis** slot. This way there will be two lines, one for *5hrs* and one for *none*, with the three levels of *caffeine* on the x-axis. Don't forget to click **add** here before clicking **continue**.

5 You can use the **Post Hoc** button to choose post hoc tests for each factor as in the one-way procedure.

6 You can choose, with the **Options** button, **Descriptive Statistics**, **Homogeneity (of variance) Tests**, **Estimates of Effect Size** and **Observed Power** among other more advanced items.

7 Notice that you can also enter a **Covariate** here and use an ANCOVA procedure.

8 Click **OK**.

With a fairly simple analysis including only descriptives, homogeneity of variance, effect size and power, you should find that the first box gives you the number of participants in each level of each factor. This is a good check on whether you have entered variables correctly. The next box gives descriptives for cells, levels, factors and the grand mean ('total', 'total'). Next comes Levene's test, which gives us the all-clear on homogeneity of variance (see p. 365) and finally the main analysis (see Figure 19.7).

Tests of between-subjects effects

Dependent variable: SKILL

Source	Type III sum of squares	df	Mean square	F	Sig.	Eta squared	Noncent. parameter	Observed power[b]
Corrected model	30.854[a]	5	6.171	2.975	.022	.262	14.874	.808
Intercept	963.021	1	963.021	464.240	.000	.917	464.240	1.000
CAFFEINE	10.292	2	5.146	2.481	.096	.106	4.961	.471
SLEEP	4.687	1	4.687	2.260	.140	.051	2.280	.312
CAFFEINE *SLEEP	15.875	2	7.938	3.826	.030	.154	7.653	.663
Error	87.125	42	2.074					
Total	1081.000	48						
Corrected total	117.979	47						

a. R squared = .262 (adjusted R squared = .174)

b. Computed using alpha = .05

Figure 19.7 SPSS output for a two-way unrelated ANOVA analysis

> **Note:** There are slight differences here from our by-hand calculations because of the decimal rounding. SPSS takes all decimals to four places throughout its calculations.

Usually you are interested only in main and interaction effects and these are provided in capital letters to the left. In our example, the main effect for caffeine was not significant ($F_{2,42} = 2.481$, $p = .096$), the main effect for sleep was not significant ($F_{1,42} = 2.226$, $p = .14$) but the interaction between caffeine and sleep was significant ($F_{2,42} = 3.826$, $p = .03$). The effect size (partial eta squared) and 'observed power' are given in the right hand columns. You should finally find a chart looking like Figure 19.7.

Exercises

1 The analysis of the students' caffeine experiment results described in this chapter could be described as a 2 x 3 between groups ANOVA with the factor **sleep** having levels *5hrs* and *no sleep* and factor **caffeine** having levels *coffee, decaff* and *none*. Describe in similar terms analyses for the following designs.

   (a) Effect of psychoanalysis, humanistic therapy *or* behaviour modification on separate groups of male and female clients.

   (b) Effect of age (old/young) on recall performance using imagery, rehearsal *and* visual cue memorising methods on each participant.

   (c) Participants are asked to perform an easy memory task and then a hard one in front of an audience *and* while alone.

   (d) Effect of either alcohol, placebo or no drink on performance of a visual monitoring task under conditions of loud, moderate, intermittent *and* no noise.

   (e) Extroverts and introverts are given a stimulant, placebo *or* tranquilliser and observed as they perform an energetic task followed by a dull one.

   (f) People with high *or* low race prejudice observe and provide a liking score for *either* a black *or* white person performing *either* a pro-social, neutral *or* hostile act.

2 Imagine that two groups of students, one vegetarian, the other meat-eating (Factor 1 – groups 1 and 2) are asked to memorise animal words, vegetable words and flower words (Factor 2 – conditions A, B and C). There's no research I know of which would predict any particular result so suppose, in each example below, that the stated results occurred. Pick out the diagram from Figure 19.4 that you think is the best fit to the results that are described. Assume that 'differences', when mentioned, are significant.

   (a) Vegetarians and meat-eaters differ. No other effect.

   (b) Vegetarians and meat-eaters do not differ but there are differences across conditions as a whole. No interaction.

   (c) There are overall differences across conditions only.

   (d) There is no overall difference between eating styles or between memory conditions.

   (e) There is at least one simple effect between groups.

   (f) There is only an interaction effect between eating style and memory condition.

   (g) There is an overall difference across conditions but this is more extreme for one of the groups.

3 Suppose the following data were obtained from a study of the sociability of boys (bold) and girls with no siblings who have or haven't attended pre-school of some kind before starting school. Calculate the two-way ANOVA and comment on the effects.

Sociability scores	
Children who attended pre-school	Children who did not attend pre-school
45 23 25 56 49 35 54 45 42 25	**9 13 24 18 15** 23 34 35 51 48

4 Suppose we measure people on a variable called 'sociability' ('S' for short). We then investigate their performance on a wiggly-wire task where touching the wire with a metal loop-on-a-stick causes a buzzer to sound and records an error. Suppose it is true that high S people perform well in front of an audience but poorly alone, and that low S people perform the other way round. Overall, high and low S people tend to perform at about the same level. What effects would you expect from ANOVA? Sketch the expected effects or choose the appropriate diagram from Figure 19.4.

Answers

1 (Note that the term 'within groups' in the answers below could also be 'repeated measures'.)

(a) 3 × 2 between groups ANOVA with factor **therapy** having levels psychoanalysis, humanistic and BM and factor **gender** having levels male and female.

(b) 3 × 2 mixed design ANOVA with between groups factor **age** having levels old and young and within groups factor **memorise** having levels imagery, rehearsal and visual cue.

(c) 2 × 2 within groups ANOVA with factor **task** having levels hard and easy, and factor **observe** having levels audience and alone.

(d) 3 × 4 mixed ANOVA with between groups factor **drink** having levels alcohol, placebo or no drink and within groups factor **noise** having levels loud, moderate, intermittent and none.

(e) 2 × 3 × 2 mixed ANOVA with between groups factor **type** having levels extrovert and introvert, between groups factor **drug** having levels stimulant, placebo or tranquilliser and within groups factor **task** having levels energetic and dull.

(f) 2 × 2 × 3 between groups ANOVA with factor **prejudice** having levels high and low, factor **ethnicity** having levels black and white and factor **act** having levels pro-social, neutral and hostile.

2 (a) d; (b) c; (c) c; (d) a (didn't say 'no interaction'!); (e) a or b; (f) a; (g) b

3 See table below.

Source of variation	Sum of squares	df	Mean sum of squares	F	Probability of F
Total	26461.05	19			
Main effects:					
School	832.05	1	832.05	6.671	.02
Gender	661.25	1	661.25	5.302	.035
Interaction					
School x					
Gender	594.05	1	594.05	4.763	.044
Error	1995.6	16	124.725		

Although main effects are significant this is clearly because of the interaction effect, which is also significant. Because the cell mean for the male group with no pre-school experience is so low this affects both the overall male score and the overall pre-school score. The descriptives show that the other three cell means are almost the same. Hence the interaction is the 'significant' finding.

4 No main effects. Significant interaction effect. Diagram (a) from Figure 19.4.

Glossary

Between groups ANOVA	ANOVA analysis where only unrelated factors are involved
Factor	Independent variable in a multi-factorial design
Interaction effect	Significant effect where effect of one factor is different across levels of another factor
Main effect	One factor alone has a significant effect across its levels, irrespective of any other factors
Mixed design ANOVA	ANOVA analysis where both related and unrelated factors are involved
Simple effect	One level of one factor alone has a significant effect across levels of another factor
Within groups ANOVA	ANOVA analysis where only related factors are involved

20 ANOVA for repeated measures designs

This chapter deals with one-way or multi-factor ANOVA when at least one of the factors is related – that is, a repeated measures or matched pairs design has been used.

- The one-way repeated measures model partials out the variation that relates to variation among the individuals in the sample – the *between subjects variation*.
- If participants all differ in the same way across conditions, i.e. between conditions, then most of the total variation will be accounted for by the *between conditions* variation and the *between subjects* variation, leaving very little residual 'error' (which is the interaction of participants with conditions – the extent to which participants do not vary consistently across conditions). When this residual error is small relative to the effect *SS*, a high value of *F* will occur.
- Data assumptions for repeated measures analyses include normality but also *sphericity*.
- In multi-factor repeated measures designs, each repeated measures main effect has its own error term, as does each interaction.
- In a mixed design, unrelated factors are dealt with as in the unrelated model dealt with earlier. Their main effects, plus interaction for the unrelated factors only, plus error, together make up the *between subjects* variation. The *within subjects* variation is made up of the main effects of the repeated measures factors plus their interaction, plus their interactions with the unrelated factors, plus the residual error for within subjects.
- A non-parametric equivalent of the one-way repeated measures ANOVA is *Friedman's test*, procedures for which are described here.
- SPSS procedures for one-way and two-way repeated measures designs, and for mixed designs, are provided.

Related designs

With our work on ANOVA up to now we have covered only designs that use independent samples throughout. We now look at 'related designs', which very often are repeated measures but which also include matched pairs. We shall look first at a repeated measures design in which a group of participants takes part in all the levels of a single independent variable. Our model study is a fictitious experiment based on an investigation of 'levels of processing', and as originally conducted by Craik and Tulving (1975). Participants are asked one of three possible questions about each of a set of presented words, which they later have to recall:

1 Is it in capitals?

2 Does it rhyme with ___?

3 Does it fit into the sentence ___?

These three conditions are known as 1. *physical*, 2. *phonetic*, 3. *semantic*, based on the assumed type of processing the participants have to perform on the presented word for each type of question. There are 45 words altogether, 15 for each type of question. The conditions are presented in a randomised manner (see p. 71). The hypothesis is that participants will recall more items at 'deeper' levels of processing. We expect $mean_{physical} < mean_{phonetic} < mean_{semantic}$. The independent variable is the question type and the dependent variable is number of items correctly recalled. The data in Table 20.1 might have been produced by such an experiment. Note that $\bar{x}_p$ is the mean of each participant's set of scores.

Type of stimulus question:

Participant	Physical	Phonetic	Semantic	$\bar{x}_p$
a	5	8	9	7.33
b	3	5	10	6
c	4	8	12	8
d	6	6	11	7.67
e	5	4	10	6.33
$\bar{x}_c$	4.6	6.2	10.4	$\bar{x}_{cp}$ = 7.07

N = 15 (= number of **scores**, not participants)
n_p = number of participants = 5 n_c = number of conditions = 3
Σx = 106 Σx^2 = 862 $(\Sigma x)^2$ = 11236

Table 20.1 Words correctly recalled by types of stimulus question

---

When to use one-way repeated measures ANOVA

Type of relationship tested	Level of data required	Design of study
Difference Between three or more levels of one within groups factor	At least interval	Related design Repeated measures or Matched pairs

Data assumptions: *sphericity* (see p. 523); data on interval scale; sampling distribution of means is normal; assumed by checking that dependent variable is normally distributed (see p. 319).

Rationale for one-way repeated measures ANOVA

Think back to the basic rationale for one-way ANOVA outlined in Chapter 18. We must again consider *all* the variation among all the scores in Table 20.1. As in Chapter 18, it can be argued that all the variation is explained by two sets of variations: the variation of scores around the mean *within* each sample (*within groups*), and the variation *between* the sample means. This is still true here, of course. However, and this is the central difference with repeated measures, we can now explain *further* the *variation within groups*. Why? Simply because the samples consist of the *same people*. We know already in part why scores differ within groups; it is because people simply differ as individuals.

Between subjects and between conditions variation

Let's try to make this clear with a graphic example. Take a look at *only* the lines A, B and C in Figure 20.1. These are meant to represent the scores of three remarkably consistent participants in the levels of processing experiment already described. Yes, the results look pretty unrealistic, but bear with me for the purposes of explanation. Let's consider the variation of all the scores for these three participants around their overall mean. We can fully explain the source of variation among their scores.

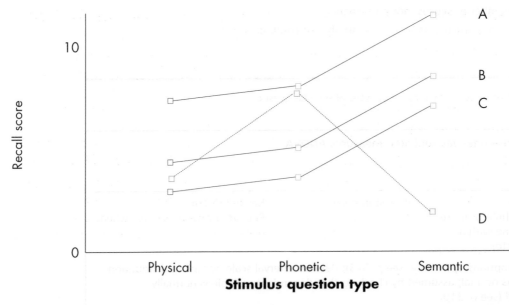

Figure 20.1 Source of error in a repeated measures design

First, there is variation attributable to the conditions of the experiment (variation BETWEEN CONDITIONS). The scores improve from physical to phonetic and then even more so to the semantic condition. Second, there is *variation among the participants themselves* – participant A is quite a bit better than participants B and C. This second source is known as the variation BETWEEN SUBJECTS.

(Note that 'subjects' is the conventional statistical term for cases, be they people, rats or schools). The important point here is that, in this example, there is no other source of variation among the scores; the variation *between conditions* and *between subjects* accounts for *all* the variation among the scores; there is no further source of 'error'. Therefore, if we could *extract* the variation attributable to the participants we would be left with the variation attributable *only* to the conditions and this is precisely what we are after.

OK, the pattern of performance for the three participants was unrealistic. Now have a look at the performance of participant D in Figure 20.1. In the context of what we have just said, here is someone mucking up our experiment. Whereas the other three participants vary in *the same way* across conditions, participant D is a maverick and varies in a *different* way. This is in fact an *interaction* of participants with conditions just as encountered in the last chapter between two factors. It is also what we can refer to as *error*. It is this unexplained error, attributable to the ways that different participants vary across conditions *other than* because of the independent variable, that we would want to keep to a minimum while keeping variation across conditions to a maximum. The central point here is that the variation among scores that is *not* attributable to conditions (what we want to keep to a minimum as in the unrelated design) can be broken up into error and variation among participants *because this is a repeated measure design*. We are reducing the 'unexplained variance' on the bottom of the standard equation for F – the smaller this is, the larger will be the F value. We reduce 'error' by explaining *some* of the variation not due to the conditions of our experiment.

The partition of sums of squares in repeated measures ANOVA

Here we are at the heart of the valuable nature of within subjects designs – we can *partial out* variance caused by differences between individuals (BETWEEN SUBJECTS VARIANCE) and leave ourselves with a better estimate of the experimental effect: the BETWEEN CONDITIONS VARIANCE. Conceptually, this is shown in Figure 20.2 where 'variation' is again measured as the sums of squares (SS) of deviations around appropriate means. The total variation is, as before, the SS of the deviations of all scores around the grand mean. The *between subjects SS* is the variation of the participants' average scores ($\bar{x}_p$). The *between conditions SS* is the variation of the condition means ($\bar{x}_c$). Notice that 'error' is, as before, the 'leftover' SS but here with the variation due to subject differences already removed.

One-way related ANOVA can be thought of mathematically as a two-way unrelated design, with the two factors being *conditions* and *subjects*. The 'cells' are, then, the individual scores by each person on each condition, so in Table 20.2 there are 15 'cells'. The 'error' term is actually the interaction of subjects with conditions – the extent to which all 'subjects' don't go the same way as each other across the conditions.

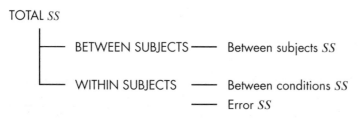

TOTAL SS

├── BETWEEN SUBJECTS ── Between subjects SS

└── WITHIN SUBJECTS ── Between conditions SS
      ── Error SS

Figure 20.2 Division of sums of squares in a one-way related ANOVA analysis

Calculation for one-way repeated measures ANOVA

We will carry out a one-way repeated measures ANOVA analysis on the data in Table 20.2. As with the two-way unrelated, I shall include the calculation steps and explanatory notes but not all the number-crunching arithmetic steps.

Procedure	Calculation/Result of steps
1 Find SS_{total} as on p. 484; note that N is all the *scores*, not participants, in repeated measures; hence $N = 15$.	$\sum x^2 - \dfrac{\left(\sum x\right)^2}{N} = 862 - \dfrac{11236}{15}$
	$= 862 - 749.07 \qquad\qquad = \mathbf{112.93}$
	Note: from here onwards $\dfrac{\left(\sum x\right)^2}{N}$ is referred to as C
2 Find $SS_{subjects}$ using $$n_c \sum \bar{x}_p^{\,2} - \dfrac{\left(\sum x\right)^2}{N}$$	$3\,(7.3333^2 + 6^2 + 8^2 + 7.6667^2 + 6.3333^2) - C$
	$= 758 - 749.07 \qquad\qquad = \mathbf{8.93}$
n_c is the number of conditions (or scores per participant), in this case 3.	Note: we are using four decimal places so that our answer will tally with SPSS
3 Find $SS_{conditions}$ using the formula above but instead of n_c use n_p the number of scores (or participants) per condition = 5. Instead of $\bar{x}_p$ use the $\bar{x}_c$ values.	$5\,(4.6^2 + 6.2^2 + 10.4^2) - C \qquad = \mathbf{89.73}$
4 Find SS_{error} using: $$SS_{error} = SS_{total} - SS_{subjects} - SS_{conditions}$$	$112.93 - 8.93 - 89.73 \qquad\qquad = \mathbf{14.27}$
5 $df_{total} = N - 1 = \mathbf{14}$ $df_{subjects} = n_p - 1 = \mathbf{4}$ $df_{conditions} = n_c - 1 = \mathbf{2}$ $df_{error} = $ remainder $= 14 - 4 - 2 = \mathbf{8}$	$MS_{conditions} = SS_{conditions}/df \qquad = 89.73/2 = \mathbf{44.865}$ $MS_{error} = SS_{error}/df \qquad\qquad = 14.27/8 = \ \ \mathbf{1.784}$
6 $F = \dfrac{MS_{conditions}}{MS_{error}}$	$F = \dfrac{44.865}{1.784} \qquad\qquad = \mathbf{25.149}$
7 Critical $F_{2,8}$ is 8.65 with $p \le 0.01$; hence our difference between means is highly significant.	

Interpreting the result

Here, our research hypothesis, that the mean numbers of words recalled in each of the three conditions (levels of processing) would differ, is strongly supported by our repeated measures analysis. H_0 (that the population means are equal) is rejected. Power and effect size should be considered (see the advice later in this chapter).

Reporting a one-way repeated measure ANOVA

This is performed in exactly the same way as for the unrelated version given on p. 486, except of course that the design would not be described as 'between subjects' but as 'repeated measures' or 'related' or 'within subjects'.

Data assumptions for repeated measures ANOVA

As with other parametric tests we should be able to assume that the dependent variable is at interval level and is normally distributed (see p. 319). In addition, we should be able to assume SPHERICITY among the variables that make up the levels of each factor. This is an important, complex concept for which it is not possible here to give a thorough definitive explanation. It has to do, however, with the fact that in a repeated measures design, scores within each condition are not independent of scores in the other conditions as they would be in an unrelated design. Basically, sphericity occurs if (1) there is *homogeneity of variance* (see p. 365 among the level variables *and* if (2) the variances of the *differences* between levels are similar to one another.[1]

To understand this last part, imagine we took the difference between your score on *physical* (level 1) and on *phonetic* (level 2) and called this d_{2-1} We then calculate the difference for each pair of scores in the sample. We then calculate d_{3-1} and d_{3-2}. Sphericity requires that the variances of each of these new (*d*) variables are similar (and assumed equal in the population). If you look back to the related *t* test, you'll recall that there we tested the *differences* between pairs of scores against the null hypothesis that their mean should be zero. Here we have two or more sets of such differences and, as with homogeneity of variance for the unrelated design, we have to be able to assume that the variances of these sets of differences are equal in the population in order to make our estimates of parameters.

Without sphericity, we can be in danger of making Type II errors and missing real effects. To check on sphericity, you could compare the variances of the variables and you could calculate all the differences between score pairs and check their variances too. However, this is laborious and it is to be hoped that you are using a computer program to calculate your related ANOVA. SPSS calculates MAUCHLY'S TEST of SPHERICITY (see the SPSS directions later on). If this test shows significance, the sphericity assumption is violated. In these conditions a value known as EPSILON can be calculated and this is multiplied by the *df* (lowering them) and *F* is evaluated on these new values. SPSS will do all this for you. If there is any anomaly you would report this with your results.

---

[1] This will happen if the correlations between variables are all similar – a condition known as *compound symmetry* if it occurs with homogeneity of variance too. Compound symmetry implies sphericity but the reverse is not true; sphericity, the weaker requirement, is adequate.

Two-way (related) design

For this, and the mixed design that follows, the calculations get rather complicated and it is difficult to conceptualise how the variation components are being accounted for. Here, then, I haven't included the equations, since they are the same as those used before. I again hope you'll have access to computer calculations of ANOVA. Though you might wish to check the calculations, the important point is to understand what the different components are telling us in the analysis. If you can understand what you have to do in these two models, and the three-way unrelated, then you can interpret all other possible combinations of the ANOVA model.

Imagine that the fictitious data in Table 20.2 are errors recorded in a hypothetical study in which students perform a short word-processing task under two conditions of temperature (factor t) – hot and cool – and three conditions of noise (factor s) – silent, moderate and loud noise. This factor is given subscript s for 'sound' in order to distinguish it from n – the symbol for sample size. Counterbalancing would be employed, of course, to even out order effects.

Temperature t	Cool				Hot				Means for sound level (s)			
	Quiet	Mod noise	Loud noise	$\bar{x}_{t1}$	Quiet	Mod noise	Loud noise	$\bar{x}_{t2}$	$\bar{x}_{s1}$	$\bar{x}_{s2}$	$\bar{x}_{s3}$	$\bar{x}_p$ subs
	$t1s1$	$t1s2$	$t1s3$		$t2s1$	$t2s2$	$t2s3$					
Pt.												
1	3	4	4	3.67	7	9	12	9.33	5	6.5	8	6.5
2	5	5	6	5.33	3	11	13	9	4	8	9.5	7.17
3	9	7	7	7.67	5	8	15	9.33	7	7.5	11	8.5
4	7	8	6	7.0	9	10	21	13.33	8	9	13.5	10.17
$\bar{x}_{ts}$	6	6	5.75		6	9.5	15.25					
Level means 8.083				5.917					10.25	6	7.75	10.5

Table 20.2 Word-processing errors made under hot and cool conditions, and under increasing conditions of noise

In this two-way repeated measures analysis the same group of participants undergo all levels of both factors – if they have the energy and stamina! Although this is often not covered in introductory texts it is, in fact, quite a common design in projects, where people may be hard to come by and you can get your friends and/or family to do, say, two versions of the Stroop test under two conditions, say fast presentation and slow.

Complications

What is new in the two-way related ANOVA calculation is the existence of a separate error term for *each* of the effects (two main and one interaction). We do with each effect what we did with the single effect in the related one-way. We look at the *interaction* of subjects with the effect – how far their scores vary across the conditions in a way contrary to the way we might expect from looking at the condition means. The subscripts here work as follows. The temperature factor (t) has two levels, 1 = *cool* and 2 = *hot*. Hence, $\bar{x}t1$ is the symbol for the mean of all scores in the cool condition – $t1s1$, $t1s2$ and $t1s3$. $\bar{x}_{s2}$ refers to the mean of hot and cool scores in the moderate noise (s) condition – that's $t1s2$ and $t2s2$.

For each factor, we calculate the SS, as before, using the overall means for each level in that factor. We then calculate an error term, which is the interaction of subjects with that factor. In Chapter 19, we saw that an interaction is calculated as $SS_{cells} - SS_{factor1} - SS_{factor2}$. Let's consider the error for temperature. We need to think of temperature as one factor, giving us SS_t, and subjects as the other factor, giving us SS_{subs}. The cells of relevance, then, are those formed by the interaction between temperature and subjects. These are the eight means under the columns $\bar{x}_{t1}$ and $\bar{x}_{t2}$ – the scores for subjects on temperature disregarding the differences across sound. $SS_{cells\,t}$ is found by using these means in the usual equation where n will be three because there are three sound level scores comprising each cell mean:

$$n\sum x_{ki}^2 - \frac{(\sum x)^2}{N}$$

, where x_{ki} means the ith mean in the kth condition and $\sum x_{ki}^2$ means add up the squares of all these means. n is 3 in each case as just explained. N is, as before, all scores *not* all participants. So the error term for the temperature factor ($SS_{error\,t}$) will be $SS_{cells\,t} - SSt - SS_{subs}$.

Calculation of two-way repeated measures ANOVA (data from Table 20.2)

Procedure	Calculation/result of steps
1. Find SS_{total} as in the one-way example	$\sum x^2 - \dfrac{(\sum x)^2}{N}$ = 1964 − 1568.17 = **395.83**
2. Find $SS_{subjects}$ using $n\sum \bar{x}_p^2 - \dfrac{(\sum x)^2}{N}$; n is 6 because there are six scores per participant	Note: C = 1568.17 $6(6.5^2 + 7.17^2 + 8.5^2 + 10.17^2) - C$ = **47.86**
3. Find SS_t using the overall $\bar{x}_t$ means; n = 12 since each mean is based on 12 scores	$12(5.917^2 + 10.25^2) - C$ = **112.71**
4. Find $SS_{cells\,t}$ (explained above)	$3(3.67^2 + 5.33^2 + 7.67^2 + 7^2 + 9.33^2 + 9^2 + 9.33^2 + 13.33^2) - C$ = **179.31**
5. Find $SS_{error\,t} = SS_{cells\,t} - SS_t - SS_{subs}$	= 179.31 − 112.71 − 47.86 = **18.74**

6. Find SS_s using the overall $\bar{x}_s$ means and $n = 8$ as there are 8 values per mean

$8(6^2 + 7.75^2 + 10.5^2) - C$ = **82.33**

7. Find $SS_{cells\ s}$ — the values in the columns headed $\bar{x}_{s1}$ etc. For each one, $n = 2$

$2(5^2 + 4^2 + 7^2 + 8^2 + 6.5^2 + 8^2 +$
$7.5^2 + 9^2 + 8^2 + 9.5^2 + 11^2 +$
$13.5^2) - C$ = **141.83**

8. Find $SS_{error\ s} = SS_{cells\ s} - SS_s - SS_{subs}$

$141.83 - 82.33 - 47.86$ = **11.64**

9. Find $SS_{cells\ ts}$; for this use the $\bar{x}_{ts}$ means for each condition ($t1s1$, $t1s2$, etc.); There are four values for each mean, so $n = 4$

$4(6^2 + 6^2 + 5.75^2 + 6^2 + 9.5^2 +$
$15.25^2) - C$ = **287.33**

10. Find $SS_{ts} = SS_{cells\ ts} - SS_t - SS_s$

$287.33 - 112.71 - 82.33$ = **92.29**

11. $SS_{error\ ts} = SS_{total} - SS_{subjects} - SS_t$
$- SS_{error\ t} - SS_s - SS_{error\ s} - SS_{ts}$

$395.83 - 47.86 - 112.71 -$
$18.74 - 82.33 - 11.64 - 92.29$ = **30.26**

12. Calculate all relevant MS and F values:

	SS	df	MS	F	p
Factor t (temperature)	112.71	1	112.71	17.98	< .05
Error t	18.74	3*	6.27		
Factor s (sound)	82.33	2	41.17	21.22	< .01
Error s	11.64	6	1.94		
Interaction $t \times s$	92.29	2	46.15	9.16	< .05
Error $t \times s$	30.26	6	5.04		

$^*df_t \times df_{subjects}$

Interpreting the result

We have significant main effects for both factors (temperature and noise) and a significant interaction effect. In fact, it is the interaction that requires scrutiny. Consulting Table 20.2, we see there is no gradual increase in errors across levels of noise, only the increase under louder noise in the hot condition. Alternatively, one could say that heat appears to have a negative effect on performance but only in the noisier conditions. Power and effect size should be considered (see the advice later in this chapter). Reporting the result would be performed as for the two-way unrelated ANOVA described on p. 511.

ANOVA mixed design – one repeated measure and one unrelated factor

Suppose the levels of processing experiment (p. 518) is conducted with two different groups. One group receives the instruction about each stimulus item in the usual way. The instruction appears underneath the item on a computer screen. The other group receives auditory instructions though headphones with the stimulus item presented visually exactly as in the first condition. The researcher here decides that the same stimulus items should be used so the two groups will have to be independent, otherwise there might be an order effect with the stimulus words more familiar in the second condition. Here we have a 3 x 2 mixed design with one related factor (*proc* = 3 levels of processing conditions) and one between groups factor (*pres* = presentation – visual or auditory).

Between groups factor *pres* ↓	Physical	Phonetic	Semantic	$\bar{x}_{pres}$	$\bar{x}_{subs}$	$(\bar{x}_{subs})^2$
		within groups factor – proc				
Visual						
Pt 1	5	8	9		7.33	53.78*
Pt 2	3	5	10		6	36
Pt 3	4	8	12		8	64
Pt 4	6	6	11		7.67	58.78
Pt 5	5	4	10		6.33	40.11
$\bar{x}_{cells}$	4.6	6.2	10.4	$\bar{x}_{visual}$ 7.067		
Auditory						
Pt 6	5	3	4		4	16
Pt 7	4	9	3		5.33	28.44
Pt 8	9	7	7		7.67	58.78
Pt 9	3	6	6		5	25
Pt 10	6	8	5		6.33	40.11
$\bar{x}_{cells}$	5.4	6.6	5	$\bar{x}_{auditory}$ 5.667		
$\bar{x}_{proc}$	$\bar{x}_{physical}$ 5	$\bar{x}_{phonetic}$ 6.4	$\bar{x}_{semantic}$ 7.7		$\Sigma(\bar{x}_{subs})^2$	420.94

*The $\bar{x}_{subs}$ values are taken to four decimal places then squared and rounded (e.g. 7.3333). This is to keep close to the SPSS result but also to avoid clutter in the table.

Table 20.3 Words recalled correctly under three (related) conditions of processing and two (unrelated) conditions of instruction presentation

Note that, in the calculations, an error term is found for both the between and within groups effects. Note, also, that any effect that includes the repeated measure factor is also counted as 'within subjects'. In this example, therefore, the interaction between *proc* and *pres* gets counted as within subjects, since it includes the within subjects *proc* factor. The data appear in Table 20.3.

Division of sums of squares

The division of sums of squares in this mixed ANOVA (one within groups and one between groups factor) is shown in Figure 20.3. Note that the within subjects error term is used both for the within conditions main effect and for the interaction. The *df* are found mostly by subtraction. There are ten participants, so between subjects *df* is 9. This is divided into 1 for the effect (two conditions) and the remainder for the error. There are 29 – 9 left for the within subjects effects, 2 for the main effect (three conditions), 2 for the interaction (between groups x within conditions) and a remainder of 16 for error.

Total $SS - SS_{total}$ $df = 29$

- Between subjects $SS - SS_{subs}$ $df = $ **9**
    - Between groups $- SS_{pres}$ $df = $ 1
    - Error between (groups) $- SS_{error\ pres}$ $df = $ 8
- Within subjects $SS - SS_{between}$ $df = $ **20**
    - Within conditions $- SS_{proc}$ $df = $ 2
    - Interaction $- SS_{pres \times proc}$ $df = $ 2
    - Error within (subjects) $- SS_{error\ proc}$ $df = $ 16

Figure 20.3 Division of SS in a mixed design (one between groups and one within groups factor)

Calculations for a mixed ANOVA – one between groups and one within groups factor

Procedure	Calculation/result of steps
1. Find SS_{total} in the usual way using all x values; n is the total number of values = 30. For all formulae here see the previous calculations (p. 525).	$SS_{total} = 1403 - 36481/30 = 1403 - 1216.03 = $ **186.97** Note: $C = 1216.03$
2. Find SS_{subs} $n = 3$ for each subject; see Table 20.3	$3(421) - C$ = **46.97**
3. Find SS_{pres} using $\bar{x}_{pres}$ and $n = 15$	$15(7.067^2 + 5.667^2) - C$ = **14.74**
4. Find $SS_{error\ pres} = SS_{subs} - SS_{pres}$	$46.97 - 14.74$ = **32.23**
5. Find $SS_{within} = SS_{total} - SS_{subs}$	$186.97 - 46.97$ = **140**
6. Find SS_{proc} using $\bar{x}_{proc}$ and with $n = 10$ (results per level of the *proc* factor)	$10(5^2 + 6.4^2 + 7.7^2) - C$ = **36.47**

7. Find SS_{cells}; see Table 20.3; $n = 5$ $5(4.6^2 + 6.2^2 + 10.4^2 + 5.4^2 + 6.6^2 + 5^2) - C$
     = 111.37

8. Find $SS_{pres \times proc} = SS_{cells} - SS_{pres} - SS_{proc}$ $111.37 - 14.74 - 36.47$ **= 60.16**

9. Find $SS_{error\ proc} = SS_{within} - SS_{proc} - SS_{pres \times proc}$ $140 - 36.47 - 60.16$ **= 43.37**

10. Calculate all relevant MS and F values:

	SS	df	MS	F	p
presentation	14.74	1	14.74	3.66	>0.05
error (pres)	32.23	8	4.03		
processing	36.47	2	18.24	6.73	< 0.01
pres × proc	60.16	2	30.08	11.1	< 0.01
error proc	43.37	16	2.71		

Interpreting and reporting the result

It looks as though level of processing has an effect but that this effect is mainly limited to the visual presentation group. There is a main effect for level of processing and a significant interaction. By inspection we can see the progression upwards of mean words recalled in the visual presentation group but not in the auditory presentation group. (These are fictitious data – if anyone actually does this study, please let me know the result!) Note that there is no main effect for presentation type, the visual group mean (7.067) not being significantly higher than the auditory group mean (5.667).

Power and effect size should be considered (see the advice later in this chapter). Reporting the result would be performed as for the two-way unrelated design.

More complex ANOVA designs

We've reached a point where it makes sense to stop. You now have the principles for any more complicated design. As I've said once or twice, I doubt you'll be calculating at this level by hand. You should now be able to interpret the terms produced when submitting your data to software analysis.

Three-way (and higher) related ANOVA

Here it is important to remember that each effect (main or interaction) has its own error term. A three-way analysis would, having found all three main effects, treat each pair of variables separately and analyse for two-way interactions as in our two-way related analysis described above. There would then remain the three-way interaction term, which would be calculated by finding $SS_{cellsAxBxC}$. SS_{AxBxC} is then $SS_{cellsAxBxC} - SS_A - SS_B - SS_C - SS_{AB} - SS_{AC} - SS_{BC}$. The error term for this interaction would be found by subtracting, from SS_{total}, SS_{subs} and the SS for all main effects, two-way interaction effects and their associated error terms.

Three-way mixed ANOVA

Where there are several between subjects variables but just one within subjects variable, work as follows. Calculate $SS_{subjects}$ and all the SS for the between subjects factors and their interactions just as in the wholly unrelated design. The error term is found by subtracting all these effects from $SS_{subjects}$. Find SS_{within} (within subjects SS) by subtracting $SS_{subjects}$ from SS_{total}. Find the within conditions factor SS and its interactions with the between subjects factors in the usual way (see above – we calculate the appropriate SS_{cells} and subtract from this the SS for the main effects involved). Finally, find the within subjects error term by subtracting from SS_{within} the SS for all the within subjects effects just calculated.

Where there is more than one repeated measures (within conditions) factor the calculation of the error terms becomes a little tricky and this is left for a higher-level text, in particular David Howell (2001).

Effect size and power

Calculating *effect size* in repeated measures designs works in exactly the same way as previously demonstrated. We use $SS_{effect}/(SS_{effect} + SS_{error})$ but we must be careful, in the more complex designs, to select the appropriate SS_{error} term for the effect of interest.

Power for the one-way related design also works just as for the one-way unrelated design using

$$\Phi' = \sqrt{\frac{\sum (\bar{x}_i - \bar{x}_g)^2}{kMS_{error}}}$$ and then converting Φ' to Φ using $\Phi = \Phi' \sqrt{n}$ where n is the number of participants.

For a mixed design when you are calculating power for the between groups factor you need to be careful when multiplying Φ' by n to get Φ. The value of n to use here is the *number of scores in the set* for each mean, not the number of participants. So, in our mixed design above, n will be 15 (scores) not 5 (participants). However, when calculating Φ for the repeated measures factor (levels of processing), n is 10.

For *two-way repeated measures designs* the same principle applies: n is the number of scores in a condition. Hence, in the temperature x noise experiment, n is 12 when calculating Φ_{temp} (since, e.g., there are 12 scores in the cool condition) but 8 in each noise condition (since, e.g., there are 8 scores in the silent condition).

A non-parametric equivalent – the Friedman test for correlated samples

When to use Friedman's test for correlated samples		
Type of relationship tested	Level of data required	Design of study
Difference	At least ordinal	Repeated measures/matched pairs
Between two or more conditions		
Data assumptions: at least ordinal level of data measurement.		
Note: non-parametric equivalent of one-way related ANOVA; Friedman's test produces a value of χ^2 which is evaluated in the usual way using $k-1$ *df*.		

If your data are related but suspect in terms of parametric test assumptions (p. 363) then the Friedman test is appropriate and is the non-parametric equivalent of a repeated measures ANOVA. The data in Table 20.4 are those from Table 20.1. We start by ranking just the scores for each participant on their own as explained below (i.e. if there are three conditions, the ranks 1, 2 and 3 are given to each participant for their three scores).

Participant	Physical	Phys rank	Phonetic	Phon rank	Semantic	Sem rank
1	5	1	8	2	9	3
2	3	1	5	2	10	3
3	4	1	8	2	12	3
4	6	1.5	6	1.5	11	3
5	5	2	4	1	10	3
Sums of ranks:		$R_1 = 6.5$		$R_2 = 8.5$		$R_3 = 15$

Table 20.4 Data from Table 20.1 arranged for a Friedman test

Calculation of Friedman's χ^2 on data in Table 20.4

Procedure	Calculation/result of steps
1 Rank each participant's set of data	See Table 20.4. Example: Participant 5's lowest score of 4 was in the phonetic condition, hence this score gets a 1; the score of 5 in the physical condition gets rank 2 and rank 3 goes to the semantic condition score of 10
2 Find the sum of ranks for each condition	See R_1, R_2 and R_3 in Table 20.
3 Insert the rank sums into the equation: $$\chi^2_F = \left(\frac{12}{Nk(k+1)} \sum R_k^2 \right) - 3N(k+1)$$ where k is the number of conditions	$$\chi^2_F = \left(\frac{12}{5 \times 3(3+1)}[6.5^2+8.5^2+15^2] \right) - 3 \times 5(3+1)$$ $$= \left(\frac{12}{60} \times 339.5 \right) - 60 = 7.9$$
4 Use as a regular χ^2 with $k - 1$ df Critical value for χ^2 with 2 df and $p \le .05$ is 5.99. Hence this result is significant.	Critical value for χ^2 with $2df$ and $p \le .05$ is 5.99, hence this result is significant.

Reporting the results of a Friedman test for related samples

Friedman's analysis of variance by ranks was used on the recognition scores in the three conditions. Differences across conditions were significant, χ^2 (2) = 7.9, $p < 0.05$. Assess effect size and power. You can proceed as for the Kruskal-Wallis and perform individual Wilcoxon tests, adjusting for error rate, and following the procedure on pp. 393–5.

The Page trend test

As with the Jonckheere test (p. 494), we might predict that a dependent variable would increase in magnitude across levels of an independent variable. We would be predicting a specific trend. The related equivalent to the Jonckheere test is the Page trend test. If you need to use this test, then please consult the companion website at: www.hodderplus.com/psychology/

SPSS procedures for repeated measures ANOVA

It is important first that you clarify for yourself what is the independent variable and how it is represented in the SPSS data sheet. As we have seen, unlike the case for unrelated designs, the levels of the independent variable in a repeated measures SPSS entry are *separate variable columns* side by side. In our levels of processing memory example there would be a column of data for the

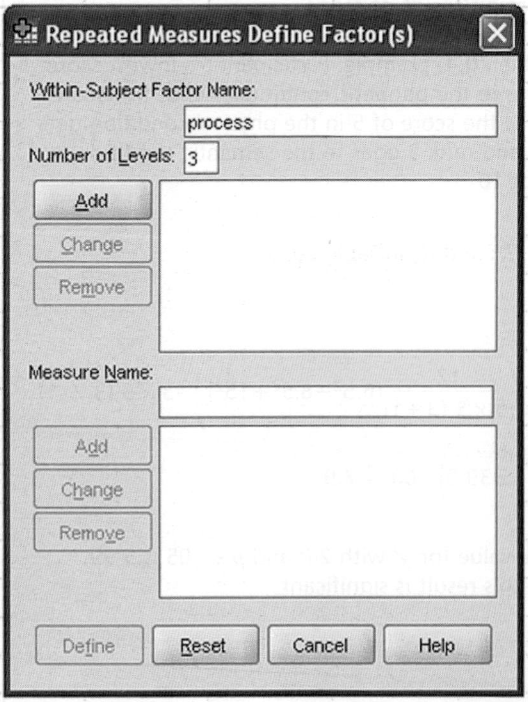

Figure 20.4 Naming the repeated measures factors and stating number of levels; it is now necessary to click 'add'

physical condition, a separate column for the phonetic condition and a third column for the semantic condition. It's easy to see why. Each participant performed in all conditions. Each participant in an SPSS data sheet is on one row. Hence we *must* be able to see each participant's three scores in their particular row of the data sheet. You must also find a generic name for your independent variable; here we might call it *'process'* with levels of *physical, phonetic* and *semantic*. These are the three columns of the datasheet so there is not in fact any place (yet) where you would enter this independent variable name, just hang on to it for now.

One-way analysis

1 Select **Analyze/General Linear Model/Repeated Measures**.

2 A dialogue box will appear which asks you to define your independent variables (see Figure 20.4). Here is where you give your generic independent variable (factor) name. Enter *process*

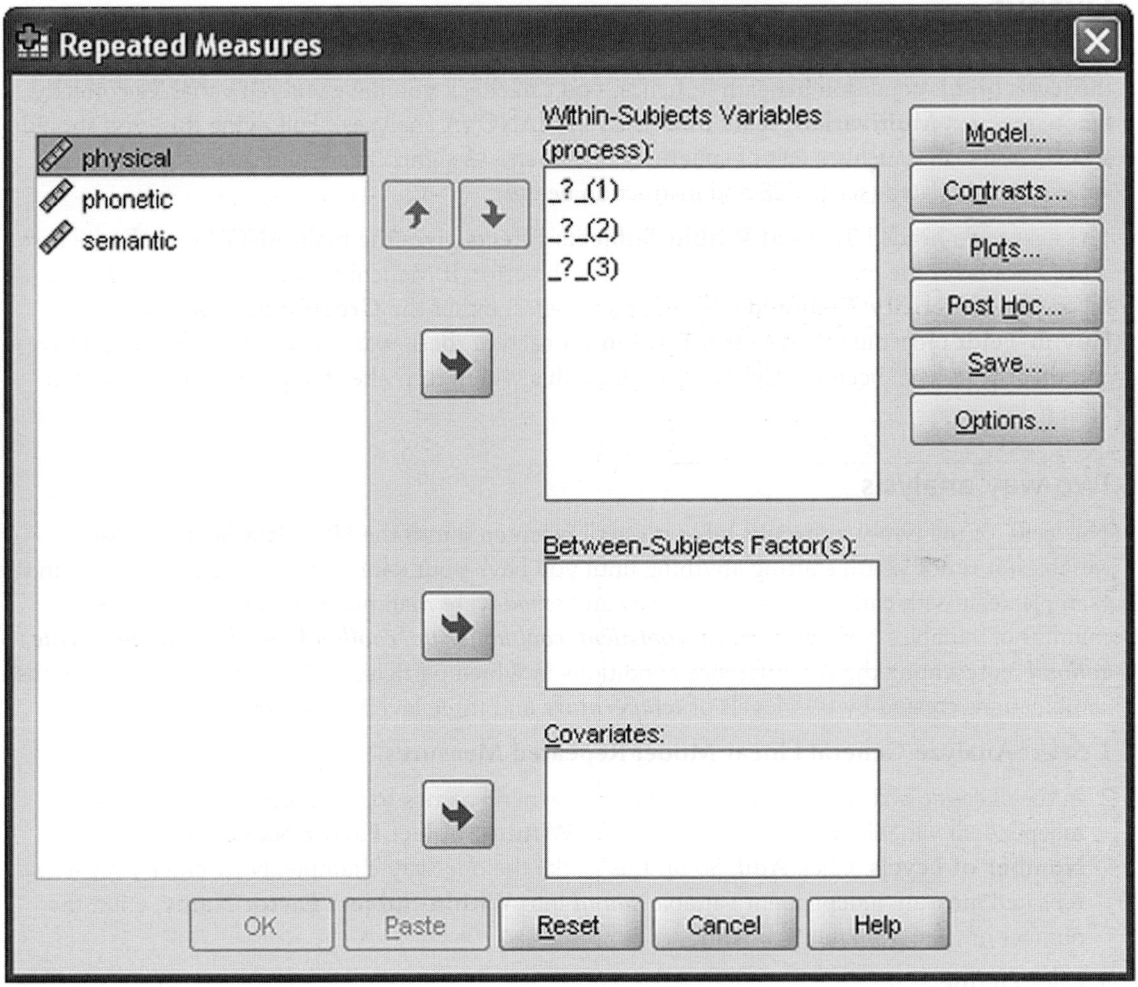

Figure 20.5 SPSS requests the levels for the repeated measures factor

under **Within-Subject Factor Name**. Then enter the **Number of Levels** this factor has (three in this case).

3 Click **Add** then **Define** (if you don't click **Add** you'll be warned you're about to lose your entry).

4 The screen now asks you to enter the three columns in SPSS which are the three levels of your factor. In our example, click over *physical*, *phonetic* and *semantic* into the slots for (1), (2) and (3) (see Figure 20.5).

5 **Options** covers a familiar selection including **Descriptives**, **Estimates of effect Size** and **Observed power**. **Contrasts** and **Post Hoc** apply only if you have a between groups factor (see the mixed analysis below).

6 Click **OK**.

Output

The first box will show your factor name at the top left-hand side with the variables that make up the levels of this condition beneath it; hence, you can check you have entered variables correctly. Ignore the next **Multivariate tests box** (used in MANOVA analyses). Following this, you should see the result of Mauchly's test of sphericity. If this shows significance then the assumption of sphericity is violated (see p. 523 and instruction below).

The next table headed **Tests of Within-Subjects Effects** gives the main ANOVA result; the first set of lines is for the effect and the lower set for the error. If Mauchly's test was not significant, follow the **Sphericity Assumed** line; otherwise select either the **Greenhouse–Geisser** or **Huynh–Feldt** procedure. Notice that **Epsilon** for each of these was calculated in the table above and that the *df* have been multiplied by epsilon; this will in turn alter the probability associated with *F*.

Two-way analysis

The 'cells' of the two-way results table must all be entered into the SPSS datasheet as separate variables. It is not worth starting anything until you have your data arranged correctly. Hence in the example dealt with earlier where *temperature* and *sound* were manipulated, you should have *six* columns of variables perhaps entitled: *coolsilent*, *coolmoderate*, *coolloud*, *hotsilent*, *hotmoderate*, *hotloud* representing the six difference conditions in which participants have performed, being the combinations created by two levels of *temperature* and three levels of *sound*.

1 Select **Analyze/General Linear Model/Repeated Measures**.

2 In the dialogue box (see Figure 20.4) give your generic names for *each* repeated measures independent variable. Enter *temperature* under **Within-Subject Factor Name**. Enter 2 into **Number of Levels**. Click **Add**. So far this is like the one-way example. Now enter your *second* repeated measure independent variable *sound* into **Within-Subject Factor Name**, enter the number of levels (3) and click **Add**.

3 Click **Define**.

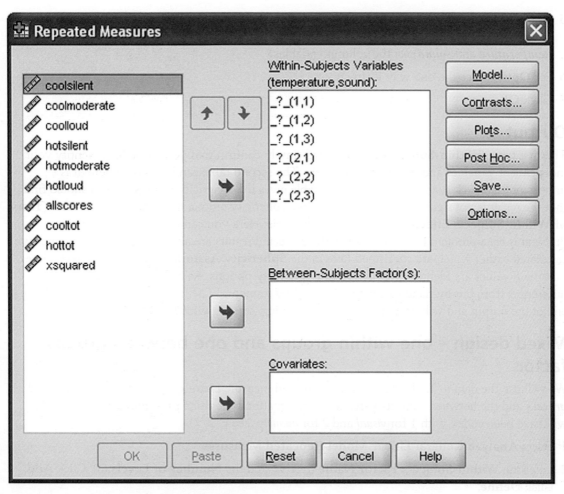

Figure 20.6 SPSS requests levels of task and sound

Now comes a seriously tricky part. If you get this wrong your analysis will be nonsensical. SPSS won't *tell* you it's nonsensical. Like Boxer in *Animal Farm*, it's a good horse and it just does what it's told without question!

4 The dialogue box (see Figure 20.6) now asks you to enter your variables according to which level of which factor they are. *Be careful!* If you entered data exactly as above, then the box will state **Within-Subjects Variables (temp, sound)** at the top right. It then asks, with a '?', for **Variable 1,1**. This means the variable that is level 1 of *temperature* and level 1 of *sound*, which is *coolsilent*. This should be followed by variable 1,2. This will be the first level of *temperature* and *second* level of *noise* so that's *coolmoderate*. *It is essential that you look at this carefully and put the appropriate variable in according to the levels requested*, otherwise your analysis will be meaningless.

5 At this point it's also a good idea to ask, under **Plots**, for your interaction chart as explained for the unrelated two-way on p. 513. Remember to enter the names of the *factors* that you created (***temperature*** and ***sound***) *not* the column variables.

6 For **Options** see the one-way instructions.

7 Click **OK**.

Output

The first table (**Within-Subjects Factors**) will simply confirm that you did indeed identify your independent variables and their levels correctly. The second table can be ignored here (it is important for MANOVA analyses. The next table gives the sphericity test result. You should find that the result is not significant so we can assume sphericity among the data. The next table (**Tests of Within-Subjects Effects**) is our main results table. Here you can see that the sphericity problem is *not* a problem in this case since the corrected results are almost identical to the ones we calculated earlier which are confirmed here in the **Sphericity Assumed** line of each effect. Note that the F values are identical throughout the sphericity options. As before, there are small differences from our by-hand calculations caused by rounding. The interaction plot appears at the end of the output and will probably need some editing, starting with the title.

Mixed design – one within groups and one between groups factor

We will use the data in Table 20.3 with the repeated measure factor of levels of processing titled ***process*** and the between subjects variable of presentation type titled ***presentation***. This variable will have been coded with 1 for *visual* and 2 for *auditory* (see p. 277).

1 Select **Analyze/General Linear Model/Repeated Measures**.

2 Enter the **Within-Subjects Factor Name** (*process*) and the **Number of Levels** (3). Click **Add**. Click **Define**.

3 Highlight the repeated measures levels (***physical***, ***phonetic*** and ***semantic***), which should all appear as separate variables. Move these over to the right-hand **Within-Subjects Variables** box.

4 Highlight the between subjects variable (***presentation***) and move this to the box marked **Between-Subjects Factors**.

5 Choose **Plots** if required as before for the interaction plot. (see p. 513)

6 In this design you can now also select **Post Hoc** tests. In this example you will see the variable ***presentation*** in the **Post Hoc Factors** box. However, moving this over is a waste of time in this example as SPSS won't do it because with only two levels there are no alternative contrasts of these levels to be made.

7 **Options** provides the choices mentioned in the one-way instructions.

8 Click **OK**.

Output

The results should appear much as for the repeated measures designs already described. The addition here will be a table marked **Tests of Between Subjects Effects**. In this example you would only be interested in the main effect for *presentation* from this table. Results displayed by SPSS (not shown here) do not exactly match our by-hand calculation results because of the usual rounding effect described earlier.

Friedman's non-parametric test for correlated samples

1 Select **Analyze/Non-parametric tests/k related samples.**

2 Move the conditions to be tested from the left side to the **Test Variables** box; click **OK**.

The **output** gives just a box with the mean rank for each level and χ^2 with df and significance.

1 As in Chapter 18, use random number tables to generate three sets of eight scores. This time, assume that the three sets are from the *same* eight people and conduct a one-way repeated measures ANOVA. Again, query the validity of significance testing with your tutor if the results are significant!

2 Produce a full outline results table, ready for entry of the results, for a mixed design where there is one repeated measures factor with three levels and one unrelated factor with four levels, eight people in each. Put values into the 'degrees of freedom' column.

3 Table 20.5 gives an incomplete fictitious results table for a 2 × 3 ANOVA analysis.

Source of variation	SS	df	MS	F	Probability of F
Between subjects		13			
Groups	14.88	1	14.88	4.55	.054
Error between	39.24	12	3.27		
Within subjects					
Conditions	16.33	2	8.17	1.32	.286
Groups × conditions	48.90	2	24.45	3.94	.033
Error within	148.76	24	6.20		

Table 20.5 Fictitious ANOVA results for exercise 3

For each statement below, choose between true/false or choose the correct answer.

   (a) There was a significant main effect for groups.

   (b) There was a significant main effect for conditions.

   (c) There was a significant interaction between groups and conditions.

(d) The design was fully unrelated.

(e) There were three groups.

(f) There were three conditions.

(g) The number of participants was: 7 21 14 (choose an answer).

(h) Total degrees of freedom were: 36 41 42 (choose an answer).

4 Mauchly's test shows a probability of .046.

(a) Should the 'sphericity assumed' line be followed, *or*

(b) should the *df* be lowered using epsilon?

5 An alternative choice in the situation described in exercise 4 would be to use (a) Friedman's test, (b) a Kruskal–Wallis test. Which?

Answers

2

	SS	df	MS	F	Prob. of F
Total		95			
Between subjects		31			
Between conditions (unrelated)		3			
Error between		28			
Within subjects		64			
Within conditions		2			
Between × within conditions		6			
Error within		56			

3 (a) False; (b) False; (c) True; (d) False; (e) False; (f) True; (g) 14; (h) 41

4 (b)

5 (a)

Glossary

Between conditions variation	The variance among data attributable to variation among the participants' overall performances
Between subjects variance	Variation, calculated in a repeated measures design, which comes from how scores vary between the conditions with the between subjects variance accounted for
Epsilon	Statistic calculated for use when the sphericity assumption is violated; df are multiplied by this statistic in order to reduce them and avoid Type II errors
Error between subjects	Error term associated with the between groups portion of the sum of squares division in a mixed ANOVA design
Error within subjects	Non-parametric rank test for significant differences between two or more related samples
Friedman's χ^2 test	Error term associated with the within subjects portion of the sum of squares division in a mixed design
Mauchly's test	Test of sphericity calculated in SPSS
Sphericity	Condition where there is homogeneity of variance among treatment variables and the variances of their differences are also similar
Within subjects variation	Variation remaining in a mixed ANOVA design when the between subjects portion has been removed from the total

Choosing a significance test for your data (and internet resources)

- This short chapter takes you through the criteria for choosing an appropriate test of significance for the data you have obtained and the effect you are investigating.
- It deals first with simple two-condition tests and reminds you about *parametric assumptions*.
- We then cover tests for more than two conditions or factors.
- Finally, some internet resources are listed and the use of computers in statistics discussed.

Choosing an appropriate test

Trying to choose an appropriate test can leave you with a floundering feeling, since there are so many tests and there can be a lot of data and several hypotheses. The first golden rule is not to panic! Stay calm. Next … have a good think about the specific hypothesis or hypotheses that you are setting out to test. These should appear very precisely stated, at the end of the introduction to your report if you have already written it. If not, just concentrate on what exactly you wanted to show, what kind of result would support the argument you are making with your study.

If your study involves just two sets of data, then the situation is relatively simple and we start with these kinds of test in just a moment. If you have a more complex set of data and hypotheses, then it makes sense to list every relationship that you want to test, giving each a number; then, for each one, you should be able to state something like 'I want to see if there is a difference between this group and that group on this variable', or 'I want to see if this variable is related to that variable [by correlation].' For more complex data, where you may be dealing with a two-way or three-way design, it is of crucial importance first to identify the dependent variable by asking 'Among these variables which is the measure of performance? Which one measures what people did?', or 'Which one is the measure of a person on which I expect groups to differ or on which I expect a difference across conditions?'

Having established this, you may well find that you expect differences on two factors (e.g. training and gender), in which case you should also be interested in the interaction of these two factors. Indeed, the prediction for your study may well be that there will be an interaction between factors. Ideally speaking, you should know, before you come to select a test, which ones you need to use since this will have been a part of your considerations when designing the study in the first place. However, it does happen that test selection is left until data are in. Whatever you do, don't just steam ahead, not really understanding what you are doing with your data and therefore reporting gobbledygook; if in doubt, ask a tutor.

Tests for two samples

The simpler tests covered in detail in this book assume you have just two samples of values and that you want to test for a difference or a correlation between them. This would include studies that produce a two-way frequency table where there may be more than two levels of either *categorical* variable. If you are in one of these positions, then you need only consult Figure 21.1 supported by the notes that follow. Tests for more than two conditions, and for more than one independent variable, are dealt with further on.

Three major decisions in choosing a two-sample test

There are, at most, three major decisions to be made in selecting a test for two samples of data or a two-way frequency table, and these are shown in Figure 21.1 as numbers 1, 2 and 3. They are:

1 Are we testing for a difference or a correlation?

2 Are our data suitable for a parametric test?

3 If testing for a difference, was the design related or unrelated?

Notes on these three major decisions

1. Difference or correlation?

Are you looking for a difference in performance or some psychological measure between two groups or conditions? If so you will be using a *t* test or its non-parametric equivalent. On rare occasions you might want a sign test; this is used only when your dependent variable is categorical. For correlation, you will be asking a question like 'Do people with a score on *X* (variable) have a similar score to what they get on *Y* (variable)? … or do they get a high score with a low score and vice versa (negative correlation)?' Note that if you have a frequency table and your variables were both categorical, use chi-square, which appears in the 'Difference' section. When used on cross-tabs tables Chi-square can be seen as a difference test or a 'test of association' (or categorical correlation). It is placed here because it tests the difference between two distributions of data. For instance, on p. 408 there are frequency data for three conditions of an experiment: 0/1 pieces of litter, 2/4 pieces and 8/16 pieces. We were looking at the difference between the frequencies for people dropping litter and the frequencies of not dropping across these three experimental conditions.

The reason Chi-square is also like a correlation is that we are often seeing whether one category of one variable is *associated* with one category of another. We can see this in a study where there are scores for each person on extroversion and on attitude to sport. If we suspected an association, we could correlate the two variables in a straightforward way. However, for some reason we might reduce our interval-level data to categorical by dividing both variables at the median (see p. 257). We would have, for each individual, whether they were extrovert or introvert and whether they were relatively positive or negative about sport. We could now perform a chi-square analysis. We would be looking for a difference between the two distributions for sport attitude, one for extroverts and one for introverts. We *could* correlate, of course, using the biserial coefficient, and obtain exactly the same overall result.

What is of crucial importance here is that you do not try to correlate the codes for a multiple category variable, such as those for marital status (married, single, cohabiting etc.) or educational level (no exam, GCSE, A Level, degree, postgraduate) with some other variable. The results here will be meaningless.

2. Data type?

You can recognise the need for a chi-square test by asking the question 'What kind of data do I have for each person?' If you have an individual score then your data can at least be treated as ordinal level. If, however, all you can say about each person's result is that they are in a category with other people, and you can't split those people on any variable, then you have frequency data and probably need chi-square. The numbers in a frequency table used to count the people in each cell are cardinal numbers but the levels of the variable themselves are categorical only. A special kind of *related* category data occurs when each person is classed as one thing or the other – e.g. improved/didn't improve; answered yes/no. Again this is the occasion for a sign test rather than a chi-square.

If data are not in categories then they will be measure on some form of *scale* – what we called in Chapter 11 a *measured variable*. If the dependent variable consists of measures on a test that has been standardised (see p. 201), then it can usually be treated as producing interval-level data. Do so unless otherwise advised. It is wise to conduct normality checks on your data anyway (see p. 319), if you wish to use a parametric test, but this is especially so if the data are in the form of scores or numbers produced by humans estimating or 'rating' events or behaviour, on some arbitrary scale, or if they are scores on an unstandardised questionnaire or opinion survey. If serious skew or kurtosis cannot be removed then an ordinal level non-parametric test is your best option. This will convert the interval level data to ordinal using ranking.

You should note that very rarely do we actually gather ordinal data directly. Normally, what we do is decide that our data are untrustworthy if treated as interval-level data and submit them to a non-parametric test which uses ranks.

Parametric assumptions: Several 'parametric data assumptions' were outlined on p. 363. You need to ask three questions of your data before assuming that a parametric level test (more correctly considered as a *distribution-dependent test*) can be employed on your data.

1 Are data really at interval level? – usually assumed so unless there are serious normality violations.

2 Is it reasonable to assume that the underlying sampling distribution is normal? – assessed by seeing whether the sample data itself is normally distributed.

3 Do we have homogeneity of variance? – applies only to unrelated difference tests.

or Do we have sphericity – applies only to related designs where the independent variable has more than two levels.

If there is serious doubt about any of these, taking into account what is said on p. 363, then you should consider carrying out a non-parametric test. In deciding to use a non-parametric test you should not feel that this is somehow an inferior approach, though many statisticians would make

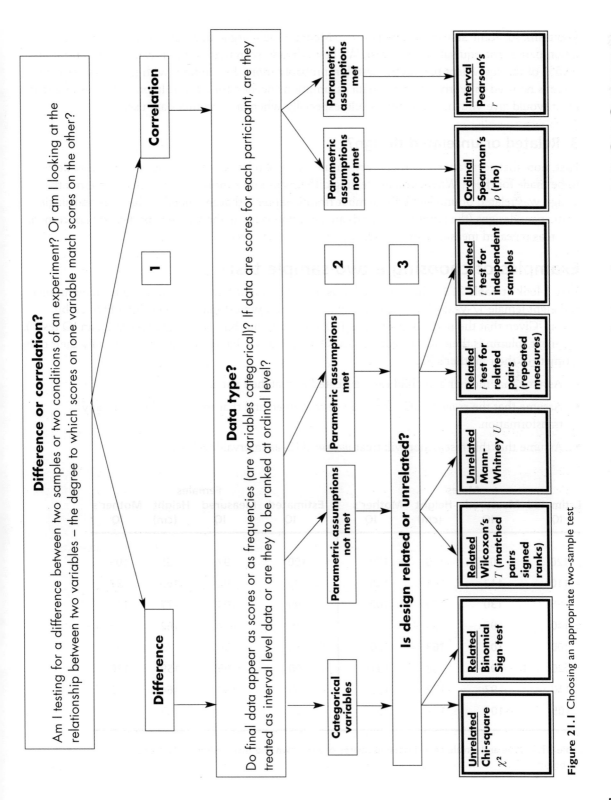

Difference or correlation?

Am I testing for a difference between two samples or two conditions of an experiment? Or am I looking at the relationship between two variables – the degree to which scores on one variable match scores on the other?

Correlation

1

Data type?

Do final data appear as scores or as frequencies (are variables categorical)? If data are scores for each participant, are they treated as interval level data or are they to be ranked at ordinal level?

| Parametric assumptions not met | Parametric assumptions met |

Ordinal
Spearman's
ρ (rho)

Interval
Pearson's
r

2

Difference

Categorical variables

Parametric assumptions not met

Parametric assumptions met

3

Is design related or unrelated?

Unrelated
Chi-square
χ^2

Related
Binomial
Sign test

Related
Wilcoxon's
T (matched pairs signed ranks)

Unrelated
Mann-Whitney U

Related
t test for related pairs (repeated measures)

Unrelated
t test for independent samples

Figure 21.1 Choosing an appropriate two-sample test

543

you think so. Some statistical theorists (e.g. Meddis, 1984) argue that very little power is lost using a non-parametric equivalent of a *t* test. We have already seen that power is calculated to be at least 95.5% of the equivalent parametric test, but probably more. In addition, with non-parametric tests there is no need to worry about the data assumptions needed for a *t* test. In practice, it is rare that a *t* test would give you an alternative result, especially when large samples are used.

3. Related or unrelated design?

First, note that correlations by their very nature, *must* be related designs. Hence there is no decision to be made for these. Where you are testing differences you simply have to decide whether the design was related or unrelated. Remember from Chapter 3 that independent samples and single-participant designs (the latter rarely used) are *unrelated* as far as the two sets of data are concerned, whereas repeated measures and matched pairs designs are *related*.

Examples of choosing a two-sample test

Take a look at Table 21.1. These are fictitious data that might have been gathered from eight male and eight female 17-year-olds. The first column is their own estimate of their IQ (obtained by asking 'Given that the national average is 100, what do you think you would score on an IQ test?'). The next column is their actual score on an IQ test, then we have their height and finally their own estimate of their mother's IQ.

- Assume that mother and child can be treated as matched pairs.
- Assume that the *estimated* IQ scores are very skewed and that this is not lost with any transformation.
- Assume that this researcher will treat *measured* IQ as interval-level data.

Males				Females			
Estimated IQ	Measured IQ	Height (cm)	Mother's IQ	Estimated IQ	Measured IQ	Height (cm)	Mother's IQ
120	107	160	100	100	97	155	105
110	112	181	105	95	92	165	97
95	130	175	102	90	104	177	115
140	95	164	97	110	112	162	96
100	104	163	120	85	130	173	100
120	92	158	131	100	95	159	120
110	97	172	115	105	107	164	102
105	101	171	96	100	101	165	131

Table 21.1 Male and female participants' estimates of their own and their mothers' IQ scores and height

Using the decision chart (Figure 21.1), try to select the appropriate test for each of the following hypotheses.

- Male IQ estimates are higher than female IQ estimates.
- Female measured IQs are higher than male measured IQs.
- The taller people are, the higher their IQ.
- Female measured IQs are higher than their mothers' IQs.

Hypothesis 1

- Decision 1: we are looking for a difference.
- Decision 2: parametric assumptions are not met.
- Decision 3: the design is unrelated; we have separate groups of males and females.

Our choice is therefore *Mann-Whitney*.

Hypothesis 2

- Decision 1: we are again looking for a difference.
- Decision 2: these data are being treated as interval-level data.
- Decision 3: the design is unrelated, as before.

A *t test for unrelated* samples is the preference but we must ensure that parametric assumptions are met:

- IQ scores can be treated as interval-level data.
- IQ tests are standardised to ensure that scores for the general population are normally distributed on them; hence, the samples come from a normally distributed population. We can always check normality of the samples anyway.
- for homogeneity of variance, we can check variances and find that S^2 male = 146.79; S^2 female = 138.54 – not too different and Levene's test (using SPSS) gives a non-significant result; this would not be a big problem anyway, since although we have an unrelated design, the numbers in each group are equal.

Hypothesis 3

- Decision 1: a positive correlation is predicted between height and IQ (we treat male and female as one group).
- Decision 2: IQ is being treated as interval-level data. Height is ratio level and, therefore, at least interval level.
- Decision 3: correlations are related designs.

Our choice is therefore *Pearson's correlation coefficient*. Parametric assumptions must be met but arguments are the same as for hypothesis 2, except that the design is related so homogeneity of variance is not relevant with only two variables; height is known to be normally distributed.

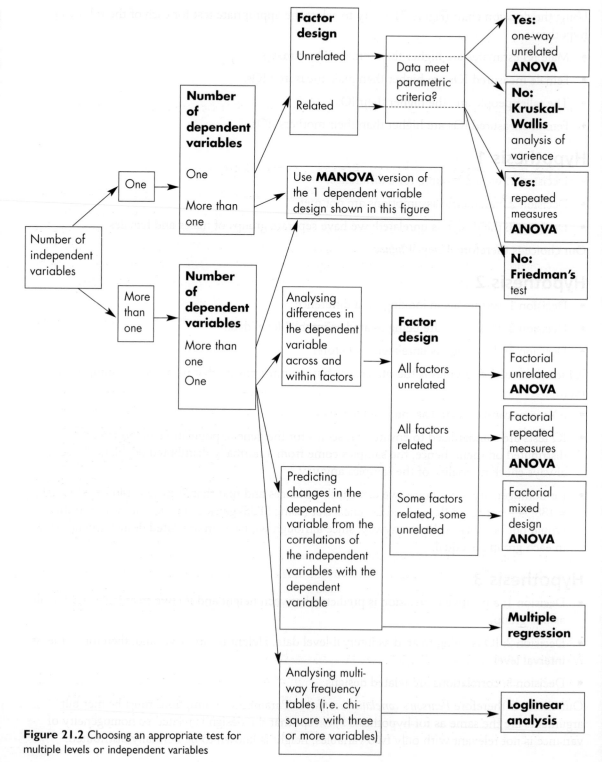

Figure 21.2 Choosing an appropriate test for multiple levels or independent variables

Hypothesis 4

- Decision 1: a difference is predicted.
- Decision 2: measured IQ is being treated as interval-level data.
- Decision 3: matched pairs are a related design.

Our choice is therefore a *t test for related samples*, but parametric assumptions must be met (as above).

Tests for more than two samples

If you have more than two sets of data, either from more than two groups or from taking measures more than twice from the same participants, then you need to think very carefully about your analysis – although, again, it should be stressed that you should normally consider the type of data analysis you will use before finalising the design of your research study. In other words, hopefully you are reading this because you are considering the types of analysis you will be able to perform when you have gathered your data and you'll adjust your study if you find that your plans at present would make data analysis either too complicated or impossible.

Following Figure 21.2, it should be possible to isolate your required design but let's just make some notes on the possible decisions.

One independent variable

If you have just the one independent variable, and are investigating differences between its levels, then you will be conducting some form of analysis of variance. If your data can be considered as being at interval level, with homogeneity of variance and underlying normality (see the earlier section) then you will perform either an unrelated ('between groups') one-way ANOVA or a repeated measures one-way ANOVA (also used for the rare case of matched threes). If your data are suspect for parametric treatment, then you'll do a Kruskal–Wallis one-way analysis of variance for unrelated data, or a Friedman test for related data. Don't forget that the acronym ANOVA refers to the parametric case and the full title is used for the Kruskal–Wallis.

If you have more than one dependent variable then properly you should perform a MANOVA test. This can be performed on one-way or multi-factorial designs; you select Analyze/GLM/Multivariate in SPSS and proceed as for the single dependent variable version except that you enter more than one dependent variable in the Dependent Variables box. However, many people skip this procedure and simply divide α by the number of univariate ANOVA tests they are performing.

More than one independent variable

If you have more than one independent variable (or 'factor'), then your choices are multi-factorial ANOVA, multiple regression or loglinear analysis. The choice of this latter test would be obvious since you would have two or more frequency tables, just as for a chi-square analysis, and this would be because you have two or more categorical variables.

If you are looking for differences in the dependent variable as a result of the manipulation of two or more independent variables, or differences *associated with* the independent variables, then you need to check each factor to see whether it is related or unrelated. This is the same as the decisions made earlier for independent variables, except that you have two or more together here. If both are repeated measures factors you have a wholly repeated measures design. You would know this is true if you have had all your participants take part in *all* your conditions. If you have entirely different participants in each condition of your study, then it is wholly unrelated (between groups). However, you might have two or more groups but on one variable you have measured all participants on each of its levels, e.g. trained or untrained participants (unrelated factor) perform both with and without coffee (related factor). In this case of a mixed design you use a repeated measures procedure, with a between groups factor, in SPSS.

Finally, if you are predicting values on or variance in a single dependent variable using several predictor variables (also known as independent variables) by combining the correlation of each independent variable with the dependent variable (or 'criterion variable') then you need multiple regression.

To avoid confusion I have not placed ANCOVA on Figure 21.2. You would probably know you were doing this since it is a planned procedure and needs a carefully considered rationale. You would use this where you wanted to analyse the effects of an independent variable (or several independent variables) on a dependent variable in the usual way, but also wanted to neutralise the effect of a likely confounding variable (e.g. we want a comparison of final performance for trainees in three different departments of a big store; however, the trainees all differ on educational experience and we want to look at the differences in performance as though these initial educational differences did not exist). The confounding variable is known as a co-variate (see p. 495).

Computers and the internet

Computers are ubiquitous, and are heaven-sent as regards doing statistical calculations. SPSS will calculate a three-way ANOVA with two co-variates in a split second – 30 years ago we had to fill out complicated tables with our data in a precise format, take them to the computer centre and wait around two weeks for the analysis! Even if you watched the process take place it would take a relatively long time for punched cards to be produced, and the calculation itself would take some minutes. However, most psychology tutors will argue that it is only by calculating at least the easier measures and tests that you come to realise just what the process is doing, why it shows what it does, what its limitations are, and so on.

By grappling (or playing) with numbers you get to realise what's going on. I would definitely recommend, therefore, that you calculate some tests to begin with and check for significance in tables. By just taking what the computer says you can end up with only a passive and superficial understanding of statistical testing, and simple mistakes can easily be missed because final results don't strike you as obviously impossible.

That said, once you do understand what's going on, I see no point in masochism. Computers in this domain are doing just what they were intended to do – not putting you out of work but leaving you free to concentrate on things that require new and creative thought. Although we do a bit of long division at school we are no longer expected to do this at work, and no one questions the use of a calculator (except Dads like me who moan 'Surely you don't need that to find 2 times 20?!'). Below, then, I've given a brief description of just one or two computer programs I know of. However, the number of cheap practical statistics software packages is increasing all the time and there are several online calculators.

If you are stuck with a statistical or methods concept, why not just simply stick it into an internet search and see what comes up? You must of course beware of charlatans and the usual nonsense that people put on there, but usually, with statistics and psychology, you will come up with interesting sites run by university lecturers and others who are often very helpful and who can explain a concept, or demonstrate it, in a way that suddenly makes sense to you. Please remember that Wikipedia is written by volunteers who could well be wrong about what they assert.

I would particularly recommend a visit to the website of the Higher Education Academy Psychology Network at www.psychology.heacademy.ac.uk/ This is the UK centre for psychology software, including quantitative and qualitative data analysis, and there is a huge range of information available here. You might have to hunt around a bit clicking links like 'resources' or putting 'data analysis' or 'psychology practicals' into their search engine. You can go from this site to many other psychology resources, including all kinds of statistical analysis packages and sites. The Network has written an extremely comprehensive guide to the internet for psychology and their own services, resource lists etc. Try its *Internet Psychologist* at www.vts.rdn.ac.uk/tutorial/psychologist/ for useful advice on where to get psychology resources and information from the web.

Other useful websites

www.stattucino.com/berrie/dsl/regression/regression.html	Fun if you're learning about correlation; it lets you put in points and instantly calculates the regression value and plots the new line.
www.bps.org.uk/index.cfm	The website of the British Psychological Society.
www.ruf.rice.edu/~lane/rvls.html	Rice virtual lab in statistics – an interactive statistics site.
www.uvm.edu/~dhowell/StatPages/StatHomePage.html	David Howell's home page (US statistics-for-psychology author).
www.bps.org.uk/about/rules5.cfm	BPS code of conduct, ethical principles for human research, etc.
www.uwsp.edu/psych/apa4b.htm#A1	APA Writing guide by M. Plonsky at University of Wisconsin.

www.intute.ac.uk/socialsciences/cgi-bin/browse.pl?id=121139	INTUTE social science – very powerful internet link database taking you to hundreds of related sites on psychology in general but this page give methods resources in particular.
www.psychology.org/links/Resources/Statistics/	Part of the Encyclopaedia of Psychology; contains links to a couple of dozen helpful statistics sites.
www.onlinepsychresearch.co.uk/	A guide to resources for conducting research online and for creating websites etc. Importantly, you can participate in many psychology experiments online and have the experience of being in an experiment run by a working psychological researcher.

Online statistical textbooks

http://trochim.human.cornell.edu/kb/contents.htm	Research Methods Knowledge Base.
http://spsp.clarion.edu/mm/RDE3/start/RDE3start	Research Design Explained.
www.statsoft.com/textbook/stathome.html	Statsoft.
www.animatedsoftware.com/statglos/statglos.htm	Internet glossary of statistical terms.
http://bmj.com/collections/statsbk/index.shtml	Statistics at Square One.
www.tufts.edu/~gdallal/LHSP.HTM	Little Handbook of Statistical Practice.
http://davidmlane.com/hyperstat/index.html	Hyperstat – a very comprehensive statistical teaching resource.
www.blackwellpublishing.com/robson/ebook.htm	This is the electronic version of a statistics textbook – *Experiment, Design and Statistics in Psychology* (3rd edn) by Colin Robson – which was a little gem in its time but still very useful indeed.
www.socialresearchmethods.net/kb/index.htm	Research methods knowledge base.
http://library.thinkquest.org/20991/alg/word.html	Maths for Morons site – friendly maths.

The following exercises are all based on tests for two samples only. Exercises involving a choice of more complex tests are included at the end of the relevant chapters (5–17).

1 Height (in cm) of girls bred on:

All Bran	Bread and dripping
172	162
181	172
190	154
165	143
167	167

The researcher was interested in whether one of the diets tended to produce taller girls. What test should be carried out on the data? Choose the most powerful test available and a simpler alternative.

2 World placings of:

Smoking and drinking players		Abstemious players	
Stephen Higgins	2	John Hendry	8
Graeme Ebdon	6	Peter Dott	1
Ronnie Williams	10	Mark O'Sullivan	5
Ken Murphy	9	Shaun Docherty	3
Stephen Junhui	4	Ding Maguire	7

In this case, we want to know whether abstemious players get higher placings. What test can be used to see whether there is a significant difference here?

3

	Jaywalkers	Non-jaywalkers
Tokyo	46	598
New York	103	524

On two similar junctions, one in New York and one in Tokyo, imagine that the data above were recorded. Do pedestrians jaywalk significantly less in Tokyo? What test will tell us?

4 20 people each perform a sensori-motor task in two conditions, one in a quiet room, alone, the other in a brightly lit room with a dozen people watching. An electronic timer takes an accurate record of the number of errors made in each condition.

    (a) What test would be appropriate for investigating the significance of the differences in performance between the two conditions?

    (b) Assume everybody deteriorates in the second condition. What test would be appropriate for seeing whether individuals tend to deteriorate to the same degree?

5 Students observe whether males or females do or don't walk under a ladder. They want to see whether one sex is more 'superstitious' than the other. What test do they need to use?

6 A psychologist claims to have a very well-standardised measurement scale. What statistical test would be used to check its test–retest reliability? What test would be used to check its validity on a criterion group that should score higher than a control group?

7 Two groups of people are selected. Scores have been used to place people in one of two groups: high 'initiative-taking' and low 'initiative-taking'. They are asked to select just one of three possible activities they would prefer to do. The choices are rock-climbing, dancing or reading a book. What test would demonstrate a significant difference between the choices of the two groups?

8 The time is recorded for the same group of participants to read out loud a list of rhyming words and a list of non-rhyming words. What test is appropriate for showing whether time differences are significant and that rhyming words take less time to read?

9 A group of management personnel undergo an intensive course on race issues. Essays written before and after the course are content-analysed and rated for attitudes to race. What test would be appropriate for demonstrating a significant change of attitude as expressed in the essays?

10 A group of people attempting to give up smoking have been assessed for their progress on two occasions separated by six months. Raw scores have been discarded and we only know for each client whether they have improved, worsened or stayed the same. What test would show any significant change over the period?

Answers

1 Unrelated *t* (most powerful); simpler alternative – Mann-Whitney.

2 A rare case of collecting ranks as raw data – Mann-Whitney.

3 Chi-square.

4 (a) Related *t*; non-parametric alternative – Wilcoxon Signed Ranks;
  (b) Pearson's correlation. Non-parametric alternative – Spearman's rho.

5 Chi-square.

6 Test–retest – Pearson correlation; Validity test – unrelated *t*.

7 Chi-square (2 × 3 table).

8 Related *t*; non-parametric alternative – Wilcoxon signed ranks.

9 Related *t* though data may well not fit normal distribution parameters in which case Wilcoxon signed ranks.

10 Sign test.

22 Analysing qualitative data

This chapter is a practical introduction to the methods employed by qualitative researchers for collecting, analysing and reporting their data, as compared with the more theoretical approach of Chapter 10. It is in the nature of qualitative research that this usually cannot be done without embedding the methodology in the epistemological arguments (about the nature of knowledge and truth) that the proponents and users of those methods have espoused. Hence this chapter also revisits and expands upon those positions.

- *Content analysis* is a conventional approach and tends to prepare qualitative data for quantitative analysis in terms of codes and frequency counts. There is, however, a contemporary form of qualitative content analysis where data are left as *qualitative*.
- Qualitative research has at least four major purposes and these are outlined as *descriptive*, *hypothesis testing*, *theory generation* and *intervention*.
- Advice is given to the student wishing to embark on a qualitative data-gathering project, first generally in terms of data sources, sampling, data gathering and analysis, and then in the form of a brief outline of three major qualitative approaches: grounded theory (GT), interpretive phenomenological analysis (IPA) and discourse analysis (DA).
- Advice is offered on the construction and form of qualitative research reports.
- The problem of evaluating qualitative research is then discussed in terms of traditional reliability and validity; various attempts to produce generalised criteria for evaluation are outlined and related to three major epistemological positions present in qualitative approaches: *scientific realist*, *contextualist* and *radical constructivist*. The criteria include *triangulation*, *respondent validation*, *fit*, *coherence*, *reflexivity*, *negative case analysis*, *transference*, *resonance* and the *data audit*.
- Brief details of computer packages for the analysis of qualitative data are given and a list of further practically oriented reading is provided. A full qualitative research article is appended.

Quantitative analysis of qualitative data – Content analysis

The bulk of this chapter is about the analysis of qualitative data *as* qualitative data; that is, research that analyses meanings in text or transcript, rather than traditional research, which defines and measures variables in quantitative fashion and tests hypotheses. (This division in research thinking and practice was discussed in Chapters 2 and 10.) For most of the last century, however, there was (and still is) a tradition of taking initially qualitative data (such as political speeches, television advertisements, reported contents of dreams, participants' descriptions of ambiguous pictures etc.) and subjecting these data to a categorisation and coding procedure, which created quantitative data.

We have met several ways of doing this already in the form of rating schedules for the assessment of stories or dream content and coding schemes for analysing reactions to TAT tests (see Chapter 8). This approach usually pre-defines what categories and themes will count for quantification, based on a mixture of prior research experience and background theory (e.g. psychoanalytic assumptions about dream symbol meanings). Research assistants are thoroughly trained in the coding of data and there is little room for creating new categories or, in the final analysis, presenting what people actually *meant* when they produced the raw data. This rating of qualitative data is in the positivist tradition of simply seeking to create measures for 'slippery' phenomena in order to bring them into the 'legitimate' arena of scientific analysis.

CONTENT ANALYSIS is a step away from this kind of pre-determination of data coding, but its roots remain firmly in a quantitative, positivist approach. Originally, the formalised method was devised for sampling and analysing messages from the media and other recorded material, such as literature, politicians' speeches or wartime propaganda. Attempts to analyse media messages can be dated back to the beginning of the twentieth century, when various writers were concerned about standards and about the influence of the press on society, crime and morals. In the 1930s and 1940s, however, content analysis became popular for providing evidence within social psychology. This growth in use was bolstered by concerns about the threat of propaganda before and during the Second World War and because the fast developing electronic media (radio, TV, film) could no longer be considered as an extension of the press. In this use it was seen as a quantifying instrument for assessing the content of communications.

It is another way of observing people, not directly, but through the messages they produce. The communications concerned were originally those already published, but some researchers conduct content analysis on materials that they *ask* people to produce, such as essays, answers to interview questions, diaries and verbal protocols (described in Chapter 6), in which case the research project becomes *reactive* (see p. 95).

Content analysis has been used on plays, folklore, legend, nursery rhymes, children's books and even popular music in order to demonstrate differences between cultures and subcultures, and within cultures over time. Books and television content, in particular, have often been analysed for race bias or sex bias. The preoccupations of various magazines, newspapers and journals have been linked, through content analysis, with the various political leanings of such publications. Changes in content have been used as indicators of change in public attitude (although they could indicate changes in the politics of the newspaper owner). Some examples of content analytic studies are given in Box 22.1.

Procedure for quantitative content analysis

Probably the first major task you face, should you decide on a content analysis project, is that of deciding just what material to *sample* from all that exists. This decision will be at the heart of your project rather than the side issue it sometimes (but wrongly) appears to be for an experiment. The sampling choice will probably depend centrally upon the hypothesis or research aim. For newspapers, this will mean making a decision based on political leaning, price, target readership,

Info Box 22.1 | Research using content analysis

Examples of analysis of existing materials

Shneidman (1963) analysed the speeches of Kennedy and Nixon in their televised presidential debates, demonstrating differences in their logical arguments.

Cumberbatch, Woods, Evans, Irvine and Lee (1990) analysed over 500 prime-time advertisements over a two-week period in 1990 involving over 200 character appearances; 75% of men but only 25% of women were judged to be over 30 years old. Men outnumbered women 2:1 and 89% of voice-overs, especially for expert/official information, were male; 50% of female voice-overs were categorised as 'sexy/sensuous'. The ratio of women to men rated as 'attractive' was 3:2. Men were as likely to be engaged in housework for friends as for their family, while females predominantly worked for their family and never friends.

An example of qualitative content analysis

Bruner and Kelso (1980) reviewed studies of 'restroom' graffiti spanning 30 years. Most studies before theirs analysed the material either at a superficial level – the overt content of statements – or at an interpretive, often psychoanalytic level. Bruner and Kelso analysed the messages *at a qualitative level*, concluding that women's graffiti were more interpersonal and interactive, tending to contain questions and advice about love, relationships and commitment. Men's graffiti tended to be egocentric and competitive, concentrating on conquests and prowess. Their messages served the function of confirming a position of control and the maintenance of power, whereas women's messages reflected the cooperation and mutual help strategies of the dominated.

Analysis of specially produced materials

Some studies use content analysis on open-ended interview data or on essays, stories or diaries written by participants. **Miller** (1997) asked college social psychology students to keep journals in which they applied course concepts to their daily social experiences. Content analysis of the entries showed evidence of the acquisition of various forms of self-knowledge, which provided tutors with a useful framework for assessing aspects of student psychosocial development.

Other examples

The range of phenomena studied using content analysis includes, for instance: identification of prevalent ideologies and myths in contemporary women's magazines; coverage of parapsychology in psychology textbooks across three decades; development and implementation of the think-aloud method in relation to fruit and vegetable purchasing behaviour; Japanese, Turkish and Israeli television content; psychotherapists' dreams about their patients; statements by 195 eminent people regarding their beliefs about the meaning of life; occurrence of cigarette-smoking images and nudity on websites accessible to young teenagers; e-mail discussion group messages between women on health issues.

Knight et al., 2003, used content analysis on responses to a semi-structured questionnaire given to young poorly controlled diabetics and recorded expressions of fear, control and acceptance. This was to assess the dependent variable in a quasi-experimental design conducted in applied health psychology where some of the adolescents received a psychological intervention programme to improve their blood sugar control.

An example of online-based content analysis comes from **Mo and Coulson** (2008) who analysed over a thousand e-messages posted on an HIV/AIDS support group website. They were interested in the kinds of social support that were offered by senders and found that most frequently offered were 'informational and emotional support, followed by esteem support and network support, with tangible assistance the least frequently offered' (p. 371).

and so on. For television, a representative sampling of programmes, times, advertising slots, and the like, must occur. Advertising is often linked to the content of adjacent programmes and to likely audiences at different times – hence all the industrial accident claims support services shown on weekday TV. Where personal ads are the target, you might want to sample different publications based on their likely readership in terms of locality, social class and so on.

Having obtained your data you will need to decide upon CODING UNITS appropriate to the kind of content that appears. Some examples are given below.

Unit:	Examples
Word:	Analyse for sex-related words in different magazines
Theme:	Analyse for occasions, in children's literature, on which boy/girl initiates and gets praised
Item:	Look for whole stories, e.g. article on Northern Ireland
Character:	Analyse types of character occurring in TV cartoons
Time and space:	Count space or time devoted to a particular issue in media

Although it is also common to decide on categories only after the data are gathered, in the traditional model the researcher presents coders with a pre-constructed system for categorising occurrences. This means that the researcher will have to become very familiar with the sort of materials likely to be encountered prior to the start of the content analysis exercise. As with observation, coders may be asked to *categorise* only. They may be asked to *rank* items – for instance, a set of participants' descriptions of themselves, ranked for 'confidence'. Alternatively, each item might be *rated*: aspects of children's drawings could be scored for 'originality'. In the interests of combating researcher bias, having developed the coding system on pilot material, the coding of the research data might be completed entirely by assistants who are unaware of the research hypothesis or aim. If this is your own project, however, you may not have the luxury of research personnel to assist you. It is also common to test for *inter-coder reliability* using correlational techniques, as for *inter-observer reliability*.

Qualitative content analysis

Below, we take a closer look at some of the popular approaches to qualitative research that were first introduced in Chapter 10. It should be noted here, however, that some researchers simply conduct a qualitative version of content analysis (see the example from Bruner and Kelso (1980) in Box 22.1). That is, they analyse the interview transcript for themes, but they do not proceed to tally these into predetermined categories. They do not conduct a quantitative analysis of extracted data; they retain the data as qualitative and in their report will illustrate each identified theme with one or more quotations from the transcript. This process is central, in fact, to most qualitative approaches and we shall now proceed to take a look at the nature of qualitative approaches that treat data at a qualitative level.

Qualitative analysis of qualitative data

We move here to what most people mean these days when they talk of 'doing a qualitative project'. However, most of the contemporary qualitative approaches are embedded in a consciously selected EPISTEMOLOGY – a philosophy of knowledge of the world, and how it is acquired or constructed. Therefore it is not possible to give any kind of fixed recipe for the analysis of qualitative data. There is far less agreement here than for quantitative methods (though even there, things are not as homogenous as they may sometimes appear). Some of the major philosophical issues involved in qualitative research approaches were discussed in Chapter 10.

All methodologies are dependent upon the underlying epistemology that drives them. Mainstream quantitative research, though, rarely stops to think about it. However, because it believes that close observation and measurement can bring us closer to the truth about the world, it is particularly concerned with the elimination of bias and sampling error. Qualitative methods that value the unique perspective of the individual will use methods that are more likely to obtain and preserve the richness of an individual account. The trouble is that there is a variety of methods and philosophies, so here we will only be able to look at general and relatively common guiding principles and some commonly used techniques associated with major approaches. First, though, I want to make a few points about doing a qualitative research project in the present academic climate.

Doing qualitative research

This chapter is not intended to give fine detail on the whole process of conducting a qualitative research project. To conduct one you will ultimately need to immerse yourself in at least one, if not several, specialised text(s) covering your chosen approach. However, since qualitative approaches to research-based assessments are becoming ever more popular on taught courses, I hope this section can prove useful in helping students decide roughly what kind of qualitative project they could conduct, and I hope it can help answer the two agonising questions I hear so often these days: 'What do I do with the data and how do I report them?' and 'What does a good qualitative report look like?'

This last question is a vexed one, even for experienced qualitative researchers, some of whom reject the very notion of fixed or conventional criteria for deciding what is *good* qualitative work. This leaves the student who wishes to do qualitative work in a disconcerting position, particularly if their tutors or supervisors are vague, unsure or dismissive about the standards to be met in qualitative reports. This can be a strong factor working against the promotion of qualitative projects, and can send students hurrying back to the safety of the known and well-documented quantitative project. A suck-it-and-see approach won't do when students have grades to think about.

The situation is not helped by a lack of texts with a very clear 'how to do it' structure, though more are now appearing and it is also easier of late to find good and accessible qualitative reports. I have included a model and relatively simple report at the end of this chapter. Because many qualitative approaches were born from a critique of and frustration with the quantitative paradigm, you will find that texts with promising 'how to do it' titles often spend much time on a rejection of positivism and scientific method in psychology with rather deep arguments that really can't be followed unless the reader is already familiar with the language of social constructionism, relativism or post-structuralism. These arguments justify the promoted approach, but one is often left screaming, 'Yes, but just tell me how you do it!' Hence the student is advised to pick carefully, following tutor advice, checking in the library, and so on, before investment.

Collecting qualitative data

Specific data-collection methods have been embedded in the methods sections earlier in this text, particularly the work on interviewing methods, but also qualitative and/or participant observation, diary studies, and so on. However, some general questions it would certainly be helpful to answer before setting out on a qualitative project are 'What is the major purpose of this project?', 'What will it attempt to achieve?' and 'How far will it go?' This is similar to thinking about the structure of measures and related data-testing issues before starting to gather quantitative data.

Purposes of qualitative projects

As for quantitative studies, qualitative studies can be carried out for a number of research purposes. A non-exhaustive list of these might include:

- descriptive/exploratory
- hypothesis testing
- theory/hypothesis generation
- intervention and change/action research.

There may be overlap between these in any particular study. Things are immediately not as clear-cut as for quantitative approaches in that some qualitative approaches involve theory generation *during* the gathering of data and a return for more, based on emergent insights and possibilities. Hence, reports do not always follow a 'this-is-what-we-did-and-here-are-the-results' format.

Descriptive studies

Some studies are purely descriptive – an attempt to start investigating an area, perhaps, or simply to record and assess experiences of a particular group or progress in a specific intervention project. There are some problems with pure description. First, qualitative approaches themselves emphasise the relativist nature of knowledge and the idea that 'facts' are social constructions. Much qualitative research is about the recognition of different perspectives, different interpretations of 'reality', and so on. Hence, a descriptive study will have to take up a position on *whose* perspective it is reporting *from*.

A more pressing problem for students new to psychology will be trying to locate the difference between an acceptable report of psychological research and a piece of journalism or anecdotal account. In Chapter 24 there is a warning about 'day at the zoo' reports. A descriptive account, standing as a psychological report, simply must find daylight between itself and what would be acceptable only for a magazine article. One danger is not to distinguish between a social problem and a psychological research problem. Hence, some (weak) psychology reports come in as 'an account of my friend's battle with anorexia' where the story may be fascinating but the reference to psychological issues, constructs, processes or relevant theory is minimal or stretched to fit. The student must ask 'In what way will this be psychology, not media reporting.' Silverman says:

How could anybody think that what we ought to do [in social science] is to go out into the field to report people's exciting, gruesome or intimate experiences? … Naïve interviewers fail to recognise what they have in common with media interviewers (whose perennial question is 'How do you/does it feel?') and with tourists (who in their search for the 'authentic' or 'different', invariably end up with more of the same). (1993: 199)

Although Silverman speaks from a sociological perspective, the issue is the same for psychology – you need a psychological research question to answer. Simply reporting what you heard or saw, from your vantage point, or only trying to reflect others' perspectives, will not advance your knowledge of psychological processes, nor anyone else's.

Reason and Rowan make the point:

Once we start to do research which does not conform to the general requirements of experimental method, we run the risk of being accused of being mere journalists; indeed we run the risk of being mere journalists. (1981: 247)

Silverman, arguing against Agar's (1986) rejection of conventional validity issues in favour of a criterion of 'intense personal involvement', among other things, states:

Immediacy and authenticity may be a good basis for certain kinds of journalism but ethnography [the particular approach under discussion] must make different claims if we are to take it seriously. (1993: 153)

Even 'purely descriptive' work needs to be related at some point either to existing theory (one might relate children's sayings to cognitive stages) or to emergent theory. In several qualitative approaches the theory 'emerges' from the data analysis, as in *grounded theory* (GT). We can see a mixture of previous research confirmation and emergent theory in the article by Knight and Barnett – see p. 643–9.

Qualitative data and hypothesis testing

In Chapter 10, Hayes' (1991) research was briefly described as an example of hypothesis testing using qualitative data. Hypothesis testing is associated strongly with the mainstream quantitative paradigm and a major critique of this paradigm has been that it stifles discovery and theory generation by concentrating only on the testing of hypotheses derived from existing theory (Henwood and Pidgeon, 1995). However, this does not mean that such hypothesis testing should be discontinued as a means to theory development; some researchers, while agreeing with some of the critiques of traditional positivism in social science (e.g. the limitations of measuring closely defined variables), nevertheless use qualitative data to check out hypotheses developed from theory. For instance, one would not need to measure narrow operationalised variables, assessed by questionnaire, in order to demonstrate that there is alienation among the workforce in one company but not in another, so long as comparable sets of workers supply the information.

Qualitative data and theory generation

Contrary to the hypothesis-testing role of qualitative data, many of the emerging methods within psychology (several have older roots in sociology) see the role of data analysis as a process in the generation and construction of theory. That is, rather than analysing data *in the light of theory*, theory is developed *from* the data during the analysis. This principle of *emergent theory* is central to the grounded theory approach discussed in Chapter 10. It implies that the researcher should approach the data with a completely open mind. No pre-conceptual explanatory schema should be imposed on the data.

Now, back in Chapter 1 it was argued that to assume we could approach any new phenomenon completely without empirically based assumptions would be conceptually naïve. We always have some ideas about what we are approaching, otherwise we wouldn't know what to approach. The idea of emergent theory is more that one should not permit initial theory to impose limits on what will be collected or on how the data will finally be organised and analysed, simply because one is expecting certain concepts or directions to emerge. Pidgeon and Henwood (1997) talk of the 'flip-flop' between known background theory and organisation of the new data. They suggest this approach might be a 'constructivist revision of grounded theory' (1997: 255).

A main aim, then, of theory-generating qualitative work is to give participants the greatest opportunity to 'tell it like it is', to gather a broad and initially untreated set of information and then to gain thorough experience of the set of data, to get immersed in it, to organise it in a way that will produce higher-order concepts ('themes') that explain, make sense of or 'fit' as much of the whole collection as possible. A major aim of grounded theory, but not all others, is to leave few, if any, 'awkward' or 'rogue' raw data out of the final analysis.

As an analogy, it's a bit like knowing something vague about psychologists and 'conditioning' (seen perhaps as 'brainwashing'), immersing oneself in the various sources of information about conditioning (textbooks, TV programmes, what psychologists and/or your tutor say) and gradually developing a fuller but never complete picture of how the various forms are conceptualised and operated in practice. The hard part is that, whereas texts are consciously and carefully produced, ordinary people will not be used to defining and discussing their views on your research topic in, say, an interview situation. Even after studying conditioning, your view will still only be a 'version', not *the truth*; but when analysing the data that ordinary people produce, most qualitative workers realise and admit that what they report is one *version* among many that are possible.

Intervention and change – action research

The student new to psychology will not usually be conducting interventions. Of course, when we investigate anything at all we must create just the slightest bit of change around us – such is everyday life. But psychologists who carry out explicit change programmes, or 'action research' (see Chapter 10), need to be professionally trained and experienced. The specific methods used in such research will, to some extent, be the same as many covered here already (interview, questionnaire, and so on), but the action researcher might also employ collaborative practices (see Chapter 10) or run training sessions – although this has little, for now, to do with our aim here of dealing with qualitative data, so we will leave this particular research purpose alone for now.

Considerations for a qualitative project

The following section attempts to raise issues that face a student contemplating a qualitative project. I've already referred briefly to the increasing number of how-to-do-it books, and this chapter cannot possibly compete with these. However, what it can do is to draw out some main features for you to consider, and direct you towards literature that might move you on in your quest. However, I hope none of the texts you move on to presents itself as an authoritative 'recipe book' for qualitative methods. Most don't. Most state early on that the methods they present are examples only and that the individual researcher must be left free, and must feel free, to adapt methodology in the light of their particular research question and circumstances. Patton states:

Qualitative analysis transforms data into findings. No formula exists for that transformation. Guidance yes. But no recipe. Direction can and will be offered, but the final destination remains unique for each enquirer, known only when – and if – arrived at. (2002: 432)

This does not mean, however, that you can shirk! Pidgeon and Henwood (1997) warn that qualitative research is, in general, 'highly labour intensive' and 'not for the faint hearted'. Such authors will also tell you that any qualitative project is an uphill struggle: there is no set formula; you gather a relatively large amount of data, and need to sift through and organise it laboriously and conscientiously until satisfied. You cannot just report a short conversation, bung in a few quotations, talk about each at a superficial level, and present your report. Well, you can, but … don't expect good marks. Your work must be thorough and in the spirit of the analytic procedure you have adopted. If you use interpretive phenomenological analysis (IPA) then you cannot just repeat or briefly summarise what your participant said. If you use grounded theory you should not simply use the GT terminology (e.g. 'axial coding') and then present only superficial category names for parts of what your participant said. You should approach 'saturation' (see Chapter 10) and you should seek higher-order explanatory categories. Note that Knight and Barnett (p. 643) approached saturation by interviewing new participants until no new information was emerging.

Students are often drawn towards doing a qualitative project because they feel unhappy with numbers and are 'not mathematical' or because they see it as an easier option. This would be one of the worst reasons I can think of for doing a qualitative project. The designing and reporting of quantitative and qualitative projects have a lot in common, including at least the use of logic and hard thinking in order to organise material and to discuss findings in the light of literature. A qualitative project requires as much concentration and clarity of thought as does the average quantitative project, but it is also very likely to take a lot longer and to deal with voluminous amounts of data. It is estimated that 15 minutes of talk can take up to three hours to transcribe and qualitative studies do not *just* report what the participants said. If, on the other hand, you have seen good examples of qualitative work and feel you understand very well the principles of your chosen analytic procedure, then you may well get a lot out of the project. Just don't be fooled into doing it as an easy option!

The research question

Questions to ask yourself when considering in what way to run your project are as follows:

- Am I looking for participants' perceptions or experiences of X (the topic)?
- Am I more interested in the ways people *construct* their perceptions or manage their talk?

- Am I interested in the concepts that underlie and explain X for people?
- Or am I trying to show that a theory or hypothesis is supported by the ways people report their experiences of or feelings about X?

The first question, answered in the positive, indicates IPA or possibly GT; the second points towards a language-oriented approach like discourse analysis (DA) or narrative analysis; the third suggests GT. The final question suggests qualitative content analysis or a thematic approach. Whatever you choose, you must be certain that you are asking a *psychological* question about phenomena and not just making a journalistic excursion into an interesting area.

Sources of data

Your data could be drawn from any of the following sources:

- participant observation field notes
- informal or semi-structured interviews
- focus group discussion
- open-ended questions (interview or questionnaire)
- in-depth case-study (mixture of interviews, observations, records)
- participants' notes and diaries
- observation of advertisements, wall paintings, graffiti, etc.

Your data will usually consist of speech but may also or otherwise include interactions, behaviour patterns, written or visual recorded material, filing systems, seating arrangements, slogans and so on. You should also keep a record of your own ideas, impressions, feelings, discoveries, blind alleys and so forth that occurred as the research project progressed.

Sampling and generalisation

There will be no simple answer to the question of how large your sample should be, nor where to obtain participants from. Qualitative studies are generally not NOMOTHETIC, which is the model for quantitative studies where we sample in order to achieve a representative group from which we can generalise to the parent population. Qualitative studies are IDIOGRAPHIC – that is, they seek to study in depth the unique characteristics of individual experience. However, this is a slippery issue. Many qualitative researchers would *like* to generalise, and indeed their discussion text often edges towards assuming that what has been uncovered applies more widely than to just the five or six people who have contributed information.

Really this is one of the nub issues that the potential qualitative researcher needs to get hold of before proceeding. Qualitative research is mostly *not* about seeing what people have in common in order to develop broad-ranging empirical laws. It is about learning from unique experience. Sure, once an experience is made public in the research community and possibly more widely, we may want to know what relevance this has for the wider population, whether there are others who may share the experience *in some (probably unique) ways* and how this all contributes to the understanding of the research phenomenon. Willig writes: 'Even though we do not know who or how many people share a particular experience, once we have identified it through qualitative research, we do know that it is available within a culture or society' (2008: 17).

We do not need to interview a lot of once-imprisoned freedom fighters in order to appreciate the powerful experiences and influence of Nelson Mandela as he worked in captivity through 27 years towards liberation from Apartheid in South Africa. We can appreciate the construction of reality experienced by just a few people with disabilities and reconstruct our own perceptions as a result. We do not need to know how *many* people felt that way in order to discover a perspective we had never considered. If you are considering a qualitative project you need to keep this notion of *discovering the other* well to the fore throughout, since otherwise you may end up superficially reporting others' talk from your own unaltered perspective. If you *do* immerse yourself in the other, then you will find that you might need only a handful of people to keep you busy throughout the assignment.

To be specific, you *could* conduct a qualitative project with only one person – a single case study – but be very careful about this approach. A case study is conducted in great depth but does not simply consist of 'all I could find out about …'. It is an analysis of data, which is organised and to some extent theoretical, just as any other project. Because you have just the one person you will be gathering substantial data and almost certainly will need to return for further questioning or observation after the first stages of your analysis in order to confirm ideas, explore unexpected directions, rule out possible explanations, and so on.

Most qualitative studies research with a *few* people and this can be from five or six to fifteen where we are getting to relatively large numbers. Smith and Osborn (in Smith, 2008) recommend no more than three interviewees for a student carrying out a first project using IPA. You will be constrained to some extent by your research question and your locality. You may find it hard to locate more than two or three people who were brought up in care, for instance. Where there are plenty of people to choose from, sampling is *purposive* (as it was really for the above examples too). Qualitative researchers select those who fit the bill – that is, are holders of relevant experience in the area of the research question. They may, for instance, be people who have just undergone heart surgery, or they may be rehabilitated alcoholics, victims of bullying, children with Asperger's syndrome whose schools have not recognised the fact, women who are managers and so on. If there are a lot of potential participants (e.g. women managers) then it makes sense to stick to the same industry, perhaps, or the same area or other demographic criteria. However, keep in mind that your project will probably only benefit from richness in the diversity of ideas and experiences that you uncover.

The data-gathering process

Techniques for gathering data have been discussed in the earlier sections of this book. What can be considered here is simply that different approaches have different implications for the specifics of the data-gathering procedure. For instance, grounded theory (at least, the full version) requires 'theoretical sampling'. This is a stage where theoretical categories have already been established but more data are required in order to affirm or complete the theoretical structure that is emerging. Gaps might appear or queries persist and the researcher goes out again, perhaps back to the original participants, in order to confirm or adjust emergent categories in the light of further findings.

Interviews and focus groups

The data-gathering technique of choice is generally the semi-structured interview for all three major approaches: GT, IPA and DA. However, versions of content analysis as well as DA might gather and analyse samples of text (e.g. personal ads, essays, graffiti) or even visual material. If the interview is chosen, then all the criteria outlined in Chapter 7 apply, including an emphasis on sensitive listening skills. If a *focus group* is used, then a few extra considerations need to be made. The product of a *focus group* is somewhere between that of an unnatural interview and naturally occurring talk. Members (of whom there would normally be no more than six) do, of course, know there's a study going on but if the topic, questions and the surroundings are arranged carefully enough, participants will forget the artificiality and get personally involved in the discussion. Hence there is a premium on preparing workable questions and on scene-setting. You might want to set up the discussion (on physical punishment, say) with a short video clip from a recently televised debate, for instance. The difference between a focus group and an interview is, of course, the presence of *interaction* between participants, which is otherwise only available from naturally occurring conversations. These interactions will usually be of interest during the data-analysis procedure.

Data analysis

Preparation – the transcript

Assuming that your project records speech (for recording issues see p. 164) you will need to *transcribe* the data into a commonly used format in order to analyse them. Several systems exist, of which by far the most popular is that devised by Jefferson (1985), which records not only the actual words used but the PARALINGUISTICS involved. This includes pauses, overlapping speech, hesitations ('um' and 'err'), speed, intonation and so on. This information is of central importance in DA, conversation analysis and some other approaches since we are then interested in the ways in which people *use* speech and how speakers interact. If your analysis only concerns the *content* of speech then doing a Jefferson transcription is unnecessary. Some central features of the Jeffersonian transcription system, along with examples of their use, are provided on the companion website at www.hodderplus.com/psychology/

Conversation analysis produced the concepts of *repair* and *self-repair*, which occur when speakers correct themselves mid-sentence or are corrected by others (including those annoying people who finish off your sentences for you). The researcher has to decide whether, Freudian-style, a slip like 'The whelk is one of my favourite orgasms … er … I mean organisms …' is of importance in the analysis that is being produced. A DA-oriented and somewhat truncated version of the Jefferson system can be found in the Appendix to Potter and Wetherell (1987).

If you are using GT, IPA or thematic analysis you may only need the verbal content without the non-linguistic features. However, depending on the nature of the project, the researcher may decide that stress and intonation are important even here, in order to capture the strength of, or difference between, certain themes or categories.

Some points about your transcript:

- it must *always* (at a student level) be included with your qualitative research report unless you are specifically instructed not to do this
- it must be absolutely verbatim – exactly what the participant said
- it may or may not include non-linguistic features (see above) but it is a very good idea to indicate laughter or other emotional accompaniments
- it should include lines from everyone, including the interviewer or focus group leader (or even someone who interrupts the group in session)
- it should contain line numbers as in:

  23 Mary: Everyone knew: she was taking the day off work … >you know to go to that

  24 transport fair thingy but< did anyone (.) you know (.2) [do anything about] it

  25 Bob: [say anything < sorry]

- as a student when you use a quotation from the transcript in the body of your report (probably in the analysis section) you should use the exact line number from the transcript; for example, if you cite Bob's interruption above, you would use line number 25 to start the quotation; do not invent a simplified line numbering system just for the report and/or analysis of results; your reader needs to be able to locate the extracted quotation in its original context.

Imposing order on the data

The next step is your analysis and this will depend precisely on the approach you have chosen to use. As has been stressed already, you really must immerse yourself in the approach if you wish to produce a good version of it in your work *without* following it recipe-style so that the product feels artificial. It is not possible to give *the* way to analyse qualitative data because a variety of approaches exists, each with different operating principles and philosophy. What appear below, then, are common and specific notes on features of the analysis for each major method; after that, direction to more specific texts will be given.

In general, you will need to read and re-read the transcript thoroughly from a dispassionate point of view. You are trying to understand the perspective and its construction rather than attempting to empathise in a particular direction at this point. Most approaches advise starting to make notes on the third reading. It is a good idea in general (and also supports a reflexive approach) to keep a journal or log of all thoughts, changes of directions, insights, plans and problems encountered along the route of your analysis (or even of the whole project from planning onwards).

Procedures in major approaches

Here are some brief notes on possible procedures in major approaches. Note that the analytic process for thematic analysis (TA) was described in some detail in Chapter 10 and so that material is not repeated here. However, for the student wishing to use a TA approach, the procedures described for theme generation in GT or IPA can be used. The article by Braun and Clarke (2006) is again recommended for this approach which is probably the most useful for the student new to qualitative analysis.

Grounded theory (GT)

Initial line-by-line coding

For each line of text, you should *code* (i.e. give a name or phrase to) each event that is happening. Smith suggests you ask yourself questions such as:

What is going on? What are people doing? What is the person saying? What do these actions and statements take for granted? How do structure and content serve to support, maintain, impede or change these actions and statements? (2008: 95)

You need constantly to be critical of what you are doing. Some codes will be *in vivo* – that is, they use phrases drawn directly from participants' speech. An example might be 'ruts', used by parents of an Asperger's syndrome (AS) child and referring to times when the child gets 'stuck in a rut' of thinking from which it is difficult to get them to break off. Others will be a description of what the person is talking about or doing with their speech at that point. A code might be 'fear of failure' for someone talking fearfully about their chances in forthcoming exams; or it might be a speech act such as apologising or forgiving.

Focused (or axial) coding

This is used as analysis proceeds, and after initial coding has led to further data gathering (in the *full* version) to expand initial ideas and directions using *purposive sampling* to re-interview existing participants or find new ones (see p. 46). It consists of starting to combine early simple codes into larger constructs that will eventually combine into explanatory *categories*. Smith (2008) gives 'avoiding disclosure' as an example of a higher-order code that summarises participants' expressions of needing to keep quiet about their illness, partly for fear of being thought to complain too much. Strauss and Corbin (1990) also encouraged the use of AXIAL CODING, which involved exploring the dimensions of a category and how each category linked to others, also using concepts of 'process' and 'change' as guiding concepts. This is the version of GT to which Glaser (1992) objected (see p. 232) and others, too (e.g. Melia, 1996; Willig, 2008), find axial coding something of a technical distraction from their analysis. Knight and Barnett (p. 643) move straight from open coding to the development of themes using constant comparison.

Categories and final analysis (selective coding)

'SELECTIVE CODING' produces the final themes and categories to be used in the overall explanatory model. Final categories are a kind of hierarchical step above substantial codes, but GT writers advise that you should not simply accept categories that appear to have emerged. They should be queried and broken down again, looking at the codes that have led to the overall concept. The early 'ruts' code might eventually contribute to a category of 'AS/normal' where parents face the constant dilemma of deciding which behaviour is AS-related and which would be expected anyway of any growing teenage child. The final analysis, as it emerges, should, ideally, comprise an explanatory framework where all categories are *saturated* (p. 232) – that is, further data do not alter them substantially and no new examples of data that don't fit can be found. The categories should subsume most, if not all, codes and sub-categories.

Memo writing

This is used to explain and justify the categories as they emerge (see Charmaz (1995) for a full account). Memos can contain reasons for forming the category, supported by raw data and argument about previous attempts, contributory codes, comparisons and links with other categories, weak points where data don't quite fit and, in general, your evidence for the category. These are a key component of a GT analysis.

Interpretive Phenomenological Analysis (IPA)

Notes

The early stages here are much like those for GT, not surprisingly. The data will be in the form of interview transcripts, or possibly of diaries or journals written by participants. A specific piece of advice is to start making notes (*after* a couple of thorough reads) in the left-hand margin, which are not the makings of codes and categories as in GT but can be any reflective notion at all: objections to what is said, knee-jerk associations, links to previous work and so on.

Themes

These are produced in the second stage (though there do not have to be just 'so many' stages; it might take a second run through notes to get started). Themes are an attempt to summarise what is going on in sections of the text. At first themes will be identified in chronological order (Smith, 2008) as you go through the transcript. Some themes will recur, and will therefore be referenced to and supported by various parts of the text. These will all be documented during this stage of the analysis. An important feature to look for is any 'transformation' of 'meaning units' (Giorgi and Giorgi, 2003). Meaning units are recognised as shifts of meaning in the text, basically when the participant delivers a new point. Each of these is summarised and then transformed. Typically, generalisation occurs as themes are developed so that, for instance, riding a bike becomes learning a skill. This is so that generalisation across cases can be made in the analysis, with comparison and contrast of themes and their usage by participants. Giorgi and Giorgi give further examples of transformation, including 'making the implicit explicit' (2003: 34) and directing the analysis towards psychological meaning. The former of these could be seen as somewhat controversial since the researcher is going beyond the information given, and perhaps this is a substantial departure from the GT position. However, as Smith (2008) explains, some interpretation of data is inevitable if we are to summarise and move towards psychological understanding.

As a fictitious example, an AS child, described by a teacher as a 'happy loner', might in fact talk of being 'lonely'. If this were coupled with later statements that concerned misunderstanding of their special interests as 'obsessions', and of their lack of deference to adults as 'disrespectful', we could summarise with a superordinate theme of *misinterpretation by professionals* (teachers), experienced as frustrating and perhaps threatening.

Structure

At some point in the previous stage the identification of themes, especially as interpretation occurs, will lead on to a potential structure for the experience. Themes will group together and some may be promoted to superordinate status. IPA aims to obtain one unified structure to cover all the data, though it seems this would often mean discarding a substantial amount in order to keep the structure unified. 'Structure' refers both to the themes and to the relationships between them. Hence the misinterpretation theme may well be intimately linked to one of avoidance of professionals.

Summary

According to Willig (2008: 63):

the presentation of results should be organised around the themes that emerged from the analysis. The aim ... is to provide a convincing account of the nature and quality of the participants' experience of the phenomenon under investigation.

Willig advises the creation of a table of themes coupled with evidence from participants in the form of referenced text quotations.

Discourse analysis (DA)

The materials of choice for DA are naturally-occurring conversation or speech (e.g. a radio broadcast). However, DA is nevertheless performed on focus group or even interview data (though the unnatural dynamics of interviewing must then be carefully borne in mind during the analysis).

Most discourse analysts I have spoken to are rather shy about setting out any clear guidelines for doing DA, which is a bit difficult for the student who would like to try it (though see Billig's procedural guide (1997: 54) and the other references below). Much of this reticence stems from a fundamental embedding of the practice of DA in its background supportive philosophy. As was hinted at in Chapter 10, the student who sets out to 'do a DA project' without fully understanding the DA construction of reality is doomed. Here's what I hope is an explanatory passage about DA from Billig (1997: 39):

It is not a set of technical procedures which can be learnt in themselves and then applied to topics, regardless of the analyst's theoretical orientation. Discourse analysis, as used in social psychology, is much more than a methodology, or set of procedures for conducting research; it is a wider, theoretical approach towards psychology. Unless the general approach is understood, then one should not attempt to conduct discourse analytic research.

Billig's procedural guide, mentioned above, has 16 steps but I have just selected steps 10–16 of these since the earlier steps concern collecting the data in ways we have already covered, transcribing them (see the Appendix to Potter and Wetherell, 1987) and reading them thoroughly, at first with no analysis so that we 'experience **as a reader** the discursive effects of the text'. (Original emphasis) (Willig, 2008: 99).

10. Keep reading them [the transcripts/data]; start looking for interesting features and developing 'intuitive hunches'

11. Start indexing for themes and discursive features

12. Read, read and read, especially to check out 'intuitive hunches' against the data; always try to look for counter-examples

13. Start writing preliminary analyses, testing your 'hunches' against the details of the data; always be critical

14. Keep drafting and re-drafting analyses, comparing different extracts, looking in detail at extracts and being aware of counter-examples

15. Keep writing, reading, thinking and analysing until you produce a version with which you are not totally dissatisfied;

16. Be prepared to return to Stage 1

Table 22.1 Steps 10–16 of Billig's procedural guide for discourse analysis (1997: 54)

Step 16 of the guidelines presented in Table 22.1 is rather disconcerting!

One of the major roots for the discursive approach (as against Foucaldian DA) has been *conversation analysis* (CA). The student thinking about doing a discursive project might do worse than read up about CA in Have (1999) and Hutchby and Wooffitt (1998). The important things about analysis to take from these readings and from discursive psychology are as follows.

• Language consists of *speech acts*; it is social action. For instance, when you say you are 'worried', you are not reporting an internal mental state but constructing a position through social discourse. We learn to use the term 'worried' by observing how others use it and in what contexts (similar to the behaviourist position on language). If I say: 'I'm worried; no, that's not the right term, perhaps bothered is better ...', this is me reconsidering what I said in a social context; perhaps not wanting to set up an image of great concern, more of being perturbed by something.

• Language, then, does not give us a direct route to internal mental states; the discourse analyst is not *interested* in mental states but in the ways in which people use language interactively to create psychological discourse in everyday conversation. It would be a mistake to use DA to investigate what you believe to be people's '*real*' emotions, or the thoughts or attitudes behind their talk.

• The emphasis is on what people *do* with language; content, though taking more prominence in some projects, is less important than the identification of ways in which people *manage their stake* in, or their accountability for, the phenomenon of interest. Managing a stake in a simple form is illustrated by the ways in which, say, politicians might rephrase titles, referring to someone as a 'freedom fighter' rather than a 'terrorist' or discussing just-announced large changes in a multi-national company as an 'opportunity to move forward and restructure' rather than a situation requiring redundancies and greater strain on the workforce.

- Language is an interaction; we look at the ways in which people interweave their comments and claims with others' speech. According to DA thinking, for instance, people construct memories together rather than holding rigid 'photocopies' of events in their minds – a point with which the early memory investigator Frederick Bartlett would no doubt agree. A memory of a party, for instance, is reconstructed as people offer instances that others then might verify or dispute.

- In analysing your text, then, you would look for devices of stake management and/or at ways in which participants in a conversation interact to construct a version of events. If you are analysing just one person's speech you might look for different versions of the same construct, or for different utterances that say the same thing. You might look for contradictions or for different 'repertoires', e.g. the kind of talk used by a participant to their mother compared with how they might talk to a friend. People often use different registers in the same session of talk because they are sometimes assuming somewhat different roles, e.g. when telling a friend what they told their mother. Repertoires may contradict to some extent as when an employee talks of a caring manager at some point, yet at another talks of them in hard-nosed terms.

Unlike grounded theory users, discourse analysts do not expect to produce a complete analysis of *all* the material in their transcripts. Their position is that any analysis is only a version. Another is always possible. As features of the text emerge to the analyst they must constantly check back, criticise and reconsider the feature in the light of further support from the text. Features themselves are often identified, according to Billig (1997), using the 'hunches' mentioned in Table 22.1. These are intuitive guesses or understandings about what the text is saying (e.g. 'Is this parent discussing their Asperger child's behaviour as that of a normal teenager with normal teenage problems or as a 'case' explained by being Asperger's? Do they realise what they're doing in their talk at some point?'). In order to keep critical, the analyst asks him/herself 'Why am I reading this text in this way?' (Willig, 2008). It might occur to the analyst that they have thought in this way because they themselves, rather than the parent, find it hard to distinguish between these two positions.

As features emerge, through hunches or otherwise, they are 'indexed' or coded. Some may emerge in later transcripts, and then it might be necessary to go back and code earlier ones on the same basis. Mostly they will emerge *during* the analysis and not a priori. Codes need not refer to explicit content; implications can be used as support or even plain omission. If a parent of an AS child never uses the term 'AS' during an interview about their child then this is important. In DA it is possible either to use a broad-brush approach, and find similarities across several participants' talk or different texts; alternatively, it is possible to concentrate on specific sections of text or perhaps on the answers to only one or two key questions. To repeat an earlier point, the emphasis can be more on content or more on the language dynamics, but topics would only be analysed according to the way in which they are presented.

To learn more about the DA approach the reader will now have to study dedicated texts such as those listed in further reading, p. 582.

Writing up the report

This is going to be putting the cart before the horse, as the chapter on report writing is yet to come. It would be best if you had read that chapter already unless you already know the general rules for psychological reports. If not, read Chapter 24 but do not pay so much attention to the quantitative aspects. What we will do here, then, is just outline the ways in which a qualitative report would differ from a quantitative one, emphasising that doing a qualitative report does not let you off all the generic features of good academic writing such as a clear abstract, an appropriately sourced and referenced introduction, clear method, organised presentation of findings, and an in-depth, coherent discussion.

Abstract and introduction

As for a quantitative report, the abstract should contain major findings. Usually these would be the major categories or themes to emerge, though this really will depend on the nature of the project. However, it would *not* do simply to state that 'Participants used a variety of discursive techniques or conversational features'.

In the purest form of GT, it has been argued that background literature should have no effect on the emergence of data from the transcripts. However, in reality there will usually be a literature to rest the present study upon and, as Willig (2008: 101) points out, although DA studies have tended to start with a critique of quantitative studies in the topic area, there should now be enough literature to be able to develop ideas from previous DA studies in an area, though not always where completely new ground is broken. Although TA may make specific testable predictions, what is otherwise common to all qualitative approaches is the absence of quantified, specific hypotheses to test, and the presence instead of the *aims* of the study. These might be in terms of an exploration of specific experiences (e.g. discovering Asperger's Syndrome in your child) or of an analysis of discursive techniques in describing one's reasons for liking *Big Brother*. One would usually also include here a rationale for using the research approach that has been selected for the study, though the detail of this might be left to the 'analytic procedure' section (below).

Method

The method section would be similar to that described on p. 618 for quantitative reports, except for the attention to precision in defining variables. DA requires only as much demographic detail of participants as is absolutely necessary, whereas an IPA approach would probably include more about the person(s) involved in order to begin painting the holistic picture. Note the way in which Knight and Barnett (p. 642) employ theoretical sampling and refer to their participants as a *snowball sample* – see p. 46.

The method section will usually contain a section that describes the ANALYTIC PROCEDURE used on the data and may be so headed. Knight and Barnett (p. 643) use the heading 'Data analysis' and describe basic procedures in grounded theory. The explanation here outlines which of the approaches has been used and provides details of the procedures. Often a justification will be given for a new or modified version of qualitative analysis. It is really important here to make clear to your reader *which version* of your chosen approach you are following: e.g. full version or abbreviated version of GT; 'pure' GT as prompted by Glaser (1992) or the more directed analysis promoted by Strauss and Corbin (1990); discursive or Foucauldian version of DA.

An important point if you are using TA is to describe precisely and in detail how the analysis was carried out, how were themes first identified, how were they finally arranged and so on. Rarely do published articles using TA do this but the student needs to convince the reader (marker) that they did not just read though and produce superficial theme labels.

Here, or at least somewhere in the report, researchers often include a section on *reflexivity*, explaining how they have accounted for this in the study. The account might be a separate section describing feelings, reactions, subjective insights, possible personal bias, and so on, or reflexivity might be integrated throughout the analysis, with the researcher commenting on each point made from their own perspective. Reflexivity also includes what Willig (2008) terms *epistemological reflexivity* (see p. 241) but these issues will usually be included in the overall discussion section.

Results, analysis, discussion

The big difference from quantitative reports occurs with what replaces the conventional results and discussion sections. Many approaches simply merge these and the analysis is reported as the data are considered. DA, in particular, argues that the researcher should not think in terms of doing the analysis then writing it up, but that the write-up itself forms part of the analysis; it is an exercise in clarifying all ideas for the reader. Whatever the approach, as the analysis progresses so quotations from the transcript *must* be included as support for claims being made. Line numbers should be given and these should be those in the original transcript so that the reader can go to the transcript and identify the surrounding context of any quotation. Some quotations are included because they 'tell it like it is'. Here are a few examples.

Management here uses the classical mushroom principle – keep 'em in the dark but pull 'em out periodically to cover 'em in crap.

It seems like central groups such as computer services or academic registry have got a life of their own and think they exist for us academics to serve them rather than supporting us in educating the students.

At six years old we thought we had a genius child; we didn't think of him as a problem.

Quotations should not be included unless a full explanation of their relevance to the present analytical point is given. As with quantitative statistics and tables, the reader should not be left guessing as to why information appears. Both IPA and GT have some ways of presenting categories and tables, together with their linkages, that have become almost conventional. The potential researcher should consult individual articles to get some idea of these. There is an example of a grounded theory model on p. 649 of the Knight and Barnett article and Table 22.2 (see overleaf) is an adaptation of an IPA-oriented table of themes.

If it is appropriate, a qualitative report can round off with a general discussion of findings, again as one might find in a quantitative report but here often limited to the general theoretical findings, spin-offs from the research, overall insights, applications and, of course, any methodological weakness or doubts about possible interpretations.

In an appendix, if you are presenting a course assignment, you would normally be required to include your entire transcript (or, for instance, all the personal ads you analysed in their original form). For published articles this is not feasible but the professional researcher is expected to be able to make their entire raw data set available to those who enquire after it.

1. *Living with an unwanted self in private*
    Undesirable behaviour ascribed to pain
    Struggle to accept self and identity — unwanted self
    Rejected as true self
    Undesirable, destructive self
    Conflict of selves
    Living with a new self

2. *Living with an unwanted self in public*
    Shame
    Lack of compassion
    Destructive social consequences of pain

3. *A self that cannot be understood*
    Lack of control over self
    Rejection of change
    Responsibility, self vs pain

4. *A body separate from the self*
    Taken for granted
    Body excluded from the self
    Body presence vs absence

Adapted from Smith and Osborn (2003); the investigation concerned the self-concept experienced by sufferers of chronic benign pain.

Table 22.2 Master table of themes for group of participants discussing chronic benign pain

How-to-do-it texts

I have included some how-to-do-it texts in the recommended readings below. However, I think that even those texts dedicated to qualitative methods will leave you feeling a little short of examples of exactly how to proceed. Of course, one always gets the mantra that there is no recipe – just proceed as you think fit; but for the inexperienced student, reliant on guidance for decent grades, this is unsatisfactory and confidence-sapping. I think there is just one good solution to this problem (unless your tutor is one of those who *does* provide a well-structured and clear set of guidelines) and that is to read as many original articles as you can. I have included a qualitative article (pp. 641–9) which is relatively easy to read and which makes clear its approach to grounded theory. For reasons of space I have omitted references but these are available on the companion website. Most students would not need to produce anything more elaborate than this, and usually something a good deal shorter, unless for a final-year thesis.

Reliability and validity – how are qualitative studies evaluated?

On hearing about how qualitative studies are conducted and reported, many researchers wedded to the quantitative way of life will throw up their arms in horror and ask forcefully 'But what about reliability and validity? How can this possibly be scientific?' (see, for instance, Morgan, 1998). Their point is that the conventional quantitative research paradigm has long-standing criteria for evaluating studies. The foundation stones of this evaluation are the concepts of the *reliability* and *validity* of psychological effects, and the associated measures used to demonstrate them (e.g. observer reliability, reliability of psychological scales, replication of studies, construct validity and so on).

In quantitative work reliability is fairly easy to demonstrate since we have a numerical measure of how closely, for instance, participants' scores agree over two testing sessions (test/re-test) or how consistent items are in a questionnaire (internal reliability). A correlate of reliability is replicability, hence the emphasis on clear definitions and standardised procedures. In order to check the reliability of an effect we must be able to replicate the demonstration of it. Although we can demonstrate reliability, this does not of course have much bearing on validity, which was earlier defined as the issue of whether an apparently demonstrated effect really is the effect it appears to be.

Realist, relativist and constructionist views of knowledge

This concept of validity belongs very much with the *realist* view of knowledge (see p. 223): that there is a single separate reality out there, which we can all agree on if only we can find the most accurate and appropriate measurement and testing instruments. That is, we are not naïve realists who believe exactly what we see but *scientific realists* who know that the world of observation is slippery but the task is to remove the camouflage caused by experimenter bias, participant expectancies, and so on. Hypothetical constructs have temporary status while we attempt to find empirical support for their actual existence.

Many qualitative researchers depart at this point because they hold a *constructionist* or at least a *relativist* version of knowledge. In the latter view, researchers hold that there are several possible versions of events (e.g. the freedom fighter's and that of the anti-terrorist police). In a constructionist view, all meanings are created through language, so even the concepts of 'reliability' and 'validity' themselves are analysed by constructionists as an aspect of the scientific discourse. This is a difficult position to appreciate fully without immersion in the literature, but it might help to consider this. Whenever we might be tempted to ask 'But how do you *know* that?' a constructionist would question what knowledge is anyway (a construction of truth versions via discourse), the ways in which knowledge is constructed and presented as fact and, for analysis, would focus on the ways in which knowledge claims are made.

The three main approaches described above (GT, IPA, DA) are explored by Madill, Jordan and Shirley (2000) in an article that considers how issues of reliability and validity can be applied across the qualitative research spectrum. They argue that grounded theory spans the realist and CONTEXTUALIST positions. By *contextualist* they mean those with a relativist view of knowledge and who reject a 'scientific realist' position (the basic quantitative position presented in this book); they would argue that qualitative research findings can only be understood as a version in a context, presented by a researcher with a 'take' on the world, hence the importance here of reflexivity.

Knowledge, they argue, is situation-dependent and provisional. It is not *expected*, therefore, that researchers should come up with identical analyses of the same material (contrary to Silverman, 1993 – see below), nor is it held that putting together the views of different sources of information will necessarily give us a composite version of 'the truth'. Nevertheless, some versions may be more important than others, depending on the research question and context. For instance, contextualists would hold that a male and female author would necessarily come up with different versions (as would any two researchers), which here depend on their gendered experience, but it may well be that a feminist version is the focus of the research project.

Madill *et al.* refer to the contemporary work of discourse analysts (e.g. Potter, Wetherell, Edwards) as arriving from a RADICAL CONSTRUCTIONIST perspective. As I tried to explain above, the focus here is always not on knowledge itself but on the *discourse of knowing*. As an example, take the radical constructionists' attitude towards researchers' attempts to present a reflexive account of their work. Madill *et al.* say:

'confessions', such as descriptions of the researcher's perspective, can be understood as a way of pre-empting and hence undermining the impact of criticism through the rhetorical management of the researcher's stake and interest (Potter, Edwards and Wetherell, 1993). (2000: 15)

In other words, DA thinking is that making an isssue of honesty about the possible biases in your own work (reflexivity) is a way of managing your research context such that you can appear perhaps a little less guilty of being biased (a bit like the ordinary conversation gambit of 'It's a terrible thing to say, I know, but …').

Different qualitative perspectives – different evaluation criteria

Madill *et al.* (2000) and others (e.g. Reicher, 2000) argue that qualitative psychology is not carried out by a unified body of psychologists. (Indeed, some of the interchanges between different 'schools' are more vitriolic than were the early critiques of positivism by qualitative researchers in general!) Hence it cannot be expected that the criteria for recognising good sound research should be equally applicable across all versions. In fact, the debate about guidelines for conducting and reporting qualitative research, and about evaluation criteria, has been vigorous and complex, with some researchers vehemently resisting what they see as the restraints of guidelines that would have the potential to become constricting conventions. Marshall and Rossman (1989) reject notions of reliability altogether, on the constructivist viewpoint, and others reject validity – for example, Agar (1986), who wants to dismiss conventional validity issues in favour of 'an intensive personal involvement', among other factors. Smith voiced the fear of qualitative researchers that:

this debate might lead to a simplistic prescriptive checklist of items, whereby a journal editor could read a qualitative paper and award it a score of, say, 7 out of 10 on quality and use that to decide whether it was publishable or not. (2003: 232)

On the other hand, as Parker states:

if qualitative research needs to refuse questions that are habitually posed in the mainstream it must at least explain why it will not address those questions, the questions being those of credibility which in the mainstream are achieved through satisfying aspects of reliability and validity. (1994a: 14)

Silverman (1993) holds that qualitative research *should* produce reliable results and argues that different researchers collecting and analysing the same data, ought to come up with the same or very similar findings.

The emergence of guidelines

Inexorably, then, over the past few years several sets of guidelines for good qualitative research and the trustworthiness of reports have emerged. Most of these are praiseworthy for attempting to assess quality across a wide range of qualitative approaches (see especially, Parker, 2004), though inevitably they will not please or satisfy everyone and every position. Coming largely from a grounded theory position but nevertheless producing width of application were Henwood and

Pidgeon (1992), who listed several criteria, some of which are discussed generically below. This goes too for the more phenomenologically oriented but well-received criteria produced by Elliott, Fischer and Rennie (1999) in the *British Journal of Clinical Psychology* and by Yardley (2000) in the area of health psychology. It is not possible here to run through all their criteria with accompanying rationale but we will discuss some, noting that the majority apply best to methods taking the contextualist position identified by Madill *et al.* (2000), whereas relatively fewer, and possibly different ones, apply to the radical constructionist position (basically DA).

Realist qualitative approaches and traditional evaluation criteria

The conventional concepts of reliability and validity (as described elsewhere in this book) will still apply where qualitative data have been content-analysed then treated in a quantitative manner. Where qualitative hypothesis-testing research has been carried out, as in qualitative content analysis and in thematic analysis, there will be no statistical checks but other standard notions of reliability and validity still apply, since the researchers are generally checking on a state of affairs assumed to be an underlying and singular reality. We can look for consistency within and between descriptions of phenomena (reliability).

Respondent validation

We can check validity, in part and where appropriate, using RESPONDENT VALIDATION. This refers to a consultation with participants to check the authenticity of the researcher's interpretations of their experiences. Not all researchers would agree that this is possible or feasible in their own projects, however, since participants may not be able to see the bigger picture the researcher has generated. Holt and Dunn (2004) refer to 'member checking' using two procedures, one an attempt to check emerging interpretations with interviewed (soccer-playing) participants, problematic because of contact difficulties, and the other a recruitment of six new and experienced 'members' who were not part of the interview procedure but who correlated emergent interpretations with their own professional soccer experience.

Triangulation

Although borrowed from the quantitative context of surveying and navigation, and used in evaluative research, triangulation has been popularly used among qualitative researchers. TRIANGULATION means comparing two (or more) different views of the same thing: interview with observational data, open with closed questions, or one researcher's analysis with another's. In most qualitative research it is also used to urge that various perspectives be compared – different participants in different roles (e.g. students, teachers), the perspectives of the researchers among one another and their views compared with the participants' views.

Here the term 'triangulation' can be unfortunately misleading in that it connotes complete accuracy – one uses two or more points in navigation to get a *perfect* 'fix' on direction. In the realist versions of qualitative research, which would include not only content and thematic analysis but also some forms of grounded theory (Silverman, 1993, Charmaz, 1995), we might expect some form of *convergence* on the same ultimate findings. However, in a contextualist approach this would *not* be expected given the approach to knowledge outlined above. 'The goal of triangulation within a contextualist epistemology is completeness not convergence,' say Madill *et al.* (2000: 10). That is, the aim is to present multiple and diverse perspectives that add up to a fuller picture than would be possible when the underlying philosophy is a search for *the* truth of a matter.

Subjectivity and reflexivity

The matter of reflexivity has probably been mentioned enough already (here and in Chapter 10) but it is worth reinforcing the point here that, whereas the positivist approach strives hard to remove what it considers to be all trace of subjectivity, proudly proclaiming to be following an 'objective' approach, qualitative researchers (e.g. Parker, 1994b), and especially feminist authors (e.g. Wilkinson, 1986), have argued that the psychological experimenter's cool detachment from 'subjects' is a distortion of human relationships and gives only a subjective impression of 'doing science'. After all, no other 'proper' science has had to think like this about its subject matter. It was psychologists' early attempts to imitate natural science that caused them to believe they had to distance themselves from human interaction with their subjects because physicists (lucky them, and without trying) already *had* this relationship with metals and gases.

Non-realist qualitative researchers, then, do not pretend to avoid subjectivity at all, but recognise it as permeating the relationship between researcher and researched. For contextualists (e.g. the Strauss and Corbin version of GT and IPA), reflexivity has been the main response to charges of subjectivity: 'Yes, you are right that we are subjective but we accept this and explain it as part of our research project.' DA, as we have seen, might see reflexivity as more research rhetoric.

Interpretations and 'fit'

Whatever is produced in the analysis (categories, themes, theory) the reader should be able to see the route from these inevitably subjective researcher interpretations back to the original data via the examples given and the rationale. This is why the writing of memos is so important in some approaches and/or the keeping of a RESEARCH DIARY. The data, by and large, should fit closely with the suggested explanatory framework and there should not be too many loose ends. Note that Knight and Barnett (p. 643) maintained a 'manuscript' which served the research diary role.

Negative case analysis

Grounded theory, in particular, argues that there should be few, if any, data left over as 'unexplained' after the analysis. This does not apply in other approaches: IPA might ditch some awkward data and DA approaches seem to pick text at will. One way of moving towards the GT position is to analyse data for cases or examples that do not fit the proposed thematic structure or explanatory framework, and then to modify as a consequence. Actually, we are not so far from the hypothetico-deductive method here, especially considering the way in which negative case analysis is described by Smith (1997) and Pidgeon and Henwood (1997). The process of looking for contradictions of one's developing theory is known as ANALYTIC INDUCTION if the motivation is to move the theory to a closer fit of all the data. This is exactly what is done by mainstream scientists and is akin to ruling out possible alternative explanations.

Potter (1996) argues that, in the discourse analysis model, a negative instance, or 'deviant case', can confirm the validity of the general pattern by demonstrating the unexpected problems produced when a deviant (i.e. 'rule-breaking') piece of discourse confuses the participants in a discussion or 'throws' them.

One problem with negative case analysis and some of the other quality checks is that they are first used as part of the analytic procedure. Hence they can't later be claimed as *checks* in the sense that one is checking the validity of reported findings, because this would mean that the tool used *during* analysis to produce results is also the tool claimed to *verify* the results. In the general qualitative view there is no independent check that results are 'right'; validity is achieved, or at least quality is enhanced, by constantly checking that the researcher is not getting carried away with a tunnel-vision perspective.

Coherence

Elliott *et al.* (1999) argue for *coherence* as a criterion. This refers not only to the obvious need to hang things together in a rational order, but also to make clear to the reader how the underlying theory or framework is integrated into a whole as far as is possible. It should be possible to appreciate how the different levels of the analysis hold together, but at the same time there should be an emphasis on retaining the idiosyncrasies of the data. Fully written memos should serve this purpose in, for instance, a grounded theory approach.

Transferability and generalisability

Pidgeon and Henwood (1997) talk of *transferability* in preference to the statistical-sounding 'generalisability' of findings, since one of the central foundations of qualitative research is its emphasis on uniqueness. Nevertheless, they say, in order to make any possible comparisons the researcher should give a full report of the context of the study.

However it is also necessary to guard against naïve empiricism here, and also not to treat context as just an adjunct to theory. In our view, rich and dense grounded theory, which is contextually sensitive to diverse levels of abstraction, will in itself suggest its own sphere or relevance and application. (1997: 271)

Resonance, impact and persuasiveness

While Pidgeon and Henwood (1997) talk of *persuasiveness*, Elliott *et al.* (1999) use the term *resonance*. The similarity in the two terms is in the idea of leaving readers with a feeling of having learned something or of having achieved new insights into the topic area. Theory should inspire and should be 'challenging, stimulating, and yet highly plausible in the sense of clearly reflecting substantive aspects of the problem domain' (Pidgeon and Henwood, 1997: 272).

To some extent, I have always felt a little edgy about the criterion of persuasiveness simply because there are plenty of theories out there that are very persuasive but plain wrong. I certainly feel this about the race and intelligence debate but that, of course, is controversial. However, there are certainly plausible and attractive practical scientific theories that are wrong – for instance, the idea that going out in the wet on a cold day will give you a cold. It doesn't matter that many people, phenomenologically speaking, hold this belief firmly in their epistemological bibles. Even discourse analysts need to distinguish between myth and virus in their daily lives.

A more extreme version of the 'impact' principle appears to be held by Billig (1997:53) who, writing on discursive analysis, says:

In going through pages of transcripts some passages seem to leap out; they might be filled with humour, irony and surprise; they might make the analyst smile. This is the sort of passage which you, the analyst, might wish to tell to your friends, for it makes a good story. And this is precisely the sort of passage to include in the analysis. If your theories are encouraging you to include the dull passages, and to omit the 'good stories', then get some better theories. After all, analysts, at all stages of qualitative research, have to back their own judgement. And can there be a better guide than the feeling that there is a good story to tell?

There could not be a better example, I think, of the difference within qualitative approaches than this advice to prospective qualitative researchers. The principle is quite contrary to that of 'fit', for instance where, in grounded theory, the aim is to fit *all* data to the categories of the analysis. Most other approaches, too, would not simply pick and mix at will, selecting just the juiciest respondent comments to 'sex up' the research report. This position does seem perilously close to mere journalism and an example of the possible lack of credibility that Reason and Rowan (1981) and Silverman (1993) warned of (see p. 560).

However, that worry aside, quantitative as well as qualitative reports have to follow several of the principles outlined in these criteria for checking the validity of qualitative reports. Quantitative reports, for instance, need to have transferability, of course, but also would need to be persuasive (otherwise journals would not accept them), to take account of negative case challenges and not to ignore aspects of data that do not fit their theory (though this last one may not be central where large data sets are gathered in survey analyses or in factor analysis investigations).

Data audit

Smith discusses Yin's suggestion (1989, in Smith 2008) that qualitative researchers can provide a validity check by organising all data so that a chain of evidence is apparent to anyone who cares to carry out an audit. Smith suggests one could go further and actually carry out the audit by asking a colleague, unrelated to the investigation, to check that the report is credible and follows a logical path, given the organised evidence. He also emphasises that the auditor is not looking to show that the report is the only one that could have been produced from the data (i.e. 'the truth'); this would be contrary to most qualitative research ideology. The audit provides verification that this account (among several possible) has been produced systematically and transparently, is coherent, exhaustive and intimately related to the raw data.

To conclude …

We have seen that validation of qualitative research is bound to depend on a varying range of commonly agreed criteria, depending largely upon the methodological principles and the epistemological basis of the particular approach taken. In addition, what has not been mentioned is the fact that the process of publication is one of interaction within human systems. Whatever you want to publish, you must find a way through the editorial board of whichever journal finally accepts your work. As Giles (2002) suggests, one way to think about achieving credibility in terms of the validity of your work (and this goes even for quite modest student projects, I would add) is to imagine you are sending off a proposal for your work to a funding body (those who might give you cash to complete your work if they find it worthy enough). He asks you to consider what you would include, knowing that the body is likely to have at least one quantitative sceptic among its advisers, who will need to be convinced that your work will produce some level of 'truth'.

There are plenty of criteria above to think about; you might discover more in your further reading and/or you may come up with your own. Whatever you do, the golden principle must be to *be clear and transparent about what you have done and what you have thought*.

Info Box 22.2	Computer software and internet links for qualitative data analysis

Full information on a number of packages, including most of those listed below and more, is available from The Psychology Network at the Higher Education Academy whose web address is www.heacademy.ac.uk/ – select the Psychology network under 'Subject Centres' or use this link if it still works: www.psychology.heacademy.ac.uk/ Some of the more popular ones are:

Software	Web address (all start with http://)
NUD*IST (a 'sexed up' title – sadly, nothing to do with nudism!!)	www.qsr.com.au
NVIVO 8 Close relative of NUD*IST	www.qsrinternational.com/products_nvivo.aspx
WINMAX	www.scolari.co.uk/winmax/winmax.htm
ETHNOGRAPH	www.QualisResearch.com
Code-A-text	www.code-a-text.co.uk/index.htm
ATLAS.ti	www.atlasti.com/
CAQDAS	www.caqdas.soc.surrey.ac.uk/
The Ethnograph	www.qualisresearch.com/

Useful websites

Online QDA – online information about many different qualitative analysis approaches. Don't worry about the title in the address this is *all* methods (27 of them in all) with links to further reading. http://onlineqda.hud.ac.uk/methodologies.php#Interpretive_Phenomenological_Analysis

The content analysis Guidebook – is what the title suggests. A comprehensive guide to content analysis with many links. http://academic.csuohio.edu/kneuendorf/content

Further reading

(Full references appear in the references section. See also the texts listed at the end of Chapter 10.)

Braun and Clarke (2006): A definitive article describing thematic analysis and giving a step by step methodological guide.

Flick (2006): A friendly general guide, fairly practical in approach. Very useful for the prospective qualitative researcher, written at an accessible level.

Flick (2008): This is the new practical hands-on volume from Flick, a leading authority on qualitative research, and takes the student through all the design, data collection and analysis stages of a project.

Giles (2002): This is a book on advanced research methods in general but contains five chapters on qualitative methods, including one each on grounded theory and DA.

Grbich (1999): Although this text is geared to health research, much of the methodological content is easily applicable to psychological research, and there are plenty of examples.

Hahn (2008): A very useful text that shows how qualitative coding can be carried out using Microsoft Word, Excel and Access

Hayes (1997): This is an extremely useful text, with several how-to and hands-on chapters. It has contributions from mainstream qualitative writers and examples of the more central approaches which students would be able to tackle in fairly early projects.

Parker (2004): Excellent and practical article discussing guidelines for good qualitative studies and therefore offering substantial criteria for quality in qualitative research.

Patton (2002): Discusses in depth the analysis of qualitative data and methods of evaluation.

Potter and Wetherell (1987): Includes a step-by-step (but of course dated) guide to discourse analysis.

Richardson (ed.) (1996): A set of edited chapters covering the qualitative—quantitative debate, and the critique of mainstream, 'old paradigm' research methods, written by mainly UK-based authors.

Robson (2002): Covers well what its title suggests (Real World Research). Describes methods for field research and includes coverage of the more mainstream qualitative methods used in contemporary social and applied psychological research, along with conventional research designs. There may be a third edition quite soon.

Silverman (2004a): Although addressing sociological research, much useful advice and how-to methodology this volume can be applied to psychological research. In particular the arguments are useful, and Silverman is not afraid to deal with numbers when appropriate, nor to call for rigour and public agreement on research findings. A particularly good discussion of reliability and validity.

Silverman (2004b): Second in a cottage industry of recent qualitative methodology books this volume is edited by Silverman and contains articles from a wide range of experts in their particular research method specialism.

Silverman (2006): Another hands-on practical methods book, including how to write up reports but aimed primarily at undergraduates doing project work.

Smith (2008): This text is also hands-on, covering much the same ground as Willig (2008), but includes narrative analysis, CA, focus groups and cooperative enquiry. Perhaps more practical and less theoretical than Willig.

Smith, Harré and Van Langenhove (eds) (1995): A central UK critical text. Very comprehensive and very influential. Mainly theoretical.

Willig (2008): A comprehensive text taking you through the way to carry out qualitative research under several approaches (IPA, GT, DA – discursive and Foucaldian), memory work, plus a discussion of quality and many research examples.

You could also take a look at a journal dedicated to qualitative research in psychology: *Qualitative Research in Psychology*, London: Sage.

Glossary

Analytic induction	Method of moving from particular to general via instances; theory is modified in the light of features of new instances
Analytic procedure	The methodological procedure used to analyse data and its epistemological justification; usually located in methods section of qualitative reports
Axial coding	Procedure following open coding in some versions of grounded theory; promoted by Glaser (1998) but seen as distracting by many (see text)
Coding unit	Item categories identified in qualitative data using content analysis
Content analysis	Search of qualitative materials (especially text) to find 'coding units' (usually words, phrases or themes); analysis often concentrates on quantitative treatment of frequencies but can be a purely qualitative approach
Contextualist	Theory of knowledge (epistemological position), which sees knowledge and truth as relative; different versions are possible depending on the context in which knowledge claims are made
Epistemology	Theory of knowledge and of how knowledge is constructed
Idiographic	Approach that emphasises unique characteristics and experiences of the individual, not common traits
Inductive analysis	Work with qualitative data, which permits theory and hypotheses to evolve from the data rather than hypothetico-deductive testing of hypotheses set before data are obtained
Nomothetic	Approach that looks for common and usually measurable factors on which individuals all differ
Paralinguistics	Body movements and vocal sounds that accompany speech and modify its meaning

Radical constructionist	Theory of knowledge (epistemological position) that sees knowledge and truth as semantic construction
Research diary	Full record of all that occurs in a research investigation, kept by the researcher throughout
Respondent validation/ Member checking	Attempt to validate findings and interpretations by presenting these to original participants for comments and verification
Selective coding	Higher order treatment of initial themes and categories where superordinate themes may emerge which bind lower categories together
Triangulation	Comparison of at least two views/explanations of the same thing(s) – events, behaviour, actions, etc.

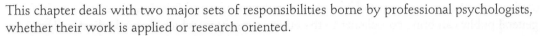

Ethical issues in psychological research 23

This chapter deals with two major sets of responsibilities borne by professional psychologists, whether their work is applied or research oriented.

- First, psychologists have responsibilities, as members of a research community, to publish only well-founded and genuine results with conventional support, open to analysis by colleagues. They also need to pay attention to the possible social effects of research results and assess these in the prevailing moral and political climate.

- Second, they need to follow strict ethical principles, such as those devised by the British Psychological Society and the American Psychological Association, when working with both research participants and clients in a professional capacity, including the recognition and promotion of equality of opportunity. Issues or procedures applying to research participants include:
  - confidentiality (of results and those who produced them)
  - anonymity
  - privacy
  - informed consent
  - deception (which can lower the public's trust in psychological research),
  - debriefing (informing participants and returning them to their pre-test state),
  - mental and physical stress and discomfort, recognition of participants' rights to withdraw
  - the special power of the investigator
  - problems with involuntary participation and intervention.

- Students, too, need to conduct their research according to these principles. There are various techniques that can be used to gain information which guarantee privacy and confidentiality, and several have been suggested for avoiding the need to deceive, but psychology has the peculiar characteristic that informing people of what is being tested has the effect of altering their likely 'natural' behaviour.

- The arguments for and against *animal research* are also outlined.

Introduction

Both the British Psychological Society (BPS) and the American Psychological Association (APA) have agreed guidelines on the ethical issues involved in psychological research. The BPS has developed its Code of Ethics and Conduct which became effective in 2006.[1] It is based on four major Ethical Principles – respect, competence, responsibility, integrity – and each of these is

[1] www.bps.org.uk/the-society/code-of-conduct/code-of-conduct_home.cfm

expanded in a Statement of Values (see Table 23.1) and then elaborated into a large and comprehensive set of 'shoulds' for practising psychologists, research or applied. To address the growing amount of research conducted over the Internet, in 2007 the BPS also introduced a set of Guidelines for Ethical Practice in Psychological Research Online.[2]

The APA's (2002) Ethical Principles of Psychologists and Code of Conduct[3] is an even more comprehensive document, which provides five General Principles for overall guidance towards 'the highest ideals of psychology'. These concern: beneficence and non-maleficence, fidelity and responsibility, integrity, justice and respect for people's rights and dignity. It also lists detailed Standards in specific areas of psychology which, unlike the General Principles, are 'enforceable'. The general public can bring complaints to the ethics committee, which then adjudicates. The psychologist concerned can be reprimanded, dismissed, or required to alter behaviour or attend relevant training. This breadth of principles and disciplinary power reflects the far wider application of psychology to the general public as consumers in the USA. Most of the major applied principles are similar to those that are relevant in the doctor–patient relationship.

The 2006 BPS Code of Ethics and Conduct brings together for the first time all the issues concerning treatment of research participants (including physical and mental protection of participants, informed consent, deception, debriefing, withdrawal from an investigation, confidentiality, anonymity) and those concerned with the treatment of clients in psychological practice (e.g. by a clinical or occupational psychologist) including the monitoring of colleagues' behaviour in the interests of the profession as a whole. Table 23.1 shows the statement of values for each of the major principles.

Respect	Psychologists value the dignity and worth of all persons, with sensitivity to the dynamics of perceived authority or influence over clients, and with particular regard to people's rights including those of privacy and self-determination.
Competence	Psychologists value the continuing development and maintenance of high standards of competence in their professional work, and the importance of preserving their ability to function optimally within the recognised limits of their knowledge, skill, training, education and experience.
Responsibility	Psychologists value their responsibilities to clients, to the general public, and to the profession and science of Psychology, including the avoidance of harm and the prevention of misuse or abuse of their contributions to society.
Integrity	Psychologists value honesty, accuracy, clarity and fairness in their interactions with all persons, and seek to promote integrity in all facets of their scientific and professional endeavours.

Table 23.1 The four Ethical Principles and associated Statements of Value from the British Psychological Society's Code of Ethics and Conduct, 2006

[2] www.bps.org.uk/downloadfile.cfm?file_uuid=2B3429B3-1143-DFD0-7E5A-4BE3FDD763CC&ext=pdf
[3] www.apa.org/ethics/code2002.html#intro

Both the British and US principles stress that psychological research should lead to better understanding of ourselves, and to the enhancement of the human condition and promotion of human welfare. Both stress the need for an atmosphere of free inquiry in order to generate the widest, most valid, body of knowledge. But both also stress that this free atmosphere requires a commitment to responsibility on the part of the psychologist in terms of competence, objectivity and the welfare of research participants.

Since 1987, the Royal Charter of the BPS has been amended, taking us some way towards the US model described above. The BPS now maintains a 'Register of Chartered Psychologists'. These are people who practise psychology either in an applied or a research capacity. Members of the register use the formal letters 'C. Psychol', can be struck off for unprofessional behaviour and, it is hoped, will become recognised as bona fide 'trademarked' practitioners whom the general public can recognise and trust. All centres (e.g. universities, hospitals) that conduct psychological research activity have in place an ethics committee to vet research proposals (of staff and some, usually postgraduate, students) for unacceptable procedures in any of the areas we are about to consider.

Publication and access to data

What gets published

Before taking a look at the rights and protection of individual participants and clients, we can consider how psychologists are expected to commit themselves to accessible and open information related to their research. In general, a psychologist cannot claim to have demonstrated an effect and then withhold raw data or information on procedures and samples used. Persons who do this are generally considered to be charlatans. Where psychologists are prepared, as most are, to be completely open with their data, they would still not allow the alleged results of their work to affect people's lives, by policy formulation for instance, before the research community has thoroughly verified, evaluated and replicated results where possible. They should not 'rush to publish' – see Box 23.1.

Info Box 23.1 **How to increase the incidence of measles**

A few years ago minimal (and now considered inadequate) research was published alleging a link between the MMR immunization and autism. Even though the theoretical connection was swiftly discredited (see e.g. Potter, 2005; Honda *et al.*, 2005) this resulted in a significant decrease in parents having their children immunized with the MMR vaccine. Consequently, recent years have seen an increase in cases of these diseases especially measles which, according to the UK's Health Protection Agency, rose by 31% from 2006 to 2007 (from 740 to 971 cases) and the increase continued into 2008[4]. Although this is not an example directly from psychological research it exemplifies the dangers of publishing tentative research on public issues which the media will report without the usual scientific reservations and to which an ill-informed public will respond.

---

[4] http://www.hpa.org.uk/webw/HPAweb&HPAwebStandard/HPAweb_C/1218093967161?p=1204186170287

There are occasions, in fact, when any scientist may feel that publication of results is potentially harmful, or even dangerous.

It was noted in Chapters 1 and 9 that there are several incidents of withholding crucial data associated with the heated debate around the extent to which 'intelligence' (often limited to the narrow construct of IQ) might be inherited. The political implications of this debate are profound. For example, do we nurture and provide compensatory support for 'slow' developers? Alternatively, do we simply accept that intellectual differences largely reflect unalterable genetic variations within society, and consequently make arrangements by, for instance, providing different 'tiers' of education?

The debate is closely linked to the hottest potato of them all: race differences in IQ, the controversy sparked by Jensen (1969) and renewed more recently by Herrnstein and Murray (1994). The debate is not just academic. Governments would like to know or, rather, would often like 'expert' support in their policies from psychologists. Sir Cyril Burt's data on the intelligence of identical twins, appeared to provide very strong evidence for the genetic role in human intellectual abilities. The early findings played a part in the political debate that produced the British '11-plus' examination and a two-tier (originally three-tier) secondary education system, wherein the successful 20% of children passing the exam received a grammar-school education. Only after Burt's death did Leon Kamin (1977) establish beyond doubt that Burt's data were inconsistent, to a degree way beyond acceptability, and probably fraudulent. Kamin demonstrated that Burt was persistently vague about the exact tests in use and had not made it at all easy to check his raw data. The cult of the 'great expert' had also inhibited investigation of Burt's work by 'lesser' researchers. Although Burt's overall work, to some degree, became rehabilitated in the psychological establishment during the 1990s, his contribution and data on IQ and inheritance will remain permanently unacceptable and controversial (e.g. see Joynson, 2003).

Burt's data have been far from the only problem in this area, however. It seems an unlikely coincidence that, in this same arena of debate, Kamin also experienced decades of resistance from Jensen in providing the data referred to in Chapter 1, and met with complete resistance from Bouchard *et al.*, who claimed (1990) remarkable similarities between identical twins 'reared apart, from birth', a theme that has advanced well beyond sober psychological research to participants in the research having agents, wide media coverage and the making of Hollywood films. Kamin questions the extent to which the 'separated' twins really saw and knew nothing of each other, yet Bouchard consistently refuses to provide detailed case histories.

Psychological researchers, and science in general, just cannot afford to work with this kind of resistance to public check. Unfortunately, the general public are not always so astute or concerned about integrity. The drama of the identical twins can swamp the academic subtleties. The lure of buying vitamins to improve their child's intelligence can blind parents to the doubts of psychologists who oppose this proposed link. Psychological researchers have an overriding responsibility to honour the scientific endeavour over the attractions of media exposure and fame.

Where to publish

Psychologists also need to exercise integrity over *where* they publish. Billig (1979) produced evidence of clear links between certain publications in which psychologists published articles during the height of the race IQ debate and extreme racist opinions and activity. *The Mankind Quarterly*, whose editorial board has included Cattell, Jensen and Lynn, the last as editor, was investigated in great detail and Billig's work is confirmed by Richards (1997). Tucker (1994) also confirms many extreme racist connections and makes clear that the journal was long supported, directly or indirectly, by the Pioneer Fund, a US white supremacist organisation, and has had a succession of far-right editors and close associations with members of neo-Nazi organisations (see Tucker, 1994). Contents have concentrated on articles stressing 'race' difference, sometimes breathtakingly global, crude and poor (see Lynn, 1991b). Hence UK psychologists would need to consider the conflict between their commitment to the British Psychological Society's multicultural and equal-opportunity principles, and support, by being published in it, of a journal with such contrary motives.

Findings on 'racial' difference (in intelligence or personality, for instance) almost always stir up controversy, which is hardly surprising. For this reason some psychologists have been led to argue that a moratorium should be held on publication. They argue that, since 'race' is always inextricably bound up with culture and socio-economic position, most responsible researchers would announce results with great qualification. However, they cannot then stop the lay racist or ignorant reader from using the unqualified information in discriminatory or abusive practices.

Psychologists have also argued that professional psychological researchers should exercise integrity over the sources of their funding, increasingly likely to come from industry or other organisations with an interest in the non-academic use of findings. The Pioneer Fund, for instance, either directly or through intermediate organisations, is alleged to have funded Jensen, Shockley, Rushton, Hans Eysenck and Lynn, all to at least six-figure sums (Connolly, 1994; Richards, 1997; Tucker, 1994).

The conduct of research with human participants

Any discussion of ethical principles in psychological research inevitably throws up Milgram's (1974) famous demonstrations of obedience fairly early on in the proceedings. Several ethical issues are involved in this study. Almost certainly, you will already have heard about the experiment but if not have a look at Box 23.2.

Info Box 23.2   Milgram – the classic experiment for ethical debate

Volunteers were introduced to another 'participant' who was actually an experimental confederate. The volunteer became a 'teacher' who was asked to administer electric shocks, increasing by 15 volts for each mistake made by the confederate; 375 volts was described as 'Danger: severe shock'. A tape recording of screams and refusals deceived the teacher-participant into believing the confederate was experiencing great pain and wished to end the session. The teacher-participant was pressured into continuing by 'prods' from the experimenter such as 'The experiment requires that you continue' and 'You have no choice but to go on.' To Milgram's surprise, 65% of participants delivered shocks to the end of the scale (450 volts) even though the confederate had ceased responding at 315 volts. Milgram had consulted 'experienced and disinterested colleagues' – psychiatrists predicted that no more than 0.1% would obey to the end. The teacher-participant often displayed extreme anxiety; one even suffered a mild seizure. Milgram (1974) wrote that an initially poised businessman was reduced within 20 minutes to a 'twitching, stuttering wreck' who was so agonised that he appeared to be approaching a nervous collapse. The results of this demonstration were used to argue that many ordinary people are capable of behaving in a manner, under pressure, that is retrospectively considered cruel. Atrocities are not necessarily carried out by purely evil persons or 'cultures'.

List the aspects of this investigation you consider to be unethical. Should the investigation have been carried out at all? Do the ends (scientific and surprising knowledge) justify the means?

Deception

Milgram's participants were grossly deceived. Not only did they believe they were shocking an innocent victim and that the victim suffered terribly, but also the whole purpose of the research was completely distorted as concerning the effects of punishment on learning.

DECEPTION, or at least the withholding of information, is exceedingly common in psychology experiments. Menges (1973) reviewed about 1000 American studies and found that 80% involved giving participants less than complete information. In only 3% of studies were participants given complete information about the independent variable, and information about the dependent variable was incomplete in 75% of cases. Ortmann and Hertwig (1997) argued that, given the ethical principles of the APA and an alleged dramatic increase in the use of deception, professional psychologists should support a complete ban on its use. Their position is challenged by Broeder (1998) and Kimmel (1998) in the interests of not completely stultifying psychological research, but some of this debate hangs on a precise definition of 'deception'. Ortmann and Hertwig (1998), for instance, did not include in the concept of deception those instances where the participant is simply not told the purpose of the experiment.

Some deception, then, seems fairly innocuous. Some participants are told a baby is male, others that it is female, and their descriptions of it are compared. Participants performing a sensori-motor task, where the true aim is to record the effect of an observer on performance, are told that the observer is present to note details of the skilled behaviour involved. Children are told not to play with a toy because it belongs to another child who is next door. Students are told their experimental rats are 'bright'. Even the use of placebos can be a deception, though participants are often informed that a placebo is possible.

Some deception is more serious. Participants have been told that test results demonstrate that they are poorly adjusted. Female participants are given feedback that they are considered attractive or unattractive by the man who will later interview them. Bramel (1962) gave male participants false feedback about their emotional reaction to photographs of men such that their responses seemed homosexually related. Participants in Latané and Darley's (1976) experiments thought they were overhearing an authentic epileptic seizure. The dependent variable was the speed or occurrence of reporting the seizure.

So what can the investigator do if deception is to be used? First, in keeping with the general principles of the Code of Ethics and Conduct, research psychologists should consult with disinterested colleagues as to the seriousness of the deception and any feasible alternatives. Second, *debriefing* should be very carefully attended to (see below). Third, in some cases it is possible to obtain permission to deceive. Volunteers can be asked to select what sort of research they would be prepared to participate in, from for instance:

- research on recognition of commercial products
- research on safety of products
- research in which you will be misled about the purpose until afterwards
- research involving questions on attitudes.

If potential participants tick the box for the third item then it can be concluded that they agree to deception though there would still be an ethical issue if the deception led to mental harm or possible humiliation.

Debriefing

In all research studies, the investigator has a responsibility to DEBRIEF each participant. The true purpose and aims of the study are revealed and every attempt is made to ensure that participants feel the same about themselves when they leave as they did when they arrived. In Johnston and Davey's (1997) experiment (described in Chapter 4), for example, the negative news tape was recognised by the researchers as possibly emotionally disturbing. For this reason they asked participants in that condition to listen to two minutes of a relaxation tape on a personal stereo before telling them all about the study and giving them their fee.

Where participants have been seriously deceived, this responsibility incurs a substantial effort in reassurance and explanation. The debriefing itself may have to involve a little more deception, as when children are told they 'did very well indeed' whatever the actual standard of their performance, and when any suspicion that a participant really is 'poorly adjusted' is not communicated to them. In Milgram's experiments, participants who went to the end of the scale were told that some people did this 'quite gleefully'. The idea was to help the obedient participants compare their own unwillingness to proceed, and their experienced anxiety, fairly favourably with the fictitious happily obedient participants. (Milgram never reported that any participant did proceed happily.) Even with this comparison, at least 26 out of 40 participants knew, when they left, that they were capable, under pressure, of inflicting extreme pain, if not death, on an innocent human being. It hardly seems possible that these people left the laboratory feeling the same about themselves as they did before they entered. The British Psychological Society has a paper on debriefing which can be found at:
www.bps.org.uk/document-download-area/document-download$.cfm?file_uuid=
1B299392-7E96-C67F-D4A092C173979F33&ext=pdf

Does debriefing work?

Milgram sent a questionnaire to his participants after the study and 84% said they were glad to have participated, whereas only 1% regretted being involved, the remainder reporting neutral feelings. A total of 80% believed more research like Milgram's should be carried out, while 75% found the experience meaningful and self-enlightening. Some writers discounted this broad range of appreciative and illuminating comments as an attempt by Milgram to justify an ethically unacceptable study.

Ring, Wallston and Corey (1970) decided to evaluate the consequences to the participant in a study which, even though the investigators were critical of Milgram, not only included the deceptions of the original study but also used a dishonest primary debriefing before a second, honest one. They showed that an initial, superficial debriefing dramatically reduces any negative participant evaluation of the research. However, they also found that one-third of participants reported residual anger and disappointment with themselves even after the second, complete, debriefing. The fact that even a few participants felt quite negative about themselves well after the experiment, and that many participants felt extremely upset during it, has led many researchers to the position that such extreme deception and stress are ethically unacceptable.

Besides the question of ethics, it is unwise of investigators to indulge in a great deal of deception. Students very often suspect that the manifest structure and explanation of a study in which they participate is false. Ring *et al.* found that 50% of their participants claimed they would be more wary and suspicious of psychology experiments in the future. As Reason and Rowan (1981) put it, 'Good research means never having to say you are sorry.'

If you won't deceive, what can you do?

Several investigators, finding gross deception of the Asch (see Chapter 4) or Milgram kind quite unacceptable, have turned to role-play or simulation. A description of successful findings by Mixon (1974), who used the heading above for his title, is given in Chapter 6.

Ring *et al.* (1970) were among the advocates of role-playing, whereas Aronson and Carlsmith (1968) argued that essential realism would be lost. Horowitz and Rothschild (1970) conducted a replication of Asch's (1956) design using a 'forewarned' group, who were told that the experiment was a fake but were asked to play the part of a naïve participant, and a 'pre-briefed' group who knew the experimental aim in detail. The forewarned group 'conformed' at a similar level to the traditionally deceived group, whereas the fully informed group did not conform at all. These latter participants seemed to behave in accordance with what most people believe would actually occur in the Asch set-up. This is, after all, why Asch's study is so renowned, gripping and well recalled by the psychology student. It defies common sense if we concentrate on the participants who went along with an obviously incorrect answer. However it is often forgotten that 68% of responses in the Asch studies were non-conforming. The prognosis for role-play, on Horowitz and Rothschild's evidence seems not so good. Informed students will not produce counter-intuitive effects. However, the capacity in normal students during role-play for aggressive authoritarianism and subservience was demonstrated convincingly and against prediction in Zimbardo's classic study (1972) described briefly below.

Stress and discomfort

There is no argument against the principle that psychological investigators should guarantee the safety of their participants, and that everything possible should be done to protect them from harm or discomfort. The difficulty comes in trying to decide what kind of stress or discomfort, physical or mental, is unacceptable. Humanists and others might argue that any traditional experimental research on 'subjects' is an affront to human dignity. At a lesser extreme, those who see value in the human experimental procedure have nevertheless criticised some investigators for going too far.

Mental stress

Examples of studies involving a possibly substantial degree of mental stress were given above. These involved deterioration of a person's self-image or the strain of feeling responsible for action in the Latané and Darley (1976) study. A further example, causing some dissent, is that in which a child was asked to guard the experimenter's pet hamster, which was then removed from its cage through a hole in the floor when the child wasn't looking.

Not all mental stress emanates from deception. Participants may be exposed to pornographic or violent film sequences. Extreme psychological discomfort, in the form of delusions and hallucinations, was experienced by participants undergoing 'sensory deprivation' (being deprived of sound, touch and sight) such that they often terminated the experience after three days (see Jolyon, 1962).

Zimbardo's (1972) simulation of authority and obedience had to be stopped after six days of the fourteen it was supposed to run. Students played the part of prison guards far too well, becoming aggressive, sadistic and brutal.[5] Their 'prisoners' (other students) became extremely passive and dependent. Within two days, and on the next few, participants had to be released, since they were exhibiting signs of severe emotional and psychological disorder (uncontrollable crying and screaming) and one even developed a nervous rash.

There is an obligation for investigators not only to debrief but also to attempt to remove even long-term negative effects of psychological research procedures. Forty of Milgram's participants were examined, one year after the experiment, by a psychiatrist who reported that no participant had been harmed psychologically by their experience. The BPS Code of Ethics and Conduct urges investigators to inform participants of procedures for contacting them should stress or other harm occur after participation.

Physical discomfort

Many psychological experiments have manipulated the variables of, for instance, electric shock, extreme noise level, food and sleep deprivation, anxiety- or nausea-producing drugs, and so on.

Watson and Rayner (1920), as is well known, caused 'Little Albert', a young infant, to exhibit anxiety towards a white rat he had previously fondled quite happily, by producing a loud, disturbing noise whenever he did so. Apparently Albert even became wary of other furry white objects. This procedure developed into that of 'aversive conditioning', which is intended to rid willing clients of unwanted or destructive behaviour.

The term 'willing' creates difficulties. In the sensitive cases that have occurred of gay men submitting themselves to aversive therapy, it has been argued that treatment is unethical, since the men are succumbing to a conventional norm structure that treats their sexual preference as undesirable or 'sick'. In general research work, a 'willing' participant may act under social pressure.

---

[5] Though, contrary to the principles of a true experiment where guards and prisoners would have started out equal, Zimbardo *briefed* his guards to make the prisoners' lives difficult. Even so only a few were truly brutal and one in particular seemed pathologically cruel, being responsible for many of the humiliating acts prisoners were asked to perform (Reicher and Haslam, 2007).

They may wish to sustain a 'real man' image, to bear as much as, or 'beat', their peers. They may feel they are ruining the experiment or letting down the experimenter. (The special power of the investigator is discussed below.) For these reasons, the investigator has a set of obligations to participants to ensure they do not suffer unduly or unnecessarily. These are outlined in the following section. In any research where discomfort might be expected the investigator is expected to seek opinion and advice from professional colleagues before going ahead.

The right to withdraw or not participate; the need for consent

In all research that involves individual participation the investigator is obliged to:

1 give the participant full information as to the likely level of discomfort, and to emphasise the voluntary nature of the exercise and the right to withdraw at any time

2 remind the participant of this right to withdraw at any point in the procedure where discomfort appears to be higher than anticipated

3 terminate the procedure where discomfort levels are substantially higher than anticipated and/or the participant is obviously disturbed to an unacceptable level.

Now we can see one of the most controversial aspects of Milgram's study. He was actually testing the power of the experimenter over the participant. His experimenter flagrantly contravened all three principles. The duty to respect the participant's right to withdraw and to remind the participant of this right are both now stressed by the APA and BPS. Contrary to this, in Milgram's study, and in a perhaps less humanistic era, each participant wishing to stop was commanded to continue in the interests of the research programme. Continuance was 'absolutely essential' and the participant had 'no choice but to go on'. The APA and BPS now also stress special vigilance when the investigator is in a position of power over the participant. This was, of course, the very position forcefully exploited and examined in the Milgram study.

It is usual to obtain the INFORMED CONSENT of research participants. As we shall see below, this isn't always possible before the research is conducted, though for laboratory experiments consent, not necessarily fully informed, can always be obtained. In research with children, the informed consent of parents or guardians must first be obtained. For obvious reasons, children cannot be subject to great stress, even in the unlikely instance that parents agree (though Little Albert's mother did). Two factors working against informed consent are the investigator's need to deceive on some occasions, and the significant power attaching to the investigator role.

The special power of the investigator

In general, then, the investigator is obliged to give the participant every chance not to participate, both before and during the experimental procedure. Working against this, as we have just said, is the position of influence, prestige and power of the investigator. Torbert says:

the unilaterally controlled research context is itself only one particular kind of social context and a politically authoritarian context at that. It should not be surprising that some of its most spectacularly well-conceived findings concern persons' responses to authoritarianism. (1981: 144)

An additional dimension to this power emerges when we consider the common position of US psychology undergraduates, who often face obligatory participation in a research project, though they may choose which one. Usually an exemption is offered but it costs one additional term paper, making the choice more apparent than real. Similar conditions now apply at several UK universities.

A further issue for ethical concern has been the practice of obtaining prison inmates or psychiatric patients for stressful experimental studies, where inducements, such as a pack of cigarettes or temporary release from daily routines, are minimal and would not normally 'buy' participation outside the institution. The Code of Ethics and Conduct places particular emphasis on the way in which consent is obtained from detained persons, and also on the special circumstances of children and adults with impairments in understanding or communication.

Confidentiality, anonymity and privacy

We turn to researchers' treatment of, and guarantees to, participants. Apart from any ethical considerations, there is a purely pragmatic argument for guaranteeing anonymity for participants at all times. If psychologists kept publishing identities along with results, the general public would soon cease to volunteer for, or agree to, research participation.

An investigator can promise ANONYMITY by guaranteeing that a participant's identity will never be revealed when data are published. This has to be carefully thought through where details of the person, even though they are not named, make it obvious who they are (e.g. in an applied project with a small company). Investigators can also request permission to identify individuals. Such identification may occur through the use of video recordings, as in Milgram's film *Obedience to Authority*. Research participants who have been seriously deceived (and in fact any others) have the right to witness destruction of any such records they do not wish to be kept. If records are kept, participants have the right to assume these will be safeguarded and used as anonymous data only by thoroughly briefed research staff.

We need to distinguish here between *anonymity* and CONFIDENTIALITY. If results (e.g. of interviews) are published then they are not confidential, but they can certainly remain anonymous. In fact, keeping data confidential would not be much use to the cause of research where data need to be accessible to other researchers. Confidentiality, then, is more a feature of psychological *practice* (keeping clients' data confidential) than it is of research and publication.

There are very special circumstances where an investigator might contravene the anonymity rule, and these are where there are clear dangers to human life. An investigator conducting participant observation into gang life would have a clear obligation to break confidence where a serious crime was about to be committed. A psychiatric patient's plan to kill himself or a room-mate would be reported. The ethical principles involved here are broader than those involved in conducting scientific research.

The participant obviously has the right to privacy, and procedures should not be planned that directly invade this without warning. Where a procedure is potentially intimate, embarrassing or sensitive, the participant should be clearly reminded of the right to withhold information or participation. Particular care would be required, for instance, where participants are being asked about sexual attitudes or behaviour.

The privacy principle is difficult to follow in the case of covert participant observation, and serious criticism has been levelled at users of this approach on these grounds (see the example of Humphreys (1970) below). In such cases it is also difficult to check out the final version of reports with participants in order to verify that an accurate account of their statements has been made.

Involuntary participation

In participant observation studies, and in naturalistic (covert) observation, the persons observed are quite often unaware of their participation. This seems fairly unobjectionable where completely unobtrusive observation is made and each person observed is just one in a frequency count; for instance, when drivers are observed in order to determine whether more males or more females stop at a 'stop' road sign. The information gathered was available to any ordinary member of the public anyway.

In participant observation, people's private lives may be invaded. Humphreys (1970) investigated the behaviour of consenting homosexuals by acting as a public washroom 'lookout'. Persons observed were completely unaware of the study and of the fact that their car registration numbers were recorded in order to obtain more background information through interviews later on.

Some field studies carried out in the public arena involve manipulations that interfere with people's lives. A street survey obviously delays each respondent, but here consent is always sought first. In Piliavin, Rodin and Piliavin's (1969) studies on bystander intervention, a person who appeared either lame or drunk 'collapsed' in a subway train. Predictably, the 'lame' person got more help than the drunk. In another version the actor bit a capsule, which produced a blood-like trickle on his chin. The 'blood' condition also had a lowering effect on helping. Piliavin *et al.*'s study, in fact, contravenes the principles of openness (no deception), stress avoidance and informed consent before participation.

Some field studies involve only a trivial effect on unwitting participants. Doob and Gross (1968) delayed drivers at a traffic light in either a very smart, new car or an older, lower-status one. Effects were predictable in that it took drivers longer to hoot at the smarter car! If these results are fairly unsurprising, couldn't willing participants simply be asked to imagine the situation and consider their likely response? Would simulation work here? Doob and Gross used a questionnaire as well, and found no difference between the times predicted by independent samples of students for hooting at either car. An odd finding occurred just among those who said they would not hoot at all at one of the cars. Of these, all six who would not hoot at the low-status car were male, and all five of those not hooting at the high-status car were female. The 'as if' findings were so different from actual behaviour that the defenders of field research seemed vindicated in their claim to more realistic data. However, by 1991, a computer simulation had been devised, and this produced results consistent with the original findings.

Intervention

Some aspects of brief INTERVENTION with naïve participants have been dealt with above. Several studies have involved intervention on a substantial scale but with willing participation. For instance, psychologists have worked with parents and children in the home in an effort to demonstrate the beneficial effects of parental stimulation on the child's learning and intellectual performance. In these studies a control group is necessary for baseline comparison. In hospital experiments with new drugs, trials are halted if success is apparent, on the grounds that it would be unethical to withhold the new drug as treatment from the placebo and control groups. Unfortunately, in psychological intervention research, even if success is apparent, there would not usually be the political power and resources to implement the 'treatment' across all disadvantaged families, for instance. Ethical issues arise, therefore, in selecting one group for special treatment.

Where intervention occurs for research purposes only, and involves the production of behaviour usually considered socially unacceptable, ethical principles need very careful consideration. Leyens, Camino, Parke and Berkowitz (1975), for instance, raised levels of aggression in boys shown a series of violent films. They were observed to be more aggressive in daily activities compared with a control group shown non-violent films. It is quite difficult to see how debriefing alone could leave the boys just where they were before the study began.

Monitoring the appropriate development of behaviour in a long term experimental study can be achieved by regularly reviewing the responses of participants to the intervention being used. Wood and Plester (2008) conducted an experiment involving groups of 9–10 year old schoolchildren who were given a mobile phone each on which to send text messages. The main aim was to demonstrate a positive effect of texting on reading and spelling ability since earlier research (e.g. Plester, Wood and Joshi, in press) had shown that those using a higher level of text message abbreviations in their messages also had higher literacy abilities. This is of course contrary to the common sense assumption of parents and teachers that text language is bound to create poor spellers. In conducting this experiment the researchers had to ensure that there was no deleterious effect on the children's literacy so the participants were tested each week using appropriate measures. In addition, the children were told that their texts would be monitored for inappropriate use such as insults or threats which could be viewed as bullying. In this way useful and relevant research could progress without incurring any harm or disadvantage to the participants.

Research with animals

There is nothing more certain of producing a lively debate among psychology students than the discussion of whether or not it is necessary or useful to experiment on defenceless animals. Many students are far more emotionally outraged about animal research than about some of the more questionable human studies, on the grounds that humans can refuse, whereas animals have no such chance.

One cannot deceive animals, though one can fool them. Nor can they give their informed consent, be debriefed or ask for a procedure to be terminated. Animals *can*, however, be subject to exploitation, extreme levels of physical pain and mental stress, though only the most callously inhumane experimenter could ignore severe suffering.

Many students, to their cost, spend the whole of an essay on psychological research ethics discussing the plight of research animals, though Milgram will often be a secondary focus of attention. I don't intend to go through the innumerable examples of animals in pitiful situations in the psychological research laboratory. To list the kinds of situation is enough:

- severe sensory deprivation
- severe to complete social deprivation
- extirpation or lesion of sections of the nervous system or body parts
- use of extremely aversive physical stimuli including electric shock, noise, poisonous or otherwise aversive chemicals, mood- or behaviour-altering chemicals
- starvation.

Why have psychologists found it useful or necessary to employ these methods?

The case for animal research

1 Animals can be used where humans can't. For instance, they can be deprived of their mothers or reared in complete darkness. This point, of course, completely begs the question of whether such procedures are ethically acceptable.

2 Great control can be exerted over variables. Animals can be made to feed, for instance, at precise intervals.

3 Several generations can be bred where species have short gestation and maturation periods. This is useful in studying genetic processes and it also means that the complete cycle of development can be observed.

4 An effect shown or insight gained in animal studies, although not directly applicable to humans, may lead to fresh and fertile theories about human behaviour. Animal studies have contributed ideas to the debate on human adult–infant bonding and maternal separation, for example.

5 Comparisons across the phylogenetic scale are valuable for showing what humans don't have or can't do (what we have probably evolved away from or out of). Comparison is invaluable in helping us develop a framework for brain analysis based on evolutionary history. A seemingly useless or mystical piece of the nervous system may serve, or may have served, a function disclosed only through the discovery of its current function in another species.

6 At a very elementary, physiological level, animals and humans have things in common. The nature of the synapse, neural connections and transmission, for instance, are similar among higher primates.

7 Skinner (e.g. 1953) argued that elementary units of learning would also be similar across most higher species. Hence, he mostly used rat and pigeon subjects in his research work, arguing that patterns of stimulus–response contingencies, schedules of reinforcement, and so on, were generalisable to the world of human behaviour.

The case against animal research

Theorists have argued that too much extrapolation from animal to human has occurred. Here are some reasons why such extrapolation is considered inappropriate.

1 Seligman (1972) argued for the concept of *preparedness*. The concept is that, through evolutionary processes, some animals are born specially prepared to learn specific behaviour patterns of survival value to the species. Likewise, some patterns are difficult or impossible to learn at all – the animal is contra-prepared. This makes comparison between one species and another hazardous, let alone comparison between human and animal.

2 Kohler (1925) demonstrated in apes what he referred to as *insight learning* – solving a novel problem with a sudden reorganisation of detail, much like we do when we spontaneously solve one of those annoying matchstick problems. If apes can do what humans certainly can, then the validity of the traditional behaviourist rat model, transferred to human learning, when the rat doesn't show anything like the same level of insight, seems questionable.

3 Ethologists have shown that quite a lot of behaviour, subject to cultural variation and slow developmental learning in humans, is instinctive in animals, demonstrated as 'fixed action patterns'. Mating preludes and territorial defence are quite rigidly organised in a large number of species, yet markedly diverse across the breadth of human cultures.

4 Ethologists, among others, have also questioned the validity of having animals do abnormal things in the laboratory and have concentrated on behaviour in the natural environment, only confronting animals in the laboratory with variations of the stimuli that would normally be encountered outside it.

5 Language, carefully defined in terms of syntax and symbol, appears to be unique to humans. Language is the vehicle for transmission of cultural values, meanings and the individual's social construction of reality. Much psychological research, consciously or not, assumes these values and meanings as integral to human awareness. The comparison with most animals seems at its weakest here, apart from the rudimentary skills that can be developed, with substantial training, in apes. Note that the vast majority of humans require no formal training at all in order to speak and understand one or more languages.

The points above are all aimed at the rejection of animal research on practical grounds. It is argued that such research will not tell us what we want to know. Other arguments take a moral or humanitarian line.

6 Some argue that it is just categorically wrong to inflict pain and suffering on any living creature.

7 A more profound argument is that the experimenter's 'attack' on nature typifies the 'controlling' model of humankind associated with the psychologist as hard, objective, neutral and distant scientist. This image of the scientist is currently rejected, not just by humanists and many other psychologists, but by many scientists across the disciplines who wish to project a model of environmental care.

Supporters of the points above would argue that kittens need not be deprived of visual experience in order to study the nature–nurture issue in perception. Field studies on children who unfortunately happen to have been so deprived would be considered more realistic and more ethical. Likewise, monkeys do not need to be deprived of their mothers; plenty of children have been. The great debate in attachment theory has been over the number and quality of bonds necessary for optimum child development, and here monkey studies can hardly help us.

Whatever the rationale for animal studies, or the fierce, impassioned objections, it seems likely they will continue as an adjunct to psychological research, though perhaps not at their earlier intensity. British research is carried out under guidelines issued by the BPS (2007[6]) to which the reader is referred in the Code of Ethics and Practice. In these, the following points are made.

- Knowledge to be gained must justify procedure; trivial research is not encouraged, alternative methods are.
- The smallest possible number of animals should be used.
- No members of endangered species should ever be used.
- Caging, food deprivation, procedures causing discomfort or pain should all be assessed relative to the particular species studied. A procedure relatively mild to one can be damaging to another.
- Naturalistic studies are preferred to laboratory ones, but animals should be disturbed as little as possible in the wild.
- Experimenters must be familiar with the technical aspects of anaesthesia, pharmacological compounds and so on; regular post-operative medical checks must be made.

The guidelines also direct the psychologist to the relevant laws under which animal research is conducted and to the need for various licences.

Conclusion

All in all, it looks difficult to conduct much research at all without running into ethical arguments. Certainly it seems impossible to proceed with anything before considering many possible ethical objections, but this is as it should be. Other sciences, too, have their associations and committees for considering social responsibility in scientific research. They argue about the use to which findings might be put or the organisations from which it would not be prudent to accept sponsorship. They consider the likely impact of their work on society as a whole. Similarly, psychology has to make these considerations. However, since humans, as individuals in society, are also the focal point of research, it is hardly surprising that psychology, as a research society, has to be particularly vigilant in spotting malpractice, abuse, thoughtlessness, charlatanism and lack of professionalism. If psychologists prefer not to have people take one step backwards at parties and say things like 'I bet you're testing me' or 'Is this part of an experiment?', they need to reassure the public constantly that some excesses of the past cannot now happen, and that deception really is only used when necessary.

The humanists and qualitative researchers appear to have gained the moral high ground on these ethical issues, not just because they put dignity, honesty and humanity first, but because they see their participative or non-directive methods as the only route to genuine, un-coerced information. According to Reason and Rowan (1981: xviii), Maslow has said, 'If you prod at people like things, they won't let you know them'.

[6] Available at: www.bps.org.uk/downloadfile.cfm?file_uuid=DA9509C9-1143-DFD0-7EE7-9D998D01F023&ext=pdf

Well, what do *you* think? You'll probably discuss quite heatedly, with co-students or colleagues, the rights and wrongs of conducting some experiments. I can't help feeling that the information from Milgram's work is extremely valuable. It certainly undermined stereotypes I had, a long time ago, about whole cultures tending to be more obedient or capable of harming others. But I also can't help thinking immediately about those participants who went all the way. Can we be so sure we'd be in the 35% who stopped? Not even all these stopped as soon as the victim was clearly in trouble. How would we feel for the rest of our lives? Should we inflict such a loss of dignity on others? I haven't made any final decision about this issue, as about many other psychological debates and philosophical dilemmas. Fortunately, I'm not in a position where I have to vote on it. But what do you think?

Exercises

What major ethical issues are involved in the following fictitious proposed research projects?

1 Researchers arrange for an actor to fall down in the street, appearing ill. They are interested in whether passers by will stop less often in this condition than in one where the actor has red liquid oozing from his mouth.

2 For her third-year project a student decides to conduct a longitudinal case study in which she covertly records the behaviour and speech of a class colleague whom she believes to be in the developmental stages of anorexia.

3 A student believes that greater use of the Internet is associated with greater depression. She asks students to complete a questionnaire on Internet use and also Beck's Depression Inventory.

4 Participants in an experiment are asked to complete a task that involves the solving of logical puzzles. Half the group are then informed that they have done well, whereas the other half are informed that they have done rather poorly. Participants are then assessed on the extent to which they make internal or external attributions for their performance in the task.

Answers

1 Involuntary participation; lack of informed consent; deception; psychological stress.

2 Lack of informed consent; involuntary participation; lack of professional expertise in the area; general lack of respect.

3 Problem of what to do if a participant scores very highly on depression. Student is not qualified to counsel or offer any kind of professional support, hence a serious debriefing problem.

4 Deception; mental stress; careful debriefing needed for the 'poor' group.

Glossary

Anonymity	Keeping participant's or client's identity away from publication or any possible inadvertent disclosure
Confidentiality	Keeping data from participants or clients away from publication
Debriefing	Informing participants about the full nature and rationale of the study they've experienced, and attempting to reverse any negative influence
Deception	Leading participants to believe that something other than the true independent variable is involved, or withholding information such that the reality of the investigative situation is masked or distorted
Informed consent	Agreement to participate in research in the full knowledge of the research context and participant rights
Intervention	Research that makes some alteration to people's lives beyond the specific research setting, in some cases because there is an intention to ameliorate specific human conditions
Invasion of privacy	Research that intrudes into people's personal lives
Involuntary participation	Taking part in research without agreement or knowledge of the study

Planning your practical and writing up your report

24

Planning your practical project

If you are devising and running your own practical work in psychology, good luck! It is highly satisfying to complete a project that was your own initial idea and that you have followed through to the presentation stage; it usually feels a whole lot more fulfilling than simply writing up a practical set by your tutor. However, *beware!* Your tutors almost certainly have a lot of experience in planning such work; you really should run all the details past them so that you do not waste your efforts and end up with useless data or find yourself running a project with hopeless snags or a completely inappropriate design.

Below I have jotted down most of the things I can think of that need attention before you start your data gathering, and to be considered while you run your study. I've almost certainly missed some things, but I hope that what I have provided here will be of some help. Nothing I've written, however, can substitute for very careful planning, preferably in a small group, before you start your data collection.

Remember that the 'practical' doesn't start when you actually begin running your trials or questioning your participants. That is a tiny part of the whole process. There is a large portion of time to spend planning and another large portion to spend analysing and (dare I say it) writing up your report!

I have written these notes with the traditional, 'tight' hypothesis test in mind. Hence there is emphasis on strict definition of variables and thinking about the system of analysis before starting. The first of these two points obviously runs counter to the tenets of qualitative research. However, most students will find that, through syllabus requirements or other forces, they will need to be familiar with this traditional design. Besides, since the 'old paradigm' is hardly likely to disappear overnight, I believe it is necessary to understand the approach fully in order to understand its weaknesses and to be able to take off in other directions. If you *are* running a qualitative project then read though these notes ignoring the more quantitative aspects, then look at the advice on qualitative report writing on pp. 572–4 and the associated further reading. Since there is generally less information available on planning good qualitative research it really is important to check thoroughly before starting out and therefore to avoid ending up with a report that is fascinating but is seen as more like the work of a 'displaced novelist' and mainly anecdotal.

The overall aim

Did the idea just pop up in your head? You will need to investigate theory that backs up your proposals. This might give you firmer ideas. Most research follows from prior findings or speculative theory based on detailed arguments. You will probably be required to 'embed' the research aims in some aspects of background theory. There is nothing wrong in principle, however, in testing a personal idea that came to you unaided – creativity is encouraging. However, it is likely that there *is* some related work on it, though perhaps hard to find. *Never* claim that no one has done work in the area you are investigating. Researching the literature has been made infinitely easier over the last decade with the development of electronic databases and the Internet. One of the best current electronic sources is *Psychinfo*. If you do not have access to this ask your tutors what there is and/or try to get access through a local university (even if you don't attend it yourself), where you may also be permitted to consult its stock of journals and textbooks. You can also write to or e-mail people in institutions where there is someone who has already researched in your area. Several journals are also now partially available on the Internet, though most require a subscription. The *Journal of Cross-Cultural Psychology* is fully available. If you visit the BPS at www.bpsjournals.co.uk/ you will find that you can select any of the dozen or so journals that they publish and view the abstract for any article. This is also true of the APA at www.apa.org/journals/. Other journals do likewise (e.g. Psychology Press at www.psypress.com/journals/), and if you just put 'psychology journals' into Google you'll be on your way to consulting academic articles on psychology that are at the epicentre of current research and thinking. Do remember that articles are published in journals and that usually you tell your tutor you read an article *not* a journal.

When considering your overall aims it is also time to state your hypotheses very carefully. Don't wait until you come to write up the report! If you think carefully about what you want to demonstrate, what effects would support your arguments, then the design, analysis and report of your study should all follow fairly logically from that. Many of my students start their very first session on planning their practical stating 'I want to use a questionnaire' to which my response is always 'Why?' and they look bemused. The point is that you can't *know* you need to use a questionnaire until you have considered what it is exactly that you want to find out, what your overall design will be and what measures you will need to use and/or develop. Your tutor might not be too amused either if, having been asked to think out the details of a project, you say something like: 'I think I'd like to do something on depression' and offer no further ideas.

Things you *should* do:

- Choose a hypothesis that is possible or feasible to test. Try to avoid difficult data collection hurdles. If you need left-handers or dyslexics, think carefully whether you will be able to find enough for a reasonably sized sample. Think *very* carefully about how your dependent variable will be measured. Independent variables are always easy to identify, but suppose you wish to test differences in 'caring attitude', 'empathy' or 'self-esteem'. How will you measure these variables?

- Check out what *can* be measured. Tutors will know of psychological scales that are available. Many (e.g. the General Health Questionnaire or Rotter's Locus of Control Scale) are accessible from textbooks and the Internet but don't use an Internet scale that doesn't tell you its scoring system. As an alternative, you may have to develop your own scale. We will talk about measures and materials later, but for now just note that you might want to alter the slant of your aims/hypotheses somewhat depending on what measures are available.

- Don't just pick up a bunch of questionnaires or scales and simply measure everyone on all of them. First, you will end up with a bewildering array of results and may not be able to handle the statistical analyses that are possible. Second, you might be inventing your hypotheses *after* gathering data, which is completely illogical. Third, you will end up FISHING. Remember that getting around one 'significant' correlation out of 20 significance tests is just what we'd expect if the null hypothesis is true for all of them. If you conduct 100 tests – the sort of thing that happens when students carry out a chi-square on every item of a questionnaire for males and females, for instance – then at least five of the 'significant' results you obtain are likely to be Type I errors, but which ones? If you do 'fish' you can only verify your results by conducting follow-up studies on the 'significant' findings. It is bad science to invent, post hoc, a 'reason' why unpredicted differences occurred, though you can speculate and then test further. Better, though, to test only the relationships that are predicted by the aims of and rationale for your study.

The design

Your design is your overall approach to structuring your study in order to answer your research question. If, for instance, you have argued that anxiety should be negatively related to self-esteem then this pretty well demands a correlational approach, and you need to find measures for the two variables, anxiety and self-esteem. You may have chosen an experimental approach, in which case do make sure it really is an experiment. For instance, showing that young children tend to say the amount of orange juice has changed in the standard Piaget routine is not an experiment; there is no independent variable – this is a *demonstration*. You can introduce an independent variable if you compare older with younger children but this is not an *experimental* variable – this will be a study of group differences (see p. 110).

Don't get carried away with independent variables

Are you dealing with too many variables for your acquired level of statistical competence? Say you wanted to see whether introverts improve on a task without rather than with an audience, whereas extroverts deteriorate. You'd like to see whether this is more true for males than for females, and perhaps whether age has an effect too. Admirable thinking on interacting variables, but the statistical analysis will be very complex; you have four independent variables and hence you'll need a four-way ANOVA. Will you be able to cope with all the effects, especially the interactions? Can you find enough participants per group?

Repeated measures

Can you use repeated measures? If so, then all the better because you remove participant variables and require fewer participants for testing overall. However, as was pointed out on p. 73, sometimes participants *must* be naïve for their condition of the experiment. If you are using vignettes and changing the values of just one variable (e.g. whether an accident had small or large consequences;

whether the driver was drunk or not) it makes no sense to use repeated measures since seeing both or all of the vignettes gives the game away completely to your participants.

Camouflaging the independent variable

On the subject of vignettes, sometimes we want to be certain that a participant has read certain crucial information that forms the levels of the independent variable. For instance, you might want to investigate whether knowing an author's gender has an effect on the evaluation of an article they have written. In this case the independent variable is manipulated simply by putting the author's name (e.g. John Coleman or Jane Coleman) at the top of the article (or at the bottom if you don't want participants to know the gender until they have read the article). Can you be sure they have the author's sex in mind as they read or that they have even noticed it? The answer is to introduce some pre-reading questions that *include* the question 'What is the gender of the author?', but that *also* include several other similar questions: 'Where did he/she live?', 'What is the word count of the article?', 'What age was the author?', etc. This way you are sure they have noted the gender of the author, but it is still unlikely that they would realise this is the sole independent variable of the experiment.

Think about your variables

Although we will discuss measures under 'materials' it is wise to think here about the level of measurement (see p. 250) of your variables. If you need to *correlate*, then it is no good selecting categorical variables (one of the commonest mistakes in student preparation for projects). It is quite pointless trying to 'correlate' marital status (single, married, divorced, etc.) with, say, happiness. Single and married are not numerical values representing levels of marital state. We can code single as '1' and married as '2', but married is not twice single! This makes no sense. We *can* correlate gender with another variable using special statistical procedures (see Chapter 17) but it's pretty pointless since what we're really doing is looking for a *difference* between two groups, male and female. Make sure, then, that if you require a variable to be at least ordinal level you use an appropriate *scale*. Instead of recording whether a driver stopped or not, perhaps you can record their speed (time to traverse two points on the road). Typically you move from asking people whether they are, for instance, pro- or anti- fox hunting, to the development of a small psychological attitude measure using a Likert scale on several pro- and anti- items. You then add up participants' overall scores. Another less elegant approach is to ask people to score on a scale where 1 = 'strongly opposed' and 10 = 'strongly support'.

Observation studies

If you want to conduct an observation study, be very careful that it does not end up as what coursework moderators like to call a 'day at the zoo study' or 'my cute baby cousin'. You must develop adequate observation schedules or coding systems and/or plan exactly what it is your observation will focus on. Almost certainly, you will need to run a pilot observation to see how hard it is to gather useful information that you can write up into a report. The closer your report comes to what a journalist or animal lover might write, the further you are away from an adequate psychological practical report.

Interviews

If you intend to use an interview but you want quantified data you need to think about how you will code the qualitative content, unless you intend only to administer a fixed-choice questionnaire (i.e. with closed questions). If you want interview content rated, think about acquiring someone to do the rating *independently* to avoid your own personal bias; you would need to create a strict coding system and train your colleague in its use.

Interviews also take a lot of time and you may need recording equipment. Consider whether this is feasible in the time available. If so, make absolutely sure you are able to use the equipment properly and without unnerving your interviewee!

Obtaining and dealing with participants

Will you be able to get enough people for your chosen design? Will you be able to match pairs appropriately? You may not be able to obtain the information you need for this (e.g. educational level). If you are going to use repeated measures, with tests on two different occasions, will everyone be available second time around? If you'd like to test children at a school then you'll need parental permission for each individual child. It really helps to know the school; better still if you were a pupil there yourself.

If you want to carry out a study of group difference(s), e.g. a sex-difference study, you need to ensure that the two groups are very carefully matched on all the possibly relevant variables you can manage (see the section on group difference studies on p. 110).

Is the interaction between researcher and participant important? Does the gender of either matter or is the interaction likely to be a problem? Some students I knew were going to say 'Hello' to passers-by under two conditions: with and without a smile. It struck them that all of them were female and that there could be a differential response from male and female passers-by!

Will conditions be equivalent? If the experimental group has longer, more intricate instructions and a more detailed introduction to their task, could this act as a confounding variable? Should the control group get equivalent but 'dummy' introduction and instructions, and/or equivalent time with the experimenters?

The sample(s)

Will you have to use the same old 'friends and acquaintances' or students in the bar? If so, will they be too well aware of your previous deceptions? Will they reveal the nature of the research to naïve participants you still wish to test? Even though the sample can't be truly random or representative, can you balance groups for sex, age, etc.? Should you ask whether they've participated in this before? You can't ask beforehand, in many cases (such as when you're showing an illusion). You'll have to ask afterwards and exclude them from the results if they weren't 'naïve'.

If you suspect some participants of 'mucking around' or of already knowing the aim and perhaps trying to 'look good', you'll have to decide, having asked them afterwards, whether it is legitimate to drop their results. You can discuss this with tutors or colleagues.

Make sure samples are of an adequate size for the job; consider power calculations for your intended statistical test and start with the information on p. 393. If they just can't be large enough, then think of another hypothesis. Some students once presented, quite seriously, the results of a project that they claimed supported their hypothesis that Northerners (in the UK) were less racist than Southerners, having used one or two questions about tolerance for racist jokes. Trouble was, they had tested just eight Northerners and five Southerners!

You can't gather a 'random sample from the population' (see p. 42) but you *can* randomly allocate your participants to conditions. A simple way to do this if, say, you have four different vignettes (possibly in a 2 x 2 experimental design) is simply to shuffle your instruction cards so that you cannot tell which condition the next participant will be in until you give them their card (see also p. 44).

The materials

In 'Think about your variables', above, we stressed that the measures you produce have a direct effect on the sort of statistical or other analysis you can perform on the data you gather. If you look back to p. 187 you'll see there that the phrasing and structure of a crucial question could have led to disaster in a student's dissertation. A slight change and she could gather data with which sensible comparisons could be made so it's a good idea to pilot your materials so that this kind of weakness is exposed *before* you gather a lot of data.

Are materials equivalent for both conditions? A group of students showed people in one group a set of terms: *intelligent, shy, confident, warm, practical, quick, quiet.* People in the other group were shown the same terms except that 'cold' was substituted for 'warm'. The participants had to judge other characteristics of the hypothetical person. In Asch's original version (1946) the warm–cold difference affected many other characteristics. One student had missed a class and had no 'cold' forms, so she changed the word 'warm' in ink and photocopied. This gave a not-too-subtle clue to her second group as to what the important word in the set was! Make sure, then, that there are no possibly confounding differences between materials apart from the difference of the independent variable.

Can two memory word lists be equivalent? Can you say that the words in each are equally frequent in normal language use, or that two sets of anagrams are equally hard to solve? You can use pre-testing of the materials to show there is no real difference or you can get hold of word frequency lists. A useful Internet source for these was provided on p. 72.

Are instructions to participants intelligible? If you're unsure of the wording in a questionnaire, do enlist the help of someone who's good with language. Respondents will not respect or take seriously a badly written questionnaire with several spelling mistakes.

If you want to construct a scale or questionnaire (see Chapter 8), remember that a test of an attitude is often made not with questions but with *statements* for people to agree/disagree with or say how far these represent their view. Don't say 'Do you believe in abortion/nuclear power/strikes?' These things exist! We want to know what people think about them. An attitude scale consists of several items, the answers to which *collectively* produce a score on, for example, attitude towards physical punishment. It doesn't make sense, then, to analyse *each item* in an attitude scale of this kind.

Several already existing measures are probably available to you one way or another. I mentioned earlier that your department may well hold copies of psychological measures, textbooks sometimes have scales, research articles often do too, and you can even write to the authors of some scales to ask for permission to use them. Remember that psychological measures are often subject to copyright restrictions and you can't just photocopy dozens of tests. You may, though, if you find the test in an article or textbook. The Internet is also a useful source, but beware of tests just put together by charlatans or amateurs, and in all cases remember that you need the *scoring system*. A good place to start for advice on how to locate tests, published or not, is the following Internet site, which is managed by the American Psychological Association: www.apa.org/science/findingtests.pdf (accessed 19 September 2008)

If all else fails, you may need to devise a scale yourself as part of your project, and at least test it for internal reliability using, for instance, Cronbach's alpha or some simple form of item analysis (see Chapter 8).

If you are focusing on a specific group of people, such as a minority ethnic group or people with a disability, then please check carefully, consulting with members of the group concerned or other experts, about your choice of language. It is easy not just to cause offence, but to show ignorance by using unacceptable, derogatory or patronising terms. This applies wherever a specific group is the focus, whether members of that group will themselves be questioned or not. In all cases, pilot! Try out materials on friends and relatives first.

The procedure

There may well be several of you going out to gather data. Make sure you standardise your procedure precisely before you start. The most common problem I have seen among a group of students doing a practical together is that they didn't have a final check that they had all got exactly the same steps of procedure. Don't be shy to ask your group-members to do a final check before they rush off after a lot of hurried changes. Don't feel stupid if you don't feel confident about exactly what you have to do. Ask your group members, or the tutor where appropriate. It's better to take a little more time, and admit you're not perfect, than to end up with results that can't be used or with having to do things over again. Also it is extremely important to remember your group-members when data are being collected. If you don't turn up, the entire project may be put on hold, making everybody late or worse with their report of the work. Because students do sometimes fail to show up with their contribution to the data it makes sense *not* to have each student collect data in one condition only. If you do this you may end up with no participants in condition 4 of a 2 x 2 design and the entire analysis is not possible. Better that all of you collect data in all conditions, then an absent colleague loses only a percentage of results for each condition.

Decide what extra data are worth recording (sex, age). These might show up a relationship that wasn't part of the original hypotheses, but that can be discussed with a view to new future research. However, don't overdo it (see p. 162 and p. 605).

Record all the information on the spot. If you decide to wait until later to record age or occupation of your interviewee, you may well forget. Then the result may be wasted. Remember to note which group a participant was in or what gender they were. If you forget, your efforts are wasted!

Be prepared to put participants at their ease and give an encouraging introduction. Work out the exact instructions to participants. Have a simulated run-through with a colleague. What have you failed to explain? What else might people need/want to know?

If your study involves a task requiring skill then it is sensible to give participants several practice trials so that they get past the early stage of making many errors. The practice should get them to a plateau of average performance before any experimental trials begin.

Decide how you will answer any questions your participants might ask. Will you have stock answers or will you ask them to wait until after the testing?

If the study is an observation, ask yourself the following questions.

- Will the observations really be unobtrusive? Check out the recording position beforehand.
- Will recording be easy? Does talking into a tape recorder attract too much attention, for instance? Does the coding system work? Is there time and ample space to make written notes?
- Will more than one person make records simultaneously in the interests of reliability?

Ethics

As a student, it is unlikely that you have been trained sufficiently to be able to conduct satisfactory debriefing sessions. Professional research psychologists themselves often argue about the adequacy of debriefing in returning people to their starting point and 'undoing' any psychological harm that may have been done. It is also unlikely that you'll have the time or resources to debrief properly. Therefore, it is extremely important that your proposed research project will not involve any of the following:

- invasion of privacy
- causing participants to lose dignity
- causing participants to think less of themselves
- deception that causes resentment or hostility (check that any deception used is absolutely necessary and is benign)
- unnecessary withholding of information
- pain or discomfort
- breaking of local prohibitions (for instance, drinking alcohol)
- anything at all about which participants feel uncomfortable.

I have come across examples, when moderating coursework assignments, that are quite unacceptable. For instance, students investigated bystander intervention in a shopping mall by falling and including the use of imitation blood. One student conducted an 'observation' by making covert notes on a class colleague, whom she described as 'disturbed and anti-social', over a period of six weeks. The notes included information on the girl's 'disruptive' class activities, including pseudo-psychiatric descriptions, and an account of the girl's apparent anorexic tendencies. Students have used questionnaires that are far too personally intrusive about, for example, sex behaviour, domestic violence, bullying. Aspects of these topics may be acceptable but students are usually much too inexperienced to be able to deal effectively with psychological and other issues that might be raised.

Public examination boards have acted sharply in recent years to ensure ethically acceptable research project behaviour and universities now have a strict vetting system for student projects. You should in any case ask your tutor to check for any ethical pitfalls you may have overlooked.

Assure participants that anonymity will be maintained, and maintain it! It is discourteous and bad practice even to talk with close colleagues in the project, or very best friends, in a derogatory manner about participants, even if anonymous. It develops an elitist, manipulative approach to people who have tried to help you in your work.

Also assure participants that they will not feel or look stupid, or reveal anything they don't wish to reveal about themselves – and make sure this, too, is true! Assure them that they can have destroyed any record of behaviour, in particular any they feel very uncomfortable about. Remind them they can stop the procedure at any time if they wish to and do remind them about this as testing progresses.

On approaching unknown members of the public, tell them who you are, where you're from and the reason for your research (it's part of your required coursework, for instance). Make sure your tutor and institution are happy about any approach to the public, since they will receive the complaints. Remember that you are, in a small way, an ambassador for your institution and for psychology, and members of the general public often already hold quite distorted views of what psychologists are about.

Writing your practical report

If you carry out some practical work, you will find yourself faced with the onerous task of writing it all up. My first piece of advice is *don't put it off*! You'll find it much harder to come back to when any initial enthusiasm you had for the project will have worn off, and you won't be able to understand why certain precautions were taken or just what certain conditions were all about. You'll find essential details of data and analysis are missing and you may need the help of your class colleagues who've now lost their raw data or are too busy to help you.

If it's any consolation, as you slog away through the small hours finishing your work, consider the general skills you are acquiring that will help you throughout your working life. Not many occupations require you to write the equivalent of essays but in many professional careers report writing is a requirement and this is something you can highlight on your CV in future job applications. Many past students have emphasised this aspect of their course, though disliked at the time, as being one of the most helpful skills they acquired in their undergraduate days. Reports are all about clear communication to others.

What is the purpose of a report?

There are two main purposes, neither of which is to do with keeping your tutor happy. First, you are telling your reader just what you did, why you did it and what you think it adds to the stockpile of knowledge and theory development. Second, you are recording your procedures in enough detail for some of those readers, who are so inclined, to replicate your work. We have seen elsewhere why this is so important to scientific method. Golden rule number one for report writing, then, is as follows.

Make sure you write with enough depth and clarity for a complete stranger of average intelligence to repeat exactly what you did in every detail.

A useful criterion for tutors who mark reports is to consider how many extra questions a naïve reader would have to ask you in order to get on with a fair replication of what you did. Think of this as you write and you really can't go far wrong. For instance, early on, when you talk about '*the* questionnaire' or '*the* vignette story', stop briefly and ask yourself, 'From the reader's point of view, would I know what that is? Have I introduced this yet?' Speaking as a marker, one of the most frustrating things is knowing that the student is not talking to a reader but is just getting things down on paper because they have to!

What are the rules?

There are no rules but there are generally accepted conventions. Most of these make sense and work in the interests of good report organisation and communication between researchers. Your tutors should in fact have issued you with a set of marking criteria so you know what is expected in your report. Yell if they don't! Have a look at journal articles in your library, on the Internet, given to you by tutors or in some edited texts. Your tutor may well have copies of old student work, though very often only the poorer work gets left (why this systematic bias?). I have included two fictitious reports of the same practical exercise, one with commentary, at the end of this chapter. These are at quite a basic level. There is a whole published qualitative article at the end of this chapter.

Psychology reports are generally presented in APA style which is detailed in the 2001 *Publication Manual of the American Psychological Association* fifth edition (Washington, DC: American Psychological Association) and which was still available in 2008 at around $28 from the APA at http://www.apa.org/. This site contains quite a few free tips and directions to other resources that will help you with writing reports. The BPS also publishes a style guide which is available free from their web site. These two guides, however, do not tell you in friendly terms how to write a report. They are concerned with the correct use of references, citations, capitals, spellings and the presentation of statistics, tables, figures, numbers, and so on.

General points

In keeping with the traditional scientific stance of separating the person from the subject matter, quantitative reports tend to be written entirely in the third person passive. Hence it is usual, instead of 'we tested thirteen participants', to write 'thirteen participants were tested...'. Qualitative reports, which tend to emphasise the personal involvement of the researcher in the research procedure, are more likely to use the first person when it is appropriate. Your report should use page numbers throughout and should be double spaced so your markers can insert useful comments.

Some useful texts on report writing for the student are listed below; for early reports in psychology the Forshaw or Harris texts are more appropriate.

- Bell, J. (2005) *Doing your Research Project: A Guide for First-Time Researchers in Education, Health and Social Science* (4th edn). Buckingham: Open University Press.
- Forshaw, M. (2004) *Your Undergraduate Psychology Project: A BPS Guide*. Chichester: Wiley Blackwell.
- Harris, P. (2008) *Designing and Reporting Experiments in Psychology* (3rd edn). Buckingham: Open University Press.
- Smyth, T.R. (2004) *The Principles of Writing in Psychology*. Basingstoke: Palgrave-Macmillan.

Plagiarism

Perhaps I was partly wrong when I said above that there are no rules. PLAGIARISM is copying directly from another's work or paraphrasing it so closely that it is recognisably similar. This includes taking other people's data. When formally published plagiarism is illegal and people can be sued for it. On academic courses, if coursework counts towards final marks, then plagiarism is exactly the same as cheating in an exam. On many courses the ruling is stiff: one substantial piece of copying fails the entire work and perhaps that whole element of coursework.

The main point is that coursework marked as individual must be entirely your *own* work. Don't attempt the 'I copied notes from an article, then didn't realise when I copied from the notes' gambit. Plagiarism is plagiarism, *intentional or not*. Copying directly from texts is, in any case, quite pointless. Educationally we learn very little from copying, as you'll know from your studies of memory and learning processes. The ethical point is that copying and reproducing is stealing. Just don't *ever* copy from texts. Copying from Internet authors is just plain daft: they don't know exactly what question was set nor the specific guidelines that the tutor outlined for this particular assignment. Besides, Google makes it so easy to locate the original source. Many universities now scan all submitted work using programmes like Turnitin which will spot anything taken from the Internet and also any copying from another student's work on the same assignment.

Of course you can't invent your ideas. Learning *is* about appreciating what has gone before then, hopefully, adding to it. However, the whole point of an assignment is to show that *you* can handle the required concepts yourself *in your own words*. The best procedure is to read, make your own notes, close any books, ask yourself questions to see how far you've understood, then attempt to write out the ideas as you now see them. If you use a direct quotation you must make this clear and you *must* give the source *and page number* of the quotation. This is just as important in the introduction and discussion sections of practical reports as in any essay. As with essays, you should not rely too much on quotations and certainly you should not use them in order to avoid defining some complex or tricky point in your own words. Your tutors want to know that *you* understand the point.

The sections of a standard report

Table 24.1 shows the standard headings of research reports. These must not be considered to be set in stone. You could pick up any journal article and find it varies from this pattern. For instance, some journals always have a 'Treatment of results' section following the presentation of descriptive statistics. Others go straight to the inferential analysis – the presentation of significant findings – and integrate the descriptives into this. Others have a different order in the method section. It all depends on the particular journal and its historical origins in, for instance, 'hard science' (e.g. cognitive neuropsychology) or elsewhere (e.g. social psychology, health psychology). However, if you are writing up a conventional quantitative report for your assignment, use Table 24.1 in lieu of any specific instructions you are provided with.

	Conventional quantitative	Qualitative
	Shaded areas common to both types of report	
	Title	Title
	Abstract	Abstract
	Introduction	Introduction
	General background to topic area	
	Relevant research	
	Argument	
	Overall aims	
	Specific hypotheses to be tested	Specific aims
	Research predictions	Justification of analytic procedure to be used
Method	Design	
	Participants	Participants
	Materials/apparatus	Development of interview questions etc.
	Procedure	Procedure
		Analytic method (and reflexive discussion)
Results	Descriptive statistics Inferential analysis*	Analysis of transcript, supporting quotations, justification of analytic themes, discussion etc., all in one section
Discussion	Discuss results; place in context of research in introduction; critique the study; conclude	General discussion section e.g. presentation of model, justification of emergent theory
References		
Appendices		

* Some results sections deliver the significance of central effects first, and integrate essential descriptives into this delivery.

Table 24.1 The standard sections of research reports

The title

This should be as concise as possible. You don't need 'An investigation to see whether ...' or similar. You just need the main variables. Very often, in an experiment, you can use the independent variable and dependent variable. For instance, 'The effect of an imagery method on recall of verbal material' will adequately describe a (probably familiar) study. For a field investigation using correlation, 'The relationship between age and attitude to environmental issues' says enough. Avoid questions and comic titles like 'Do boys exaggerate their IQ?' or 'Watching the detectives'. If you really can't resist such a pre-title then make sure you add a fully informative second half after a colon, such as 'Gender differences in self-estimation of IQ' or 'Content analysis of stereotype assumptions in television police-based drama series'. The golden rule here, as so often in report writing, is: *make sure your reader can grasp the exact content from what you write*. With all sections about which you are unsure, you can always ask a non-psychology student friend or your grandmother to read the section and see if they understand without any extra explanation from you. If the extra explanation *is* needed then, unless this concerns psychology jargon, you probably need to write some more detail.

Abstract

Your abstract should stand out from the rest of the report by being in a different font and/or indented. It is a skeleton of the main features of the work, 'abstracted' from it, in around 200 words at most. You do not need any detail of methods, just the theory on which your research is based, main design, central findings (usually verbal and not numerical), and any major emergent critical points or conclusions. Because you have already written the report it is very tempting here to refer to items in the report as if your reader is already familiar with them. Remember, this is the *first* thing your marker reads so do not refer to 'the questionnaire' 'the practice session' unless you have introduced them in your abstract. Have a look at the 'good report' example below (pp. 635–41). Abstracts may also be called the 'Summary' and it is very hard indeed to learn to write them.

Why on earth do we have a summary at the beginning? Well, suppose you were interested in whether anyone had done work on your proposed topic: anxiety and jogging behaviour in red-bearded vegetarian East Londoners. As you flip through dozens of journals looking for related work, how much easier it is to see the summary of findings right at the beginning of the article, without having to wade through to the end. Electronic databases give you the abstract of contemporary articles but not necessarily of older ones.

Introduction

I like to think of this as shaped like a funnel:

> Start with the general psychological topic area. Discuss theory
> and research work that is relevant to the research topic,
> especially your rationale. Move from the research
> findings to an argument for conducting
> *your* research study. Generally
> introduce it and, using
> earlier findings, relate
> your study to the
> hypothesis (or
> hypotheses)
> under test
> by making
> specific
> RESEARCH PREDICTION(S).

The discussion of relevant research work is often referred to as a LITERATURE REVIEW. Your research prediction(s) must follow from an argument that depends on the results of prior research or existing theory reported in that review. This is also true of the aims in most qualitative research. You *must* support each empirical claim you make with a published reference. You cannot, for instance, claim that 'most people are fairly obedient' without citing research evidence or academic argument to this effect. Your sources are likely to be research articles, textbooks, electronic databases and the Internet. Be sure to make a note of every reference you use since you must include them in a list at the end of your work. It is sometimes painful to try to track them down a long time after you have read them (as all book authors will agree!).

As an example of the funnelling argument required, let's run through the introduction to our experiment to test the hypothesis that an audience inhibits performance, described briefly in Chapter 3. The introduction to a study testing this hypothesis should *not* contain a five-page essay on social influence. The hypothesis test belongs within a specialised area of social influence research, the issue of whether social facilitation occurs from an audience when the task performed is complex. We can move our reader through the introduction in the following steps.

- Evidence that an audience tends to facilitate performance on a simple task.
- Locate history of the study of audience effects in early studies on competition.
- Allport's (1924) finding that participants not competing but working in the presence of each other perform better.
- General social facilitation effects.

- Zajonc and Sales' (1966) more complex theory that an audience improves well-learned responses but impairs the learning of new skills.

- Zajonc's explanation that an audience increases arousal which, enhances performance, but introduces more errors on a complex task because there is added arousal from the task itself.

- Hence, according to this theory and past research, and since the wiggly wire task is highly complex (and probably even more arousing), an audience has a detrimental effect on people performing a complex task, including the wiggly wire one.

We have argued through to our hypothesis. Note that the 'average' report, which starts on p. 627, is rather rambling in its introduction, whereas the better one (from p. 635) is more tightly arranged around relevant literature. It only remains now to state our specific research prediction(s) in the clearest terms so there can be no doubt about what is the expected outcome.

The hypothesis

Although conventional quantitative studies do test hypotheses, what is usually given at the end of a report's introduction is a *research prediction*. What we are testing in the audience experiment, for instance, is the general hypothesis that an audience worsens performance on a complex task. However, in order to be specific as to how that hypothesis is to be tested we set up a design, then predict, or at least outline, what should happen if the hypothesis is to be supported. On some courses you may be asked to write out specifically what the 'hypothesis' is, but most research articles include research predictions in the final paragraph of the introduction as part of the normal prose progression of the article. There should not be a separate heading for 'The hypothesis'. For instance, in our audience effect practical our last paragraph might run:

Zajonc and Sales (1966) argued that a more complex task worsens performance because the task itself involves arousal. Whereas moderate levels of arousal improve performance, high levels are likely to provoke more errors and therefore worsen performance. Since the task in this experiment is particularly difficult and clearly heightens arousal and frustration, it was expected that participants in the audience condition would produce more errors and take longer to complete the task than those in the alone condition.

Notice that *two* predictions are being made here, one about time and the other about errors, both of which can be quantitatively tested. One could demand that the word 'significantly' be inserted here before 'more' and 'longer', but it is taken for granted that the difference will be tested and that the usual rules of significance testing will be followed before claiming evidence for an effect. There is a tradition, which you may encounter, of attempting to write out the 'null hypothesis' at this point. This is an odd requirement. Almost all 'null hypotheses' written here in student work are not null hypotheses at all but the research prediction as described above with the word 'not' inserted somewhere. The null hypothesis, should you be required to write it, is not a prediction of what *will* happen but a *claim about underlying populations*, often that population means are equal or that the population correlation is zero. Re-read Chapter 14 if necessary in order to reinforce this concept. If you *are* asked to write out the null hypothesis you might just grin and bear it or you could show your tutors this book and the arguments in Chapter 14.

What is *essential* here is that your prediction is made absolutely clear *in operationalised terms*. Remember, your inferential results analysis must relate back directly to the exact predictions made here. It will be uninformative to say 'people will remember better after caffeine'. You must state how 'remembering better' is *defined*, e.g. increased number of words correctly recalled from a list. Neither should the hypothesis or prediction contain the underlying rationale. For instance, we do not say 'There will be a correlation between self-esteem and academic achievement because people feel better when they are successful'; this is more a description of the aim of the study. We simply hypothesise or predict a correlation between self-esteem scores and a precise measure of academic achievement (say, number of GCSE and A level passes). Sometimes it would be awkward, in your hypothesis, to spell out exactly what will be the operational definition of a construct to be measured. In such cases, psychologists refer to the term specifically but leave detailed operationalisation until the 'design' or 'materials' section of their description of the method.

As an example, Fisk and Pidgeon (1997: 5) said: 'Relative to a control group receiving no training, participants trained in the extension rule [will] commit fewer conjunction errors.' They make quite clear what their dependent variable is, but the detailed description of their measure of a 'conjunction error' will appear in the 'Method' section of their report.

Table 24.2 contains loosely and tightly worded research predictions appropriate to some of the exercises at the end of Chapter 21. The exercise numbers are given to the left. You might like to try writing out column two while only looking at column one.

Loosely worded prediction	Research prediction
4. People will be worse on a sensori-motor task in front of an audience.	Participants will make more errors on the sensori-motor task in the audience condition than when working alone.
7. High-initiative participants will prefer more dynamic activities.	Frequencies for the high-initiative group would be expected to increase from reading through dancing to rock climbing, whereas frequencies for the low-initiative group would be expected to decrease.
8. Non-rhyming words are harder to read.	The mean time to read rhyming words is expected to be lower than the mean for non-rhyming words.
9. Participants will be less racist on the second test because the training is intended to reduce prejudice.	The mean score on the second test will be lower than the mean score on the first test.

Table 24.2 Making tight predictions

The method

It is customary and convenient, but not absolutely necessary, to break the method used down into the following four sub-headings. Materials (or 'apparatus') and procedure may often be one heading. As stated earlier, different research journals have very different traditions for their methods sections.

Design

This describes the 'skeleton' outline of the study – its basic framework. For instance, is it an experiment or not? If it is, what design is used (repeated measures, etc.)? How many groups are used? What is the purpose of each group (control, placebo etc.)? In many cases, describing the groups will be a way of describing the independent variable. In any case and where appropriate, the independent variable, its levels and the dependent variable should be specified exactly here. In more complex ANOVA designs you would identify each factor and its levels. In multiple regression you would identify the predictors and the criterion variable.

In addition, it might be relevant to identify any further controls, such as counterbalancing, though this can otherwise be dealt with in the procedure section. In our experiment on audience effects we could say:

An independent samples design was used. One group of participants performed a wire and loop sensori-motor task in front of an audience while a second group performed the task whilst alone in a soundproof room. Participants were allocated to conditions at random. Two dependent variables were measured: time taken to complete and number of errors made.

… and that's enough. You don't need to give any details of procedure or materials used, otherwise you'll find yourself laboriously repeating yourself later on.

If the study is non-experimental, its overall approach (e.g. observational) can be stated along with design structures such as longitudinal, cross-sectional etc. There may be independent and dependent variables that are uncontrolled, such as number of pedestrians waiting at a crossing and whether a driver stops or not. Controls, such as measures of inter-observer reliability, may have been incorporated. Don't mention details here, just that the control was employed.

Participants

Give numbers, including how many in each group, and other details relevant to the study. If someone wishes to replicate your findings about 'adolescents' and their self-concepts, it is important for them to know exactly what age and sex your participants were. These variables are less important in technical laboratory tasks, though general age range is usually useful and handedness may be relevant. Other variables, such as social class or occupation, might be highly relevant for some research topics. Certainly important is how naïve participants were to psychology. Otherwise, keep details to a minimum. How were participants obtained? How were they allocated to the various experimental groups (if not covered in your 'design')? *Never* be tempted to say that you drew a 'random sample'. If, however, it was haphazardly drawn, say so. The description 'opportunity sample' is useless; it gives no information about selection *at all* other than that participants were conveniently available. Give *some* information about how participants were obtained, even if it was just by grabbing who was around at the time plus your parents and boyfriend. It is usually also useful to say where participants came from (e.g. 'third-year undergraduate students at Utopia University').

Materials/apparatus

At various workshops for teachers I have observed Cara Flanagan liken the process of writing the materials and procedure sections to writing the recipe for a cake: the materials are the ingredients and the procedure is how you put them together. A golden rule here is: *give enough detail for a full replication to be possible.* This means giving specifications of constructed equipment (finger-maze, illusion box) and source (manufacturer, make, model) of commercial items (stopwatches, computer software, heart rate monitor). Exact details of all written materials should be given here or in an appendix if substantial, including: word lists, questionnaires, lists people had to choose from, vignettes, pictures and so on. You don't need to give details of blank paper or pencils!

Do not simply write out a list of materials: the materials section should be just like any other, written in normal English prose. It may also be useful to include a diagram or photo of an experimental set-up or seating arrangements, but don't go overboard; only do this *if necessary*. There are no Brownie points available for artistic merit!

In our audience study we would describe the wiggly wire apparatus giving overall size, length of wire, nature of the loop and handle, battery type, error counter, timing mechanism or stopwatch type and so on. A diagram might be useful in this case.

A reference must be provided for any published psychological measures that you have used (e.g. "Rotter, 1966" if using his original Locus of Control scale); the full reference should appear in your references section. If questionnaires are 'home-grown', then there should be a description of how the measure was developed and any information, if possible, on its reliability or validity, such as Cronbach's alpha for your scale. A sample questionnaire can be included in an appendix, unless it is a very well-known instrument.

Procedure

The rule here is simple. Describe exactly what happened *from start to finish* of the testing; think of the cake-making recipe. It is a good idea to go through the procedure from a participant's perspective in chronological order. The account must be enough for good replication. Any standardised instructions should be included here or in an appendix, including any standard answers to predicted questions from participants. The exact wording used in training participants to use imagery in our memory experiment should be included, together with instructions for the reading condition and any practice trials included.

It might be tempting to skim the rather dry and descriptive methods section. However, marks are available here for what is an essential piece of communication, so don't rush this bit. Have a good look afterwards to make sure that a psychologically naïve friend of yours could do exactly what you did. If they can't, you haven't finished yet!

Results

Description

It is very important to realise that one's description of results at this point carries on the prose style of the previous sections of the report. You tell your reader, *in words*, what you found. Tables and charts are *supplementary* aids to communication. You cannot simply present a table of data as 'The results'. Raw data go in an appendix, if anywhere. A *summary* table of these (only) is presented, including frequencies or means and standard deviations or their equivalents. You should not include every measure of central tendency and dispersion you can think of. Marks are awarded for *appropriate* selection of statistical summaries, not for a shotgun approach. The mean *or* the median *or* the mode but not *all* will be appropriate, depending on how you have gathered and treated/arranged your data. If you present means then the appropriate measure of dispersion to accompany them is the standard deviation. With medians it might be the interquartile range.

Any tables (appearing here or in the appendix) should be well headed and labelled. For instance, a summary of our experimental results as in Table 24.3 is inadequate. What do the numbers measure? We need a fully informative heading like 'Mean time (seconds) taken to complete the wire task" or "Mean number of errors". The units of measurement (such as seconds) should always be stated. Note that your reader should understand what the table or figure is telling them without reference to the text. Hence it is not appropriate to label one of your columns 'Group 1', for instance.

	Audience	Alone
Mean	12.4	8.3
SD	1.5	1.1

Table 24.3 Inadequate results table (no heading or information about measures)

Tables and charts should occur in the text of the report where they are relevant, not in an appendix. Tables are numbered separately from Figures, i.e. you can have Table 24.1 *and* Figure 24.1. The number goes with the title. Note that charts are 'figures'; *tables* of data (like the inadequate Table 24.3) are not 'figures'.

Charts with more than one group or variable need a fully informative legend. Again don't go overboard; don't litter your work with charts looking at the data from various angles. Only one chart is usually useful in a simple experiment, one that demonstrates the main effect found. Why should the reader be interested in a chart showing a column for each individual's score (see p. 288)? Why would they want to see a pie chart, bar chart and line chart of the same data? Why would they want to see the distribution of all scores unless this is referred to in parametric screening? Ask yourself 'What does my reader *need*?', not 'How can I make the report look as stunning or pretty as possible?' Markers will not give extra marks for superfluous charts. Most simple reports do not include a chart and may not even need a table so long as the results are clear in the main text. Charts drawn by computer will need editing so that they don't, for instance, have an axis labelled 'Variable 0001' when using SPSS. You will need to edit to include full title and appropriate labels. Tables produced in SPSS are also not to be trusted. They will, for instance, give values to five decimal places! I would say *never* copy and paste a table directly from SPSS unless you are going to seriously edit it.

Analysis or 'treatment' of results

It is best to tell your reader when you've finished describing your data and are about to analyse them, e.g. by using an inferential statistical test. If there are several hypotheses to test, or different treatments, take one at a time in separate paragraphs. State which statistical test is being applied to which data. You don't need to justify your choice of statistical test unless your tutors ask you to in which case use the sorts of decision procedure outlined in Chapter 21. This might include giving details of why a non-parametric test is used in preference to a parametric one – for instance, normality violations or heterogeneity of variance. *Never* say 'the results were tested …'. State exactly *which* results. The simplest table of data can be tested in several ways. Say, for instance, 'The difference between the mean completion times of the audience and alone conditions was tested with an independent sample *t* test.'

State the result of the test clearly and compare this with the appropriate critical value, if not using a statistical analysis program. Justify the choice of this critical value, including N or degrees of freedom, number of tails, and the corresponding level of probability under H_0 (e.g. '$p \leq .05$'). If you are using SPSS *never* state that the difference is significant with '$p = .000$'. It is true that SPSS gives such values but this is only because it does not calculate to more than three places of decimals. Such a result should be reported as $p < .01$, or possibly $p < .001$. Box 24.1 is a quick exercise in noting what can be missing from statements of significance. Remember that it is now usual to report the *exact* value of p if known. Note that, for each test presented in this book, there is an accompanying demonstration of the accepted way of reporting such a result.

Info Box 24.1	Incomplete significance statements
Significance statements	**What's missing**
'The *t* test showed that differences were significant.'	*Which* difference? Significant at what level? How many degrees of freedom? One- or two-tailed test? Only *one* difference at a time can be tested with a *t* test.
'There was a strong correlation between the two variables.'	*Which two*? Positive or negative? What value? Was it significant? If so, at what level? One- or two-tailed?
'There was a significant difference between the two conditions at the 1% level.'	*Which* conditions? One- or two-tailed? Why not $p \leq .01$?

If required, state whether the null hypothesis is being rejected or retained. If there are a number of test results, these could be presented in a clear summary table. Calculations of your tests, if you wish to include them, should appear *only* in an appendix. Many calculations these days will be performed by computer or dedicated calculator. The software used is usually not relevant so long as you have a result.

Actual journal articles never show calculations or include raw data, and rarely justify the statistical test chosen. However, this information is always available through private correspondence.

Students are often asked to substitute for the real-life situation by including these as appendices, and by explaining why they have chosen their particular significance test.

In more complex ANOVA designs it is acceptable to report significant effects and to integrate with this the reporting of the means and standard deviations, rather than presenting descriptive statistics *before* the analysis; see, for instance, p. 486. With complex ANOVA designs you *must* report means for each significant effect reported. Say you test people on memory with loud/soft/no noise and concrete/abstract words, expecting only an interaction, with the loud noise disrupting abstract word learning. You might obtain an unexpected *overall* main effect for noise. If you report this then you *must* also report the *overall* means for the levels in the noise condition, along with the cell means that you must report if the interaction is significant.

Discussion

Do not be tempted to give brief attention to your findings here then revert to another essay on your topic. In general, very little, if any, new research or background theory should be introduced into your discussion. You should rely on what you have written in your introduction. Here you discuss your findings in the light of the argument in the introduction. On occasion, because of what has shown up in your study, or as an overall comment, you might include a new reference, but these should be absolutely minimal.

Summarising the findings

The first step here is to explain in non-statistical language just what has happened in the results section and how this relates to what you predicted. These results must then be related to the hypotheses you set out to test, and to the original aims of the research. These in turn are then related to the background theory, showing support or a need to modify theory in the light of contradictory or ambiguous findings. Unexpected findings or 'quirks' in the results, such as extreme 'rogue' scores or unexpected effects, can also be discussed as a secondary issue. From time to time, such 'oddities' lead in novel research directions. You can try to offer some explanations of these if you have good reasons.

Evaluating the method

The conscientious researcher always evaluates the design and method, picking out flaws and areas of weakness. This isn't just to nitpick. A reader of the report might well come back and accuse the researcher of not considering such weaknesses. The researcher can forestall such criticism by presenting a good argument as to why the potential weakness should not have serious effect. The emphasis of the evaluation depends partly on the outcome, as shown below.

- If we got the result we expected, we should look carefully at the design for possible confounding variables or causes of Type I error. If we were expecting to find no difference (e.g. to reject an earlier finding of difference), we should look for ways in which the design and procedures may have hidden differences or relationships.

- If we failed to get a predicted difference, we should look for sources of random variables or negative confounding (though research with a successful outcome may also have been affected by these). What aspects of the design, procedures and materials used did we find unsatisfactory? We should also look for any *confounding* variable that might have acted in a direction that obscures our predicted effect.

You should never present a discussion that is a litany of faults in your design and that is longer than the section you spend on findings and implications for theory. If such a report were presented for publication the editor would wonder why on earth you submitted it in the first place. Not everything in an experiment or investigation can be perfect. There is no need to talk about not controlling temperature or background noise unless there is good reason to suppose that variation in these could have seriously affected results. Usually this is quite unlikely – remember Hovey (1928) in Chapter 4.

Suggest modifications and extensions

Most research leads on to more research. From the considerations made so far you should be able to suggest modifications to this design: first, in order to check the critical points made and, second, to follow up speculations and suggestions for new directions with the research topic.

If you find yourself stuck for something to say, do avoid the knee-jerk reaction of 'We should have tested more participants'. This is often said under a misapprehension of the purpose and nature of experiments and sampling. Chapter 2 explains why, to some extent, larger samples aren't always better. If you tested 30 participants in two conditions of a tightly controlled experiment then you shouldn't require more, especially if you did get a significant effect. If you do say you needed more participants then you should explain exactly *why* you think so, possibly relating this to arguments about statistical power. The same goes for the suggestion that a sex difference for the effect should now be investigated or that 'people from different cultures' should now be tested. This latter statement begs the question of *which* culture the author is assuming he/she, the participants *and* the reader are all from; the most important point in this context, though, is the question '*Why?*' Why would any such difference be expected? Unless you can think of a good *reason* to extend the study in this way it is better not to appear to be padding out your discussion because you can't think of anything else!

Conclusion

Your discussion should end up with a final comment, though a heading for this last paragraph is not usually required. Avoid repeating the summary, abstract or findings at this point. What you can do is to make some summarising comment in terms of their implications for existing models or theories, and for the future. Try not to over-blow your findings by claiming for instance that 'A new effect has been found' or 'This result should be useful to all clinical psychologists …'.

References

Completing the end list of references can be a fiddly job, especially if you've referred to a lot of different research in your work. Referencing is usually something of a shock to first year undergraduates but it is also the section that will infuriate tired marking tutors if omitted or done poorly. There is often a lot of confusion over what exactly counts as a publication reference.

Exactly what should be included? The golden rule is:

If you referred to it somewhere in your text, include it. If you didn't refer to it, don't include it!

If you read Gross (2007) in order to familiarise yourself with the topic area, but you did not refer to Gross directly in your text, then Gross is *not* a 'reference' – you didn't refer to it! Such items belong, if anywhere, in a 'bibliography' but these are not required in psychology essays and reports. Box 24.2 gives specific advice on referencing.

Info Box 24.2	How to reference

Primary source

If you cite in your text "Burr, 1995" then you're saying you have actually read this book and your entry in the final reference list should be:

> Burr, V. (1995) *An introduction to social constructionism.* London: Routledge.

Note that we have name(s), initials, date, *title*, place of publication, publisher.

Note where there is an italic font and that *town* of publication (*not* country) comes before the publisher.

An article reference ('Hancock and Rhodes, 2008' in the text) might be:

> Hancock, K.J. and Rhodes, G. (2008) Contact, configural coding and the other-race effect in face recognition. *British Journal of Psychology, 99,* 1, 45–56.

The order here is: name(s), initials, date, title, *journal, volume,* part, pages
If you are quoting exact words, then you *must* give the page number(s) in your in-text citation, e.g. "Burr (1995: 12) states that...."

Secondary source

If you read about Burr's work in Smith (2008) you would write in your text: "Burr (1995, in Smith, 2008)" and Smith is a SECONDARY REFERENCE for your primary source. This is important because Smith might not faithfully represent Burr's views and you cannot claim to have read Burr directly. Your end reference would now be just the reference for Smith (2008) but note that for the Harvard system (see below) you include both together.

Electronic sources

Mostly these will be internet sources and these are tricky. Consult the various guides and your university or college's advice on this but the main features to include are:

> Name (if given if not the corporate site), date*, title, page number (if used) and then you write: 'Available at [web address], [give the date you last looked at the source].

*The date is not always obvious. You can estimate it writing "Hyperstat c. 2005" or you can state that the date was unavailable by writing, e.g. "Science buddies, n.d."

Here is an example:

> The Research Methods Knowledge Base (2006) *Variables.* [Online] available at: www.socialresearchmethods.net/kb/variable.php>, [accessed 23 September 2008].

Websites and other electronic sources differ so much that to some extent you will often need to use your own judgement about what to include but the most important aspects are the web address and the date of access.

Use of 'et al.'

This really is simple. You *cannot* use 'et al.' (the full term means 'and others') unless you have *first* introduced all the names, e.g. "Morgan, Pear and Blanchard, 2005", *but* if there are more than five authors you may use 'et al.' at the first citation.

APA vs Harvard style

The style just described (I have only given the central points) is that advocated by the American Psychological Association which is a version of the Harvard system. Some institutions might ask student to use the standard Harvard style instead. There are three main differences from APA style:

- Where you are paraphrasing or summarising an author's argument, even though you are not quoting, give the page number(s) – as in "Burr (1995:12) has argued that ……"
- The part number appears in brackets in the end list: ….*Cognition,* 43 (2), 32–38.
- The reference for the *primary* source is given with the secondary as in:

Burr, V. (1995) *An introduction to social constructionism.* London: Routledge. Cited in Smith, J.A. (2008) *Qualitative psychology: A practical guide to research methods.* London: Sage.

Appendices

These might contain: calculations, instructions given to participants, memory list items, questionnaires, and so on. Separate topics go in separate, numbered and headed appendices ('Appendix 1', 'Appendix 2', etc.). Normal page numbering is continued throughout.

Glossary

Bibliography	A list of sources used, *but not cited*, in the preparation of an essay or report. Not required in psychology reports
Literature review	A review of relevant literature on the topic of the report. This must be used in the argument towards the hypotheses, predictions or aims
Plagiarism	Claiming that other authors' work is your own, e.g. by not providing quotation marks or appropriate references. Plagiarism occurs *whether or not* the writer knew they were using another author's exact words
Primary reference	An original source which the writer has not read but about which they have obtained information in a *secondary source*
Secondary reference	Source in which the writer obtained information about an original or *primary source*

Comments on a student practical report

What you see below are two fictitious student reports. The first is not a good report, so please use it carefully as a model, taking into account all the comments I've made on it. My reasoning was this. If I comment on a perfect report, the recent newcomer to psychology and its practical writing conventions would have little clue as to what typically goes wrong in report writing. To include all possible mistakes would be to produce an unreadable piece of work serving little purpose. You should also note that I have avoided spelling and grammatical errors but that student reports usually do have a few of these, if not many. Where there *are* many errors it is perfectly correct for your tutors to ask impatiently that you use a spellchecker or dictionary and writing guide. Demanding good spelling and grammar is *not* being fussy; errors make your work hard to read and it really is worth practising while you are a student (and can sort of get away with it) so that your job applications do not let you down, and you are not embarrassed or penalised in employment when other people have to read your work.

I have also included a 'good' version of the report and this follows the 'average' version. I resisted demands for this for a while because I was concerned that the 'good' version might be seen as *the* model, with tutors having constantly to explain that, although a student's report follows all the points in the 'good' version, it still has faults in the context of the particular assignment that has been set. So please see this as a fair example for specific circumstances and not a gold standard that can serve all purposes.

The 'average' report below might just scrape a 2:2 at degree level and is not particularly good even at levels below this (by the standards with which I am familiar). Hence I've refrained from assessing it formally. It contains quite a lot of omissions and ambiguities, but few outright mistakes. Too many of these might be misleading. I have coded comments as follows:

✓ a good point

✗ an error, omission, ambiguity; in general, a point that would count cumulatively to lower the overall mark for the report

? an ambiguity or odd point that would not lower the mark on its own but could contribute to an overall lower mark if it were repeated. This is also used for grammatical and conventional style points which, again, are not terribly bad on their own but which may accumulate into a feeling of 'not quite so good' (but this does depend on your level of study).

Assume that materials mentioned as being in appendices were included (often they aren't!). Superscript numbers refer to the marker's comments which follow the report on p. 632.

An experiment to show whether people are[1] affected by knowing a writer's sex when they judge a piece of writing

Abstract

We[2] set out to see whether people make sexist assumptions about an author when they read their writing. We asked 39 participants to read an article and told half of them (19) that the author was a man and the others that it was a woman. We did this by making the writer's name 'John Kelly' for one version of the article and 'Jean Kelly' for the other.[3] Because of stereotyping we expected the 'Jean Kelly' group to think worse of the article's quality.[4] Results were not significant[5] and the null hypothesis was kept. It was thought that the article was too neutral and women might have voted lower on a technical article and men lower on a child-care article. If results were valid this could be interpreted as a change in attitude since Goldberg's (1968) work.[6]

Introduction

People use stereotypes when they look at other people. When we perceive people it's like looking at things in the world. We look through a framework of what we've learnt and we don't see the real thing but our impressions of it are coloured by what we expect and our biases.[7] Bruner (1957) said we 'go beyond the information given';[8] we use what's there as 'cues' to what we interpret is really there. For example, when we see a car on the road and a mountain behind it, the mountain might look only twice as high as the car but because we know how far away the mountain is we can estimate what size it really is. When we take a picture of a pretty sight we often get telephone wires in the way because we've learnt not to see what isn't important. Also, we take a shot of Uncle Arthur on the beach and he comes out really small because we thought he looked much bigger in the viewfinder because he's important to us. Bruner and his friends started the 'new look' in perception where they experimented with perception to show that we're affected by our emotions, motivation and 'set'. In one experiment they showed sweet jars to children that were either filled with sand or sweets.[9] The children saw the jars with sweets as larger, so we are affected by our past experience and what we want. (Dukes and Bevan, 1951.)[10]

To show that a small bit of information affects our judgement of persons, Asch (1946, in Brewer and Crano, 1994)[11] gave some people some words to describe a person. The words were the same except that 'warm' and 'cold' were different. This even works when the person is real because Kelley (1950) introduced students to a 'warm' or 'cold' person and they liked the 'warm' one more. The 'warm' person was seen quite differently from the 'cold' one.

Sex differences are a myth.[12] Condry and Condry (1976) showed people a film of a nine-month-old child reacting to a jack-in-the-box. If they were told he was a boy the reaction was thought of as 'anger' but for a 'girl' it was thought of as 'fear'. Deux (1977) reviewed several studies and found females often explain their performance as luck, even if they do well, but men say their ability helped them. This was where the task they did was unfamiliar. This means that men and women accept their stereotype and go along with it in their lives.[13] Maccoby and Jacklin's experiment[14] in 1974 showed that males describe themselves with independent terms (e.g. intelligent, ambitious) but females use more social terms (e.g. co-operative, honest).

A psychologist called[15] Goldberg (1968) got female students to read articles written by a man or a woman (they thought). The articles written by a man were rated as better. This is the experiment we're doing here.[16] If gender stereotypes affect our judgments we would expect that participants told an author is male will think some articles are better written than participants told the author is female.[17]

Method[18]

Design

The experiment used an independent samples design.[19] There were two groups. The independent variable was the sex of the author and the dependent variable was the way they judged the article.[20]

Participants

We used a random sample of 39 participants from the college canteen.[21] Originally there were 20 in the male author condition and 20 in the female author condition but the results for one in the male author condition went missing. The participants were all students except for one who was a friend of one of the students.

Materials

We used an article from *The Guardian Weekend* magazine about travelling in Tuscany. This is in Appendix 1. It was 908 words long and was printed on two sheets of A4 paper. We also used a rating sheet (in Appendix 2) where participants recorded their rating of the article for quality and interest on a 10-point scale.[22,23] This also had some questions on it to make sure the participants had noticed the name of the author.[24]

Procedure

We sat each participant down and made them feel at ease. We told them there would be no serious deception and that they would not be 'tested' or made to feel stupid in any way. We said we just wanted their opinion of something and that their opinion would be combined with others, their results would be anonymous and that the exact aims of the research would later be explained.[25] We then gave them the instructions shown below. All this was done in a standardised way.[26]

We would like you to read the article we are about to give you. Please read it once quickly, then again slowly. When you have done that, please answer the questions on the sheet which is attached to the article. Try to answer as best you can but please be sure to answer all questions in the order given.[27]

If the participant's number was odd they received the female author where the article was written by 'Jean Kelly'. The other participants were given 'John Kelly' sheets. In one case this order was reversed by mistake.[28]

Participants were then left to read the article and no questions were answered by the experimenters unless they did not concern the reading at all, for instance, if they wanted the light turned on or heater turned off. Questions about the reading were answered 'Please answer as best you can and we can talk about ('that problem') after you've finished. That way, all our participants do exactly the same thing. Thank you for your co-operation.' The experimenters kept a watchful eye to ensure that instructions were followed in the correct order.

Results

The results from the two groups were collected and organised into the table of raw data shown in Appendix 3. The averages and standard deviations were calculated and these are shown in Table 1.[29]

		Sex of author	
		Female	Male
Quality			
	Mean	6.7	6.3
	sd	1.5	2.3
Interest			
	Mean	4.3	5.2
	sd	1.1	1.3

Table I

You can see from this Table[30] that the male got a lower rating on quality but a higher rating on interest. This may be because people think men can write more interestingly, in general, but women are more likely to be accurate and are generally better with language and the rules of grammar.[31]

We decided to use an unrelated *t* test on this data to test for differences between the male and female quality and interest means since we had interval data and an unrelated design[32]. *t* tests are parametric and therefore the data were checked for normality. Levene's test was not significant and there were no violations of skew or kurtosis.[33, 34]

Our *t* was 0.97 for quality and 1.43 for interest. Neither of these is significant and in both cases we retained the null hypothesis.[35]

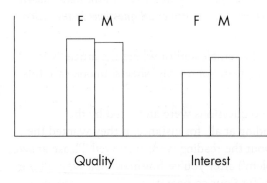

Discussion

As we see above, there were small differences between the male and female author groups but the tests showed there was no significance. It could be that there is a difference but our design has failed to show this.[37] Or else[38] there really is no difference in the way people judge this article according to the sex of the author. If this is true then we have contradicted Goldberg's results but these were done in 1968. Perhaps things have changed and people no longer judge according to sex of writer. However, there are several technical reasons why we might not have shown Goldberg's effect.[39]

We asked participants to answer some 'dummy' questions so that we could be sure they'd noticed the sex of the author before they rated the article.[40] When we thought about it afterwards, we decided perhaps we should have got them to do the questions (or some of them) *before* they read the article so that they would be aware of the author's sex while they were reading it. This might have made a difference and we could do another study like this sometime.[41] We didn't take any notice of the sex of our participants but obviously this might make a difference. Perhaps males would downrate[42] female authors and maybe vice versa. In a future study we could take groups of men and women separately.[43] Another problem was that not everybody would use our scale in the same way. 'Good' might be 7 to one person and 9 to another. We could perhaps have standardised by getting them to rate something else first and then discussing the points on the scale with them.[44] Also, we should have used more participants[45] and participants may have guessed what was going on and there may have been demand characteristics.[46]

We felt that the article used was on a very neutral subject. Goldberg used a selection of articles. Some were on traditionally male subjects and some of the subjects would be more associated with females. We could do the study again using, perhaps, an article on car maintenance and one on child-care to see whether this made a difference, like Mischel did.[47,48]

If our result is genuine then perhaps times have changed since 1968. These days there are female bus drivers, fire-fighters and even boxers. According to Gross (1992; p.696), Bem sees sex stereotypes as a 'straight-jacket'[49] and argues that society would improve with a shift towards 'androgyny'. This is where a person has the strengths of both traditional sex-roles. In order to 'discover' androgyny, it was necessary to see masculinity and femininity as not mutually exclusive but as two independent dimensions and to incorporate this into a new sort of test which would produce two logically independent scores. Bem developed such a test (1974).[50] It has been shown that people scoring high on Bem's Sex Role Inventory report higher levels of emotional well-being than others (Lubinski *et al.*, 1981) and show higher self-esteem (Spence *et al.*, 1975)[51]. Perhaps, from our results, we have shown that people are less likely today to take sex into account when judging the quality of writing because androgyny is more acceptable.[52]

References[53]

Asch, S.E. (1946) Forming impressions of personality. *Journal of Abnormal and Social Psychology, 4,* 258–90.

Bem, S.L. (1974) The measurement of psychological androgyny. *Journal of Consulting and Clinical Psychology, 42*(2), 155–62.

Brewer, M.B. and Crano, W.D. *Social psychology.* St Paul, MN: West Publishing Company.

Bruner, J.S. (1957) Going beyond the information given. In *Contemporary approaches to cognition: a symposium held at the University of Colorado.* Cambridge, MA: Harvard University Press.

Condry, J. and Condry, S. (1976) Sex differences: A study in the eye of the beholder. *Child Development, 47,* 812–19.

Deux, K. (1977) The social psychology of sex roles. In L. Wrightsman, *Social Psychology,* Monterey, CA: Brooks/Cole.

Dukes, W.F. and Bevan, W. (1951) Accentuation and response variability in the perception of personally relevant objects. *Journal of Personality, 20,* 457–65.

Goldberg, P. (1968) Are women prejudiced against women? *Transaction,* April.

Gross, R.D. (1992) *Psychology: The science of mind and behaviour* (second edition). London: Hodder and Stoughton Educational.

Kelley, H.H. (1950) The warm–cold variable in first impressions of people. *Journal of Personality, 18,* 431–9.

Lubinski, D., Tellegen, A. and Butcher, J.N. (1981) The relationship between androgyny and subjective indicators of emotional well-being. *Journal of Personality and Social Psychology, 40,* 722–30.

Maccoby, E.E. and Jacklin, C.N. (1974) *The psychology of sex differences.*[54]

Spence, J.T., Helmreich, R.L. and Stapp, J. (1975) Ratings of self and peers on sex-role attributes and their relation to self-esteem and concepts of masculinity and femininity. *Journal of Personality and Social Psychology, 32,* 29–39.

Rogers, W.S. (2003) *Social psychology: Experimental and critical approaches.* Maidenhead: OUP.[55]

Comments on the text

1 ? Don't need 'An experiment to show …'; title could be shorter: 'The effect of author's sex on evaluation of an article'.

2 ? Conventional reports are written in passive not personal mode; e.g. 'The theory was tested that author's sex affects judgement of writing.' 'Thirty-nine participants were asked …'.

3 ✓ Independent variable is clearly described.

4 ✗ Dependent variable is not defined. How was 'thinking worse of' measured? (It was rated, we find out later on.)

5 ✗ Results very poorly reported. What data were tested and how?

6 ✓ Some brief statement of conclusions included.

7 ✗ Several wide claims; no evidence offered.

8 ✓ Quoted phrase is in quote marks and attributed to an author, with date – this must be referenced at the end of the report. It's a small quotation but technically the page number should be provided (✗).

9 ? (Poor children! You wouldn't think they'd let psychologists do that sort of thing!)

10 ? A broad start about factors that affect judgement in perception. This is kind of relevant but the report could start much closer to *social* perception.

11 ✓ An appropriate secondary reference. The writer obtained the information from Brewer and Crano, and doesn't have access to the original. Only Brewer and Crano should therefore appear in the final reference list (APA style; both in Harvard).

12 ✗ A gigantic and unjustified assumption made here; there are *some* differences (e.g. reading development rate); the claim needs qualifying with the use of 'some', 'many' or examples and trends.

13 ✗ Another grand assumption here, following a very specific result; needs qualification.

14 ✗ It wasn't an experiment; it was a review of mostly post facto studies.

15 ? Don't need 'A psychologist called …'; simply delete these words here.

16 ✗ The leap into the hypothesis is far too sudden here; we lurch from fair background description straight into the hypothesis without some introduction to the current study and a rationale for it.

17 ✗ Research prediction is vague. The research prediction states the independent variable but should also specify the dependent variables of 'quality' and 'interest' which have not yet been mentioned. Hence there should be *two* specific predictions.

18 ✓ Good that all sections of the method are present and correctly titled.

19 ✓ Correct design and this *is* an experiment.

20 ✗ Again, dependent variable *still* not specified; it doesn't need complete description here but there should be an operational definition of the measure – 'quality was measured by scores given on a ten-point scale' or similar. Other controls have not been specified.

21 ✗ Almost certainly not a 'random' selection from the canteen. If it *was* random, explain how this was achieved; no mention of participant gender and this *is* relevant given the topic and aims of this study.

22 ✓ Materials well described so far.

23 ✗ Notice that tucked away here is the first mention of the precise dependent variables. We still don't know which way the scale runs – is 10 high or low?

24 ✗ The technique of asking questions, including dummy ones, in order to ensure participants noticed the sex of the author, deserves clearer explanation. We are not told here, or (more correctly) in the procedure, that participants *first* answer the pre-reading questions, which include sex of the author but also others as camouflage (see p. 606 above), *then* read the main article and rate it for quality and interest. That is, the *purpose* of these questions is never given.

25 ✓ Ethical considerations well implemented.

26 ? Ambiguity; was the initial rapport session standardised, or just the instruction-giving?

27 ✓ Instructions used are included here. These could also be paraphrased.

28 ? This system of allocation of participants might have been mentioned in the 'participants' section; good that the mistake was reported, however.

29 ✗ Table has no title. The title should state that the values are the 'Means and standard deviations of quality and interest ratings by sex of author'.

30 ? Should describe and summarise *for* the reader, not refer to them in this personal style.

31 ✗ This kind of interpretation or speculation belongs in the 'Discussion' section; here, just the factual results should be reported.

32 ✓ Correct but you would not usually be required to justify the use of your test in such detail. Here assume the tutors made it a criterion of the assignment since it is first year work.

33 ✓ Good that data checking has been reported.

34 ✗ Hasn't stated that Levene's test is for homogeneity of variance; value of p not given

35 ✗ t not reported in conventional form; no df, no values for p; was the test two-tailed?

36 ✗ Chart has no title; 'M' and 'F' have no key (yes, it's obvious what they mean but clarity is the keyword here); the vertical scale has no values; the chart is correctly drawn as a clustered bar chart. However, it is not referred to anywhere in the text of the report.

37 ✓ Recognition that a Type II error could have occurred and (in the next line) that the outcome, if genuine, needs interpretation in the light of its contradiction of other work.

38 ? Grammar! Can't start a sentence this way.

39 ✓ Deals with Type II error possibility i.e. looks critically at the method to see what might have prevented the demonstration of an effect.

40 ? Again, role of dummy questions should have been made clear earlier but we have already taken this weakness into account in our assessment – not a double penalty.

41 ✓ Suggests modifications based on an analysis of the present study's outcomes and weaknesses.

42 ? Is there such a word? Use the dictionary!

43 ✓ Recognises that gender might be a relevant variable and suggests further research.

44 ✓ A pity this wasn't done then. Why only report it now as a weakness? The point could also have been used to justify a non-parametric statistical test.

45 ? Should avoid this knee-jerk point, unless there is a good reason to include it; there was a fair number of participants and with no reason given this is rather an empty point, 'thrown in'.

46 ✗? A difficult one; is the point that people may have guessed *and* there could have been 'demand characteristics'? If so, there should be an explanation of why the effect of demand characteristics is suspected; in what way? If people's guessing was meant *as* a demand characteristic, is this feasible? It must always be remembered in independent samples designs of this kind that *you* know what the independent variable is but how can the participants know? Why should they suspect that another author will be a different sex? One needs to see the participant's perspective here.

47 ✓ Good extension of study proposed, though the new design would involve two-way ANOVA.

48 ✗ 'Mischel' has no date and does not appear in the reference list.

49 ✓ Has quoted and acknowledged, with page number, Gross's specific term here.

50 ✗!!! Alarm bells ring for markers when they encounter such a suddenly technical and academic sounding piece of text, compared to most of the rest of the report. Most markers, after only a little experience, can spot this kind of change and will reach for Google or the most likely textbooks to check for plagiarism. It is, in fact, cribbed straight from Gross (1992), page 696 – a little clue is given just above! This really would be a shame in an otherwise fair report.

51 ✗ You do not use '*et al.*' on the first mention of a publication unless it has more than five names. *After* that you may use '*et al.*'.

52 ✓ Good attempt to feed the result into general context. ? However, some of these findings are over 30 years old. It would be better to try to find some later work.

53 ✓ Good references, put in conventional style and most in alphabetical order. ✗ However, Mischel (****) should appear here too.

54 ✗ No place of publication or publisher.

55 ✗ 'Allo, 'allo! What's this one doing here? It's not in alphabetical order and it wasn't referred to in the text of the report at any time. It's probably been read to do the report but it isn't a reference. It could be included as 'background reading' but isn't necessary at all unless it was the source of evidence or some of the apparently 'primary' references.

A better report of the same practical

Effect of author's apparent sex on assessment of a written article

Abstract

In an attempt to assess current effects of sex-role stereotyping on judgement of writing skill, Goldberg's (1968) study was partially replicated. Twenty five participants were asked to read an article. Twelve participants were told the author was male whilst 13 were told the author was female. It was found that the 'male' author was rated significantly higher than the 'female' author on 'interest'. The 'female' author was rated higher on quality than was the 'male' author but this difference was not significant. The neutrality of the assessed article is discussed and the suggestion made that judgements might vary according to author's sex if the supposed authored articles had themselves been sex-typed (e.g. technical or child-care related). The result offered only partial support for a change in social attitude since Goldberg's work.

Introduction

Just as our perception of the physical world is affected by the subjective, interpretive and constructive nature of perception, so is our perception of people. In Bruner's words (1957:12) we 'go beyond the information given' in constructing our perceptual world of objects. It is of interest whether our perception and impressions of people are affected by the same sorts of processes as are our perceptions of the physical world. To show that varying a small piece of information can affect our judgement of persons, Asch (1946) gave some people a list of terms which described an imaginary person. In two conditions the word lists were identical except for the replacement of 'warm' by 'cold'. The imaginary person described by the words was judged quite differently in the two conditions, with the word 'cold' apparently producing a more negative appraisal on quite a number of other characteristics. Asch argued that the warm-cold trait was a central characteristic which coloured perception of several others.

Sex (or gender) can be seen as a very central character which affects people's judgments of many other characteristics which are stereotypically related to sex. In a classic study, Goldberg (1968) showed that female students rated several articles more highly when the article indicated a male author than when the apparent author was female. Mischel (1974) found that participants of both sexes rated a male author more highly on a male-dominated topic and a female author more highly on a female-dominated topic. This raises the issue of whether these participants *consciously* used the gender of author information when making their assessments. This is unlikely since they would not have known that male or female author was the independent variable for the experiment. However, work by Devine (1989) suggests that even non-prejudiced people have popular cultural stereotypes available and though they would suppress these when consciously expressing attitudes and beliefs, it is possible that judgements are affected by them at a pre-conscious level. Studies of stereotyping effects have continued but in more specific and applied areas. For instance, Johanson (2008) found that the more masculine participants perceived a face to be the more they attributed initiation of structure (a typically masculine leadership style), rather than consideration (a feminine style) and vice versa. In a cross-cultural study, Prime, Jonsen, Carter & Maznevski (2008) showed that among Nordic and Anglo groups in particular, male participants' stereotypes of women's leadership skills were disparaging where the skills in question were those they most valued in leadership assessment.

It has been suggested that stereotypical knowledge might affect judgements more when these judgements are made under pressure and/or with minimal information available. Fiske and Taylor (1991) argued for a *continuum model* of impression formation. They suggest that initially, on encountering someone or hearing about them, we make a simple initial categorisation. If we are not going to interact further then there is no more analysis. However, if we have to interact with or make some judgement about them then we seek further information. If there is a popular, well permeated stereotype for this category then the characteristics of this stereotype might pervade until we find contradictory information which might force us to re-categorise (e.g. a 'hard' businessman who nevertheless sets up childcare facilities for his staff); alternatively we might simply find our stereotype information reinforced (we meet a politician who *is* boring and spin-oriented). Evidence for this position is plentiful, including the finding that judgements of people are more stereotype-based when made in a hurry rather than when relaxed (Pratto and Bargh, 1991). In addition, Nelson, Acker and Manis (1996) asked participants to judge whether someone was a nursing or engineering student and provided traits consistent with them being male or female. Some participants were motivated to make non-stereotypical judgements (they would have to justify their judgements publicly) or were warned that knowledge of a person's gender was not helpful in making the judgement. This information had the effect of lessening the degree of stereotypical judgement but did not reduce it completely.

The continuum model predicts that participants in Goldberg's study *would* be affected by the gender information since they have minimal information about the person (just their name and the article they have written), yet they are asked to make a judgement about that person's ability or at least the work they have produced. To discover whether this effect might still occur 30 years on, a partial replication of this study was attempted using just one 'gender-neutral' article, where Goldberg had used several, some more male-oriented and some more female-oriented. His participants were all female whereas we involved both male and female students. Participants were made aware of the author's sex whilst judging the article by asking what sex the author was but this question was camouflaged among several other 'dummy' questions. Participants were asked to rate the article on both 'quality' and on 'interest'. If popular gender stereotypes are still available to students, and are more powerful when judgements have to be made swiftly and with minimal information, then it would be expected that participants told the author was male would give higher mean ratings for interest and quality of the article than participants told the author was female.

Method

Design

An independent samples experimental design with two groups was employed. The independent variable, being apparent sex of the author, was manipulated so that one group was informed that the author was male while the other group was informed that the author was female. Dummy questions were used to ensure that the participant was made aware of the sex of the author (via their name). The dependent variables were ratings of quality and interest of the article, both assessed on a 10-point scale.

Participants

Thirty-nine participants from the students' union were asked to participate, selected as haphazardly as possible. There were 12 males and eight females in the male author condition and nine males and 10 females in the female author condition. Participants were allocated to conditions on an alternate basis, as selected, and were all students except for one who was a friend of one of the students. Numbers in each condition were originally equal but one participant's results were subsequently mislaid.

Materials

We used an article from *The Guardian Weekend* magazine about travelling in Tuscany. This is provided in Appendix 1. It was 908 words long and was printed on two sheets of A4 paper. One version gave the author's name as 'John Kelly' while the other version used 'Jean Kelly'. We also used a rating sheet (in Appendix 2) where participants recorded their rating of the article for quality and interest on a 10-point scale where '1' was designated as 'low' and '10' as high. We also used a sheet asking the author's name but with several other dummy questions (such as the title of the article, the number of pages and so on). This was to ensure that participants were aware of the name, and therefore the sex, of the author, when they were making their assessments but were not alerted to this as the specific independent variable.

Procedure

Each participant was asked to sit down and an attempt was made to make them feel at ease. They were told that there would be no deception and that they would not be 'tested' or made to feel stupid in any way. They were assured that the researchers simply wanted their opinion on something and that their opinion would be combined with others and their results would be anonymous. The full aim of the study would be explained to them after the testing session. The instructions (given below) were then administered. The instructions and all statements used in the preliminary briefing were standardised.

We would like you to read the article we are about to give you. Please read it once quickly, then again slowly. When you have done that, please answer the questions on the sheet which is attached to the article. Try to answer as best you can but please be sure to answer all questions in the order given.

If the participant's number was odd they received the female author version where the article was written by 'Jean Kelly'. The other participants were given 'John Kelly' sheets. In one case this order was reversed by mistake. Participants were then left to read the article and no questions were answered by the experimenters unless they did not concern the reading at all, for instance, if participants wanted the light turned on or heater turned off. Questions about the reading were answered 'Please answer as best you can and we can talk about that (problem) after you've finished. That way, all participants do exactly the same thing. Thank you for your co-operation.' The experimenters monitored participants and checked that instructions were followed in the correct order.

Results

The results from the two groups were collected and organised into the table of raw data shown in Appendix 3. Summary statistics are given in Table 1. The male author received a lower mean rating (M 6.3, SD 2.3) than the female author (M 6.7, SD 1.5) on quality, but the male author mean on interest (M 5.2, SD 1.3) was higher than for the female author (M 4.3; SD 1.1). The mean values are also displayed in Figure 1.

Both dependent variable measures were relatively skewed (quality: skew = 0.933, se = 0.441; interest skew = 0.612, se = 0.231). To test for differences between the male author and female author conditions on quality and interest a non-parametric Mann-Whitney analysis was

	Apparent sex of author	
	Female	Male
Quality		
Mean	6.7 (1.5)	6.3 (2.3)
Interest		
Mean	4.3 (1.1)	5.2 (1.3)

Table 1 Mean (and sd) of quality and interest ratings for female and male author conditions

consequently used on the unrelated data reduced to ranks. Median ranks for quality were female author 6.2, male author 6.1, and for interest, female author 4.5, male author 5.2.

For quality of the article, U (N_a, 20, N_b, 19) = 183, p > .05. For interest of the article, U (N_a = 20, N_b,19) = 164, p = .043. Hence, a significant effect in favour of the male author was found for interest but not for quality.

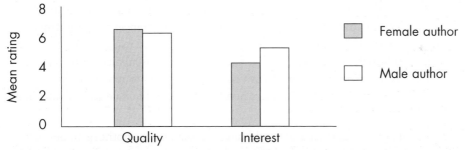

Figure 1 Mean ratings on quality and interest for female and male author conditions

Discussion

This result partially supports Goldberg in that a significantly higher 'interest' mean was found for the male author condition compared with the female but this difference did not occur for 'quality'. Goldberg's effect was found only with female students whereas here members of both sexes were tested. If the effect is genuine it is subtle since being an interesting author is not an obvious aspect of the male stereotype. As with Goldberg's finding, participants appear to act under a generalised more favourable response to the male author, or possible a less favourable one to the female author. It is unclear why the effect did not occur for 'quality' but, in a sense, it is even less clear why participants should rate the male author higher than the female on 'interest'. According to Fiske and Taylor's (1991) model however, the 'interest' finding is consistent with participants in this experiment having only superficial knowledge of the person they were judging and hence the employment of a generalised stereotype in the absence of further information. The participants in this study were not acting in a hurry but were not told that their results would be publicly viewed and hence the apparent privacy of the response might enhance the knee-jerk resort to stereotype. The picture is left unclear however by the occurrence of only one significant effect. The failure to support Goldberg on 'quality' may be related to real changes in the effects of sex-role stereotyping since the time of his study. It could also be that, although Pratto and Bargh (1991) and Nelson *et al.* (1996) did demonstrate effects, the original Goldberg effect may now be too subtle given heightened public sensitivity to gender stereotypes over three decades of feminist publication and an equal opportunity climate. On the other hand, it may well be that our design has failed to identify a difference for quality.

We asked participants to answer some 'dummy' questions so that we could be sure they had noticed the sex of the author before they rated the article. In fact, this does not ensure that participants' stereotype schemas are operating *while* they read and interpret the article, only when they are asked to *assess* it. An amendment might be to present some of the dummy questions, including the crucial author name item, *before* participants read the article so that they would be aware of the sex during the reading.

Goldberg's stimulus materials were student essays and so his participants, being female college students, might well have judged these on a peer evaluation basis. Since we used a travel article the author was an 'authority' and the subject matter might have been responsible for an interaction effect. Perhaps the article had some kind of 'male' flavour. There could also be an interaction here between author sex and the apparent masculinity or femininity of the article's content. The article did feature a rather 'masculine' car and several references to quite dangerous activities. Following Mischel's (1974) finding the study could be repeated using an additional more female oriented article. Although no measure of the 'femininity' or 'masculinity' of the article content was used, it would have been possible to ask other participants to rate it on this dimension or to investigate any difference in ratings between male and female participants in a control group not given any author name.

In this study it was unlikely that participants could have guessed the hypothesis under test since they took part in only one condition and were asked several questions about the article and author's characteristics, their sex being only one of these. The scale was not standardised and may have been used differently by each participant; one person's 'low' might be another's 'moderate'. However, the appearance of one out of the two differences as significant seems to justify the assumption that each group, as a whole, used the scale differently from the other.

As feminism started to make its impact on psychology in the 1970s, Bem (1975) argued that society would improve with a shift towards 'androgyny' – the adaptation to both masculine and feminine personalities by both men and women. Perhaps, from our results, we might tentatively speculate that such a shift may now have occurred, at least for the 'quality' variable, or at least that people are less likely today to take sex into account when judging the quality of writing. However, there may have been no shift but simply a weakening of the strength of sex-stereotyped assumptions in snap judgements. The result for 'interest' supports the still active role of sex bias and there is still plenty of evidence (e.g. Johanson, 2008; Prime, Jonsen, Carter and Maznevski, 2008) that sex role assumptions have a differential effect on people's behaviour towards the different sexes in everyday working life.

References
Assume they were perfect!

Appendix to Chapter 22

ANTHROZOÖS   VOLUME 21.   ISSUE 1   PP 31-42
REPRINTS AVAILABLE DIRECTLY FROM THE PUBLISHERS
PHOTOCOPYING PERMITTED BY LICENSE ONLY

Justifying Attitudes toward Animal Use: A Qualitative Study of People's Views and Beliefs

Sarah Knight and Louise Barnett
Department of Psychology, University of Portsmouth, UK

ABSTRACT "Animal use" is a contentious topic that refers to practices involving the utilization of non-human animals by human beings. These practices often evoke strong and emotional reactions from opposing parties, and individuals can hold incongruent views concerning different ways in which animals are used. Yet previous research in this area has tended to portray attitudes toward animal use as uni-dimensional (rather than distinguishing between different types of use), and the field has been dominated by quantitative approaches that focus on participant characteristics such as gender, age, and so on, in order to explain variance in people's views on this topic. The present study assumed that attitudes are not uni-dimensional and applied Grounded Theory Methodology in order to determine psychological factors that underlie people's views concerning animal use issues. Eight participant-led interviews explored the factors that people consider when rationalizing their attitudes toward the use of animals, and interview transcripts were analyzed with an aim to understanding why attitudes vary depending upon the type of animal use in question. Three key themes were identified, labelled as "type of animal used," "purpose of animal use," and "knowledge of animal use." These represent beliefs concerning animals and animal use, and help explain why people can support some animal use practices whilst opposing others. We conclude that taking a psychological approach in order to further examine the beliefs that underlie attitudes provides a way forward for future research.

Keywords: animal use, attitudes, beliefs

Attitudes and beliefs are of interest to sociologists and psychologists alike; they are influenced by societal values and norms and can determine how individuals and groups respond to many aspects of everyday life (Davey et al. 2004). We use the word "attitude" to describe the way people view many aspects of their social world, such as issues, groups, people, objects, and so on (Baron, Byrne and Branscombe 2006); attitudes can be positive, negative, and neutral, and vary in intensity and strength. One topic that can evoke a diversity of responses is that of "animal use." This term describes a wide range of practices that involve the utilization of non-human animals[1] by human beings, for example, keeping animals for companionship, hunting for sport, invasive medical research, and so on. Such practices can lead to strong emotional reactions from some people whilst others remain indifferent to the subject. Further, individuals present seemingly disparate opinions concerning different animal use practices (Knight et al. 2003; Knight et al. 2004); for example, an individual may express great affection for some species, object to animal cloning, but support invasive medical procedures that cause pain and death to animal subjects. Yet previous research, whilst measuring levels of support for different types of animal use, has analyzed and reported attitudes as uni-dimensional (e.g., Armstrong and Hutchins 1996). Instead, the present study acknowledges that people's views might vary depending upon the type of animal use in question. We aimed to develop what is known about attitudes toward animal use by exploring how people justify ostensible inconsistencies in their views. It is proposed that by identifying psychological factors that underlie these attitudes, seemingly incongruent views can be understood.

Research that examines attitudes toward the utilization of animals can inform social scientists about the society in which we live, since how we view and treat animals can reflect individual differences, group norms, and cultural values, and can also reflect how we view and treat our fellow human beings (Ascione 1992; Taylor and Signal 2005). The study of attitudes toward animal use is a relatively new area of research, with a growth of interest in this area emerging in the 1980s. This has been prompted in part by an increase in our concern for animal well-being in recent years (Broom and Johnson 1993; Clough and Kew 1993; Wells and Hepper 1997), coupled with technological advances that have led to an increase in animal use in research, industry, and agriculture. Research in this area has mainly examined relationships between people's views on the subject and participant characteristics. For example, gender (Furnham and Pinder 1990; Rajecki, Rasmussen and Craft 1993; Pifer, Shimizu and Pifer 1994; Plous 1996), experience of animals (Paul and Serpell 1993; Wells and Hepper 1997), and religious orientation (Bowd and Bowd 1989; Flynn 2001), have all been found to relate to people's views toward the use of animals, and such factors together account for a significant, but small (around 5-10%), amount of the variance in attitudes. Instead, more recent research has found beliefs concerning the mental abilities of animals ("belief in animal mind") to impact more on attitudes toward animal use than do gender and experience of animals (Herzog and Galvin 1997; Knight et al. 2004).

The present study aimed to further explore factors such as belief in animal mind and identify other psychological variables that might explain why people do not hold uni-dimensional attitudes toward animal use. Previously, research methods employed for conducting studies interested in people's views on animal use were mostly quantitative, yet a qualitative approach is especially appropriate when little is known about a topic. Qualitative methodology can provide researchers with rich and detailed information from which to develop models and theory (Robson 2002). In particular, Grounded Theory Methodology (GTM) can enable researchers to construct theory that can describe and explain data (Knight et al. 2003). GTM was the approach chosen for the present study since relatively little is known about the psychological factors that underlie attitudes toward animal use. Moreover, some people are ambivalent about the topic, perhaps because they have never needed to consider their attitudes regarding animal use; hence, the present research involved participant-led interviews in order to encourage participants to explore in-depth their views (Knight et al, 2003), Participants discussed the issues that they perceived to be relevant, rather than being asked about constructs seen as important by researchers. GTM was applied throughout data collection and analysis, with an aim toward identifying central themes that help explain people's views concerning the use of animals by human beings.

Methods

Participants

Herzog (1993) claimed that qualitative research methods can be used to study smaller samples more intensively, where participants are selected on the basis of their familiarity with the interview topic and ability to describe their experiences, rather than the usual method of random sampling. In the present research, sampling was purposive (see Patton 1990), with an aim to illuminating the study question and increasing the richness of data, rather than seeking data that are representative of a population. A sample of eight participants (4 female, 4 male, aged 22-65 years) were recruited via a snowball method. The first two participants were known to colleagues of the researchers, one was involved in wildlife conservation, and the other was involved in fox hunting. These participants provided contact names of other people who they anticipated would hold different views to themselves concerning animal use issues. Theoretical sampling led to a group of participants who had a range of attitudes toward animal use. Occupations included: teaching, midwifery, catering, conservation work, farming, clerical, and unskilled labor. The sample size was dictated by the concept of "saturation" (see Guest, Bunce and Johnson 2006), that is, a number of interviews were conducted until new information and understanding ceased to emerge.

Procedure

In-depth interviews were participant-led, via a flexible format that encouraged participants to explore the issues they believed to be important and unimportant concerning their ideas about animals and animal use practices.[2] Each interview opened with the interviewer requesting the participant to identify different ways in which animals are used and to consider their views on these. Participants were encouraged to question, explain, and justify their attitudes and discuss the issues that were believed to be relevant concerning their views on this subject. Each interview lasted between 45-90 minutes and all were audio-recorded. As is usual when using GTM, during the process of data collection interview recordings were transcribed and analysis commenced, so that interviews were being conducted and analyzed in parallel. In total there were 274 pages of transcripts.

Data Analysis

The researcher used constant comparative methods to analyze the data (see Glaser and Strauss 1967; Turner 1981; Strauss and Corbin 1990). After the initial read through of all transcripts (several times), "open-coding" began, where transcripts were examined, line-by-line, and each line or paragraph was broken down into smaller pieces of information. Each statement was considered in relation to the question "what does this represent?" and ideas that addressed this question were noted next to each piece of data. For example, text that read "humans have always eaten animals . . . they need to eat meat," was recorded as one chunk of data, and notes such as "meat eating is natural," and "meat eating is necessary" were made alongside the text. Once open coding had been applied to all data, constant comparison methods allowed the identification of similarities and differences between chunks of data; this led to the emergence of themes and identification of relationships between these. Therefore, if two participants made similar statements regarding the reasons why humans eat meat, these statements were grouped together under the same heading. Hence, once text was deconstructed into a large number of small chunks, similarities, differences, and patterns in the data then allowed the development of a model that represented the reconstruction of the text.

The analysis required the reading and re-reading of transcripts, during which a manuscript was kept, comprising ideas concerning emerging themes and sub-themes, patterns and relationships, similarities and differences, key quotes, and so on. This manuscript provided the basis of the results presented below, and acted as a paper trail to support the emerging picture as the text was first deconstructed, then reconstructed. Hence, the manuscript was evidence that analysis was conducted with rigor, and ensured that findings were grounded in the data.

Results and Discussion

Three central themes emerged from the data that were labeled: "type of animal used," "purpose of animal use," and "knowledge of animal use." In general, views varied depending upon the type of animal being discussed. Less support was shown for the use of animals that were perceived as high in mental capabilities, aesthetically pleasing, and those that participants had more experience with. Participants were more in favor of animal use when they believed the purpose to be necessary and beneficial to humans, and when no alternatives were available. Participants felt uninformed about animal use practices and procedures, and believed that if their knowledge increased they might be more opposed to such issues. Overall, results showed that participants were least in favor of animal use for personal decoration (e.g., cosmetics testing, wearing fur), whilst the majority of participants approved of the use of animals for medical research when this is likely to lead to high value benefits such as a cure for serious human disease. The three central themes are now discussed in detail with the use of quotes extracted from the transcripts to demonstrate that the theory is grounded in the data.

Type of Animal Used

When rationalizing their attitudes toward animal use, participants discussed their views in relation to different types of animal. Some participants proposed that all animals should be treated equally, whilst others admitted that their views varied according to the type of animal in question:

> . . . You can't differentiate – you can't turn round and say that's okay to do that to those [types of animal] but you can't do that to them [another type of animal] . . .

> But I might [differentiate] between a cow and an insect, and an ant, and maybe unfairly so . . . Yes, I do, I categorize the insects into a different category than mammals and so forth . . .

The latter view tends to support findings from previous research that revealed different levels of support for the use of different species such as rats, monkeys, or dogs (Driscoll 1992). In the present study, participants explained this variance in their views in terms of the psychological and physical characteristics of animals.

Most participants believed in the existence of animal mind, to varying degrees depending upon the type of animal in question. The possibility of animals experiencing thoughts and emotions was discussed: The general opinion was that animals are capable of cognitive processes and feeling, but not necessarily in the way that humans are:

> My take on it is that animals do think . . . not necessarily the same cognitive processes or affective processes that a human uses though . . .

The notion of animal mind refers to their capacity to experience feelings and emotions and to have cognitive abilities such as intelligence, problem solving skills, and self-awareness (Herzog and Galvin 1997; Knight et al. 2003). Belief in the notion of animal mentality is referred to in the literature as "belief in animal mind" (Hills 1995) and leads to moral questions concerning the admissibility of animal use. That is, if we believe that animals are capable of mental experience, especially sentience (the capacity to experience pain), then animal use presents us with an uncomfortable dilemma, especially if practices cause suffering and/or death to those animals involved (Herzog and Galvin 1997). Indeed, high levels of belief in animal mind are associated with increased likelihood that people will condemn animal use, and vice versa (Hills 1995; Knight et al. 2004), This is supported by data from the present research. One participant who supported hunting animals for sport justified the activity by denying animal mind:

> I don't think they [foxes] do [have a mind] but if I did I think that would put me off [fox hunting] . . .

Yet the same participant described one particular fox as being intelligent and calculating, having escaped hunters over a long period of time. Admiration was expressed for this particular animal's survival skills, and the participant stressed that he would not like to see this one be caught during the hunt. This is an example of how individual animals can be singled out for having special abilities and/or qualities, whilst others, even of the same species, can be viewed and treated differently (Herzog 1988). Arluke (1988) revealed similar disparity in his ethnographic research in biomedical research environments. Workers responsible for caring for laboratory animals treated animals simultaneously as objects and pets: some were objectified whilst others were accorded special privileges including liberation from the research establishment. Arluke claimed that objectification permits violation by minimizing the emotional discomfort that comes with killing laboratory animals: This same mechanism may be how the participant in the present study admired individual animals yet continued to participate in hunting for sport. Low levels of belief in animal mind, especially regarding their capacity to suffer, reduces potential discomfort in people who might be directly or indirectly involved with animal use procedures. For example, people tend to rate farm animals as less capable mentally compared with other animals such as dogs and cats; hence, they feel comfortable about using animals such as cattle, pigs, and sheep for food. Yet the notion of eating dogs and cats is met with repulsion by persons in the UK (Podberscek 2005), The same phenomenon can apply to other types of animal use, for example, the use of mice and rats in invasive medical research is more likely to be supported than if the same procedures involved primates or dogs (Knight et al. 2003). Conversely, if we consider animals to be similar to ourselves in terms of their mental experiences then we are more likely to show concern for them and oppose animal use (Pious 1993; Knight et al. 2004).

People tend to rank different animals on a continuum according to their perceived mental complexity, with larger brained mammals and primates at the top of the scale, smaller brained animals, invertebrates, and fish near the bottom, and other animals somewhere in the middle (Eddy, Gallup and Povinelli 1993; Herzog and Galvin 1997). Since different kinds of animals are likely to be associated with different mental capacities, this explains why attitudes toward animal use can differ for different types of animals. The use of those animals associated with high mental capacities (e.g., primates), will lead to strong opposition, whilst the use of "lower" animals (e.g., rat, mice) is perceived as more acceptable:

> . . . I have very, very, very strong misgivings about using primates for any research, because I think they're just too close to us . . . mentally, I mean

> . . . But I would respond differently to something that doesn't seem to have a personality as such . . . I mean – rats and mice in labs, I have less of a problem with that . . .

Another factor concerning type of animal that influences attitudes toward animal use is the physical appearance of animals. Animals perceived as attractive were more likely to evoke negative reactions to their use, whilst animal use was deemed more acceptable for those animals perceived as less attractive:

> But they [dogs] are so lovely I don't know how people could do that to them [discussing the use of dogs for food in Korea]. They're so pretty – how could they do that to them?

> Well I have to admit, I wouldn't agree to them using chimps or monkeys [for medical research], but rats – they give me the creeps, so I wouldn't care as much . . .

Clearly, the way animals look affect how people view animal use. This is supported by other research that has found opposition to the use of animals perceived as "attractive" or "cute" (Herzog and Galvin 1997; Hagelin, Carlson and Hau 2003). Hence, the use of animals that are perceived to be aesthetically more pleasing, and higher in mental abilities and sentience, is more likely to evoke negative attitudes than is the use of those animals perceived as unattractive or less capable mentally.

Participants' views and perceptions of different types of animals were influenced by whether they had personal experience of such animals, and this in turn impacted on their opinions concerning animal use practices. Previous research agrees that personal experience such as pet ownership is influential on our attitudes toward animal use (Wells and Hepper 1997), for example, pet owners tend to oppose animal research more than non-owners (Driscoll 1992). In this present study, the same conclusions were drawn, in that participants who had experience of animals at some stage in their lives were more inclined to oppose animal use:

> I've always had animals around, and so it seems wrong to support these kinds of things [animal use practices], I just don't like to think about what goes on . . .

However, it is important to note that this relationship is species-specific; a person who has experience of one type of animal may not oppose the use of another type of animal. So, for example, a dog owner may oppose the use of dogs for cosmetics testing or for their fur, but support the use of animals for sports such as fox hunting (Wells and Hepper 1997):

> I just can't bear to think of those poor animals [in research] because I can't remember life without cats, so part of it was that I'd always been around cats . . . my world and existence always had a cat in it. But I guess if you are asking about rats – then I would accept that.

It is believed that pet owners form an attachment with their animals, which reinforces a positive attitude towards animals in general (Bowd 1984; Furnham and Heyes 1993; Paul and Serpell 1993). Experience with animals is likely to affect how animals are perceived; therefore the relationship between factors such as experience of animals, the perceived mental abilities of animals, and the perceived attractiveness of animals is interactive and fluid. Furthermore, it is not only present pet owners who are affected by this factor; people who have had past experiences with animals in their childhood are also more inclined to be concerned about animal welfare (Serpell 1993). Hence, experience of animals has a lasting effect on people's attitudes toward ways in which we as humans treat them.

Attitudes toward animal use are therefore influenced by the type of animal involved, in terms of the animal's perceived mental capacity, its appearance, and whether the person has prior experience with this particular type of animal.

Purpose of Animal Use

Kellert (1980) proposed an attitude typology that comprised ten different perceptions of animals, the most prevalent being "humanistic," "moralistic," "utilitarian," and "negativistic." In simple terms, these represent two broad and conflicting dimensions of attitudes toward animals, allowing for a diversity of views and potential conflict within society. Basically, moralistic and utilitarian points-of-view clash in terms of human exploitation of animals, with the former opposing, and the latter endorsing, the utilization of animals for human benefit. Negativistic and humanistic viewpoints conflict in terms of affection for animals, with the former rejecting the notion of loving animals, whilst the latter involving affection for animals. Kellert emphasized that researchers should not attempt to categorize individuals into one of the ten categories, but suggested that the typology describes elements of individuals attitudes toward animals that are embedded in general wildlife values. Hence, whilst type of animal used will impact on levels of support for animal use, other factors such as whether animal use will benefit human beings will mediate people's views.

In the present research, the main purposes of animal use as discussed by participants were using animals for medical research, for food, for personal decoration (e.g., testing cosmetics and wearing fur), and for entertainment (e.g., hunting for sport and animals in zoos); the former two deemed most acceptable. All participants indicated the purpose of animal use to be important when they rationalized their views on this topic; this supports previous research that recognized this as an influencing factor (Pifer, Shimizu and Pifer 1994).

The majority of participants agreed with using animals for medical research, due to the benefits that they associated with such practices:

> I mean, if we can find a cure for cancer, for AIDS, that would just be fantastic. . . . So we have to use animals for research . . .

Another element to support for medical research was that participants perceived there to be few alternatives to using animals:

> I have very mixed feelings about animals being made to suffer for the sake of treatments for us, if there is an alternative.

Participants who believed there were alternatives were less supportive of such practices, for example, those who proposed human volunteering as a viable substitute for research on animals:

> I think wherever there are human volunteers, I think that should always be your preferred option . . .

The general view seemed to be that if alternatives existed, these should be used to replace animals, and that the medical community has a responsibility to work on developing such alternatives.

Pifer, Shimizu and Pifer (1994) suggested that public support for using animals in medical research is on the decrease, perhaps because people no longer recognize this practice to be necessary in order to make imperative discoveries in medical research. However, the present research (and that of Knight et al. 2003, 2004) does not support this notion; at present, the UK public seem to remain firm in their support for using animals in medical research.

Participants also tended to find acceptable the use of animals for food. Participants on the whole believed that eating meat is natural for humans. However, it was frequently stated that animals should be given an adequate life beforehand, in terms of farming practices, and should be killed humanely:

> I think that's what we're designed to do, to eat meat. But I do think that farming can be done in a humane way, and should be done in a humane way. And I do believe that we can give animals a reasonable life, and you can kill them humanely . . .

Previous research revealed that people tend to hold adverse views regarding using animals for non-medical research purposes such as cosmetic and product testing (Wells and Hepper 1997). This finding was supported by the present study, with all participants expressing opposition toward the use of animals for personal decoration purposes, since these were perceived as unnecessary. Unlike using animals for medical research, there were no high value benefits associated with using animals for personal decoration, and alternatives were perceived to exist. This helps explain why attitudes toward animal use are not uni-dimensional in nature; a person can support the use of animals for medical research and food due to the perceived benefits and necessity of such practices, whilst at the same time opposing the use of animals for personal decoration or entertainment purposes such as hunting animals for sport. Indeed, most participants disapproved of animals being used for hunting. They believed that hunting for sport or entertainment purposes was unjustified and unnecessary and therefore unacceptable:

> Hunting animals for the fun of it . . . I wouldn't agree with . . .

> Why kill a fox? . . . I can't see any sense in that . . .

Recently in the UK, legislation banning hunting with dogs has been introduced, leading to controversy and public flouting of the law. Yet research has shown high levels of support for some kinds of hunting across time and countries (Heberlein and Willebrand 1998). Kellert (1980) stressed that attitudes toward hunting are dependent upon the purpose of the activity; traditional native hunting, for recreation and meat, or for recreation and sport. Approval is highest for the former and lowest for the latter (as found also by Heberlein and Willebrand 1998).

In the present study, hunting was justified by one participant who claimed that it was necessary in order to control the number of predators in the wild. It was believed that fox populations had become excessive and that hunting could help maintain the balance between species in the wild:

> It's a question of balance – I'd certainly hate to see no predators – you need predators, you need a balance.

> I've always been involved in shooting I suppose, or hunting . . . you have to make sure the predators are kept under control . . .

It seemed that if people are directly involved in certain practices, they can find justification for such. Indeed, another participant who opposed fox hunting supported fishing; a sport that they regularly participated in. Research has shown also that rural residence and ties are strongly related to pro-hunting attitudes (Decker and Mattfield 1988) and that support for hunting is woven into the social fabric of the community (Mehmood, Zhang and Armstrong 2003). The participant referred to here lived in a rural community and had strong ties with the countryside. Clearly people's views on animal use are influenced not only by purpose but also by personal involvement in animal use practices. Hence, attitudes vary for very specific types of animal use; using animals for sport will evoke different reactions depending upon the type of practice in question. This variance indicates that researchers using questionnaires to gain data on the attitudes of people need to ask very specific questions in order to generate valid and reliable findings, otherwise such subtleties will likely be lost.

Knowledge of Animal Use

The present research revealed a general lack of knowledge concerning animal use procedures and practice, and this lack of knowledge was perceived to prevent informed evaluation of animal use issues:

> I don't know enough about it [animal research] to really know how I feel about what goes on . . .

Some participants stated that they did not want to know the procedures involved in animal use; in fact, they actively avoided accessing this kind of information. Reasons for this were two-fold: it was anticipated that such information would be distressing, and it was acknowledged that such distress might likely threaten their enjoyment of certain activities such as eating meat:

> Yes, and if there are things in the paper about it [factory farming], I won't read it, it's just too upsetting . . .

Research that compared medical and non-medical students showed that medical students who have participated in research on animals were more likely to oppose animal use compared with non-medical students without such experience (Broida et al. 1993). Lack of knowledge in this area causes people to be more ambivalent about animal use compared with those who have an understanding of what animal research entails (Pifer, Shimizu and Pifer 1994). Indeed, the present study suggests that more knowledge is likely to be associated with lower levels of support for animal use, and vice versa. However, this is not always the case. For example, the participant who regularly participated in fox hunting had a clear understanding of what was involved. Perhaps this is why this particular participant held disparate beliefs concerning animal mentality, as discussed earlier. When a person benefits from an animal use practice, but recognizes that the practice has unpleasant consequences for the animals involved, this constitutes a dilemma. Justification such as rejecting the notion of animal mind minimizes any discomfort experienced due to a perceived discrepancy between one's views and one's actions. This is the basis of cognitive dissonance theory (Festinger 1957; Baumeister 1982), and may explain how others avoid inner conflict. For example, the person who is fond of animals but is involved in animal use practices on a daily basis is likely to hold beliefs that minimize discomfort experienced as a result of their involvement with animal use. They might reject the notion of animal mind, objectify certain animals, and/or stress the benefits of using animals whilst minimizing the costs.

Summary and Conclusions

The present study revealed that attitudes toward animal use are influenced by factors relating to views and beliefs concerning the type of animal involved, the purpose of animal use, and knowledge of animal use practices. Findings overlap with previous research and reflect themes identified by other research (Knight et al. 2003). This previous study described four themes: "attitudes toward animals," "knowledge of animal use procedures," "cost-benefit analysis," and "perceptions of choice." The first of these overlaps with "type of animal used," and both themes comprise components that acknowledge the influence of belief in animal mind, perceived attractiveness, and experience of animals on how people view ways in which humans use animals. Knowledge of animal use procedures, and people's avoidance of information regarding animal use, are also recognized as important by both studies. "Purpose of animal use" (in the present research) incorporates elements of both "cost-benefit analysis" and "perceptions of choice;" that is, the present research combines these themes under one heading, whilst Knight et al. (2003) described these as separate themes. We propose that the present study lends further weight to the psychological factors that underlie attitudes toward animal use, as proposed originally by Knight et al. (2003). The results show that attitudes toward animal use are not uni-dimensional, as suggested by previous research; they are rich and complex and influenced by a range of factors. The themes described in both studies effectively explain why people's views vary according to type of animal use in question, therefore adding to our understanding of this subject.

Whilst previous research has focused on participant characteristics to explain variance in attitudes toward the use of animals, the present study highlights the beliefs (i.e., psychological factors) that underlie people's views. Participant characteristics, as previously identified, do influence people's views, but individual differences such as personal experience of animals, belief in animal mind, and the perceived purpose of animal use are factors that also have impact, as shown in Figure 1. For example, if a person has experience of animals, they are likely to experience a bond with animals, and may also have witnessed animal behavior that is perceived as evidence for mentality. This may lead to opposition to animal use practices that cause distress and pain to animals. Further, this opposition may be stronger if the person is female because females more easily empathize with animals; therefore compared with males, females show higher levels of belief in animal mind (Herzog, Betchart and Pittman 1991). Belief in animal mind also, however, depends upon the type of animal being discussed, and its impact on attitudes toward animal use is therefore species-specific. Hence, people may support animal use practices involving one type of animal, but oppose the exact same practice when it involves another type of animal. Moreover, the benefits associated with animal use sometimes outweigh the impact of factors such as belief in animal mind, for example, in the case of using animals for medical research.

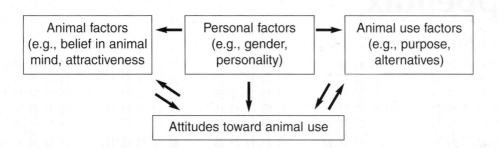

Figure 1. Beliefs that underlie attitudes toward animal use.

People's attitudes toward animal use are therefore influenced by factors relating to the individual, the animal, and the animal use. The same animal use scenario can evoke different responses from different individuals, depending upon their preconceived beliefs and perceptions regarding animals and animal use. It is also important to note that the relationship between these factors and attitudes is fluid; behavior is not always based on the rational consideration of relevant factors. A person who enjoys behaving in a certain way that is to the detriment of animals (for example, by using animals for food), may seek to rationalize or defend their behavior in order that they can continue to act in this way (for example, by arguing that human consumption of meat is natural or necessary). As a consequence, attitude and action are consonant and cognitive dissonance is resolved (Festinger 1957). Future research needs to examine this relationship further, gain quantitative evidence for the themes identified here, and compare the relative impact of these on attitudes toward animal use. Findings from research in this area can inform social scientists who are especially interested in the human-animal relationship, the nature of attitudes, and the attitude-behavior relationship.

Acknowledgements

We would like to thank the Economic and Social Research Council for their financial support (PTA-030-2003-00903 and PTA-026-27-1488), and also two anonymous reviewers for their feedback and comments.

Notes

1. From this point onward referred to simply as "animals," meaning all animals other than humans.
2. A popular criticism of qualitative methodology is that researchers might impose their views and beliefs on the interview situation and on later analysis. The authors of this article propose that by taking a participant-led approach to interviews, and ensuring that evidence is grounded in the data, subjectivity has been minimized.

References

References are available on the companion website, www.hodderplus.com/psychology.

Address for correspondence: Dr Sarah Knight, Department of Psychology, King Henry Building, King Henry I St, Portsmouth PO1 2DY, UK. E-mail: sarah.knight@port.ac.uk

Appendix

Table I Random numbers

03 47 43 73 86	39 96 47 36 61	46 98 63 71 62	33 26 16 80 45	60 11 14 10 95
97 74 24 67 62	42 81 14 57 20	42 53 32 37 32	27 07 36 07 51	24 51 79 89 73
16 76 62 27 66	56 50 26 71 07	32 90 79 78 53	13 55 38 58 59	88 97 54 14 10
12 56 85 99 26	96 96 68 27 31	05 03 72 93 15	57 12 10 14 21	88 26 49 81 76
55 59 56 35 64	38 54 82 46 22	31 62 43 09 90	06 18 44 32 53	23 83 01 30 30
16 22 77 94 39	49 54 43 54 82	17 37 93 23 78	87 35 20 96 43	84 26 34 91 64
84 42 17 53 31	57 24 55 06 88	77 04 74 47 67	21 76 33 50 25	83 92 12 06 76
63 01 63 78 59	16 95 55 67 19	98 10 50 71 75	12 86 73 58 07	44 39 52 38 79
33 21 12 34 29	78 64 56 07 82	52 42 07 44 38	15 51 00 13 42	99 66 02 79 54
57 60 86 32 44	09 47 27 96 54	49 17 46 09 62	90 52 84 77 27	08 02 73 43 28
18 18 07 92 46	44 17 16 58 09	79 83 86 16 62	06 76 50 03 10	55 23 64 05 05
26 62 38 97 75	84 16 07 44 99	83 11 46 32 24	20 14 85 88 45	10 93 72 88 71
23 42 40 64 74	82 97 77 77 81	07 45 32 14 08	32 98 94 07 72	93 85 79 10 75
52 36 28 19 95	50 92 26 11 97	00 56 76 31 38	80 22 02 53 53	86 60 42 04 53
37 85 94 35 12	83 39 50 08 30	42 34 07 96 88	54 42 06 87 98	35 85 29 48 38
70 29 17 12 13	40 33 20 38 26	13 89 51 03 74	17 76 37 13 04	07 74 21 19 30
56 62 18 37 35	96 83 50 87 75	97 12 25 93 47	70 33 24 03 54	97 77 46 44 80
99 49 57 22 77	88 42 95 45 72	16 64 36 16 00	04 43 18 66 79	94 77 24 21 90
16 08 15 04 72	33 27 14 34 90	45 59 34 68 49	12 72 07 34 45	99 27 72 95 14
31 16 93 32 43	50 27 89 87 19	20 15 37 00 49	52 85 66 60 44	38 68 88 11 80
68 34 30 13 70	55 74 30 77 40	44 22 78 84 26	04 33 46 09 52	68 07 97 06 57
74 57 25 65 76	59 29 97 68 60	71 91 38 67 54	13 58 18 24 76	15 54 55 95 52
27 42 37 86 53	48 55 90 65 72	96 57 69 36 10	96 46 92 42 45	97 60 49 04 91
00 39 68 29 61	66 37 32 20 30	77 84 57 03 29	10 45 65 04 26	11 04 96 67 24
29 94 98 94 24	68 49 69 10 82	53 75 91 93 30	34 25 20 57 27	40 48 73 51 92
16 90 82 66 59	83 62 64 11 12	67 19 00 71 74	60 47 21 29 68	02 02 37 03 31
11 27 94 75 06	06 09 19 74 66	02 94 37 34 02	76 70 90 30 86	38 45 94 30 38
35 24 10 16 20	33 32 51 26 38	79 78 45 04 91	16 92 53 56 16	02 75 50 95 98
38 23 16 86 38	42 38 97 01 50	87 75 66 81 41	40 01 74 91 62	48 51 84 08 32
31 96 25 91 47	96 44 33 49 13	34 86 82 53 91	00 52 43 48 85	27 55 26 89 62
66 67 40 67 14	64 05 71 95 86	11 05 65 09 68	76 83 20 37 90	57 16 00 11 66
14 90 84 45 11	75 73 88 05 90	52 27 41 14 86	22 98 12 22 08	07 52 74 95 80
68 05 51 18 00	33 96 02 75 19	07 60 62 93 55	59 33 82 43 90	49 37 38 44 59
20 46 78 73 90	97 51 40 14 02	04 02 33 31 08	39 54 16 49 36	47 95 93 13 30
64 19 58 97 79	15 06 15 93 20	01 90 10 75 06	40 78 78 89 62	02 67 74 17 33
05 26 93 70 60	22 35 85 15 13	92 03 51 59 77	59 56 78 06 83	52 91 05 70 74
07 97 10 88 23	09 98 42 99 64	61 71 62 99 15	06 51 29 16 93	58 05 77 09 51
68 71 86 85 85	54 87 66 47 54	73 32 08 11 12	44 95 92 63 16	29 56 24 29 48
26 99 61 65 53	58 37 78 80 70	42 10 50 67 42	32 17 55 85 74	94 44 67 16 94
14 65 52 68 75	87 59 36 22 41	26 78 63 06 55	13 08 27 01 50	15 29 39 39 43

Abridged from R. A. Fisher and F. Yates, *Statistical Tables for Biological, Agricultural and Medical Research*, (6th ed.) Longman Group UK Ltd (1974).

Table 2 Areas under the normal distribution

The left-hand column in each set of three shows the particular z-value. The centre column shows the area contained between the mean and this z-value. The right-hand column shows the area left in the whole distribution to the right of this z-value. The whole area is one unit and values shown are decimal portions of it. These are also the probabilities of finding a value within the area concerned. For percentages, multiply all area values by 100. For areas between −z and +z, double the values shown.

z	0 z	0 z	z	0 z	0 z	z	0 z	0 z
.00	.0000	.5000	.40	.1554	.3446	.80	.2881	.2119
.01	.0040	.4960	.41	.1591	.3409	.81	.2910	.2090
.02	.0080	.4920	.42	.1628	.3372	.82	.2939	.2061
.03	.0120	.4880	.43	.1664	.3336	.83	.2967	.2033
.04	.0160	.4840	.44	.1700	.3300	.84	.2995	.2005
.05	.0199	.4801	.45	.1736	.3264	.85	.3023	.1977
.06	.0239	.4761	.46	.1772	.3228	.86	.3051	.1949
.07	.0279	.4721	.47	.1808	.3192	.87	.3078	.1922
.08	.0319	.4681	.48	.1844	.3156	.88	.3106	.1894
.09	.0359	.4641	.49	.1879	.3121	.89	.3133	.1867
.10	.0398	.4602	.50	.1915	.3085	.90	.3159	.1841
.11	.0438	.4562	.51	.1950	.3050	.91	.3186	.1814
.12	.0478	.4522	.52	.1985	.3015	.92	.3212	.1788
.13	.0517	.4483	.53	.2019	.2981	.93	.3238	.1762
.14	.0557	.4443	.54	.2054	.2946	.94	.3264	.1736
.15	.0596	.4404	.55	.2088	.2912	.95	.3289	.1711
.16	.0636	.4364	.56	.2123	.2877	.96	.3315	.1685
.17	.0675	.4325	.57	.2157	.2843	.97	.3340	.1660
.18	.0714	.4286	.58	.2190	.2810	.98	.3365	.1635
.19	.0753	.4247	.59	.2224	.2776	.99	.3389	.1611
.20	.0793	.4207	.60	.2257	.2743	1.00	.3413	.1587
.21	.0832	.4168	.61	.2291	.2709	1.01	.3438	.1562
.22	.0871	.4129	.62	.2324	.2676	1.02	.3461	.1539
.23	.0910	.4090	.63	.2357	.2643	1.03	.3485	.1515
.24	.0948	.4052	.64	.2389	.2611	1.04	.3508	.1492
.25	.0987	.4013	.65	.2422	.2578	1.05	.3531	.1469
.26	.1026	.3974	.66	.2454	.2546	1.06	.3554	.1446
.27	.1064	.3969	.67	.2486	.2514	1.07	.3577	.1423
.28	.1103	.3897	.68	.2517	.2483	1.08	.3599	.1401
.29	.1141	.3859	.69	.2549	.2451	1.09	.3621	.1379
.30	.1179	.3821	.70	.2580	.2420	1.10	.3643	.1357
.31	.1217	.3783	.71	.2611	.2389	1.11	.3665	.1335
.32	.1255	.3745	.72	.2642	.2358	1.12	.3686	.1314
.33	.1293	.3707	.73	.2673	.2327	1.13	.3708	.1292
.34	.1331	.3669	.74	.2704	.2296	1.14	.3729	.1271
.35	.1368	.3632	.75	.2734	.2266	1.15	.3749	.1251
.36	.1406	.3594	.76	.2764	.2236	1.16	.3770	.1230
.37	.1443	.3557	.77	.2794	.2206	1.17	.3790	.1210
.38	.1480	.3520	.78	.2823	.2177	1.18	.3810	.1190
.39	.1517	.3483	.79	.2852	.2148	1.19	.3830	.1170

Table 2 Continued

z	0 z	0 z		z	0 z	0 z		z	0 z	0 z
1.20	.3849	.1151		1.60	.4452	.0548		2.00	.4772	.0228
1.21	.3869	.1131		1.61	.4463	.0537		2.01	.4778	.0222
1.22	.3888	.1112		1.62	.4474	.0526		2.02	.4783	.0217
1.23	.3907	.1093		1.63	.4484	.0516		2.03	.4788	.0212
1.24	.3925	.1075		1.64	.4495	.0505		2.04	.4793	.0207
1.25	.3944	.1056		1.65	.4505	.0495		2.05	.4798	.0202
1.26	.3962	.1038		1.66	.4515	.0485		2.06	.4803	.0197
1.27	.3980	.1020		1.67	.4525	.0475		2.07	.4808	.0192
1.28	.3997	.1003		1.68	.4535	.0465		2.08	.4812	.0188
1.29	.4015	.0985		1.69	.4545	.0455		2.09	.4817	.0183
1.30	.4032	.0968		1.70	.4554	.0446		2.10	.4821	.0179
1.31	.4049	.0951		1.71	.4564	.0436		2.11	.4826	.0174
1.32	.4066	.0934		1.72	.4573	.0427		2.12	.4830	.0170
1.33	.4082	.0918		1.73	.4582	.0418		2.13	.4834	.0166
1.34	.4099	.0901		1.74	.4591	.0409		2.14	.4838	.0162
1.35	.4115	.0885		1.75	.4599	.0401		2.15	.4842	.0158
1.36	.4131	.0869		1.76	.4608	.0392		2.16	.4846	.0154
1.37	.4147	.0853		1.77	.4616	.0384		2.17	.4850	.0150
1.38	.4162	.0838		1.78	.4625	.0375		2.18	.4854	.0146
1.39	.4177	.0823		1.79	.4633	.0367		2.19	.4857	.0143
1.40	.4192	.0808		1.80	.4641	.0359		2.20	.4861	.0139
1.41	.4207	.0793		1.81	.4649	.0351		2.21	.4864	.0136
1.42	.4222	.0778		1.82	.4656	.0344		2.22	.4868	.0132
1.43	.4236	.0764		1.83	.4664	.0336		2.23	.4871	.0129
1.44	.4251	.0749		1.84	.4671	.0329		2.24	.4875	.0125
1.45	.4265	.0735		1.85	.4678	.0322		2.25	.4878	.0122
1.46	.4279	.0721		1.86	.4686	.0314		2.26	.4881	.0119
1.47	.4292	.0708		1.87	.4693	.0307		2.27	.4884	.0116
1.48	.4306	.0694		1.88	.4699	.0301		2.28	.4887	.0113
1.49	.4319	.0681		1.89	.4706	.0294		2.29	.4890	.0110
1.50	.4332	.0668		1.90	.4713	.0287		2.30	.4893	.0107
1.51	.4345	.0655		1.91	.4719	.0281		2.31	.4896	.0104
1.52	.4357	.0643		1.92	.4726	.0274		2.32	.4898	.0102
1.53	.4370	.0630		1.93	.4732	.0268		2.33	.4901	.0099
1.54	.4382	.0618		1.94	.4738	.0262		2.34	.4904	.0096
1.55	.4394	.0606		1.95	.4744	.0256		2.35	.4906	.0094
1.56	.4406	.0594		1.96	.4750	.0250		2.36	.4909	.0091
1.57	.4418	.0582		1.97	.4756	.0244		2.37	.4911	.0089
1.58	.4429	.0571		1.98	.4761	.0239		2.38	.4913	.0087
1.59	.4441	.0559		1.99	.4767	.0233		2.39	.4916	.0084

Table 2 Continued

z	0 z	0 z		z	0 z	0 z		z	0 z	0 z
2.40	.4918	.0082		2.72	.4967	.0033		3.04	.4988	.0012
2.41	.4920	.0080		2.73	.4968	.0032		3.05	.4989	.0011
2.42	.4922	.0078		2.74	.4969	.0031		3.06	.4989	.0011
2.43	.4925	.0075		2.75	.4970	.0030		3.07	.4989	.0011
2.44	.4927	.0073		2.76	.4971	.0029		3.08	.4990	.0010
2.45	.4929	.0017		2.77	.4972	.0028		3.09	.4990	.0010
2.46	.4931	.0069		2.78	.4973	.0027		3.10	.4990	.0010
2.47	.4932	.0068		2.79	.4974	.0026		3.11	.4991	.0009
2.48	.4934	.0066		2.80	.4974	.0026		3.12	.4991	.0009
2.49	.4936	.0064		2.81	.4975	.0025		3.13	.4991	.0009
2.50	.4938	.0062		2.82	.4976	.0024		3.14	.4992	.0008
2.51	.4940	.0060		2.83	.4977	.0023		3.15	.4992	.0008
2.52	.4941	.0059		2.84	.4977	.0023		3.16	.4992	.0008
2.53	.4943	.0057		2.85	.4978	.0022		3.17	.4992	.0008
2.54	.4945	.0055		2.86	.4979	.0021		3.18	.4993	.0007
2.55	.4946	.0054		2.87	.4979	.0021		3.19	.4993	.0007
2.56	.4948	.0052		2.88	.4980	.0020		3.20	.4993	.0007
2.57	.4949	.0051		2.89	.4981	.0019		3.21	.4993	.0007
2.58	.4951	.0049		2.90	.4981	.0019		3.22	.4994	.0006
2.59	.4952	.0048		2.91	.4982	.0018		3.23	.4994	.0006
2.60	.4953	.0047		2.92	.4982	.0018		3.24	.4994	.0006
2.61	.4955	.0045		2.93	.4983	.0017		3.25	.4994	.0006
2.62	.4956	.0044		2.94	.4984	.0016		3.30	.4995	.0005
2.63	.4957	.0043		2.95	.4984	.0016		3.35	.4996	.0004
2.64	.4959	.0041		2.96	.4985	.0015		3.40	.4997	.0003
2.65	.4960	.0040		2.97	.4985	.0015		3.45	.4997	.0003
2.66	.4961	.0039		2.98	.4986	.0014		3.50	.4998	.0002
2.67	.4962	.0038		2.99	.4986	.0014		3.60	.4998	.0002
2.68	.4963	.0037		3.00	.4987	.0013		3.70	.4999	.0001
2.69	.4964	.0036		3.01	.4987	.0013		3.80	.4999	.0001
2.70	.4965	.0035		3.02	.4987	.0013		3.90	.49995	.00005
2.71	.4966	.0034		3.03	.4988	.0012		4.00	.49997	.00003

SOURCE: R. P. Runyon and A. Haber, *Fundamentals of Behavioral Statistics*, 3rd Ed. Reading, Mass.: McGraw-Hill, Inc. (1976) Artwork from R. B. McCall. Fundamental Statistics for Psychology, Second Edition, New York: Harcourt Brace Jovanovich, Inc. (1975).

Table 3 Critical values of t

	Level of significance for a one-tailed test			
	.05	.025	.01	.005
	Level of significance for a two-tailed test			
	.10	.05	.02	.01
Degrees of freedom				
1	6.314	12.706	31.821	63.657
2	2.920	4.303	6.965	9.925
3	2.353	3.182	4.541	5.841
4	2.132	2.776	3.747	4.604
5	2.015	2.571	3.365	4.032
6	1.943	2.447	3.143	3.707
7	1.895	2.365	2.998	3.499
8	1.860	2.306	2.896	3.355
9	1.833	2.262	2.821	3.250
10	1.812	2.228	2.764	3.169
11	1.796	2.201	2.718	3.106
12	1.782	2.179	2.681	3.055
13	1.771	2.160	2.650	3.012
14	1.761	2.145	2.624	2.977
15	1.753	2.131	2.602	2.947
16	1.746	2.120	2.583	2.921
17	1.740	2.110	2.567	2.898
18	1.734	2.101	2.552	2.878
19	1.729	2.093	2.539	2.861
20	1.725	2.086	2.528	2.845
21	1.721	2.080	2.518	2.831
22	1.717	2.074	2.508	2.819
23	1.714	2.069	2.500	2.807
24	1.711	2.064	2.492	2.797
25	1.708	2.060	2.485	2.787
26	1.706	2.056	2.479	2.779
27	1.703	2.052	2.473	2.771
28	1.701	2.048	2.467	2.763
29	1.699	2.045	2.462	2.756
30	1.697	2.042	2.457	2.750
40	1.684	2.021	2.423	2.704
60	1.671	2.000	2.390	2.660
120	1.658	1.980	2.358	2.617
∞	1.645	1.960	2.326	2.576

Calculated t must EQUAL or EXCEED the table (critical) value for significance at the level shown.
SOURCE: Abridged from R. A. Fisher and F. Yates, *Statistical Tables for Biological, Agricultural and Medical Research*, (6th ed.) Longman Group UK Ltd (1974).

Table 4 Power as a function of δ and significance level (α)

δ	.1	.05	.02	.01
		α for two-tailed test		
1.00	.26	.17	.09	.06
1.10	.29	.20	.11	.07
1.20	.33	.22	.13	.08
1.30	.37	.26	.15	.10
1.40	.40	.29	.18	.12
1.50	.44	.32	.20	.14
1.60	.48	.36	.23	.17
1.70	.52	.40	.27	.19
1.80	.56	.44	.30	.22
1.90	.60	.48	.34	.25
2.00	.64	.52	.37	.28
2.10	.68	.56	.41	.32
2.20	.71	.60	.45	.35
2.30	.74	.63	.49	.39
2.40	.78	.67	.53	.43
2.50	.80	.71	.57	.47
2.60	.83	.74	.61	.51
2.70	.85	.77	.65	.55
2.80	.88	.80	.68	.59
2.90	.90	.83	.72	.63
3.00	.91	.85	.75	.66
3.10	.93	.87	.78	.70
3.20	.94	.89	.81	.73
3.30	.95	.91	.84	.77
3.40	.96	.93	.86	.80
3.50	.97	.94	.88	.82
3.60	.98	.95	.90	.85
3.70	.98	.96	.92	.87
3.80	.98	.97	.93	.89
3.90	.99	.97	.94	.91
4.00	.99	.98	.95	.92
4.10	.99	.98	.96	.94
4.20	–	.99	.97	.95
4.30	–	.99	.98	.96
4.40	–	.99	.98	.97
4.50	–	.99	.99	.97
4.60	–	–	.99	.98
4.70	–	–	.99	.98
4.80	–	–	.99	.99
4.90	–	–	–	.99
5.00	–	–	–	.99

Taken from Howell, D. C. (1992) *Statistical Methods for Psychology*, 3rd edn. PWS-Kent, p. 644.

Table 5 Critical values of T in the Wilcoxon Signed Ranks test

	Levels of significance for a one-tailed test			
	.05	.025	.01	.001
	Levels of significance for a two-tailed test			
Sample size	.1	.05	.02	.002
$N = 5$	$T \leqslant 0$			
6	2	0		
7	3	2	0	
8	5	3	1	
9	8	5	3	
10	11	8	5	0
11	13	10	7	1
12	17	13	9	2
13	21	17	12	4
14	25	21	15	6
15	30	25	19	8
16	35	29	23	11
17	41	34	27	14
18	47	40	32	18
19	53	46	37	21
20	60	52	43	26
21	67	58	49	30
22	75	65	55	35
23	83	73	62	40
24	91	81	69	45
25	100	89	76	51
26	110	98	84	58
27	119	107	92	64
28	130	116	101	71
29	141	125	111	78
30	151	137	120	86
31	163	147	130	94
32	175	159	140	103
33	187	170	151	112

Calculated T must be equal to or less than the table (critical) value for significance at the level shown.
SOURCE: Adapted from R. Meddis, *Statistical Handbook for Non-Statisticians*, McGraw-Hill, London (1975).

Table 6a Critical values of U for a one-tailed test at .005; two-tailed test at .01* (Mann-Whitney)

n_2 \ n_1	1	2	3	4	5	6	7	8	9	10	11	12	13	14	15	16	17	18	19	20
1	—	—	—	—	—	—	—	—	—	—	—	—	—	—	—	—	—	—	—	—
2	—	—	—	—	—	—	—	—	—	—	—	—	—	—	—	—	—	—	0	0
3	—	—	—	—	—	—	0	0	0	0	0	1	1	1	2	2	2	2	3	3
4	—	—	—	—	0	0	0	1	1	2	2	3	3	4	5	5	6	6	7	8
5	—	—	—	0	0	1	1	2	3	4	5	6	7	7	8	9	10	11	12	13
6	—	—	—	0	1	2	3	4	5	6	7	9	10	11	12	13	15	16	17	18
7	—	—	0	0	1	3	4	6	7	9	10	12	13	15	16	18	19	21	22	24
8	—	—	0	1	2	4	6	7	9	11	13	15	17	18	20	22	24	26	28	30
9	—	—	0	1	3	5	7	9	11	13	16	18	20	22	24	27	29	31	33	36
10	—	—	0	2	4	6	9	11	13	16	18	21	24	26	29	31	34	37	39	42
11	—	—	0	2	5	7	10	13	16	18	21	24	27	30	33	36	39	42	45	48
12	—	—	1	3	6	9	12	15	18	21	24	27	31	34	37	41	44	47	51	54
13	—	—	1	3	7	10	13	17	20	24	27	31	34	38	42	45	49	53	56	60
14	—	—	1	4	7	11	15	18	22	26	30	34	38	42	46	50	54	58	63	67
15	—	—	2	5	8	12	16	20	24	29	33	37	42	46	51	55	60	64	69	73
16	—	—	2	5	9	13	18	22	27	31	36	41	45	50	55	60	65	70	74	79
17	—	—	2	6	10	15	19	24	29	34	39	44	49	54	60	65	70	75	81	86
18	—	—	2	6	11	16	21	26	31	37	42	47	53	58	64	70	75	81	87	92
19	—	0	3	7	12	17	22	28	33	39	45	51	56	63	69	74	81	87	93	99
20	—	0	3	8	13	18	24	30	36	42	48	54	60	67	73	79	86	92	99	105

* Dashes in the body of the table indicate that no decision is possible at the stated level of significance.

For any n_1 and n_2 the observed value of U is significant at a given level of significance if it is equal to or less than the critical values shown.

SOURCE: R. Runyon and A. Haber (1976) *Fundamentals of Behavioural Statistics* (3rd ed.) Reading, Mass.: McGraw Hill, Inc.

Table 6b Critical values of U for a one-tailed test at .01; two-tailed test at .02* (Mann-Whitney)

n_2 \ n_1	1	2	3	4	5	6	7	8	9	10	11	12	13	14	15	16	17	18	19	20
1	—	—	—	—	—	—	—	—	—	—	—	—	—	—	—	—	—	—	—	—
2	—	—	—	—	—	—	—	—	—	—	—	—	0	0	0	0	0	0	1	1
3	—	—	—	—	—	—	0	0	1	1	1	2	2	2	3	3	4	4	4	5
4	—	—	—	—	0	1	1	2	3	3	4	5	5	6	7	7	8	9	9	10
5	—	—	—	0	1	2	3	4	5	6	7	8	9	10	11	12	13	14	15	16
6	—	—	—	1	2	3	4	6	7	8	9	11	12	13	15	16	18	19	20	22
7	—	—	0	1	3	4	6	7	9	11	12	14	16	17	19	21	23	24	26	28
8	—	—	0	2	4	6	7	9	11	13	15	17	20	22	24	26	28	30	32	34
9	—	—	1	3	5	7	9	11	14	16	18	21	23	26	28	31	33	36	38	40
10	—	—	1	3	6	8	11	13	16	19	22	24	27	30	33	36	38	41	44	47
11	—	—	1	4	7	9	12	15	18	22	25	28	31	34	37	41	44	47	50	53
12	—	—	2	5	8	11	14	17	21	24	28	31	35	38	42	46	49	53	56	60
13	—	0	2	5	9	12	16	20	23	27	31	35	39	43	47	51	55	59	63	67
14	—	0	2	6	10	13	17	22	26	30	34	38	43	47	51	56	60	65	69	73
15	—	0	3	7	11	15	19	24	28	33	37	42	47	51	56	61	66	70	75	80
16	—	0	3	7	12	16	21	26	31	36	41	46	51	56	61	66	71	76	82	87
17	—	0	4	8	13	18	23	28	33	38	44	49	55	60	66	71	77	82	88	93
18	—	0	4	9	14	19	24	30	36	41	47	53	59	65	70	76	82	88	94	100
19	—	1	4	9	15	20	26	32	38	44	50	56	63	69	75	82	88	94	101	107
20	—	1	5	10	16	22	28	34	40	47	53	60	67	73	80	87	93	100	107	114

* Dashes in the body of the table indicate that no decision is possible at the stated level of significance.

For any n_1 and n_2 the observed value of U is significant at a given level of significance if it is equal to or less than the critical values shown.

SOURCE: R. Runyon and A. Haber (1976) *Fundamentals of Behavioural Statistics* (3rd ed.) Reading, Mass.: McGraw Hill, Inc.

Table 6c Critical values of U for a one-tailed test at .025; two-tailed test at .05* (Mann-Whitney)

n_1

n_2	1	2	3	4	5	6	7	8	9	10	11	12	13	14	15	16	17	18	19	20
1	—	—	—	—	—	—	—	—	—	—	—	—	—	—	—	—	—	—	—	—
2	—	—	—	—	—	—	—	0	0	0	0	1	1	1	1	1	2	2	2	2
3	—	—	—	—	0	1	1	2	2	3	3	4	4	5	5	6	6	7	7	8
4	—	—	—	0	1	2	3	4	4	5	6	7	8	9	10	11	11	12	13	13
5	—	—	0	1	2	3	5	6	7	8	9	11	12	13	14	15	17	18	19	20
6	—	—	1	2	3	5	6	8	10	11	13	14	16	17	19	21	22	24	25	27
7	—	—	1	3	5	6	8	10	12	14	16	18	20	22	24	26	28	30	32	34
8	—	0	2	4	6	8	10	13	15	17	19	22	24	26	29	31	34	36	38	41
9	—	0	2	4	7	10	12	15	17	20	23	26	28	31	34	37	39	42	45	48
10	—	0	3	5	8	11	14	17	20	23	26	29	33	36	39	42	45	48	52	55
11	—	0	3	6	9	13	16	19	23	26	30	33	37	40	44	47	51	55	58	62
12	—	1	4	7	11	14	18	22	26	29	33	37	41	45	49	53	57	61	65	69
13	—	1	4	8	12	16	20	24	28	33	37	41	45	50	54	59	63	67	72	76
14	—	1	5	9	13	17	22	26	31	36	40	45	50	55	59	64	67	74	78	83
15	—	1	5	10	14	19	24	29	34	39	44	49	54	59	64	70	75	80	85	90
16	—	1	6	11	15	21	26	31	37	42	47	53	59	64	70	75	81	86	92	98
17	—	2	6	11	17	22	28	34	39	45	51	57	63	67	75	81	87	93	99	105
18	—	2	7	12	18	24	30	36	42	48	55	61	67	74	80	86	93	99	106	112
19	—	2	7	13	19	25	32	38	45	52	58	65	72	78	85	92	99	106	113	119
20	—	2	8	13	20	27	34	41	48	55	62	69	76	83	90	98	105	112	119	127

* Dashes in the body of the table indicate that no decision is possible at the stated level of significance.

For any n_1 and n_2, the observed value of U is significant at a given level of significance if it is equal to or less than the critical values shown.

SOURCE: R. Runyon and A. Haber (1976) *Fundamentals of Behavioural Statistics* (3rd ed.) Reading, Mass.: McGraw Hill, Inc.

Table 6d Critical values of U for a one-tailed test at .05; two-tailed test at .10* (Mann-Whitney)

n_2 \ n_1	1	2	3	4	5	6	7	8	9	10	11	12	13	14	15	16	17	18	19	20
1	—	—	—	—	—	—	—	—	—	—	—	—	—	—	—	—	—	—	—	0
2	—	—	—	—	0	0	0	1	1	1	1	2	2	2	3	3	3	4	4	4
3	—	—	0	0	1	2	2	3	3	4	5	5	6	7	7	8	9	9	10	11
4	—	—	0	1	2	3	4	5	6	7	8	9	10	11	12	14	15	16	17	18
5	—	0	1	2	4	5	6	8	9	11	12	13	15	16	18	19	20	22	23	25
6	—	0	2	3	5	7	8	10	12	14	16	17	19	21	23	25	26	28	30	32
7	—	0	2	4	6	8	11	13	15	17	19	21	24	26	28	30	33	35	37	39
8	—	1	3	5	8	10	13	15	18	20	23	26	28	31	33	36	39	41	44	47
9	—	1	3	6	9	12	15	18	21	24	27	30	33	36	39	42	45	48	51	54
10	—	1	4	7	11	14	17	20	24	27	31	34	37	41	44	48	51	55	58	62
11	—	1	5	8	12	16	19	23	27	31	34	38	42	46	50	54	57	61	65	69
12	—	2	5	9	13	17	21	26	30	34	38	42	47	51	55	60	64	68	72	77
13	—	2	6	10	15	19	24	28	33	37	42	47	51	56	61	65	70	75	80	84
14	—	2	7	11	16	21	26	31	36	41	46	51	56	61	66	71	77	82	87	92
15	—	3	7	12	18	23	28	33	39	44	50	55	61	66	72	77	83	88	94	100
16	—	3	8	14	19	25	30	36	42	48	54	60	65	71	77	83	89	95	101	107
17	—	3	9	15	20	26	33	39	45	51	57	64	70	77	83	89	96	102	109	115
18	—	4	9	16	22	28	35	41	48	55	61	68	75	82	88	95	102	109	116	123
19	0	4	10	17	23	30	37	44	51	58	65	72	80	87	94	101	109	116	123	130
20	0	4	11	18	25	32	39	47	54	62	69	77	84	92	100	107	115	123	130	138

* Dashes in the body of the table indicate that no decision is possible at the stated level of significance.

For any n_1 and n_2 the observed value of U is significant at a given level of significance if it is equal to or less than the critical values shown.

SOURCE: R. Runyon and A. Haber (1976) Fundamentals of Behavioural Statistics (3rd ed.) Reading, Mass.: McGraw Hill, Inc.

Table 7 Critical values in the Binomial Sign Test

Level of significance for a one-tailed test

Level of significance for a two-tailed test

N	.05 / .10	.025 / .05	.01 / .02	.005 / .01	.0005 / .001
5	0	—	—	—	—
6	0	0	—	—	—
7	0	0	0	—	—
8	1	0	0	0	—
9	1	1	0	0	—
10	1	1	0	0	—
11	2	1	1	0	0
12	2	2	1	1	0
13	3	2	1	1	0
14	3	2	2	1	0
15	3	3	2	2	1
16	4	3	2	2	1
17	4	4	3	2	1
18	5	4	3	3	1
19	5	4	4	3	2
20	5	5	4	3	2
25	7	7	6	5	4
30	10	9	8	7	5
35	12	11	10	9	7

Calculated S must be equal to or less than the table (critical) value for significance at the level shown.
SOURCE: F. Clegg, *Simple Statistics*, Cambridge University Press, 1982.

Table 8 Critical values of χ^2

	Level of significance for a one-tailed test					
	.10	.05	.025	.01	.005	.005
	Level of significance for a two-tailed test					
	.20	.10	.05	.02	.01	.001
df						
1	1.64	2.71	3.84	5.41	6.64	10.83
2	3.22	4.60	5.99	7.82	9.21	13.82
3	4.64	6.25	7.82	9.84	11.34	16.27
4	5.99	7.78	9.49	11.67	13.28	18.46
5	7.29	9.24	11.07	13.39	15.09	20.52
6	8.56	10.64	12.59	15.03	16.81	22.46
7	9.80	12.02	14.07	16.62	18.48	24.32
8	11.03	13.36	15.51	18.17	20.09	26.12
9	12.24	14.68	16.92	19.68	21.67	27.88
10	13.44	15.99	18.31	21.16	23.21	29.59
11	14.63	17.28	19.68	22.62	24.72	31.26
12	15.81	18.55	21.03	24.05	26.22	32.91
13	16.98	19.81	22.36	25.47	27.69	34.53
14	18.15	21.06	23.68	26.87	29.14	36.12
15	19.31	22.31	25.00	28.26	30.58	37.70
16	20.46	23.54	26.30	29.63	32.00	39.29
17	21.62	24.77	27.59	31.00	33.41	40.75
18	22.76	25.99	28.87	32.35	34.80	42.31
19	23.90	27.20	30.14	33.69	36.19	43.82
20	25.04	28.41	31.41	35.02	37.57	45.32
21	26.17	29.62	32.67	36.34	38.93	46.80
22	27.30	30.81	33.92	37.66	40.29	48.27
23	28.43	32.01	35.17	38.97	41.64	49.73
24	29.55	33.20	36.42	40.27	42.98	51.18
25	30.68	34.38	37.65	41.57	44.31	52.62
26	31.80	35.56	38.88	42.86	45.64	54.05
27	32.91	36.74	40.11	44.14	46.96	55.48
28	34.03	37.92	41.34	45.42	48.28	56.89
29	35.14	39.09	42.69	49.69	49.59	58.30
30	36.25	40.26	43.77	47.96	50.89	59.70
32	38.47	42.59	46.19	50.49	53.49	62.49
34	40.68	44.90	48.60	53.00	56.06	65.25
36	42.88	47.21	51.00	55.49	58.62	67.99
38	45.08	49.51	53.38	57.97	61.16	70.70
40	47.27	51.81	55.76	60.44	63.69	73.40
44	51.64	56.37	60.48	65.34	68.71	78.75
48	55.99	60.91	65.17	70.20	73.68	84.04
52	60.33	65.42	69.83	75.02	78.62	89.27
56	64.66	69.92	74.47	79.82	83.51	94.46
60	68.97	74.40	79.08	84.58	88.38	99.61

Calculated value of χ^2 must be equal to or exceed the table (critical) values for significance at the level shown.
Abridged from R.A. Fisher and F. Yates, *Statistical Tables for Biological, Agricultural and Medical Research*, (6th ed.) Longman Group UK Ltd (1974).

Table 9 Critical values of Pearson's r

Level of significance for a one-tailed test				
	.05	.025	.005	.0005
Level of significance for a two-tailed test				
	.10	.05	.01	.001
df $(N-2)$				
2	.9000	.9500	.9900	.9999
3	.805	.878	.9587	.9911
4	.729	.811	.9172	.9741
5	.669	.754	.875	.9509
6	.621	.707	.834	.9241
7	.582	.666	.798	.898
8	.549	.632	.765	.872
9	.521	.602	.735	.847
10	.497	.576	.708	.823
11	.476	.553	.684	.801
12	.475	.532	.661	.780
13	.441	.514	.641	.760
14	.426	.497	.623	.742
15	.412	.482	.606	.725
16	.400	.468	.590	.708
17	.389	.456	.575	.693
18	.378	.444	.561	.679
19	.369	.433	.549	.665
20	.360	.423	.537	.652
25	.323	.381	.487	.597
30	.296	.349	.449	.554
35	.275	.325	.418	.519
40	.257	.304	.393	.490
45	.243	.288	.372	.465
50	.231	.273	.354	.443
60	.211	.250	.325	.408
70	.195	.232	.302	.380
80	.183	.217	.283	.357
90	.173	.205	.267	.338
100	.164	.195	.254	.321

Calculated r must equal or exceed the table (critical) value for significance at the level shown.

SOURCE: F. C. Powell, *Cambridge Mathematical and Statistical Tables*, Cambridge University Press (1976).

Table 10 Critical values of Spearman's r_s ρ

	Level of significance for a one-tailed test			
	.05	.025	.01	.005
Level of significance for a two-tailed test				
	.10	.05	.02	.01
$N = 4$	1.000			
5	.900	1.000	1.000	
6	.829	.886	.943	1.000
7	.714	.786	.893	.929
8	.643	.738	.833	.881
9	.600	.700	.783	.833
10	.564	.648	.745	.794
11	.536	.618	.709	.755
12	.503	.587	.671	.727
13	.484	.560	.648	.703
14	.464	.538	.622	.675
15	.443	.521	.604	.654
16	.429	.503	.582	.635
17	.414	.485	.566	.615
18	.401	.472	.550	.600
19	.391	.460	.535	.584
20	.380	.447	.520	.570
21	.370	.435	.508	.556
22	.361	.425	.496	.544
23	.353	.415	.486	.532
24	.344	.406	.476	.521
25	.337	.398	.466	.511
26	.331	.390	.457	.501
27	.324	.382	.448	.491
28	.317	.375	.440	.483
29	.312	.368	.433	.475
30	.306	.362	.425	.467

Calculated r_s must equal or exceed the table (critical) value for significance at the level shown.

For $n > 30$, the significance of r_s can be tested by using the formula:

$$t = r_s \sqrt{\frac{n - 2}{1 - r_s^2}} \qquad df = n - 2$$

and checking the value of t in Table 3.

SOURCE: J. H. Zhar, *Significance testing of the Spearman Rank Correlation Coefficient*, Journal of the American Statistical Association, 67, 578–80.

Table 11 Critical values of F at the 5% level of significance

Degrees of freedom for the numerator v^1

v^2	1	2	3	4	5	6	7	8	9	10	12	15	20	24	30	40	60	120	∞
1	161.4	199.5	215.7	224.6	230.2	234.0	236.8	238.9	240.5	241.9	243.9	245.9	248.0	249.1	250.1	251.1	252.2	253.3	254.3
2	18.51	19.00	19.16	19.25	19.30	19.33	19.35	19.37	19.38	19.40	19.41	19.43	19.45	19.45	19.46	19.47	19.48	19.49	19.50
3	10.13	9.55	9.28	9.12	9.01	8.94	8.89	8.85	8.81	8.79	8.74	8.70	8.66	8.64	8.62	8.59	8.57	8.55	8.53
4	7.71	6.94	6.59	6.39	6.26	6.16	6.09	6.04	6.00	5.96	5.91	5.86	5.80	5.77	5.75	5.72	5.69	5.66	5.63
5	6.61	5.79	5.41	5.19	5.05	4.95	4.88	4.82	4.77	4.74	4.68	4.62	4.56	4.53	4.50	4.46	4.43	4.40	4.36
6	5.99	5.14	4.76	4.53	4.39	4.28	4.21	4.15	4.10	4.06	4.00	3.94	3.87	3.84	3.81	3.77	3.74	3.70	3.67
7	5.59	4.74	4.35	4.12	3.97	3.87	3.79	3.73	3.68	3.64	3.57	3.51	3.44	3.41	3.38	3.34	3.30	3.27	3.23
8	5.32	4.46	4.07	3.84	3.69	3.58	3.50	3.44	3.39	3.35	3.28	3.22	3.15	3.12	3.08	3.04	3.01	2.97	2.93
9	5.12	4.26	3.86	3.63	3.48	3.37	3.29	3.23	3.18	3.14	3.07	3.01	2.94	2.90	2.86	2.83	2.79	2.75	2.71
10	4.96	4.10	3.71	3.48	3.33	3.22	3.14	3.07	3.02	2.98	2.91	2.85	2.77	2.74	2.70	2.66	2.62	2.58	2.54
11	4.84	3.98	3.59	3.36	3.20	3.09	3.01	2.95	2.90	2.85	2.79	2.72	2.65	2.61	2.57	2.53	2.49	2.45	2.40
12	4.75	3.89	3.49	3.26	3.11	3.00	2.91	2.85	2.80	2.75	2.69	2.62	2.54	2.51	2.47	2.43	2.38	2.34	2.30
13	4.67	3.81	3.41	3.18	3.03	2.92	2.83	2.77	2.71	2.67	2.60	2.53	2.46	2.42	2.38	2.34	2.30	2.25	2.21
14	4.60	3.74	3.34	3.11	2.96	2.85	2.76	2.70	2.65	2.60	2.53	2.46	2.39	2.35	2.31	2.27	2.22	2.18	2.13
15	4.54	3.68	3.29	3.06	2.90	2.79	2.71	2.64	2.59	2.54	2.48	2.40	2.33	2.29	2.25	2.20	2.16	2.11	2.07
16	4.49	3.63	3.24	3.01	2.85	2.74	2.66	2.59	2.54	2.49	2.42	2.35	2.28	2.24	2.19	2.15	2.11	2.06	2.01
17	4.45	3.59	3.20	2.96	2.81	2.70	2.61	2.55	2.49	2.45	2.38	2.31	2.23	2.19	2.15	2.10	2.06	2.01	1.96
18	4.41	3.55	3.16	2.93	2.77	2.66	2.58	2.51	2.46	2.41	2.34	2.27	2.19	2.15	2.11	2.06	2.02	1.97	1.92
19	4.38	3.52	3.13	2.90	2.74	2.63	2.54	2.48	2.42	2.38	2.31	2.23	2.16	2.11	2.07	2.03	1.98	1.93	1.88
20	4.35	3.49	3.10	2.87	2.71	2.60	2.51	2.45	2.39	2.35	2.28	2.20	2.12	2.08	2.04	1.99	1.95	1.90	1.84
21	4.32	3.47	3.07	2.84	2.68	2.57	2.49	2.42	2.37	2.32	2.25	2.18	2.10	2.05	2.01	1.96	1.92	1.87	1.81
22	4.30	3.44	3.05	2.82	2.66	2.55	2.46	2.40	2.34	2.30	2.23	2.15	2.07	2.03	1.98	1.94	1.89	1.84	1.78
23	4.28	3.42	3.03	2.80	2.64	2.53	2.44	2.37	2.32	2.27	2.20	2.13	2.05	2.01	1.96	1.91	1.86	1.81	1.76
24	4.26	3.40	3.01	2.78	2.62	2.51	2.42	2.36	2.30	2.25	2.18	2.11	2.03	1.98	1.94	1.89	1.84	1.79	1.73
25	4.24	3.39	2.99	2.76	2.60	2.49	2.40	2.34	2.28	2.24	2.16	2.09	2.01	1.96	1.92	1.87	1.82	1.77	1.71
26	4.23	3.37	2.98	2.74	2.59	2.47	2.39	2.32	2.27	2.22	2.15	2.07	1.99	1.95	1.90	1.85	1.80	1.75	1.69
27	4.21	3.35	2.96	2.73	2.57	2.46	2.37	2.31	2.25	2.20	2.13	2.06	1.97	1.93	1.88	1.84	1.79	1.73	1.67
28	4.20	3.34	2.95	2.71	2.56	2.45	2.36	2.29	2.24	2.19	2.12	2.04	1.96	1.91	1.87	1.82	1.77	1.71	1.65
29	4.18	3.33	2.93	2.70	2.55	2.43	2.35	2.28	2.22	2.18	2.10	2.03	1.94	1.90	1.85	1.81	1.75	1.70	1.64
30	4.17	3.32	2.92	2.69	2.53	2.42	2.33	2.27	2.21	2.16	2.09	2.01	1.93	1.89	1.84	1.79	1.74	1.68	1.62
40	4.08	3.23	2.84	2.61	2.45	2.34	2.25	2.18	2.12	2.08	2.00	1.92	1.84	1.79	1.74	1.69	1.64	1.58	1.51
60	4.00	3.15	2.76	2.53	2.37	2.25	2.17	2.10	2.04	1.99	1.92	1.84	1.75	1.70	1.65	1.59	1.53	1.47	1.39
120	3.92	3.07	2.68	2.45	2.29	2.17	2.09	2.02	1.96	1.91	1.83	1.75	1.66	1.61	1.55	1.50	1.43	1.35	1.25
∞	3.84	3.00	2.60	2.37	2.21	2.10	2.01	1.94	1.88	1.83	1.75	1.67	1.57	1.52	1.46	1.39	1.32	1.22	1.00

Degrees of freedom for the denominator v^2

Values of F that equal or exceed the tabled value are significant at or beyond the 5% level.

SOURCE: Radford, J. & Govier, E. Textbook of Psychology (2nd ed.) Routledge (Abridged from Table 18 of The Biometrika Tables for Statisticians, Vol. I, edited by Pearson, E. S. and Hartley, H. O. with the permission of E. S. Pearson and the trustees of Biometrika.)

Table 12 Critical values of F at the 1% level of significance

	Degrees of freedom for the numerator v^1																		
	1	2	3	4	5	6	7	8	9	10	12	15	20	24	30	40	60	120	∞
1	4052	4999.5	5403	5625	5764	5859	5928	5982	6022	6056	6106	6157	6209	6235	6261	6287	6313	6339	6366
2	98.50	99.00	99.17	99.25	99.30	99.33	99.36	99.37	99.39	99.40	99.42	99.43	99.45	99.46	99.47	99.47	99.48	99.49	99.50
3	34.12	30.82	29.46	28.71	28.24	27.91	27.67	27.49	27.35	27.23	27.05	26.87	26.69	26.60	26.50	26.41	26.32	26.22	26.13
4	21.20	18.00	16.69	15.98	15.52	15.21	14.98	14.80	14.66	14.55	14.37	14.20	14.02	13.93	13.84	13.75	13.65	13.56	13.46
5	16.26	13.27	12.06	11.39	10.97	10.67	10.46	10.29	10.16	10.05	9.89	9.72	9.55	9.47	9.38	9.29	9.20	9.11	9.02
6	13.75	10.92	9.78	9.15	8.75	8.47	8.26	8.10	7.98	7.87	7.72	7.56	7.40	7.31	7.23	7.14	7.06	6.97	6.88
7	12.25	9.55	8.45	7.85	7.46	7.19	6.99	6.84	6.72	6.62	6.47	6.31	6.16	6.07	5.99	5.91	5.82	5.74	5.65
8	11.26	8.65	7.59	7.01	6.63	6.37	6.18	6.03	5.91	5.81	5.67	5.52	5.36	5.28	5.20	5.12	5.03	4.95	4.86
9	10.56	8.02	6.99	6.42	6.06	5.80	5.61	5.47	5.35	5.26	5.11	4.96	4.81	4.73	4.65	4.57	4.48	4.40	4.31
10	10.04	7.56	6.55	5.99	5.64	5.39	5.20	5.06	4.94	4.85	4.71	4.56	4.41	4.33	4.25	4.17	4.08	4.00	3.91
11	9.65	7.21	6.22	5.67	5.32	5.07	4.89	4.74	4.63	4.54	4.40	4.25	4.10	4.02	3.94	3.86	3.78	3.69	3.60
12	9.33	6.93	5.95	5.41	5.06	4.82	4.64	4.50	4.39	4.30	4.16	4.01	3.86	3.78	3.70	3.62	3.54	3.45	3.36
13	9.07	6.70	5.74	5.21	4.86	4.62	4.44	4.30	4.19	4.10	3.96	3.82	3.66	3.59	3.51	3.43	3.34	3.25	3.17
14	8.86	6.51	5.56	5.04	4.69	4.46	4.28	4.14	4.03	3.94	3.80	3.66	3.51	3.43	3.35	3.27	3.18	3.09	3.00
15	8.68	6.36	5.42	4.89	4.56	4.32	4.14	4.00	3.89	3.80	3.67	3.52	3.37	3.29	3.21	3.13	3.05	2.96	2.87
16	8.53	6.23	5.29	4.77	4.44	4.20	4.03	3.89	3.78	3.69	3.55	3.41	3.26	3.18	3.10	3.02	2.93	2.84	2.75
17	8.40	6.11	5.18	4.67	4.34	4.10	3.93	3.79	3.68	3.59	3.46	3.31	3.16	3.08	3.00	2.92	2.83	2.75	2.65
18	8.29	6.01	5.09	4.58	4.25	4.01	3.84	3.71	3.60	3.51	3.37	3.23	3.08	3.00	2.92	2.84	2.75	2.66	2.57
19	8.18	5.93	5.01	4.50	4.17	3.94	3.77	3.63	3.52	3.43	3.30	3.15	3.00	2.92	2.84	2.76	2.67	2.58	2.49
20	8.10	5.85	4.94	4.43	4.10	3.87	3.70	3.56	3.46	3.37	3.23	3.09	2.94	2.86	2.78	2.69	2.61	2.52	2.42
21	8.02	5.78	4.87	4.37	4.04	3.81	3.64	3.51	3.40	3.31	3.17	3.03	2.88	2.80	2.72	2.64	2.55	2.46	2.36
22	7.95	5.72	4.82	4.31	3.99	3.76	3.59	3.45	3.35	3.26	3.12	2.98	2.83	2.75	2.67	2.58	2.50	2.40	2.31
23	7.88	5.66	4.76	4.26	3.94	3.71	3.54	3.41	3.30	3.21	3.07	2.93	2.78	2.70	2.62	2.54	2.45	2.35	2.26
24	7.82	5.61	4.72	4.22	3.90	3.67	3.50	3.36	3.26	3.17	3.03	2.89	2.74	2.66	2.58	2.49	2.40	2.31	2.21
25	7.77	5.57	4.68	4.18	3.85	3.63	3.46	3.32	3.22	3.13	2.99	2.85	2.70	2.62	2.54	2.45	2.36	2.27	2.17
26	7.72	5.53	4.64	4.14	3.82	3.59	3.42	3.29	3.18	3.09	2.96	2.81	2.66	2.58	2.50	2.42	2.33	2.23	2.13
27	7.68	5.49	4.60	4.11	3.78	3.56	3.39	3.26	3.15	3.06	2.93	2.78	2.63	2.55	2.47	2.38	2.29	2.20	2.10
28	7.64	5.45	4.57	4.07	3.75	3.53	3.36	3.23	3.12	3.03	2.90	2.75	2.60	2.52	2.44	2.35	2.26	2.17	2.06
29	7.60	5.42	4.54	4.04	3.73	3.50	3.33	3.20	3.09	3.00	2.87	2.73	2.57	2.49	2.41	2.33	2.23	2.14	2.03
30	7.56	5.39	4.51	4.02	3.70	3.47	3.30	3.17	3.07	2.98	2.84	2.70	2.55	2.47	2.39	2.30	2.21	2.11	2.01
40	7.31	5.18	4.31	3.83	3.51	3.29	3.12	2.99	2.89	2.80	2.66	2.52	2.37	2.20	2.20	2.11	2.02	1.92	1.80
60	7.08	4.98	4.13	3.65	3.34	3.12	2.95	2.82	2.72	2.63	2.50	2.35	2.20	2.12	2.03	1.94	1.84	1.73	1.60
120	6.85	4.79	3.95	3.48	3.17	2.96	2.79	2.66	2.56	2.47	2.34	2.19	2.03	1.95	1.86	1.76	1.66	1.53	1.33
∞	6.63	4.61	3.78	3.32	3.02	2.80	2.64	2.51	2.41	2.32	2.18	2.04	1.88	1.79	1.70	1.59	1.47	1.32	1.00

Degrees of freedom for the denominator v^2

Values of F that equal or exceed the tabled value are significant at or beyond the 1% level.

SSOURCE: Radford, J., & Govier, E. *Textbook of Psychology* (2nd ed.) Routledge (Abridged from Table 18 of The Biometrika Tables for Statisticians, Vol. I, edited by Pearson, E. S. and

Table 13 Power values for the F test

Power = 1 − (table entry)

df_e	α	.50	1	1.2	1.4	Φ 1.6	1.8	2	2.2	2.6	3
						$df_t = 1$					
2	.05	.93	.86	.83	.78	.74	.69	.64	.59	.49	.40
	.01	.99	.97	.96	.95	.94	.93	.91	.90	.87	.83
4	.05	.91	.80	.74	.67	.59	.51	.43	.35	.22	.12
	.01	.98	.95	.93	.90	.87	.83	.78	.73	.62	.50
6	.05	.91	.78	.70	.62	.52	.43	.34	.26	.14	.06
	.01	.98	.93	.90	.86	.81	.75	.69	.61	.46	.31
8	.05	.90	.76	.68	.59	.49	.39	.30	.22	.11	.04
	.01	.98	.92	.89	.84	.78	.70	.62	.54	.37	.22
10	.05	.90	.75	.66	.57	.47	.37	.28	.20	.09	.03
	.01	.98	.92	.87	.82	.75	.67	.58	.49	.31	.17
12	.05	.90	.74	.65	.56	.45	.35	.26	.19	.08	.03
	.01	.97	.91	.87	.81	.73	.65	.55	.46	.28	.14
16	.05	.90	.74	.64	.54	.43	.33	.24	.17	.07	.02
	.01	.97	.90	.85	.79	.71	.61	.52	.42	.24	.11
20	.05	.90	.73	.63	.53	.42	.32	.23	.16	.06	.02
	.01	.97	.90	.85	.78	.69	.59	.49	.39	.21	.10
30	.05	.89	.72	.62	.52	.40	.31	.22	.15	.06	.02
	.01	.97	.89	.83	.76	.67	.57	.46	.36	.19	.08
∞	.05	.89	.71	.60	.49	.38	.28	.19	.12	.04	.01
	.01	.97	.88	.81	.72	.62	.21	.40	.30	.14	.05
df_e	α					$df_t = 2$					
2	.05	.93	.88	.85	.82	.78	.75	.70	.66	.56	.48
	.01	.99	.98	.97	.96	.95	.94	.93	.92	.89	.86
4	.05	.92	.82	.77	.70	.62	.54	.46	.38	.24	.14
	.01	.98	.96	.94	.92	.89	.85	.81	.76	.66	.54
6	.05	.91	.79	.71	.63	.53	.43	.34	.26	.13	.05
	.01	.98	.94	.91	.87	.82	.76	.70	.62	.46	.31
8	.05	.91	.77	.68	.58	.48	.37	.28	.20	.08	.03
	.01	.98	.93	.89	.84	.78	.70	.61	.52	.34	.19
10	.05	.91	.75	.66	.55	.44	.34	.24	.16	.06	.02
	.01	.98	.92	.88	.82	.74	.65	.55	.45	.26	.13
12	.05	.90	.74	.64	.53	.42	.31	.22	.14	.05	.01
	.01	.98	.91	.86	.80	.71	.61	.51	.40	.22	.09
16	.05	.90	.73	.62	.51	.39	.28	.19	.12	.04	.01
	.01	.97	.90	.84	.77	.67	.57	.45	.34	.16	.06
20	.05	.90	.72	.61	.49	.36	.26	.17	.11	.03	.01
	.01	.97	.90	.83	.75	.65	.53	.42	.31	.14	.04
30	.05	.90	.71	.59	.47	.35	.24	.15	.09	.02	. 00
	.01	.97	.88	.82	.72	.61	.49	.37	.26	.10	.03
∞	.05	.89	.68	.56	.43	.30	.20	.12	.06	.01	.00
	.01	.90	.86	.77	.66	.53	.40	.28	.18	.05	.01

Table 13 Continued

Power = 1 − (table entry) Φ

df_e	α	.5	1	1.2	1.4	1.6	1.8	2	2.2	2.6	3
						$df_t = 3$					
2	.05	.93	.89	.86	.83	.80	.76	.73	.69	.60	.52
	.01	.99	.98	.97	.96	.96	.95	.94	.93	.90	.88
4	.05	.92	.83	.77	.71	.63	.55	.47	.39	.25	.14
	.01	.98	.96	.94	.92	.89	.86	.82	.77	.67	.55
6	.05	.91	.79	.71	.62	.52	.42	.33	.24	.11	.04
	.01	.98	.94	.91	.87	.82	.76	.69	.61	.44	.29
8	.05	.91	.76	.67	.57	.46	.35	.25	.17	.06	.02
	.01	.98	.93	.89	.84	.77	.68	.59	.49	.30	.16
10	.05	.91	.75	.65	.53	.41	.30	.21	.13	.04	.01
	.01	.98	.92	.87	.80	.72	.62	.52	.41	.22	.09
12	.05	.90	.73	.62	.50	.38	.27	.18	.11	.03	.01
	.01	.98	.91	.85	.78	.69	.58	.46	.35	.17	.06
16	.05	.90	.71	.60	.47	.34	.23	.14	.08	.02	.00
	.01	.97	.90	.83	.74	.64	.51	.39	.28	.11	.03
20	.05	.90	.70	.58	.45	.32	.21	.13	.07	.01	.00
	.01	.97	.89	.82	.72	.60	.47	.35	.24	.08	.02
30	.05	.89	.68	.55	.42	.29	.18	.10	.05	.01	.00
	.01	.97	.87	.79	.68	.55	.42	.29	.18	.05	.01
∞	.05	.88	.64	.50	.36	.23	.13	.07	.03	.00	.00
	.01	.97	.84	.73	.59	.44	.30	.18	.10	.02	.00
df_e	α					$df_t = 4$					
2	.05	.94	.89	.87	.84	.81	.77	.74	.70	.62	.54
	.01	.99	.98	.97	.97	.96	.95	.94	.93	.91	.88
4	.05	.92	.83	.78	.71	.64	.55	.47	.39	.25	.14
	.01	.98	.96	.94	.92	.89	.86	.82	.78	.67	.56
6	.05	.92	.79	.71	.62	.52	.41	.31	.23	.10	.04
	.01	.98	.94	.91	.87	.82	.76	.68	.60	.43	.28
8	.05	.91	.76	.66	.55	.44	.33	.23	.15	.05	.01
	.01	.98	.93	.89	.83	.76	.67	.57	.47	.28	.14
10	.05	.91	.74	.63	.51	.39	.27	.18	.11	.03	.01
	.01	.98	.92	.86	.79	.70	.60	.49	.37	.19	.07
12	.05	.90	.72	.61	.48	.35	.24	.15	.08	.02	.00
	.01	.98	.91	.85	.76	.66	.55	.42	.31	.13	.04
16	.05	.90	.70	.57	.44	.31	.19	.11	.06	.01	.00
	.01	.97	.89	.82	.72	.60	.47	.34	.23	.08	.02
20	.05	.89	.68	.55	.41	.28	.17	.09	.04	.01	.00
	.01	.97	.88	.80	.69	.56	.42	.29	.18	.05	.01
30	.05	.89	.66	.52	.37	.24	.14	.07	.03	.00	.00
	.01	.97	.86	.77	.64	.50	.35	.22	.13	.03	.00
∞	.05	.88	.60	.45	.29	.17	.08	.04	.01	.00	.00
	.01	.96	.81	.68	.53	.36	.22	.11	.05	.01	.00

Taken from Howell, D. C. (1992) *Statistical Methods for Psychology*, 3rd edn. PWS-Kent, pp. 641–642.

Table 14 Power in multiple regression as a function of λ, u (= v_1) and v (= v_2) with α = .05

v_1	v_2	$\lambda =$ 2	4	6	8	10	12	14	16	18	20	24	28	32	36	40
1	20	27	48	64	77	85	91	95	97	98	99	*				
	60	29	50	67	79	88	92	96	98	99	99	*				
	120	29	51	68	80	88	93	96	98	99	99	*				
	∞	29	52	69	81	89	93	96	98	99	99	*				
2	20	20	36	52	65	75	83	88	92	95	97	99	*			
	60	22	40	56	69	79	87	91	95	97	98	*				
	120	22	41	57	71	80	87	92	95	97	98	*				
	∞	23	42	58	72	82	88	93	96	97	99	*				
3	20	17	30	44	56	67	75	82	87	91	94	97	99	*		
	60	19	34	49	62	73	81	87	92	95	97	98	*			
	120	19	35	50	64	75	83	89	93	95	97	99	*			
	∞	19	36	52	65	76	84	90	93	96	98	99	*			
4	20	15	26	38	49	60	69	76	83	87	91	95	98	99	*	
	60	17	30	44	57	68	77	83	89	92	95	98	99	*		
	120	17	31	46	58	70	78	85	90	93	96	98	99	*		
	∞	17	32	47	60	72	80	87	91	94	96	99	*			
5	20	13	23	34	44	54	63	71	78	83	87	93	96	98	99	*
	60	15	27	40	52	63	72	80	86	90	93	97	99	*		
	120	16	29	41	54	65	75	82	87	91	94	98	99	*		
	∞	16	29	43	56	68	77	84	89	93	95	98	99	*		
6	20	12	21	30	40	50	59	66	73	79	84	91	95	97	99	*
	60	14	25	37	48	59	68	76	83	87	91	96	98	99	*	
	120	14	27	39	50	62	71	79	85	89	93	97	99	99	*	
	∞	15	27	40	53	64	74	81	87	91	94	97	99	*		
7	20	11	19	28	37	46	54	62	69	75	80	88	93	96	98	99
	60	17	24	35	45	56	65	73	80	85	89	94	97	99	99	*
	120	13	25	37	47	59	68	76	82	87	91	96	98	99	*	
	∞	14	25	38	50	61	71	79	85	89	93	97	99	99	*	
8	20	10	18	26	34	42	50	58	65	71	76	85	91	94	97	98
	60	12	23	33	43	52	62	70	77	83	87	93	97	98	99	*
	120	12	24	35	45	55	65	73	80	85	89	95	98	99	*	
	∞	13	24	36	48	59	68	77	83	88	92	96	99	99	*	

Taken from Cohen, J. (1988) *Statistical Power Analysis for the Behavioral Sciences*. Hillsdale, NJ: LEA, pp. 420–421.

Table 15 Critical values of Bonferroni Multiple Comparison test

$\alpha = .05$

| df | \multicolumn{9}{c}{Number of comparisons} |
	2	3	4	5	6	7	8	9	10
5	3.16	3.53	3.81	4.03	4.22	4.38	4.53	4.66	4.77
6	2.97	3.29	3.52	3.71	3.86	4.00	4.12	4.22	4.32
7	2.84	3.13	3.34	3.50	3.64	3.75	3.86	3.95	4.03
8	2.75	3.02	3.21	3.36	3.48	3.58	3.68	3.76	3.83
9	2.69	2.93	3.11	3.25	3.36	3.46	3.55	3.62	3.69
10	2.63	2.87	3.04	3.17	3.28	3.37	3.45	3.52	3.58
11	2.59	2.82	2.98	3.11	3.21	3.29	3.37	3.44	3.50
12	2.56	2.78	2.93	3.05	3.15	3.24	3.31	3.37	3.43
13	2.53	2.75	2.90	3.01	3.11	3.19	3.26	3.32	3.37
14	2.51	2.72	2.86	2.98	3.07	3.15	3.21	3.27	3.33
15	2.49	2.69	2.84	2.95	3.04	3.11	3.18	3.23	3.29
16	2.47	2.67	2.81	2.92	3.01	3.08	3.15	3.20	3.25
17	2.46	2.65	2.79	2.90	2.98	3.06	3.12	3.17	3.22
18	2.45	2.64	2.77	2.88	2.96	3.03	3.09	3.15	3.20
19	2.43	2.63	2.76	2.86	2.94	3.01	3.07	3.13	3.17
20	2.42	2.61	2.74	2.85	2.93	3.00	3.06	3.11	3.15
21	2.41	2.60	2.73	2.83	2.91	2.98	3.04	3.09	3.14
22	2.41	2.59	2.72	2.82	2.90	2.97	3.02	3.07	3.12
23	2.40	2.58	2.71	2.81	2.89	2.95	3.01	3.06	3.10
24	2.39	2.57	2.70	2.80	2.88	2.94	3.00	3.05	3.09
25	2.38	2.57	2.69	2.79	2.86	2.93	2.99	3.03	3.08
30	2.36	2.54	2.66	2.75	2.82	2.89	2.94	2.99	3.03
40	2.33	2.50	2.62	2.70	2.78	2.84	2.89	2.93	2.97
50	2.31	2.48	2.59	2.68	2.75	2.81	2.85	2.90	2.94
75	2.29	2.45	2.56	2.64	2.71	2.77	2.81	2.86	2.89
100	2.28	2.43	2.54	2.63	2.69	2.75	2.79	2.83	2.87
∞	2.24	2.39	2.50	2.58	2.64	2.69	2.73	2.77	2.81

Taken from Howell, D.C. (1992) *Statistical Methods for Psychology*, 3rd edn. PWS-Kent, p. 652.

References

Abrahamsson, K.H., Berggren, U., Hallberg-Lillemor, R.M. and Carlsson, S.G. (2002) Ambivalence in coping with dental fear and avoidance: a qualitative study. *Journal of Health Psychology*, *7*, 6, 653–64.

Acklin, M.W., McDowell, C.J., Verschell, M.S. and Chan, D. (2000) Interobserver agreement, intraobserver reliability, and the Rorschach comprehensive system, *Journal of Personality Assessment*, *74*, 1, 15–47.

Adair, J.G. and Schachter, B.S. (1972) To cooperate or look good? The subjects' and experimenters' perceptions of each other's intentions. *Journal of Experimental Social Psychology, 8*, 74–85.

Agar, M. (1986) Speaking of ethnography. *Qualitative Research Methods Series*, No. 2. London: Sage.

Ainsworth, M.D.S., Beli, S.M. and Stayton, D.J. (1971) Individual differences in strange situation behaviour of one-year-olds. In Schaffer, H.R. (ed.) *The origins of human social relations*. London: Academic Press.

Allport, F.H. (1924) *Social Psychology*. Boston: Houghton Mifflin.

Allport, G.W. (1940) The psychologist's frame of reference. *Psychological Bulletin*, *37*, 1, 1–28.

American Psychological Association (2002) *Ethical principles of psychologists and code of conduct*. Washington, DC: American Psychological Association.

Anderson, C. (1987) Temperature and aggression: effects on quarterly, yearly, and city rates of violent and nonviolent crime. *Journal of Personality and Social Psychology*, *52*, 1161–73.

Araújo, D., Davids, K. and Passos, P. (2007) Ecological validity, representative design, and correspondence between experimental task constraints and behavioral setting: comment on Rogers, Kadar, and Costall (2005). *Ecological Psychology, 19*, 1, 69–78.

Archer, J. (2000) Sex differences in aggression between heterosexual partners: a meta-analytic review. *Psychological Bulletin, 126,* 651–80.

Argyle, M. (1994) *The psychology of social class*. London: Routledge.

Aronson, E. and Carlsmith, J.M. (1968) Experimentation in social psychology. In G. Lindzey and E. Aronson (eds) *Handbook of social psychology*, (2nd edn) Reading, MA: Addison-Wesley.

Asch, S.E. (1946) Forming impressions of personality. *Journal of Abnormal and Social Psychology, 41*, 258–90.

Asch, S.E. (1956) Studies of independence and submission to group pressure, 1. A minority of one against a unanimous majority. *Psychological Monographs*, *70*, 9 (whole No. 416).

Awosunle, S. and Doyle, C. (2001) Same-race bias in the selection interview. *Selection Development Review*, *17*, 3, 3–6.

Bakeman, R. and Gottman, J.M. (1997) *Observing interaction: an introduction to sequential analysis*. Cambridge: Cambridge University Press.

Baker, K., Curtice, J. and Sparrow, N. (2003) Internet poll trial: research report. ICM with the *Guardian* as sponsor; available at: http://www.icmresearch.co.uk/reviews/2002/Internet-polling-paper-jan-03.htm, accessed 9 January 2003.

Bandura, A. (1965) Influence of models' reinforcement contingencies on the acquisition of imitative responses. *Journal of Personality and Social Psychology*, *1*, 589–95.

Bandura, A. (1977) *Social learning theory*. Englewood Cliffs, NJ: Prentice-Hall.

Banyard, P. and Hunt, N. (2000) Reporting research: something missing? *The Psychologist*, *13*, 2, 68–71.

Beloff, H. (1992) Mother, father and me: our IQ, *The Psychologist*, *15*, 7, 309–11.

Bem, S. and Looren de Jong, H. (1997) *Theoretical issues in psychology*. London: Sage.

Benedict, R. (1934) *Patterns of culture*. Boston: Houghton Mifflin.

Ben-Porath, Y.S., Almagor, A., Hoffman-Chemi, A. and Tellegen, A. (1995) A cross-cultural study of personality with the Multi-dimensional Personality Questionnaire. *Journal of Cross-Cultural Psychology*, *26*, 360–73.

Berry, J.W. (1989) Imposed etics-emics-derived etics: the operationalization of a compelling idea. *International Journal of Psychology*, *24*, 721–35.

Billig, M. (1979) *Psychology, racism and fascism*. Birmingham: AF & R Publications.

Billig, M. (1997) Rhetorical and discursive analysis: how families talk about the royal family, in N. Hayes (ed.) *Doing qualitative analysis in psychology*. Hove: Psychology Press.

Bishop, M. and Slevin, B. (2004) Teachers' attitudes towards students with epilepsy: results of a survey of elementary and middle school teachers. *Epilepsy and Behaviour, 5*, 308–15.

Block, N.J. and Dworkin, G. (1974) IQ – heritability and inequality. *Philosophy and Public Affairs*, *3*, 331–407.

Bouchard, T.J., Lykken, D.T., McGue, M., Segal, N.L. and Tellegen, A. (1990) Sources of human psychological differences: the Minnesota study of twins reared apart. *Science*, *250*, 223–8.

Bowlby, J. (1953) *Child care and the growth of love*. Harmondsworth: Penguin.

Bracht, G.H. and Glass, G.V. (1968) The external validity of experiments. *American Educational Research Journal*, *5*, 437–74.

Bradley, D.R. (1991) Anatomy of a DATASIM simulation: the Doob and Gross horn-honking study. *Behavior Research Methods, Instruments & Computers, 23, 2*, 190–207.

Bramel, D.A. (1962) A dissonance theory approach to defensives projection. *Journal of Abnormal and Social Psychology*, *64*, 121–9.

Braun, V. and Clarke, V. (2006) Using thematic analysis in psychology, *Qualitative Research in Psychology*, *3*, 77–101

Breakwell, G.M. and Fife-Schaw, C.R. (1992) Sexual activities and preferences in a UK sample of 16–20 year olds. *Archives of Sexual Behaviour*, *21*, 271–93.

Brody, G.H., Stoneman, Z. and Wheatley, P. (1984) Peer interaction in the presence and absence of observers. *Child Development*, *55*, 1425–28.

Broeder, A. (1998) Deception can be acceptable. *American Psychologist*, *53*, 7, 805–6.

Bromley, D.B. (1986) *The case study method in psychology and related disciplines*. Chichester: Wiley.

Brown, R. (1988) *Group processes: dynamics within and between groups*. Oxford: Blackwell.

Bruner, E.M. and Kelso, J.P. (1980) Gender differences in graffiti: a semiotic perspective. *Women's Studies International Quarterly*, *3*, 239–52.

Bruner, J.S. (1973) *Beyond the information given*. New York: Norton.

Brunswik, E. (1947) *Systematic and unrepresentative design of psychological experiments with results in physical and social perception*. Berkeley: University of California Press.

Bryman, A. and Burgess, R.G. (eds) (1994) *Analyzing qualitative data*. London: Routledge.

Burns, J.L. (1974) Some personality attributes of volunteers and of non-volunteers for psychological experimentation. *Journal of Social Psychology, 92*, 1, 161–2.

Camilli, G. and Hopkins, D. (1978) Applicability of chi-square to 2 3 2 contingency tables with small expected cell frequencies. *Psychological Bulletin*, *85*, 1, 163–7.

Campbell, D.T. (1970) Natural selection as an epistemological model. In R. Naroll and R. Cohen (eds) *A handbook of method in cultural anthropology*. New York: Natural History Press, 51–85.

Carlsmith, J., Ellsworth, P. and Aronson, E. (1976) *Methods of research in social psychology*. Reading, MA: Addison-Wesley.

Cartwright, A. (1988) Interviews or postal questionnaires? Comparisons of data about women's experiences with maternity services. *Millbank Quarterly, 66,* 1, 172–89.

Chapman, D.S. and Rowe, P.M. (2001) The impact of videoconference technology, interview structure, and interviewer gender on interviewer evaluations in the employment interview: a field experiment. *Journal of Occupational and Organizational Psychology*, *74*, 3, 279–98.

Charlesworth, R. and Hartup, W.W. (1967) Positive social reinforcement in the nursery school peer group. *Child Development*, *38*, 993–1002.

Charlton, T., Panting, C., Davie, R., Coles, D. and Whitmarsh, L. (2000) Children's playground behaviour across five years of broadcast television: a naturalistic study in a remote community. *Emotional & Behavioural Difficulties*, *5*, 4, 4–12.

Charmaz, K. (1995) Grounded theory. In J.A. Smith, R. Harré and L. Van Langenhove (eds) *Rethinking psychology*. London: Sage.

Cialdini, R.B., Reno, R.R. and Kallgren, C.A. (1990) A focus theory of normative conduct: recycling the concept of norms to reduce litter in public places. *Journal of Personality and Social Psychology*, *58*, 1015–26.

Clark-Carter, D. (1997) *Doing quantitative psychological research: from design to report*. Hove: Psychology Press.

Cochran, W.G. (1954) Some methods for strengthening the common $x2$ tests. *Biometrics*, *10*, 417–51.

Cohen, J. (1962) The statistical power of abnormal-social psychological research: a review. *Journal of Abnormal and Social Psychology*, *65*, 145–53.

Cohen, J. (1988) *Statistical power analysis for the behavioral sciences*. San Diego, CA: Academic Press.

Cohen, J. (1992) A power primer. *Psychological Bulletin*, *112*, 1, 155–9.

Connolly, J. (1994) Of race and right. *Irish Times*, 6 December.

Cook, S. and Wilding, J. (2001) Earwitness testimony: effects of exposure and attention on the face overshadowing effect. *British Journal of Psychology*, *92*, 4, 617–29.

Cook, T.D. and Campbell, D.T. (1979) *Quasi-experimentation: design and analysis issues for field settings*. Chicago: Rand McNally.

Coolican, H. (2004) *Research methods and statistics in psychology* (4th edn). London: Hodder.

Craik, F. and Tulving, E. (1975) Depth of processing and the retention of words in episodic memory. *Journal of Experimental Psychology* (General), *104*, 268–94.

Crawford, J., Kippax, S., Onyx, J., Gault, U. and Benton, P. *Emotion and gender: Constructing meaning from memory*. London: Sage.

Csapo, B. (1997) The development of inductive reasoning: cross-sectional assessments in an educational context. *International Journal of Behavioral Development, 20,* 4, 609–26.

Cumberbatch, G., Jones, I. and Lee, M. (1988a) Measuring violence on television. *Current Psychology Research and Reviews, 7,* 1, 10–25.

Cumberbatch, G., Lee, M. and Jones, I. (1988b) Measuring violence on television. *Current Psychological Research and Reviews, 7,* 8–23.

Cumberbatch, G., Woods, S., Evans, O., Irvine, N. and Lee, M. (1990) *Television advertising and sex role stereotyping: a content analysis* (working paper IV for the Broadcasting Standards Council), Communications Research Group, Aston University.

Darwin, C. (1877) A biographical sketch of an infant. *Mind, 2,* 285–94.

David, S.S.J., Chapman, A.J., Foot, H.C. and Sheehy, N.P. (1986) Peripheral vision and child pedestrian accidents. *British Journal of Psychology, 77,* 4, 433–50.

Davie, R., Butler, N. and Goldstein, H. (1972) *From Birth to Seven.* London: Longman.

De Waele, J.-P. and Harré, R. (1979) Autobiography as a psychological method. In G.P. Ginsburg (ed.) *Emerging strategies in social psychological research.* Chichester: Wiley.

DeBono, K.G. and Packer, M. (1991) The effects of advertising appeal on perceptions of product quality. *Personality and Social Psychology Bulletin, 17,* 2, 194–200.

Diesing, P. (1972) *Patterns of discovery in the social sciences.* London: Routledge & Kegan Paul.

Dineen, R. and Niu, W. (2008) The effectiveness of western creative teaching methods in China: an action research project. *Psychology of Aesthetics, Creativity, and the Arts, 2,* 1, 42–52.

Doob, A.N. and Gross, A.E. (1968) Status of frustration as an inhibitor of horn-honking responses. *Journal of Social Psychology, 76,* 213–18.

Douglas, J.D. (1972) *Research on deviance.* New York: Random House.

Dunn, O.J. (1961) Multiple comparisons among means. *Journal of the American Statistical Association, 56,* 52–64.

Durrant, J.E. (1999) Evaluating the success of Sweden's corporal punishment ban. *Child Abuse and Neglect, 23,* 5, 435–48.

Durrant, J.E. (2000) Trends in youth crime and well-being since the abolition of corporal punishment in Sweden. *Youth and Society, 31,* 4, 437–55.

Earley, P.C. (1989) Social loafing and collectivism: a comparison of the United States and the People's Republic of China. *Administrative Science Quarterly, 34,* 565–81.

Ebbinghaus, H. (1913) *Memory: a contribution to experimental psychology.* New York: Teachers College, Columbia University.

Eden, D. (1990) Pygmalion without interpersonal contrast effects: whole groups gain from raising manager expectations, *Journal of Applied Psychology, 75,* 4, 394–8.

Edwards, D. and Potter, J. (1992) *Discursive psychology.* London: Sage.

Ehrlichman, H. and Halpern, J.N. (1988) Affect and memory: effects of pleasant and unpleasant odours on retrieval of happy and unhappy memories. *Journal of Personality and Social Psychology, 55,* 5, 769–79.

Elliott, R., Fischer, C. and Rennie, D. (1999) Evolving guidelines for publication of qualitative research studies in psychology and related fields. *British Journal of Clinical Psychology, 38,* 215–29.

Ericsson, K.A. and Simon, H.A. (1984) *Protocol analysis: verbal reports as data*. Cambridge, MA: MIT Press.

Exner, J.E. Jr (1993) *The Rorschach: a comprehensive system,* Vol. 1: *Basic foundations* (3rd edn). Oxford: Wiley.

Eysenck,, H.J. (1970) *The Structure of Human Personality.* London: Methuen.

Eysenck, H.J. and Eysenck, S.B.G. (1975) *Manual of the Eysenck Personality Questionnaire*. London: Hodder & Stoughton.

Eysenck, M.W. and Keane, M.T. (1995) *Cognitive psychology: a students handbook*. Hove: LEA.

Ferguson, G.A. and Takane, Y. (1989) *Statistical analysis in psychology and education*. New York: McGraw-Hill.

Festinger, L., Riecken, H.W. and Schachter, S. (1956) *When prophecy fails*. Minneapolis: University of Minnesota Press.

Fife-Schaw, C.R. (1995) Surveys and sampling issues. In G.M. Breakwell, S. Hammond and C.R. Fife-Schaw (eds) *Research Methods in Psychology.* London: Sage.

Fischer, C.S., Hout, M., Jankowski, M.S., Lucas, S.R., Swidler, A. and Voss, K. (1996) *Cracking the bell curve myth*. Princeton, NJ: Princeton University Press.

Fischer, R. and Chalmers, A. (2008) Is optimism universal? A meta-analytical investigation of optimism levels across 22 nations. *Personality and Individual Differences*, *45*, 5, 378–82.

Fisk, J.E. and Pidgeon, N. (1997) The conjunction fallacy: the case for the existence of competing heuristic strategies. *British Journal of Psychology*, *88*, 1, 1–27.

Flick, U. (2006) *An introduction to qualitative research.* London: Sage.

Flick, U. (2008) *Designing qualitative research (Qualitative Research Kit)*. London: Sage.

Flick, U. (1998) *An introduction to qualitative research*. London: Sage.

Fraser, S. (ed.) (1995) *The bell curve wars: race, intelligence, and the future of America*. New York: Basic Books.

Friedman, N. (1967) *The social nature of psychological research*. New York: Basic Books.

Gabrenya, W.K., Wang, Y.E. and Latané, B. (1985) Social loafing on an optimizing task: cross-cultural differences among Chinese and Americans. *Journal of Cross-Cultural Psychology*, *16*, 223–42.

Gannon, T.A., Keown, K. and Polaschek, D. (2007) Increasing honest responding on cognitive distortions in child molesters: the bogus pipeline revisited. *Sexual Abuse: Journal of Research and Treatment*, *19*, 1, 5–22.

Gibson, E.J. and Walk, R.D. (1960) The "visual cliff." *Scientific American*, *202*, 67–71.

Giles, D. (2002) *Advanced research methods in psychology*. Hove: Routledge.

Gilligan, C. (1982) *In a different voice: psychological theory and women's development*. Cambridge, MA: Harvard University Press.

Giorgi, A. and Giorgi, B. (2003) Phenomenology. In J.A. Smith, *Qualitative psychology: a practical guide to research methods*. London: Sage.

Gittelsohn, J., Shankar, A.V., West, K.P., Ram, R.M. and Gnywali, T. (1997) Estimating reactivity in direct observation studies of health behaviours, *Human Organization*, *56*, 2, 182–9.

Glaser, B.G. (1992) *Emergence vs forcing: basics of grounded theory analysis*. Mill Valley, CA: Sociology Press.

Glaser, B.G. (1998) *Doing grounded theory: issues and discussions:* Mill Valley, CA: Sociology Press.

Glaser, B.G. and Strauss, A.L. (1967) *The discovery of grounded theory: strategies for qualitative research*. Chicago: Aldine.

Godden, D. and Baddeley, A.D. (1975) Context-dependent memory in two natural environments: on land and under water. *British Journal of Psychology*, *66*, 325–31.

Gordon, R., Bindrim, T., McNicholas, M. and Walden, T. (1988) Perceptions of blue-collar and white-collar crime: the effect of defendant race on simulated juror decisions. *Journal of Social Psychology*, *128*, 2, 191–7.

Gould, S.J. (1997) *The mismeasure of man*. London: Penguin.

Gould, S.J. (1999) *The mismeasure of man* (2nd edn). London: Penguin.

Govier, E. and Feldman, J. (1999) Occupational choice and patterns of cognitive abilities. *British Journal of Psychology*, *90*, 1, 99–108.

Gravetter, F.J. and Wallnau, L.B. (1996) *Statistics for the behavioural sciences*. New York: West Publishing Company.

Grbich, C. (1999) *Qualitative research in health*. St Leonards, NSW: Sage.

Green E.G.T., Deschamps, J. and Páez, D. (2005) Variation of individualism and collectivism within and between twenty countries: a typological analysis. *Journal of Cross-Cultural Psychology*, *36*, 321–39.

Gregor, A.J. and McPherson, D.A. (1965) A study of susceptibility to geometric illusion among cultural sub-groups of Australian Aborigines. *Psychologia Africana*, *11*, 1–13.

Gregory, R.L. (1966) *Eye and brain*. New York: McGraw-Hill.

Gregory, R.L. and Wallace, J.G. (1963) *Recovery from early blindness*. Cambridge: Heffer.

Gross, R.D. (2001) *Psychology: the science of mind and behaviour* (4th edn). London: Hodder & Stoughton Educational.

Gross, R.D. (2003) *Key studies in psychology* (4th edn). London: Hodder & Stoughton Educational.

Grossman, L.S., Wasyliw, O.E., Benn, A.F. and Gyoerkoe, K.L. (2002) Can sex offenders who minimize on the MMPI conceal psychopathology on the Rorschach? *Journal of Personality Assessment*, *78*, 3, 484–501.

Guardian (1996) Poor believe honesty is the best policy (by Stuart Miller), 17 June.

Gulian, E. and Thomas, J.R. (1986) The effects of noise, cognitive set and gender on mental arithmetic and performance. *British Journal of Psychology*, *77*, 4.

Haber, R.N. (1983) The impending demise of the icon: a critique of the concept of iconic storage in visual information processing. *Behavioral and Brain Sciences*, *6*, 1–11.

Hahn, C. (2008) *Doing qualitative research using your computer*. London: Sage

Hall, B.L. (1975) Participatory research: an approach for change. *Convergence, an International Journal of Adult Education*, *8*, 2, 24–32.

Halliday, S. and Leslie, J.C. (1986) A longitudinal semi-cross-sectional study of the development of mother–child interaction. *British Journal of Developmental Psychology*, *4*, 3, 221–32.

Hammer, M. (1970) Preference for a male child: Cultural factor. *Journal of Individual Psychology*, *26*, 1, 54–6.

Hammersley, M. and Atkinson, P. (1983) *Ethnography: principles in practice*. London: Routledge.

Hammersley, M. and Atkinson, P. (1994) *Ethnography: principles in practice* (2nd edn). London: Routledge.

Hammond, K.R. (1948) Measuring attitudes by error-choice: an indirect method. *Journal of Abnormal Social Psychology*, *43*, 38–48.

Hammond, K.R. (1998) *Ecological Validity: Then and Now*. University of Colorado [online] available at: www.albany.edu/cpr/brunswik/notes/essay2.html Accessed 23.9.2008.

Harcourt, D. and Frith, H. (2008) Women's experiences of an altered appearance during chemotherapy: an indication of cancer status. *Journal of Health Psychology*, *13*, 5, 597–606. Available online at http://www.thepsychologist.org.uk/archive/archive_home.cfm/volumeID_20-editionID_150-ArticleID_1225

Harcum, E.R. (1990) Guidance from the literature for accepting a null hypothesis when its truth is expected. *Journal of General Psychology*, *117*, 3, 325–44.

Haug, F. (ed.) (1987) *Female sexualization*. London: Verso.

Have, P. (1999) *Doing conversation analysis*. London: Sage.

Hayes, N. (1997) *Doing qualitative analysis in psychology*. Hove: Psychology Press.

Hayes, N.J. (1991) Social identity, social representations and organisational cultures. PhD thesis, CNAA/Huddersfield.

Hays, W.L. (1973) *Statistics for the social sciences*. London: Holt Rinehart Winston.

Heather, N. (1976) *Radical perspectives in psychology*. London: Methuen.

Henderson, V.R. (2007) Longitudinal associations between television viewing and body mass index among White and Black girls. *Journal of Adolescent Health, 41*, 6, 544–50.

Henwood, K.I. and Pidgeon, N.F. (1992) Qualitative research and psychological theorizing. *British Journal of Psychology*, *83*, 97–111.

Henwood, K. and Pidgeon, N. (1995) Grounded theory and psychological research, *The Psychologist*, *8*, 3, 115–18.

Herrnstein, R.J. and Murray, C. (1994) *The bell curve: intelligence and class structure in American life*. New York: Free Press.

Hess, R., Azuma, H., Kashiwagi, K., Dickson, W.P., Nagano, S., Holloway, S., Miyake, K., Price, G., and Hatano, G. (1986) Family influences on school readiness and achievement in Japan and the United States: an overview of a longitudinal study. In H. Stevenson, H. Azuma and K. Hakuta (eds) *Child development and education in Japan*. New York: Freeman.

Hinckley, E.D. (1932) The influence of individual opinion on construction of an attitude scale. *Journal of Social Psychology*, *3*, 283–96.

Hofling, C.K., Brotzman, E., Dalrymple, S., Graves, N. and Pierce, C.M. (1966) An experimental study in nurse-physician relationships. *Journal of Nervous and Mental Disease*, *143*, 171–80.

Hofstede, G. (1980) *Culture's consequences: International differences in work-related values*. Beverley Hills, CA: Sage.

Hollway, W. (1991) *Work psychology and organizational behaviour*. London: Sage.

Holt, N.L. and Dunn, J.G.H. (2004) Towards a grounded theory of the psychosocial competencies and environmental conditions associated with soccer success. *Journal of Applied Sport Psychology, 16*, 199–219.

Honda, H., Shimizu, Y. and Rutter, M. (2005) No effect of MMR withdrawal on the incidence of autism: a total population study. *Journal of Child Psychology and Psychiatry*, *46*, 6, 572–9.

Horowitz, I.A. and Rothschild, B.H. (1970) Conformity as a function of deception and role-playing. *Journal of Personality and Social Psychology*, *14*, 224–6.

Hovey, H.B. (1928) Effects of general distraction on the higher thought processes. *American Journal of Psychology*, *40*, 585–91.

Howell, D.C. (1992) *Statistical methods for psychology*. Boston: PWS-Kent.

Howell, D.C. (2001) *Statistical methods for psychology* (2nd edn). Boston: PWS-Kent.

Howitt, D. and Owusu-Bempah, J. (1994) *The racism of psychology*. Hemel Hempstead: Harvester Wheatsheaf.

Humphreys, G.W. and Riddock, M.J. (1993) Interactions between object and space systems revealed through neuropsychology. In D.E. Myer and S.M. Kornblum (eds) *Attention and performance* (Vol. XIV). London: MIT Press.

Humphreys, L. (1970) *Tearoom trade*. Chicago: Aldine.

Hutchby, I. and Wooffitt, R. (1998) *Conversation analysis*. Malden, MA: Blackwell.

Ingham, A.G., Levinger, G., Graves, J. and Peckham, V. (1974) The Ringelmann Effect: Studies of group size and group performance. *Journal of Experimental Social Psychology*, *10*, 371–84.

Jacob, T., Tennenbaum, D., Seilhamer, R. and Bargiel, Kay. (1994) Reactivity effects during naturalistic observation of distressed and non-distressed families. *Journal of Family Psychology*, *8*, 3, 354–63.

Jacoby, R. and Glauberman, N. (eds) (1995) *The bell curve debate*. New York: Times Books.

Jansen, V.A.A., Stollenwerk, N., Jensen, H.J., Ramsay, M.E., Edmunds, W.J. and Rhodes, C.J. (2003) Measles outbreaks in a population with declining vaccine uptake. *Science*, *8*, 301, 804.

Jefferson, G. (1985) An exercise in the transcription and analysis of laughter. In T. van Dijk (ed.) *Handbook of discourse analysis*, Vol. 3. London: Academic Press.

Jensen, A.R. (1969) How much can we boost IQ and scholastic achievement? *Harvard Educational Review*, *39*, 1–123.

Johnston, W.M. and Davey, G.C.L. (1997) The psychological impact of negative TV news bulletins: the catastrophizing of personal worries. *British Journal of Psychology*, *88*, 85–91.

Jolyon, L. (1962) *Hallucinations*. Oxford: Grune and Stratton.

Jones, E. (1931) The problem of Paul Morphy: a contribution to the psycho-analysis of chess. *International Journal of Psycho-Analysis*, *12*, 1–23.

Jones, E.E. and Sigall, H. (1971) The bogus pipeline: a new paradigm for measuring affect and attitude. *Psychological Bulletin*, *76*, 349–64.

Jones, F. and Fletcher, C.B. (1992) *Transmission of occupational stress: a study of daily fluctuations in work stressors and strains and their impact on marital partners*. VIth European Health Psychology Society Conference (presented as poster) University of Leipzig (August).

Jones, J.S. (1981) How different are human races? *Nature*, *293*, 188–90.

Joravsky, D. (1989) *Soviet psychology*. Oxford: Blackwell.

Jowell, R. and Topf, R. (1988) *British social attitudes*. London: Gower.

Joynson, R.B. (2003) Selective interest and psychological practice: a new interpretation of the Burt affair. *British Journal of Psychology*, *94*, 3, 409–26.

Jung, C.G. (1921) *Collected works of C.G. Jung*. Princeton, NJ: Princeton University Press.

Jung, C.G. (1930) Your Negroid and Indian behaviour. *Forum*, *83*, 4, 193–9.

Kalton, G. (1983) *Introduction to survey sampling*. Newbury Park, CA: Sage.

Kamin, L. (1977) *The science and politics of IQ*. Harmondsworth: Penguin.

Kamin, L. (1981) *Intelligence: the battle for the mind: Eysenck vs Kamin*. London: Pan.

Kamin, L.J. (1995) Lies, damned lies and statistics. In R. Jacoby and N. Glauberman (eds) *The bell curve debate*. New York: Times Books.

Karau, S.J. and Hart, J.W. (1998) Group cohesiveness and social loafing: effects of a social interaction manipulation on individual motivation within groups. *Group Dynamics: Theory, Research, and Practice*, 2, 3, 185–91.

Karau, S.J. and Williams, K.D. (1993) Social loafing: a meta-analytic review and theoretical integration. *Journal of Personality and Social Psychology, 65*, 681–706.

Keller, E.F. (1986) *Reflections on gender and science*. New Haven, CT: Yale University Press.

Kenrick, D.T. and MacFarlane, S.W. (1986) Ambient temperature and horn honking: a field study of the heat/aggression relationship. *Environment & Behavior, 18*, 2, 179–91.

Kidder, L.H. (1981) *Selltiz Wrightsman and Cook's research methods in social relations* (4th edn). New York: Holt, Rinehart & Winston.

Kidder, L.H. and Fine, M. (1987) Qualitative and quantitative methods: when stories converge. In M.M. Mark and L. Shotland (eds) *New directions in programme evaluation*. San Francisco: Jossey-Bass.

Kimmel, A.J. (1998) In defense of deception. *American Psychologist, 53*, 7, 803–5.

Kline, P. (2000) *Handbook of psychological testing*. London: Routledge.

Knight, K.M., Bundy, C., Morris, R., Higgs, J.F., Jameson, R.A., Unsworth, P. and Jayson, D. (2003) The effects of group motivational interviewing and externalizing conversations for adolescents with Type-1 diabetes. *Psychology, Health and Medicine, 8*, 2, 149–58.

Kohlberg, L. (1976) Moral stages and moralisation. In T. Likona (ed.), *Moral development and moral behaviour*. New York: Holt, Rinehart & Winston.

Kohlberg, L. (1981) *Essays on moral development*. New York: Harper & Row.

Kohler, W. (1925) *The mentality of apes*. New York: Harcourt Brace Jovanovich.

Koluchová, J. (1976) Severe deprivation in twins: a case study. In A.M. Clarke and A.D.B. Clark (eds) *Early experience: myth and evidence*. London: Open Books.

Kraut, R., Patterson, M., Lundmark, V., Kiesler, S., Mukophadhyay, T. and Scherlis, W. (1998) Internet paradox: a social technology that reduces social involvement and psychological well-being? *American Psychologist, 53*, 9, 1017–31.

Kuhn, T. (1962) *The structure of scientific revolutions*. Chicago: University of Chicago Press.

Kvavilashvili, L., and Ellis, J. (2004) Ecological validity and real-life/laboratory controversy in memory research: A critical and historical review. *History of Philosophy and Psychology, 6*, 59–80.

Langdridge, D. (2007) *Phenomenological psychology: theory, research and method*. London: Pearson Prentice Hall.

Latané, B. and Darley, J.M. (1976) *Help in a crisis: bystander response to an emergency*. Morristown, NJ: General Learning Press.

Lawn, S.J. (2004) Systemic barriers to quitting smoking among institutionalised public mental health service populations: a comparison of two Australian sites. *International Journal of Social Psychiatry, 50*, 3, 204–15.

Leahy, W. and Sweller, J. (2004) Cognitive load and the imagination effect. *Applied Cognitive Psychology, 18*, 7, 857–75.

Leary, M.R. (1995) *Introduction to behavioural research methods* (2nd edn). Pacific Grove, CA: Brooks/Cole.

Lehmann, E.L. (1998) *Nonparametrics: statistical methods based in ranks*. Upper Saddle River, NJ: Prentice Hall.

Levin, R.B. (1978) An empirical test of the female castration complex. In S. Fisher, S. and R.P. Greenberg, (eds) *The scientific evaluation of Freud's theories and therapy*. New York: Basic Books.

Lewis, G., Croft-Jeffreys, C. and David, A. (1990) Are British psychiatrists racist? *British Journal of Psychiatry*, *157*, 410–15.

Leyens, J., Camino, L., Parke, R.D. and Berkowitz, L. (1975) Effects of movie violence on aggression in a field setting as a function of group dominance and cohesion. *Journal of Personality and Social Psychology*, *32*, 346–60.

Likert, R.A. (1932) A technique for the measurement of attitudes. *Archives of Psychology*, *140*, 55.

Lindsay, D.S. (1990) Misleading suggestions can impair eyewitnesses' ability to remember event details. *Journal of Experimental Psychology: Learning, Memory and Cognition*, *16*, 1077–83.

Linton, M. (1975) Memory for real world events. In D.A. Norman and D.E. Rumelhart (eds) *Explorations in cognition*. San Francisco: Freeman.

Lippmann, W. (1922) The abuse of the test. In N.J. Block and G. Dworkin (eds) *The IQ controversy*. New York: Pantheon, 1976.

Loewenthal, K.M. (2001) *An introduction to psychological tests and scales* (2nd edn). London: UCL Press.

Loftus, E.F. and Palmer, J.C. (1974) Reconstruction of automobile destruction: an example of the interaction between language and memory. *Journal of Verbal Learning and Verbal Behaviour*, *13*, 585–9.

Lonner, W.J. and Berry, J.W. (1986) *Field Methods in cross-cultural research*. Beverley Hills, CA: Sage.

Luria, A.R. (1969) *The mind of a mnemonist*. London: Jonathan Cape.

Lynn, R. (1991a) Race differences in intelligence: a global perspective. *Mankind Quarterly*, *31*, 254–96.

Lynn, R. (1991b) The evolution of racial differences in intelligence. *Mankind Quarterly*, *32*, 99–121.

Lyons, E. and Coyle, A. (2007) *Analysing qualitative data in psychology*. London: Sage

MacRae, A.W. (1995) Statistics in A level psychology: a suitable case for treatment? *The Psychologist*, *8*, 8, 363–6.

Madge, J. (1953) *The tools of social science*. London: Longman

Madill, A., Jordan, A. and Shirley, C. (2000) Objectivity and reliability in qualitative analysis: realist, contextualist and radical constructionist epistemologies. *British Journal of Psychology*, *91*, 1–20, 238.

Malinowski, B. (1929) *The sexual life of savages*. New York: Harcourt Brace & World.

Maltby, N., Kirsch, I., Mayers, M. and Allen, G.J. (2002) Virtual reality exposure therapy for the treatment of fear of flying: a controlled investigation. *Journal of Consulting and Clinical Psychology*, *70*, 5, 1112–18.

Manfredi, C., Cho, Y.I., Crittenden, K.S. and Dolecek, T.A. (2007) A path model of smoking cessation in women smokers of low socio-economic status. *Health Education Research*, *22*, 5, 747–56.

Marshall, C. and Rossman, G. (1989) *Designing qualitative research*. London: Sage.

Martin, S.L. and Klimowski, R.J. (1990) Use of verbal protocols to trace cognitions associated with self- and supervisor-evaluations of performance. *Organizational Behaviour and Human Decision Processes*, *46*, 1, 135–54.

Masling, J. (1966) Role-related behaviour of the subject and psychologist and its effect upon psychological data. In D. Levine (ed.) *Nebraska symposium on motivation*. Lincoln, NE: University of Nebraska Press.

Matsumoto, D. (1999) Culture and self: an empirical assessment of Markus and Kitayama's theory of independent and interdependent self-construals. *Asian Journal of Social Psychology*, *2*, 289–310.

McEwan, R.T., Harrington, B.E. and Bhopal, R.S. (1992) Telling or writing? A comparison of interview and postal methods. *Health Education Research, 7,* 2, 195–202.

Meddis, R. (1984) *Statistics using ranks: a unified approach*. Oxford: Blackwell.

Melia, K.M. (1996) Rediscovering Glaser, *Qualitative Health Research*, *6*, 3, 368–78.

Menges, R.J. (1973) Openness and honesty versus coercion and deception in psychological research. *American Psychologist*, *28*, 1030–4.

Meyer, G.J., Hilsenroth, M.J., Baxter, D., Exner, J.E. Jr, Fowler, J.C., Piers, C.C. and Resnick, J. (2002) An examination of interrater reliability for scoring the Rorschach comprehensive system in eight data sets, *Journal of Personality Assessment*, *78*, 2, 219–74.

Milgram, S. (1963) Behavioural study of obedience. *Journal of Abnormal and Social Psychology*, *67*, 371–8.

Milgram, S. (1974) *Obedience to authority*. New York: Harper & Row.

Miller, S. (1997) Self-knowledge as an outcome of application journal keeping in social psychology. *Teaching of Psychology*, *24*, 2, 124–5.

Mixon, D. (1974) If you won't deceive what can you do? In N. Armistead (ed.) *Reconstructing social psychology*. London: Penguin Education.

Mixon, D. (1979) Understanding shocking and puzzling conduct. In G.P. Ginsburg (ed.) *Emerging strategies in social psychological research*. Chichester: Wiley.

Mo, P.K.H. and Coulson, N.S. (2008) Exploring the communication of social support within virtual communities: a content analysis of messages posted to an online HIV/AIDS support group *CyberPsychology & Behavior*, *11*, 3, 371–4.

Montagu, A. (1975) *Race and IQ*. Oxford: Oxford University Press.

Morgan, M. (1998) Qualitative research … science or pseudo-science? *The Psychologist*, *11*, 481–3.

Murphy, K.R. and Myors, B. (1998) Statistical power analysis. Mahwah, NJ: LEA.

Murray, M. (2008) Narrative psychology In J. Smith (ed) *Qualitative psychology: a practical guide to research methods*. London: Sage

Musselwhite, K., Cuff, L., McGregor, L. and King, K.M. (2007) The telephone interview is an effective method of data collection in clinical nursing research: a discussion paper. *International Journal of Nursing Studies, 44,* 6, 1064–70.

Neisser, U. (1978) Memory: what are the important questions? In M.M. Gruneberg, P.E. Morris and R.N. Sykes (eds) *Practical aspects of memory*. London: Academic Press.

Niles, S. (1998) Achievement goals and means: a cultural comparison. *Journal of Cross-Cultural Psychology*, *29*, 5, 656–67.

Nisbet, R. (1971) Ethnocentrism and the comparative method. In A. Desai (ed.) *Essays on modernisation of underdeveloped societies* (Vol. 1, 95–114). Bombay: Thacker.

Olson, C.K., Kutner, L.A. and Warner, D.E. (2008) The role of violent video game content in adolescent development: boys' perspectives. *Journal of Adolescent Research*, *23*, 1, 55–75.

Olson, R., Hogan, L. and Santos, L. (2006) Illuminating the history of psychology: tips for teaching sudents about the Hawthorne studies. *Psychology Learning and Teaching*, *5*, 2, 110–18.

Ora, J.P. (1965) Characteristics of the volunteer for psychological investigations. *Office of Naval Research Contract 2149 (03)*, Technical Report 27.

Orne, M.T. (1962) On the social psychology of the psychological experiment: with particular reference to demand characteristics and their implications. *American Psychologist*, *17*, 776–83.

Orne, M.T. and Scheibe, K.E. (1964) The contribution of non-deprivation factors in the production of sensory deprivation effects: the psychology of the 'panic button'. *Journal of Abnormal and Social Psychology*, *68*, 3–12.

Ortmann, A. and Hertwig, R. (1997) Is deception acceptable? *American Psychologist*, *52*, 7, 746–7.

Ortmann, A. and Hertwig, R. (1998) The question remains: is deception acceptable? *American Psychologist*, *53*, 7, 806–7.

Osgood, C.E., Suci, G.J. and Tannenbaum, P.H. (1957) *The measurement of meaning*. Urbana, IL: University of Illinois.

Oswald, D.G. and Blanchflower, A.J. (2008) Is well-being U-shaped over the life cycle? *Social Science and Medicine, 66*, 1733–49.

Pallant, J. (2004) *SPSS survival manual*. Buckingham: Open University Press.

Pallant, J. (2007) *SPSS survival guide*. Buckingham: Open University Press.

Paludi, M.A. (2001) *The psychology of women*. Englewood Cliffs, NJ: Prentice-Hall.

Parker, I. (1994a) Qualitative research, in P. Bannister, A. Burman, I. Parker, M. Taylor and C. Tindall (eds) *Qualitative methods in psychology: a research guide*. Buckingham: Open University Press.

Parker, I. (1994b) Reflexive research and grounding of analysis: social psychology and the psy-complex. *Journal of Community and Applied Social Psychology*, *4*, 239–52.

Parker, I. (2004) Criteria for qualitative research in psychology. *Qualitative Research in Psychology, 1*, 2, 95–106.

Patton, M.Q. (2002) *Qualitative research and evaluation methods*. Thousand Oaks, CA: Sage.

Paunonen, S.V. and Ashton, M.C. (1998) The structured assessment of personality across cultures. *Journal of Cross-Cultural Psychology*, *29*, 1, 150–70.

Penfield, W. and Rasmussen, T. (1950) *The cerebral cortex of man: a clinical study of localization of function*. Oxford: Macmillan.

Peronne, V., Patton, M.Q. and French, B. (1976) *Does accountability count without teacher support?* Minneapolis: Centre for Social Research, University of Minnesota.

Piaget, J. (1936) *The origins of intelligence in the child*. London: Routledge & Kegan Paul.

Pidgeon, N. and Henwood, K. (1997) Using grounded theory in psychological research. In N. Hayes (ed.) *Doing qualitative analysis in psychology*. Hove: Psychology Press.

Pike, K.L. (1967) *Language in relation to a unified theory of the structure of human behavior*. The Hague: Mouton.

Piliavin, I.M., Rodin, J. and Piliavin, J.A. (1969) Good Samaritanism: an underground phenomenon? *Journal of Personality and Social Psychology*, *13*, 289–99.

Pirsig, R.M. (1999) *Zen and the art of motorcycle maintenance* (25th Anniversary edn). London: Vintage.

Plester, B., Wood, C. and Joshi, P. (2009) Exploring the relationship between children's knowledge of text message abbreviations and school literacy outcomes. *British Journal of Development Psychology, 27*, 1.

Pliner, P. and Steverango, C. (1994) Effect of induced mood on memory for flavours. *Appetite*, *22*, 2, 135–48.

Pooler, W.S. (1991) Sex of child preferences among college students. *Sex Roles, 25*, (9–10), 569–76.

Popper, K.R. (1959) *The logic of scientific discovery*. London: Hutchinson.

Potter, D. (2005) Review of MMR and autism: what parents need to know and MMR science and fiction. *Autism*, *9*, 5, 553–5.

Potter, J. (1996) *Representing reality: discourse rhetoric and social construction*. London: Sage.

Potter, J., Edwards, D. and Wetherell, M. (1993) A model of discourse in action. *American Behavioral Scientist*, *36*, 383–401.

Potter, J. and Wetherell, M. (1987) *Discourse and social psychology: beyond attitudes and behaviour*. London: Sage.

Presby, S. (1978) Overly broad categories obscure important differences between therapies. *American Psychologist*, *33*, 514–15.

Quine, L. (2002) Workplace bullying in junior doctors: questionnaire survey. *British Medical Journal*, *324*, 7342, 878–9.

Rabinowitz, F.E., Colmar, C., Elgie, D., Hale, D., Niss, S., Sharp, B. and Sinclitico, J. (1993) Dishonesty, indifference, or carelessness in souvenir shop transactions. *Journal of Social Psychology, 133*, 1, 73–9.

Rabrenovic, G., Levin, J. and Oliver, N.M. (2007) Promoting respect for difference on the college campus: the role of interdependence. *American Behavioral Scientist, 51*, 294–301.

Rachel, J. (1996) Ethnography: practical implementation. In J.T.E. Richardson (ed.) *Handbook of qualitative research methods for psychology and the social sciences*. Leicester: BPS Books.

Rafetto, A.M. (1967) Experimenter effect on subjects' reported hallucinatory experiences under visual and auditory deprivation. Master's thesis, San Francisco State College.

Rank, S. and Jacobson, C. (1977) Hospital nurses' compliance with medication overdose orders: a failure to replicate. *Journal of Health and Social Behaviour*, *18*, 188–93.

Reason, P. and Riley, S. (2008) Co-operative enquiry: an action research practice. In J.A. Smith, *Qualitative psychology: a practical guide to research methods*. London: Sage.

Reason, P. and Rowan, J. (eds) (1981) *Human enquiry: a sourcebook in new paradigm research*. Chichester: Wiley.

Regan, P.C and Llamas, V. (2002) Customer service as a function of shoppers' attire. *Psychological Reports*, *90*, 1, 203–4.

Reicher, S. (2000) Against methodolatry: some comments on Elliott, Fischer and Rennie. *British Journal of Clinical Psychology*, *39*, 1–6.

Reicher, S. and Emmler, N. (1986) Managing reputations in adolescence: the pursuit of delinquent and non-delinquent identities. In H. Beloff (ed.) *Getting into life*. London: Methuen.

Reicher, S. and Haslam, A. (2007) Is evil banal? *Psychology Review*, *13*, 1, 2–6.

Reinharz, S. (1983) Experiential analysis: a contribution to feminist research. In G. Bowles and R. Dueli Klein (eds) *Theories of women's studies*. London: Routledge & Kegan Paul.

Reyner, L.A. and Horne, J.A. (2000) Early morning driver sleepiness: effectiveness of 200 mg caffeine. *Psychophysiology, 37*, 2, 251–6.

Rice, A.K. (1958) *Productivity and social organisations: the Ahmedabad experiment*. London: Tavistock Publications.

Richards, G. (1997) *'Race', racism and psychology*. London: Routledge.

Richardson, J.T.E. (ed.) (1996) *Handbook of qualitative research methods for psychology and the social sciences*. Leicester: BPS Books.

Riecken, H.W. (1962) A program for research on experiments in social psychology. In N.F. Washburen, (ed.) *Decisions, values and groups*, Vol. 2. New York: Pergamon Press.

Ring, K., Wallston, K. and Corey, M. (1970) Mode of debriefing as a factor affecting subjective reaction to a Milgram-type obedience experiment: an ethical inquiry. *Representative Research in Social Psychology, 1,* 67–88.

Ritov, I. and Baron, J. (1990) Reluctance to vaccinate: omission, bias and ambiguity. *Journal of Behavioral Decision Making, 3,* 263–77.

Robson, C. (2002) *Real world research*. Oxford: Blackwell.

Roethlisberger, F.J. and Dickson, W.J. (1939) *Management and the worker*, Oxford: Harvard University Press.

Rosenberg, M.J. (1969) The conditions and consequences of evaluation apprehension. In R. Rosenthal and R.L. Rosnow (eds) *Artifact in behavioral research*. New York: Academic Press.

Rosenhan, D.L. (1973) On being sane in insane places. *Science, 179,* 250–8.

Rosenthal, R. (1966) Covert communication in the psychological experiment. *Psychological Bulletin, 67,* 356–67.

Rosenthal, R. and Fode, K. (1963) The effects of experimenter bias on the performance of the albino rat. *Behavioral Science, 8,* 183–9.

Rosenthal, R. and Jacobson, L. (1968) *Pygmalion in the classroom*. New York: Holt.

Rosnow, R.L., Goodstadt, B.E., Suls, J.M. and Gitter, A.G. (1973) More on the social psychology of the experiment: when compliance turns to self-defense. *Journal of Personality and Social Psychology, 27,* 337–43.

Rosnow, R.L. and Rosenthal, R. (1997) *People studying people: artifacts and ethics in behavioral research*. New York: W.H. Freeman.

Rosnow, R.L. and Rosenthal, R. (1999) *Beginning behavioural research: a conceptual primer*. Upper Saddle River, NJ: Prentice Hall

Ross, H.L., Campbell, D.T. and Glass, G.V. (1973) Determining the social effects of a legal reform: the British 'breathalyser' crackdown of 1967. *American Behavioral Scientist, 13,* 493–509.

Rotter, J.B. (1966) Generalized expectancies for internal versus external control of reinforcement. *Psychological Monographs, 30,* 1, 1–26.

Rubin, D.L. and Greene, K.L. (1991) Effects of biological and psychological gender, age cohort, and interviewer gender on attitudes toward gender-inclusive language. *Sex Roles, 24,* 7–8, 391–412.

Rule, B.G., Taylor, B.R. and Dobbs, R.A. (1987) Priming effects of heat on aggressive thoughts. *Social Cognition, 5,* 2, 131–43.

Rushton, P. (1990) Race differences, r/K theory, and a reply to Flynn. *The Psychologist, 3,* 5, 195–8.

Russell, B. (1976) *The impact of science on society*. London: Unwin Paperbacks.

Ryle, G. (1949) *The concept of mind*. London: Hutchinson.

Sacks, H. (1992) *Lectures on conversation*. Oxford: Blackwell.

Sears, R.R., Maccoby, E. and Levin, H. (1957) *Patterns of child rearing*. Evanston, IL: Row, Petersen & Co.

Sedlmeier, P. and Gigerenzer, G. (1989) Do studies of statistical power have an effect on the power of studies? *Psychological Bulletin*, *105*, 309–16.

Segall, M.H., Campbell, D.T. and Herskovit, M.J. (1968) The influence of culture on visual perception. In H. Toch and C. Smith, *Social perception*. New York: Van Nostrand & Reinhold.

Seligman, M. (1972) *Biological boundaries of learning*. New York: Appleton-Century-Crofts.

Selwyn, N. (2008) An investigation of differences in undergraduates' academic use of the Internet. *Active Learning in Higher Education, 9*, 1, 11–22.

Shadish, W.R., Cook, T.D. and Campbell, D.T. (2002) *Experimental and quasi-experimental designs for generalized causal inference*. Boston: Houghton Mifflin.

Shaffer, D.R. (1985) *Developmental psychology: theory, research and applications*. Pacific Grove, CA: Brooks/Cole.

Shikanai, K. (1978) Effects of self-esteem on attribution of success-failure. *Japanese Journal of Experimental Social Psychology*, *18*, 47–55.

Shneidman, E.S. (1963) Plan 11. The logic of politics. In L. Arons and M.A. May (eds) *Television and human behaviour*. New York: Appleton-Century-Crofts.

Shotland, R.L. and Yankowski, L.D. (1982) The random response method: a valid and ethical indicator of the 'truth' in reactive situations. *Personality and Social Psychology Bulletin*, *8*, 1, 174–9.

Sieber, J.E. (1999) What makes a subject pool (un)ethical? In G.D. Chastain and R.E. Landrum (eds) *Protecting human subjects: departmental subject pools and institutional review boards*. Washington, DC: American Psychological Association.

Sigal, H., Aronson, E. and Van Hoose, T. (1970) The cooperative subject: myth or reality? *Journal of Experimental Social Psychology*, *6*, 1–10.

Silverman, D. (1993) *Interpreting qualitative data*. London: Sage.

Silverman, D. (2000) *Doing qualitative research: a practical handbook*. London: Sage.

Silverman, D. (2004a) *Doing qualitative research: a practical handbook* (2nd edn). London: Sage

Silverman, D. (2004b) *Qualitative research: theory, method and practice* (2nd edn). London: Sage.

Silverman, D. (2006) *Interpreting qualitative data: methods for analyzing talk, text and interaction* (3rd edn). London: Sage.

Sims, D. (1981) From ethogeny to endogeny: how participants in research projects can end up doing action research on their own awareness. In P. Reason and J. Rowan (eds) *Human enquiry: a sourcebook in new paradigm research*. Chichester: Wiley.

Skinner, B.F. (1953) *Science and human behaviour*. New York: Macmillan.

Smith, G. (1975) Reception class: the individual language follow-up programme. In G. Smith (ed.) *Education priority*, Vol 4, *the West Riding Project*. London: HMSO.

Smith, J.A. (1995a) Evolving issues for qualitative psychology. In J.T.E. Richardson (ed.) *Handbook of qualitative research methods for psychology and the social sciences*. Leicester: BPS Books.

Smith, J.A. (1995b) Semi-structured interviewing and qualitative analysis. In J.A. Smith, R. Harré and L. Van Langenhove (eds) *Rethinking methods in psychology*. London: Sage.

Smith, J.A. (1997) Developing theory from case studies; self-reconstruction and the transition to motherhood. In N. Hayes (ed.) *Doing qualitative analysis in psychology*. Hove: Psychology Press.

Smith, J.A.. (2003) *Qualitative psychology: a practical guide to research methods*. London: Sage.

Smith, J.A. (2008) *Qualitative psychology: a practical guide to research methods*. London: Sage.

Smith, J.A., Harré, R. and Van Langenhove, L. (eds) (1995) *Rethinking methods in psychology*. London: Sage.

Smith, J.A. and Osborn, M. (2003) Interpretive phenomenological analysis. In J.A. Smith (ed.) *Qualitative psychology: a practical guide to research methods*. London: Sage.

Smith, M.L. and Glass, G.V. (1977) Meta-analysis of psychotherapeutic outcome studies. *American Psychologist*, *32*, 752–60.

Smith, N.E.I., Rhodes, R.E. and Naylor, P. (2008) Exploring moderators of the relationship between physical activity behaviors and television viewing in elementary school children. *American Journal of Health Promotion, 22*, 4, 231–6.

Smith, P.B. and Bond, M.H. (1998) *Social psychology across cultures: analysis and perspectives*. London: Harvester Wheatsheaf.

Solso, R.L. and Johnson, H.H. (1998) *Experimental psychology: a case approach* (6th edn). New York: HarperCollins.

Spelke, E.S., Hirst, W.C. and Neisser, U. (1976) Skills and divided attention. *Cognition*, *4*, 215–30.

Sprinthall, R.C. (2003) *Basic statistical analysis*. Boston: Allyn & Bacon.

Steelman, L.M., Assel, M.A., Swank, P.R., Smith, K.E. and Landry, S.H. (2002) Early maternal warm responsiveness as a predictor of child social skills: direct and indirect paths of influence over time. *Journal of Applied Developmental Psychology*, *23*, 2, 135–56.

Stephenson, P.H., Wolfe, N.K., Coughlan, R. and Koehn, S.D. (1999) A methodological discourse on gender, independence, and frailty: applied dimensions of identity construction in old age. *Journal of Aging Studies*, *13*, 4, 391–401.

Stevens, M.J. and Gielen, U.P. (eds) (2007) *Toward a global psychology: theory, research, intervention and pedagogy.* Hove: Psychology Press.

Stewart, S., Riecken, T., Scott, T., Tanaka, M. and Riecken, J. (2008) Expanding health literacy: indigenous youth creating videos. *Journal of Health Psychology, 13*, 2, 180–9.

Stipek, D. (1998) Differences between American and Chinese in the circumstances evoking pride, shame and guilt. *Journal of Cross-Cultural Psychology*, *29*, 5, 616–29.

Storms, M.D. (1973) Videotape and the attribution process: revising actors' and observers' points of view. *Journal of Personality and Social Psychology*, *27*, 165–75.

Strauss, A.L. and Corbin, J.A. (1990) *Basics of qualitative research; grounded theory procedures and techniques*. Newbury Park, CA: Sage.

Sturges, J.E. and Hanahan, K.J. (2004) Comparing telephone and face-to-face qualitative interviewing: a research note. *Qualitative Research, 4,* 107.

Tandon, R. (1981) Dialogue as inquiry and intervention. In Reason, P. and Rowan, J. (1981) *Human inquiry: a sourcebook in new paradigm research*. Chichester: Wiley.

Tavris, C. (1993) The mis-measure of woman. *Feminism and Psychology*, *3*, 2, 149–68.

Thigpen, C.H. and Cleckley, H. (1954) A case of multiple personality. *Journal of Abnormal and Social Psychology*, *49*, 175–81.

Thurstone, L.L. (1931) The measurement of social attitudes. *Journal of Abnormal and Social Psychology*, *26*, 249–69.

Titchener, E.B. (1901) *Experimental psychology, a manual of laboratory practice*: Vol. I, *Qualitative Experiments*, Part I, Student's Manual, Part II, Instructor's Manual. New York: Macmillan.

Titchener, E.B. (1905) *Experimental psychology, a manual of laboratory practice*: Vol. II, *Quantitative Experiments*, Part 1, Student's Manual, Part II, Instructor's Manual. New York: Macmillan.

Torbert, W.R. (1981) Why educational research has been so uneducational: the case for a new model of social science based on collaborative enquiry. In P. Reason and J. Rowan, J. (eds) *Human inquiry: a sourcebook in new paradigm research*. Chichester: Wiley.

Tran, M. (1998) 'Loneliness of virtual living', *Guardian*, 31 August.

Trist, E.L. and Bamforth, K.W. (1951) Some social and psychological consequences of the longwall method of coal-cutting. *Human Relations*, *4*, 1, 3–38.

Tucker, W.H. (1994) *The science and politics of racial research*. Chicago: University of Illinois Press.

Tukey, J.W. (1977) *Exploratory data analysis*. Reading, MA: Addison-Wesley.

Uetake, K., Hurnik, J.F. and Johnson, L. (1997) Effect of music on voluntary approach of dairy cows to an automatic milking system. *Applied Animal Behaviour Science*, *53*, 3, 175–82.

Vidich, A.J. and Bensman, J. (1958) *Small town in mass society*. Princeton, NJ: Princeton University Press.

Vrij, A. (1991) *Misunderstandings between police force and immigrants: the socio-psychological aspects of suspicion*. Amsterdam: V U Uitgeverij.

Wagenaar, W.A. (1986) My memory: a study of autobiographical memory over six years. *Cognitive Psychology*, *18*, 225–52.

Wardle, J. and Watters, R. (2004) Sociocultural influences on attitudes to weight and eating: results of a natural experiment. *International Journal of Eating Disorders 35*, 4, 589–96.

Watson, J.B. and Rayner, R. (1920) Conditioned emotional reactions. *Journal of Experimental Psychology*, *3*, 1–14.

Weber, S.J. and Cook, T.D. (1972) Subject effects in laboratory research: an examination of subject roles, demand characteristics and valid inference. *Psychological Bulletin*, *77*, 273–95.

Weich, S., Blanchard, M., Prince, M., Burton, E., Erens, B. and Sproston, K. (2002) Mental health and the built environment: cross-sectional survey of individual and contextual risk factors for depression, *British Journal of Psychiatry*, *180*, 5, 428–33.

Whyte, W.F. (1943) *Street corner society: the social structure of an Italian slum*. Chicago: University of Chicago Press.

Wilkinson, S. (1986) *Feminist social psychology*. Milton Keynes: Open University Press.

Willig, C. (2008) *Introducing qualitative research in psychology*. Maidenhead: Open University Press.

Wilson, S.R., Brown, N.L., Mejia, C. and Lavori, P. (2002) Effects of interviewer characteristics on reported sexual behavior of California Latino couples. *Hispanic Journal of Behavioral Sciences*, *24*, 1, 38–62.

Wolf, S. (1985) Manifest and latent influence of majorities and minorities. *Journal of Personality and Social Psychology*, *48*, 4, 899–908.

Wood, C. and Plester, B. (2008) Coventry University, Personal communication, 17 September.

Woolgar, S. (1988) *Science: the very idea*. London: Tavistock.

Woolgar, S. (1996) Psychology, qualitative methods and the ideas of science. In J.T.E. Richardson (ed.) *Handbook of qualitative research methods for psychology and the social sciences*. Leicester: BPS Books.

Word, C.H., Zanna, M.P. and Cooper, J. (1974) The non-verbal mediation of self-fulfilling prophecies in interracial interaction. *Journal of Experimental Social Psychology, 10*, 109–20.

Wright, R.L.D. (1976) *Understanding statistics*. New York: Harcourt Brace Jovanovich.

Yardley, L. (2000) Dilemmas in qualitative health research. *Psychology and Health, 15*, 215–28.

Yardley, L. (2008) Demonstrating validity in qualitative psychology. In J.A. Smith, *Qualitative psychology: a practical guide to research methods.* London: Sage.

Yin, R.K. (1989) *Case study research: design and methods.* London: Sage.

Yin, R.K. (1994) *Case study research: design and methods* (2nd edn). London: Sage.

Zajonc, R.B. and Sales, S.M. (1966) Social facilitation of dominant and subordinate responses. *Journal of Experimental Social Psychology, 2, 2*, 160–8.

Zegoib, L.E., Arnold, S. and Forehand, R. (1975) An examination of observer effects in parent–child interactions. *Child Development, 46*, 509–12.

Zimbardo, P.G. (1972) Pathology of imprisonment. *Society*, April, 4–8.

Index

Note: page numbers in **bold** refer to glossary entries.

A

α (alpha) 322, 339, 340, **348**
   in ANOVA 488
   Cronbach's 195–7, **204**
   relationship to power 386–7, 388
β (beta) 341, **348**, 470, **473**, 462
δ (delta), Cohen's 389–90, **396**
η^2 (eta squared) 389, 395, **396**
   in ANOVA 485
K (Kappa), Cohen's 129
μ (mu, population mean) 263
ρ (rho) **348**
   see also Spearman's rho rank correlation
Σ (sigma) 285
φ (phi) 406–7, **427**, 457, **473**, **500**
   in ANOVA 491–2
V (Cramer's phi) 407, **426**
χ^2 *see* chi-square test

A

a priori comparisons, ANOVA 487, 488–90, **499**
ABBA gambit 452–3
Abrahamsson, K.H., Berggren, U., Hallberg-Lillemoe, R.M.
   and Carlsson, S.G. 224
abstracts 615
   qualitative reports 572
accuracy 164
action research 238–9, **245**, 561
active role-playing 133
Adair, J.G. and Schachter, B.S. 95
age effects, interviews 153
Ainsworth, M.D.S., Beli, S.M. and Stayton, D.J. 118, 129, 132
Allport, G.W. 7, 225
alpha (α) 322, 339, 340, **348**
   in ANOVA 488
   Cronbach's 195–7, **204**
   relationship to power 386–7, 388
alternative explanations 57–9
alternative hypothesis (H_1) 326, **348**
American Psychological Association (APA)
   Ethical Principles of Psychologists and Code of Conduct
   586
   report style guide 612
analysis 23, **26**
analytic induction 578, **583**

analytic procedure **583**
ANCOVA (analysis of covariance) 495, **499**, 548
Anderson, C. 57, 60
animal research 597–600
anonymity 160, 595, **602**, 611
ANOVA (analysis of variance) 475, 480, **499**
   a priori comparisons 487, 488–90
   Bonferroni t tests 488
   calculation 483–5
   complex designs 529–30
   data assumptions, repeated measures designs 523
   division of deviation 481–2
   effect size 485
   error concept 480–1
   error rates 487–8
   F statistic 482–3
   indications for use 546, 547
   mixed design 527–9
   one-way 477–9
   post hoc comparisons 487, 488, 490–1
   power estimation 491–2
   reporting of results 486
   report writing 623
   SPSS procedures 495–7
   three-way 512–13
   with two or more independent variables 501–2
   see also one-way repeated measures ANOVA; two-way
   between groups ANOVA; two-way repeated measures
   ANOVA
animal use, views and beliefs 641–9
APA (American Psychological Association), convention for
   reporting results 357
appendices to reports 626
Araújo, D., Davids, K. and Passos, P. 99
Archer, J. 3
archival data 146, **148**
area of histograms 293
area under normal distribution curve 310–11, 651–3
Aristotle 8
Aronson, E. and Carlsmith, J.M. 94, 592
artificiality, laboratory experiments 117
Asch, S.E. 112, 116, 592, 608
asymmetrical order effects 70, **79**
asymptotes 310
attention-placebo treatment 63
attitude scales 177–8, **204**, 225–6, 608–9
   Likert-type scales 179–80, 183–4
   semantic differential scale 180–1